ASPEN CASEBOOK SERIES

Payment Systems and Other Financial Transactions

Cases, Materials, and Problems

Seventh Edition

Ronald J. Mann
Professor of Law and Co-Chair,
Charles E. Gerber Transactional Studies Program,
Columbia Law School

Published by Wolters Kluwer in New York.

Wolters Kluwer Legal & Regulatory U.S. serves customers worldwide with CCH, Aspen Publishers, and Kluwer Law International products. (www.WKLegaledu .com)

To contact Customer Service, e-mail customer.service@wolterskluwer.com, call 1-800-234-1660, fax 1-800-901-9075, or mail correspondence to:

Wolters Kluwer
Attn: Order Department
PO Box 990
Frederick, MD 21705

Printed in the United States of America.

1 2 3 4 5 6 7 8 9 0

ISBN 978-1-5438-0451-5

Library of Congress Cataloging-in-Publication Data
Names: Mann, Ronald J., author.
Title: Payment systems and other financial transactions : cases, materials,
   and problems / Ronald J. Mann.
Description: Seventh edition. | New York : Wolters Kluwer, 2019. | Includes
   bibliographical references and index. | Summary: "Payment Systems and
   Other Financial Transactions provides a comprehensive introduction to
   the mechanisms that people use to make payments. The audience is law
   school students taking courses on Payment Systems, Negotiable
   Instruments, or Commercial Paper" — Provided by publisher.
Identifiers: LCCN 2019027597 (print) | LCCN 2019027598 (ebook) | ISBN
   9781543804515 (hardcover) | ISBN 9781543815160 (ebook)
Subjects: LCSH: Payment — United States. | Credit — Law and
   legislation — United States. | LCGFT: Casebooks (Law)
Classification: LCC KF957.M36 2019 (print) | LCC KF957 (ebook) | DDC
   346.73/096 — dc23
LC record available at https://lccn.loc.gov/2019027597
LC ebook record available at https://lccn.loc.gov/2019027598

About Wolters Kluwer Legal & Regulatory U.S.

Wolters Kluwer Legal & Regulatory U.S. delivers expert content and solutions in the areas of law, corporate compliance, health compliance, reimbursement, and legal education. Its practical solutions help customers successfully navigate the demands of a changing environment to drive their daily activities, enhance decision quality and inspire confident outcomes.

Serving customers worldwide, its legal and regulatory portfolio includes products under the Aspen Publishers, CCH Incorporated, Kluwer Law International, ftwilliam.com and MediRegs names. They are regarded as exceptional and trusted resources for general legal and practice-specific knowledge, compliance and risk management, dynamic workflow solutions, and expert commentary.

For Allison

— R.J.M.

Summary of Contents

Contents

Part Three
Liquidity Systems   423

Acknowledgments

My debt to Jay Westbrook, University of Texas School of Law, is evident in every page of this book, not only for the inspiration of his teaching when I was a law student more than three decades ago, but also for his role in developing the *Debtor-Creditor* materials with Elizabeth Warren that are the precursor to the approach used in these materials. Accordingly, it should be no surprise that I also am indebted to Elizabeth Warren for her part in that development, as well as her advice on these materials, which she provided at both a "big-picture" and a "fine-print" level. I also owe special thanks to Dan Keating, who provided detailed comments on each of the assignments within days of its initial drafting, and to Bob Rasmussen, whose comments based on his teaching of the original version of the materials went far beyond the call of professional courtesy.

I also received invaluable feedback from several other professors who taught from portions of earlier versions of these materials: Amelia H. Boss, Temple University School of Law; Jean Braucher, University of Arizona College of Law; Tracey E. George, University of Missouri-Columbia School of Law; John P. Hennigan, Jr., St. John's University School of Law; Curtis R. Reitz, University of Pennsylvania Law School; Howard P. Walthall, Cumberland School of Law of Samford University; and Jane Kaufman Winn, University of Washington School of Law. Finally, Avery Katz provided useful suggestions on the materials related to guaranties. I am indebted to them and their students, and to my own students at Columbia, Texas, Michigan, and Washington University in St. Louis, for improving the book and for putting up with my errors, both substantive and typographical.

Numerous people who work in the commercial systems discussed in this book were kind enough to answer my questions about the systems and otherwise provide information. They include Buddy Baker (from ABN/Ambro); James J. Ahearn, Richmond W. Coburn, Janet L. Haley, Carol A. Helmkamp, and Linda Jenkins (all from NationsBank, formerly the Boatmen's National Bank of St. Louis); Paul Easterwood and Tom McCaffrey (from Dow, Cogburn & Friedman, P.C.); Mary Binder, Dale R. Granchalek, James Hinderaker, David Machek, Kevin Meyer, Mark A. Ptack, and Frank Ricordati (all from NBD, formerly First National Bank of Chicago); Mary-Ann Novinsky and Frank Trotter (from Mercantile Bank, formerly Mark Twain Bancshares); John Powell (from National Cachecard); Joe DeKunder (from NationsBank of Texas, N.A.); and Margie Bezzole (from Phoenix International).

Joanne Margherita and Gail Ristow have assisted me since the beginning of this project several years ago, both working in capacities too numerous to mention, ranging from desktop publisher to manuscript organizer to sales representative. Without their tireless, careful, and thoughtful work, the book would not be what it is. I also owe special thanks to David Murrel for his skillful preparation of many of the figures in the book. Rebecca Berkeley, Bob Droney,

Judson Hoffman, Laurel Kolinski, Jennifer Marler, Paul Nalabandian, and David Royster provided valuable assistance with research.

The following are acknowledged and have my appreciation for granting permission to reprint:

Middlebrook, Stephen T., "Bitcoin for Merchants: Legal Considerations for Businesses Wishing to Accept Bitcoin as a Form of Payment." Republished with permission of the American Bar Association, from Business Law Today, Stephen T. Middlebrook, November 2014, copyright © 2014 by the American Bar Association. Permission conveyed through Copyright Clearance Center, Inc.

Preface to the Seventh Edition

Payment Systems and Other Financial Transactions provides a comprehensive introduction to the mechanisms that people use to make payments. The systems of credit cards, checks, and wire transfer are a few examples of financial systems designed to support payment transactions. The guiding principle of this book is the idea that law students learn best from materials that present this area of law as an integral element in a system that includes not only abstract legal rules, but also people who engage in payment transactions; the contracts designed to guide those transactions; and the physical tools, such as filing systems and check sorters, that implement and record payment transactions. To understand the significance and effectiveness of the legal rules, it is necessary to understand the commercial and financial frameworks in which they are applied.

My examination of these systems has had a pervasive effect on the texture of the assignments that constitute the problem-based pedagogy of this book. First, to get a sense of how the rules of commercial law operate in context, I have conducted dozens of interviews with business people and lawyers who use the various systems in their daily work. Second, to give students a feel for how those systems operate in practice, the book incorporates a substantial number of sample documents and forms used in business transactions. Finally, because the casebook is organized according to the systems in which commerce operates — rather than by the sections into which statutes are divided, or by the categories of legal doctrine — the presentation frequently cuts across the arbitrary legal standards that divide commercially similar activities.

I want students to see the deep structural similarities of all the different payment systems in our economy, such as the parallel roles of guaranties and standby letters of credit and the effectiveness of negotiability and securitization as substitute devices for enhancing the liquidity of payment obligations. If students can understand the connections among those different topics, they will be better prepared to grasp the issues raised by the new institutions and systems that will develop during the course of their careers.

I am firmly committed to the view that the best way for students to understand how systems operate is by working through problems that require them to formulate legal strategies. This method encourages a teaching approach in which students are asked to work through the problems on their own; the issues and ramifications raised in the assignments form the basis for class discussion.

My interest in fostering an understanding of real-world commercial transactions influences the types of issues included in the book. The problems are designed to present students with real controversies that could arise between real people. The assignments do not require students to consider issues that rarely arise in practice. For the same reason, some of the more obscure details of the UCC and other statutory materials have been omitted. My attention to nondoctrinal aspects of commercial transactions is reflected in my use of narrative text and case summaries that provide the background necessary for working through the problems. Given the choice of asking a student to read a lengthy opinion that resolves a difficult legal problem or providing a concise summary of the key points of analysis, I choose the concise analysis every time. My goal is to maximize the pedagogical value of each page and to minimize the time students spend poring over the details of cases that do not directly advance an understanding of the system at hand. Consequently, the exposition is more extensive compared with some traditional casebooks, while excerpts from cases are considerably less extensive.

My goal at all points is to provide two things: the ability to see the grand structure of the existing systems covered in the book and the ability to pick up and use new systems that will develop in the years to come.

The last few two editions have implemented the most substantial revisions made to the book since the first edition. The novelty of that original version of this text was its stripped-down attention to negotiability. Instead of the conventional lengthy opening chapters about the details of Article 3, it began with a lengthy discussion of checks that largely ignored the basic principles of negotiability. During the intervening years, though, the role of checks in the payment system has declined steadily, to the point where it can only be anachronistic to design a text that opens with checks as the "paradigmatic" payment system. Accordingly, this book has changed the order of the material considerably, presenting payment cards as the first and paradigmatic payment system. I am cognizant of the difficulty it presents to new users for the edition to change so substantially. But I am equally cognizant of the ever-more pressing need to update the organization of the text to match modern realities.

A word about the editing is appropriate. Because this book is intended for pedagogical use, rather than direct scholarly engagement, I have taken unusual liberties in my editing of cases and other materials. Specifically, I have freely (that is, without any indication in the affected text) deleted brackets, citations, emphasis, ellipses, parallel citations, and quotation marks, as appropriate to smooth the reading experience for the student. I of course continue to indicate any revisions I make to the text that I do present. I trust that the benefits of readability outweigh any potential for confusion.

I welcome the opinions of users (and students) about the success of this new organizational arrangement. I am most grateful to the users of the book who have sent suggestions for emendations and improvements of previous editions. As in the last edition, I single out for their particularly useful and detailed suggestions Kenneth Kettering, Jim Rogers, and Paul Shupack.

RONALD J. MANN

April 2019
New York, New York

Payment Systems and Other Financial Transactions

Part One
Payment Systems

Introduction to Part One

The three parts of this book discuss systems used to make, support, and facilitate payment transactions. Those transactions occur in a wide variety of contexts, but for present purposes it is valuable to distinguish two broad classes of transactions. The first class is typical sales transactions, in which a seller receives payment at the time of the transaction. The second class is credit enhancement transactions, in which a third party enhances the reliability of the primary obligor by committing to make the payment. Part One of this book generally focuses on the different systems for completing the first class of transactions, simple payments. Part Two generally focuses on the second class, credit enhancement transactions. Part Three discusses negotiability and securitization, two systems that facilitate both payment and credit transactions.

The first topic, then, is how purchasers pay for the things they wish to buy. When they use cash, payment is simple: The purchaser provides cash, with which the seller can buy whatever the seller wishes. For a variety of reasons, however, many transactions are not settled with cash. Although it is easy to imagine many reasons a person might not use cash in a particular situation, the most general reason is the practical difficulty of transporting and using cash securely. Most of us find it impractical or imprudent to carry a sufficient amount of cash to complete all of our payment transactions. Some think it inconvenient to go to a bank or an automatic teller machine to get the cash. Others worry that the cash might be stolen. Finally, thoughtful purchasers might worry that a payment of cash would limit the leverage purchasers have if they use some other method of payment that is less final than cash (such as a credit card).

Those problems are particularly important in large transactions. For example, in the consumer context, few individuals ordinarily carry enough cash to complete purchases of major items such as furniture or stereo equipment. But the use of cash has steadily declined even in small, everyday transactions. Cash is used for less than 20 percent of the value of retail purchases, and its share is steadily declining. In commercial transactions, the use of cash is extraordinarily uncommon. Only the most unreasonable party would insist on a tender of cash to close a substantial commercial transaction: Imagine the spectacle of armored cars transporting the funds necessary to close a large commercial transaction.

The easiest way to satisfy a seller's desire to be paid without actually providing cash is to convince the seller that it can obtain payment from some financially reliable third party, usually a bank or other financial institution. Indeed, although we may not think of it when we make purchases, all of the most significant noncash payment systems used in this country — checks, credit cards, debit cards, wire transfers, and letters of credit — function by convincing the seller to rely on the expectation of prompt payment from a bank.

The substantive parts of this book differ from most law-school texts in placing great emphasis on the practical details of the various payment systems and relatively little emphasis on the abstract doctrinal rules that do not affect how the systems work in practice. That is not to say that the doctrinal details are unimportant: far from it. The role of the lawyer is to understand how the legal rules that set boundaries for each system apply in specific situations. It is to say, however, that the legal rules make sense only in the context of a practical and operating system. Nevertheless, because the first part of the book discusses so many different payment systems, it is useful before discussing the details of any particular system to provide some relatively abstract generalizations about the types of payment systems and how they differ from each other.

Typologies of Payment Systems

Cash and Noncash.   To generalize, payment systems can be cash or noncash systems. Cash is widely accepted as a payment device by both individuals and businesses. Indeed, to say it is legal tender is to say that a creditor acts wrongfully if the creditor refuses cash when offered to discharge an existing obligation. When a purchaser pays for an item with cash, the seller receives immediate and final payment, in a form that the seller can immediately use to make other payments, without further processing or transformation.

Cash also has the benefit of being anonymous. Cash payments often leave no trail from which subsequent investigators or data profiteers might discover the payment. The privacy benefits of cash have led technologists to complex efforts to provide similarly anonymous electronic payment solutions, but to date the efforts have not been fruitful. This benefit, of course, raises a corollary concern that people will prefer to pay cash when they wish to avoid the notice of law enforcement authorities that might have an interest in the subject matter of the transaction or taxing authorities that might wish to tax the transaction.

Many transactions, however, are not settled with cash. As Figure I.1 shows, cash is used for less than a fifth of the value of retail transactions in this country. The reasons are obvious. Cash is difficult to transport and use securely. In addition, the finality of a cash payment induces some purchasers to use noncash payment systems. Although it is difficult to quantify the effect, some of us use checks or credit cards solely to obtain the "float" that we gain when we can purchase an item today in return for a withdrawal from our deposit account that occurs some days later. Similarly, though doubtless less common, the robustly strategic among us should use credit cards when we deal with merchants of dubious reliability, because of legal attributes of the credit-card system that give purchasers a right to withhold payment unparalleled in other modern systems. Finally, in some cases, a merchant or individual may wish to leave a paper trail that proves the payment has been made. Few of us, for example, use cash to pay reimbursable expenses.

Noncash payment systems respond to that set of costs and benefits by convincing the seller to rely on its ability to obtain payment from a reliable third party, usually a bank or other financial institution. A check, for example, offers the hope—certainly not a promise—of payment from funds the purchaser has deposited with a bank. A credit card, in contrast, offers payment from the financial institution that has issued the card. The key point, however, is that all noncash payment systems depend for their success on credible arrangements to facilitate collection of claims in a timely and inexpensive manner.

Figure I.1
2015 U.S. Noncash Payments

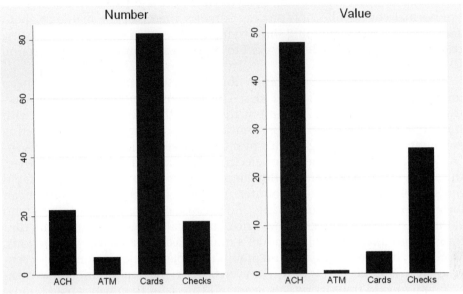

Paper and Electronic. Another important fault line lies between paper-based and electronic systems. For example, after we deposit funds in a checking account, we can make payments through the largely paper-based checking system or through the mostly electronic automated clearinghouse system that facilitates direct debits and direct credits to our banking accounts. Only in recent years have the procedures for using and collecting on checks begun to divorce themselves from an outdated focus on the tangible object. Compared to procedures that manage information electronically, paper-based check-collecting procedures were quite costly, perhaps in the range of two to three dollars per check (including the costs of handling the item by the payor, the payee, and the various banks that process it). The procedures also were quite slow, typically requiring a period of days to determine whether a check ultimately would be paid by the bank on which it is drawn. The delays required by such procedures hindered the efficiency of the system. Less obvious but just as serious, the paper-based procedures raised costs by increasing the potential for fraud. The long period between the time of deposit and the time at which the bank of deposit discovered whether the check would be honored presented a salient opportunity for a variety of creative schemes to steal money from the bank at which the check was first deposited. As Figure I.1 shows, check transactions by 2012 had fallen below 20 billion (from a high a few decades earlier of about 60 billion).

Responding to the high costs of paper-based processing, the American banking industry for decades has supported a variety of efforts to foster the use of electronic technology as a means for controlling and reducing costs in the checking system. Most recently, for example, the industry supported the

Check Clearing in the 21st Century Act of 2003 (commonly known as Check 21). The principal purpose of that statute is to foster check truncation, in which electronic systems replace the need to transport the paper check through the normal check collection process. A major theme of the materials about checking will be the ongoing shift from paper-based to electronic processing and the struggles of the legal system to support, accommodate, and respond to that shift.

By contrast, payment card transactions (at least in this country) have been processed electronically for decades. The settlement process has been electronic since the early 1970s, and in the 1990s the industry dispensed with the use of paper credit card slips. Thus, the cost of processing and collecting payments has been falling steadily over the last few decades, as part of the general increase in the efficiency of electronic information systems. Moreover, the ability to transmit information electronically often facilitates more rapid transactions at the checkout counter. That is beneficial both because it can lower labor costs for the merchants and because it can attract customers who value the shorter wait in checkout lines. Empirical evidence suggests that card transactions already are about a half a minute faster than check transactions. Moreover, if contactless cards and mobile card-based devices gain wide acceptance, it is probable that they will be even faster at the retail counter than cash.

Payment card transactions also generally are safer than paper-based transactions. Because the information on the card can be read electronically, the system can verify the authenticity of the card in real time. The terminal that reads the information on the card transmits that information to the issuer while the customer is at the counter, so that the issuer can decide whether to authorize transactions. Although that system certainly is not impervious to fraud, it plainly is more efficient than the checking system, which relies for verification primarily on a manual signature or presentation of a photo-bearing identification card. To be sure, the system depends on a reliable and inexpensive telecommunications infrastructure, but this country has had such an infrastructure throughout the relevant period. As Figure I.1 shows, there now are more than 80 billion payment card transactions a year in this country.

The shift from paper-based to electronic systems also has a substantial policy component, because at least in the United States, it is a shift from government-subsidized systems, provided exclusively by pervasively regulated financial institutions, to wholly private systems, provided by entities less subject to the control of public authorities. That attribute will undergird the materials on those topics, as they present card-based systems, in which most of the basic rules are established as private profit-seeking decisions of the large card networks, contrasting with the checking system, in which most of the basic rules are a matter of public legislation.

In-Person and Remote.   A third way to think about payment systems is to consider the difference between face-to-face and long-distance transactions. The rise of Internet retailing, in particular, focuses attention on the advantages of the payment card in long-distance transactions. The preexisting Visa and Mastercard networks, and the widespread distribution of cards to consumers in the United States, gave credit-card issuers a built-in nationwide payment network available when Internet commerce began. Other payment systems that existed at the time were not useful in the Internet setting. For example, cash is entirely impractical in a remote transaction unless the consumer has some reliable way to send the cash to the merchant. Even if some hypothetical consumer were willing to mail cash for an Internet purchase, the merchant would not receive the cash for several days until it came in the mail. Similarly, a commitment to pay by check gives the merchant nothing for several days while the merchant waits for the check (except a promise that "the check is in the mail"). Finally, when Internet commerce began, online retailers could not accept ACH transfers. A system for such payments now exists, but the move to ACH Internet payments is happening only after the system is to some degree "locked in" to reliance on credit-card payments. Thus, the most perceptible shifts in the payments patterns for maturing Internet retailers are not from credit cards to wholly separate systems, but from credit cards to debit and other developing card-based products that for the most part clear through the locked-in Visa and Mastercard networks.

Universal and Networked.   Cutting across all of the functional categories discussed previously is the question of whether a payment system is universal or limited to members of a network. Checks and cash are functionally universal, in the sense that they can be presented to almost any person or business. To send the check, you must know the address to which you wish to send the check. To collect the check, the person who receives it, at least theoretically, need not even have a bank account. They do not have to be a merchant approved by a credit-card network or have a contract with a member of the ACH network or some other collection system. To be sure, quite a number of people do not have bank accounts, which makes it somewhat harder to collect a check, particularly if an individual rather than a business writes it. In particular, persons without bank accounts are almost certain to pay fees to collect a check, even if they go to the bank that issued the check (a task that will be inconvenient for most of us). Yet, the key point is that, at least with respect to in-person transactions, a large number of payees accept checks more readily than other noncash payment systems. For example, almost all individuals will be compelled by social custom to accept a check in payment of an obligation. To succeed in that market, a new payment must devise some method of collection that is generally available to payees. PayPal, for instance, was successful in developing an Internet-based payment system that depends on payees having a combination of an e-mail address and a checking account into which PayPal can disburse funds. But at the same time it was much less successful with its original goal — to establish an electronic substitute for cash in small dollar payments between individuals.

By contrast, payment cards are unlikely to become a universal payment system. Rather, they depend directly on networks of participants, economically motivated by the structure of the system to make a voluntary decision to join the network. The banks that issue the cards do so because they believe they will profit from the fees and interest that they can charge. The customers that use the cards think they are a better vehicle for payment or borrowing than the alternatives available to them—the central focus of the first three chapters of the book. The merchants that accept them believe that customers will make additional and larger transactions with cards, the profits from which will more than offset the fees they must pay. The institutions that acquire the transactions and process them from the merchants believe that the fees they charge the merchants will exceed the costs of their processing. Persons or entities that do not make those decisions do not participate in the network.

The distinction between networked and universal payment systems is important as a policy matter because of the need to maintain a menu of payment systems that includes at least some universal payment systems for most important payments.

Developing Payment Systems

For each of the distinctions discussed previously, the increasing effectiveness of information technology offers the potential to unseat incumbent systems. Use of cash sinks lower each year as noncash payment systems penetrate the markets of merchants with smaller and smaller transactions: The passage of McDonald's from the list of cash-only merchants presages the desuetude of that category for substantial chain merchants. Use of checks sinks each year as more consumers use debit cards and Internet banking systems for transactions that formerly would have required a check.

Moreover, as more and more payments shift to Internet mechanisms each year, the possibility grows ever greater that some wholly new electronic payment system could arise to reorder the traditional markets. For example, a portable currency, capable of being stored on a card or other device (such as a cellular telephone or a personal digital assistant), could have a number of useful applications. Current applications in the arena of gift cards and payroll cards show particular promise. The market niche of that technology would be the ability to store an indicator of value directly on the card. That feature would obviate the need for a contemporaneous authorization of the transaction to confirm that an account holds funds for the transaction—a central feature of the dominant credit and debit card networks today. Rather, the transaction could be completed entirely based on an interaction between the merchant's terminal and the card itself. In a hybrid model now being deployed in the United Kingdom, cards include authorization information—the limit on the card and some information to allow the merchant to verify that the card is being used by the account holder—and the system approves most transactions without real-time authorization by the issuer. Surprisingly, despite the abandonment of real-time assessment by the issuer, that system probably is more secure than the long-standing U.S. system. Only in 2015 did the United States begin the shift to the more modern "chip-and-PIN" cards.

Stored-value cards also have the potential to limit the risk of violent crime against cardholders, at least if they are deployed broadly enough to lower the amount of cash that cardholders carry. If the thief that steals the card is unable to use the value on the card for the thief's own purposes, there is little point in stealing the card. Finally, stored-value cards are not tied to a bank account or line of credit, and thus can be used by individuals that do not have bank accounts. For that reason, they have been a persistent object of government policymakers attempting to develop cheaper—that is, electronic—methods of disbursing benefits to the unbanked.

The last major electronic product on the horizon is the bank transfer, or the *giro*, which is common in many foreign markets (particularly Japan and countries in continental Western Europe). Functionally, this is the equivalent of the ACH transfer that is used in the United States to make direct debits (for recurring payments such as mortgages or car loans) and direct credits (for recurring income items like salary). Bank transfer systems—"A2A" payments in the conventional terminology—result in a payment directly from one bank account to another. A2A payments have not been important in Internet commerce to date, largely because until 2001 the ACH network did not permit consumers to authorize nonrecurring transactions on the network. But the search of NACHA (the main proprietor of the ACH network) for new market niches, coupled with continuing merchant dissatisfaction about the high costs of accepting credit cards, led NACHA in 2001 to permit a new Web entry that permits such payments. Since that time, consumer ACH payments have become routine. That single product was used in 2013 for more than 3 billion payments worth more than a trillion dollars. That figure is dwarfed, though, by the massive use of ACH for business applications such as dispensing salary and reimbursements to employees. As Figure I.1 shows, there are currently about 20 billion ACH transactions each year in this country, worth about $50 trillion.

This book begins with payment cards, which in their ever-burgeoning manifestations have become the dominant retail payment system in the United States and most of the developed world. Accordingly, the best way to illustrate the general operation of payment systems is to examine the payment card, a task undertaken in Chapter 1 (Assignments 1 through 4). With that framework in place, Chapter 2 (Assignments 5 through 7) discusses electronic consumer payments. Chapter 3 (Assignments 8 through 10) discusses checks, and Chapter 4 (Assignments 11 through 14) discusses payments by "wire."

Before moving forward with the substantive materials, one final threshold point about statutory references is important. The Uniform Commercial Code has been revised and amended several times in the last few decades, and many of those amendments and revisions have not been uniformly adopted. To limit confusion, references in this book to the Uniform Commercial Code, or the UCC, refer to the official text promulgated by the American Law Institute and the Uniform Law Commission, as of January 1, 2019.

Chapter 1. Paying with a Card

Assignment 1: The Credit-Card System

Payment cards quickly are becoming the system of choice in the American economy, and credit cards — the original payment card — are still the most widely used of all payment cards. To get a sense for the size of the system, at the end of 2016, Americans were using credit cards in about 37 billion transactions worth about three-and-a-quarter trillion dollars each year. This assignment discusses the institutions on which that system rests and the mechanics of how that system completes payment transactions. Assignment 2 discusses the losses that arise from error or fraud in those transactions.

A. The Issuer-Cardholder Relationship

The system involves four major participants: a purchaser that holds a credit card, the issuer that issues the credit card, a merchant that makes a sale, and an acquirer that collects payment for the merchant. (The acquirer is so named because it "acquires" the transaction from the merchant and then processes it to obtain payment from the issuer.) The credit card reflects a relationship between the cardholder and an issuing bank. The cardholder can make purchases on the account either by using the card directly or by using the number without the card. The issuing bank commits to pay for purchases that the cardholder makes in accordance with the agreement between the issuer and the cardholder. What that means, among other things, is that the merchant that accepts a credit card ordinarily gets paid even if the cardholders ultimately fail to pay their bills.

Although those four parties are the nominal parties to the transaction, lurking behind them in most cases is the network under which the card has been issued (usually Visa or Mastercard). Although credit cards originated in the 1920s as proprietary cards issued by department stores to save the time of evaluating the credit of purchasers on a purchase-by-purchase basis, they have gone far beyond that. By the 1950s, a few national organizations (entities such as American Express, Diner's Club, and Carte Blanche) developed cards designed to allow travelers to pay for meals and lodging in remote locations without the uncertainty of writing a check. But more recently the market has come to be dominated by the familiar "universal" card, which aspires to universal acceptance for all purchases of any item anywhere. For those types of cards, Visa and Mastercard are the clear market leaders. As explained below, however, Visa and Mastercard do not participate directly in the transactions using the cards that bear their names and insignia. Rather, they operate more as facilitators, providing the technology and marketing to keep the system operating.

There is no general statute or set of common-law doctrines that governs the mechanics of credit-card transactions. Rather, for the most part the rules for the transactions come from a set of (often private) contracts among the institutional players in the market, with only a smattering of occasional intervening regulation that sets limits on the structures of those privately designed institutions. On that point, the principal legal regulation of the credit-card system comes from the federal Truth in Lending Act (TILA) and from Regulation Z (12 C.F.R. Part 1026), supervised by the federal Consumer Financial Protection Bureau. TILA is codified at 15 U.S.C. §§1601-1667e, as Title I of the Consumer Credit Protection Act, 15 U.S.C. §§1601-1693r. For clarity, citations in this book to TILA use the section numbers of the Consumer Credit Protection Act instead of the U.S. Code section numbers.

TILA and Regulation Z do not focus on the payment aspect of a credit card (the function that provides substantially immediate payment to sellers). Instead, they focus on the credit aspect (the function that allows a purchaser to pay a seller now in return for a commitment by the purchaser to repay the card issuer in the future). Specifically, TILA includes a series of rules that apply to any "credit card," which it defines in §103(k) as "any card . . . or other credit device existing for the purpose of obtaining money, property, labor, or services on credit." Thus, TILA applies not only to the most common credit cards issued by banks (Visa cards and Mastercards) but also to general-purpose cards issued by nonbank entities such as American Express or Discover, and even to limited-purpose cards issued by department stores and gasoline retailers (among others). The body of TILA might suggest that charge cards are not covered: TILA is limited to credit "payable by agreement in more than four installments or for which the payment of a finance charge is or may be required," TILA §103(f)(1). But Regulation Z defines "credit card" to include a charge card even if "no periodic rate is used to compute a finance charge." Regulation Z, §1026.2(a)(15); see also Regulation Z, §1026.2(a)(17)(iii) (defining "[c]reditor" for purposes of the credit card regulations to include a card issuer that "extends . . . credit that is not subject to a finance charge and is not payable by written agreement in more than 4 installments").

Appearing as it does in the Consumer Credit Protection Act, it comes as no surprise that TILA for the most part is limited to consumer transactions. Specifically, with one minor exception discussed in Assignment 2, TILA is limited to credit extended to individuals, TILA §104(1), Regulation Z, §1026.3(a)(2), and does not apply to credit extended "primarily for business, commercial, or agricultural purposes," TILA §104(1). It also does not apply to transactions involving more than $50,000. TILA §104(3).

The key to any credit-card arrangement is the relationship between the cardholder and the card issuer. Although the law leaves many of the aspects of the ongoing relationship to the parties, the legal regime does impose significant constraints on the practices that card issuers use to acquire customers, generally out of a concern that consumers will become overburdened with debt that they did not intentionally incur. Among other things, §132 of the Truth in Lending Act prohibits banks from issuing credit cards to consumers "except in response to a request or application." See Regulation Z, §1026.12(a) (same). Similarly, Regulation Z requires that a bank issuing a credit card provide the consumer a "clea[r] and conspicuou[s]" written disclosure that summarizes the applicable legal rules. Regulation Z, §1026.5(a)(1). Those rules are enforceable by a private right of action that the cardholder can bring in federal court. See TILA §130. Issuers with more than 10,000 cardholders must file their cardholder agreements with the CFPB and post them online. Regulation Z, §1026.58.

As a contractual matter, the basic relationship between an issuer and a cardholder is a simple one. The issuer commits to pay for purchases made with the card, in return for the cardholder's promise to reimburse the issuer over time. That relationship is exactly the opposite of the common banking relationship, where the customer normally must deposit funds *before* the bank will honor debit-card purchases or checks. Of course that distinction is not universal, because some checking customers have overdraft arrangements with their banks under which their banks honor debit-card transactions and checks even if they exceed the amount of the funds that the customer previously has deposited. Conversely, some credit cards issued to persons of doubtful credit strength require the cardholders to limit their purchases to amounts the cardholder previously has deposited with the issuer.

Even in those cases, however, the issuer cannot simply offset the charges against predeposited funds, as it does with checking accounts (or with debit cards that draw on those accounts). The most that the credit-card issuer can do is periodically deduct an amount from the funds to pay a prearranged portion of the charges. TILA §169(a); Regulation Z, §1026.12(d)(3). For example, a common arrangement grants the issuer an advance authorization to make a monthly ACH deduction from the customer's checking account equal to 3 percent of the customer's outstanding credit-card balance. (Chapter 2 discusses ACH transactions in detail.)

The buy-first, pay-later aspect of most credit-card relationships shapes the underlying economics of the system. Banks that provide checking accounts can earn profits by investing the funds that customers have placed in their accounts. A credit-card issuer does not have that option because most cardholders do not deposit funds before they make purchases on their cards. The profit for the typical card issuer comes predominantly from the interest income that the issuer earns on the balances that its cardholders carry on their cards from month to month. Although issuers commonly earn the majority of their income from fees of various kinds, interest revenues are essential to the profitability of the product.

The dependence on interest revenues produces an odd irony. The consumers that pay their credit-card balances every month — so-called convenience users — generally are the most creditworthy individuals in the system, but are more difficult customers for issuers that depend on interest income to fund the system. Issuers respond to that problem in various ways, primarily by imposing annual fees on cards unlikely to generate interest revenues and by targeting products to convenience users that are likely to be used frequently. If the cards are used frequently, they will produce revenue from interchange (discussed below) sufficient to make them profitable for the issuer. To give a sense of the frequency of the different customer types, the Federal Reserve's Survey of Consumer Finances reports (as of 2016) that 43 percent of *all*

Americans were carrying credit-card balances at any given time. And those that do carry balances carry staggering amounts of debt. Outstanding credit-card balances at the end of 2016 on general-purpose credit cards in the United States totaled more than $860 billion, more than $2,600 for each person in the entire population. That sum provides an ample base for interest and late charges sufficient to motivate issuers to participate in the credit-card system.

One last point about the relationship between the bank and the cardholder touches on the relation between the credit card and other products the bank might offer. For obvious reasons, cardholders sometimes have bank accounts at the banks that issue their credit cards. Among the reasons for that might be the ability of the bank where an individual has a bank account to acquire significant information about an individual's creditworthiness that gives that bank an advantage in assessing the individual as a credit-card customer. That relationship also could give the bank a fortuitous advantage when the card-holder fails to make payments required under the terms of its card agreement because the bank could obtain payment by offsetting its claim under the credit-card agreement against funds of the customer on deposit at the bank. TILA §169(a), however, strictly limits the issuer's right to obtain payment through an offset against the cardholder's bank account. First, an issuer can obtain payment through such an offset only if the cardholder consents in writing in connection with a plan for the bank to obtain automatic monthly payments on the card (a practice discussed above). TILA §169(a)(1). Second, even if the cardholder enters into such an agreement with the issuer, the issuer cannot deduct such a payment from the cardholder's bank account if the payment is for a charge that the cardholder disputes and if the cardholder requests the bank not to make such a deduction. TILA §169(a)(2).

B.   Using the Credit-Card Account

From the cardholder's perspective, payment with a credit card is simple. In a face-to-face transaction, the merchant normally swipes the card on a machine and produces a slip for the consumer to sign a few moments later, on which the cardholder promises to pay the transaction amount. In a transaction that is completed over the telephone (or the Internet) rather than face to face, the cardholder provides the card number to the merchant, and the transaction proceeds. The only difference is that the merchant does not have a signed slip as evidence that the cardholder in fact authorized the transaction.

Several significant things happen during the moments just after the card-holder provides its card to the merchant. First, the merchant's card terminal reads the magnetic stripe on the back of the card (or interrogates the chip on the card). The stripe ordinarily includes a magnetic description of the cardholder's issuing bank and account number, as well as a "card verification" value or code designed to confirm that the card is authentic. If the terminal is equipped to interrogate the chip, the chip sends a cryptogram, unique to the transaction, that more reliably confirms the card's authenticity.

Next, the merchant's terminal uses that information to conduct an authorization transaction. In that transaction, the terminal contacts the merchant's financial institution and sends an encrypted message that includes information about the transaction such as the card number, card verification value, expiration date, transactions amount, location, and Standard Industry Classification (SIC) code of the merchant; in chip-verified transactions, the cryptogram passes with that message. The acquirer then routes the message to processing computers at the card network (assume that it is Visa, for convenience). Visa then routes the message in accordance with the issuer's directions, either to the issuer itself or to a third party that processes credit-card authorizations on the issuer's behalf.

The recipient of the message (assume that it is the issuer, for convenience) then determines whether the account number reflects a valid card and whether the amount of the transaction is within the card's authorized credit limit. The issuer also examines the card verification value and the cryptogram (in a chip-verified transaction) to determine whether the card is counterfeit. Finally, the issuer considers the overall package of information about the transaction to determine whether there is an undue risk that the transaction is fraudulent. Large issuers use neural-network products designed to recognize out-of-pattern behavior that suggests a likelihood of fraud. The merchant's SIC code is crucial to the use of that software because it provides a general identification of the type of item being purchased. For example, three separate transactions on the same day purchasing jewelry and stereo components in a city 800 miles from the billing address are much more likely to reflect fraud than three separate transactions purchasing meals in the same location. If the transaction appears to be legitimate, the issuer (only seconds after receiving the incoming message) sends an encrypted message back to the merchant authorizing the transaction.

C. Collection by the Payee

1. *The Mechanics of Collection*

After the cardholder leaves the counter, the merchant is left with the authorized credit-card "slip" (which only rarely will be represented by a piece of paper). To turn that slip into money, the merchant must collect the slip through the network associated with the card that was used in the transaction. Visa and Mastercard are the largest networks; they each have more than 20,000 members and together cover about 70 percent of the general-purpose credit-card market in this country. The Visa and Mastercard entities are not themselves financial institutions. Rather, they are loosely organized cooperative organizations composed of banks that participate in the industry. Their main purposes are operating a clearance network (which includes setting the prices for use of the network) and coordinating advertising and research on technology and other issues important to the credit-card system.

To collect payments made by a credit card, a merchant must have an agreement with a member of the applicable network, normally referred to as the acquirer or acquiring bank. Thus, to collect a Visa receivable, a merchant must have an agreement with an acquirer that is a member of the Visa network. One of the principal topics of such an agreement is regulation of the merchant's relation with its customer, the cardholder. For example, the agreements establish a tier of discount rates that give the merchant a strong incentive to act with care in deciding whether to accept a credit card. Among other things, those rates make the transaction cheaper for the merchant if the merchant obtains the appropriate authorization from the issuer *before* completing the transaction.

At one time, those agreements also included provisions that prevented merchants from offering discounts to customers that paid with cash. A merchant might have an incentive to offer a cash discount because cash sales would allow the merchant to obtain payment without losing the portion of the sales price that the acquirer charges to process payment for the merchant (as discussed below). Given the tough competition in the credit-card market, it would be plausible to expect that the profits merchants could make by offering cash discounts eventually would induce acquirers to offer agreements that did not contain such restrictions. As it happens, however, it was positive law, not competition, that drove out those agreements. Specifically, §167 of TILA now prohibits those agreements and leaves merchants free to offer any cash discounts they find appropriate. Regulation Z, §1026.12(f).

After completing the transaction with the cardholder, the merchant delivers the slips to the acquirer, usually on a daily basis. Ordinarily, the same terminal that conducted the authorization transaction stores information about all the merchant's transactions. At the end of the day (if not more frequently), the terminal transmits a single mass ("batched") message to the acquirer that describes all of the transactions since the last transmission. It is possible for the process to be conducted based on the paper slips, rather than electronic messages, but that is now quite rare and tends to be significantly more expensive (about one-and-a-half times as costly per transaction from the merchant's perspective). Although the details depend on the particular agreement, the acquirer ordinarily gives a provisional credit to the acquirer's account for the charges processed that day. The funds become available a few days later, subject only to the acquirer's limited right (discussed below) to charge back funds if a cardholder declines to pay.

The amount of the credit that the acquirer provides the merchant is less than the gross amount of the slips because the acquirer deducts a small discount to cover the services that it is providing. The discount ordinarily has two components, a percentage of each transaction and a small per-item fee (in the range of 10 cents per transaction). In most contexts, the merchant receives a net credit in the range of 95 to 98 percent of the gross amount of the charges. The amount of the discount is negotiated as a key term of the agreement between the acquirer and the merchant, with the final amount depending on several factors. The most important factors are the volume and size of the transactions for which the merchant accepts credit cards. A local pharmacy with relatively few, relatively small transactions pays a much higher discount than a national department-store chain, with thousands of relatively large transactions each day.

Another important factor is whether the merchant sells face to face or online. Acquirers charge higher discounts for mail-order transactions because of the increased potential for fraud in transactions where the parties do not meet. Similarly, the agreements often include a separate (higher) charge that applies in "nonqualifying" transactions, those in which merchants type in a card number instead of swiping the whole strip or inserting the chip. The failure to swipe the card (or insert the chip) deprives the network of the ability to use security features that appear only on the stripe or chip (such as the card verification value). Accordingly, because there is a higher risk that such a transaction is fraudulent, the acquirer charges more to process payment for the merchant.

The acquirer promptly passes the slips along to obtain payment from the bank that issued the card. Ordinarily, it sorts all of the messages into on-us charges (charges on cards issued by the acquirer) and into separate piles for each network (Visa, Mastercard, and the like). It then sends a batched message describing all of its transactions to each network in which it participates. The network assesses an interchange fee on those transactions as well as a relatively small network fee of its own and then credits each acquirer for the difference: the face amount of the transactions (the amount the consumers promised to pay), reduced by the interchange fee and the network fee. The amount of those fees is slightly lower than the amount of the merchant discounts, so that the amount credited to the acquirer (gross amount, less interchange fee) is slightly higher than the amount the acquirer gave the merchant (gross amount, less the merchant discount). That relationship is not a coincidence; the business of acquiring credit card transactions would not be profitable unless the acquirer set its merchant discounts at a rate that exceeds its expenses. Ordinarily, the network credits the acquirer for 98 to 99 percent of the charges, depending on the type of transaction (card fully processed; face to face, but card not processed; remote transaction). The credit is applied to a designated account of the acquirer, typically the acquirer's account at its Federal Reserve bank.

Finally, the network sorts the transactions by issuer and debits each issuer for the amounts credited to acquirers for transactions on that issuer's cards. Thus, the issuers are charged only the net amount of the charges (the face amount reduced by the interchange fees). The issuers, in turn, sort the transactions reported to them, post them to the separate accounts, and bill for them on a monthly basis.

When the process is complete, the credit-card account of the purchaser/cardholder has been charged the face amount of the purchase. If all goes well, the issuer has revenues of 1 to 2 percent of the transaction: The issuer has been charged for 98 to 99 percent of the transaction and has obtained a right to collect 100 percent from its cardholder. Visa has charged a slight network fee. The acquirer has a profit as well, although often much less than the issuing bank: It has received a credit for 98 to 99 percent of the transaction and passed on to its merchants some negotiated, but slightly smaller amount (usually between 95 and 98 percent). Finally, the merchant has received that 95 to 98 percent as payment for its transaction with the purchaser. Its profit (if it has

Figure 1.1:
Payment by Credit Card

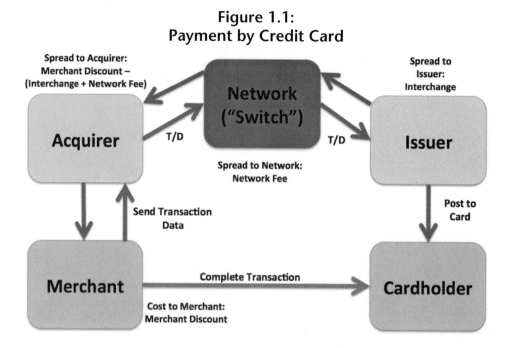

one) has to come from its having sold the product for an amount that exceeds its costs by more than the 2 to 5 percent it expended in obtaining payment through the credit card system. Figure 1.1 illustrates the process.

2.   Finality of Payment

One of the most distinctive features of the credit-card system is that it gives the consumer a right to cancel payment that is much broader than the consumer's rights in any of the competing systems. For example, under the checking system (which you will study in Chapter 3), a consumer's right to cancel payment is relatively limited. The consumer technically has the right to stop payment on a check, but that right is effective only if the consumer acts before the check is honored by the payor bank, which will be at most a matter of days and might be only a matter of hours. Similarly, debit-card payments (which you will study in Assignment 3) are final at the moment of sale, leaving the consumer no later opportunity to stop payment. That does not mean that a consumer who pays with a check or debit card has lost the ordinary contract-law right to rescind the transaction. But it does mean that the merchant already has the money while the cardholder is pursuing that right. As a result, it may be more difficult for the cardholder to challenge the transaction.

In the credit-card system, however, the issuing bank's obligation to pay does not become final at the time of the initial payment to the acquirer. Rather, TILA §170(a) grants a cardholder the right to withhold payment on the basis of any defense that it could assert against the original merchant. For example, suppose that Cliff Janeway uses a credit card to purchase some books as a gift for a friend, relying on the merchant's assurance that the books are rare first editions. If Cliff later discovers that the books in fact are not first editions, TILA §170(a) allows Cliff to refuse to pay the charge on his credit-card account. Specifically, he can assert against the issuer his ordinary contract-law defense that the goods fail to conform to the underlying sales contract.

Standing alone, that provision would wreak havoc with credit cards as a payment system. Issuers as a class would be in a difficult position if they could collect credit-card charges only when they could prove that the merchant had performed properly on the underlying sales contract. Furthermore, a system that allowed merchants to pass to the issuer any risk that the cardholder would refuse to pay because of nonperformance would leave merchants with an inadequate incentive to satisfy their customers. The card-issuing networks solve that problem by adopting rules that pass that risk back to the merchant. Thus, when a cardholder raises a defense against the issuer under TILA §170(a), the issuer can charge the challenged slip back to the acquirer. The charge-back is accomplished in the same way as the forward processing of the slip when the transaction first occurred: The issuing bank sends an item through the Visa network, seeking to recover the appropriate funds from the acquirer and, if all goes as it should, receives a credit from the Visa clearinghouse in the daily entry into the issuing bank's bank account at its Federal Reserve bank. Similarly, the acquirer's agreement with the merchant allows the acquirer to charge back the same transaction to the merchant. Thus, the acquirer removes the funds from the merchant's account (just as it would remove funds from a dishonored check that the merchant had deposited). In the end, the merchant bears the burden of obtaining payment from the disgruntled cardholder.

Several qualifications limit the cardholder's right to challenge payment. The first cuts off the right as the cardholder pays the bill. The cardholder's right under TILA §170(a) is only a right to withhold payment from the issuer; it does not include a right to seek a refund from the issuer or the merchant. Accordingly, the right dissipates as the cardholder pays off the credit-card balance generated by the transaction in question. See TILA §170(b) (limiting challenge right to "the amount of credit outstanding with respect to the transaction"); see also Regulation Z, §1026.12(c) (same). That limitation should not trouble cardholders significantly because of the likelihood that defects in the purchased goods or services would be evident before the cardholder received the bill and paid it.

Another minor limitation is the requirement in TILA §170(a)(1) that the cardholder "ma[k]e a good faith attempt to obtain satisfactory resolution of [the] disagreement . . . from the [merchant] honoring the credit card." That also is not a significant problem. Few cardholders will challenge items on their credit-card bill if they easily can resolve the dispute directly with the merchant in question.

The most significant—and oddest—limitation relates to the location of the transaction. Specifically, TILA §170(a) prevents cardholders from withholding payment on transactions that occur both outside the state where the cardholder resides and more than 100 miles from the cardholder's billing address. Under that rule, the only transactions that the cardholder can challenge are transactions that occur either in the state of the cardholder's residence or within 100 miles of the cardholder's billing address. As the following case suggests, the frequency with which consumers use credit cards while at locations remote from their homes brings that provision into play with some regularity.

Hyland v. First USA Bank

1995 WL 595861 (E.D. Pa. Sept. 28, 1995)

Giles, District Judge.

In February, 1994, First USA Bank issued a Gold Visa Card to the Plaintiffs. In May, 1994, Plaintiffs traveled to Greece for a vacation, where they purchased an oriental carpet ("the carpet") from Aris Evangelinos, the owner of an antique store in Nauplia, Greece. Plaintiffs paid US $2,070.57 for the carpet with the Visa Card issued by the Bank.

Plaintiffs contend that in order to induce Plaintiffs to purchase the carpet, Evangelinos made express warranties that the carpet was an antique Kilim, circa 1930, that it was woven and embroidered with pure silk with a cotton warp, and that it had been colored with vegetable dyes. Upon inspection by a United States carpet expert, Plaintiffs discovered that these express warranties were false. The Plaintiffs contacted the Bank and the merchant to obtain a credit.

Plaintiffs allege that the Bank directed them to return the carpet to the merchant. They did so via Federal Express. However, the carpet was intercepted by Greek Customs, who informed Plaintiffs that a duty of approximately US $1,240 would have to be paid before the carpet could be released. Plaintiffs refused to pay the duty, and notified the Bank that they would hold the Bank responsible for the loss of the carpet. The carpet was ultimately confiscated by Greek Customs.

Plaintiffs maintain that the Bank repeatedly assured them that it would assist the Plaintiffs in resolving the matter if Plaintiffs (1) returned the carpet to Evangelinos; and (2) provided a return receipt to the Bank. Plaintiffs contend that they relied on the Bank's assurance of assistance, and ceased personal efforts to obtain a refund. The Bank later informed Plaintiffs that consumer protection does not exist for purchases made outside of the United States. Accordingly, the Bank refused to accept liability for the loss of the carpet. . . .

Plaintiffs allege that Evangelinos made certain express warranties regarding the authenticity of the carpet. The formation of an express warranty is governed by statute: Any affirmation of fact or promise made by the seller to the buyer which relates to the goods and becomes part of the basis of the bargain creates an express warranty that the goods shall conform to the affirmation or promise. [UCC §2-313(a)(1).] Breach of warranty claims serve to protect buyers from loss where the goods purchased do not meet commercial standards or affirmations. In the present case, Plaintiffs clearly allege that the carpet did not conform to the affirmations of authenticity made by Evangelinos.

However, Plaintiffs have chosen not to sue Evangelinos directly. Instead, Plaintiffs allege that under [TILA §170], and Regulation Z, 12 C.F.R. §[10]26.12(c), Plaintiffs are permitted to assert against the Bank, as card issuer, the claim for breach of warranty that they are entitled to assert against Evangelinos. Plaintiffs further allege that the Bank has waived and is estopped from asserting any limitations or defenses to liability on the Truth in Lending Act claim. The Bank asserts that under [TILA §170](a)(3) . . . it cannot be held liable for the loss of the carpet because the transaction did not occur in the state of, or within 100 miles of, Plaintiffs' mailing address. In addition, the Bank contends that it has not waived its right to assert the geographic limitation as a defense.

As a general rule, the Truth in Lending Act provides that "a card issuer who has issued a credit card to a cardholder . . . shall be subject to all claims (other than tort claims) and defenses arising out of any transaction in which the credit card is used as a method of payment or extension of credit." [TILA §170](a). However, a card issuer is liable for such claims only if "the place where the initial transaction occurred was in the same State as the mailing address previously provided by the cardholder or was within 100 miles from such address. . . ." [TILA §170](a)(3). In the present case, Plaintiffs purchased the carpet in Greece, a foreign country that is neither in the same state nor within 100 miles of the Plaintiffs' mailing address. Therefore, the allegations in the Plaintiffs' complaint do not satisfy the geographical limitation provided by [TILA §170](a)(3). However, Plaintiffs also allege that the Bank waived the protection granted by this geographical limitation. Plaintiffs allege that by initially agreeing to assist Plaintiffs in an international dispute, the Bank knowingly waived its right to assert the geographical limitation as a defense.

A waiver is a voluntary and intentional relinquishment or abandonment of a known right. In the present case, Plaintiffs allege that they "specifically asked the BANK whether the BANK could assist them in obtaining reimbursement from a seller who was located not merely out of state but, in fact, abroad, in Greece." Plaintiffs contend that the Bank responded by assuring them that the Bank "could be of assistance." The complaint further alleges that Plaintiffs spoke frequently with the Bank by telephone, and referred the Bank's customer service representative to the charge statement which showed that the purchase had been made in Greece. According to Plaintiffs, the Bank repeatedly agreed to assist them.

Reading the complaint liberally, and viewing the allegations in the complaint in a light most favorable to Plaintiffs, we conclude that Plaintiffs have adequately alleged waiver of the geographic limitation by the Bank sufficient to survive a motion to dismiss.

It is difficult to assess the practical effects of the 100-mile limitation. On the one hand, the increasing nationalization of the economy and the rapid growth of Internet and mail-order businesses selling goods by credit cards have increased the share of nonlocal transactions. Furthermore, *Hyland* might give an exaggerated impression of the cardholder's rights. Many courts would not be as generous as the *Hyland* court, and many issuers would hesitate to offer assistance on transactions for which the 100-mile limit gives them immunity. On the other hand, it is not clear whether the 100-mile limitation applies to online or mobile transactions; cases considering the location of a credit-card transaction made by telephone reached conflicting results, with some concluding that the transaction takes place at the consumer's location and others concluding that the transaction takes place at the merchant's location.

Perhaps more importantly, a variety of considerations can lead issuing banks to forgo a strict reliance on their rights under the 100-mile limitation. For example, as in most of the systems discussed in the first few chapters of the book, the transaction costs to the bank of contesting the customer's claim readily could exceed the amount in dispute, especially on small charges. Finally, in an increasingly competitive market for credit-card business, issuers may be reluctant to alienate customers that are, after all, free to take their credit business to another issuer. Presumably for reasons of that sort, the network rules for the major networks permit issuers to charge back transactions without regard to the distance limitations. Thus, issuers have no monetary incentive to enforce those limitations against their customers. In sum, the right to withhold payment gives credit-card users an advantage much broader than anything they would have under the other payment systems readily available to consumers. Having said that, the following case shows that at least some issuers are policing the limits on the provision.

CitiBank (South Dakota), N.A. v. Mincks

135 S.W.3d 545 (Mo. Ct. App. 2004)

JEFFREY W. BATES, J.

CitiBank (South Dakota), N.A. ("CitiBank") sued defendant Mary Mincks ("Mary") for breach of contract after Mary refused to make any further payments on her CitiBank credit card account.

Mary defended on the ground that: (1) the only unpaid charges on the account related to merchandise which was never delivered by the merchant; and (2) since her CitiBank credit card was used to order the merchandise, she was entitled to assert the defense of non-delivery against CitiBank in its action to recover the balance due on her credit card account. After a bench trial, judgment was entered in Mary's favor. On appeal, CitiBank argues that the trial court's judgment should be reversed because it was . . . based on an erroneous application of the provisions of the Truth in Lending Act, 15 U.S.C. 1601, *et seq*. We affirm. . . .

II.FACTUAL AND PROCEDURAL HISTORY

. . . On September 18, 1999, Mary applied to have a credit card issued to her by CitiBank. She filled out a document called a "CitiBank Platinum Select Acceptance Form," which appears to be a typical application for personal credit. Nothing on the application indicates that credit was being sought by either a business or by an individual who intended to use the credit card for business purposes. The application listed Mary as the cardholder and showed her home address as the billing location. The form asked for the normal personal information (*e.g.*, mother's maiden name, social security number, income) found in such personal applications. Mary applied for credit for herself, and she requested that her husband, Chuck, also be authorized to use her credit card account. The application contained the familiar exhortation, typically found in consumer credit applications, offering an introductory period of very low interest.

Mary's application was accepted, and CitiBank issued a credit card to her with an $8,000 line of credit. On October 26, 1999, Mary transferred the existing balances from two other credit cards, totaling $7,213.50, to her CitiBank account. There is no indication in the record that these balance transfers were comprised of purchases for anything other than personal, family or household purposes.

Between November 1999 and January 2000, Mary purchased a few additional items with her credit card and made several payments on her account. Once again, nothing in the record demonstrates that these purchases were made for anything other than personal, family or household purposes. On January 27, 2000, Mary made a large payment on her account that reduced the outstanding balance to approximately $20.00.

In February 2000, Chuck received a solicitation to order merchandise from Purchase Plus Buyers Group ("PPBG"). PPBG sold products like mailing cards, telephone cards and other similar items which could be used to promote a home business. After reviewing the solicitation, Chuck decided to order some high-definition, high-color postcards that he could use to contact potential customers for a home business that he had started about three months earlier. On February 24, 2000, Chuck placed an order with PPBG for 4,000 postcards. The order form was sent by fax from Lamar, Missouri, to PPBG's office in Westerville, Ohio. Chuck used Mary's CitiBank credit card to pay the $7,600 purchase price for the postcards. The charge for this purchase first appeared on Mary's CitiBank statement in March 2000.

Four weeks after placing the order, Chuck contacted PPBG by telephone to find out why he had not yet received the postcards. He was told that the merchandise was on backorder and would not be available for another month. Having no reason to doubt that explanation at the time, he waited another month. When he still had not received the postcards, he contacted PPBG again by telephone. The persons with whom he spoke were very positive and continued to assure him that he would receive the postcards in time. Thereafter, he called PPBG "innumerable times" by telephone, and PPBG personnel kept reiterating that he would ultimately receive the postcards he ordered. In mid-May 2000, Chuck first learned from PPBG that the type of postcards he ordered had been discontinued in December 1999, even though the product continued to be offered for sale until April 2000. On May 18, 2000, he faxed a letter to PPBG requesting that he be given some other type of product that he could use since the postcards he wanted were no longer available. He received no response. He faxed the same letter to PPBG's executive committee on July 13, 2000, and again received no response.

Around August 1, 2000, Chuck decided he was never going to receive the postcards he ordered from PPBG. On August 4, 2000, he faxed a written demand for a full refund to PPBG because the company had failed to deliver either the postcards or a satisfactory alternative product. He sent this fax because he still believed he could get a refund for the undelivered merchandise. This belief changed on September 1, 2000, when he received a fax from PPBG stating the company had ceased operations and permanently closed its doors that day. Chuck knew then he would not be able to get a refund from PPBG.

On September 28, 2000, the Mincks sent a letter to CitiBank. In sum, the letter provided CitiBank with the following information: (1) Chuck's $7,600 postcard order from PPBG had never been delivered; (2) the charge for this order first appeared on Mary's March 2000 statement; (3) the facts showing that Chuck had made a good faith effort to resolve the issue with PPBG were recounted with considerable specificity and detail; (4) PPBG committed a breach of contract and fraud by failing to deliver the ordered merchandise and by continuing to sell a discontinued product; and (5) the Mincks were invoking their rights under Regulation Z of the federal Truth in Lending Act to have their account credited in the amount of $7,600 and to have this sum charged back to PPBG.

On October 9, 2000, CitiBank responded in a letter sent to Mary. CitiBank took the position that it was not able to assist the Mincks because it had not received their letter "within 60 days of the disputed charge." CitiBank advised the Mincks to pursue the matter with the merchant or through some alternative means available to them.

After receiving the October 9, 2000, letter from CitiBank, the Mincks continued to use Mary's credit card. They made a few additional purchases with the card, and they continued to make payments on the account. That changed in February 2002, when the Mincks stopped making any payments on the CitiBank account. The outstanding account balance at this time was comprised solely of the remaining amount due for the undelivered postcards ordered from PPBG, plus accrued interest and late charges.

On October 7, 2002, CitiBank sued Mary for breach of contract and sought to recover the $9,048.49 then due, accrued interest at the rate of 24.99% per annum and a 15% attorney fee. Insofar as pertinent to the issues here, the petition alleged that: (1) CitiBank had issued a credit card to Mary; (2) by acceptance and use of the credit card, Mary had agreed to make the monthly payments described in the CitiBank Card Agreement attached to the petition; (3) CitiBank had advanced credit to Mary, through the use of the credit card, to certain persons or firms shown on her account statements; (4) CitiBank had made demand on Mary to pay the amount due on her account, but she refused to do so for more than 25 days; and (5) CitiBank had "paid valuable consideration to each of said issuers of the credit to Defendant [Mary], and that as consideration therefore [sic] each of said issuers of credit has assigned to Plaintiff [CitiBank] the rights to receive payment evidenced in each of the transactions making up the balance due. . . . " Thus, it is apparent from CitiBank's petition that it was suing as the assignee of the individual merchants from whom Mary or Chuck had made purchases using Mary's CitiBank credit card. It is also undisputed that the entire account balance which CitiBank sought to recover from Mary resulted from the direct and collateral charges associated with the single $7,600 transaction in which PPBG was the merchant. In Mary's answer, she specifically asserted non-delivery of the merchandise ordered from PPBG as a defense against CitiBank's claim.

At trial, the sole dispute was whether Mary was entitled to assert PPBG's non-delivery as a defense against CitiBank, which sought to recover the purchase price of the postcards as PPBG's assignee. CitiBank argued that the non-delivery defense should not be permitted on two grounds. First, the PPBG postcard order, which was the only transaction at issue, was not within the scope of Regulation Z since this specific purchase was for a business or commercial purpose. Second, even if Regulation Z did apply, non-delivery of merchandise constitutes a "billing error" within the meaning of the regulation. According to CitiBank, Mary lost the ability to assert non-delivery as a defense in this lawsuit because she did not give CitiBank notice of this "billing error" within 60 days after the charge first appeared on her credit card statement. In response, Mary argued that Regulation Z imposed no time limit that precluded her from asserting non-delivery as a defense in CitiBank's lawsuit against her, and she denied that this was a "billing error" within the meaning of the regulation. At the conclusion of the case, the trial court made the following ruling from the bench:

> I think that Reg Z does apply, and I don't think this is a—a billing error. And I think that the provision of Reg Z that allows the cardholder to assert any . . . defenses that they could assert against the provider of the product is against the—the credit card company. Court's going to find the issues in favor of the Defendant and enter a judgment for the Defendant against the Plaintiff.

Judgment was entered in accordance with the trial court's pronouncement, and CitiBank appealed.

III.   DISCUSSION AND DECISION

CitiBank's appeal presents two points for us to decide. Each point relied on is a rescript of the arguments CitiBank made below.

POINT I

In CitiBank's first point, it contends the trial court erred in permitting Mary to assert PPBG's non-delivery as a defense in CitiBank's breach of contract action. Specifically, CitiBank argues that the trial court's judgment is . . . based on a mis-application of the law because "Regulation Z" should not have been applied in this lawsuit, in that the PPBG transaction was primarily for a business or commercial purpose. CitiBank's argument is grounded upon two implicit premises: (1) the Truth in Lending Act and its implementing regulations do not apply to this lawsuit if the single PPBG transaction at issue was for a business purpose; and (2) Mary's ability to assert non-delivery as a defense against CitiBank in this contract action is derived solely from the Truth in Lending Act and Regulation Z. CitiBank's first point fails because neither implicit premise is correct.

The Truth in Lending Act and Regulation Z Do Apply to Mary's Open End Consumer Credit Plan

The overall purpose of the Truth in Lending Act is "to assure a meaningful disclosure of credit terms so that the consumer will be able to compare more readily the various credit terms available to him and avoid the uninformed use of credit, and to protect the consumer against inaccurate and unfair credit billing and credit card practices." [TILA §102](a). As a remedial act, the Truth in Lending Act must be strictly construed against creditors and liberally construed in favor of consumers.

The Truth in Lending Act governs a number of different types of consumer credit, including one type described as an "open end consumer credit plan." *See* [TILA §127]. This phrase is derived from a combination of two other statutory definitions found in [TILA §103]:

> (h) The adjective "consumer," used with reference to a credit transaction, characterizes the transaction as one in which the party to whom credit is offered or extended is a natural person, and the money, property, or services which are the subject of the transaction are primarily for personal, family, or household purposes.

> (i) The term "open end credit plan" means a plan under which the creditor reasonably contemplates repeated transactions, which prescribes the terms of such transactions, and which provides for a finance charge which may be computed from time to time on the outstanding unpaid balance. A credit plan which is an open end credit plan within the meaning of the preceding sentence is an open end credit plan even if credit information is verified from time to time.

The designation of an extension of credit as an "open end consumer credit plan" is significant because the Truth in Lending Act and its implementing regulations specify both the nature and timing of required disclosures that must be made to the consumer before such a plan can be established. *See* [TILA §127](a) (identifying the required disclosures which the creditor must make "before opening any account under an open end consumer credit plan"); 12 C.F.R. §[10]26.5(b)(1) (requiring the creditor to "furnish the initial disclosure statement required by §[10]26.6 before the first transaction is made under the plan"); 12 C.F.R. §[10]26.6 (identifying what must be included in the creditor's initial disclosure statement). . . . We find th[e] evidence sufficient to support the conclusion that Mary's account was an open end consumer credit plan within the meaning of the Truth in Lending Act. Furthermore, CitiBank's counsel forthrightly conceded during oral argument that Mary's account was this type of plan.

Since Mary's open end consumer credit plan involved the use of a credit card, the Truth in Lending Act specifically preserves her right to assert defenses against CitiBank arising out of the PPBG transaction. . . .

At the trial, Mary presented substantial evidence proving that she met each statutory element necessary to successfully assert the defense of non-delivery against CitiBank under the Truth in Lending Act claims and defenses rule:

1. The defense arose out of the PPBG transaction, and Mary's credit card was used as the method of payment for that purchase.
2. The Mincks made a good faith attempt to resolve the issue with PPBG.
3. The amount of this transaction greatly exceeded the $50 minimum.
4. The PPBG transaction occurred in Missouri, which is the same state as the mailing address shown on Mary's billing statements from CitiBank.
5. The non-delivery defense was used solely to extinguish the remaining indebtedness on Mary's CitiBank account resulting from the single PPBG transaction at issue.

Therefore, we hold that the trial court committed no error in concluding Mary was entitled to assert the non-delivery defense against CitiBank. The Truth in Lending Act claims and defenses rule authorized Mary to assert non-delivery as a defense because her CitiBank credit card account was an open end consumer credit plan, and her credit card was used to make the PPBG purchase at issue.

In so holding, we have given due consideration to CitiBank's assertion that the Truth in Lending Act claims and defenses rule does not apply because the single PPBG purchase was for a business or commercial purpose. CitiBank's argument is based on [TILA §104](1), which defines what transactions are exempted from the scope of the Truth in Lending Act. This statute states, in pertinent part:

> This subchapter [i.e., the Truth-in-Lending Act] does not apply to the following:
>   (1) Credit transactions involving extensions of credit primarily for business, commercial, or agricultural purposes, or to government or governmental agencies or instrumentalities, or to organizations.

We find this argument unpersuasive for two reasons.

First, CitiBank's argument is inconsistent with the plain language of [TILA §170]. When an open end consumer credit plan is involved, this statute explicitly authorizes a cardholder (*i.e.*, Mary) to assert a defense against the card issuer (*i.e.*, CitiBank) "arising out of any transaction in which the credit card is used as a method of payment or extension of credit . . . ." [TILA §170](a). Since we are required to liberally construe this language in Mary's favor, we interpret the phrase, "any transaction," to mean exactly what it says. So long as a credit card was used to make a purchase on an open end consumer credit plan, the claims and defenses rule in [TILA §170] applies to "any transaction" meeting the other requirements set forth in the statute. Any less expansive interpretation of this phrase would constitute a strict, rather than a liberal, construction of this remedial statute. We decline CitiBank's invitation that we do so.

Second, CitiBank's argument ignores the fact that the relevant "transaction" here was the initial extension of credit to Mary when her CitiBank account was opened, rather than the specific transaction involving the postcard purchase from PPBG. We find the initial transaction controlling because it resulted in the creation of an open end consumer credit plan for Mary. It was this occurrence which inexorably led us to conclude that Mary was authorized by statute and regulation to assert non-delivery as a defense against CitiBank in its lawsuit.

We believe this result is entirely consistent with the discussion of the Truth in Lending Act by the United States Supreme Court in American Express Company v. Koerner, 452 U.S. 233 (1981), upon which CitiBank relies. In *Koerner*, the Supreme Court acknowledged that there can be an extension of consumer credit when an open end consumer credit account is created or renewed, as well as when individual credit card transactions occur. For the purpose of determining when the provisions of the Truth in Lending Act apply, the Supreme Court described three possible alternative tests:

> The language of [TILA §161] does not distinguish between the two types of transactions included in the definition of "credit" or indicate which of them must satisfy the definition of "consumer" in order for the section to be applicable. There are several possibilities. The relevant extension of credit may be only the creation or renewal of the account. Under this view, . . . if an account is opened by a natural person, its overall purpose must be considered. If the account is opened primarily for consumer purposes, [TILA §161] applies, even if the cardholder uses the card for an occasional nonconsumer purchase. On the other hand, the language might be interpreted to call for a transaction-by-transaction approach. With such an approach, [TILA §161] would apply if the transaction that is the subject of the dispute is a consumer credit transaction, regardless of the overall purpose of the account. A third alternative would be to combine the two approaches by holding [TILA §161] applicable to all disputes that arise under an account that is characterized as a consumer credit account as well as to any dispute concerning an individual transaction that is an extension of consumer credit, even if the overall purpose of the account is primarily a business one.

The Supreme Court, however, was not required to decide which approach should be used because it determined there had not been an extension of consumer credit under any of the alternative tests.

In the case at bar, we do reach the issue which was deferred in *Koerner* and conclude that the first of the three alternatives, which we denominate the "overall purpose" test, is the one that should be used when an open end consumer credit plan is involved. Under this test, the overall purpose of an account opened by a natural person must be considered. If the account was opened primarily for consumer purposes, the statutory and regulatory framework of the Truth in Lending Act applies, even if the cardholder occasionally uses the card for a non-consumer purchase.

We find support for this conclusion in the Official Staff Interpretations of Regulation Z. The Official Staff Commentary dealing with 12 C.F.R. §[10]26.3 (exempt transactions) notes that a creditor must determine in each case whether the extension of credit "is primarily for an exempt purpose." "Examples of business-purpose credit include: . . . A business account used occasionally for consumer purposes. Examples of consumer-purpose credit include: . . . A personal account used occasionally for business purposes." Therefore, we disagree with CitiBank's contention that the use of Mary's CitiBank credit card account to purchase non-consumer goods on one occasion prevents her from taking advantage of the Truth in Lending Act's claims and defenses rule in this case.

Mary's Use of Non-delivery as a Defense Against CitiBank Also Is Authorized by State Law

Even if we accepted CitiBank's argument in Point I that the Truth in Lending Act does not apply, our decision would not change. Like Ulysses' unfortunate sailors in *The Odyssey*, CitiBank would successfully navigate past the Charybdis of federal law only to be devoured by the Scylla of state law.[1] Expressed in less metaphorical terms, the trial court's decision to enter judgment for Mary is still correct, based exclusively on Missouri common law and statutory principles. . . .

CitiBank brought a breach of contract action against Mary for failing to pay her credit card account. The only unpaid charge on Mary's account was the PPBG purchase. As the petition expressly acknowledged, CitiBank was suing Mary as PPBG's assignee.

Missouri law is well-settled that an assignee acquires no greater rights than the assignor had at the time of the assignment. As a result, CitiBank stands in PPBG's shoes and can occupy no better position than PPBG would if it sued Mary directly. These common law principles compel the conclusion that any defense valid against PPBG is valid against its assignee, CitiBank.

Assuming PPBG had sued Mary for breach of contract and sought to recover the cost of the postcards, would she have had a valid defense against that claim? We answer this question affirmatively because PPBG never delivered the merchandise for which Mary was charged. This defense is just as effective against CitiBank as it would have been against PPBG.

---

1. Homer, *The Odyssey*, Book XII. A more homespun Homer from the Ozarks might describe CitiBank's situation as being caught between a rock and a hard place.

Regardless of whether the trial court's decision is reviewed by using the federal Truth in Lending Act or state law standards, the judgment is correct. The trial court committed no error by ruling in Mary's favor and denying CitiBank any recovery on its action for breach of contract. CitiBank's first point is denied.

POINT II

In CitiBank's second point, it contends the judgment is . . . based on a misapplication of the law because, even if Regulation Z does apply, PPBG's non-delivery of the postcards constituted a "billing error" within the meaning of the regulation. Assuming that to be true, CitiBank then argues Mary could not avoid responsibility for the PPBG purchase unless she gave CitiBank notice of the error within 60 days after the charge first appeared on her credit card statement. According to CitiBank, failure to invoke the billing error provisions of the Truth in Lending Act prohibits a consumer from thereafter relying on the claims and defenses rule if he or she is sued on the debt by the creditor.

The relevant statutory and regulatory provisions of the Truth in Lending Act dealing with billing errors are found in [TILA §161] and 12 C.F.R. §[10]26.13. Hereinafter, we generically refer to the consumer protections contained in this statute and regulation as the "billing error rule." The billing error rule gives a consumer the right, upon proper written notice, to request correction of billing errors. The notice must be received within 60 days after the creditor has sent the consumer a statement reflecting a billing error. *See* [TILA §161](a); 12 C.F.R. §[10]26.13(b). . . .

The trial court concluded that PPBG's failure to deliver the postcards did not constitute a "billing error" within the meaning of [TILA §161] and 12 C.F.R. §[10]26.13. We interpret this decision to be a rejection of CitiBank's position that the 60 day time limit for giving written notice began running in March 2000 when the PPBG charge first appeared on Mary's statement because the Mincks did not know, during any portion of this 60 day period, that they would never receive the postcards, an acceptable substitute product, or a refund from PPBG. In order to dispose of CitiBank's second point on appeal, however, it is unnecessary for us to decide whether this ruling was in error. Assuming PPBG's non-delivery of the postcards did constitute a "billing error" within the meaning of the Truth in Lending Act, Mary still was entitled to invoke the claims and defenses rule in [TILA §170] and 12 C.F.R. §[10]26.12(c). This statute and regulation are stand-alone provisions that operate independently of [TILA §161] and 12 C.F.R. §[10]26.13, which give a consumer separate and distinct rights and remedies when seeking to correct a billing error. We find support for our conclusion through a textual analysis of [TILA §161] and an examination of the Official Staff Interpretations of Regulation Z.

The only obligation imposed upon a consumer by [TILA §161] is the transmittal of an adequate written notice to the creditor within 60 days after receiving a statement containing a billing error.

Once the billing error process is properly initiated, the consumer may withhold payment of the disputed sum and obtain an abatement of collection and adverse reporting activity while the creditor investigates the issue. Nothing in the statute affirmatively imposes any penalty on the consumer for failing to take advantage of the benefits of this statute. The only penalty which can even be inferred is the loss of the abatement rights contained therein. We accept as accurate the way in which the Texas Court of Appeals summed up the purpose of [TILA §161]:

> The purpose of the protections afforded a consumer under [TILA §161] is not, after all, to change the substantive law with regard to his liability for the underlying debt, but to protect him from the intimidating process of bargaining over a disputed debt with a creditor in a superior bargaining position. Without such protections, the creditor may use that bargaining power to encourage payment of even an illegitimate debt by threatening to force the consumer to expend substantial time and money to protect his rights.

Dillard Department Stores, Inc. v. Owens, 951 S.W.2d 915, 918 (Tex. App. 1997).

In contrast, the statute does affirmatively impose a penalty upon a creditor that ignores the provisions of this statute. This conclusion follows from [TILA §161](e), which states:

> (e) Effect of noncompliance with requirements by creditor. Any creditor who fails to comply with the requirements of this section or [TILA §162] of this title forfeits any right to collect from the obligor the amount indicated by the obligor under paragraph (2) of subsection (a) of this section, and any finance charges thereon, except that the amount required to be forfeited under this subsection may not exceed $50.

Thus, [TILA §161] only affects the amount of the debt in the event of a creditor's noncompliance with the statute. When this occurs, however, the creditor may still sue on the debt if there is a remaining balance due after subtracting the $50 forfeiture sum. If we were to accept CitiBank's argument, it would mean that a consumer who failed to utilize this billing error statute—through ignorance, inadvertence, or purposeful action—would completely forfeit his right to contest the debt owed in a collection lawsuit. The creditor, on the other hand, could knowingly and willfully ignore its responsibilities under this statute and only be penalized a maximum of $50. In our view, this interpretation of the statute leads to an absurd result and turns topsy-turvy our duty to liberally construe the Truth in Lending Act in a consumer's favor. Again, we decline to do so.

Our construction of how the billing error rule operates also is supported by the Official Staff Interpretations of Regulation Z . . . . In this very specialized area of law governing commerce in credit, we believe the Federal Reserve Board's interpretation of the Truth in Lending Act and its implementing regulations are entitled to substantial deference as we analyze the issues presented in CitiBank's appeal.

The regulation dealing with a consumer's right to correct billing errors is 12 C.F.R. §[10]26.13. The regulation dealing with a consumer's right to assert claims and defenses is 12 C.F.R. §[10]26.12. The Official Staff Commentary for 12 C.F.R. §[10]26.12 states, in pertinent part:

> 12(c) Right of cardholder to assert claims or defenses against card issuer.
>
> 1. *Relationship to §[10]26.13*. The §[10]26.12(c) credit card "holder in due course" provision deals with the consumer's right to assert against the card issuer a claim or defense concerning property or services purchased with a credit card, if the merchant

has been unwilling to resolve the dispute. Even though certain merchandise disputes, such as non-delivery of goods, may also constitute "billing errors" under §[10]26.13, that section operates independently of §[10]26.12(c). The cardholder whose asserted billing error involves undelivered goods may institute the error resolution procedures of §[10]26.13; but whether or not the cardholder has done so, the cardholder may assert claims or defenses under §[10]26.12(c). Conversely, the consumer may pay a disputed balance and thus have no further right to assert claims and defenses, but still may assert a billing error if notice of that billing error is given in the proper time and manner. An assertion that a particular transaction resulted from unauthorized use of the card could also be both a "defense" and a billing error.

Thus, the Federal Reserve Board recognizes that the claims and defenses rule operates independently of the billing error rule. As the Board's analysis of the proper relationship between these two different rules and their respective remedies is not demonstrably irrational, we accept it as dispositive here.

For all of the foregoing reasons, we reject CitiBank's argument that a consumer's failure to give a creditor timely notice of a billing error precludes the consumer from later invoking the claim and defense provisions of [TILA §170] and 12 C.F.R. §[10]26.12(c) if the creditor sues on the debt. CitiBank's second point is denied.

IV. CONCLUSION

Mary was entitled to assert non-delivery as a valid defense against CitiBank in its action for breach of contract. The use of this non-delivery defense was authorized both by the Truth in Lending Act and by state law. Furthermore, the use of this defense was not precluded by the billing error rule found in the Truth in Lending Act. Therefore, the trial court ruled correctly when it denied CitiBank any recovery and entered judgment in Mary's favor. The judgment is affirmed.

Problem Set 1

1.1. Ben Darrow (your banker client from First State Bank of Matacora (FSB), a small rural bank) stopped by late yesterday afternoon to show you a "bizarre" letter that he received in the mail yesterday. He mentions that because of a recent consolidation he now oversees his bank's credit-card issuing operations, even though he has little experience in the area. The letter is from one of FSB's cardholders and describes a $475 mountain bike that the cardholder recently purchased using an FSB Visa card. The letter explains that the bike's gear-shifting mechanism does not function properly and asks FSB to "refund" to the customer the amount shown on the customer's current Visa statement for the purchase of the bike. The letter encloses payment for $100 (the amount of the other charges shown on the statement).

Ben tells you that he is completely befuddled. "Why should I care whether the stupid bike works? If she doesn't like it, let her take it up with the merchant.

My only job is to make sure I pay the merchant for her charges and then to make sure that she pays me. What does she think I am, some kind of traveling Better Business Bureau? Can you believe the nerve of some people?" Do you share Ben's assessment of the "nerve" of the letter writer? Is the writer entitled to a refund? To anything? Do you need to know anything about the charges on her statement to ascertain Ben's obligations to her? TILA §170; Regulation Z, §1026.12(c). Would it matter to you if the charge was made on the cardholder's American Express card (issued to her by the cardholder's employer) as opposed to her personal card?

1.2.   Your friend Willie McCarver runs a struggling computer-services company. Talking to you over dinner, Willie tells you that he has gotten into a tight spot with some of his most important suppliers. If he does not pay them $10,000 in the next week, they are going to stop shipping goods to him, which would finish his business in a matter of days. Willie thinks that some highly profitable orders are "just around the corner." In the meantime, he thinks that he has hit on a way to keep his suppliers satisfied and wants your advice. Fortuitously, he received a new credit card in the mail yesterday, with a credit limit of $10,000. He plans to use the card to pay the suppliers $10,000 to reduce the amount that he owes for past shipments. Mindful of some advice you gave him several years ago about his rights on credit-card charges, he figures that he can dispute the charges (perhaps claiming that the goods were defective) and defer payment to the credit-card issuer indefinitely. He wants to know if you think the scheme will work and how he can design it to hold off the creditors as long as possible. TILA §§104(1), 170; Regulation Z, §1026.12(c).

1.3.   A few hours after your discussion with Ben in Problem 1.1, Ben calls back to ask you how he would be able to respond to a cardholder's defenses in cases where the cardholder could assert those defenses. "How am I supposed to prove that her mountain bike works? I don't sell mountain bikes. I drive a car to work. I haven't ridden a bicycle since I was 15 years old. Do I just have to give her the money?" What do you tell Ben?

1.4.   Jodi Kay from CountryBank calls to discuss a troubling article that she read in this morning's newspaper. The article reports that a client of hers named CompUPlus recently filed for bankruptcy in the face of rampant consumer complaints about CompUPlus's newest line of laptop computers. Jodi thinks that she is in good shape because (she says) she has never made any loans to the client. The only service that she has provided has been as an acquirer processing CompUPlus's mail-order credit-card sales. Those sales recently have been substantial: $150,000 over the last three months. Does that relationship put her employer, CountryBank, at risk? TILA §170; Regulation Z, §1026.12(c).

1.5.   Cliff Janeway (a book dealer and frequent client of yours) drops in to discuss a difficulty he is having with Bulstrode Bank, the acquirer that clears credit-card transactions for him. Cliff found out this morning that Bulstrode has bounced several checks of Cliff's during the last week. Cliff is unhappy because the checks should have been covered easily by funds deposited into his account several days earlier in the form of credit-card receivables from his business. When Cliff called Bulstrode to complain, Bulstrode explained that it had adopted a new policy with respect to credit-card services. Under that policy, Bulstrode plans to place a hold on Cliff's credit-card deposits for 45 days after the date that Cliff deposited them to protect against the possibility that Bulstrode will be obligated to disgorge funds to card issuers if cardholders challenge any of the relevant transactions. Cliff wants to know if the bank can do this. "Isn't there some law requiring the bank to release the funds to me in just a few days?" UCC §§4-104(a)(9), 4-214(a), 4-215(e); Regulation CC, §§229.10-229.12; TILA §170; Regulation Z, §1026.12(c).

Assignment 2: Error and Fraud in Credit-Card Transactions

The credit-card system is as vulnerable to mistake and chicanery as any other payment system. Given its large place in the economy, though, it should come as no surprise that the system has well-developed institutions for dealing with those problems. Despite recent well-publicized problems, the system's resistance to fraud is impressive: 6 cents of fraudulent transactions out of every $100 of transaction volume as of 2015. This assignment discusses two general problems: erroneous charges and unauthorized charges.

A. Erroneous Charges

The simplest problem is the erroneous charge: an item that appears on a credit-card statement that does not reflect an actual transaction on the account. In addition to the right to withhold payment set out in TILA §170 (described in Assignment 1), TILA §161 sets out detailed provisions for resolving alleged billing errors related to credit cards (indirectly at issue in *Mincks*). See also Regulation Z, §1026.13 (offering details on procedures for resolving billing errors). To challenge a billing error under TILA, the cardholder must provide written notice to the issuer within 60 days of the date on which the creditor sent the relevant statement to the cardholder. TILA §161(a).

The statute gives a broad meaning to the term "billing error," so that it includes not only claims that the cardholder did not make the charge in question but also claims that the merchant failed to deliver the goods and services covered by the charge in question, and even requests for additional clarification about the charge. TILA §161(b); Regulation Z, §1026.13(a). Thus, if Cliff's statement shows a charge for a purchase from Amazon.com, Cliff could use the billing-error procedures not only to press a claim that he never made the purchase, but also in cases where he did purchase the books so long as he can claim that the seller never delivered the books or that he wants further information justifying the charge.

If the cardholder sends the proper notice, the creditor must send a written acknowledgment of the notice within 30 days and must resolve the claim within two billing cycles. If the cardholder alleges that the merchant failed to deliver the goods or services covered by the charge, the issuer cannot reject the claim without first "conduct[ing] a reasonable investigation and determin[ing] that the property or services were actually delivered . . . as agreed." Regulation Z, §1026.13(f) n.31; see TILA §161(a)(3)(B)(ii). If the issuer does not accept the cardholder's allegation, the issuer must (within the two-billing-cycle period) give the cardholder a written explanation of the issuer's reason for not correcting the charge. TILA §161(a); Regulation Z, §1026.13(c)(2), (f). Most important from the cardholder's perspective, the creditor is barred from closing or restricting the cardholder's account for failure to pay the disputed amount during the pendency of the dispute. TILA §161(d); Regulation Z, §1026.13(d). The issuer can, however, accrue a finance charge against the disputed amount. The finance charge would be due only if the dispute is resolved against the card-holder. Regulation Z, §§1026.13(d)(1) n.30, 1026.13(g)(1). Finally, the statute provides a modest penalty for failure to follow the procedures, requiring the creditor to forfeit the first $50 of the charge in dispute. TILA §161(e).

The following case illustrates how those provisions operate in practice.

Belmont v. Associates National Bank (Delaware)

119 F. Supp. 2d 149 (E.D.N.Y. 2000)

Trager, District Judge.

Plaintiff Peter Belmont, an attorney licensed to practice in the State of New York, but acting pro se in this matter, brought this suit against Associates National Bank (Delaware) ("Associates") under the Truth in Lending Act ("TILA" or the "Act"), 15 U.S.C. §1601 et seq., and Regulation Z thereunder, 12 C.F.R. §[10]26.13, for failure to properly respond to a notice of billing error and for having threatened to make adverse credit reports while the billing error remained unresolved.

Peter Belmont alleges that on a monthly statement dated May 5, 1998, he was improperly billed for charges made on his son's Associates Mastercard credit card account. While Associates maintained that Peter Belmont was a co-obligor on his son's account and was thus liable for charges on the account after his son filed for bankruptcy, Peter Belmont questioned whether he was an obligor and demanded documentary proof of his obligation. Peter Belmont claims that Associates failed to comply with the requirements of TILA in responding to his notice.

Associates has moved for dismissal of, or in the alternative, for summary judgment on, all claims brought by Peter Belmont. Peter Belmont filed a cross-motion for summary judgment in response.

BACKGROUND

Associates alleges that its records indicate that on September 21, 1987, Peter Belmont and his son, Jeremy Belmont, opened a Boatmen's Bank of St. Louis ("Boatmen's") Mastercard credit card account which was later purchased by Associates. Peter Belmont acknowledges that in September 1987 he did co-sign for a credit card account with his son, but does not recall doing so with either Boatmen's or Associates and states that he no longer has a copy of the credit card application. [Ed.: It is apparent that neither Boatmen's nor Associates has a copy either.]

On April 6, 1992, Peter Belmont sent a letter entitled "NOTICE OF REVOCATION OF CO_SIGNER_SHIP" to Consumer Loan Center, P.O. Box 9101, Boston, MA 02209-9101, regarding a Mastercard account numbered 5417-6710-0001-9848, in which he stated that he wished to be removed as a co-signer on his son's account. In the letter, Peter Belmont noted that the account was "in arrears in the amount of $48.00 and going into a 30-day late status." Id. He further stated: "I no longer wish to guarantee borrowing against this account or to have my credit-worthiness affected by the failure of the account's holder, Mr. Jeremy Belmont, to pay his bills in timely fashion." With the letter, Peter Belmont sent a check, dated April 5, 1992, for $48.00 to "The Massachusetts Co." with "Jeremy Belmont 5417 6710 0001 9848 M/C" specified on the check's memo line. See id. On the canceled check, cashed at the Texas Commerce Bank-Dallas on April 11, 1992, the account number was crossed-off on the memo line and replaced by the account number "5419312700002648," the Associates account number held by Jeremy Belmont from January 1993 until October 1995.

Associates denies ever having received Peter Belmont's April 1992 letter and avers that the Consumer Loan Center address specified in the letter was never an address used by Associates. Associates, however, offers no explanation of how its account number came to be placed on the check Peter Belmont enclosed with the letter.

At any rate, the Associates statements on the account sent to Jeremy Belmont at his addresses in Massachusetts and California from January 1993 through April 1998 continued to list Peter Belmont as an addressee. The elder Belmont, however, has resided at 166 Columbia Heights, Brooklyn, N.Y. 11201-2105 since September 1992. . . .

Then, on April 28, 1998, Associates removed Jeremy Belmont from the account when he filed for bankruptcy. Associates claims that his son's default made Peter Belmont the primary cardholder on the account and thus, solely responsible for payment of the debt. As a result, Associates sent the next monthly statement, dated May 5, 1998, to "Peter A Belmont, 166 Columbia Heights, Brooklyn, N.Y. 11201-2105." This statement showed that the account had been assessed finance charges and a late charge that brought the balance owed to $1,895.49 and stated that a minimum payment of $413.49 was due on May 30, 1998.

On May 15, 1998, Peter Belmont sent Associates a six-page letter (dated May 13, 1998) by certified mail, return receipt requested, with the caption "NOTICE OF BELIEVED BILLING ERROR AND REQUEST FOR DOCUMENTARY EVIDENCE OF CONSUMER INDEBTEDNESS." Associates received the letter on May 19, 1998. In the letter, Peter Belmont stated that he did not admit to being an obligor on the account and believed the bill for $1,898.49 was in error because he had no contractual obligation to pay any amount borrowed under the account. Specifically, Peter Belmont wrote: "The listing on this BILL of my name and address is, I believe, a computational or similar billing error of an accounting nature." Further, Peter Belmont stated that if he were proven to be obligated in some way, he would continue to challenge the amount due as a billing error, because he had never had prior correspondence from Associates, such as billing statements or other documents detailing the charges. Finally, Peter Belmont demanded that Associates provide him with documentary evidence, including contracts, agreements and applications executed by him for the account, as well as copies of any written communications sent to him by Associates or any other lender pertaining to the account.

On June 23, 1998, Peter Belmont sent by certified mail, return receipt requested, a second letter to Associates, that was "substantially identical" to his May 13, 1998 letter, Am. Compl. ¶8. Associates received this second letter on June 30, 1998.

On June 25, 1998—thirty-seven days after Peter Belmont's first letter was received—Associates sent Peter Belmont a letter . . . , which stated:

> We have made several attempts to reach you [apparently not in writing] but have been unsuccessful. Our goal is to work out a solution for your delinquent balance and help bring your account to a current status. . . . Do not allow this situation to become more serious. Protecting your credit is important to you both today and in the future.

Enclosed with the letter was another billing statement showing that the account balance was now $1,959.88, with a total amount due of $266.00.

On July 20, 1998—sixty-two days after Peter Belmont's first letter was received and twenty days after his second letter was received—Associates sent Peter Belmont a letter [that stated]: "We have received your recent correspondence regarding the above-referenced account. We have ordered additional information in order to respond to your correspondence properly."

Associates sent Peter Belmont a second letter . . . also dated July 20, 1998, stating that the account had been opened on September 21, 1987 in the names of Peter Belmont and Jeremy Belmont, and adding that plaintiff became the primary cardholder on the account when Jeremy Belmont filed for bankruptcy. The letter stated that Associates was unable to find a copy of the original application and further advised Peter Belmont that if he wanted a copy of the original application, he would have to contact Boatmen's. [Ed.: Boatmen's had merged into NationsBank in 1996.]

On July 22, 1998, Associates sent Peter Belmont [yet] another letter . . . which was identical to its June 25th letter, except that the amount due was specified as $316.00 and the account balance had risen to $2,024.29. This letter also included the same warning regarding Peter Belmont's credit.

On July 29, 1998, Peter Belmont sent Associates a third letter bearing the caption "NOTICE OF BELIEVED BILLING ERROR AND REQUEST FOR DOCUMENTARY EVIDENCE OF CONSUMER INDEBTEDNESS." In the letter, Peter Belmont wrote that he believed the entire balance on the account—$1,959.88 (which included the $1,895.49 he had previously contested, as well as $29.00 in additional late charges and $35.39 in finance charges which were newly billed on the statement for the period ending June 5, 1998)—was erroneously billed. Peter Belmont referenced his previous letters to Associates and stated that the July 20, 1998 letter signed by Patrick Wilson "failed to satisfy [his] demand for documentation in any respect." Finally, Peter Belmont stated that he believed that his April 6, 1992 letter to Consumer Loan Center absolved him of responsibility for Jeremy Belmont's credit card debts.

On August 5, 1998, Associates sent Peter Belmont another monthly billing statement for the Mastercard account. The statement showed that no payment had been made, but a finance charge of $37.79 and a late charge of $18.00 had been assessed, raising the balance to $2,080.08, with a minimum payment of $748.08 due on August 30, 1998. Finally, this statement advised: "Your account is seriously past due. Send in the total amount due immediately."

On August 10, 1998, Associates sent Peter Belmont another letter . . . , which reiterated information from the second July 20th letter, and again asserted that Peter Belmont was the sole obligor on the account because of his son's bankruptcy filing. The letter also responded to Peter Belmont's belief that his 1992 request to be removed as a joint cardholder applied to the Associates account by stating:

> [O]ur records do not indicate that your name was ever removed as a primary card holder on this account. Please forward supporting documentation from Boatmen's . . . confirming that your name was removed from this account . . . and we will adjust our records accordingly. Unfortunately, we are not legally obligated to provide you a copy of your original application. In order to obtain a copy of your original application, you will need to contact Boatmen's. . . .

[The record also indicates that a credit report issued in August 1988 for Peter Belmont by Trans Union, a national credit reporting firm, reported the delinquency in question.]

On June 18, 1999, Peter Belmont filed his original complaint in this action, seeking relief under 15 U.S.C. [TILA §§130](a)(2)(A), 1[3]0(a)(3) and 16[1](e). On that same day, Associates sent Peter Belmont a letter, signed by Todd Mitchell, an Associates vice president, which advised that Associates had deleted the "tradeline from all credit reporting agencies. Nothing is due." . . .

DISCUSSION

. . .

(1)

Peter Belmont brought this action under [TILA §130], alleging that Associates failed to comply with the billing-error correction provisions of TILA, 15 U.S.C. §§1666-1666a. Peter Belmont claims that defendant made a billing error when it sent him the May 5, 1998 billing statement for the Mastercard account numbered 5457-1500-5024-6016 because he had never borrowed on the account, and because he believed that his 1992 letter released him of responsibility for his son's debts. Peter Belmont further claims that Associates's response to his May 13, 1998 Notice of Billing Error did not comply with the provisions of TILA. . . .

Associates argues that Peter Belmont's letter of May 13, 1998 is not a billing error notice within the meaning of [TILA §161]—and hence did not trigger Associates's statutory obligation to respond—for two reasons. First, defendant contends that the "Wrong-Person Error" alleged by Peter Belmont does not constitute a "billing error" under [TILA §161](b). Second, defendant argues that even if the error alleged by Peter Belmont does constitute a billing error, his Notice of Billing Error did not conform to the requirements of [TILA §161](a). Each of defendant's arguments is considered in turn below.

a.   Billing Error . . .

Peter Belmont contends that a creditor's demand for payment on an account from someone who is (allegedly) not an obligor on the account, which he describes as a "Wrong-Person Error," qualifies as a billing error under paragraphs (1), (2), and (5) of [TILA §161](b). In response, Associates argues that [TILA §161] by the plain meaning of its language, simply does not cover alleged errors of personal identification. Associates characterizes [TILA §161] as "a transaction dispute statute. It is not a statute that applies to questions of who is obligated to pay correct billing charges to the account." . . .

[T]his case presents an issue which appears to be one of first impression in the federal courts, namely whether the "Wrong-Person Error" alleged by plaintiff is encompassed by [TILA §161](b). It is necessary, therefore, to look first to the language of the statute. In doing so, it must be remembered that TILA is a remedial act intended to protect consumers, see [TILA §102] (a) . . . and, as such, its provisions are to be construed liberally in favor of consumers.

In this light, the "Wrong-Person Error" alleged by plaintiff can be deemed to fall under paragraphs (1) and (2) of [TILA §161](b). Under paragraph (1) of [TILA §161](b), a billing error includes "a statement of credit which was not made to the obligor or, if made, was not the amount reflected on such statement." [TILA §161](b)(1). Under TILA, "credit" simply refers to a right that a creditor grants a debtor to defer payments of debt, whereas an "extension of credit" occurs when an individual opens or renews an account that lets him do so. Here, although it appears that Peter Belmont opened a credit account and gained an "extension of credit" in 1987, he contended in his May 13, 1998 letter to Associates that he was not an obligor on the Associates account and, thus, implied that Associates never extended credit to him in the amount stated on the May 5, 1998 billing statement, viz., the entire amount of the statement, $1,898.49.[6] Nothing in paragraph (1) indicates that its scope is limited to particular charges to the account, as opposed to the entire account itself. Thus, plaintiff's "Wrong-Person Error" falls within the language of paragraph (1), liberally construed.

For similar reasons, plaintiff's "Wrong-Person Error" also qualifies as a billing error under [TILA §161](b)(2). Peter Belmont's May 13, 1998 letter clearly requested clarification, including documentary evidence, regarding whether Associates had, in fact, extended him the credit reflected on the May 5, 1998 statement, viz., the entire balance of $1,898.49.

Whether, as argued by plaintiff, the "Wrong-Person Error" could also qualify as a "computation error or similar error of an accounting nature" under [TILA §161] (b)(5) presents a more difficult question of interpretation, which need not, and will not, be addressed given that the error alleged by Belmont clearly falls within the language of paragraphs (1) and (2), liberally construed.

---

6. Although it remains an open issue whether plaintiff was in fact an obligor on the account after his 1992 letter, the disposition of that question has no bearing on the legal issue of whether a notice that alleges that the plaintiff is not an obligor qualifies as a notice of "billing error" under [TILA §161] (b). Section [161]'s requirements that a creditor promptly respond to consumer inquiries is triggered upon receipt of a timely notice of "billing error" regardless of whether the consumer who sent the notice was correct in his belief that an error had been made. Simply put, the fact that a TILA plaintiff was incorrect in his belief that a billing error had occurred is not a defense to an action under §[130].

b.   Sufficiency of Plaintiff's Notice of Billing Error

Associates argues in the alternative that even if Peter Belmont's claims qualify as a billing error, it had no obligation to respond to his letters because Belmont did not comply with the notice requirements of [TILA §161]. . . .

Peter Belmont's May 13, 1998 "Notice of Billing Error" letter, which Associates received on May 19, 1998—well within the sixty-day period following the May 5, 1998, statement—(1) repeatedly stated his name and account number, and (2) indicated the reason he believed a billing error occurred, as well as (3) the amount of such error. In point of fact, after examining Peter Belmont's letter (which is couched throughout in language mirroring that of [TILA §161]), it is doubtful that Associates has ever received a more perspicuous notice of billing error or one that adheres more closely to the requirements of [TILA §161].

Associates's suggestion that plaintiff's letter was not recognizable as, and is not, a valid notice of billing error—despite the all-capitals heading on the first page which read "NOTICE OF BELIEVED BILLING ERROR AND REQUEST FOR DOCUMENTARY EVIDENCE OF CONSUMER INDEBTEDNESS"—appears to be simply a transparent, post-hoc excuse for its tardy and incomplete compliance with TILA. In this regard, it should be noted that there is absolutely nothing in the correspondence between Associates and Peter Belmont that suggests that defendant did not recognize Peter Belmont's May 13, 1998 letter, or either of his two, equally meticulous subsequent letters, for what they manifestly were: notices of billing error under [TILA §161].

Nonetheless, Associates contends that the plaintiff's May 13, 1998 letter did not indicate that he was disputing a particular charge or alleging a "particular billing error" and the amount of such error. However, Peter Belmont's letter clearly indicates at several different points that he believed the amount of the billing error to be $1,895.49; indeed, the heading of the letter's second paragraph reads "*The amount for which I was billed, and which ENTIRE AMOUNT I believe to be erroneously billed, as to me, is: $1,895.49.*" . . .

(2) . . .

In this case, Associates received Peter Belmont's first Notice of Billing Error on May 19, 1998, but did not send any correspondence to Peter Belmont regarding the notice until July 20, 1998—sixty-two days later. Associates's July 20, 1998 correspondence to Belmont consisted of two letters, the first of which appears to be a form response letter, while the second more directly responds to his notice(s) of billing error. On its face, defendant's response violates [TILA §161](a)(3)(A), which requires a creditor to acknowledge the receipt of a notice of billing error within thirty days.

In its defense, Associates contends: "Both letters were mailed to the plaintiff within . . . [the] two complete billing cycle period allowed by [TILA §161](a)(B) [*sic*]. Indeed, at least one was mailed within the 30 days required by [TILA §161](a)(A) [*sic*]." However, Associates's argument is again based on an untenable interpretation of the statute. Although it is true that Associates's July 20th correspondence came within two complete billing cycles of the May 5, 1998 statement, [TILA

§161](a)(3)(B) states a requirement in addition to, not in lieu of, [TILA §161](a)(3)(A), which sets forth the 30-day written acknowledgment requirement.

Finally, Associates's defense that at least one letter was sent within the thirty-day period of [TILA §161](a)(3)(A) appears to be based on the fact that Associates's July 20th letters were sent within thirty days of Belmont's *second* Notice of Billing Error. However, the fact that Associates's response would have been timely as to Peter Belmont's second letter, does not excuse Associates for not responding to his initial notice until sixty-two days after it was received.

Moreover, even if the July 20th letters had been preceded by a timely acknowledgment of receipt of Peter Belmont's May 13th notice, they still would not have complied with [TILA §161](a)(3)(B). [TILA §161](a)(3)(B) is not satisfied simply by showing that the creditor sent any response at all to the notice of billing error; rather, it requires that the creditor either (1) make the appropriate corrections to the account, thereby remedying the billing error, or (2) send a written explanation or clarification, including copies of any documentary evidence requested. See [TILA §161](a)(3)(B). Associates's July 20th correspondence did neither.

On this point, Associates contends that "one of the [response] letters ... provides a written explanation as to why defendant Associates believes the plaintiff was liable for the undisputed charges on the account. This is all that is required by [TILA §161](a)(B)(ii) [*sic*]." On the contrary, what is required by [TILA §161](a)(3)(B)(ii) in this case is that "copies of documentary evidence of the obligor's indebtedness" be provided in accord with plaintiff's request. [TILA §161](a)(3)(B)(ii). No such documentation was provided with the July 20th letters, and while it may be that the pertinent documentary evidence rested with Boatmen's or some other prior holder of the account, even that would not release Associates of its statutory obligation. Therefore, Associates did not comply with the "procedure upon receipt of notice [of billing error] by creditor" prescribed by [TILA §161](a)(3).

Nonetheless, Associates argues that even if their response letters were not sufficient for timely compliance with [TILA §161], it still has established a good faith defense under [TILA §130](f). Section [130](f) states that no liability under the Act shall apply "to any act done or omitted in good faith in conformity with any rule, regulation, or interpretation thereof by the [Federal Reserve] Board." [TILA §130](f). However, nowhere does Associates assert that it mistakenly relied on any rule, regulation or interpretation of the Federal Reserve Board in fashioning its response to plaintiff's Notice of Billing Error. Accordingly, Associates's argument under §[130](f) has no merit.

Because Associates manifestly did not comply with the 30-day written acknowledgment requirement of [TILA §161](a)(3)(A) and because it has not established its entitlement to a good faith defense under §[130](f), its actions in failing to respond to Peter Belmont's May 13, 1998 letter until July 20, 1998, constitute a violation of [TILA §161](a)(3).

(3)

Peter Belmont also claims that Associates violated [TILA §162](a) and 12 C.F.R. §[10]26.13(d)(2) when it made or threatened to make an adverse credit report while his Notice of Billing Error remained unresolved.

Peter Belmont alleges that Associates threatened his credit rating during the pendency of his billing error dispute in its letters dated June 25, 1998 and July 22, 1998. On June 25, 1998, Associates, despite having received Peter Belmont's Notice of Billing Error on May 19, 1998, wrote: "Do not allow this situation to become more serious. Protecting your credit is important to you both today and in the future." Then, on July 22, 1998, after having received two additional notices of billing error that reported the same believed billing error, but before it had complied with its obligations under [TILA §161](a)(3)(B)(ii) to provide plaintiff with the documentary evidence he requested, Associates sent another letter to Peter Belmont that contained the same warning. Finally, while all three notices of billing error remained outstanding, Associates notified a credit agency, Trans Union, of Belmont's allegedly delinquent payments. It is, therefore, clear that Associates made an adverse credit report during Peter Belmont's pending billing error dispute.

Associates proffers no explanation or defense, other than those discussed and found unavailing above, for its actions with respect to Peter Belmont's credit rating. Because Associates's two letters constitute implicit threats to Belmont's credit rating, and the evidence indicates that Associates actually did make an adverse credit report to Trans Union after receipt of a valid notice of billing error, but before complying with its obligations under [TILA §161](a)(3), Associates violated [TILA §162].

(4)

Finally, Associates argues that if Belmont was not obligated on the account (as he at one time claimed and possibly still does claim), then he is not eligible for the protections accorded to "obligor[s]" by [TILA §§161-162]. Given the remedial nature of TILA, Congress's intent to protect consumers, and the courts' mandate that TILA be liberally construed, the term "obligor[s]" must necessarily be construed to include those whom the creditor claims are obligors, as well as individuals who are in fact obligors in the contract law sense. Otherwise, there would be a lacuna in the statute, and an important area in the statute's remedial scheme would be left unprotected. A consumer who believes that he is not obligated under a credit account, and promptly notifies the creditor of the mistake through a proper notice of billing error, deserves the broad protections that Congress intended under the Act.

The need for such protections [is] particularly illustrated by Associates's actions in this case and its ability to harm Peter Belmont's credit even if he is not an obligor and was not obligated to Associates at the time of the May 5, 1998 statement. Associates chose to treat Peter Belmont as if he were an obligor, threatened his credit and, indeed, was even able to carry out its threats, as evidenced by the Trans Union credit report which detailed adverse information about Peter Belmont. Thus, whether or not Peter Belmont is actually obligated on the account has no bearing on whether he has standing to bring this action under TILA. Accordingly,

Peter Belmont does have standing to bring this suit under TILA to the extent that he is alleging a "Wrong-Person Error."

(5)

Having found that Associates violated TILA and that Peter Belmont has standing to invoke the Act's remedies, it is necessary to determine the appropriate TILA remedy.

Defendants argue that even if violations occurred, Peter Belmont should not be awarded penalties under the Act. Associates argues that the penalty provision applicable under the facts of this case is [TILA §161](e), which provides that a creditor who fails to comply with the requirements of [TILA §161] forfeits any right to collect on the amount contested in the notice of billing error or any associated finance charges, except that the amount forfeited is not to exceed $50. See [TILA §161](e). As defendant would have it, if Peter Belmont's April 6, 1992 letter was insufficient to remove him from the account and he is deemed liable for the $1,895.49 or any other sum on the account, Associates, then, could collect whatever total sum was found due after $50 was subtracted in accord with [TILA §161](e). Associates, however, contends that because it has "forgiven" the $1,895.49 debt owed by plaintiff, "the plaintiff has already recouped any amount he may have been entitled to under these provisions."

Associates's argument is flawed in two respects. First, it is not entirely clear whether Associates's letter of June 18, 1999 stating that "[n]othing is due," constitutes a binding forgiveness of debt. In light of defendant's argument, however, and to avoid unnecessarily reaching the question of whether Peter Belmont is still an obligor on the Associates account, Associates will be enjoined from collecting from Peter Belmont the first $50 on the account in accordance with [TILA §161](e).

Second, the forfeiture provision of [TILA §161](e) is not the sole remedy for Associates's violations in this case. Associates gives short shrift to the penalty provision of [TILA §130](a)(2)(A) which provides a penalty of "twice the amount of any finance charge in connection with the transaction . . . except that the liability . . . shall not be less than $100 nor greater than $1,000" for violations of [TILA §§161 and 162]." [TILA §130](a)(2)(A). Associates argues that Peter Belmont is not entitled to recoup a finance charge because he has not paid one.

The purpose of TILA, however, is not solely for plaintiffs to recoup finance charges wrongfully paid; rather, it is to assure that creditors comply with TILA's provisions, including those regarding the proper handling of billing errors. See [TILA §102](a). The goals of TILA—to provide for prompt disclosure of the basis for charges and to enable consumers to resolve disputes without fear that the creditor will make adverse credit reports during the pendency of such disputes—would not be served if the only protection offered to consumers was that they were forgiven finance charges that they were never obligated to pay, or refunded finance charges that they should not have paid because they were erroneously billed. Thus, even if a particular obligor is incorrect in his belief that a billing error has

occurred, he is still entitled under the Act to a prompt response from the creditor disclosing the basis of his liability. Indeed, the irrelevance of actual damages
is what makes §[130](a)(2)(A) a *penalty* provision. Therefore, regardless of what
Peter Belmont's obligor status is and regardless of whether he actually paid any
finance charges, Peter Belmont is entitled to recovery of twice the finance charge
in the transaction under the penalty provision of §[130](a).[11]

In this case, when Associates erroneously billed Peter Belmont $1,895.49 on
May 5, 1998, that amount included finance charges which had accrued over the
history of the account for which it asserted Belmont was responsible as an obligor.
The question thus becomes: What is the "finance charge in the transaction" under
the facts of this case? . . .

Taking into consideration that the account was fully paid, i.e., had a zero
balance and no finance charges, from January 1994 until April 1995, it seems
most reasonable to consider the finance charges accumulated on the account
from April 1995 until May 1998, when the alleged billing error occurred, in cal-
culating the applicable penalty. The total accumulated finance charges from April
1995 to May 1998 amount to $769.13. This accumulated total finance charge
on the account, when doubled, exceeds the maximum of $1,000 allowed by
§[130](a). Therefore, the $1,000 maximum shall be granted to Peter Belmont as a
penalty for Associates's failure to comply with [TILA §§161 and 162].

(6)

Peter Belmont also seeks an award of reasonable attorney's fees pursuant to [TILA
§130](a)(3). . . .

Although TILA is remedial legislation intended to protect consumers, its
attorney's fee provision does not extend to attorneys who bring claims as pro se
litigants. While the issue of the availability of attorney's fees to a pro se attorney
in TILA actions is another matter of first impression, Supreme Court and appeals
court precedents on similar fee-shifting provisions of other federal remedial statutes
compel this result. [I omit a lengthy discussion of that question.]

There is, however, no corresponding case law limiting the availability of an
award of costs under §[130](a). Accordingly, Peter Belmont is entitled to an award
of his costs in this action.

The provisions of TILA directly delay the issuer's right to collect from a
cardholder that questions the correctness of the charge. As with the right to
withhold payment discussed in Assignment 1, implementation of that provision standing alone would place a significant burden on the issuer because
the issuer ordinarily is not in a position to demonstrate the correctness of the
charge. The most that the issuer is likely to know is that the issuer received the

---

11. Although Associates violated TILA on several occasions by continuing to send Peter Belmont
billing statements after it received his notices of billing error and by threatening and then damaging
his credit history, Peter Belmont is foreclosed by statute from recovering separate penalties for each
violation. See [TILA §130](g).

charge from the acquirer acting on behalf of the merchant. The credit-card networks solve that problem just as they do the analogous problem arising from the right to withhold payment: They allow the issuer to pass the disputed charge back to the acquirer. The acquirer, in turn, has a right to pass the charge back to the merchant, putting the onus on the merchant to justify the charge.

B.   Unauthorized Charges

Erroneous charges may be irritating and occur with some regularity, but they do not present a serious problem for the system because they tend to reflect innocent errors, rather than the loss of money to parties outside the system. Unauthorized charges, on the other hand, are a more serious matter because they reflect attempts by interlopers to obtain goods and services without paying for them, leaving participants in the credit-card system to bear the cost of those purchases. Although they have declined in recent decades, losses from unauthorized charges remain quite large: Industry fraud losses amount to more than a billion dollars a year in the United States alone.

The most significant feature of the system is the strong protection for cardholders on whose accounts unauthorized charges are made. Specifically, TILA §133(a)(1)(B) limits the cardholder's liability for unauthorized charges to a maximum of $50. Under TILA, that $50 limit is an absolute ceiling. Nothing in TILA contemplates a greater loss for the cardholders, even if they know that their card has been stolen and never bother to notify the issuer of the theft. See Regulation Z, §1026.12(b)(1) (regulatory restatement of the same rule). Although issuers ordinarily have been relatively lenient in accepting the credibility of claims that transactions were unauthorized, there are, as the case below illustrates, cognizable limits on that leniency.

Roundtree v. Chase Bank USA, N.A.
2014 WL 794800 (W.D. Wash. 2014)

Marsha J. Pechman, District Judge.
This matter comes before the Court on [cross motions for summary judgment.] . . . The Court DENIES Mr. Roundtree's Motion for Summary Judgment and GRANTS in part and DENIES in part Chase's Motion for Partial Summary Judgment. . . . Genuine issues of material fact, however, exist as to Mr. Roundtree's Fair Credit Banking [*sic*, should be Billing] Act ("FCBA") . . . claims.

BACKGROUND

This case involves credit card charges on Mr. Roundtree's Chase credit card. He used his Chase credit card for travel and entertainment. The Parties dispute whether these charges were authorized and if Mr. Roundtree is obligated to pay them.

A.   MR. ROUNDTREE'S NIGHT AT THE BAGDAD IN SPAIN

Mr. Roundtree was in Barcelona for a business conference in early 2012. He and a few others went to an Irish pub, where he had at least two drinks. The group then went to dinner, where he had two glasses of wine. The group went to a nightclub for a while but left because they could not get a drink.

Mr. Roundtree, along with Mr. Roution and Mr. Choy, decided to go to the Bagdad [sic], a strip club, around midnight. Mr. Roundtree ordered a gin and tonic, a round of drinks for his business associates, and one bottle of champagne for some women who worked at the club. He used his HSBC credit card to pay for these drinks, which cost approximately 300 Euros. Mr. Roundtree states he authorized the payment by signing an electronic pad.

Mr. Roundtree claims he felt dizzy and tired after taking a sip of his gin and tonic. He passed out within five to ten minutes and woke up with a mouth full of vomit. He then passed out again. Briefly regaining consciousness, he recalled seeing the bartender and the credit card machine. He said one of the girls at the club grabbed his hand to place it on the card reader on which he scribbled something and passed out again. He also remembers waking up in a dark room while holding the electronic credit card reader and then passing out again. Mr. Roundtree woke early in the morning and was handed a receipt that had his passport number on it. He immediately left.

Mr. Roundtree's HSBC credit card was charged three times for a total of $3,833.83. He says the HSBC charges were authorized. Mr. Roundtree's Chase credit card was also charged three times for the following amounts: $25,727.97, $4,743.97, and $12,156.43. However, Mr. Roundtree says he never took his Chase card out of his pocket and the signatures on the transaction slips are forged.

Mr. Roundtree did not file a formal police report regarding his alleged drugging and unauthorized credit card charges. He did, however, speak to a Spanish police officer and to an English-speaking security guard at the conference he was attending about the night at the Bagdad.

B.   MR. ROUNDTREE'S INITIAL RESPONSE TO THE CHARGES

Mr. Roundtree called Chase later that day when he remembered seeing the receipt in front of him with a high dollar amount. Chase said three charges were pending from the Bagdad for approximately $42,000. According to Mr. Roundtree, Chase told him, "It's all taken care of. Don't worry about it." The employee also told Mr. Roundtree to call back. Mr. Roundtree closed his Chase account.

Mr. Roundtree claims his Chase credit card has a spending limit of $26,500, thus making him not responsible for at least approximately $15,000 of the allegedly unauthorized charges. The Chase card, however, does not have a spending limit; instead, it has a credit access line. The Cardmember Agreement states the cardholder is responsible for balances on the account including those charged in excess of the credit access line.

C.   CHASE'S INVESTIGATION

Chase initiated an investigation following Mr. Roundtree's call. Chase noted Mr. Roundtree said he was at a restaurant called the Bagdad and the charge should have only been 220 Euros. In a later call, Mr. Roundtree stated he was drugged and the charges were not authorized. He also told Chase his card was taken out of his pocket. As part of its investigation, Chase contacted the Bagdad and Barcelona police. The police said Mr. Roundtree never filed a police report. Chase was unable to obtain any information from the Bagdad. Chase compared the signatures on the transaction slips from the Bagdad with those on file and concluded the signatures were the same. Chase sent Mr. Roundtree a letter concluding the charges were authorized.

. . .

ANALYSIS

To succeed on an FCBA claim, Mr. Roundtree must show (1) the existence of a billing error, (2) timely notification of the billing error, and (3) failure of the bank issuing the card to comply with the procedural requirements of 15 U.S.C. §1666 (2011). Mr. Roundtree argues Chase failed to comply with the FCBA's procedural requirements.

First, Mr. Roundtree argues Chase never sent a written acknowledgement or its conclusions about his claim within the required 30 days. 12 C.F.R. §[10]26.13(c) states Chase is required to deliver to the consumer within 30 days of receiving a billing notice a written acknowledgment unless Chase complied with the resolution procedures outlined in (e) and (f) of the section within the 30-day period. Mr. Roundtree sent a Confirmation of Unauthorized Use to Chase on April 24, 2012. Chase argues it sent a finality letter stating the charges were authorized on May 4, 2012, but this letter is not in the record before the Court. Thus, questions of fact remain as to whether a letter of acknowledgment was sent within 30 days.

Second, Mr. Roundtree argues Chase did not conduct a reasonable investigation, also in violation of the FCBA. 12 C.F.R. §[10]26.13(f) states:

> If, *after conducting a reasonable investigation*, a creditor determines that no billing error occurred or that a different billing error occurred from that asserted, the creditor shall within the time limits in paragraph (c)(2) of this section: (1) Mail or deliver to the consumer an explanation that sets forth the reasons for the creditor's belief that the billing error alleged by the consumer is incorrect in whole or in part.

Comments to this regulation outline what constitutes a reasonable investigation:

> A. Reviewing the types or amounts of purchases made in relation to the consumer's previous purchasing pattern.
> B. Reviewing where the purchases were delivered in relation to the consumer's residence or place of business.
> C. Reviewing where the purchases were made in relation to where the consumer resides or has normally shopped.

D. Comparing any signature on credit slips for the purchases to the signature of the consumer (or an authorized user in the case of a credit card account) in the creditor's records, including other credit slips.

E. Requesting documentation to assist in the verification of the claim.

F. Requiring a written, signed statement from the consumer (or authorized user, in the case of a credit card account). For example, the creditor may include a signature line on a billing rights form that the consumer may send in to provide notice of the claim. However, a creditor may not require the consumer to provide an affidavit or signed statement under penalty of perjury as a part of a reasonable investigation.

12 C.F.R. §[10]26.12(b)(3), Supp. I, cmt. 3. Generally, deciding whether an investigation was reasonable is not appropriate on summary judgment, but summary judgment is not precluded when the jury could come to one conclusion about the investigation's reasonableness.

The record before this Court shows Chase undertook many of the FCBA's listed steps in investigating Mr. Roundtree's claims. For instance, Chase employees in the fraud unit concluded the signatures "on the sales draft for these transactions [were] similar to his signatures" from other transactions. Chase attempted to fax the Bagdad for information regarding the claim, but it did not respond. Chase also contacted law enforcement in Spain and discovered Mr. Roundtree did not file a police report. Chase also noted Mr. Roundtree never filed a police report when he got back to the U.S. Finally, Chase looked at the discrepancies in the phone calls from Mr. Roundtree: when Mr. Roundtree first called Chase on February 26, 2012, he said he was charged more than the amount authorized and mentioned nothing about being drugged.

However, questions of fact as to the reasonableness of the investigation remain. First, a genuine issue of material fact exists as to whether Chase really did review "the types or amounts of purchases made in relation to the consumer's previous purchasing pattern." 12 C.F.R. §[10]26.12(b)(3), Supp. I, cmt. 3. Mr. Shrock states Chase would have analyzed Mr. Roundtree's spending patterns, but nothing from Chase's documentation of the investigation reveals that anyone looked into Mr. Roundtree's spending patterns. The only high-spending transaction Chase refers to from Mr. Roundtree's credit card statements is the $22,500 liposuction. The transaction at issue is about twice the amount of the liposuction.

Second, a genuine issue of material fact exists as to whether Chase requested all pertinent "documentation to assist in the verification of the claim." 12 C.F.R. §[10]26.12(b)(3), Supp. I, cmt. 3. Although Chase contacted law enforcement in Spain, the investigative record does not indicate whether Chase contacted the security officer Mr. Roundtree allegedly spoke to at the conference he was attending.

The Court DENIES summary judgment on the FCBA, finding genuine factual disputes as to the investigation exist for trial.

You might worry that protecting the cardholder so broadly from unauthorized charges deprives cardholders of any incentive to give notice to the issuer when they lose their credit card. On the contrary, because the cardholder is absolutely immune from unauthorized charges that occur after the card issuer has been notified of a loss or theft of the card, the cardholder can cut off liability (even below the $50 threshold) by sending notice to the issuer. TILA §133(a)(1)(E). Moreover, at least as of the date that this assignment was written, that incentive is enhanced for cards issued by Mastercard and Visa by voluntary policies stating that the cardholders will be completely free from responsibility for unauthorized charges if they report the lost card within two business days of the date that the card was lost, even if the unauthorized charges were made before the cardholder reported the loss of the card.

In addition to the incentive cardholders have to keep their liability below the $50 limit and the ever-present incentive to avoid the hassle of dealing with unauthorized charges, a prudent cardholder also should worry—notwithstanding TILA—that a court will conclude that their conduct was so negligent that it should bear responsibility for charges beyond the $50 limit.

Azur v. Chase Bank, USA, N.A.

601 F.3d 212 (3d Cir. 2010)

Fisher, Circuit Judge.

Francis H. Azur filed suit against Chase Bank, USA, alleging violations of 15 U.S.C. §§1643 and 1666 of the Truth in Lending Act (TILA) and a common law negligence claim after Azur's personal assistant, Michele Vanek, misappropriated over $1 million from Azur through the fraudulent use of a Chase credit card over the course of seven years. The District Court granted Chase's motion for summary judgment, and Azur appealed. . . . First, we must determine whether §1643 of the TILA provides the cardholder with a right to reimbursement. Second, we must evaluate whether Azur's §§1643 and 1666 claims are precluded because Azur vested Vanek with apparent authority to use the Chase credit card. For the reasons stated herein, we will affirm, on partly different grounds, the District Court's order granting Chase's motion for summary judgment.

I.

A.

ATM Corporation of America, Inc. (ATM) manages settlement services for large national lenders. Azur, the founder of ATM, served as its president and chief executive officer from 1993 until September 2007, when ATM was sold. In July 1997, ATM hired Vanek to be Azur's personal assistant. Vanek's responsibilities consisted of picking up Azur's personal bills, including his credit card bills, from a Post Office Box in Coraopolis, Pennsylvania; opening the bills; preparing and presenting checks for Azur to sign; mailing the payments; and balancing Azur's checking and savings accounts at Dollar Bank. According to Azur, it was Vanek's job alone to review Azur's credit card and bank statements and contact the credit card company to discuss any odd charges. Azur also provided Vanek with access to his credit card number to enable her to make purchases at his request.

From around November 1999 to March 2006, Vanek withdrew without authorization cash advances of between $200 and $700, typically twice a day, from a Chase credit card account in Azur's name. Azur was the sole cardholder and only authorized user on the account. Although Azur recalls opening a credit card account in or around 1987 with First USA, Chase's predecessor, Azur was unaware that he had a Chase credit card.

Each fraudulent transaction included a fee of approximately $2.00 and a finance charge that corresponded to the amount withdrawn, ranging from $4.00 for a $100 advance, to $21.06 for a $700 advance. The fraudulent charges were reflected on at least 65 monthly billing statements sent by Chase to Azur, and Vanek paid the bills by either writing checks or making on-line payments from Azur's Dollar Bank checking account. When writing checks, Vanek forged Azur's signature. Over the course of seven years, Vanek misappropriated over $1 million from Azur.

The transactions occasionally triggered Chase's fraud strategies. On April 16, 2004, Chase detected its first potentially fraudulent transaction, made outbound calls to the account's home telephone number, and left an automated message on the number's answering machine. Chase received no response. On April 23, 2004, one week later, Chase detected a second potential problem and left another automated message at the same telephone number. Three days later, Chase received a call from someone that was able to verify the account's security questions and validate the card activity. Although Chase's records indicate that the caller was female, Chase did not use voice recognition or gender identification as a means of security verification. Finally, on May 14, 2005, approximately one year later, Chase detected a third potentially fraudulent transaction and called the home telephone number. As before, five days later, a return caller once again verified the account activity. The account was paid in full without protest after each incident.

On or about March 7, 2006, Azur discovered a suspicious letter requesting a transfer of funds from his checking account. After investigating, Azur and ATM discovered Vanek's fraudulent scheme and terminated her employment. On March 8, 2006, Azur notified Chase by telephone of the fraudulent use of the Chase account and closed the account. Thereafter, Azur sent Chase [correspondence disputing the charges in question.]

B.

On February 22, 2007, Azur filed an amended complaint against Chase under §§1643 and 1666 of the TILA, 15 U.S.C. §§1601 *et seq.* (2006). On April 8, 2008, Chase filed under seal a motion for summary judgment seeking dismissal of all . . . of Azur's claims.

[The trial court granted that motion.]

. . .

III.

Azur appeals the District Court's order granting Chase's motion for summary judgment. . . .

A.   Right to Reimbursement

Chase argues that Azur cannot recover the money already paid to Chase under §1643 of the TILA. We agree. Section 1643 does not provide the cardholder with a right to reimbursement. This is clear from the statute's language: "A cardholder shall be liable for the unauthorized use of a credit card only if . . . ." 15 U.S.C. §1643(a). "Liable" means "[r]esponsible or answerable in law" or "legally obligated." *Black's Law Dictionary* 998 (9th ed. 2009). *See also Webster's Third New Int'l Dictionary* 1302 (1993) (defining "liable" as "bound or obliged according to law or equity"). Accordingly, the statute's plain meaning places a ceiling on a cardholder's obligations under the law and thus limits a card issuer's ability to sue a cardholder to recover fraudulent purchases. The language of §1643 does not, however, enlarge a card issuer's liability or give the cardholder a right to reimbursement.

. . .

B.   Apparent Authority

Vanek's alleged apparent authority is a more difficult issue. Relying on three cases, Minskoff v. American Express Travel Related Services. Co., Inc., 98 F.3d 703 (2d Cir. 1996), DBI Architects, P.C. v. American Express Travel-Related Services. Co., Inc., 388 F.3d 886 (D.C. Cir. 2004), and Carrier v. Citibank (S.D.), N.A., 383 F. Supp. 2d 334 (D. Conn. 2005), the [district court] dismissed Azur's §1643 claim. On appeal, Azur argues that whether he clothed Vanek with apparent authority is an issue of fact to be decided by a jury.

The application of both §§1643 and 1666 of the TILA depend, in part, on whether the fraudulent user had apparent authority to use the credit card. As stated above, §1643 provides that "[a] cardholder shall be liable for the unauthorized use of a credit card" in certain circumstances. 15 U.S.C. §1643(a). The term "unauthorized use" is defined as the "use of a credit card by a person other than the cardholder who does not have actual, implied, or apparent authority for such use and from which the cardholder receives no benefit." Id. §1[03](o). Relatedly, §[161](a) sets forth the procedures a creditor must follow to resolve alleged billing errors. Like the phrase "unauthorized use," the phrase "billing error" includes "[a] reflection on or with a periodic statement of an extension of credit that is not made to the consumer or to a person who has actual, implied, or apparent authority to use the consumer's credit card or open-end credit plan." 12 C.F.R. §[10]26.13(a)(1).

To determine whether apparent authority exists, we turn to applicable state agency law. *See* 12 C.F.R. Pt. 1026, Supp. I ("Whether such [apparent] authority exists must be determined under state or other applicable law."); *Minskoff*, 98 F.3d at 708 ("Congress apparently contemplated, and courts have accepted, primary reliance on background principles of agency law in determining the liability of cardholders for charges incurred by third-party card bearers."). In this case, the parties do not refute the application of Pennsylvania law. Citing the Restatement (Second) of Agency, the Pennsylvania Supreme Court has explained as follows:

> Apparent authority is power to bind a principal which the principal has not actually granted but which he leads persons with whom his agent deals to believe that he has

granted. Persons with whom the agent deals can reasonably believe that the agent has power to bind his principal if, for instance, the principal knowingly permits the agent to exercise such power or if the principal holds the agent out as possessing such power.

Revere Press, Inc. v. Blumberg, 246 A.2d 407, 410 (1968). Similarly, we have stated that under Pennsylvania law "[t]he test for determining whether an agent possesses apparent authority is whether a man of ordinary prudence, diligence and discretion would have a right to believe and would actually believe that the agent possessed the authority he purported to exercise." In re Mushroom Transp. Co., Inc., 382 F.3d 325, 345 (3d Cir. 2004).

Although the articulation of the proper agency law standard is fairly easy, the application of that standard is difficult. Two decisions of the Second and D.C. Circuits, respectively, are instructive. In both cases, the Second and D.C. Circuits held that a cardholder's negligent omissions clothed the fraudulent card user with apparent authority under facts similar to those present in the instant case.

The Second Circuit in *Minskoff* was the first court of appeals to address this issue. Minskoff served as the president and chief executive officer of a real estate firm. In 1988, the firm opened an American Express corporate credit card account and issued one card in Minskoff's name. In 1992, Minskoff's assistant, whom the firm had recently hired, applied for and obtained an additional card to the account in her own name without Minskoff's or the firm's knowledge. From April 1992 to March 1993, the assistant charged a total of $28,213.88 on the corporate card. During this period, American Express sent twelve monthly billing statements to the firm's address; each statement listed both Minskoff and the assistant as cardholders and separately itemized their charges. At the same time, American Express was paid in full by a total of twelve forged checks drawn on bank accounts maintained by either Minskoff or the firm at Manufacturers Hanover Trust (MHT), which also periodically mailed statements to the firm showing that the payments had been made. The assistant used the same system to misappropriate another $300,000 after applying for a platinum account. After discovering the fraud, Minskoff filed suit against American Express under the TILA.

In determining whether or not the assistant had apparent authority to use the credit card, the Second Circuit began by differentiating between the acquisition and use of a credit card obtained through fraud or theft: "[W]hile we accept the proposition that the *acquisition* of a credit card through fraud or theft cannot be said to occur under the apparent authority of the cardholder, [that] should not . . . preclude a finding of apparent authority for the subsequent *use* of a credit card so obtained." Then, noting that "[n]othing in the TILA suggests that Congress intended to sanction intentional or negligent conduct by the cardholder that furthers the fraud or theft of an unauthorized card user," the court held that "the negligent acts or omissions of a cardholder may create apparent authority to use the card in a person who obtained the card through theft or fraud." Applying that reasoning to the facts before it, the Second Circuit found that Minskoff's and the firm's failure to examine any of the credit card or bank statements created, as a matter of law, "apparent authority for [the assistant's] continuing use of the cards, especially because it enabled [the assistant] to pay all of the American Express statements with forged checks, thereby fortifying American Express' continuing impression that nothing was amiss with the Corporate and Platinum Accounts."

In *DBI Architects*, the D.C. Circuit took a narrower approach. DBI was a corporation with an AMEX credit card account. In 2001, DBI appointed a new account manager of its D.C. and Virginia offices. Soon thereafter, the new manager requested that AMEX add her as a cardholder on DBI's corporate account without DBI's knowledge, although AMEX sent DBI an account statement reflecting the change. From August 2001 to May 2002, the manager charged a total of $134,810.40 to the credit card. As in *Minskoff*, AMEX sent DBI ten monthly billing statements — each listing the manager as a cardholder and itemizing her charges — and the manager paid AMEX with thirteen DBI checks. Most of the checks were signed or stamped in the name of DBI's president; none were signed in the manager's own name. Like Minskoff, DBI eventually filed suit against AMEX under the TILA.

Acquainted with the Second Circuit's decision in *Minskoff*, the D.C. Circuit decided its case on narrower grounds. Rather than fault the cardholder for merely failing to inspect monthly credit card statements, the court focused on the cardholder's continuous payment of the fraudulent charges without complaint:

> DBI is correct that its failure to inspect its monthly billing statements did not clothe [the manager] with apparent authority to use its corporate AMEX account. [However,] AMEX is correct that DBI clothed [the manager] with apparent authority to use its corporate AMEX account by repeatedly paying without protest all of [the manager's] charges on the account after receiving notice of them from AMEX.

The court later explained its reasoning as follows:

> By identifying apparent authority as a limit on the cardholder's protection under §1643, Congress recognized that a cardholder has certain obligations to prevent fraudulent use of its card. DBI's troubles stemmed from its failure to separate the approval and payment functions within its cash disbursement process. [The manager] had actual authority both to receive the billing statements and to issue DBI checks for payment to AMEX. While DBI did not voluntarily relinquish its corporate card to [the manager], it did mislead AMEX into reasonably believing that [the manager] had authority to use the corporate card by paying her charges on the corporate account after receiving AMEX's monthly statements identifying her as a cardholder and itemizing her charges.

Although the [*DBI*] court acknowledged that payment might not always create apparent authority, it held that such authority existed as a matter of law in that case:

> [T]his is not a case involving an occasional transgression buried in a welter of financial detail. [ ]Nor is this a case involving payment without notice, as might occur when a cardholder authorizes its bank to pay its credit card bills automatically each month. Where, as here, the cardholder repeatedly paid thousands of dollars in fraudulent charges for almost a year after monthly billing statements identifying the fraudulent user and itemizing the fraudulent charges were sent to its corporate address, no reasonable juror could disagree that at some point the cardholder led the card issuer reasonably to believe that the fraudulent user had authority to use its card.

Ultimately, the court remanded the case to determine at what point the manager's apparent authority began.

We agree with the D.C. Circuit's more nuanced analysis. "Apparent authority is power to bind a principal which the principal has not actually granted but which he leads persons with whom his agent deals to believe that he has granted." *Revere Press,* 246 A.2d at 410. A cardholder may, in certain circumstances, vest a fraudulent user with the apparent authority to use a credit card by enabling the continuous payment of the credit card charges over a period of time. As the D.C. Circuit reasoned, by identifying apparent authority as a limitation on the cardholder's protections under §1643, Congress recognized that the cardholder is oftentimes in the best position to identify fraud committed by its employees.

Here, Azur's negligent omissions led Chase to reasonably believe that the fraudulent charges were authorized. Although Azur may not have been aware that Vanek was using the Chase credit card, or even that the Chase credit card account existed, Azur knew that he had a Dollar Bank checking account, and he did not review his Dollar Bank statements or exercise any other oversight over Vanek, his employee. Instead, Azur did exactly what the D.C. Circuit in *DBI Architects* cautioned against: he "fail[ed] to separate the approval and payment functions within [his] cash disbursement process." Had Azur occasionally reviewed his statements, Azur would have likely noticed that checks had been written to Chase. Because Chase reasonably believed that a prudent business person would oversee his employees in such a manner, Chase reasonably relied on the continuous payment of the fraudulent charges.

Many of Azur's counter-arguments are beside the point. Azur asserts that *Minskoff* and *DBI Architects* are distinguishable because the fraudulent users in those cases were cardholders on the accounts. This distinction is irrelevant: Chase's belief that the fraudulent charges were authorized did not depend on whether the fraudulent charges were made by a second cardholder; Chase's belief was contingent upon the continuous payment of the fraudulent charges—regardless of which card they were on—without objection. Azur also focuses on Chase's failure to identify the fraud. The issue, however, is whether Azur led Chase to believe that Vanek had authority to make the charges, not whether Chase's fraud-detecting tools were effective. Moreover, Vanek's ability to answer the account security questions over the telephone and the fact that Chase's fraud-detecting tools identified relatively few problems reinforce the conclusion that Chase was reasonable in believing, and did in fact believe, that the charges were authorized. In short, none of the arguments Azur has advanced persuade us to disturb the District Court's apparent authority determination.

Accordingly, we hold that Azur vested Vanek with apparent authority to use the Chase credit card, thus barring his §§1643 and 1666 claims.

New Century Financial Services v. Dennegar

928 A.2d 48 (N.J. Super. Ct. App. Div. 2007)

Before Judges Wefing, C.S. Fisher, and Messano.
The opinion of the court was delivered by Fisher, J.A.D.
In this appeal, we consider whether defendant was properly held liable for a credit card debt despite his contention that he never applied for or used the credit

card. Because the evidence supported the trial judge's determination that defendant either expressly applied for the card, or authorized his roommate—to whom he ceded authority over his finances—to apply for and use the card, we affirm the judgment entered in plaintiff's favor.

I

The testimony revealed that AT & T Universal (AT & T) issued a credit card in the name of defendant Lee Dennegar (defendant) on or about February 1, 2001, that it thereafter sent monthly statements to defendant's home, and that $14,752.93 was due and owing when the debt was eventually assigned to plaintiff New Century Financial Services, Inc. (plaintiff) [a prominent debt collector].

Defendant asserted that he had no knowledge of this account. The evidence revealed that defendant lived in West Orange with a Mark Knutson from 1999 to 2000; they subsequently moved to 55 Thompson Street in Raritan in 2000. This home was owned by defendant. Knutson had no funds or income, and defendant's funds were used to pay the mortgage on the Raritan home, and all other household expenses, as they had been in West Orange.

Defendant testified that he had suffered a nervous breakdown in September 2001 and had been hospitalized for a period of time as well. Prior to his breakdown and until Knutson's death on June 22, 2003, defendant had allowed Knutson to manage their household's financial affairs and the "general office functions concerned with maintaining the house." Defendant admitted during his testimony that he allowed Knutson "to handle all the mail" and "left to [Knutson's] discretion to open [the mail] and to do with it as he chose." As a result, Knutson wrote out checks for defendant to sign, although defendant testified that he "rarely signed checks at all." In fact, defendant testified that he then knew that "Knutson was signing [defendant's] name to many of the checks," and that he had no objection to this course of conduct.

Once Knutson died, defendant learned that Knutson had incurred obligations in his name of which he was not previously aware. Not long thereafter, plaintiff commenced this suit in the Special Civil Part to collect from defendant the amount of the outstanding debt. At the conclusion of the trial, the judge found that "defendant created the situation where someone else would utilize his financial resources to pay for the joint expenses." He held that either defendant or Knutson had opened this account in February 2001 and that defendant was liable for the debt that thereafter accrued. Judgment was entered in favor of plaintiff in the amount of $14,752.93 plus costs. . . .

We . . . find no merit in defendant's assertion that he could not be found liable through the application of either (a) common law principles, or (b) the Truth in Lending Act.

A

Because plaintiff could not affirmatively demonstrate that defendant entered into an agreement with AT & T, plaintiff was left with attempting to prove that

Knutson was defendant's agent and acted within the scope of that agency relationship or, if Knutson exceeded his authority through forgeries or other fraudulent conduct, that defendant—having placed Knutson in the position to abuse his authority—should bear the risk of loss. [Ed.: Again, it is apparent that the plaintiff does not have a copy of the agreement in question.]

The trial judge found that defendant had authorized Knutson to conduct the financial affairs of their household prior to the time that the AT & T account was opened and until Knutson's death in 2003, by which time the AT & T account had gone into default. We discern from the judge's decision that he found that defendant, as principal, had appointed Knutson as his agent for the conducting of his financial affairs. See Restatement (Second) of Agency, §26 (observing that "authority to do an act can be created by written or spoken words or other conduct of the principal which, reasonably interpreted, causes the agent to believe that the principal desires him so to act on the principal's account").

Although the finding of Knutson's authority to deal with household bills through the utilization of defendant's funds does not necessarily compel a finding that Knutson was authorized to borrow funds or make purchases based on defendant's credit, we conclude that the judge implicitly and correctly found that Knutson was authorized to act in this latter respect as well.

The judge found that defendant admitted having "a poor memory" and "it may well be that his memory with regard to this account is just not allowing him to remember" the circumstances of its formation, or even whether it was defendant himself who entered into the relationship with AT & T. Moreover, even if defendant did not expressly open the AT & T account, the judge found that "it seems that Mr. Knutson was given authority to open this account [for defendant's] benefit." The evidence amply supports this finding. As defendant testified, Knutson was authorized to open defendant's mail, to attend to the mail as he saw fit, to make out checks on defendant's checking account, and to even sign defendant's names to those checks.

In addition, defendant acknowledged that some of the charges on the account were the type of purchases that Knutson was authorized to make for the household. And the monthly statements, which were mailed by AT & T to defendant's home, reveal that payments were periodically made. Although a complete record of these statements was not moved into evidence, monthly statements ranging from February 2002 to January 2003 were available and were admitted into evidence. They reveal that payments were made to AT & T against the outstanding balance on April 3, 2002, May 8, 2002, May 21, 2002, September 10, 2002, October 10, 2002, November 8, 2002, and December 10, 2002. This evidence fairly supports the inference the judge implicitly drew that either defendant or Knutson obtained the credit card from AT & T; and, if the latter, the evidence of the activity on the AT & T account, together with the surrounding circumstances of defendant having ceded his authority over incoming mail, his checkbook, and his finances, amply supported the judge's finding that Knutson was authorized by defendant to obtain and use the credit card. . . .

The general rule is that a principal is accountable for the conduct of his agent acting within the scope of his authority even though the conduct is unauthorized and the principal receives no benefit from it. The reason for the rule is that though the agent may have deceived the principal as well as the victim, since the principal placed the agent in the position where he had the power to perpetuate the wrong, the principal rather than the innocent third party should bear the loss.

Because the trial judge found as a fact that Knutson was authorized by defendant either to enter into the credit relationship with AT & T or, assuming defendant himself actually entered into the relationship, that Knutson was authorized to utilize the credit card, the consequence of any misuse or fraudulent use by Knutson is to be borne by defendant, not AT & T or its assignee. And, despite defendant's forceful argument to the contrary, it does not matter whether defendant gained a benefit from Knutson's actions.

B

Defendant lastly argues that the TILA precluded the entry of a judgment against him for the balance due on this account. We find no merit in this contention. Congress enacted the credit card provisions of the TILA in large measure to protect credit cardholders from unauthorized use. As a result, the TILA credit card provisions were designed to strictly limit the cardholder's liability for "unauthorized" charges, [TILA §133](a)(1), by, among other things, placing the burden of establishing cardholder liability on the card issuer, [TILA §133](b), and imposing criminal sanctions for the fraudulent use of credit cards, [TILA §134]. . . .

As indicated earlier, we interpret the trial judge's findings here as consistent with a determination that defendant either obtained the credit card on his own, or that he authorized Knutson to enter into the relationship with AT & T. Although the judge did not make specific findings regarding the TILA's provisions, the only rational findings permitted by the evidence, as interpreted by the judge in his oral decision, was that defendant was, at best, careless or negligent with regard to his finances. . . . [W]e conclude that the proper application of the TILA's provisions requires a determination that the debt in question had been permitted to accrue through defendant's intentional, careless or negligent conduct, and that, as a result, the TILA imposes no obstacle to plaintiff's recovery.

Cases like *Minskoff* and *DBI* implicitly reflect one unusual aspect of the provisions of TILA that protect cardholders from paying unauthorized charges: They apply not only in consumer transactions, but also in business and commercial transactions. In the business context, however, the issuer and the cardholder can contract out of the statutory allocation of loss from unauthorized charges. Specifically, TILA §135 permits any business that issues credit cards to at least ten of its employees to accept liability for unauthorized charges without regard to the provisions of TILA §133, so long as the business does not attempt to pass on to the individual employees any liability greater than the liability permitted under TILA §133. See Regulation Z, §§1026.3(a) n.4, 1026.12(b)(5) (regulatory explanation of TILA §135). The credit-card network rules treat claims that charges are unauthorized differently than they treat other cardholder claims. At least in face-to-face transactions, the issuer bears the loss from unauthorized charges as long as the merchant followed the requisite procedures (that is, verifying the signature and obtaining the appropriate authorization for the transaction). Thus, if the merchant incurs charges by accepting a card proffered by a thief, the network rules do not permit the issuer to pass those charges back to the acquirer or the merchant. In remote transactions (sales by telephone or, increasingly, over the Internet), however, the risk of loss is left with the merchant. Thus, a merchant that does not deal face to face has to accept the risk that its customers subsequently may disavow the transactions.

Moreover, several common situations remain in which true strangers execute transactions that plainly are not authorized by cardholders. For example, at one point in time, never-received cards—cards intercepted before they reached the cardholder—amounted for half of all losses to fraud in the credit-card system. Those losses have almost been eradicated in the intervening decades through card-activation programs, under which cardholders must contact the issuer to activate the card.

Losses from counterfeit cards have proved more intractable. The reason is easy to identify: The technology available to create false cards has improved significantly at a time when the major issuers have been slow to upgrade the security features of their cards that would make it harder to counterfeit cards. The main difficulty is that the most effective security features would require merchants to upgrade the terminals that they use to process credit cards. The desire to hold down the cost of credit-card transactions to the merchant has slowed the networks significantly in adopting more sophisticated security procedures. Although a few new card-based security features—holograms on the face and special printing on the signature stripe—have limited counterfeit-card losses by increasing the costs of manufacturing plausible counterfeits, it is doubtful that those kinds of minor improvements can deter counterfeiters in the long run. The only plausible long-term deterrent is to increase the amount and sophistication of the encrypted data on the card. Significant advances on that front should come in the next few years, as the United States moves to the chip-and-PIN technology so common in other countries.

More recently, identity theft has come on the scene as a significant mechanism for credit-card fraud. An identity thief takes over the credit identity of an affluent individual and then uses the financial strength associated with that identity to execute fraudulent financial transactions. For example, in a common scheme, the thief would start with the theft of a credit-card statement (or even better, a preapproved credit-card application) from the victim's mailbox. With that statement, the identity thief could call the issuer and ask to have the mailing address and telephone number for the card changed so that the victim would not receive mail or telephone calls related to the card. If the issuer is vigilant, that step might require knowledge of the victim's mother's maiden name or some similar piece of information; but a talented thief would have acquired that information from the victim's publicly available birth certificate. At that point, the thief could use the card at will, without making any payments, at least until the issuer cuts off the card for nonpayment. By that time, of course, the victim's credit-card accounts—accounts that the thief took over and new accounts that the thief opened while "in possession" of the victim's identity—are likely to have thousands of dollars of unauthorized charges for purchases made by the thief.

Although losses from identity theft have remained relatively modest to date, identity theft poses a serious threat to the system because of the identity thief's ability to operate on information (such as credit-card numbers, Social Security numbers, and birth information) that is becoming readily available through electronic sources. Industry and legislative policymakers are considering a variety of reforms that would make it more difficult for identity thieves to acquire the information necessary for them to succeed. None of those reforms, however, appears likely to respond to the central problem — the ease with which information alone can be used to fool the system into authorizing a credit-card transaction. Until the system adopts an authorization mechanism that requires more than information alone (most likely a biometric mechanism based on fingerprint or retinal characteristics), identity theft is likely to increase.

Although TILA narrowly confines the ability of the card issuer to pass losses from unauthorized transactions to card purchasers, it imposes no restraints at all on the ability of card networks to shift those losses from issuers to merchants. The baseline rule of the system traditionally has been that the issuers bear those losses. But over the last few decades several exceptions have undermined the generality of that proposition. The first was with the rise of mail-order and telephone-order (MOTO) transactions. Because mail-order and telephone-order merchants could not readily obtain signatures to verify transactions, they could not obtain the signatures necessary to process transactions in the conventional way. Eventually, though, the networks agreed to accept transactions in the MOTO channel without signatures, but on the condition that the merchants accept the risk that the transactions were unauthorized. The system, at that time, proceeded on the assumption (which you might regard as dubious) that the signature was a valuable tool in demonstrating the purchaser's authorization to use the card.

That is not to say that all transactions without signatures pass the risk of unauthorized card use to the merchant. In recent years, the card networks have relaxed the signature requirement in a number of areas, starting with fast-food restaurants (the so-called QSR or "quick-service restaurant" sector). In those venues, the transaction is verified with a mere swipe (or insertion) of the card, typically without either a signature or a PIN. The networks accept the transactions without the signature and the issuers accept the risk that the transactions are not authorized.

More recently, the introduction of chip cards in 2015 has complicated the picture still further. In the post-chip world, merchants that have not upgraded to chip-compatible terminals now bear the risk of all unauthorized transactions that involve chip-bearing cards. If they have upgraded to chip-compatible terminals, though, those risks return to their ordinary state, with the issuer generally bearing the risk that a transaction is unauthorized.

Problem Set 2

2.1. When Cliff Janeway returned to his home in Denver this weekend, he called to tell you that he has discovered that he lost his Iridium Mastercard, which has a $20,000 limit. It now has been more than a week since he lost it. Does that give him anything to worry about? TILA §§133, 170(a); Regulation Z, §1026.12(b), (c). Would it matter if a thief's use of the card was in New York (as opposed to Denver)? What if Cliff paid the bill without noticing unauthorized charges on the bill? What if he did not notice unauthorized charges for several months?

2.2. You will recall from Problem Set 1 that issuers commonly charge back transactions in which card purchasers complain that merchants have failed to perform without performing any investigation into the validity of the cardholder's claims. Why didn't the issuer in Roundtree do the same thing?

2.3. While he has you on the phone, Cliff tells you that he is about to start selling books by mail order, in an effort to build volume for his business. He is worried about accepting payment by credit cards because the cardholders won't be signing any slips.

   a. Does that mean the cardholders will have a greater right to get out of the transactions? TILA §§103(p), 133(a), 170; Regulation Z, §1026.12(b), (c), Interp. 12(b)(2)(iii).
   b. Would your opinion change if he also stopped requiring signatures for retail transactions?

2.4. Cliff's last question for you relates to a trip he had planned to take to London. Several weeks ago he bought tickets to fly to London on Great Atlantic Air. Yesterday Great Atlantic Air stopped flying. This morning's paper reports that the assets of Great Atlantic Air are being liquidated in bankruptcy. Cliff purchased his ticket on his Mastercard. Can he get the money back? What do you need to know to answer Cliff's question? TILA §§161, 170; Regulation Z, §§1026.12(c), 1026.13.

2.5. Ben Darrow meets you for breakfast this morning to discuss a problem with some credit cards that FSB recently issued. As part of a general initiative to provide more services to small businesses, FSB has a program that provides credit cards for small businesses at low costs, with no annual fee and an interest rate that is two points lower than FSB's standard rate. As part of the program, however, the cardholding small business must sign an agreement accepting responsibility for any unauthorized charges that are made with a stolen card.

Ben got in a dispute this week with Carol Long (one of the first people to sign up for the program) after a thief came through her offices at lunch and stole three of the five credit cards she had issued to her employees. Although Carol called Ben to report the theft by the end of the day, the thief already had charged about $500 on each of the three cards. Based on Carol's agreement with Ben, Carol was not surprised to see the unauthorized charges on the statements for the employees. Because she had agreed to accept responsibility for those charges, she proposed to deduct them from the next paycheck due to each employee whose card was stolen. One of the employees, however, protested, arguing that Carol could not make him pay an unauthorized charge on the credit card. In response to that claim, Carol called Ben. She wants to know if the employee is right. Moreover, if the employee is right, she thinks that Ben should bear the charge, not her. What should Ben tell her? TILA §§133(a)(1), 135; Regulation Z, §1026.12(b)(5).

2.6.   Your friend Tony Tedeschi forgets his credit card on the table as he leaves a restaurant. A thief picks up the card and uses it for several months before Tedeschi happens to notice the fraudulent charges on his statements. Can the card issuer force Tedeschi to pay for those charges? UCC §3-406(a); TILA §133. Would your answer change if he paid his bill in full each month?

Assignment 3: Debit Cards

Debit cards have grown rapidly in use in the last decade, now being used for almost twice as many retail transactions as credit cards (about 60 billion in 2015). Thus, the issues related to debit cards, and the differences in legal treatment from credit cards, are gaining rapidly in importance.

This assignment proceeds in two parts. The first part discusses the mechanics of making payment with a debit card. The second part discusses how the debit-card system deals with the inevitable problems of error and fraud.

A. Payment with a Debit Card

A debit card is physically almost indistinguishable from a credit card, with a magnetic stripe on the back that technologically is quite similar to the stripe on a credit card. Sometimes a debit card may go by a different name—some banks call theirs ATM cards or banking cards—but whatever the name, the feature that distinguishes a debit card for purposes of this discussion is that a debit card always serves as an adjunct to a checking (or savings) account. Thus, unlike a credit card, a debit card does not reflect an independent source of funds. Rather, it is a device to facilitate the customer's access to funds that either are already in an account or are available through an overdraft feature of that account.

Although it is now quite rare, there is no reason the credit and debit features cannot be combined on the same piece of plastic. See, e.g., Regulation E, 12 C.F.R. §1005.12 (outlining regulatory requirements for dual-purpose cards). When cards combine the two features, the mechanisms for completing payment transactions made with the card depend on whether the customer pays with the debit feature or the credit feature. Thus, a transaction using the debit feature would be governed by the rules and practices discussed in this assignment, but a transaction using the credit feature would be completed as described in Assignment 1. See Regulation E, §1005.12(a); Regulation Z, §1026.12(g).

The key to the debit-card system is that it replaces the paper check with an electronic impulse that directs the bank to transfer funds to the customer (when the card is used to withdraw cash at an ATM) or to transfer funds to a third party (when the card is used in a sales transaction). The use of the electronic impulse removes the need for the check and thus many of the cumbersome problems raised by a paper-based checking system (which Chapter 3 discusses). Just as important for our purposes, the use of that impulse to obtain funds directly from an account causes the transaction to qualify as an electronic funds transfer regulated by the federal Electronic Funds Transfer Act (EFTA).

62

15 U.S.C. §§1693 et seq. The EFTA is Title IX, §§901-920, of the Consumer Credit Protection Act (the same statute in which TILA appears as Title I). As EFTA §903(7) states, the EFTA applies to any "transfer of funds . . . initiated through an electronic terminal so as to order . . . a financial institution to debit . . . an account." The term "account" is broadly defined to include not only checking accounts but also savings accounts and even money-market or securities accounts held by broker-dealers. EFTA §903(2). Thus, the EFTA (together with its regulatory counterpart, Regulation E, 12 C.F.R. Part 1005) applies to all cards that can be used to make electronic withdrawals from any such account.

1. Establishing the Debit-Card Relationship

The law related to debit cards is pervaded with a deep-seated suspicion that consumers are not sophisticated enough to understand the nature of a debit card. For starters, although no law regulates the way in which a bank can initiate a checking-account relationship, the EFTA imposes two significant procedural requirements that complicate a bank's efforts to update its checking-account relationships to include debit cards. First, EFTA §911 generally allows a bank to send an unsolicited debit card to a customer only if the card is sent in an unvalidated condition. Hence, a bank cannot mail a debit card out to a customer hoping that the customer will begin to use it. Rather, it has to convince the customer either to request the card before the bank sends the card or cause the customer to validate the card when the customer receives it. Depending on the issuer's technology, validation might require some online interaction, a telephone call, or a visit to the bank. EFTA §911(b).

The second restriction is the disclosure requirement set forth in Regulation E. That regulation requires the bank to provide the consumer a detailed up-front disclosure of the terms and conditions that will govern use of the card. Regulation E, §1005.7(a). To its credit, the regulation states that the disclosure must be "in a readily understandable written statement that the consumer may retain." Unfortunately, like the analogous regulations discussed in earlier assignments, the regulation reduces the likelihood that the disclosure will be "readily understandable" by imposing a requirement that the disclosure include ten specified items, which require not only a summary of much of the EFTA and the substantive provisions of Regulation E but also a detailed 300-word disclosure about the procedures for resolving disputes over transactions made with the card. The result should surprise nobody. The typical bank produces an attractive booklet — prominently displaying the bank's logo or trademark — for the bank officer to give the customer when it opens the account. The booklet usually contains about 30 to 40 pages setting forth the "agreement" of the parties related to the checking account. Toward the back of the booklet are three to five pages of single-spaced ten-point type setting forth the disclosures required by Regulation E, often in the form of model clauses set out in Appendix A to Regulation E. The typical large bank may promulgate aspirational procedures suggesting that the officer should go over the specific disclosures with the customer and even highlight important provisions. The reality, however, is that the busy consumer is unlikely ever to open the booklet, much less read (or understand) the dense legalese that describes the rules governing use of the debit card. As you consider the effect of the consumer-protection rules discussed later in this assignment, you should keep in mind the limited likelihood that the average consumer will be aware of those rules, much less understand how they differ from the analogous rules for credit cards or checks.

2. Transferring Funds with a Debit Card

There are two basic uses of a debit card. The first use is where the cards initially became popular: depositing and withdrawing money from an account without the burden of going to the bank and waiting to see a teller during regular banking hours. In that use, a debit card allows a customer to go to an ATM and perform any of the transactions that the customer could perform directly with a teller at the bank: withdrawing funds, depositing funds, inquiring about balances, or transferring funds among different accounts. Those functions do not involve payments to third parties; rather, they are limited to adjustment of the relationship between the customer and the bank where the customer maintains its account. Thus, they are not the sort of substitute-check transactions that involve use of the debit card as a payment system.

For purposes of the payment system, the important function is a different one: the ever-burgeoning use of debit cards in point-of-sale (POS) transactions. In those transactions, a customer can use the card at the point of sale as a substitute for a check. From the customer's perspective, payment with a debit card is simple. The customer or the merchant swipes the debit card through a machine that reads the magnetic stripe (or chip) on the card to verify the customer's bank and account. Depending on the type of card or terminal, the customer may be asked to type in a personal identification number (PIN) and verify the amount of the transaction; alternatively the customer might sign to authorize the transaction. Finally, EFTA §906(a) requires that consumers be provided written documentation for each transaction that they initiate. Accordingly, if all goes well, a printer produces a paper record of the transaction a few seconds later, and the customer is free to go.

3. Collection by the Payee

As with a point-of-sale credit-card transaction, the apparently simple and straightforward swiping of the card hides a considerably more convoluted arrangement between the merchant/payee and the ultimate payor bank. In order to collect funds through debit-card transactions, a merchant must enter into a contract, either directly with the bank that issued the card or indirectly through a network that processes debit-card transactions for the card-issuing bank.

On the other side, the cardholder must have a contract with a bank that can deduct funds from a bank account; almost invariably the card is issued by the bank at which the cardholder has an account. With those arrangements in place, the process is quite similar to the process summarized for credit-card transactions in Assignment 1. The merchant's terminal first sends an authorization message. If the issuer authorizes the transaction, it then proceeds and the merchant sends the payment data to its acquirer and through the network for settlement. The only difference is what happens on the issuer's side. Instead of assessing the creditworthiness of the cardholder at the authorization stage, the issuer examines the account balance and places a hold on the funds needed for the transaction. Then, when the payment data arrive, the issuer simply removes the funds from the account (or, which is much the same thing, grants an overdraft to the cardholder).

The interchange fees for debit-card transactions traditionally have been considerably lower than those for credit-card transactions, in part because of the relatively low risk of loss and in part because of the even lower interchange fees that were common in the debit-card transactions conducted by regional ATM networks before the spread of the Visa and Mastercard debit cards that dominate the present market. Still, merchants for many years have complained that the interchange fees for debit-card transactions remain excessive. Although the processing is quite similar, the key difference between a credit-card transaction and a PIN-less debit-card transaction cleared through a credit-card network is finality. As a legal matter, debit-card transactions are electronic fund transfers; they are not credit-card transactions governed by Regulation Z and TILA. Accordingly, from the consumer's perspective, payment is as a practical matter final at the time of the transaction. The consumer has none of the TILA-based rights to challenge payment at a later time.

B.   Error and Fraud in Debit-Card Transactions

Because the debit-card system allows the merchant/payee to determine at the time of the transaction that the payor bank will honor the transfer request and because the customer has no substantial right to stop payment, the risk of non-payment is much less substantial in debit-card transactions than it is in traditional checking transactions. That leaves two other possible sources of loss for the system to address: erroneous transactions and fraudulent transactions.

1.   Erroneous Transactions

It is easy to see how the electronic portions of the debit-card processing system could make a variety of errors in handling payment transactions: The system could make an improper withdrawal (a withdrawal of the wrong amount or from the wrong account), or the system could fail to make a withdrawal that it should have made. Happily, those types of mistakes have not yet caused any significant losses. That is mostly because many of the common ways that the electronic system could fail ordinarily would not result in losses.

In the debit-card context, the merchant is unlikely to allow the customer to complete the transaction unless the merchant's terminal receives the authorization from the payor bank agreeing to make the withdrawal. When the authorization system goes offline, the merchant normally refuses to accept debit cards for transactions completed before the system appears to be functioning again. Similarly, at least in the absence of a serious processing failure, the payor bank is unlikely to send a signal committing to pay money to the merchant and then fail to charge some account for the funds it has agreed to pay.

Similarly, it is possible that the payor bank could send a signal committing to make the payment, but then charge the wrong account. In that event, the payor bank would have to recredit the incorrectly charged account, but it then could charge the correct account and pursue the customer for any deficiency. That problem, however, is unlikely to leave the bank with any significant losses. In most cases, banks should find that the accounts contain funds sufficient to bear the correct charges. How many customers would try to use a debit card against insufficient funds on the negligible chance that the system would slip up and let them get away with it?

2.   Fraudulent Transactions

The most serious risk of loss in the debit-card context is the risk from false authorizations: debit-card transactions that the customer in fact has not authorized. For example, in one early case, an aide to a District of Columbia Council member made about $11,000 of unauthorized withdrawals on the council member's ATM card; the aide stole the card from the council member's office and guessed that the PIN would be the last four digits of the council member's home telephone number. See United States v. Miller, 70 F.3d 1353 (D.C. Cir. 1995) (affirming the thief's conviction for federal bank fraud). A more enterprising criminal used funds from fraudulent credit-card transactions to construct a false ATM (complete with a device to read and store the information on consumers' cards). He installed the ATM in a shopping mall, without any connection to a bank whatsoever. He then disabled the other ATM in the mall to increase usage of his false machine. Using that device, he created hundreds of counterfeit cards, with which he successfully stole more than $100,000. See United States v. Greenfield, 44 F.3d 1141 (2d Cir. 1995) (reviewing the sentence for Greenfield's conviction).

Several features of the debit-card system operate to minimize losses from fraud. First, the rules preventing unsolicited mailing of activated debit cards and the practice of mailing PINs separately from the cards should limit fraud from cards stolen without the customer's knowledge. Second, both the authorization request from the merchant to the bank and the bank's reply travel in an encrypted format that makes it relatively difficult to obtain funds through transmission of false messages: Even if an interloper intercepted and copied the message (an event usually described as a "man in the middle" attack), the encryption would make it difficult for the interloper to use the message to design forged messages or to alter the genuine message to call for payment to the interloper's account. Third, the PIN pads at the point of sale include software designed to prevent theft of the encryption protocol by destroying the encryption protocol if someone tampers with the pads.

The encryption technology used for debit cards is not at the highest level of sophistication. It is not, for example, nearly as secure as the technology used in the stored-value cards and electronic-money systems developed in recent years. Banks have resisted upgrading the technology for quite some time, based on concerns about the costs of requiring all merchants to purchase replacement terminals that would operate with more sophisticated encryption systems. Banks are particularly sensitive to those costs because merchants' concerns about high equipment costs were for many years one of the main obstacles to growth of debit-card networks. Whatever has been true in the past, however, that problem should pass in the near future, when American terminals are converted to chip-and-PIN technology.

Although the relatively low level of technology in the current system has not been a major problem, it has not been impervious to attack. The rate of loss from unauthorized transactions on PIN-based debit cards, for example, has persisted at about 0.3 cent per $100, one-twentieth of the analogous rate on credit cards (typically about 6 cents per $100). For example, in one 1997 incident, hackers managed to access a computer program used to encode information on debit cards and succeeded in manufacturing and using a dozen false debit cards before the scheme was uncovered. Nevertheless, it is a testament to the clarity and effectiveness of the system that there is almost no reported litigation in this area. An overwhelming majority of the recent reported cases discussing debit cards involve criminal convictions of the malfeasors for various types of criminal conduct that are much more direct than attempts to compromise the technological protections of the system. See, e.g., Garner v. State, 1996 WL 9600 (Tex. Ct. App.—Houston (1st Dist.) 1996) (affirming a conviction for aggravated robbery after defendant forced the victim into a car at gunpoint and forced her to withdraw cash from an ATM); State v. Knight, 909 P.2d 1133 (Haw. 1996) (affirming a conviction for murder committed after defendant forced the victim at knifepoint to reveal his PIN); State v. Fortune, 909 P.2d 930 (Wash. 1996) (en banc) (affirming a conviction for murder after defendant beat the victim to death with a sledgehammer, stole his debit card, and then used the card to empty the victim's bank account).

In fact, statistics indicate that more than 99 percent of fraud on PIN-based debit cards results from card usage by close acquaintances of the cardholder (relatives, friends, and the like). Although banks have difficulty documenting the identity of the user in POS transactions, they have been quite successful in using cameras at ATM and retail locations to defeat those claims. Most claims of unauthorized ATM usage are resolved when the customer, after reviewing the photograph of the allegedly unauthorized user, acknowledges that the user is not an unknown thief, but a close acquaintance of the customer.

Of course, the rapidly growing use of PIN-less debit cards issued through the major credit-card networks leaves the system much more exposed to fraud. Accordingly, although the credit-card networks can be expected to work to minimize losses, there is every reason to believe that the credit-card-related debit cards will become subject to fraudulent transactions much more frequently than debit cards have been. And that problem poses a serious threat to the success of the system because consumers react much more negatively to a surprise discovery that their bank account has been emptied (after a debit card has been stolen) than they do to a surprise discovery that their credit-card line has been exhausted (after a credit card has been used up). In the credit-card case, consumers need only notify the issuer that the charges are unauthorized, pull different cards from their wallets, and go about their business. By contrast, when consumer bank accounts have been depleted upon a debit-card theft, consumers face a much more serious problem unless they can get the funds recredited immediately (something Regulation E does not require).

Turning to that problem, the system must resolve two questions when losses arise from false authorizations on debit cards. The first is deciding who bears a loss as between the merchant that accepts payment based on a stolen debit card and the bank on which the card draws. For example, if a merchant operating a POS system sells goods to somebody who pays with a stolen debit card, can the bank recover the funds that it paid to the merchant based on that sale?

Because there is not yet any significant legal regulation of that issue, that question currently is answered by the contractual arrangements of the different systems. Ordinarily, the network rules allocate that loss to the bank, relying on the notion that the bank is in a much better position to mitigate those losses than the merchant. It is the bank, after all, that maintains the system for authorizing withdrawals and has the ability to design the cards so as to limit the possibility of counterfeiting and incorrect identifications. To be sure, the system could rely on the merchant to limit losses through signature-verification or photograph requirements, but those devices are notoriously unsuccessful at limiting fraudulent authorizations. Thus, the merchant is entitled to payment from the bank even if the customer was not entitled to draw on the account.

The second problem for the legal system is deciding who bears the loss as between the bank on which the card draws and the customer whose card has been stolen. On that point, positive law provides an answer that protects the cardholder considerably even apart from the parties' own agreements. Specifically, federal law provides two separate protections related to unauthorized transactions, as well as a set of specified procedures for determining whether a particular transaction in fact was authorized.

The first set of rules establishes a threshold requirement that a card have some minimal security feature for confirming transactions, whether by PIN or by some other method (such as a photograph, signature, or fingerprint). EFTA §909(a). In the absence of such a feature, the EFTA bars any imposition on the consumer of liability for unauthorized use. Traditionally, that requirement has posed little difficulty: PIN-based transactions use PINs, and PIN-less transactions commonly rely on signatures.

The important part of the EFTA framework is its limitation of consumer liability even in cases in which the card does have a security feature. Those limitations appear in the complex and poorly drafted provisions of EFTA §909(a). Essentially, that section establishes three separate rules that a bank can use to impose liability on the consumer when the consumer's card is lost or stolen.

Although EFTA §909(a) seems to establish a rule limiting the customer's loss from each unauthorized transfer, the Federal Reserve has interpreted the rules in §909(a) to apply to any "series of related unauthorized transfers." Regulation E, §1005.6(b). Thus, if a debit-card thief uses the card ten times, the dollar limits in §909(a) describe the consumer's exposure for the entire incident, not the exposure for each of the ten unauthorized transactions.

The first rule appears in the second sentence of EFTA §909(a), which begins with "In no event." That rule allows the bank to hold the consumer responsible for up to $50 of unauthorized transfers that occur before the financial institution learns of the consumer's loss of the card. See 12 C.F.R. §1005.6(b)(1). That rule applies without regard to fault or diligence on the part of the consumer. Thus, the consumer can be held responsible for losses under that rule even with respect to transactions made before the consumer knows that the card has been stolen.

The second rule appears in the fourth sentence of EFTA §909(a), which begins with "In addition." The second rule is a fault-based notice rule that allows the bank to charge the consumer for losses if the consumer does not promptly notify the bank after it discovers that the card has been lost. That rule operates on the assumption that the consumer should notify the bank within two business days after the time that the consumer learns of the theft and allows the bank to charge the consumer for all losses that occur more than two business days after the consumer learns of the theft, but before the financial institution learns of the loss of the card. The maximum amount that the consumer can be charged under the notice rule is $500. That $500 includes the $50 that could have been charged the consumer under the first rule. Thus, assuming that the consumer was aware of the theft from the moment that it occurred, the consumer would be responsible for a total of only $500 if $50 were charged on the first two days after a card was stolen and $500 on the third and fourth days. See 12 C.F.R. §1005.6(b)(2).

The third rule is a bank-statement rule that appears in the third sentence of EFTA §909(a), which begins with "Notwithstanding the foregoing." Under that rule, consumers must review their statements to identify unauthorized transactions that appear on the statements. Under the EFTA, the consumer has a (relatively generous) 60 days to review the statements (starting on the date they are sent). EFTA §909(a). If the consumer fails to report an unauthorized transaction within that 60-day period, the consumer bears responsibility for any subsequent unauthorized transactions that would have failed had the consumer identified the unauthorized transactions on the statement and advised the bank of the problem. EFTA §909(a); Regulation E, §1005.6(b)(3). The consumer's liability under the bank-statement rule is entirely separate from the liability under the two previous rules and has no maximum dollar limit.

The federal rules described above establish a floor of risk that banks must accept, but they permit states to limit the consumer's share of the loss even more narrowly. See EFTA §919 (stating that the EFTA does not preempt state laws that "affor[d] any consumer [protection that] is greater than the protection afforded by [the EFTA]"). Some states have responded to that invitation by extending the EFTA deadlines. See Kan. Stat. Ann. §9-1111d (allowing four days rather than two to notify the bank of the loss). Others lower the amount of the consumer's exposure in cases in which the consumer fails to give the notice. See, e.g., Colo. Rev. Stat. §11-6.5-109(2) (absolute limitation of customer's responsibility to $50); Kan. Stat. Ann. §9-1111d ($300, rather than $500, exposure); Mass. Gen. L. ch. 167B, §18 (absolute limitation of customer's responsibility to $50).

Perhaps more surprisingly, a recent rash of publicity regarding the $500 potential loss rule under the EFTA has motivated the major debit-card networks (Mastercard and Visa) to alter their network rules to limit the consumer's exposure to losses from unauthorized transactions. Specifically, both networks voluntarily have agreed that the banks issuing their cards will limit consumer liability for unauthorized transactions to $50, *even if* the consumer fails to notify the issuer of the theft of the debit card and fails to identify the fraudulent transaction within the 60-day EFTA period.

The EFTA also establishes a framework for resolving disputes about whether particular transactions were authorized. To invoke that framework, a customer must give oral or written notice of transactions claimed to be unauthorized within 60 days after the bank mails documentation of the transaction to the customer. EFTA §908(a). When a bank receives such a notice, it must investigate the error and provide the customer a written explanation of its conclusion. The bank must respond within ten business days or give the customer a provisional recredit for the disputed amount. Recognizing the importance to consumers of the date that funds return to a customer's account, Visa and Mastercard (in connection with their voluntary agreement to limit cardholder exposure to unauthorized losses to $50) have agreed that the recredit deadline for banks issuing their cards will expire after five days, instead of the ten days permitted under the EFTA.

Even if the bank provides a provisional recredit, it still must proceed to investigate the customer's complaint. Under the EFTA, it must complete its investigation within 45 days after receiving the customer's 60-day notice. The statute backs up its procedural requirements by allowing a federal court to impose treble damages on any bank that (a) fails to recredit an account within the ten-day period when required to do so or (b) unreasonably rejects a customer's claim of error. EFTA §908; Regulation E, §1005.11(c)(3).

In some cases, account holders unable to recover under those provisions have sought relief under the Uniform Commercial Code rules related to checks (the subject of Chapter 3). As the case that follows illustrates, those efforts are unlikely to succeed. As you study the case, consider the reasons why the account holder did not attempt to rely on the EFTA.

Hospicomm, Inc. v. Fleet Bank, N.A.

338 F. Supp. 2d 578 (E.D. Pa. 2004)

SURRICK, District Judge.

Presently before the Court is Defendant Fleet Bank, N.A.'s Motion to Dismiss. . . . For the following reasons we will grant Defendant's motion. . . .

BACKGROUND

Plaintiff Hospicomm, Inc. is a Pennsylvania corporation with its principal place of business in Philadelphia, Pennsylvania. Plaintiff provides data processing, marketing, operations management, and other services to healthcare providers. Defendant Fleet Bank, N.A., is a bank incorporated in Rhode Island with its principal place of business in Boston, Massachusetts.

Pursuant to an agreement reached on November 21, 2002, Plaintiff began performing all day-to-day management services for Hamilton Continuing Care Center ("Hamilton"). On behalf of Hamilton, Plaintiff established numerous bank accounts with Defendant. Access to these accounts was limited to authorized account signatories and authorized account managers. Defendant issued "transfer cards" to these authorized persons, to allow them to transfer funds between the accounts. . . .

On or about April 15, 2003, Plaintiff terminated an employee named Guillermo A. Martinez. Martinez had been employed as a financial analyst and his duties included bookkeeping for facilities managed by Plaintiff, including Hamilton. After terminating Martinez, Plaintiff discovered bank statements for one of the accounts held by Defendant that indicated that ATM withdrawal transactions had been processed through the account. Plaintiff determined that Martinez, an employee without access to the accounts, gained access when he requested and received a "VISA ATM" card. Over the course of an eight-month period, Martinez allegedly used the ATM card issued to him by Defendant to make more than 400 transactions and/or cash withdrawals from the accounts totaling in excess of $148,000.

After reimbursing Hamilton for the funds converted by Martinez, Plaintiff filed the instant action against Defendant. Plaintiff alleges that Defendant issued Martinez the ATM card without "prior notification, consultation, or approval" from Plaintiff or Hamilton; Defendant failed to detect these "highly suspect transactions and irregular withdrawals"; and Defendant failed to take any action or notify Plaintiff about the issuance of the ATM card or the suspicious activity connected to the account. On the basis of these allegations Plaintiff filed the instant Complaint, in the Court of Common Pleas in Philadelphia County, alleging [among other things, breach of the duty of] good faith in violation of Article 4 of the Uniform Commercial Code ("UCC"). Defendant removed the case pursuant to 28 U.S.C. §1441.

Defendant subsequently filed the instant motion to dismiss. Defendant contends that the entire Complaint should be dismissed because . . . Plaintiff's UCC Article 4 claim must be dismissed because Article 4 does not apply to ATM cards. . . .

DISCUSSION . . .

UCC Article 4

Plaintiff contends that Defendant violated various duties Defendant owed it under Article 4 of the UCC. Defendant contends that this claim should be dismissed because Article 4 does not apply to ATM transactions. . . .

. . . Defendant's sole argument is that Plaintiff's claim is insufficient because transactions related to the use of an ATM card are not covered by Article 4 of the

UCC. Article 4 only applies to "items" as defined in [UCC §4-104]. Item is defined as "[a]n instrument or a promise or order to pay money handled by a bank for collection or payment. The term does not include a payment order governed by [Article] 4A (relating to funds transfers) or a credit or debit card slip." Defendant argues that based on the definitions of "instrument," "promise," and "order" it is apparent that an ATM transaction is not contemplated by the definition of item. See [UCC §§3-103, 3-104]. Plaintiff contends that an ATM card replaces money, such that it can be considered an instrument as defined by the UCC.

There are no federal or state cases in Pennsylvania that address the extent to which Article 4 of the UCC covers electronic withdrawals of funds. Numerous cases in other jurisdictions have considered the question of whether Article 4 covers electronic fund transfers ("EFTs"). Each of the cases that have considered the issue ha[s] found that the UCC does not apply to EFTs. The issue presently before us—whether Article 4 applies to electronic withdrawals—has not been thoroughly analyzed. The Supreme Court of Kansas in the case of Sinclair Oil Corp. v. Sylvan State Bank, 254 Kan. 836, 869 P.2d 675 (1994), discussed an issue similar to the one currently before us. In *Sinclair Oil*, the plaintiff was paid for products it delivered by "making electronic debits" from its customer's bank account. [Ed.: The case involved ACH debits of the type discussed in Assignment 5.] On one such occasion, the defendant bank returned the debited funds to the customer's account because after the electronic debits the customer's account was left with insufficient funds. Plaintiff alleged that the return of the debited funds was late under the Article 4 of the Kansas Uniform Commercial Code. Ultimately, the court was forced to consider whether electronic debits are excluded from UCC coverage. The court initiated its analysis by noting that other courts had excluded EFTs from UCC coverage because: (1) electronic debits are not "items" within the meaning of Article 4; (2) the UCC does not specifically address the problems of electronic fund transfers; and (3) the UCC drafters never contemplated electronic transactions when developing the Code.

The court first analyzed what "item" meant under Article 4. An item is an "instrument." An "instrument" under the UCC is defined as a "negotiable instrument." A "negotiable instrument," is defined as "'any writing' that was signed by the maker, containing an unconditional promise to pay a sum certain, payable on demand or at a definite time to order or to bearer." The court went on to recognize that the 1990 statute adopting that definition identified the writings that complied with the section to include drafts, checks, certificates of deposit, and notes. "An EFT is not a writing and is not within the specific list of writings that are 'instruments.'"

The court moved on to consider the intent behind the adoption of Article 4. It noted numerous ways in which the concept of electronic transfers is not contemplated by the UCC. These reasons include: (1) Article 4A specifically excludes so called "debit transfers," where the order to pay is given by the person receiving payment; (2) electronic fund transfers were not in the contemplation of the Article 4 drafters, as Article 4 is

a direct outgrowth of the American Bankers Association Bank Collection Code, drafted in the early 1920s to govern check collection; and (3) the ideas in Articles 3 and 4 of the UCC . . . depend upon bankers looking at particular words and numerals on the face of a particular instrument. In the case of EFTs, the medium of communication is the computer. . . .

Though the financial transactions at issue in this case are alleged unauthorized ATM withdrawals rather than electronic debits from one bank account sent to another, we are satisfied that the rationale of *Sinclair Oil* applies equally here. By its very definitions, Pennsylvania's adoption of Article 4 does not contemplate electronic withdrawals. The statute defines "item" as "[a]n instrument or a promise or order to pay money handled by a bank for collection or payment. The term does not include a payment order governed by [Article] 4A (relating to funds transfers) or a credit or debit card slip." [UCC §4-104]. In the instant case, Martinez allegedly withdrew funds using a Visa ATM card issued by Defendant. As in *Sinclair Oil*, Article 4 was meant to apply only to traditional written instruments, rather than electronic means of transferring and withdrawing funds. Nowhere in Article 4 are ATM withdrawals discussed. Rather, a review of the text supports the conclusion that Article 4 was meant to apply to checks and traditional, written, monetary instruments.

Our conclusion that Article 4 does not cover ATM withdrawals is buttressed by the federal law in this area. While focusing on Defendant's liability under Article 4 of the UCC, neither party addressed the fact that Congress enacted legislation covering ATM withdrawals when it enacted the Electronic Fund Transfer Act ("EFTA"), 15 U.S.C. §1693 *et seq.* The EFTA was enacted "to provide a basic framework establishing the rights, liabilities, and responsibilities of participants in electronic fund transfer systems." 15 U.S.C. §1693. The statute was designed to specifically cover withdrawals made from an ATM. See 15 U.S.C. §1693a (defining "electronic fund transfer" to mean "any transfer of funds . . . which is initiated through an electronic terminal, telephonic instrument, or computer or magnetic tape so as to order, instruct, or authorize a financial institution to debit or credit an account. Such term includes . . . automated teller machine transactions . . . ."). See also United States v. Goldblatt, 813 F.2d 619, 622 (3d Cir. 1987) (criminal case discussing applicability of EFTA to ATM withdrawals). Moreover, the EFTA enacted a defined process for a consumer to bring a claim against a bank for an alleged "unauthorized fund transfer." See 15 U.S.C. §§1693c-h.

The EFTA has an anti-preemption clause specifically allowing states to enforce consumer credit protections that go beyond the protections of the EFTA that are not inconsistent with EFTA. 15 U.S.C. §1693q; Metrobank v. Foster, 193 F. Supp. 2d 1156, 1159 (S.D. Iowa 2002). Article 4A of the UCC specifically states that "this division does not apply to a funds transfer any part of which is governed by the [EFTA]." [UCC §4A-108; see also UCC §4A-108 comment] ("The effect of section 4A-108 is to make Article 4A and EFTA mutually exclusive."). Though this text seems to suggest that in Pennsylvania the EFTA is the exclusive remedy for claims relating to ATM transactions, nowhere in the statute are ATM transactions explicitly removed from the application of Article 4. Even assuming, *arguendo*, that Article 4 of the UCC does in fact apply to ATM transactions, we believe it still would be preempted by the EFTA. The EFTA constructs a process for consumers wishing to contest unauthorized transfers, with clear burdens that must be satisfied in any suit. See 15 U.S.C. §§1693c-h. Under the circumstances, we conclude that in

Pennsylvania, a cause of action for an unauthorized use of an ATM card should be brought under the EFTA, rather than Article 4 of the UCC.

Problem Set 3

3.1.   The ever forgetful Cliff Janeway (your bookseller friend, most recently from Problem Set 2) calls you one afternoon from the airport in Albuquerque, where he just got off a plane to visit some local booksellers. He is frantic because he left his checkbook on the seat next to him when he left the plane. He is pretty sure that his debit card was stuffed inside the checkbook, and he is sure that his personal identification number is written on the inside cover of the checkbook. His account has about $12,000 in it because he planned to purchase several expensive books while in Albuquerque. He wants to know what he should do. Does he have anything to worry about? For example, what would happen if the thief used the debit card to spend $3,000 on the day that the card is stolen, but Cliff doesn't report the theft for two weeks? Would it be different if the $3,000 charge occurred a week after the theft instead of the next day? Why should that matter? EFTA §§908, 909.

3.2.   Archie Moon comes by this morning and insists that he has to see you without an appointment. He tells you that about a month ago he purchased a new printing press. As it happens, he is completely dissatisfied with the printing press because it does not perform nearly as well as the salesperson promised him. Accordingly, he decided that he wanted to withhold payment. Remembering some advice you gave him several years ago, he did not write a check for the press; instead, he paid for it with his bank card. When Archie called his bank officer last week to tell her that he did not wish to pay for the press and identified the transaction, his bank officer told him that he could not challenge the transaction because he had purchased the press with a debit card.

Archie has looked at the card in his wallet and the information from his bank and tells you that the card contains two features, a PIN-less debit card feature (a Mastercard, as it happens), and a PIN-based debit card (NYCE). He can't remember whether he punched the "credit" or the "debit" button, but he knows that he usually pushes the credit button. Putting aside any right that Archie might have against the merchant and assuming that Archie is right about what happened, can Archie force his bank to refund the money to him? EFTA §§903(7), 909; TILA §170(a).

3.3.   Luck being what it is, Archie calls you a few weeks later to report that in the course of reviewing his bank statements in connection with the transaction discussed in Problem 3.2, he noticed quite a number of unauthorized transactions. The transactions go back over a year and total $3,000. (The thief did not get greedy, but took only $250 each month.) For how much of the $3,000 is Archie responsible? (For purposes of the problem, assume that the theft occurred on March 1, that on the first day of each month the bank mails a statement that includes all of the previous transactions, and that the thefts occurred in individual $250 transactions on the fifteenth of each month.)

    a.   First, assume that Archie called his bank the instant that he lost his card about a year ago. EFTA §909(a); Regulation E, §§1005.6(b), 1005.12(a).

    b.   Second, assume that Archie never called his bank about the loss of his card at all.

3.4.   Same facts as Problem 3.3, but now change the date of the $250 March 15 theft to March 2 and assume that the May 15 theft did not occur.

3.5.   Would your answers change if Archie told you that he received and read (but ignored) a text message from the bank reporting the March 2 $250 theft to him at the moment that it occurred?

3.6.   Same facts as Problem 3.3, but now assume that all of the transactions were made with a contact-less debit card, for which neither a signature nor a PIN is required. What if some of the transactions caused an overdraft, but were honored under the overdraft agreement that Archie had with his bank? EFTA §909(a); Regulation E, §1005.6(a); Reg. E Interp., ¶6(a); Reg. Z Interp., ¶¶2(a)(15), 12(b)(2)(iii).

3.7.   Just after you get off the phone with Bill, you discover that Cliff Janeway is waiting to see you. He explains that in response to the advice that you gave him in Problem 3.1, he promptly went to his bank to report the unauthorized transactions. That visit occurred on Monday March 1, the same day that he learned that the card had been lost. Based on a review of charges that had been posted to his account at that time, he reported a total of $1,000 of unauthorized charges, all of which apparently were used to purchase beer and wine at a nearby liquor store that accepts debit cards. Assuming that the problem had been dealt with, Cliff went about his business.

Much to his surprise, ten days later on March 11, Cliff got a telecopy from one of his suppliers advising Cliff that the supplier was canceling its contract with Cliff because Cliff's bank had bounced the check Cliff had written to that supplier on March 6. On inquiry, Cliff discovered that the bank bounced the check on the morning of March 9 because it had not yet determined how to respond to Cliff's claim that the beer-and-wine debit-card transactions were unauthorized. Does Cliff have a right to complain about the bank's dishonor of his check? UCC §4-402; EFTA §908(c); Regulation E, §1005.11(c).

3.8.   Joe Willie ("Bill") Robertson is a long-time friend of yours who operates a chain of independent cleaners in Houston, Texas. He has always resisted taking debit cards or credit cards, but is now seriously considering it. His bank has just come to him with a proposal that he start accepting debit cards under a PIN-based system at his stores. The bank tells Bill that his account will be credited with funds much more rapidly on debit-card transactions than it is on traditional checking transactions, which should bring him additional interest income on an annual basis of about $160,000. Bill also hopes that it will save him a substantial amount on bad-check expenses; he currently has to write off about 1.5 percent of all receipts that come in the form of checks, either because the checks are uncollectible or because collecting them through litigation is too expensive. These cost savings far exceed the cost of the equipment that Bill would have to buy to implement the debit-card system, even taking account of the 15- to 35-cent discount Bill will have to pay his bank on each transaction.

Notwithstanding those possible benefits, Bill is skeptical about the bank's proposal for two reasons. He doubts the reliability of the computer technology, and he has a policy of always worrying when his banker claims to be doing something for his benefit. Bill asks you whether he faces any significant risks of loss if he starts accepting the cards. What if people present forged cards? What if they use stolen cards? Does it matter if they enter a PIN or sign? What if they do neither (which, according to his banker, seems to be an option)?

Assignment 4: Prepaid Cards

The most recent development in the payment card industry is the "prepaid" card, formerly known as the "stored-value" card. Like the debit card, the pre-paid card is a product that was around, at least conceptually, for many years before it finally gained market traction and broad usage. Since the last years of the twentieth century, card professionals in this country have assumed that consumers soon would be using sophisticated stored-value cards on which consumers could store money in the form of encrypted packets of electronic information. By the turn of the millennium, however, those expectations had been doused by a continuing series of market disappointments for such products. Among other things, numerous high-profile tests of chip-enabled stored-value cards (in the United States and elsewhere) were characterized by a startling inability to generate consumer acceptance.

In the early years of this century, a stripped-down, simplified version of that technology began to gain traction. Two major applications (discussed in more detail below) drove the initial adoption by a sufficient nucleus of issuers and cardholders to give the product mainstream acceptance: gift cards and payroll cards. Building on those initial successes, stored-value cards are now ubiquitous, available off the shelf at retailers and convenience stores. By 2016, they were being used in more than 9 billion transactions a year, worth almost $320 billion.

A.   Mechanics

In its most basic form, a prepaid card (to use the modern term) is a card that accesses value that the cardholder (or some third party) previously has paid to the issuer. That description makes the product sound just like a debit card. The difference is that the stored-value card ordinarily is not linked to a bank account. Rather, the issuer simply keeps track of the funds it has received from each cardholder, so that it can tell how much is "on" the card at any given time. This is crucial, because it makes the cards available to individuals without bank accounts, easing the ability of low- and moderate-income households to participate in the modern card-based payments economy.

Another distinctive feature is that the indicator of value can but need not be carried directly on the card. Thus, unlike a credit card, at least in theory (though rarely in practice) there is no need for a contemporaneous authorization of the transaction to confirm that an account holds funds for the transaction. Rather, the transaction could be completed entirely based on an interaction between the merchant's terminal and the card itself.

Conceptually, writers (and occasionally legislators, as discussed below) often refer to the "value" as "residing" on the card — as if value were a tangible object with a specific location. The concept of value being located in a tangible object might make some sense for currency — which passes from hand to hand without any realistic prospect of redemption. But in this context, where each transaction is likely to involve almost immediate collection of funds from the issuer of the card, it makes more sense to recognize that the "value" involved in a prepaid card is an obligation of the issuer, which does not have any specific physical location.

Some of the earliest uses of prepaid cards did involve something more akin to value "stored" "on" the card; the paradigm was as a substitute for cash in small-dollar contexts where it was inconvenient to pay cash for each transaction. For example, mass-transit farecards and copier cards long have provided two successful applications for primitive stored-value cards. Those cards also limit the risk of violent crime against cardholders by lowering the amount of cash that cardholders are carrying — at least to the extent that the thief who steals the card is unable to use the value on the card for the thief's own purposes (often not the case for farecards and copier cards).

The technology behind the earliest stored-value cards was quite simple. Those cards carried a simple magnetic stripe that maintained a balance of value that was reduced by each subsequent use of the card. There was no significant encryption of the cards; the value was indicated by the number of magnetic impulses on the card. Moreover, the value was easily lost if the card was placed next to an object with a strong magnetic field.

Those cards are likely to continue in contexts where the attractiveness of theft is limited either by the low value of the amounts that can be stored on the card or by the limited use to which the funds can be put (such as subway rides in a particular city or on a particular line, or gift certificates to be redeemed at a particular store). In other contexts, however, two products that have more robust protections against fraud have replaced them: prepaid cards that verify transactions contemporaneously, and chip-enhanced "smart" cards that can verify their own transactions.

Mass-market prepaid cards have grown rapidly since their 2001 introduction by Mastercard; this is the market that produces the billions of transactions per year mentioned at the beginning of the assignment. The basic concept of this product is to have the value that is to be placed on the card collected by the person that sells the card: An employee at a 7-11 might sell a $50 prepaid Mastercard, take the cash (plus a commission), and dispense the card to the customer. The most visible early success doubtless was the Starbucks card, which debuted to wide acclaim in 2002. Starbucks now loads more than a billion dollars per quarter onto those cards, which offer the convenience of a tap-and-pay transaction (always important in the long lines at Starbucks), as well as an easy method for tracking rewards.

The other early use of the modern prepaid card was the payroll card. In that context, the product offers substantial savings to employers trying to pay employees that do not have bank accounts. When employees have bank accounts, their employers can pay them with direct deposit (a type of ACH transaction, discussed below in Chapter 2), at a cost of pennies per pay period.

When they do not have a bank account, employers formerly paid with a paper check, at a cost approaching $10 per pay period. Now, giving employees a prepaid card, the employers can load payments on to the card each pay period at a cost similar to the cost of direct deposit payments. Those cards currently are used for about $50 billion of salary payments a year. That product got a major boost when the federal government decided that it would no longer issue checks for any of its benefits programs. All of those programs are being moved to a series of prepaid cards, generally under the name of Direct Express.

Those cards typically include a unique card number on a magnetic stripe that can be used in an authorization transaction much like the authorization transaction for a conventional credit- or debit-card transaction. The general-purpose cards commonly used for the payroll card and Direct Express applications are now almost always Visa and Mastercard products. What that means, of course, is that the cards can be used at all the retail locations that commonly accept Visa and Mastercard products; this is a far cry from the stigma associated with using food stamps, money orders, and the like in previous decades.

Those cards (referred to as "host-based" or "hosted" cards because a record for the value of the card is maintained at a host) often are marketed by third-party processors, which maintain databases for all cards issued by their clients and verify the individual transactions. Cards often can be reloaded, either at a participating merchant or by telephone or Internet (drawing on a credit card, debit card, or ACH transfer).

A more visionary product is the chip-enhanced smart card. That product carries a tiny microprocessor on the card that includes an electronic record of the value on the card. Those cards interact with readers at the merchant's terminal, so that no contemporaneous authorization is necessary. In this country, they remain relatively uncommon, limited for the most part to closed environments like university and corporate campuses. For example, the most prominent deployment in recent times is the various stored-value applications that the Department of the Treasury operates for the United States military, the most prominent of which are NavyCash and EagleCash. Because the military already requires soldiers to carry a chip-enhanced Common Access Card, it has been easy to add a stored-value function to those cards, responding to the desire for Navy vessels to be cashless environments, as well as the need for military personnel to make reliable payments in military contexts in which access to conventional card-processing networks is impractical.

Smart prepaid cards are much more common overseas, generally because the infrastructure for conventional telephonic authorization of payment-card transactions is much less satisfactory. In that context, there is much to be gained from a product that permits reliable authorization without the need for a contemporaneous telephonic connection. The value to be gained overseas from sophisticated local authorization is underscored by circumstances in the United Kingdom, where *all* card users have migrated to smart cards, generally to cure intractable problems with fraud, attributable at least in part to relatively low rates of telephonic authorization of conventional credit-card transactions.

Another benefit of that product is that the transactions can be entirely anonymous: Without a host maintaining a record of each card, there is no central record from which transaction data can be compiled for individuals who use the system. As discussed below with respect to electronic money, that privacy concern has not been an important driver of payment preferences in this country, but it may be more important overseas, where these products have been more successful.

A typical product is the Octopus card widely used in Hong Kong. There are about 10 million cards in circulation (in a country with a population of about 7 million), used for 8 million transactions a day. Originally developed to simplify the process of collecting fares for mass transit, the card is now accepted widely at convenience stores, fast-food restaurants, and other outlets with low average checks. Tellingly, the Web site for the card emphasizes to users that the card is completely anonymous.

B.   Legal Issues

1.   EFTA

The legal framework that governs stored-value cards in this country is remarkably unstable. In the terms of the EFTA, the fundamental question that the cards present is whether transactions that use the card involve an "electronic fund transfer" governed by the EFTA. To understand that question, three definitions from the statute are important. First, an electronic fund transfer is defined in §903(7) as any "transfer of funds . . . which is initiated through an electronic terminal . . . so as to order, instruct, or authorize a financial institution to debit . . . an account." An account, in turn, "means a demand deposit (checking), savings, or other consumer asset account held directly or indirectly by a financial institution." Regulation E, §1005.2(b)(1). Finally, the term "financial institution" is defined broadly to include "a State or National bank, a State or Federal savings and loan association . . . or any other person who, directly or indirectly, holds an account belonging to a consumer." EFTA §903(9).

For a host-based card like the ones discussed above, it would be plausible to characterize the card sponsor as a financial institution, holding a "consumer asset account" for each consumer to which it has issued a card. Then, it would be plausible to say that each transaction using the card is a transfer, initiated through an electronic terminal, instructing the sponsor to debit that account (and pay the money to the appropriate merchant through the Visa or Mastercard network, as the case may be). That view gains significant weight from a decision by the FDIC under which banks that hold such funds would be able to treat them as deposits (to which deposit insurance would apply and against which banks must hold reserves).

If the EFTA applied, that would have several ramifications for the industry. Among other things, issuers would be responsible for unauthorized transactions and would have to refund amounts previously loaded on cards that are lost. Presently, the most that can be said is that recent amendments to Regulation E bring payroll cards explicitly within the statute. See Regulation E, §§1005.2(b)(2), 1005.18(a).

Many, but not all, issuers already provide such protections. Application of the EFTA would make protection universal. Also, many of the protections that apply—such as the Visa and Mastercard "zero liability" policies—have loopholes that could not continue if the statute applied. For example, Mastercard's policy does not apply if there are multiple unauthorized transactions in a single year, if the cardholder has failed to use reasonable care to safeguard the card, or if the cardholder is delinquent in payments on the account. The EFTA includes no such restrictions.

At the same time, application of the EFTA to many other common applications seems dubious. For example, the Direct Express cards are not payroll cards, nor are Starbucks cards or the increasingly ubiquitous gift cards. The occasional "smart" prepaid cards are even more clearly outside the statute. In contrast to host-based cards, the only record of value for those cards often is on the card itself. In that case, it is difficult to view use of the card as a "transfer," because the "financial institution" seems to hold no "account" out of which funds are being transferred. The CFPB recently has promulgated regulations that require disclosures and limit fees for most of these cards, but they do not bring them within the regulation for purposes of the protections against unauthorized transactions. 12 C.F.R. §1005.20. After numerous delays, the CFPB finally adopted new regulations that extend substantially all of Regulation E to substantially all prepaid cards. See 12 C.F.R. §§1005.2(b)(3) (defining "account" to include payroll cards, government benefit cards, and other general-purpose prepaid cards), 1005.18 (establishing specialized rules for disclosure and dispute resolution on prepaid cards).

2. Other Issues

The rise of prepaid cards also has generated controversy in several other areas. For example, there has been considerable discussion of the applicability of the money-transmitter laws most states have enacted. At least some of those laws rather clearly apply to the host of a stored-value system. See, e.g., Uniform Money Services Act §102(14) (defining "Money transmission" to include "selling or issuing . . . stored value").

Similar regulations in the European Union, issued under its Electronic Money Directive, apply to many of these products. Article 1 of that Directive defines "electronic money" to include monetary value as represented by a claim on the issuer which is:

(i) stored on an electronic device;
(ii) issued on receipt of funds of an amount not less in value than the monetary value issued;
(iii) accepted as means of payment by undertakings other than the issuer.

As discussed in the opening pages of this assignment, that definition relies on the notion that the "value" involved in stored value resides in some particular location. However difficult it might be to apply that definition in some situations—as with the host-based products common in this country—it quite naturally extends to the chip-enhanced "smart" stored-value cards that are more common in Europe. For institutions that issue those cards, the Directive imposes minimum capitalization requirements (Article 4), investment limitations (Article 5), and auditing requirements (Article 6) much like the requirements that the Uniform Money Services Act and similar statutes impose on money transmitters in the United States.

In some states, however, older statutes are being updated to ensure that they reach the variety of prepaid card models described above. Again, those laws typically do not regulate the transactions directly by protecting the user against an improper use of the funds. Rather, they focus on regulation of the host—rules to prevent the funds from disappearing through financial irresponsibility of the host before the cardholder can get an opportunity to spend them.

Another issue relates to unused funds on the cards. Many systems impose fees for inactivity or otherwise provide that the funds revert to the issuer if they are not spent within a certain time. (Starbucks, for example, initially included a $2.00 fee for inactive cards, but ultimately rescinded the fee before ever charging it.) Motivated in part by the rapid rise of prepaid cards, most states now have statutes that ban such provisions, at least for gift cards. Because the statutes vary in their details—most do not apply, for example, to cards issued by financial institutions—the significance of those statutes is difficult to gauge.

The cards also raise a final set of problems related to the question whether they can be sold anonymously. For example, the USA Patriot Act requires a bank to verify its account holders against lists of known terrorists and take steps to ensure that its products are not being used to support terrorism. If the purchase of a prepaid card establishes an "account" under 31 U.S.C. §5318 (which includes "a formal . . . business relationship established to provide regular services, dealings, and other financial transactions"), then the financial institution might be subject to those obligations with respect to persons about whom it knows nothing. More broadly, even a nonbank issuer might be covered if its activities involve sufficient conduct to make it a "financial institution" under applicable definitions. See 31 U.S.C. §5312(a)(2)(R) (including "a licensed sender of money or any other person who engages as a business in the transmission of funds, including any person who engages as a business in an informal money transfer system or any network of people who engage as a business in facilitating the transfer of money domestically or internationally outside of the conventional financial institutions system"). Similar issues arise under the Bank Secrecy Act, which generally requires reports of large financial transactions conducted either through banks or through "money servicing businesses," a term defined in 31 C.F.R. §103.11 specifically to include parties that send or redeem stored value.

For years, the prepaid card industry opposed regulation, fearing that regulation would stifle developing business models. That attitude seems to be rapidly shifting, as the growth of large businesses has made the level of uncertainty in the interpretation of existing law such that clarity now seems preferable.

Supplemental Reading: Liran Haim & Ronald Mann, *Putting Stored-Value Cards in Their Place*, 18 Lewis & Clark L. Rev. 989 (2014).

Problem Set 4

4.1. The ever forgetful Cliff Janeway (your bookseller friend, most recently from Problem 3.1) calls you again to mention that his son believes he left his payroll card on the same plane. What should his son do? Does he have anything to worry about? Consider how your answer might change if it were any prepaid card you happen to find in your wallet, a Starbucks card, or a Direct Express card? Any other types of prepaid cards that occur to you? Regulation E, 12 C.F.R. §§1005.2(b)(3), 1005.15, 1005.18(a), 1005.20; EFTA §§903, 908, 909.

4.2. a. Same facts as Problem 3.4, but now assume that the transactions occurred on your client's Mastercard branded, reloadable stored-value card. Also, you should assume that the issuer does not send periodic statements, but rather posts information about the transactions in an accessible location online, and that the cardholder does not ever view the information. 12 C.F.R. §1005.2(b)(3), 1005.18(c)(1) & (e)(1).

b. Would your answer change if it was a Direct Express card issued to disburse federal benefits? Proposed 12 C.F.R. §1005.15(d)(1) & (e).

c. What if it was a Starbucks card?

4.3. When your daughter goes off to college, you pay for a meal plan for her first semester in a single lump sum. She accesses the value with a meal card the university issues her, which she can swipe on a terminal at any of the food-service locations on the campus. You get a 20 percent discount on the cost of her meals by prepaying. Should you worry about putting all her money on the card? Do you want to know anything further about the details of the card system to answer that question? If so, why should the details of the technology affect the answer to such a simple and practical question? Regulation E, 12 C.F.R. §§1005.2(b), 1005.18(a), 1005.20; EFTA §§903, 908, 909; Proposed 12 C.F.R. §§1005.2(b)(3), 1005.18.

4.4. You have a meeting this morning with a new client, Mike McLaughlin, who runs a sporting goods store near the local university. Because many of his customers are students, he signed up to join the university's stored-value-card program (called I-Card). His problem arises from a series of transactions totaling several thousand dollars that occurred over a three-day period last week, all from students who live at a single fraternity house near his store. The first day's transactions went through fine last Tuesday night, but the second day's transactions were rejected when he tried to send them in for collection last Wednesday and Thursday night.

As best as he can understand based on his conversations with the university's I-Card office, the students at the fraternity appear to have discovered a way to create false value on their I-Cards—an amusing prank in the view of the fraternity members, but not in the view of the I-Card administrators (or, it seems,

Mike). The students apparently used information one of them took from I-Card computers when he worked at the I-Card office as an intern last semester.

It appears that none of the transactions in question involved funds that actually had been deposited on the cards. The I-Card administrators haven't paid Mike for the bulk of the transactions, and have told him they may ask him to refund money from the Tuesday night transactions for which he already has been paid. He doesn't understand why this should be his problem. "It's their equipment — the terminal, the software, the cards, everything. I did everything exactly like they said, running the cards in the readers, having them type in the PINs. How can they refuse to pay?" What do you tell him? Is there anything you would like to know?

4.5.   Another new client this afternoon is Kate Raven. She works for a local technology company that is trying to market a stored-value card product for corporate campuses. Largely because of what she perceives to be the attraction to users of the ability to have their transactions be anonymous, the product would not involve any host-based records of the accounts. She contemplates allowing employees to put up to $100 on the card at any given time, expecting them to spend the money at vending machines, the corporation's onsite dining facilities, and gift shops (which sell typical corporate paraphernalia). As a legal matter, do you foresee any difficulty with her plan? What would be the benefits of changing her product to involve a host that would maintain records of the payments? EFTA §§903, 909, Regulation E, §§1005.2(b)(3), 1005.3, 1005.6, 1005.18.

4.6.   Seattle's Finest Coffee introduces a new prepaid card product, competing with the Starbucks card. The card is host-based, so that Seattle's Finest can add rewards points to the balance on the card for frequent users. After a rash of claims for lost cards, Seattle's Finest adopted a rule that it would not replace lost cards. Is this permissible? Are there any other ways that Seattle's Finest can protect itself against losses from lost cards? EFTA §§903, 909; 12 C.F.R. §§1005.2(b)(3), 1005.18.

4.7.   Same facts as the previous problem, but Seattle's Finest now wants to issue a card to employees without bank accounts so that it can deposit their salaries directly to the card. See Regulation E, 12 C.F.R. §1005.18.

4.8.   Your last call of the day is from Congresswoman Pamela Herring, who is interested in regulation of stored-value cards. Her specific concern relates to the fees. She is considering a statute that would set out a schedule of maximum fees issuers could charge. She is interested in your views on that proposal as a matter of policy. What do you tell her? You might consider 12 C.F.R. §1005.20 as a possible point of reference.

4.9.   Pleased with your analysis of the fee question, Congresswoman Herring asks your view as to the policy propriety of the broad expansions of EFTA coverage in the provisions of 12 C.F.R. §§1005.2(b)(3) & 1005.18 extending Regulation E to prepaid cards. What do you say?

Chapter 2.   Electronic Consumer Payments

In the electronic age, it seems almost quaint to use a tangible object to complete a payment transaction. Accordingly, it should come as no surprise that major developments over the last few decades have escalated the ease of consumer payments that are made by some wholly electronic method. This chapter breaks down those developments into three separate topics: automated clearing house (ACH) payments, Internet payments, and virtual currencies.

Assignment 5:   Automated Clearing House Payments

This assignment discusses the development of electronic transfers to and from bank accounts through the ACH system.

A.   The Basics of ACH Transfers

Banks have been making electronic transfers to and from consumer accounts for decades. With respect to commercial accounts, those transfers normally are made through specialized systems covered by Article 4A, the subject of Chapter 4. See UCC §4A-108 and comment (explaining that Article 4A does not apply to transactions that involve transfers to consumer accounts). With respect to consumer accounts, those payments frequently are made through a separate network, known as the Automated Clearing House (ACH) network. Although the ACH payment is not a widely known device, it is in fact quite common. During 2016, for example, the ACH network cleared more than 20 billion payments worth more than $40 trillion. (ACH transactions closely resemble the bank transfers and "giro" transactions that are common in Japan and those parts of Europe where checks were never used frequently.)

The ACH network is a nationwide computerized counterpart to the checking system, parallel to (but separate from) the networks used for transactions on credit cards or on debit (and ATM) cards. The network is used for electronic transfers between accounts at American financial institutions—most commonly for automated deposits of salaries and for automated payments of recurring bills (mortgages, car payments, and the like).

The network generally is governed by the Operating Rules issued by NACHA (formerly known as the National Automated Clearing House Association), a not-for-profit association of 36 regional clearinghouse associations. Those associations, in turn, are composed of the roughly 13,000 depositary institutions that participate in the network. The network also is closely associated with the Federal Reserve system, if only because (as described in more detail below) ACH payments generally are cleared through accounts at Federal Reserve banks and because communications to make payments on the ACH network are made over the communication system of the Federal Reserve. The financial institutions that participate in the network agree to those rules as a condition of their ability to send or receive entries on that network.

The other important source of law is the Electronic Fund Transfers Act (commonly known as the EFTA). The statute generally applies to "electronic fund transfers," which EFTA §903(7) defines to mean "any transfer of funds, other than a transaction originated by check, . . . which is initiated through an electronic terminal, telephonic instrument, or computer so as to order, instruct, or authorize a financial institution to debit or credit an account." Because all ACH transfers involve such a transfer, the EFTA applies to all ACH transfers into or out of a consumer account.

To understand how those payments work, four topics are useful points of discussion: the basic terminology of ACH transfers, the mechanics of ACH entries, the various types of ACH entries, and issues related to finality, errors, and fraud.

1.   The Basic Terminology

The ACH network is quite flexible, contemplating transactions in which the initial instruction can come either from the payor or from the payee. That instruction—an "entry" in NACHA terminology, NACHA Rules §8.37—can be either a credit entry initiated by the payor (asking the payor's institution to credit the account of the recipient) or a debit entry initiated by the payee (asking the payee's institution to debit the account of the recipient).

In the terminology of the NACHA rules, each ACH transfer involves (at least) five participants, as follows:

Originator: The party that makes the entry (or communication) that initiates the transaction. NACHA Rules §8.68. In a credit transfer that is the payor; in a debit transfer that is the payee.

Originating Depository Financial Institution (or ODFI): The financial institution of the Originator. NACHA Rules §8.68. Normally this is the location of the account from which payment is to be made in a credit entry, or the account to which payment is to be made in a debit entry.

Automated Clearing House Operator or ACH Operator: The party that carries communications (and funds) from the ODFI to the RDFI (described below). NACHA Rules §8.11. Except in the New York Federal Reserve District, this is the local Federal Reserve bank. In transfers between different Federal Reserve districts, there will be an Originating ACH Operator (normally the Federal Reserve bank in the district in which the ODFI is located) and a Receiving ACH Operator (normally the Federal Reserve bank in the district in which the RDFI is located).

Receiving Depository Financial Institution (or RDFI): That is the location of the Recipient. NACHA Rules §8.83. Normally this is the location of the account to which payment is to be made in a credit entry, or the account from which payment is to be made in a debit entry.

Receiver: The party to which the entry is directed. NACHA Rules §8.81. In a credit transfer, that is the payee; in a debit transfer, that is the payor.

2.   The Mechanics

The ACH network is a computerized alternative to the checking system. Thus, it relies entirely on electronic messages to convey the information that paper checks convey in the conventional checking system. The process of an ACH transfer starts with a message from the Originator to the ODFI. That message—an entry for each transaction—is likely to be sent to the ODFI as part of a large volume of messages (a "batch" or in NACHA terminology a "file"), which the ODFI will process in due course. Each entry is in a standardized format that defines the type of entry and includes the specific information necessary for the ODFI to process the particular type of entry. (The next section of this assignment includes more information about the various types of specialized entries that are possible.)

When the ODFI receives a batch of data, it examines the data to ensure that all of the data is in a comprehensible format so that the ODFI can process the requested transactions. It directly processes entries for which it is the RDFI ("on-us" entries). It then merges the remaining valid entries with data from other originators and transmits the data to its ACH Operator. When it transmits the data to the ACH Operator, it binds itself to pay the ACH Operator for all credit transfers included in the data (with the actual funds to be taken from the Federal Reserve account of the ODFI, NACHA Rules §7.3). So, for example, if an employer processed the direct-deposit portion of its payroll through the ACH system, the employer (as Originator) would send a file of credit entries to its bank (the ODFI). That bank would charge the employer's account for the total amount of

Figure 5.1
ACH Credit Entry

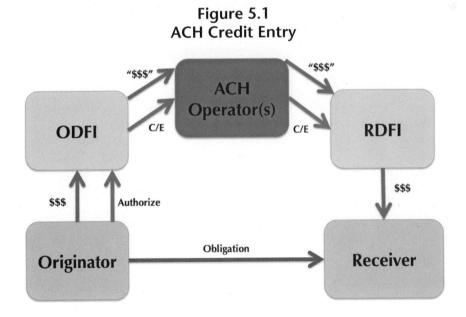

the payroll, keep data for employees that were its own customers, and send the remaining data on to the local Federal Reserve bank (as the ACH Operator).

The ACH Operator engages in a similar process. It sorts the transactions by region (to determine the appropriate Receiving ACH Operator). It retains transactions for which it is the Receiving ACH Operator, but transmits to the appropriate entity all transactions from other regions (for which some other entity would be the Receiving ACH Operator). At the same time, it is receiving transactions from other ACH Operators for which it is the Receiving ACH Operator. It sorts all of those transactions — that is, both the intra-region and inter-region transactions for which it is the Receiving ACH Operator — to produce separate batches of entries for each of the local institutions. Then, it transmits to each of those institutions (the respective RDFIs) a file reflecting the transactions that it has received for that institution. In our employer hypothetical, the Receiving ACH Operator would send back to all of the banks in its district the data for all of the employees that use a bank in the same Federal Reserve district as their employer. Data for remote employees would be sent to the Federal Reserve bank in the relevant district.

Finally, the RDFIs sort the data by account, post the transactions to the respective accounts, and provide the relevant notice to the holders of the accounts (the respective Receivers for the various entries). Thus, continuing our example, each of those banks would credit the employees with the appropriate funds. When the Receiver receives the funds for credit entries (on the settlement date of those entries), it must give the Originator credit for the payment as of that date. NACHA Rules §3.3.1.1. Thus, for example, if an Originator makes an ACH payment to its electric company to pay its electric bill, the electric company as Receiver must give its customer, the Originator, credit for the payment as of the settlement date of the payment, without regard to the electric company's internal procedures for processing payments.

Figure 5.2
ACH Debit Entry

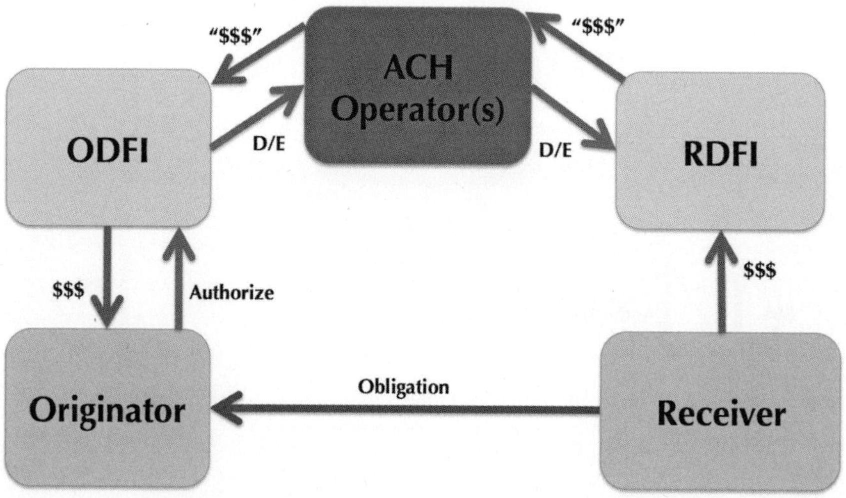

Because many of the payments made by ACH transfer fulfill obligations to make payments on a specific date (such as the obligation of an employer to pay its employees), the system uses a "value-dating" mechanism. With that mechanism, each entry specifies a settlement date on which the funds are to be transferred among the relevant accounts. The funds transfers are made on that date through net entries on designated Federal Reserve bank accounts of the participating depositary institutions. The entries also normally are posted on that same date to the accounts of the Originator and Receiver. The principal exception is for smaller institutions that have less expeditious methods of communicating with their ACH Operators; in that case the RDFI may not receive information about the transaction in time to credit the account of the Receiver until a few days after the settlement date.

A final question is how far in advance a payment can be entered. Under rules promulgated by the Federal Reserve, a debit entry must be transmitted by the ODFI the day before the settlement date; a credit transaction typically can be transmitted either on the day before the settlement date or two days before the settlement date. That rule has several ramifications. For one thing, it means that financial institutions cannot send entries long periods in advance and expect the receiving ACH Operators and financial institutions to hold onto them and process them on the appropriate day. More importantly, it effectively means that ACH entries cannot (like debit cards) be used to provide immediate payment in retail transactions (which might be desirable for POP or WEB entries, both discussed below), because a transaction will not in any event settle until the business day after the date on which it is transmitted. As NACHA continues in its efforts to make ACH a payment system of general desirability, there may be pressure to move to systems that permit more contemporaneous payment.

3.   Types of ACH Entries

Although ACH transfers are used in contexts that involve only businesses, the focus here is on their use for payments to or from consumers. In that context, the typical and most common ACH transfer (about 6 billion a year) is a credit entry sending payment from an employer to an employee (a "direct deposit" in common parlance). Probably the second most common ACH transfer (more than 4 billion a year) is a pre-authorized debit entry, in which a consumer agrees that a payee periodically can deduct funds to pay a bill. For example, it is common for mortgage payments to be made by a pre-authorized ACH transaction in which the lender is the Originator and the homeowner is the Receiver.

There also are a variety of specialized types of ACH entries used in particular contexts. Most of those have been created recently, as NACHA struggles to come up with products that allow it to retain (or increase) its market share in a vigorous competition against payment cards. For example, several of the new products are designed to remedy a variety of common problems in the check-collection process. For example, if a check is lost in the course of processing, it often is possible for the depositary bank to collect the check by sending a "destroyed check entry" (an XCK entry in the terminology of the NACHA

Rules) to the payor bank. NACHA Rules §8.29. Similarly, if a check bounces, a depository bank that wants to make a second attempt at collection can do so by the expeditious method of submitting an ACH entry called an RCK entry (instead of sending the physical check a second time through the normal channels for check processing). NACHA Rules §§2.5.13 and 8.80 (discussing those entries). You will notice that in the limited context of those problems, the NACHA Rules permit debit entries against consumer accounts without the prior consent of the Receiver. NACHA Rules §2.5.13.2.

Later sections of this assignment discuss POP entries (for point-of-purchase check conversion, often called "POS" or point-of-sale entries) and TEL entries (for telephone transactions) in detail. You also will increasingly see WEB entries (used for Internet transactions) and ARC entries (accounts-receivable conversion), used to convert remittance payments to ACH entries (especially by credit-card issuers and other high-volume payees).

4. Finality, Error, and Fraud in ACH Transfers

Because ACH transfers are governed by the NACHA Rules, those rules for the most part define the obligations of the parties to those transactions. The most distinctive attribute of those rules involves the finality of the payments: the possibility that an entry sent forth by the Originator in fact will not result in payment. With respect to credit entries, finality has two aspects: the point at which the RDFI loses its right to return the item (the analogue to final payment of a check) and the point at which the Originator and ODFI lose their right to retract the item (the analogue to losing the right to stop payment on a check). On the first point, the ACH system (like the checking system) imposes no general substantive constraint on the right of the RDFI to reject any entry. See NACHA Rules §3.8 (permitting return "for any reason"). The most important constraint (parallel to the midnight deadline in UCC Article 4) is that the return must be made in time to be received by the ODFI by the opening of business on the second banking day following the settlement date. NACHA Rules §3.8; see NACHA Rules §8.15 (defining banking day). Thus, if the RDFI wishes to return a credit entry that was to be paid on Wednesday March 31, it must get the return back to the ODFI by Friday April 2. As long as it returns the entry within that time period, it need not have any particular reason for the return.

Of course, it is not as easy to see why an RDFI would reject ACH entries as frequently as payor banks would reject checks drawn on them. For one thing, credit entries are transmissions of funds to the RDFI, not requests that the RDFI disburse funds. Accordingly, the customers of the RDFI have little reason to complain of those entries. Only if the entries are debit entries is there a possibility of rejection for insufficient funds. The rules above permit such a rejection easily. What they do not permit, however — and here they differ, for example, from the payment-card systems discussed in Chapter 1 — is any later rejection for reasons such as dissatisfaction with the underlying performance by the Originator of a debit entry. The principal exception is a procedure for an "extended return," which permits a customer to challenge an unauthorized transaction as much as two months later. NACHA Rules §§3.11-3.13.

From the other side, the ACH system has a much more limited right of retraction and stopping payment than other systems. Specifically, a consumer who wants to stop payment on such an entry normally must provide notice to the RDFI three banking days before the scheduled transfer date.

With respect to debit entries, the right to stop payment is much different, generally resembling the rules in Article 4 for stopping payment on checks. Thus, the Receiver of a debit entry (the party from whom payment is to be taken) can stop payment on the entry by providing notice to the RDFI "at such time and in such manner as to allow the RDFI a reasonable opportunity to act upon the stop payment order before acting on the debit entry." NACHA Rules §3.7.2. Compare UCC §4-403(a) (similar rule for stopping payment on a check). Debit entries against consumer accounts are treated slightly differently. Specifically, although the same rule applies to a variety of specialized debit entries (RCK, POP, WEB, and TEL entries, all discussed above), a consumer who wants to stop payment on a "normal" entry must provide notice to the RDFI three banking days before the scheduled transfer date. NACHA Rules §3.7.1.1.

Although the NACHA Rules discussed above create a payment that is final in a relatively firm way (at least as compared to payment cards), they do include a variety of procedures to deal with innocent or fraudulent mistakes in ACH entries. The simplest preventative is a procedure that allows the Originator to test the efficacy of an ACH entry before actually sending the entry. To use that procedure, the Originator sends a "pre-notification" through the ODFI to the RDFI, describing the entries that the Originator plans to initiate with regard to a Receiver's account. After sending a pre-notification, the Originator must wait six banking days before it can initiate entries to the Receiver's account. During that period, the RDFI has an opportunity to transmit a "Notification of Change" (NOC), identifying any errors in the information sent by the Originator. If the ODFI receives an NOC, it can initiate the entries in question only if it complies with the NOC. NACHA Rules §§2.6.2 and 2.11.

The NACHA Rules recognize that one of the most typical problems of all electronic systems is the problem of duplicate files or entries—correct transmissions that are sent more than once. The NACHA Rules include specific rules that permit the ODFI to reverse such transactions, whether they are whole files (batches of entries) or individual entries. Under the NACHA Rules, the ODFI can reverse an entire file if it acts within five banking days of the settlement date of the file in question, but no later than 24 hours after discovery of the duplication or other error. NACHA Rules §2.8.3. Any such request obligates the reversing ODFI to indemnify all participating financial institutions and ACH Operators for all losses related to their compliance with either the original or reversing instructions. NACHA Rules §2.8.4.

By contrast, if an Originator wishes to reverse a single entry (rather than an entire file of entries), the Originator must notify the Receiver not later than five days after the settlement date for the entry claimed to be erroneous. NACHA Rules §2.9.1. Moreover, even if it acts in a timely manner, it must, as in the case of reversing an entire file, provide a broad indemnity to the relevant financial institutions and ACH Operators. NACHA Rules §2.9.2. The following case aptly illustrates the problems that can arise when banks make errors in attempting to reverse entries.

In re Ocean Petroleum, Inc.
(Fleet Bank, N.A. v. Business Alliance Capital Corp.)

252 B.R. 25 (Bankr. E.D.N.Y. 2000)

DOROTHY EISENBERG, Bankruptcy Judge.

Fleet Bank N.A. ("Fleet") brought this adversary proceeding to recover a sum of money from Business Alliance Credit Corp. ("BACC") who provided revolving credit and asset-based lending to the Chapter 7 Debtor, Ocean Petroleum Corp. (the "Debtor"). In its complaint, Fleet claims that it mistakenly paid BACC in connection with a series of Automated Clearing House debit transactions initiated by BACC against a Fleet deposit account established by the Debtor for the benefit of BACC.

Fleet has moved for summary judgment claiming that the equitable doctrine of mistaken payment requires BACC to return the sum of money that was mistakenly paid to it. BACC cross-moved for summary judgment on the grounds that the [NACHA Rules] barred such an action. . . .

FACTS

BACC is a Delaware corporation engaged in the business of providing revolving credit and asset-based lending to businesses in exchange for a security interest in their assets, including inventory and accounts receivable.

Fleet is a national banking association with its principal place of business in Jersey City, New Jersey.

On May 8, 1996, BACC entered into a Loan and Security Agreement with the Debtor pursuant to which BACC agreed to provide the Debtor with a revolving line of credit secured by the Debtor's accounts receivable and other collateral. Under the Loan Agreement, the Debtor was entitled to receive advances from BACC, not exceeding its credit line. On September 1, 1998, the Debtor's available line of credit was $2,000,000.00.

In order to implement this borrowing arrangement, the Debtor and BACC entered into an agreement ("the Blocked Account Agreement") with Fleet Bank whereby a blocked deposit account ("the Blocked Account") was created in the name of the Debtor but solely for the benefit of and exclusively controlled by BACC. The Debtor made payments to BACC under the revolving line of credit by depositing its collections into the Blocked Account pursuant to the Blocked Account Agreement. BACC would then initiate Automated Clearing House ("ACH") debit transfers and wire transfers from the Blocked Account so that it could transfer the money to its own accounts as it saw fit. In order to initiate ACH debit transfers, BACC had a direct computer link with its Bank [First Union,] so that BACC could initiate a debit request from Fleet, through First Union, directly from a PC in its office.

In a typical transaction, the Debtor prepared a Borrowing Base Certificate in order to request an advance against its credit line from BACC. This statement set forth the Debtor's alleged sales, its collections and a calculation as to its eligibility and availability under the credit line so as to justify a request for an advance. Historically, the Debtor prepared a Borrowing Base Certificate and requested an advance nearly every day.

The certification as to the Debtor's collections on the Borrowing Base Certificate was critically important to BACC as the Debtor was supposed to have deposited these collections directly into the Blocked Account. Relying upon the Debtor's Borrowing Base Certificate and the representations as to deposits made therein, BACC chose to routinely wire advances to the Debtor despite the fact that it would be unable to verify that such deposits had actually been made until the next business day.

On the next business day, the Debtor would forward to BACC a statement produced by Fleet known as the Fleet AM Fax, which listed all of the Debtor's deposits made into the Blocked Account during the previous business day. The AM Fax reported all deposits made on a given day under the heading of "Ending Balance." It also clearly and unequivocally reported an "Available Balance" reflecting that portion of the funds in the ending balance which had actually cleared and had been collected. It also clearly listed the dollar amount of "Funds Pending" which reflected the dollar amount of funds that had been deposited into the account by the Debtor but had not actually been cleared and collected. Nevertheless, BACC would initiate ACH debit requests from the Blocked Account based upon the Ending Balance as reported on the Fleet AM Fax.

In the two-week period prior to the Debtor's bankruptcy filing, BACC was unable to initiate ACH debit transfers from the Blocked Account due to complications with its own bank, First Union. Notwithstanding BACC's inability to withdraw from the Blocked Account, it continued to make advances to the Debtor in the amount of $6,071,000.00 based upon the Debtor's representations in its Borrowing Base Certificates that it had deposited $6,091,789.41. On Friday, November 20, 1998, the date of the Debtor's bankruptcy filing, BACC advanced to the Debtor an additional $550,000.00 in reliance upon $597,194.78 reported by the Debtor in its November 20, 1998 Borrowing Base Certificate.

On the same day the Fleet AM Fax showed the Ending Balance in the Blocked Account as $6,089,483.86, the available balance as $5,305,062.16, and Funds Pending in the account as $784,424.00. Based on this figure, and BACC's renewed ability to withdraw from the account, BACC initiated a $5.8 million ACH transfer from the Blocked Account through its bank First Union.

On Monday, November 23, 1998, the $5.8 million ACH debit initiated by BACC was settled at the Federal Reserve Bank, which charged Fleet's account to the credit of First Union. On the same day, the $5.8 million was posted as a debit to the Debtor's Blocked Account by Fleet. However, on that date the Blocked Account at Fleet had uncollected and/or insufficient funds available to cover the $5.8 million ACH debit request by BACC. Accordingly, on November 24, 1998 the $5.8 million debit request initiated by BACC was returned as uncollected by Fleet's own system and credited back to the Blocked Account by Fleet as part of the process to return the ACH debit request initiated by BACC. Although the $5.8 million debit should have also been reversed by Fleet through an automatic return file sent to the Federal Reserve, due to a computer glitch related to a computer upgrade taking place at Fleet during the weekend of November 20, 1998, the ACH return was never initiated by Fleet to the Federal Reserve and the transaction was ultimately deemed final at Fleet's Federal Reserve Account and thus became final within the ACH system.

Upon learning of the Debtor's bankruptcy filing on November 23, 1998, BACC initiated an ACH debit transfer in the amount of $800,000.00. On November 24, 1999, BACC [e]ffected a wire transfer from the Blocked Account in the amount of $741,000.00. Upon the settlement of these three transactions, BACC received funds into its First Union account totaling $7,341,000.00 despite the fact that there was only $5,934,310.72 in collected funds available for withdrawal. The remaining $1,406,689.28 BACC received were not funds of the Debtor but rather funds from Fleet's own Federal Reserve Account.

Significantly, Robert J. Flynn, the officer handling the Blocked Account on behalf of BACC, testified in his deposition before trial that he knew as early as November 23, 1998 that $516,000 in deposits made by the Debtor on November 20, 1998 had not cleared the Blocked Account.

On December 14, 1998, twenty two days after the $5.8 million debit item had settled, John Dell'Orso of Fleet Bank contacted Steve Caroll of BACC and advised him that the $5.8 million ACH debit item presented for payment on November 20, 1998 should have been returned for insufficient and/or uncollected funds. This was due to the fact that in the days prior to the bankruptcy filing, the Debtor had deposited checks into the account that did not clear. As a result, the Blocked Account had a deficiency of $1.4 million. Fleet demanded return of the $1.4 million it paid to BACC out of its own Federal Reserve Account, however, BACC declined to return the money.

. . .

On April 14, 2000, Fleet commenced the instant action alleging, *inter alia*, that it was entitled to the return of the $665,689.28 based upon the theories of mistaken payment, restitution and unjust enrichment. BACC answered, claiming Fleet was barred from asserting that it was entitled to the monies paid to BACC since Fleet had failed to timely return the mistaken payment within the two-day deadline for return of a debit item for insufficient funds pursuant NACHA Operating Rule 5.1.2. [Ed.: Current version at NACHA Rules §3.8.]

DISCUSSION

The ACH Network is a processing and delivery system that provides for the distribution and settlement of electronic credits and debits among financial institutions. The ACH Network is governed by the NACHA Operating Rules. . . . In the transactions at issue BACC was the Originator, the Debtor was the Receiver, Fleet was the RDFI, the Federal Reserve Bank was the ACH Operator and First Union was the ODFI.

NACHA Rule 5.1.2 [Ed.: Current version at NACHA Rules §3.8] states in relevant part:

> [E]ach return entry must be received by the RDFI's ACH Operator by its deposit deadline for the return entry to be made available to the ODFI no later than the opening of business on the second banking day following the Settlement day of the original entry.

Pursuant to the foregoing, Fleet was required to return the $5.8 million ACH debit transfer initiated by BACC "no later than the opening of business on the second banking day following the Settlement date of the original entry."

Fleet admits that it failed to comply with the time limitations set forth in the NACHA rules but contends that based on Rule 2.11 [Ed.: Current version at NACHA Rules §7.4], it is not precluded from seeking the return of the money under New York state common law.

Rule 2.11 provides

Effect of Settlement

Settlement of entries does not preclude a Participating DFI from pursuing any available legal rights or remedies concerning any entry, adjustment entry or return entry including without limitation any right or remedy arising out of a return entry or adjustment entry, transmitted after the time limits established by these rules.

Despite the expansive language of Rule 2.11, BACC argues that Fleet may not maintain an action under state common law since allowing it to do so would render the NACHA rules meaningless.

ISSUES

Before this Court may reach the merits of Fleet's mistaken payment claim, it must determine an issue of first impression. Specifically, whether the ACH Rules foreclose a party who has failed to timely request a reverse entry from seeking other relief or put another way, whether NACHA Operating Rule 2.11 allows a participating institution to pursue its remedies under the common law, despite its failure to comply with the deadline set forth in Rule 5.1.2.

A plain meaning interpretation of Rule 2.11 supports the conclusion that Fleet may pursue a common law claim against BACC for the return of the mistaken payment despite the fact that it failed to comply with the two-day deadline for the return of debit entries as set forth in Rule 5.1.2.

Contrary to BACC's assertions, such an interpretation of the NACHA rules does not render them meaningless. On the contrary, the interpretation is consistent with other rules aimed at the settlement of disputes arising out of ACH transactions.

In addition to Rule 2.11, the NACHA Rules and the NACHA Operating Guidelines provide, in numerous instances, for the resolution of disputes regarding ACH transactions outside of the ACH network. For instance, the NACHA rules specifically state that in cases where an ODFI contests a dishonored return and an RDFI disputes the ODFI's protests,

an ODFI may not contest a contested dishonored return received by an RDFI by reinstating the entry. *Any further action concerning the dishonored return must be pursued outside of ACH* [emphasis supplied [by court].]

NACHA Operating Rule 5.2.6.2 [Ed.: Current version at NACHA Rules §2.12.5.2]. *See also* NACHA Operating Guidelines, Sec. III, Ch. III at OG62.

The NACHA Operating Guidelines actually require DFIs, in certain cases, to seek relief outside of the ACH system. The section entitled *Untimely Entries* states, in relevant part:

Once an ODFI receives a Contested Dishonored Return for an entry that it claimed was returned late, *that ODFI must look to procedures outside of the ACH system to settle any further dispute with the RDFI* [emphasis supplied [by court].]

NACHA Operating Guidelines Sec. III, Ch. III, at OG65.

In fact, the NACHA Operating Guidelines provide that in cases where an Originator seeks to dishonor an untimely return and fails to utilize the Dishonored Return process as set forth in the NACHA rules, "such failure does not preclude its right to seek recovery against an RDFI outside of the ACH process for a late return."

Finally, the NACHA Guidelines provide that ACH participants may resolve disputes through its own arbitration procedures. However, arbitration is not mandatory and each member must agree to submit the dispute to arbitration prior to the filing of the complaint. NACHA Operating Guidelines Sec. IV, Ch. V at OG105.

A plain meaning interpretation of Rule 2.11 and a reading of other rules regarding the settlement of disputes arising out of ACH transactions, supports the conclusion that the NACHA rules do not prohibit institutions from pursuing rights and remedies arising out of ACH transactions, outside of the NACHA system. Accordingly, this Court finds that Fleet may pursue its common law claim against BACC for the return funds under the theory of mistaken payment.

FLEET'S COMMON LAW CLAIM

Under New York law it is well settled that a party who has made a mistaken payment to another based upon a unilateral mistake of fact may recover the payment unless that payee has changed his position to his detriment in reliance upon the mistaken payment. Money paid under mistake of fact may be recovered back however negligent that party paying may have been in making the mistake.

In the instant case, BACC does not dispute that Fleet paid BACC by mistake. On that fact alone, absent a valid affirmative defense, Fleet is entitled to the return of the mistaken payment.

BACC's main defense to Fleet's mistaken payment claim is that BACC detrimentally relied on Fleet's mistaken payment by making advances to the Debtor from November 6, 1998—November 20, 1998. BACC claims that in making such advances, it relied on the fact that the Debtor had made deposits into the Blocked Account as confirmed by Fleet's AM Fax. Although the mistaken payment was not credited to BACC's account until November 23, 1998, BACC alleges that based upon the borrowing history between BACC and the Debtor, BACC was required to rely on "the Debtor's Borrowing Base Certificates and the Debtor's promises therein to immediately deposit all of its collections into the Blocked Account," and also to rely on the Fleet AM Fax Ending Balance in deciding whether to make advances to the Debtor.

BACC's argument defies logic and does not establish that BACC did anything more than rely on the *representations made by the Debtor* that it had made good deposits into the Blocked Account. The Fleet AM Fax, which BACC allegedly relied upon in lending to the Debtor showed an Ending Balance, which included all of the deposits that had been made into the Blocked Account. However, the same document clearly and unequivocally reported . . . an Available Balance reflecting that portion of the funds in the Ending Balance which had actually "cleared" and been collected and the amount of "Funds Pending" which reflected the dollar amount of funds that had been deposited into the account by the Debtor but had not actually been cleared and collected. The fact that BACC chose to rely on the Ending Balance and therefore rely upon the representations of the Debtor that those deposits would eventually clear and be available for withdrawal at a later date, is of no consequence, and cannot be attributed to Fleet's actions.

Furthermore, in the transactions at issue, BACC received all of the funds to which it was entitled. Indeed, BACC received into its accounts all of the funds the Debtor had deposited into the Blocked Account, which were ultimately collected. The funds at issue are solely those that were debited from Fleet's own Federal Reserve Account, and BACC has no rightful claim to these funds.

Significantly, the testimony of Robert Flynn, BACC's manager of the Blocked Account[,] demonstrates that BACC knew of the mistaken payment as early as November 23, 1998. Despite this knowledge, BACC chose to remain silent and retain funds which were not the Debtor's while the November 25, 1998 deadline for return of the debit item pursuant to Rule 5.1.2 expired.

This Court finds that BACC did not detrimentally rely on Fleet's mistaken payment and therefore, Fleet is entitled to the return of the remaining balance of its own funds it mistakenly paid to BACC.

The biggest problem for erroneous or fraudulent transmissions is not an erroneous credit entry — in which an Originator mistakenly sends funds to a third party — if only because the party most likely to be inconvenienced is the party that has erroneously sent the transmissions. The more serious problem occurs when a debit entry is sent that withdraws funds from the account of a Receiver that has not authorized such a transaction. In that context, the NACHA Rules grant consumers a specific right to have their account recredited. The Receiver that wants to get the funds back from an allegedly erroneous debit entry must act within 60 calendar days of the date that the RDFI sends a statement showing the debit, and must provide an affidavit "in the form required by the RDFI" declaring that the entry was not in fact authorized. NACHA Rules §§3.11.1 and 3.11.2.1. When the consumer Receiver complies with those requirements, the RDFI must credit the consumer's account "promptly." NACHA Rules §3.11.1. See also NACHA Rules §§3.11.2.1 (requiring an RDFI to recredit a consumer's account promptly if the RDFI honors an RCK or POP entry despite a proper stop-payment request from the consumer). As the case that follows shows, however, it will not be easy even for consumers with creative lawyers always to gain a return of the funds.

Clinton Plumbing and Heating v. Ciacco

2010 WL 4224473 (E.D. Pa. 2010)

CYNTHIA M. RUFE, Judge.

In this case, Plaintiffs Clinton Plumbing and Heating of Trenton, Inc. ("CPH") and Peter and Nancy Pelicano ("Pelicanos"), bring multiple claims against Defendants, all relating to Stephen Anthony Ciacco's alleged fraudulent scheme to make unauthorized transfers from Plaintiff[s'] bank accounts to Ciacco's outstanding credit balance held by Defendant Capital One Bank ("Capital One"). Presently before the Court is Defendant Capital One's Motion to Dismiss Counts II, VII, and XI of the First Amended Complaint. For the reasons that follow, Capital One's Motion will be GRANTED.

I.   FACTUAL AND PROCEDURAL BACKGROUND

A.   Procedural Background

Plaintiff Peter Pelicano is the president and sole shareholder of Plaintiff CPH, a corporation that provides plumbing and heating services in New Jersey and Pennsylvania. Defendants are Stephen Ciacco ("Ciacco"), his wife, Nicole Marie Ciacco, and Capital One, the national bank that allegedly held Ciacco's outstanding credit balance and initiated the unauthorized debits from CPH's accounts.

. . . The amended complaint describes a scheme by Ciacco to defraud CPH and the Pelicanos by misrepresenting himself as authorized to initiate transfers from CPH's bank account to his outstanding balance at Capital One. Capital One is alleged to have participated, albeit unwittingly, in Ciacco's scheme by carrying out the unauthorized transactions. . . .

Defendant Capital One has moved to dismiss Plaintiffs' claims against it for computer fraud . . . and breach of warranty. The Court has considered the Motion, Response in Opposition, Reply and Sur-reply, and this matter is now ready for disposition.

B.   Factual Background

Stephen Ciacco is the sole proprietor of Krash Enterprises ("Krash"), a computer repair and management company. On November 21, 2007, Ciacco, acting through Krash, entered into a service agreement with CPH. Pursuant to that contract, Ciacco was responsible for installing and managing CPH's network servers and office management software—which included the software for managing payables and receivables.

Allegedly, Ciacco soon sought greater responsibility for managing the accounts receivable software from CPH. Plaintiffs claim they promoted Ciacco to comptroller of CPH because he told them he required greater access to their bank accounts in order to manage the complexity of the software and difficulties arising from its installation. As comptroller, Ciacco was responsible for managing CPH's payables and receivables and was given access to CPH's bank accounts. Ciacco also set up CPH's computer system so that he could remotely access CPH's account information from his home and personal computer. However, Plaintiffs allege that Ciacco's authorized access was limited to monitoring the daily status of those accounts. Plaintiffs also claim the Pelicanos had sole authority to authorize payments from the CPH accounts and to authorize automatic clearing house ("ACH") debit transfers on behalf of CPH.

In March of 2008, Ciacco allegedly began making unauthorized transfers from CPH's bank accounts to his personal Capital One credit card account. Plaintiffs claim that Ciacco initiated the ACH debit transfers using Capital One's online credit card payment site. Upon receiving Ciacco's transfer request, Capital One debited the funds from CPH's bank accounts and applied them to Ciacco's outstanding credit balance. Although the Pelicanos terminated Ciacco from his position as Comptroller in August 2008, he allegedly continued to remotely access the CPH servers and accounts until November 2008.

In November 2008, the Pelicanos discovered the electronic withdrawals by Capital One. They immediately cut off Mr. Ciacco's access to their bank accounts, suspended all remote access to CPH's computers, changed the passwords for their bank accounts, and informed Capital One of the improper withdrawals. Capital One responded by advising the Pelicanos that it would investigate the allegations. Although Capital One has since provided Plaintiff with statements regarding the Capital One account, it refuses to reimburse CPH for the amounts withdrawn from their accounts.

. . .

III.   DISCUSSION

A.   Count II: Computer Fraud Claim Under 18 U.S.C. §1030

[After extended discussion, the court dismisses the claim based on the Computer Fraud and Abuse Act (CFAA), 18 U.S.C. §1030.]

C.   Count XI: Breach of Warranty

Plaintiffs allege that under the National Automated Clearing House Association ("NACHA") rules, Capital One warranted to CPH that it would not debit accounts without authorization. Therefore, when Capital One carried out the unauthorized debit transfers (Automatic Clearing House ("ACH") transactions), it breached its warranty. In response, Capital One argues that Plaintiffs do not have standing to assert a breach of warranty claim because the warranty provisions of the NACHA Rules apply only to the obligations between banks.

The NACHA Rules establish the contractual obligations between the parties to ACH transactions. The ACH is a national network of banks and financial institutions which transfers funds electronically to and from bank customers' accounts. In a typical transaction, the *Originator* is any individual that initiates entries into the ACH network. Here, the originator was Ciacco, who fraudulently initiated the

ACH transfer from CPH's bank account. Ciacco sent his request to Capital One, the *Originating Depository Financial Institution* ("ODFI"). A financial institution is an ODFI if it agrees to originate ACH entries at the request of its customers. After receiving Ciacco's (the originator's) response, Capital One (the ODFI) sent a request for a debit transfer to the *ACH*, who processed the request and forwarded it to CPH's bank, the *Receiving Depository Financial Institution* ("RDFI"). Because CPH had entered into ACH agreements authorizing its Bank (the RDFI) to honor ACH requests to debit its account, it was categorized as a *Receiver*. A *Receiver* is the consumer whose account is accessed. Therefore, the bank (the RDFI) approved Capital One's (the ODFI) debit requests and debited CPH's (the receiver's) account.

Here, an important precondition to any ACH transfer—authorization—was missing. But Capital One relied on the Ciaccos' (the originator's) representation that the transfer was authorized and carried out the transaction. When this type of unauthorized ACH transfer occurs, the NACHA Rules protect *certain* parties by requiring: "[e]ach ODFI sending an entry [to] warrant[] the following to each *RDFI*, *ACH Operator*, and *Associations:*

> §2.2.1.1 [Ed.: Current version at NACHA Rules § 2.4.4.1] . . . each entry transmitted by the ODFI to an ACH Operator is in accordance with *proper* authorization provided by the Originator and that is in accordance with proper authorization provided by the Originator and the Receiver; [and]

> §2.2.6.2 [Ed.: Current version at NACHA Rules §2.4.5.1] Each ODFI breaching any of the preceding warranties [here, §2.4.1.1] shall indemnify each *RDFI*, *ACH Operator*, and *Association* from and against any and all claim, demand, loss, liability, or expense, including attorney's fees and costs, that result directly or indirectly from the breach of warranty or the debiting or crediting of the entry to the receivers account.

Plaintiffs do not have standing to raise a breach of warranty claim pursuant to the *NACHA Rules.* Neither section creates an authorization warranty that runs to any party outside the RDFI, ACH Operator, and Associations. Plaintiffs direct the Court to consider Security First Network Bank v. C.A.P.S., Inc., where an Illinois federal district court considered a breach of warranty claim directly analogous to the one raised by Plaintiffs. In that case, Joseph Sykes, using the name Marvin Goldman, opened a deposit account at Security First Bank in Chicago. Security First was unaware of Sykes' true identity at the time. Using the Goldman alias, Sykes was able to fraudulently debit accounts held by two companies at other banks in the Chicago area and transfer the funds into his Goldman account at Security First. One of the accounts debited was Consolidated Artists Payroll Service, Inc. ("CAPS"), an Illinois firm that used electronic fund transfers to provide payroll services to its customers. The other account that Sykes defrauded was a Saks Fifth Avenue ("Saks") payroll account held at LaSalle Bank.

Both Saks and CAPS alleged that they entered into agreements with their banks for ACH services, and that the agreements incorporated the *NACHA Rules.* Security First argued that neither company could enforce the NACHA warranty provisions because they run only to RDFIs and ACH operators, and not to receivers. The court began by drawing a distinction between §§2.2.1.1 and 2.2.6.2.1. Although it agreed that Saks could not enforce the warranty provisions under §2.2.6.2 because "it [was] an agreement *to indemnify* an RDFI, ACH Operator or Association for the breach of the warranty in §2.2.1.1," it interpreted §2.2.1.1 to create a direct warranty between Saks (the receiver) and Security First (the OFDI). Accordingly, the court allowed the breach of warranty claim to survive the Motion to Dismiss.

The Court does not find the reasoning of *Security First* persuasive. First, the *Security First* court apparently ignored the clear text of the warranty provision, which limits its reach to RDFIs, ACH Operators, and Associations. Sections 2.2.1.1 and 2.2.6.2 fall under that limitation, so it is unclear how the *Security First* court interpreted §2.2.1.1 to have a broader reach than §2.2.6.2. Second, NACHA clarified its own rules in a 2008 Amendment entitled "Beneficiaries of the Rules," which states that:

> §1.9 Nothing in these rules is intended to, and nothing in these rules shall be implied to, give any legal or equitable right, remedy, or claim to other entity, including to any Originator, *Receiver*, Third-Party Service Provider, or Third-Party Sender.

Notably, the *Security First* decision predates the rule clarification offered in §1.9. In this case, Capital One was an ODFI, Plaintiffs' banks were RDFIs, and CPH was a receiver. Since CPH has receiver status, it does not have standing to bring a breach of warranty claim under NACHA.

IV. CONCLUSION

Based on the foregoing discussion, the Court finds that Plaintiff has failed to sufficiently allege that Defendant Capital One violated the CFAA . . . or the terms of a warranty owed to Plaintiffs. Accordingly, Capital One's Motion to Dismiss is GRANTED in full.

B. POS Conversion

As originally designed, ACH transfers were a useful substitute for transactions in which consumers previously might have sent checks through the mail: An ACH debit entry substitutes for the monthly mortgage check. More recently, NACHA has developed entries that substitute for conventional retail payments. The first of those transactions was the conversion at the point of sale of a check to an electronic-payment transaction. Confusingly enough, this normally is referred to as a POS conversion (for point of sale), although the NACHA entry is called a POP entry (for point of purchase). Although that transaction in legal contemplation is an electronic funds transfer, it works from the consumer's perspective much like a conventional check transaction. The consumer writes a check and hands it to the retail clerk (at a grocery store, for example). The clerk takes information from the check's MICR line (ordinarily by passing the check through a reader designed to collect that information), marks the check as void, and then hands the check back to the consumer. NACHA Rules §2.5.10.4. The merchant then sends that information to its bank, which uses it to process an ACH transaction taking money for the transaction from the consumer's account at its own bank. In any event, POS conversion to automated-clearinghouse transactions has been highly successful. In 2013, it was used for more than 400 million checks. Its use has been declining in recent years both because of the decline in use of checks by consumers (more on that in the next chapter) and because of the adoption in 2007 of the BOC (Back-Office Conversion) entry (about 200 million entries a year), which allows retailers to convert the check not at the retail counter, but later in the back office. This avoids the problems retailers have faced of retail clerks unable to identify which checks were suited for conversion and also of consumers confused by the return of their check to them at the retail counter.

When POS conversions first appeared, the speed of the transactions seemed problematic to many consumer advocates. Because the transactions are cleared electronically, the funds are likely to be removed from the consumer's account on the next business day if the transaction involves conversion to an ACH transaction. If the consumer had paid with a conventional check, the consumer might have relied on the "float," expecting the check not to clear for a number of days.

For several reasons, that problem probably will not be a major obstacle for POS conversion. First, as a practical matter, consumers at the check-out counter are not likely to object in any significant way to the conversion process based on the speed of clearing: After all, they can't really object if the merchant is simply trying to get paid sooner for goods that the consumer already has taken from the merchant's store. For another thing, although it has not always been true, it now is the case that checks a consumer writes locally are likely to be collected by the next business day anyway. If the great majority of retail checks that consumers write are to merchants in the same metropolitan area as the consumer's bank, then the substitution of POS conversion for conventional checks will not significantly alter the float available to consumers. More generally, consumers are unlikely to object because they are unlikely to understand the nature of the transaction (i.e., the difference from a conventional check) and the legal rules that govern the transaction.

A similar issue relates to the consumer's right to stop payment. Under UCC Article 4, a check-writer has the right to stop payment by giving notice to the bank on which the check is drawn, if the notice arrives in time to permit the bank on which the check is drawn to refuse to pay the check. UCC §§4-303 and 4-403. As discussed above, NACHA Rules ordinarily require any stop-payment order to be sent at least three days before the payment is to be made. NACHA Rules §3.7.1.1; see EFTA §907 (same requirement). Because that would bar any stop-payment right in POS conversions, NACHA has adopted a special rule for POS conversions, which tracks UCC §4-303 in permitting the customer to stop payment if the consumer sends notice at a time that allows the bank a reasonable opportunity to act before it becomes obligated on the item. NACHA Rules §3.7.1.1. Because the transactions are cleared electronically, even that right will last only a short time, certainly less than one business day. Again, however, because the relevant universe is local retail payments, that rule does not put the customer at a significant disadvantage compared to conventional check transactions. Those transactions also tend to clear very quickly, so the customer normally has less than a full business day to stop payment in those transactions as well.

The most important difference for the parties to a POS conversion is the risk of fraud. For conventional check transactions, the payor bank ordinarily bears the risk of loss if it pays an item that is unauthorized (not signed by the purported drawer). See UCC §4-208(a)(3) (permitting a payor bank to recover for an unauthorized item only if the depositary bank knew that the purported customer had not authorized the item). Thus, with a check, the merchant bears the loss if the check bounces, but the payor bank bears the loss if the fraud is sufficiently skillful to trick the payor bank into honoring the fraudulent item.

Under NACHA Rules, however, the bank that originates an ACH transaction (normally the merchant's bank) bears that responsibility. NACHA Rules §2.4.1.1 (including a warranty that "[t]he Entry has been properly authorized by the Originator and the Receiver"). And, in that context, there is every reason to believe that the merchant's bank will require the merchant to bear that risk. Thus, merchants who take fraudulent checks bear the risk in the conversion transactions even if the payor bank honors the item. Hence, POS conversions to ACH transactions place a much greater burden of security on the merchants and their banks. NACHA strongly urges those parties to take substantial precautions to identify the parties that purport to send transactions—because the merchants and their banks will bear the losses if the transactions are fraudulent.

That burden is mitigated somewhat by the speed of POS conversions, because the items are likely to be returned to the depositary bank and the merchant much more rapidly than conventional checks. Thus, at least if the payor bank identifies the problem when the item is first processed, the merchant who takes a POS conversion will learn that the item has been dishonored quite a bit sooner (probably on the second business day) than the merchant who takes a paper check. Experience suggests several reasons why losses from bad checks are mitigated significantly as the speed of response increases: because the customer will have less time to stop payment on the check; because of the greater likelihood that funds will remain in the account if the check is processed more promptly; and because the merchant will have greater success at collecting the bounced check if it starts its efforts more promptly. Of course, those advantages will not help the merchant if the payor bank fails to notice the problem at the time—because the return will come much later, at the end of the month when the purported drawer challenges the item on its monthly statement.

C. Telephone-Initiated Payments

The final subject of this assignment is the telephone-initiated payment, which has become controversial in recent years because of its frequent use to defraud consumers. The situation arises when a payee obtains consent for a transaction completed over the telephone. If the payee wants to use a telephone check to obtain payment, it will induce the customer (the drawer of the check) to recite (from the bottom of one of the customer's conventional checks) the routing number for the customer's bank and the account number of the customer. The payee (typically a bill-collection service or a telemarketer) then will use that information in one of two ways. Not so many years ago, the most common approach would be, using software readily available on the Internet, to print a check drawn on the customer's account. The check of course would not include a manual signature by the customer but would suggest in some way that a signature is not required (for example, by a stamp that might say "AUTHORIZED BY DRAWER" or (with even less sincerity) "SIGNATURE ON FILE"). More recently, using an ACH TEL entry, the payee might use the bank account information to initiate an ACH entry (almost 500 million entries a year).

Under applicable FTC regulations, the payee must retain a "verifiable authorization" of such a transaction for 24 months. 16 C.F.R. §310.5(a)(5). That authorization could be in writing or it could be a tape recording of an oral authorization. 16 C.F.R. §310.3(a)(3). Given the purpose of the system — to allow payees to obtain payment without waiting for the payor to transmit a written check — it is not surprising that the companies that have designed telephone-check software recommend that their customers rely on oral authorizations.

As the existence of the FTC regulation suggests, some of the businesses that use telephone checks have come under fire for processing checks that have not been authorized by their customers (or, in some cases, checks in amounts larger than the amounts authorized by their customers). Canada, indeed, has gone so far as to ban all telephonically initiated checks. No legislature in this country has yet gone so far, but the UCC and Regulation CC create warranty liability for the bank that accepts such items for deposit. See UCC §§3-416(a)(6), 3-417(a)(4), 4-207(a)(6), 4-208(a)(4); 12 C.F.R. §229.34(b). The premise of those provisions is that in that context at least the possibility of fraud is better policed by action on the part of the depositary bank. For example, depositary banks that accept deposits of telephone checks might be induced to monitor the activities of those customers or require them to provide financial assurances of the authenticity of the items, lest the depositary bank be left holding the bag on warranty claims for unauthorized items.

Those provisions do not apply to TEL entries, at least directly, because they do not involve checks governed by Article 4. Thus, when the telemarketer uses a TEL entry, the transaction is governed by the EFTA and by the standard NACHA Rules discussed above, which place responsibility for fraud and error on the bank that originated the incorrect or fraudulent entry. EFTA protections are not available for telephone-initiated check transactions, because the Federal Reserve has concluded that those do not constitute electronic fund transfers under the applicable statutory provisions. Regulation E, Interp. ¶3(c)(6).

Problem Set 5

5.1.   Suppose that your bill for Internet service at your home each month is paid by an automatic deduction from your bank account. You agreed to this when you signed up for Internet service with your Internet Service Provider (ISP), and at that time provided to your ISP information about your bank so that the ISP could arrange for the payments.

a.   Is this most likely a credit entry or debit entry?
b.   Assuming that you reside in Chicago and that the ISP is located in Washington state (near the Seattle Federal Reserve bank), identify the most likely parties to the transaction and the roles they would play under applicable NACHA Rules.
c.   Assuming that the next payment is due on Monday April 1, what would you need to do to cancel that payment and what is the latest date on which you could act to do so in a timely manner? EFTA §907; 12 C.F.R. §1005.10(c); NACHA Rules §§3.7.1.1, 8.96.

5.2.   Suppose that you pay your credit-card bill through an Internet bill-payment service offered by your bank, through which you can direct your financial institution to pay bills using ACH transfers. Using that service, you direct a transfer to pay a $7,000 credit-card bill in its entirety. Suppose that you change your mind the next day. Is there anything that you can do to prevent the payment from being made? NACHA Rules §§2.7, 2.9.

5.3.   Your old friend Cliff Janeway mentions a small problem to you over lunch one day. He explains that he customarily pays for his groceries with checks. Starting last month, his grocery store has a new system under which it marks his checks void and hands them back to him at the register. Although he was worried at first that the grocery store was making a mistake and would not be paid (because the check was marked void), the clerks assured him that the charges would show up on his monthly statement. To his surprise, the charges did show up. Indeed, he was charged twice for one of them — his statement showed two transactions at Kroger's on February 14, each at the same time and each for $92.26. Cliff understandably thinks he should pay only once.

a.   What should he do? EFTA §§908(a), 909; Regulation E, §1005.11; NACHA Rules §3.11.2.1, 3.11.3.
b.   What if the transaction resulted from a telephone conversation between Cliff and a telemarketer, in which he ultimately declined to make a purchase, but the telemarketer still created a TEL entry to draw funds from Cliff's account? EFTA §909; NACHA Rules §§1.9, 2.4.1.1, 3.11.1.
c.   Who will bear the loss in each of those transactions? NACHA Rules §§1.9, 2.4.1.1; EFTA §909; UCC §§4-207, 4-208, 4-401.

5.4.   Your friend Jodi Kay has some questions about payments she receives on home mortgages that her bank services. The mortgages are all set up to have recurring payments. She has two questions for you.

a.   First, she has heard that customers in some cases can retract their monthly mortgage payment even after she has received it. Is that correct? Does it depend on what paperwork Jodi got at the time of the original loan? Does it depend on whether the customers are willing to lie? NACHA Rules §§2.3, 3.11, 3.12.

b.   Second, as the economy has gotten worse, she has had an increasing number of her pre-arranged debit payments "bounce," from the lack of sufficient funds in the consumer's account. Once the authorized recurring payment bounces, what can she do to recover payment? Does she need new authorization from the customer? NACHA Rules §2.12.4.

5.5.   Your friend Bill Robertson drops by one day to ask some questions about new payment methods. His bank suggested that he might start accepting ACH payments from customers paying their monthly bills. What he wants to know is what risks he will face if he does so. The banker tells him these transactions will cost him a lot less than credit cards and he is happy to avoid the expenses of collecting the checks that they mail to him. But he is always wary, as he has all too often had charges on credit cards reversed by customers claiming some imagined problem with his service. What do you tell him? TILA §§133, 161, 170; EFTA §§908, 909; NACHA Rules §§2.7, 2.9, 3.11-3.13. Does it matter if his customers are willing to lie?

5.6.   Jodi Kay has started to worry about the increasing volume of ACH transfers she is processing for her merchants: ARC, POP, BOC, and even TEL. She is particularly worried about the TEL entries, because she has encountered some fraudulent behavior there in the past. She holds back the funds to protect herself until she is sure that the entries have cleared, but what she wants to know is whether the entries can be charged back to her if the customer becomes dissatisfied with the purchase. This has happened to her frequently with credit-card transactions. She wants to know if she faces the same risk here. TILA §§133, 161, 170; EFTA §§908, 909; NACHA Rules §§3.7.1, 3.7.2.

Assignment 6:   Internet Payments

It certainly would come as a surprise to those who watched the Internet in its infancy, but consumers still pay for most retail Internet purchases with credit cards. There has been some shift to debit (and prepaid) cards processed by Visa and Mastercard (which take advantage of their existing networks) and a more recent shift in favor of ACH transfers, but at least for now, those three products are the principal vehicles for making retail Internet payments. The assignment closes with a brief discussion of foreign and mobile payments.

A.   Credit Cards on the Internet

With the rise of Internet retailing, the advantages of the credit card as a payment system are obvious. The preexisting Visa and Mastercard networks, and the widespread distribution of cards to consumers in the United States, gave credit-card issuers a built-in nationwide payment network available when Internet commerce began. Other payment systems that existed at the time were not as easily transferred to the Internet setting. For example, cash is entirely impractical in a remote transaction unless the consumer has some reliable way to send the cash to the merchant. Even if some hypothetical consumer were willing to mail cash for an Internet purchase, the merchant would not receive the cash for several days until it came in the mail. Similarly, a commitment to pay by check gives the merchant nothing for several days while the merchant waits for the check (except a promise that "the check is in the mail"). Finally, when commerce on the Internet began, there was no system by which online retailers could accept ACH transfers. That has changed—as you will see in the discussion below—but the change is slow and is happening only after the system is to some degree "locked in" to reliance on credit-card payments.

1.   Processing the Transactions

Although some merchants (and third-party security providers) are developing creative ways to enhance the authenticity of their online credit-card transactions, the typical process requires nothing more than that the consumer enter a credit-card number, verification value (CVV) from the back of the card, and billing address on the merchant's checkout page. Indeed, in many cases of repeat purchases (or for those using an intermediary like PayPal) the information might be entered automatically. As discussed below, a merchant concerned about fraud might request some additional information, but the need for that information is unlikely to delay the completion of the transaction more than a few seconds beyond the time necessary to provide the information to the merchant's checkout software.

With respect to unauthorized transactions, the cardholder that purchases on the Internet often is not responsible even for $50. The relevant provision of TILA conditions the cardholder's responsibility for $50 on the issuer's having provided some method for the cardholder to identify itself as the authorized user of the card (such as a signature, photograph on the card, or the like). TILA §133(a)(1)(F); Regulation Z, §1026.12(b)(3). At least in the view of the responsible regulators, an Internet transaction that verifies the customer's identity solely by asking for the card number and billing address has not identified the customer adequately. Accordingly, the Federal Reserve concluded in its commentary to Regulation Z, cardholders have no responsibility at all in unauthorized transactions that are conducted based solely on card numbers. Regulation Z, Official Staff Interpretation 12(b)(2)(iii). In any event, the ability to impose the $50 on cardholders has diminishing practical relevance, because both Visa and Mastercard generally waive the $50 of liability that the statute permits, at least if the cardholder notifies the issuer promptly after discovering the loss of control of the card (or its number).

2.   Problems

Despite its current dominance, the credit card faces a number of problems as a long-term vehicle for Internet purchases. Thus, it remains to be seen whether it can retain its first-mover advantage in the long run. The following sections discuss the three most salient obstacles to continued use of credit cards as the dominant Internet payment system: fraud, privacy, and the need to facilitate micropayments.

   (a)   Fraud.   The most obvious problem is the astonishing rate of fraud perpetrated through the relatively insecure system of credit-card authorization as it currently exists for Internet transactions. In a face-to-face credit-card transaction, the merchant can swipe the card. When that is done, the terminal on which the card is swiped transmits to the card issuer (or its agent) data on the back of the card (unknown to the cardholder) that allows the issuer to verify that the card in fact is physically present. Although it is possible to forge a card, it is relatively difficult, especially with the advent of chip cards.

By contrast, in an Internet transaction (included in the industry within the category known as card-not-present transactions), the merchant often will proceed with no information other than the numerical items described above (the idea being that it is harder for a malefactor to obtain a billing address and the verification value from the back of the card than it is to obtain the card number alone). As it happens, it is not difficult for malefactors to obtain the credit-card number and verification value, either by examination of the card itself or by hacking into the records of Internet merchants from whom cardholders have made purchases. The billing address of course ordinarily can be obtained from public records (such as a telephone book or Internet database). The ease of obtaining that information has led to a rash of so-called identity thefts, in which malefactors masquerade for a considerable period of time as another individual, often even obtaining new credit cards in the name of other individuals. For many years, those thefts were a more or less endemic problem on the Internet (where, of course, the risk of being caught is relatively small). In 2014, though, the incidence and size of card-data hacking mushroomed, leading to a situation in which most of us can be sure that our card data has been stolen from one retailer or another; whether that will lead to an increase in identity theft remains to be seen.

The problem is exacerbated by the ease with which cardholders can disavow an Internet transaction in which they in fact did participate. That seems to be particularly common for merchants that sell information that is delivered over the Internet. (It is harder for cardholders to disavow transactions in which tangible goods were delivered to their home or office.) Online merchants try to counter that activity through a variety of responses, which collectively consume 1 to 2 percent of their revenues. Many merchants use some form of a "hot list," which identifies card numbers known to be stolen. Others use sophisticated analysis of transaction information to identify transactions that match profiles of fraudulent behavior. Finally, a newer response is geolocation technology, which examines the ISP through which the purchaser is connecting to assess the likelihood that the purchaser would be contacting the merchant from that location. But even with those products, the costs of fraud are high. Fraud in the early days of the commercial Internet ranged as high as 5 to 15 percent of all transactions, but persistent technological advances have brought the rate down to about 33 basis points (one-third of 1 percent), about five times the rate for face-to-face transactions.

For legal and historical reasons, losses from unauthorized transactions on the Internet are not treated the same way as losses from unauthorized transactions in conventional face-to-face retail transactions. As discussed above, issuers absorb losses from unauthorized transactions in the conventional face-to-face setting. Because the risk of fraud in transactions where the card is not present is so high, for many years the major credit-card networks excluded mail-order and telephone-order (MOTO) transactions from their networks. With the rise of the credit card as a major payment device of the American consumer, it became increasingly important to mail-order and telephone-order merchants that they be permitted to accept credit cards. So, after discussions with the credit-card networks, MOTO merchants began conducting card-not-present transactions, but they agreed to accept the risk that those transactions would be unauthorized. When Internet merchants began accepting credit cards, they became subject to the same card-not-present rules developed for MOTO transactions.

For legal and historical reasons mentioned briefly in Assignment 2, losses from fraud, credit-card issuers have a strong incentive to respond to fraud losses: If fraud losses remain as high as they have been to date, Internet merchants will have a powerful incentive to encourage their customers to use other payment systems that are more secure. The simplest possibility for the credit-card issuers would be to disseminate some PIN-like password authentication system. This is an almost revolutionary step, because for years only the debit-card system has relied on personal identification numbers (PINs); the credit-card system (as well as the debit-card systems promulgated by Visa and Mastercard) stubbornly relied on the signature and account number alone as adequate for authentication. In the fall of 2001, though, Visa and Mastercard introduced such products. The first step in getting those products deployed was to persuade individual issuing banks to implement systems to issue and check passwords. That process was successful; more than 90 percent of Visa issuers, for example, participate in the "Verified by Visa" program. Mastercard's parallel program is called SecureCode.

The second step is to persuade merchants to modify their check-out software to require the consumer to enter the password. Merchants obviously have an incentive to keep their check-out procedures as simple as possible — data indicate that a substantial number of Internet purchases are lost from consumer frustration caused by lengthy check-out procedures. Nevertheless, to date merchants have been cooperative, at least in making the systems available to their customers. The incentive has been the willingness of the major networks to consider transactions authorized through the new PIN systems as card-present transactions: The issuers of the cards accept the risk of loss on those transactions. (The experience with debit-card transactions in the offline world suggests that fraud in those transactions will be quite low. Retail fraud on PIN-based cards is about one-twentieth the rate of fraud on signature-authorized cards.)

The problem, however, has been to persuade customers to sign on to those systems. The consumer is not liable in either event, so the consumer has little incentive to go to the trouble of collecting a PIN from the consumer's issuer for credit-card transactions. Thus, unless the issuer or the merchant *forbids* Internet transactions without a PIN (which no merchant or issuer has done to date), it is not at all obvious why any consumer would use the system.

A more dramatic possibility is that credit-card issuers could deploy "smart" cards, which hit the United States in 2015. In this context, "smart" cards or "chip" cards refer to credit cards enhanced with an integrated-circuit chip. That chip includes a microprocessor and storage device that allows the card to perform a variety of functions, including — crucially for security reasons — a card-authentication function.

At least potentially, internet merchants could take advantage of the chip's technology to authenticate the card by requiring the cardholder to insert the card in a reader for use in a card-not-present transaction; such a reader well might be integrated into desktop or laptop computers in the years to come, but that had not yet occurred as this edition went to press. With the card in the reader, the issuer can verify with considerable certainty that an authentic card is present. If the issuer could not verify the card, it would decline the transaction. Generally speaking, that process (like the parallel process at retail) would largely eradicate fraud that relies on forged cards or stolen card numbers (the vast majority of internet-based fraud).

The biggest obstacle to that solution is in getting the cards and readers disseminated to cardholders. Credit-card issuers have been looking for ways to use smart-card technology for years, without success. Several times in the last decade major American issuers have initiated widely advertised programs to issue general-purpose credit cards enhanced with such a chip, with American Express's Blue card being the most prominent. No issuer, however, has yet succeeded in shifting a substantial portion of its Internet purchases to that technology. In that case, the readers would go a long way toward proving that the card was authentic, but help not at all in establishing that the user was the cardholder.

Deployment of smart cards has been much more successful in other countries, but the driving force in most cases (as in the UK "chip-and-PIN" program) has been brick-and-mortar fraud, not Internet transactions, which are much less important to overseas issuers than they are to American issuers. Thus, even in those countries in which consumers have chip-enhanced smart cards, they do not appear to use them commonly to make Internet purchases.

Looking even farther ahead, the "holy grail" of fraud prevention would be some form of "biometric" identification, which would authenticate transactions based on verification that certain physical characteristics (retina, fingerprint, or the like) of the individual presenting the card match the previously recorded physical characteristics of the person to whom the card was issued. For example, a smart card might store a record of the cardholder's fingerprint and prevent use of the card without entry of a matching fingerprint into a fingerprint pad connected to the computer through which the card was being used. Biometric technology has struggled for a variety of reasons, including not only technical difficulties but also consumer resistance. That technology received a big boost first from government initiatives that forced the development of technology for use in passports and other identification documents, and then more recently from private initiatives involving phones, which have made fingerprint and facial identification seem much more routine and less intrusive than it did just a few years earlier.

(b)   Privacy.   Even if the fraud problems are resolved, credit cards still face other serious issues, which continue to undermine the use of credit cards for Internet purchases. The most important of those issues surely is the privacy problem. For this context, the privacy problem has two manifestations. The first is the prospect, mentioned above, that interlopers will steal data from Internet merchants. In several widely publicized incidents, malefactors have succeeded in stealing large volumes of consumer data from prominent Internet merchants. The prospect that their transaction data will be compromised is likely to trouble some consumers even apart from the burden they will face in convincing their issuers to credit them for any unauthorized transactions that may result.

A more serious problem for consumers is the likelihood that the merchants and issuers themselves will make use of the data for reasons that trouble consumers. As a greater share of consumer purchases drift into online venues, the possibility continuously grows of aggregating individual consumer profiles at greater levels of detail. Consumers find it chilling to contemplate a database in the hands of direct marketers (or investigative reporters) that describes in detail the kinds of books, music, clothes, and information they tend to purchase.

It is difficult to assess the seriousness of that problem. For many years, privacy concerns were thought to be a substantial obstacle that would keep consumers from using credit cards on the Internet and foster the development of more anonymous payment systems, such as so-called electronic-money systems. But the rapid growth of Internet retail transactions and the dominance of credit cards in those transactions suggest that the privacy issue may trouble consumers less than many observers expected.

The industry also has developed a technological response in the form of disposable credit-card numbers that inhibit the aggregation of payment information. Those systems (pioneered by Orbiscom, but now widely available) provide software to the purchaser's personal computer. The software generates a new credit-card number for each transaction. When the merchant sends the number through to the issuer, the number is valid only for that transaction. Thus, the merchant is no longer in a position to aggregate information based on the credit-card number (which will differ in each transaction). The only party in a position to aggregate information is the issuer (or, depending on the structure of the system, a third party generating the disposable numbers). Again, consumer disinterest has slowed the growth of those systems.

Thus, at least for the time being, it seems unlikely that privacy concerns will pose a substantial obstacle to the continued primacy of credit cards as a vehicle for Internet retail payments. However serious the concerns might be, the available technological solutions should solve the problem without significant disruption.

(c)   Micropayments.   Another problem that has confronted credit cards is that of micropayments. Because of their relatively high fixed costs, merchants traditionally found credit cards unsuitable for transactions much below $10 in amount. In the early days of the Internet, it was expected that much of Internet commerce would involve information merchants selling information piece by piece for very small amounts — 25 cents or less in the near future, perhaps even fractions of a cent in decades to come. Those transactions could not occur, however, unless merchants could find a practical way to obtain payment. If credit cards could not provide that, then some other alternative would be necessary. As with the privacy issue, observers thought that the natural solution was a purely electronic payment system.

As it happens, however, the market has developed quite robustly without such a system, relying for payment on a variety of relatively conventional devices, most but not all of which rely on credit cards or checks in some way. First, most existing information merchants (primarily newspapers and sports-information sources) do not charge piece by piece, but instead charge a monthly subscription fee in an amount adequate to justify conventional credit-card payment. Economists studying the issue suggest that the piece-by-piece pricing model will be useful in many fewer contexts than observers originally had expected. Generally, they reason that the development of sophisticated bundling techniques by merchants, together with customer aversion to piece-by-piece pricing plans, has lessened the importance of the issue. Of course, it is entirely possible that customer aversion was caused not by piece-by-piece pricing models, but by the "clunky" software available for such programs several years ago. Software programs available now, not surprisingly, work much more smoothly and simply, and thus might be more acceptable to consumers.

Moreover, even when merchants do charge piece by piece, the problem has been resolved by one of a variety of payment aggregators that have arisen. Those aggregators provide software that gathers up a large number of a consumer's small transactions and then uses a conventional payment system to charge the consumer for the transactions periodically (normally once a month). For example, a consumer might receive a single monthly bill for all Internet information purchases, which the consumer could pay with a conventional check or credit card. The provider typically provides the consumer a PIN to help ensure authenticity of the transactions. Yet another model (used most prominently by MicroCreditCard) aggregates a number of charges and then when the aggregate amount reaches a certain point (perhaps $8 to $10), charges the aggregate amount to the customer's credit card.

Variations on that model, pioneered by companies like NTT DoCoMo in Japan but spreading widely in Europe and now routine for purchases of cellphone apps, work through an Internet or wireless service provider to obtain a reliable identification of the payor from the payor's point of access to the Internet or wireless network: The Internet service provider and wireless service provider invariably are able to identify in a reliable way the account of the person accessing their systems. (At least theoretically, that person might not be the account holder, but that seems to be a relatively small problem under current conditions.) Relying on that identification, those systems can dispense with the PIN requirement, which makes the transactions simpler to execute. Those systems then charge for the transactions either by applying them to a pre-arranged card account or by adding the appropriate charges to the monthly bill for Internet or wireless access.

Finally, in recent years the card networks have revised their interchange schedules to provide markedly lower minimum interchange fees for small-dollar transactions. This has made it much easier for Internet merchants to accept payment cards even for single-item information transactions.

In sum, although it is much too early to identify what response will resolve the problem definitively in the long run, the technological responses discussed above have solved the micropayment problem quite adequately for the time being. They might result in the insertion of an intermediary between credit-card issuers and merchants, but it is not clear that they will result in a major shift of Internet payments away from the credit card.

B.   Debit Cards on the Internet

In the early days of the Internet, credit cards had an appreciable advantage over debit cards largely because debit cards were relatively uncommon at the time. Debit cards, however, have made major advances in the United States since 1999, so that they now are used almost as frequently as credit cards. Moreover, because about 20 percent of American consumers do not have a credit card (including many teens and elderly persons who might be ideal customers for Internet retailers), Internet retailers that accept both credit cards and debit cards have access to a broader customer base than those that accept only credit cards.

Several other reasons apparent from the discussion above also motivate Internet merchants to accept debit cards. First, Internet merchants also prefer debit cards because of the smaller interchange fee they pay. Second, Internet merchants should prefer the finality of debit cards. As discussed above, credit-card transactions have been plagued with charge-backs. The more limited charge-back rights of debit cards should be particularly attractive to merchants.

Given those advantages, it is not surprising that online retailers prefer debit-card transactions. To date debit-card transactions on the Internet overwhelmingly are conducted with signature-based debit cards (Visa Check and Master Money cards). Because those cards do not require a PIN, they can be used at most major online retailers in precisely the same way consumers use credit cards. Merchants would prefer that their customers be able to use PIN-based cards, both because of the diminished risks of fraud and because the charges they would pay for the transactions would be smaller as well. As it happens, however, it has been harder than expected to develop an Internet version of the debit card that would allow consumers to make PIN-protected debit transactions from the personal computer.

C. ACH Transfers (WEB Entries)

The last advance in Internet payments has been the development of an ACH transfer that can be used to make retail Internet purchases. Those transactions have grown exponentially in the years since the promulgation in early 2001 of new NACHA Rules governing "Internet-Initiated Entries" — WEB entries in the NACHA terminology. In 2016, customers initiated more than 4.5 billion of those transactions (more than 25 for every salaried employee in the United States).

The NACHA Rules make WEB systems generally available to all banks that participate in the ACH system, which in turn should facilitate merchants in incorporating those systems into their Web sites so that consumers can use them. Because about one in five consumers in the United States lacks a credit card, the availability of this system offers merchants a way to serve those customers. Although it is still much smaller than card-based usage, it has grown rapidly, as many major merchants now accept those payments.

If the buyer wishes to purchase an item using one of the ACH-check systems, a check-like form appears on the buyer's screen. The buyer fills out the form, except for the signature line (which typically is marked "No Signature Required"). When the buyer confirms the information on the form, the software encrypts the information and transmits it to the service provider. The service provider then generates a WEB ACH debit entry based on the information and clears that information through the normal ACH system discussed above. That entry is processed and cleared in much the same way a typical ACH transaction is cleared. Thus, the buyer's account is debited one or two business days later, and the merchant receives the funds at that time (or perhaps a few days later, depending on the system's specific features). Those transactions functionally are quite similar to debit-card transactions: They result in a contemporaneous transfer of funds from the purchaser's bank account to the seller, and the EFTA and Regulation E govern them. The principal difference is the information that the purchaser must provide: normally information that identifies the customer's bank account. Interestingly, it appears that one of the main obstacles to uptake of the ACH payments is the considerable consumer resistance to providing that information to a retailer; although the legal and practical risks are not in fact very different, consumers are much more willing to provide their credit- or debit-card number to an Internet merchant than the information from the bottom of a check that identifies their bank account.

As with all ACH transactions, the system places fraud risks on the party that sends the entry to the system. Thus, if a transaction is fraudulent, the provider that is a member of the ACH system and entered the entry will bear the loss: It will have to return the funds to the account from which they were taken and will be left with a right to pursue the malefactor. Again, NACHA strongly urges those providers to use robust methods of identifying parties that enter transactions.

When the buyers are consumers (rather than businesses), those transactions are subject to all of the protections of the EFTA. Thus, as discussed above, the consumer ordinarily will have the right to disavow any transaction that is unauthorized and the benefit of the EFTA dispute-resolution mechanism.

D.   Foreign and Cross-Border Payments

Because consumers in countries other than the United States use credit cards much less frequently, credit cards are not as dominant for Internet retail purchases in other countries. They are, however, the leading method of paying for Internet retail purchases. Interestingly, jurisdictions outside the United States generally have statutory protections for the users of those cards that are much less protective than those in the TILA/Z regime discussed above. There is a great deal of variety among the specific protections, but often there are no protections at all, and where protections exist, they often have more exceptions than the rules in TILA and Regulation Z. Thus, disputes about payments in those countries are much more likely to be resolved under the contracts between the issuer and the cardholder or between the issuer, the merchant, and the merchant's financial institution.

In the absence of a substitute for the credit card, one consequence has been to make it more common in other countries to pay for an Internet purchase with an offline payment method—a check sent through the mail or cash on delivery. In Japan, for example, to this day a common model involves the retailer mailing the goods to a convenience store near the purchaser's home. The purchaser can obtain the goods by going to the convenience store and paying for them at that location. Although cash on delivery has long been an option at mainstream retailers like Amazon.com, few U.S. online shoppers have ever used that method.

In the absence of credit cards, retailers that wish to establish a presence in foreign markets have strong incentives to accept alternative forms of payment. Technology is still developing, but the most common denominator among developing alternative systems is some form of bank transfer or giro (the functional equivalent of an ACH transfer in the United States), which would result in a payment directly from the consumer's bank account to the merchant. The problem with that system is that it generally involves a separate transaction between the consumer and the consumer's financial institution, followed by a payment from the financial institution to the merchant and only at that point by shipment of the product. Given the common use of bank transfers in so many countries, it seems highly likely that an important payment product eventually will be one in which (1) a consumer can request a bank transfer directly from the merchant's site, (2) the merchant can verify the transfer in real time, and (3) shipment can be made immediately. Such a transaction would not differ in any substantial way from an online debit-card transaction in this country, except that the information entered by the consumer would be bank account information rather than a debit-card number. Such systems are not, however, widely deployed at this time.

At this time, cross-border payments are an even smaller market than foreign payments. Because most of the major retailers operate a number of country-specific sites, the great majority of Internet retailing occurs on a "national" basis. To date, transactions that occur across borders are predominantly settled by Visa, Mastercard, American Express, UnionPay, or JCB, because those are the only major card brands with substantial cross-border clearance networks. The law that applies to domestic purchases by the cardholder usually would govern payments in those transactions. The agreement between a card issuer and cardholder establishes the cardholder's obligations, and TILA and the EFTA limit those obligations, regardless of whether the card is used to buy something from Amazon.co.uk, from a brick-and-mortar retailer in London or Tokyo, or a restaurant in the United States. The principal difference is that the right to withhold payment under TILA §170 does not technically apply to transactions overseas. (Indeed, strictly speaking it does not apply to transactions more than 100 miles from, or outside the state of, the cardholder's residence. In practice, most issuers do not enforce any geographical limitation on rights under that section.)

The credit card is likely to face serious competition for cross-border payment systems that can affect transfers directly from bank accounts. In the absence of international bank-clearance systems—something that the industry is only beginning to develop—those payments are not likely to be generally available for some time. They do, however, have considerable potential within closely integrated economies like the member states of the European Union or NAFTA, where those kinds of clearing networks already are developing.

E.   A Note on Mobile Payments

Although Internet retail transactions have been growing steadily over the last few years, the most rapid growth has been in mobile transactions — transactions where the purchase is made over a cellphone or other mobile electronic device. M-commerce transactions in 2015 were estimated to total more than $100 billion, more than 30 percent of all e-commerce transactions.

Industry specialists for years pressed the idea that mobile payments should be an attractive convenience for consumers, but it was not until the second decade of this century that they began to penetrate the U.S. market substantially. For present purposes, it is useful to distinguish two separate classes of payments — "in-band" and "out-of-band."

By far the most common are so-called in-band or content payments, normally payments for information or content delivered directly to the telephone. For example, the first successful m-commerce application was the I-mode service provided by Japan's DoCoMo, which is used primarily to download "character" information. From that start, the variety of "apps" available for modern cellphones is staggering.

The second class is "out-of-band" payments — purchases in which a telephone is used to purchase something that cannot be delivered to the telephone. By far the most successful example here is Starbucks. By 2016 it was processing almost 10 million mobile payments per week; its mobile application alone is producing more than 20 percent of all orders placed at United States retail locations. It remains to be seen whether Apple Pay or some competing product from PayPal or Google will make a substantial dent in those numbers.

Although the methods of collecting for those payments are likely to develop over time, presently two methods dominate. The first is the aggregation method discussed for micropayments above. In the early days of mobile commerce, this often was used for in-band payments. For example, charges for i-Mode usage always have been added to the monthly mobile-phone bill; payments can be forwarded from the telephone company to the appropriate content provider. The second is for the merchant to use information sent from the telephone to conduct a contemporaneous credit- or debit-card transaction. In recent years, that method has come to dominate both in-band and out-of-band transactions: purchases from the App Store on iPhones, from Starbucks for out-of-band transactions, and the like. To the extent there is any variation, it is that in some cases the device is linked not directly to a payment card, but to a "wallet" that itself is linked to a variety of payment devices (PayPal, Google Checkout, and Apple Pay). Whether direct or indirect, though, all of those payment methods are transmitting payments over the payment-card system (discussed in the first three assignments) or the ACH system (discussed in Assignment 5). In practice, all of them function in just the same way as a conventional retail Internet purchase.

Problem Set 6

6.1.   Cliff Janeway (your book-dealer client) comes to see you to talk about developments in his industry. He finds that many of the people from whom he buys books now have many of the items he needs available for sale over the Internet. The three sites that he has examined so far accept both credit cards and debit cards. He has heard a lot about fraudulent transactions on the Internet, and he particularly remembers recent press coverage about credit-card numbers being stolen from Web merchants. As a result, he is worried that if he starts making such purchases he will expose himself to a significant risk. What do you tell him about his risks of being charged for unauthorized transactions on his credit card? Would it matter if the retailer from whom he made the purchase forced him to enter a PIN or the CVV from the back of his card? Would your advice be any different for his debit card?

What if he made the purchase with a WEB entry? Does it make sense that those things should change the outcome? TILA §133; EFTA §§903(5), 909; Regulation E, §1005.6; Regulation Z, §1026.12.

6.2.   A few days later, Cliff comes to you, surprised to tell you that his banker is now pressing him to accept ACH payments on his site. He wants to know what risks he will face if he accepts those payments: In what circumstances could he be forced to return those payments?

6.3.   Consider the facts of Problems 6.1 and 6.2 in the mobile context. Would your answer be different if the purchaser used a cellphone application (such as Apple Pay) to communicate with and received information from the merchant instead of an Internet connection? Consider the following scenarios, and whether TILA, the EFTA, or the NACHA Rules would apply to each:

(a) The application provides the merchant information to access a credit-card account.
(b) The application provides the merchant information to use a debit-card number to access a demand-deposit account.
(c) The application provides the merchant access to a prepaid card, such as an American Express gift card.
(d) The application provides the merchant routing information to a demand-deposit account.
(e) The application provides the merchant access to a merchant's own payment devices (such as a Starbucks card).
(f) The application makes an in-app purchase (tied to an account linked to the device itself, such as iTunes or Google Wallet).

6.4.   Consider the Venmo payment system as it is used in the following transactions between Cioffi and Fang.

(a) Cioffi sends Fang a payment of $100. Does Venmo use debit entries or credit entries? What credit risk does Venmo take if it lets Fang withdraw the funds?
(b) Fang hacks into Cioffi's Venmo account and sends a message, using Cioffi's credentials, asking Venmo to send $100 to Fang. Venmo complies. Must Venmo return the funds to Cioffi? 12 C.F.R. §1005.14.

Assignment 7: Virtual Currencies

The final topic for this chapter is the development of virtual currencies, or electronic money. In the early days of the Internet, it was widely assumed that some form of electronic money soon would become the dominant method of payment for Internet purchases. By the turn of the millennium, however, those expectations had been doused by a continuing series of market disappointments for such products. Despite the fascinating technological details of Internet-capable electronic money, the years continue to pass without the widespread deployment of such a product; the most prominent early developer (DigiCash) filed for bankruptcy. More recently, a group of companies (Beenz.com and Flooz.com being the most obvious) that tried to build forms of electronic money founded on gift certificates and loyalty points failed dismally, like so many other Internet startups in the second half of 2001.

In the last few years, however, the rise of Bitcoin has brought this issue back to the fore; its increasing use has brought regulatory attention from federal and state regulators, as well as initiated the process for a uniform state law on the topic. Perhaps the most salient feature of the rise of Bitcoin is the "point" of the system. The early developers of electronic money were heavily concerned with the problem of micropayments — a problem that existing systems largely have resolved over the last decade through advances in aggregation and increased flexibility in interchange rate schedules.

Bitcoin, however, is driven almost entirely by a distrust of governmental supervision. This means that anonymity is at the heart of its design, and central to its attractiveness. Unfortunately, this also means that a substantial part of its use has been for money laundering or for untraceable payments in illicit transactions. Thus, the rise of regulatory attention in this area has little or nothing to do with consumer protection. It is, instead, largely an effort to develop some window into the system that will stifle its illicit use. If that cannot readily be done (and I for one am doubtful that it can), it may well be that federal and state regulators will bring the system down in the relatively near term.

A. The Mechanics of Bitcoin

The following excerpt provides an excellent overview of how Bitcoin works.

Stephen T. Middlebrook, Bitcoin for Merchants: Legal Considerations for Businesses Wishing to Accept Bitcoin as a Form of Payment

Business Law Today, November 2014

Bitcoin is an Internet-based virtual currency which can be used to transfer value between parties. It is often classified as a "cryptocurrency" because it relies on cryptography to authenticate transactions. A bitcoin has no physical presence and no central authority administers the currency. It is not backed by any government and is not legal tender in any jurisdiction. It is not issued by or redeemable at any financial institution. A bitcoin only has value because other participants in the ecosystem ascribe value to it. The authenticity of any particular bitcoin may be verified by consulting a master database of bitcoins (called the "block chain") which is maintained over a peer-to-peer network on the Internet. The entities which provide the hardware and software to host the database and authenticate transactions are called "miners" and they are periodically rewarded for their public service by being given a few bitcoins. This is how new units of the virtual currency come into existence.

Bitcoin users are identified by their "public key" which is essentially a very large number. The public key is cryptographically associated with another large number, the "private key" which the user keeps confidential and uses to mathematically sign transactions. Because keeping track of these large numbers can be cumbersome, users typically employ a special piece of software called a "wallet" to manage their public and private keys. That software may be located on a personal computer or smartphone or hosted in the cloud by a service provider. While bitcoin is sometimes described as an anonymous currency, every transaction is recorded in the publicly accessible block chain and is associated with a public key. Tying a particular public key to an individual or company may be difficult, but it can be done. Bitcoin users, and merchants in particular, should assume that their bitcoin transactions are public knowledge.

To make a payment, a person uses his or her cryptographic credentials to sign a transaction transferring some amount of bitcoin to another person and submits it to the block chain. The miners perform the mathematic calculations necessary to verify the transaction, and if it is deemed authentic, update the block chain to indicate the transfer of ownership. The whole process takes a couple of minutes maximum. Once written to the block chain, the transaction is not reversible.

The price of a bitcoin relative to the U.S. dollar has fluctuated dramatically over time. In the early days of the virtual currency, it was worth only a few cents. As its fame increased and speculators began to invest, the price increased dramatically, reaching a high of $1,162 on November 30, 2013. The exchange rate has since retreated from that peak, falling to around $300 in early October 2014. Volatility is likely to be an aspect of the bitcoin market for the foreseeable future and consequently should be a consideration for businesses which engage in transactions denominated in bitcoin.

B.   Legal Issues

As suggested above, concerns about the use of Bitcoin to facilitate illicit activity have plagued the system as it has grown in the last few years. For example, when federal authorities in 2013 shut down the Web site Silk Road — a clandestine site used for the sale of illegal drugs and the like — they confiscated about 175,000 bitcoins, worth about $30 million at that time. It did not help matters when federal officials a few months later arrested the CEO of BitInstant (then a prominent Bitcoin exchange), charging him with conspiracy to launder money for customers of Silk Road. The currency suffered another major public relations problem a few months later when another exchange (MtGox) acknowledged that hackers had stolen 850,000 bitcoins from the site. To get a sense of the importance of those events, the coins seized in connection with Silk Road amounted to about 1.5 percent of the entire universe of then-outstanding bitcoins (around 12 million); the coins hacked from MtGox about 7 percent of that supply.

The most prominent issue for Bitcoin and the exchanges where users can obtain (or redeem) coins is the applicability of conventional moneytransmitter legislation. As those statutes are currently written, it seems likely that any exchange in the business of managing the supply of those coins is covered by that legislation. See Uniform Money Services Act §102(14) (defining "Money transmission" to include "receiving money or monetary value for transmission"). The failure of MtGox, together with the rampant illicit use of bitcoins, has spurred efforts to impose licensing regimes that would remove the anonymity of those marketplaces. At the same time, it seems unlikely that merchants or consumers whose sole activities are to spend or receive the coins in transactions have little basis for concern about those regimes; indeed, the purpose of those regimes would be to ensure the "safety and soundness" of those intermediaries, with a goal of protecting the users from the losses they suffer when exchanges like MtGox "lose" their (virtual) funds.

A second obvious issue is protection and allocation of liability among participants in those transactions. For now, at least, because the coins themselves are the repository of value, transactions that use the coins do not involve an "account" and thus are for that reason difficult to bring within the EFTA. Still, the CFPB in 2014 issued a proposed regulation that creates a new category of "prepaid accounts" to which Regulation E would extend protection. Because a bitcoin is a token of value that a user acquires on a prepaid basis, available for use in transactions, it is at least possible that the regulation will extend protections to those transactions.

The following case illustrates the regulatory openings related to bitcoin in its current usage.

Florida v. Espinoza

No. F-14-2923 (Fla. Cir. Ct. July 22, 2016)

THIS CAUSE came before the Court on Defendant, MICHELL ABNER ESPINOZA's multiple Motions to Dismiss the Information Pursuant to Florida Rule of Criminal Procedure 3.190(c)(4). This Court . . . hereby FINDS as follows:

BACKGROUND

Detective Ricardo Arias is a detective of the Miami Beach Police Department who worked in conjunction with the United States Secret Service's Miami Electronic Crimes Task Force (hereinafter "Task Force"). The Task Force is a team led by the Secret Service that is comprised of state and local agents. Prior to his encounter with the Defendant, Detective Arias attended a meeting at the United States Secret Service relating to virtual currencies. In his deposition, Detective Arias stated that he "became intrigued of the possibility" of initiating a local investigation into virtual currencies. He therefore reached out to Special Agent Gregory Ponzi from the United States Secret Service, which led to the Task Force's investigation into the purchase and sale of Bitcoin in South Florida.

On December 4, 2013, Detective Arias and Special Agent Ponzi accessed the Internet website https://localbitcoins.com seeking to purchase Bitcoin. Localbitcoins.com is a peer-to-peer Bitcoin exchange which defines itself as a marketplace where users can purchase and sell Bitcoin. Users who wish to sell Bitcoin create an advertisement containing the amount of Bitcoin they are offering and their asking price. Potential buyers browse the site and make arrangements to purchase Bitcoin with any seller they choose. The transaction can take place online, or, as in the instant case, the buyer and seller can agree to a local, face-to-face trade.

Detective Arias found multiple sellers of Bitcoin on the website, including the Defendant, whose username on the website was "Michelhack." The Defendant advertised that his contact hours were anytime and his meeting preferences were a Starbucks coffee store, internet café, restaurant, mall, or bank. The Defendant's posted advertisement, which Detective Arias found similar to a Criagslist.com advertisement, stated, "You will need to bring your wallet and your smartphone or the address the Bitcoin will be deposited to . . . " and further specified that interested buyers will have to pay in cash and in person. Based upon Defendant's username and advertisement, the Task Force determined that the Defendant might be engaged in unlawful activity and decided to initiate a Bitcoin trade with him. Although the Task Force specifically selected to investigate the Defendant, there were no previous reports that the Defendant was engaged in any illicit criminal activity and it appears that the Defendant was selected for the investigation based on his username, his 24-hour availability, and his desire to meet in public places.

On December 4, 2013, Detective Arias, acting in an undercover capacity as an interested buyer, contacted the Defendant by sending a text message to the Defendant's listed phone number. The Defendant responded to Detective Arias and agreed to meet with him the following day. On December 5, 2013, Detective Arias met with the Defendant at a Nespresso Café located at 1105 Lincoln Road, Miami Beach, Florida 33139. At this meeting, the Defendant agreed to sell .40322580

Bitcoin to Detective Arias in exchange for five hundred dollars ($500) in cash. The Defendant also explained to Detective Arias how the Bitcoin market worked, since Detective Arias claimed to be a new-time purchaser and inquired about the process. The Defendant explained to Detective Arias how he made a profit of eighty-three dollars and sixty-seven cents ($83.67) on this sale. Defendant further explained that he purchased the Bitcoin at ten percent (10%) under market value and sold the Bitcoin at five percent (5%) above market value. There was no discussion of illegal activity or stolen credit cards at this meeting. Detective Arias made several comments to the Defendant, none of which amounted to a direct statement that the Bitcoin were to be used for an illicit purpose. Detective Arias made it clear to the Defendant that he wanted to remain anonymous, and that the people he engaged in business with did not accept cash. Thereafter, the Defendant was followed by an undercover surveillance team to Citibank where he later completed the transaction.

On January 10, 2014, Detective Arias contacted the Defendant to arrange a second purchase. Detective Arias purchased one (1) Bitcoin in exchange for one thousand dollars ($1,000) at a Häagen-Dazs ice cream store located in Miami, Florida. At this meeting, Detective Arias told the Defendant that he was in the business of buying stolen credit card numbers from Russians and the Bitcoin would be used to pay for the stolen credit cards. Detective Arias did not show the Defendant any stolen credit cards or credit card numbers. Detective Arias asked the Defendant if the Defendant would be willing to accept stolen credit cards numbers as a trade for Bitcoin in their next transaction and the Defendant allegedly replied that "he would think about it." Despite the Defendant's purported indecisive response to Detective Arias' illicit proposal, there exists no evidence that the Defendant accepted stolen credit card numbers as payment for any subsequent Bitcoin transaction between the parties.

On January 30, 2014, Detective Arias again contacted the Defendant through a text message to arrange a purchase of more Bitcoin. The entire sale was conducted through text message communication. Detective Arias purchased five hundred dollars ($500) in Bitcoin. The money was deposited into the Defendant's bank account. Detective Arias informed the Defendant through a text message that he wanted to purchase thirty thousand dollars ($30,000) worth of Bitcoin in the future.

On February 6, 2014, Detective Arias met the Defendant with the intent of conducting a fourth Bitcoin transaction in the amount of thirty thousand dollars ($30,000) and effectuating an arrest. The parties met in the lobby of a hotel where the Task Force had a hotel room wired with cameras that was being used for their operation. After a brief meeting in the lobby, Detective Arias brought the Defendant to the hotel room in order to complete the transaction and make the arrest. The meeting in the hotel room was filmed. At this meeting, Detective Arias and the Defendant discussed the illicit credit card operation that Detective Arias had fabricated as part of his cover for the investigation. Detective Arias explained to the Defendant that he was engaged in the activity of buying stolen credit cards wholesale to resell at a higher price. Detective Arias also produced a "flash roll" of hundred dollar bills purportedly containing the thirty thousand dollar ($30,000) payment. The money was in fact undercover funds that were counterfeit. The Defendant inspected the currency and immediately became concerned that the money was counterfeit. The Defendant told Detective Arias he had to take the money to five different banks because he purchased the Bitcoin from five different sellers. According to Detective Arias' deposition, the Defendant wanted to bring portions of the money to the bank "a little at a time" in order to verify its authenticity. The Defendant never took possession of the counterfeit money and was subsequently arrested.

The Defendant was charged with one (1) count of unlawfully engaging in business as a money services business, to wit, a money transmitter, in violation of §560.125(5)(a), Fla. Stat. (Count I); and two (2) counts of money laundering, in violation of §896.101(5)(a) and (5)(b), Fla. Stat. (Counts II and III).

On September 17, 2015, the Defendant filed his initial Motion to Dismiss the Information. . . . Both parties submitted Memorandums of Law.

I. UNAUTHORIZED MONEY TRANSMITTER

In Count I, the Defendant was charged with violating §560.125(5)(a), Fla. Stat. Section 560.125(1), (5)(a) and (5)(b) states, in pertinent part, as follows:

> (1) A person may not engage in the business of a money services business or deferred presentment provider in this state unless the person is licensed or exempted from licensure under this chapter . . . .
> (5) A person who violates this section, if the violation involves:
>
>> (a) Currency or payment instruments exceeding $300 but less than $20,000 in any 12-month period, commits a felony of the third degree . . . .
>> (b) Currency or payment instruments totaling or exceeding $20,000 but less than $100,000 in any 12-month period, commits a felony of the second degree . . . .

§560.125.

The State contends that the Defendant is operating as an unlicensed "money services business." Section 560.103(22) defines "money services business" as a person "who acts as a payment instrument seller, foreign currency exchanger, check casher, or money transmitter." The term "money transmitter" means "a corporation, limited liability company, limited liability partnership, or foreign entity qualified to do business in this state which receives currency, monetary value, or payment instruments for the purpose of transmitting the same by any means, including transmission by wire, facsimile, electronic transfer, courier, the Internet, or through bill payment services or other businesses that facilitate such transfer within this country, or to or from this country." §560.103(23).

Initially, the State charged the Defendant as operating a "money services business, to wit a money transmitter." During the course of the last hearing, however, the State orally amended the Information to include a "payment instrument seller." A "payment instrument seller" is defined as "a corporation, limited liability company, limited liability partnership, or foreign entity qualified to do business in this state which sells a payment instrument." §560.103(30). A "payment instrument" means "a check, draft, warrant, money order, travelers check, electronic instrument, or other instrument, payment of money, or monetary value whether or not negotiable. The term does not include an instrument that is redeemable by the issuer in merchandise or service, a credit card voucher, or a letter of credit." §560.103(29).

When construing the meaning of a statute, the courts must first look to its plain language. Defendant's sale of Bitcoin does not fall under the plain meaning of Section 560.125(5)(a). Firstly, the Defendant did not receive currency for the purpose of transmitting same to a third party. If one goes by the plain meaning of Section 560.125, a "money transmitter" would operate much like a middleman in a financial transaction. The term "transmit" means "to send or transfer (a thing) from one person or place to another." Black's Law Dictionary (10th ed. 2014). Defendant's actions do not meet the definition of "transmit." Defendant was not a middleman. A money-transmitting business, such as Western Union, fits the definition of "money services business." For example, Western Union takes money from person A, and at the direction of person A, transmits it to person B or entity B. See, e.g., U.S. v. Elfgeeh, 515 F.3d 100, 108 (2d Cir. 2008) (where an FBI agent's testimony in court compared a Hawala to a Western Union because "it's a money transfer operation . . . [a] business used to send money from one location to another.").

In this case, the Defendant was a seller. According to the Arrest Affidavit, the Defendant told Detective Arias that he purchases Bitcoin for ten percent (10%) under market value and sells them for five percent (5%) over market value. The Defendant explained to Detective Arias that this fifteen percent (15%) spread is the method by which the Defendant yields a profit on his Bitcoin transactions. The Defendant purchases Bitcoin low and sells them high, the equivalent of a day trader in the stock market, presumably intending to make a profit.

Secondly, the Defendant does not fall under the definition of "payment instrument seller" found in §560.103(29) because Bitcoin does not fall under the statutory definition of "payment instrument." The federal government, for example, has decided to treat virtual currency as property for federal tax purposes (See I.R.S. Notice 2014-2, https://www.irs.gov/pub/irs-drop/n-14-21.pdf). "Virtual Currency" is not currently included in the statutory definition of a "payment instrument;" nor does Bitcoin fit into one of the defined categories listed.

Thirdly, the State alleges that the Defendant charged a commission or fee for the Bitcoin transaction, and therefore, the Defendant's actions meet the definition of a "money transmitter." Case law requires that a fee must be charged to meet all the elements of being a money transmitting business. "A money transmitting business receives money from a customer and then, for a fee paid by the customer, transmits that money to a recipient." United States v. Velastegui, 199 F.3d 590, 592 (2d Cir.1999). In the case at bar, the Defendant did not charge a fee for the transaction. The Defendant solely made a profit. In his deposition, Special Agent Ponzi acknowledged as much, noting that the Defendant made a profit of $83.67 on the $500 Bitcoin sale. "Commission" is defined as "an amount of money paid to an employee for selling something." Merriam-Webster's Dictionary (11th ed. 2016). The Defendant was not selling the Bitcoin for an employer. The Defendant was selling his personal property. The difference in the price he purchased the

Bitcoin for and what he sold it for is the difference between cost and expenses, the widely accepted definition of profit.

Nothing in our frame of reference allows us to accurately define or describe Bitcoin. In 2008 a paper was posted on the internet under the name Satoshi Nakamoto (thought to be a pseudonym for a person or group of people) which described a way to create a peer-to-peer network for electronic transactions which did not rely on trust. Satoshi Nakamoto, A Peer-to-Peer Electronic Cash System (2008). The network came into existence in 2009 when this network created the first block of Bitcoin. Subsequent Bitcoins are created by a process called "mining," essentially a record keeping process. To accrue Bitcoins, the miner must use open source software which allows their computer processors to catch and record peer-to-peer transactions. Bitcoins are bits of data that the miner receives in exchange for the use of their computer processor.

Bitcoin may have some attributes in common with what we commonly refer to as money, but differ in many important aspects. While Bitcoin can be exchanged for items of value, they are not a commonly used means of exchange. They are accepted by some but not by all merchants or service providers. The value of Bitcoin fluctuates wildly and has been estimated to be eighteen times greater than the U.S. dollar. Their high volatility is explained by scholars as due to their insufficient liquidity, the uncertainty of future value, and the lack of a stabilization mechanism. With such volatility they have a limited ability to act as a store of value, another important attribute of money.

Bitcoin is a decentralized system. It does not have any central authority, such as a central reserve, and Bitcoins are not backed by anything. They are certainly not tangible wealth and cannot be hidden under a mattress like cash and gold bars.

This Court is not an expert in economics, however, it is very clear, even to someone with limited knowledge in the area, that Bitcoin has a long way to go before it is the equivalent of money.

The Florida Legislature may choose to adopt statutes regulating virtual currency in the future. At this time, however, attempting to fit the sale of Bitcoin into a statutory scheme regulating money services businesses is like fitting a square peg in a round hole. This Court finds that the Defendant's sale of Bitcoin to Detective Arias does not constitute a "money services business" for all the reasons stated above. The Motion to Dismiss is granted as to Count I.

II. MONEY LAUNDERING

In Counts II and III, Defendant is charged with money laundering in violation of §896.101(3)(c). "Money laundering" is commonly understood to be the method by which proceeds from illicit activity ("dirty money") becomes legitimized. There are numerous ways through which this can occur, but it generally begins with money that is "dirty." The portion of the money laundering statute which the Defendant is charged under is not so straightforward. Section 896.101(3)(c) makes it illegal for an individual to conduct or attempt to conduct a financial transaction involving property or proceeds that a law enforcement officer has represented came from, or are being used to conduct or facilitate a specified unlawful activity, when the person's conduct is undertaken with the intent to: (1) promote the carrying on of specified unlawful illicit activity; (2) to control or disguise the illicit proceeds, or (3) to avoid reporting requirements. §896.101(3)(c).

The Defendant argues that the money laundering counts should be dismissed because the sale of Bitcoin does not meet the definition of "financial transaction" or "monetary instruments" under §896.101(2)(d) and (e). "Monetary instrument" is defined as "coin or currency of the United States or any other country, travelers' checks, personal checks, bank checks, money orders, investment securities in bearer form or otherwise in such form that title thereto passes upon delivery, and negotiable instruments in bearer form or otherwise such form that title thereto passes upon delivery." §896.101(2)(e). "Virtual currency" is not separately included as a category in that definition, nor does Bitcoin fall under any of the existing categories listed.

The definition of "financial transaction" is found in §896.101(2)(d). A "financial transaction" is a "transaction . . . involving one or more monetary instruments, which in any way or degree affects commerce . . . ." If the statute is read to mean that in the transaction, the Defendant must be the party who uses the monetary instruments then the money laundering statute would not apply in this case, because Bitcoins, as previously discussed, are not monetary instruments.

The more likely interpretation of the statute is that as long as one party to the transaction, in this case the law enforcement officer, is using a monetary instrument, a financial transaction has occurred. Therefore, any sale of property for cash is a financial transaction. Potentially any sale of property for cash could be a violation of the money laundering statute.

In this case, Detective Arias did not represent that the cash was the proceeds of an illegal transaction. Detective Arias did represent to the Defendant, in so many words, that he was planning to trade what he was buying from the Defendant (Bitcoin) for stolen credit card numbers. The statute requires that the officer as buyer merely make the representation that what was in this case, legally purchased Bitcoin is being used to facilitate or conduct illegal activity; it does not require any affirmative acknowledgement or action from the seller. Presumably the officer/buyer would be using the stolen credit cards to further engage in some kind of identity theft or fraudulent purchases, though they did not make this clear.

The statute does go on to require that the Defendant charged under this statute undertake the transaction with the intent to promote the carrying on of the illegal activity (Sections B and C do not apply here). §896.101(3)(c)1. The usage of the word "promote" in §896.101(3)(c)1 is troublingly vague. It is not clear to this Court what conduct is proscribed and what conduct is permitted. The term "promoter" is defined in Black's Law Dictionary as "someone who encourages or incites." Black's Law Dictionary 1333 (10th ed. 2014). The term "incite" is defined in Merriam-Webster Dictionary as "to cause (someone) to act in an angry, harmful, or violent way." Merriam-Webster's Dictionary (11th ed. 2016). The term "encourage" is defined as "to make (something) more appealing or more likely to happen." Is it criminal activity for a person merely to sell their property to another, when the buyer describes a nefarious reason for wanting the property? Does "promoting" require that there be more of an affirmative act or does the mere act of selling constitute promoting? Has a seller crossed into the realm of "promoting" by virtue of simply hearing the illicit manner in which the buyer intends to use what's been purchased? There is unquestionably no evidence that the Defendant did anything wrong, other than sell his Bitcoin to an investigator who wanted to make a case. Hopefully, the Florida legislature or an appellate court will define "promote" so individuals who believe their conduct is legal are not arrested.

This Court is unwilling to punish a man for selling his property to another, when his actions fall under a statute that is so vaguely written that even legal professionals have difficulty finding a singular meaning. Without legislative action geared towards a much needed update to the particular language within this statute, this Court finds that there is insufficient evidence as a matter of law that this Defendant committed any of the crimes as charged, and is, therefore, compelled to grant Defendant's Motion to Dismiss as to Counts II and III.

WHEREFORE, it is ORDERED AND ADJUDGED that the Motion to Dismiss the Information is hereby GRANTED.

Problem Set 7

7.1.   Your client is a merchant who has been approached by an entity that says it can arrange for merchants to receive bitcoins as payments. It will provide a software interface for the merchant to accept the bitcoins, and will purchase them at 98.5 percent of their market value as of the end of the business day on which the merchant accepts them. The software will convert her regular prices to bitcoin equivalents based on the real-time price at the time of the transaction, increased by 2 percent. This will be invisible to the customer, who will simply see a price; in effect, it is no different than the system by which the merchant accepts euros, except that the merchant has that arrangement with its bank. The question for you is whether the merchant needs to be concerned about falling under regulatory schemes for money transmitters and the like. What do you say? Uniform Money Services Act §§102(11)-(14) & comments 8-11, 201, 301, 401.

7.2.   Before she leaves, the client comments that she has heard a lot about bitcoins being connected with organized crime and money laundering. She asks whether, if she receives a bitcoin in payment that is the product of criminal activity, the government can confiscate it. 18 U.S.C. §1963(c).

7.3.   You have a great opportunity to represent an executive at your firm's largest bank client. He has been given the task of setting up a group that will issue a "BitCard," which he describes to you as a credit card on which all payments will be made in bitcoins. The card also will offer the option to make payments in bitcoins to merchants that accept them. Will this endeavor require licensing under the UMSA? UMSA §103.

7.4.   How would your answers to the preceding problem change if the business were operated by Elon Musk, the billionaire co-founder of PayPal and current CEO of SpaceX? If licenses are required, will he need them in every state in which cardholders reside? To which he sends payments? UMSA §§102, 201, 204.

7.5.   In Problem 7.4, to what degree would Musk be able to attract customers by promising absolute anonymity for purchases made using the BitCard?

Chapter 3.   Paying with Paper (Checks)

Assignment 8:   The Basic Checking Relationship

A.   The Basic Relationship

When we turn to payments with paper checks, we enter an area characterized at once by an immense and detailed body of law on just about every aspect of the system and at the same time by rapid technological advances that have changed just about everything about the way the system works in practice. Those technological advances have accompanied a marked decline in check usage, from more than 40 billion checks in 2000 to less than 17 billion checks in 2015. At the same time, the decline in total checks reflects a shift toward business use: About 70 percent of all checks are now written by businesses, as consumer use steadily dwindles.

To understand how the checking system works, it is best to start by identifying the parties that appear at the various steps of a checking transaction. If Cliff Janeway writes a check to Archie Moon to buy a book, that check is "drawn" on Cliff's account at Rocky Mountain Bank. That makes Rocky Mountain the "drawee" or the "payor bank." UCC §§3-103(a)(2), 4-104(a)(8), 4-105(3). Cliff, the person who directs the payment by writing the check, is called the "drawer" or "issuer." UCC §§3-103(a)(3), 3-105(c). Archie, the person to whom the check is written ("issue[d]," to use the statutory term, UCC §3-105(a)), is the "payee." Assuming that Archie does not have an account at Rocky Mountain Bank, the process of collecting on the check will involve one or more intermediaries between the payee and the payor bank. For example, Archie is most likely to deposit the check in his account at Colorado National Bank. That makes Colorado National the "depositary bank." UCC §4-105(2). Finally, if other banks (such as the Federal Reserve Bank in Denver) handle the check before it gets from the depositary bank to the payor bank, all of those banks — intermediaries between the depositary bank and the payor bank — are "intermediary bank[s]." UCC §4-105(4). The subsequent assignments discuss the various processes for collecting the check in detail, but it is important even at this early stage to understand the identity and role of the various parties that handle a check as it passes from the drawer that writes the check to the bank on which it is drawn.

A checking account basically is a two-step arrangement between the bank and the customer, under which the customer deposits money with the bank and the bank then disposes of the money in accordance with the customer's directions. In that regard, it is structurally much like the debit card discussed in Chapter 1 — except that the authorization of payment in this case is (at least initially) tangible rather than electronic.

The operations of the checking system are much more a product of positive law than those of the payment-card systems, which are largely governed by the private contractual arrangements of the card networks. The rules of the checking system, by contrast, include (in addition to customers' agreements with their bank) an entire Article of the Uniform Commercial Code (Article 4) devoted to the subject, large portions of another Article (Article 3 on negotiable instruments), and federal laws such as the Expedited Funds Availability Act and the Check Clearing for the 21st Century Act (universally known as Check 21). For the most part, this assignment discusses the rules for processing of paper checks; discussion of the increasingly routine processing of electronic images (rather than the paper checks themselves) is deferred to Assignment 10. This chapter emphasizes the rules of Article 4 and the applicable federal laws; discussion of the more technical details of negotiability is deferred to Chapter 7.

B.   The Bank's Right to Pay

From the perspective of the customer depositing its money with the bank, nothing is more central to the checking relationship than the rules that determine when the bank can give the customer's money to third parties and what happens if the bank does so improperly. The two issues are separate.

1.   When Is It Proper for the Bank to Pay?

On the first point, the text of the UCC offers little guidance, stating only that it is proper for the bank to charge a customer's account for any "item that is properly payable." UCC §4-401(a). The comments to that section explain the concept more clearly, indicating that an item is properly payable "if the customer has authorized the payment." UCC §4-401 comment 1. In the checking context, the most common way (although not the only way) for the customer to authorize payment is by writing a check, which authorizes the bank to use funds in the customer's account to pay the amount of the check to the payee. Accordingly, if the payee presents the check to the customer's bank (the payor bank, as discussed previously), it would be proper for the payor bank to "honor" the check. If the payor bank does honor the check, it gives funds in the amount of the check to the payee and charges the customer's account for the amount of the check. Thus, for example, if Archie presented Cliff's check to Rocky Mountain, it would be proper for Rocky Mountain to pay the check and charge Cliff's account.

In most cases, the payee does not take the check directly to the payor bank. Instead, the payee obtains payment from an intermediary, such as the payee's own bank or a check-cashing outlet. As long as the payee properly transfers the check to the intermediary (a topic discussed in detail below), the intermediary becomes, in the terms of UCC §3-301, a "person entitled to enforce" the check; at that point the intermediary is just as entitled to payment of the check as the original payee. See UCC §1-201(b)(25), (27) ("person" in the UCC includes not only natural individuals but also organizations such as corporations, partnerships, trusts, and other legal or commercial entities).

Conversely, if the check is stolen through no fault of Archie's and presented by a party that does not have any right to enforce the check, it is not proper for Rocky Mountain to pay the check. See UCC §4-401 comment 1, sentences 5-7. The idea is simple: When customers write checks to specific individuals, they intend to authorize payment to those payees and at least implicitly authorize payment to parties that acquire the checks from the named payees, but they have no intention — explicit or implicit — to authorize payment to thieves that steal the checks before payment.

(a)   Overdrafts.   A variety of problems can complicate the bank's entitlement to pay a check even in cases in which the customer actually wrote the check and in which the party seeking payment is the proper holder of the check. The most common problem arises when the customer authorizes payment by writing a check, but the account does not have enough funds to cover the check when it arrives at the payor bank. The answer in that situation is simple, if not intuitively obvious: The payor bank is free to pay the check or dishonor it as the bank wishes. That is, the payor bank can charge the account, but (absent some specific agreement) it also is free to dishonor the check and refuse to pay it. UCC §§4-401(a), 4-402(a).

McGuire v. Bank One, Louisiana, N.A.

744 So. 2d 714 (La. Ct. App. 1999)

STEWART, J.

Lottie M. McGuire ("McGuire") filed suit against Bank One Louisiana ("Bank One") for damages after Bank One paid a check drawn by McGuire and thereby created an overdraft in the amount of $188,176.79. Bank One filed an exception of no cause of action which the trial court sustained. McGuire now appeals the dismissal of her suit for damages. We affirm.

FACTS

. . . [O]n the morning of August 26, 1996, Timothy P. Looney ("Looney"), an acquaintance representing himself as an investment broker, approached [McGuire] with an offer to sell $200,000 in bonds due to mature on October 31, 1996 for $206,400. McGuire told Looney that she would think about it and let him know. Later that day, McGuire informed Looney that she would buy the bonds for $200,000. Looney agreed to come by later to pick up McGuire's check.

McGuire maintained both a checking account and an investment account with Bank One in Shreveport, Louisiana. Bank One's trust department administered McGuire's investment account. McGuire contacted Harvey Anne Leimbrook, an account officer in Bank One's trust department, and instructed her to [take the steps necessary to move funds from the investment account] to the checking account. Leimbrook informed McGuire that it would take two or three days for the money to be transferred.

Later that same day, Looney went to McGuire's house, and McGuire presented him with a check for $200,000 payable to his company, Paramount Financial Group. The check was dated August 26, 1996. McGuire gave Looney "strict instructions" not to present the check for payment until Wednesday, August 28, 1996, so as to insure that the transfer of funds would be complete. Looney did not heed McGuire's instructions, but instead he immediately deposited the check at Commercial National Bank ("CNB").

CNB then presented McGuire's check for payment to Bank One on August 27, 1996. Bank One, without notifying McGuire, honored the check even though the amount of money in McGuire's checking account was "grossly insufficient" to cover the check. Bank One did mail an overdraft notice to McGuire the next day informing her that her checking account was overdrawn in the amount of $188,198.79 and that an overdraft fee of $22 was charged to her account. McGuire received the overdraft notice on Friday, August 30, 1996.

Unfortunately, Looney did not purchase the bonds with McGuire's money. Instead, Looney converted the money for his own benefit. Looney subsequently pled guilty to mail fraud and was sentenced to serve time in a federal penitentiary. McGuire alleges that if Bank One had informed her on August 26 or 27 that her check had been prematurely presented for payment contrary to her explicit instructions to Looney, then she would have become suspicious of Looney and stopped payment on the check. McGuire seeks damages for Bank One's negligence in failing to exercise ordinary care in paying the check and creating the overdraft.

In response to McGuire's petition for damages, Bank One . . . asserted that McGuire's check was properly payable and that pursuant to [UCC §]4-401, it was authorized to honor the check even though an overdraft resulted. The trial court [ruled in favor of Bank One.]

DISCUSSION

. . . According to the facts alleged in her petition, McGuire seeks damages from Bank One because a substantial overdraft resulted when Bank One honored a check drawn by McGuire on her own checking account. . . . McGuire does not dispute that her check was properly payable. However, McGuire argues that the bank's authority to honor a check creating an overdraft is discretionary under [UCC §4-]401(a) and that, as a matter of policy, this statutory right should be tempered by some standard of due care in compliance with the general usage and customs of the banking industry. As an alternative to reversal of the trial court, McGuire seeks leave to amend her petition to add additional pleadings regarding the duty of ordinary care owed by banks and the general banking customs and practices in this area. . . .

. . . The language of [Section] 4-401 permits a bank to charge a properly payable check against a customer's account even though an overdraft results. No showing of good faith is required to justify the bank's action. However, under the provisions of [UCC §]4-103, a bank is required to exercise ordinary care. Bank One asserts that it exercised ordinary care in paying McGuire's check and charging payment to her account. We agree. . . . Payment of a properly payable item creating an overdraft is an action approved by [Section] 4-401(a). Therefore, such action by a bank is the exercise of ordinary care. General banking usage, customs, or practices would have no bearing on whether Bank One did or did not exercise ordinary care since its payment of McGuire's check, even though an overdraft resulted, was expressly authorized by [Section] 4-401(a) and is *per se* the exercise of ordinary care under [Section] 4-103(c). Therefore, we find, as did the trial court, that McGuire's petition fails to state a cause of action against Bank One. . . .

. . . Bank One had authority to pay McGuire's check even though it created an overdraft. The check was properly payable. The fact that a substantial overdraft resulted does not override the bank's authority under [UCC §]4-401(a). The allegations in McGuire's petition indicate that she drew the check knowing that she had insufficient funds in her checking account to cover the check. It is unfortunate that McGuire was the victim of fraud. However, her loss is not one for which Bank One can be found liable under the circumstances of this case.

Although it might seem unduly deferential to give the payor bank unguided discretion to decide whether to pay the check, it does make more sense than a mandatory legal rule that takes away that discretion and establishes a fixed course of action for such checks. Consider first a possible rule that would *require* banks to dishonor overdraft checks. That rule would be much worse for customers than the present discretionary rule. Most customers would prefer for their banks to honor their checks even if their accounts contain insufficient funds, if only to protect the customers from the difficulties they face when their checks bounce: monetary charges by those to whom they wrote the checks, possible criminal liability, and more general harm to the customers' reputations. Conversely, it would be unreasonable to require banks to honor checks even when accounts do not contain enough funds to cover the checks. That rule would expose banks to the risk of loss in any case in which the customer did not voluntarily reimburse the bank for the amount of the check.

As it happens, most banks are willing to agree to pay overdrafts for their customers (at least for some of their customers) by providing "overdraft protection." Thus, for a fee, banks agree in advance that they will honor checks up to a preset limit even if the checks are drawn against insufficient funds. That agreement overturns the standard Article 4 rule and leaves the bank obligated to pay the checks when they appear. See UCC §§4-402(a) (stating that "a bank may dishonor an item that would create an overdraft *unless it has agreed to pay the overdraft*" (emphasis added)), 4-103(a) (stating that "[t]he effect of the provisions of this Article may be varied by agreement").

Another major topic of dispute relates to the order in which banks process checks for payment. Banks often pay the largest checks first and smaller checks later (that is, by descending order of amount). On a day when the account contains insufficient funds to pay all of the checks presented against it, that procedure can lead to a larger number of bounced checks (and thus a greater amount of bounced-check fees) than a policy that paid checks by increasing order of amount. Banks have defended those policies by pointing out that the largest checks often are items such as mortgage and car payments — for which consumers are most likely to suffer serious damage from payor-bank dishonor. Consumer advocates — skeptical of the sincerity of the bank's professed interest in customer welfare — have filed a number of suits challenging such policies, but those suits to date have foundered on the statement in UCC §4-303(b) that banks can pay items "in any order." E.g., Smith v. First Union Nat'l Bank, 958 S.W.2d 113 (Tenn. Ct. App. 1997); Hill v. St. Paul Federal Bank, 768 N.E.2d 322, 325-327 (Ill. App. Ct. 2002). Similarly, efforts to revise the statute to provide a uniform policy failed because of the opposition of the banking industry.

(b)   Stopping Payment.   A second problem regarding the bank's right to pay a check arises when customers change their minds after writing checks and decide that they no longer want the payments to be made. That could happen for several reasons, ranging from dissatisfaction with the goods or services purchased with the check to completely unrelated financial distress (such as loss of a job) that alters the customer's willingness to pay. A notable feature of the checking system is that the customer's decision to pay does not become final at the time that the customer issues the check. Rather, Article 4 gives the customer that changes its mind the right to "stop" payment. Specifically, a check ceases to be properly payable if the customer gives the payor bank timely and adequate notice of the customer's desire that the payor bank refuse to pay the check. Hence, at least if the customer manages to send a timely and effective notice, the bank loses its right to charge the customer's account for the item even if the item initially was authorized by the customer. UCC §4-403 & comment 7.

Three major considerations, however, limit the practicality of the customer's right to stop payment. First, the customer must act promptly to exercise the right. UCC §4-403(a) provides that a stop-payment notice is effective only if it is "received at a time and in a manner that affords the bank a reasonable opportunity to act on it before any [final] action by the bank with respect to the item." As the later assignments explain, current check-collection systems usually result in final action on a check within a few days, or even hours, after the check is deposited for collection. Accordingly, any attempt to stop payment that does not follow closely upon the original transaction is unlikely to be effective under UCC §4-403.

The second problem relates to the duration of the stop-payment order. Under UCC §4-403(b), a stop-payment order is valid only for six months. To be sure, the drawer can renew the stop-payment order every six months if it wishes to keep the check permanently unpayable, but as a practical matter few drawers remember to renew the stop-payment order every six months. Accordingly, it is easy enough for the savvy holder of a stopped check to wait out the six-month period and present it shortly after the termination of that period. Experience (and occasional litigation on the topic) suggests that banks readily honor items presented shortly after the expiration of the statutory six-month period. The six-month limit is particularly odd because it is so obviously contrary to the typical intent of a customer seeking to stop payment — can you imagine wanting to stop payment on a check *now* but intending for your bank to pay the check *six months later*? Still, efforts to revise the statute to remove the six-month limit failed because of opposition of the banking industry, which contends that it would be unduly difficult to design computer software that would treat stop-payment requests as permanently effective.

The third problem with a customer's effort to stop payment arises from the underlying obligation for which the check was written. When somebody satisfies a payment obligation with a check, the payee has two separate rights to payment: the right to enforce the check and the right to pursue the check writer on the underlying transaction. The right to enforce the check arises under Articles 3 and 4; the right on the underlying transaction arises under the law that governs that transaction, which might be the rules in Article 2 that govern sales, the terms of a lease if the check is issued to pay rent, or common-law rules governing promissory notes if the check is issued to make a payment on a note.

Section 3-310 of the UCC articulates a set of rules to govern the two rights of the payee, the general purpose of which is to enhance the likelihood that the payee will be paid once, and only once. For present purposes, two of those rules are crucial. First, to prevent the payee from obtaining double payment by collecting both on the check and on the underlying obligation, the UCC "suspend[s]" the payee's right to pursue the customer on the underlying transaction when the payee accepts the customer's check. See UCC §3-310(b). Second, to ensure that the payee is not prejudiced by accepting a check that goes unpaid, the statute provides that the suspension ends if the check is dishonored. See UCC §3-310(b)(1). The termination of the suspension leaves the payee back where it started, with its right to pursue the check writer on the underlying transaction. Thus, even if a check writer succeeds in causing its bank to stop payment on a check, the check writer remains liable to the payee on the underlying obligation.

2.   Remedies for Improper Payment

Sometimes a bank pays a check that was not, in the terms of UCC §4-401, properly payable. The most likely problems are (a) that the customer in fact did not write the check, (b) that payment was made after a forged indorsement (and thus was not made to the payee or some other person entitled to enforce the check), or (c) that the bank failed to comply with a valid order to stop payment. The basic remedy for an improper payment is simple and intuitively obvious. The bank must reverse the improper transaction. Specifically, because the item was not properly payable, the bank cannot sustain the charge on the customer's account based on that item. Accordingly, the bank must recredit the customer's account with the funds improperly paid out, so that the balance in the customer's account will be the same as it would have been if the bank had not made the improper payment. Moreover, as discussed in more detail below, the statute even provides a form of consequential damages in cases in which the charge to the account leads the bank to dishonor other checks. In that event, the bank not only must return any fees it charged in connection with those dishonored checks, but also must pay any damages to the customer that follow proximately from the dishonor. See UCC §4-402(b).

However generous the obligation to recredit might appear at first glance, its practical import is limited sharply by UCC §4-407. That provision "subrogates" the bank to the rights of the payee of the check, so that the bank can assert the payee's rights against the drawer as a defense to the bank's obligation to recredit the account. Returning to the previous example, suppose that Cliff changed his mind about buying the books after he wrote the check to Archie and properly stopped payment before Archie presented the check to Rocky Mountain (the payor bank). If Rocky Mountain mistakenly paid Archie anyway, Rocky Mountain's right of subrogation would allow the bank to refuse to recredit Cliff's account *even though the check was not properly payable.* By subrogation to Archie's rights, the bank would be entitled to assert Archie's right to payment. Assuming that Cliff was obligated to pay for the books even though Cliff changed his mind (a plausible assumption), then the bank would be entitled to payment just as much as Archie was (because the bank already paid Archie on the check). Thus, the bank would not have to recredit the account. If that rule seems fundamentally unfair at first glance to the party that attempted to stop payment, it is worth considering matters from the perspective of the payee, a perspective well illuminated by the case that follows.

McIntyre v. Harris
709 N.E.2d 982 (Ill. App. Ct. 1999)

Justice LYTTON delivered the opinion of the court:

The plaintiff, Brian P. McIntyre, filed a complaint against the defendants, Twin Oaks Savings Bank (Bank) and Robert E. Harris (Harris), the Bank's executive vice-president. McIntyre alleged that the defendants coerced him into signing a $2,000 personal note made payable to the Bank after the Bank had erroneously paid out a check over McIntyre's valid stop payment order. The defendants counterclaimed, demanding payment on the overdue note. After a bench trial, the court found in favor of the defendants. . . . We affirm.

In mid-October 1996 McIntyre's company, Total Home, placed a telemarketing call to Sandra Bennett. As a result, Ray Archie visited Bennett's home and quoted her a price to repair her roof. McIntyre testified that since his company did not repair roofs, he referred the job to Archie. . . .

Around October 19, 1996, McIntyre visited Bennett and told her that in order to complete the job, it was necessary for her to give Archie $2,000 for the materials. Bennett wrote a check to Total Home for $2,000 that day. In return, McIntyre wrote Bennett a check for $2,000 and postdated it to October 28, 1996. Bennett said that McIntyre told her that she could cash his check if her roof was not repaired by October 28, 1996. McIntyre cashed Bennett's check and deposited it in his business account at the Bank. . . .

McIntyre admitted that Bennett's roof was not repaired by October 28, 1996. Nevertheless, on November 14, 1996, he ordered the Bank to stop payment on the check to Bennett.

Around November 27, 1996, the Bank erroneously paid out on McIntyre's check over his stop payment order. After McIntyre learned that the Bank had withdrawn the $2,000 from his business account, he spoke with Harris and told him that the withdrawal would cause his account to be overdrawn. He then went to the Bank and signed an agreement to pay the Bank $2,000 plus interest due by July 1, 1997. In return, the Bank agreed to leave the $2,000 in his account. McIntyre admitted that he never paid on the note and at the time of trial he was currently 2 months overdue on it. . . .

The judge [concluded that] the Bank was subrogated to the rights of Sandra Bennett and could recover the money from McIntyre. The court then found in favor of the defendants. . . .

I

A. UNJUST ENRICHMENT

McIntyre first contends that the Bank is not entitled to a $2,000 reimbursement. . . .

Section 4-407 of the UCC provides that if a payor bank has paid an item over the stop order of the drawer or maker, the bank may become subrogated to the rights of other parties in order to prevent unjust enrichment to the extent necessary to prevent loss to the bank by reason of its payment of the item. . . . When a bank pays out a check over a valid stop payment order, the ultimate burden of proof as to loss is on the customer.

Since the Bank paid out over McIntyre's valid stop payment order, we must determine whether the Bank can become subrogated to the rights of another party to prevent unjust enrichment. McIntyre admitted that Bennett wrote a $2,000 check to Total Home and that he deposited it in his business account at the Bank. He did not dispute Bennett's testimony that he told Bennett she could cash his check to her if her roof was not completed by October 28, 1996. He agreed that the roof was never completed. Therefore, McIntyre deposited $2,000 of Bennett's money in his account for work that was never performed. Under these facts, the trial court properly . . . found that McIntyre was unjustly enriched. Thus, the Bank is entitled to repayment if it can subrogate itself to the rights of a proper party under the UCC.

[The court then considered whether Bennett was a proper party. Ultimately, it concluded that it did not matter whether Bennett was a holder in due course (a topic discussed in Chapter 7):] [U]nder 4-407(2), even if Bennett were not a holder in due course, the Bank would still be subrogated to her rights as a payee. Under subsection (2), Bennett, as the payee of the instrument, even as a mere holder, obtained the right to pursue McIntyre. A payor Bank is subrogated to the rights "of the payee or any other holder . . . against the drawer . . . on the item or under the transaction out of which the item arose." The Bank was properly subrogated to Bennett's interest as the holder of McIntyre's check. [Ed.: Bennett plainly qualifies as a holder of the item under UCC §1-201(b)(21).] . . .

The judgment of the circuit court of La Salle County is affirmed.

If the bank relied on subrogation to justify a refusal to recredit, the result doubtless would disappoint Cliff (who, after all, followed the correct steps to stop payment). It is justified, however, by the unfairness of allowing the drawer to have its account recredited when the drawer in fact is obligated to pay for the books. In the absence of subrogation (or some similarly equitable remedy such as restitution), the result would be that Cliff would get to keep the books without paying for them.

C.   The Bank's Obligation to Pay

For the checking system to work, the payor bank's obligation to pay must be sufficiently certain to convince sellers to accept checks as a method of payment. Accordingly, the rules establishing when a bank must pay the customer's funds to another party are central to the success of the checking system. Those rules fall into two classes: rules obligating the bank to pay and rules establishing remedies for the bank's failure to pay as required.

1.   When Are Funds Available for Payment?

As discussed above, a bank has the option to pay any item that is properly payable from the customer's account. The flip side of that, however, is that the bank has an affirmative obligation to pay the item when the account has funds "available" to cover the item. To be sure, as discussed later, that obligation runs only to the bank's customer (the drawer), not to the payee or any subsequent holder of the check. Thus, even if funds are available to pay the item at the time the item comes to the bank, the payee has no claim against the bank if the customer prevents the bank from paying the check by withdrawing those funds or otherwise stopping the bank from paying the check. But from the customer's perspective, the bank's obligation to pay is central because the reliability of that obligation is what makes it useful for the customer to make payments with checks.

Surprisingly, the question of how much money the customer has in its account to cover checks at any time is relatively complicated, with several sections of the United States Code and pages of Federal Reserve Board regulations providing a network of rules that limit the bank's discretion to decide that question for itself. The complexity of those rules is an artifact of the modern checking system. In a simpler world, there would be no need for complicated rules about funds availability. For example, if all deposits to checking accounts were made in cash, there would be no need for disputes about the date when the deposited funds would be available for payment of checks written by the customer: As soon as the bank received the cash and noted the deposit on its records — probably by the next business day after the date of the deposit — the bank would be safe in disbursing the funds to pay checks written by the customer. See 12 C.F.R. §229.10(a) (requiring payor banks to make funds available by the next business day after the deposit if the funds are deposited in cash with a teller at the bank).

As it happens, however, many of the deposits to checking accounts are made not in the form of cash or some other immediately verifiable means of payment (such as the wire transfers discussed in the next chapter), but in the form of checks. Again, there would be no problem if all checks were deposited at the payor bank: Whenever a customer deposited a check to its account, the bank could refer to its records for the account on which the check was drawn to see if there was enough money to pay the check; if there was, the depositary bank safely could credit the customer's account and debit the drawer's account at the same time. See 12 C.F.R. §229.10(c)(1)(vi) (requiring payor banks to make funds available by the next business day after the deposit if the funds are deposited in the form of a check drawn on a local branch of the depositary bank).

In reality, of course, there are thousands of different banks in this country, and thus banks receive deposits containing a prodigious number of checks that are drawn on other banks. Accordingly, a bank into which a check is deposited cannot tell from its own records whether it safely can allow the depositor to withdraw the funds represented by the check. Thus, if Bank A wants to be safe in deciding whether to honor a check based on funds that its customer has deposited in the form of a check drawn on an account at Bank B, Bank A will have to wait until it finds out whether Bank B will honor the deposited check. If Bank A grants immediate access to the funds, Bank A will have a problem if Bank B later dishonors the check after Bank A's customer has already withdrawn the money. Accordingly, depositary banks have an incentive to limit their customers' access to funds deposited by check until they can be certain that the deposited checks will be honored by the banks on which the checks are drawn. If Bank A does not limit that access, it exposes itself to fraud by a customer that might withdraw the funds even if the customer knows that the account at Bank B on which the deposited check was drawn does not contain sufficient funds to cover the deposited check.

For many years, the only legal rule governing the bank's evaluation of funds availability was the rule set forth in UCC §4-215(e) (and its predecessors). That statute grants the depositary bank unfettered discretion to protect itself by permitting the bank to limit the customer's access to funds deposited by check until the depositary bank can determine whether the check will be honored. The practices of banks under that rule eventually became intolerably onerous to consumers. As the Supreme Court has explained:

> [Under the UCC], the check-clearing process too often lagged, taking days or even weeks to complete. To protect themselves against the risk that a deposited check would be returned unpaid, banks typically placed lengthy "holds" on deposited funds. Bank customers, encountering long holds, complained that delayed access to deposited funds impeded the expeditious use of their checking accounts.
>
> In 1987, Congress responded by passing the Expedited Funds Availability Act, [which] requires banks to make deposited funds available for withdrawal within specified time periods, subject to stated exceptions.

Bank One Chicago, N.A. v. Midwest Bank & Trust Co., 516 U.S. 264, 266-267 (1996).

The Expedited Funds Availability Act (EFAA), 12 U.S.C. §§4001-4010, has been implemented by the Board of Governors of the Federal Reserve System under Regulation CC, 12 C.F.R. Part 229. Regulation CC establishes a framework of deadlines within which a depositary bank must release funds that its customers deposit by check. Unlike UCC §4-215, those deadlines apply even if the depositary bank does not determine by the deadline if the payor bank will honor the check in question. The deadlines in Regulation CC mirror deadlines required in the text of the EFAA itself. To avoid duplication, this text discusses only the more detailed regulatory provisions.

Although the regulations contain plenty of special provisions and exceptions (several of which are discussed below), the general framework that they establish is not hard to follow. Until 2010, that framework had separate rules for local and nonlocal checks — which depended on whether the check was deposited in the check processing region of the bank on which it was drawn. But the rise of electronic processing has led to rapid consolidation of check processing, and in early 2010 the Federal Reserve announced that there henceforth would be only a single check-processing region. Thus, although the EFAA and Regulation CC continue to articulate rules for nonlocal checks, all checks are now local. Thus, the most important distinction now in assessing funds availability is whether the customer wishes to use those funds indirectly (by writing checks against them) or directly (by withdrawing cash). On that point, the regulations give banks more time before they must make funds available in cash, on the theory that individuals trying to defraud banks are more likely to withdraw funds in cash than by check.

(a) Noncash Withdrawals.   This is the quickest way for funds to become available. In this situation, the bank must make $200 available on the first business day after the banking day on which the funds are deposited. Regulation CC, §229.10(c)(1)(vii); 12 U.S.C. §4002(a)(2)(D) (as amended by the Dodd-Frank Wall Street Reform and Consumer Protection Act). The rest of the funds must be available for withdrawal no later than the second business day. Regulation CC, §229.12(b).

(b) Cash Withdrawals.   If the customer wants to withdraw the funds by cash (rather than by check), the regulations permit the bank to defer for still another day the availability of all sums beyond the first $600. Regulation CC, §229.12(d). Thus, the bank still must make $200 available on the first business day and must make an additional $400 available on the second business day (for a total of $600), but the bank can defer the availability of any remaining amount until the third business day. Regulation CC, §229.12(b) & (d).

(c) Low-Risk Items.   To complicate that basic framework, Regulation CC includes a set of special rules for a group of particularly low-risk items. Instead of the $100 next-day availability discussed above, those rules generally require the bank to make the entire amount of funds from such items available on

the first business day after the banking day on which the funds are deposited. Regulation CC, §229.10(c)(1).

It is important to examine one other introductory matter, Regulation CC's scheme for counting days. The Regulation CC deadlines employ distinct concepts of banking days and business days, with all of the deadlines running from the "banking day" on which an item is deposited, rather than the "business day" on which it is deposited. Under the regulation, banking days are a subset of business days, specifically those business days on which the bank is open "for carrying on substantially all of its banking functions." Regulation CC, §229.2(f). Business days, by contrast, are all calendar days other than Saturdays, Sundays, and federal holidays. Regulation CC, §229.2(g). The relevant point is that business days on which a bank is not open (perhaps the day after Thanksgiving) are not banking days that start the running of the availability deadlines.

Although the Regulation CC deadlines might seem unreasonably long to a customer waiting to use money that it gave to its bank several days earlier, they are short enough to put banks at some risk of loss, largely because of the possibility that the deadline will arrive — requiring the depositary bank to permit disbursement of the funds before the depositary bank discovers whether a payor bank will honor a check. For example, a depositary bank must release funds on the second business day after deposit, even though banks frequently will not know by that time whether the check will be honored. Because of the recent consolidation of check processing regions, the likelihood that dishonored checks will fail to return to the depositary bank before the applicable EFAA deadline is quite real, at least for paper checks.

To get a sense of the susceptibility of the system, consider a common scheme that takes advantage of the interplay between the funds availability rules and the mechanics of deposits at remote locations (usually ATMs). If a thief learns the hours at which a bank collects deposits from a remote location (often less frequently than once a day), the thief can go to the ATM and use an ATM card to feign a deposit transaction. The thief punches in the numbers for a deposit transaction and even deposits an envelope into the machine: The envelope, however, is empty. Because of the infrequency with which the deposit envelopes are collected, the funds from the deposit often become available before the envelope is collected and examined. For example, if the envelope is deposited at one o'clock Monday afternoon at a machine from which envelopes are collected at noon each day, some of the funds from the deposit often would become available for withdrawal on Tuesday morning. The knowledgeable thief could withdraw the (falsely deposited) funds the next morning and leave before the bank even retrieved the empty envelope from the machine!

Three general considerations, however, provide at least a partial justification for prompt funds-availability requirements notwithstanding the risk of loss that they impose. First, Regulation CC does not unconditionally obligate the bank to release funds immediately. It has a number of detailed exceptions describing circumstances in which a depositary bank can limit access even beyond the deadlines described above. For example, the bank can limit severely the availability of funds in a new account (which the regulation defines as any account less than 30 days old. See Regulation CC, §229.13(a)(2)). Among other things, the two-day schedule does not apply to deposits made by checks that exceed $5,000 on any single banking day, even if the deposits include government-issued checks or other low-risk items. See Regulation CC, §229.13(b). The bank also can defer availability of funds if the funds are deposited in accounts that have had repeated overdrafts in the last six months, Regulation CC, §229.13(d) or, even more generally, if the bank "has reasonable cause to believe that the check is uncollectible," id. §229.13(e).

The second consideration is convenience. Many customers have important needs for their funds immediately at the time of deposit. It is plausible to argue that those needs, coupled with the fact that well over 99 percent of checks deposited in banks clear without incident, justify allowing prompt access to funds deposited by check, even if the check has not yet cleared. A rule making that money available might result in occasional losses that otherwise could be prevented, but it is arguable that the benefit to customers of that access exceeds the cost to the system of modest losses.

The third consideration is the most important: the likely long-term effects of giving banks the risk of loss that they face if the deadlines force them to release funds without determining whether a check will clear. By putting that risk on banks, the system gives banks the incentive to speed up the system to limit the frequency with which the deadlines arrive before information about the validity of the check. Thus, as new technology and systems develop to accelerate the check-clearance system, the risk of loss that the deadlines impose on the banks should decrease. As discussed above, banks in the pre-EFAA era tended to defer availability for long periods of time, often exceeding a week. As I explain later in the chapter, the industry has developed systems for clearing checks that can provide prompt certainty about clearing. It is possible that competitive forces would have produced the same result without regulation, but it is hard to be sure of that.

One interesting twist about funds availability policies is evidenced by the extent to which banks have gone beyond their Regulation CC obligations. However much the deadlines might have spurred banks into action to develop faster procedures for clearing checks, the result is a process in which the regulatory deadlines have become irrelevant in many contexts. Presently, most banks offer availability much sooner than Regulation CC requires. One recent Federal Reserve study (conducted before the demise of nonlocal check rules) indicated that more than a quarter of all banks offered same-day availability for local checks and that 85 percent offered second-day availability even for nonlocal checks; less than 10 percent of all banks held funds as long as the law permits.

2. Wrongful Dishonor: What Happens If the Bank Refuses to Pay?

The reliability of the checking system is a function of the likelihood that banks will honor checks in accordance with their agreements with their customer. Unfortunately, banks, like all other actors in the economy, sometimes fail to perform as promised. When a bank violates its agreement with its customer by failing to pay a check that it was obligated to pay, it commits "wrongful dishonor." Recognizing the seriousness of that offense to the system, the UCC imposes a relatively onerous penalty. Specifically, the customer is entitled to all of the "damages proximately caused by the wrongful dishonor." UCC §4-402(b). That provision may not strike the first-time reader as notably generous to the customer. As it happens, though, UCC §4-402(b)'s remedy is considerably more generous than the remedy available in many contexts in the checking system, which frequently caps damages against a bank at the amount of the check. See UCC §4-103(e) (damages for failure to exercise ordinary care); Regulation CC, §229.38(a) (damages for failure to return dishonored checks within Regulation CC deadlines).

The generosity of the statute's damage formulation is particularly important because wrongful dishonor presents a context in which that formulation matters: The damages caused by wrongful dishonor often exceed the amount of the dishonored check. For example, when a bank dishonors a business's check, the bank's mistake might harm the business's reputation with its suppliers: The suppliers might be reluctant to continue to ship goods to a customer on favorable credit terms if they believe that the customer is bouncing checks. Similarly, in the individual context, an individual who bounces a check might be subject to arrest or prosecution. Article 4 expressly states that the customer can recover consequential damages for those types of losses. It rejects prior judicial holdings that limited the damages available for wrongful dishonor. UCC §4-402(b); see UCC §4-402 comment 3.

Problem Set 8

8.1. Terry Lydgate comes to you with a problem about a $1,500 check that he wrote recently. The account contained only $50 at the time, and Terry had declined to purchase overdraft protection from the bank at which he maintained the account. Still, the bank honored the check and has now written Terry a letter threatening unspecified "serious consequences" if he does not reimburse the bank for the amount of the check. Is Terry liable for the check? UCC §§4-401(a) & 4-401 comment 1.

8.2. One Monday afternoon Ben Darrow calls from FSB to ask you about a problem that has arisen at his bank. Darrow explains that his problem relates to a $900 check drawn by his customer Jasmine Ball, which Darrow's bank received for payment on Monday January 22. The check was payable to Checks2Cash (a local payday lender) and dated January 31 of the current year. Because his bank's brand-new automated check-processing system does not examine the dates on checks, the bank honored the check. The problem, though, is that two days later the bank bounced the check that Ball had written for her car payment. Ball is outraged, because her $1,000 paycheck was deposited on January 30 and would have been adequate to cover the item written to Checks2Cash. She contends that the bank should have dishonored the Checks2Cash check because it was presented too early. Has Darrow's bank acted improperly? What should Ball have done? UCC §§3-113(a), 4-401(c), 4-401 comment 3, 4-403(b).

8.3. Pleased with your advice in Problem 8.2, Darrow calls you again a few days later. Because of a clerical error, the bank paid a check in contravention of a written stop-payment order. The check was written by Albert "Bud"

Lassen and payable to Carol Long in the amount of $150,000, apparently for some cooking equipment. Shortly after Bud got home with the equipment, he decided that he did not want it because it was slightly larger than he had understood. As a result, the equipment was too big for the space in his kitchen. Carol refused to take back the equipment. Bud immediately came to the bank and filled out the bank's stop-payment form, identifying the account number, as well as the number, amount, and date of the check. Unfortunately, a clerk incorrectly entered the information supplied by Bud. As a result, the system did not recognize the check to Carol when she came in and cashed it the next day. Bud is furious and insists that the bank recredit his account. Darrow wants to know if he must recredit Bud's account. If he does recredit Bud's account, will the bank lose the money? UCC §§4-401(a), 4-403(a) & (b), 4-407(2) & (3), 4-407 comments 2 & 3.

8.4.   What would have happened if the bank had complied with Bud's stop-payment order and had refused to honor Bud's check? Could Carol force Bud to pay for the equipment? UCC §3-310(b)(1), (3), & comment 3.

8.5.   One day a friend named Caleb Garth calls you with a question about his checking account. Upon examining one of his checks that the payor bank recently honored, Caleb noticed that the check was dated last summer (about seven months ago). Caleb thinks it ridiculous that the bank honored a check so stale. Can you do anything for Caleb? UCC §§4-404 & comment, §1-201(b)(20).

8.6.   Early this week your client Jodi Kay called seeking advice about problems at some branches she manages for CountryBank. Several of those branches have received checks (often quite large) drawn on nonlocal banks that the payor banks eventually have refused to honor. Those branches have lost a substantial sum of money on those checks in cases in which the customers withdrew the funds and closed their accounts before CountryBank learned that the checks would not be honored. Jodi mentions that a large share of the problems occurred in cases that involved recently opened accounts or accounts on which overdrafts had been frequent past occurrences. Jodi wants to know if there is anything that she can do about that problem. In particular, she wants to extend to six business days the hold that the bank puts on all nonlocal checks deposited at the problem banks. What do you recommend? Regulation CC, §229.13(a), (b), (d), (e).

8.7.   While Jodi is with you, she mentions a litigation matter she is bringing you. Out of a misguided desire to accommodate a fellow banker, one of her account officers declined to make funds from a cashier's check available until a week after the customer deposited the cashier's check. The officer explained to Jodi that the bank on which the cashier's check had been drawn called and asked Jodi's officer to put a hold on the funds while the bank that issued the cashier's check tried to find a way to justify dishonoring the cashier's check. The customer that deposited the cashier's check is threatening to sue Jodi's bank. She mentions to you that the item was very large ($50,000) and also that she had reason to doubt that the bank on which it was drawn would honor it. She assumes that you easily can take care of this problem for her. What do you tell her? Regulation CC, §§229.10(c)(1)(v), 229.13(g).

Assignment 9:   Risk of Loss in the Checking System

Any functioning payment system will produce losses, either because of errors in the process of completing transactions or because of misconduct connected with the transactions. The checking system is by no means immune from that problem. Indeed, if anything its reliance on paper would seem to make it more vulnerable than the electronic systems discussed in the preceding chapters. As a legal matter, the checking system includes a detailed, two-tier framework that addresses those issues. The first tier is a basic framework that distributes losses based on generalized assumptions about the relative abilities of the parties to prevent certain types of losses. The second tier consists of several situation-specific exceptions to the general first-tier rules.

A.   The Basic Framework

The first tier of the framework relies on two major legal theories to distribute losses, indorsement liability and warranty liability. The sections that follow use those theories to describe the basic rules for distributing losses in three situations: nonpayment, forgery, and alteration.

1.   Nonpayment

Losses from nonpayment are the simplest place to start. Two fundamental elements of the checking system make those losses relatively common: the payee's inability to know when it takes a check whether the payor bank will honor it, and the relatively long delay between the time that the payee receives the check and the time that the payee finds out whether the check will be honored. Indorser liability under UCC §3-415 is the principal statutory mechanism for allocating these losses. To understand that concept, it is necessary to work through a few of the UCC's rules regarding indorsements.

The basic role of indorsement in the checking system is to provide a simple method for transferring checks. A check starts out being payable to the payee to whom the drawer issues it. If the payee wants to transfer the check (perhaps to the bank where it has a bank account, perhaps to a check-cashing business of some kind, perhaps to a friend), the simplest way to proceed is to indorse the check to the party acquiring it. The payee could sell the check without indorsing it (just as the payee could sell any other type of personal property), but under principles of negotiability discussed in a later chapter, the transferee acquires greater rights in the check if the transferee acquires the check by indorsement. Thus, most transfers of checks are made with indorsements.

The indorsement itself need be nothing more than a signature by the person selling the check. UCC §3-204. That type of signature-only indorsement — a "blank" indorsement for purposes of Article 3 — has the legal effect of making the check "bearer paper," so that any party that subsequently is in possession of the check (even a thief) would be entitled to enforce it. UCC §3-205(b). If the indorser wants to make the paper payable to a particular person (such as the person cashing the check), it would add a statement identifying that person ("Pay to Otto's Check-Cashing Outlet") above the signature. That would be a "special" indorsement, which would make the check "order paper." Order paper, unlike bearer paper, can be enforced only by the identified party (Otto's Check-Cashing Outlet in the example). UCC §3-205(a). The payee also might wish to indorse the check "for deposit only" or "for collection." Those are "restrictive indorsements," which restrict the right of later parties to transfer the check except in accordance with the indorsement. UCC §3-206.

Indorsement, however, does more than confer a right to enforce an instrument. It is important in this assignment because it carries with it a form of liability that shifts the loss that arises when a payor bank refuses to pay a check. Under UCC §3-415, each party that indorses a check makes an implied contract with subsequent parties that acquire the check. (Technically, the contract runs only to a "person entitled to enforce the instrument," a term discussed in detail in the materials on negotiability in a later chapter. For now, it is enough to know that it excludes parties that acquire the check by theft or similar misconduct.) That contract obligates the indorser to pay the check if the payor bank dishonors it. Because each party that indorses the check is liable on its indorsement and because each party's liability runs to all subsequent owners of the check, the rule results in a chain of liability under which each party can pass a dishonored check back up the chain to the last person in the chain (the earliest indorser) that is able to pay. Although the rule's chain of responsibility appears convoluted at first, the result is sensible: It leaves the loss with the party that made the imprudent decision to purchase the check from an insolvent entity (presumably the payee). The underlying principle is simple: Be careful when you purchase financial instruments from parties of questionable financial strength.

To see how the rule works, consider the following example. A drawer writes a hot check on an account at SecondBank and gives it to an insolvent payee. The payee then indorses the check and cashes it at Otto's, which in turn cashes the check at FirstBank. FirstBank presents the check to SecondBank without indorsing it. No indorsement is necessary for the transaction between FirstBank and SecondBank because that transaction does not involve a transfer of the instrument from one party to another; it is a request from one party (the owner of the check) for payment from another party (in this case the drawee or payor bank). Now suppose that SecondBank dishonors the check and returns it to FirstBank. UCC §3-415's indorser-liability rule entitles FirstBank (the depositary bank) to pursue either Otto (the check casher) or the payee. At this stage, the indorser liability parallels the bank's right of chargeback under UCC §4-214. As discussed in more detail later in the chapter, that section allows a collecting bank to which a dishonored item is returned to recover any funds it advanced to its customer. If FirstBank chooses to pursue the check casher, the check casher would, in turn, be entitled to pursue the payee. Because the payee is insolvent, the loss eventually is borne by Otto (the one that dealt with the insolvent payee).

The fact that Otto is liable does not suggest that the drawer is free from responsibility. In addition to the indorser-liability rule in UCC §3-415, Article 3 also imposes liability on the drawer of the check. See UCC §3-414(b). If the check has been dishonored, however, there is a considerable likelihood that the check will not be paid: People whose checks are dishonored often are insolvent. Accordingly, in many cases, Otto's liability on the indorsement will result in Otto bearing the loss when a check is dishonored, in the sense that Otto pays the payee for the check but cannot recover from the drawer, the payee, or the payor bank.

The last important point about indorser liability is that it is not mandatory. Indorsement liability is only an implied contract. The UCC provides an easy mechanism for an indorser to disclaim indorser liability if the indorser does not wish to accept that responsibility. All the indorser must do to disclaim the liability is to add the phrase "without recourse" to the indorsement. If an indorsement is made "without recourse," subsequent owners of the check cannot sue the indorser even if the check is dishonored. UCC §3-415(b).

2.   Forged Signatures

Another issue that all payment systems must confront is the problem of forgery. The reason for the high incidence of fraud in the checking system is not hard to identify. The checking system's reliance on low-tech authorization mechanisms — pieces of paper and ordinary written signatures — leaves the system an easy target. Moreover, continuing advances in the anti-fraud mechanisms used in competing payment systems like payment cards have enhanced the relative attractiveness of the low-tech checking system as a target for those who practice fraud.

The major instrument for fraud in the checking system is a forged or unauthorized signature of one kind or another. Thus, the legal system's main response to fraud in the checking system is to devise rules related to false signatures. The first response of the system is the obvious one that the unauthorized signer — the thief — should be responsible for all losses caused by the forgery. It is likely, however, that most thieves will be unwilling or unable to accept that responsibility: The thief might be insolvent or simply have moved without leaving a forwarding address. The difficult task is to devise rules to determine who among the innocent parties should bear the losses when the thief is unavailable. To see how the system allocates those losses, it is necessary to distinguish two different problems: false drawers' signatures and false indorsements.

One introductory point bears emphasis before turning to the specific rules for those problems. Much of the present discussion proceeds on the assumption that none of the parties is negligent and that no special circumstances justify a departure from the basic rules. As the next section explains, in many cases negligence or other circumstances do justify a departure from the basic rules set out in this section. Accordingly, while studying these materials, you should consider the possibility that a result that appears inappropriate at first glance might be altered by one of the special rules discussed below.

(a) Forged Drawers' Signatures and the Rule of Price v. Neal. Turning to the specific rules, the first problem arises when a check is a complete forgery, not even signed by the purported drawer. For example, a thief might steal someone's checkbook and successfully purchase goods and services with checks written from the stolen checkbook. Alternatively, the forger might obtain a single valid check and use copying or printing equipment to fabricate a convincing duplicate check. In either case, the allocation of losses from that kind of forgery depends on whether the payor bank (a) is duped into paying the check or (b) notices the forgery and dishonors the check.

(i) What If the Payor Bank Pays the Forged Check? A time-honored rule, dating to the famous eighteenth-century case of Price v. Neal, 97 Eng. Rep. 871 (K.B. 1762) (per Mansfield, C.J.), holds that a payor bank bears the loss if it fails to notice the forgery and honors the check. From the modern statutory perspective, the result follows from the idea that the check was not properly payable from the account of the purported drawer because that person did not authorize the check. Thus, the payor bank had no right to charge the drawer's account. UCC §4-401(a) & comment 1. The UCC does, though, set out two statutory exceptions that allow the payor bank in limited circumstances to shift that loss back to some earlier party in the collection process.

First, UCC §3-418(a)(ii) allows the payor bank to seek recovery from "the person to whom or for whose benefit payment was made." That provision does not apply, however, against a person that took the instrument "in good faith and for value." UCC §3-418(c). Thus, if the depositary bank (the person to whom the payor bank made payment) took the check from the forger knowing that the check was a forgery, the payor bank could recover from the depositary bank under UCC §3-418. But in the ordinary case the payor bank will not be able to prove bad faith or failure to pay value on the part of any of the parties involved in collection of the check. Accordingly, in that situation, the payor bank's remedy will be limited to the forger. Given the likelihood that the forger will be insolvent or unavailable, that framework tends to leave the loss on the payor bank.

The payor bank also could claim that some earlier party in the chain of collection breached a presentment warranty. UCC §4-208 creates a series of implied presentment warranties in favor of the payor bank. If any of those warranties is false, the payor bank can recover from the party that presented the check to the payor bank or from any previous transferor in the chain of collection of the check. (I defer to the materials on negotiability a more detailed discussion of what it means to be a "transferor" for purposes of those warranties.) The last of those warranties (set forth in UCC §4-208(a)(3)) imposes warranty liability if the transferor had "knowledge" that the signature of the drawer was unauthorized. Unfortunately for the payor bank, however, the statute requires "knowledge," rather than mere "notice." That means that the payor bank will be able to recover on this warranty only if some party took the check with actual knowledge that the check was unauthorized. See UCC §1-202 (distinguishing between "knowledge" and "notice"). Again, in the absence of some conspiracy between the forger and a solvent party, no solvent party will breach this warranty. Thus, like UCC §3-418, the presentment warranty ordinarily leaves that type of loss with the payor bank.

Although those rules inevitably cause payor banks to lose money on transactions in which they were not involved in the fraud, it often makes some sense to allocate that risk to the payor bank because the payor bank's preexisting relationship with the drawer can give it a greater ability to prevent those losses than any other party in the collection chain.

To be sure, it is impractical for the payor bank to examine checks on a case-by-case basis to detect forgeries, which gives even the most primitive forgeries a substantial chance of success. Moreover, many forgeries would go undetected even if the payor bank did examine each check by hand. For example, one of the most common current methods of fraud develops utterly bogus checks from a single legitimate check. Consider a fraud-minded individual that receives a refund check from Sears. At this point in time, it is easy to produce a replica of that check, including the facsimile signature, which would pass a cursory visual inspection. It is only marginally more difficult to encode the MICR line at the bottom of the check so that the check passes through the system and is honored without incident. If the checks are written in relatively small amounts, to a number of different payees, and deposited in differing accounts, visual inspection of the checks by Sears's bank is unlikely to catch the forgeries. But visual inspection is not the only way to catch forgery. The payor bank's relationship with the drawer gives it considerable ability to prevent losses through the development of systems that recognize unauthorized withdrawals without visual inspection of the checks or of the signatures on them. One common approach relies on expert-system pattern-recognition software, which is designed to identify unusual transactions through algorithms analogous to those the payment-card networks have used to identify fraudulent transactions for decades. Another common technique, especially for business customers, involves "positive-pay" systems. Those systems rely on software that the customer uses to provide an electronic record of all authorized checks. The customer transmits that record to its bank each day. The bank's sorters are designed to recognize any check drawn on such a positive-pay account and to route each such check for comparison with the information provided by the customer in its previous daily transmissions. The bank honors checks only if those transmissions indicate that the check actually was issued by the purported drawer. Customers like those systems because they often provide faster access to more accurate information about disbursements. Although that system cannot prevent all forgeries (because the customer's positive-pay employees could forge checks and include them in the transmissions), it does appear to make considerable inroads on the problem. Neither pattern-recognition software nor positive-pay systems are perfect solutions. But they do make it harder for forgers to succeed in getting unauthorized checks through the system. And a legal rule that puts the losses from forged checks on payor banks gives payor banks every incentive to work to develop institutions that limit losses from forged checks. The relatively rapid development and implementation of those systems make it plausible to believe that the incentive imposed by that legal rule is strong enough to have a beneficial effect on the system.

(ii)   What If the Payor Bank Dishonors the Forged Check?   If the payor bank notices the forgery and dishonors the check, then the party that presented the check to the payor bank (usually a collecting bank) is left holding the uncollectible check. In that case, the presenting bank seeks to pass its loss (the sum that it paid for the check) on to some earlier party in the transaction. The UCC contains two legal rules on which the presenting bank can rely. The first is the indorser-liability rule discussed above. That rule allows the presenting bank faced with dishonor to pass the loss up the chain to the earliest solvent party that indorsed the check without disclaiming liability.

Although the preceding paragraph suggests a relatively simple legal distinction between the rights of the payor bank and the rights of other banks in the collection chain, the statute implements that distinction in an indirect way. Specifically, to ensure that the rights of the payor bank are less than the rights of other parties in the chain — to reflect the rule of Price v. Neal — the statute takes two steps: (1) it creates a special set of warranties that limit claims about forged drawer's signatures, and (2) it limits payor banks to pursuing that limited set of warranties. As the foregoing discussion suggests, step 1 (the limitation of the presentment warranty) appears in the qualification of the warranty regarding the drawer's signature that permits a payor bank to complain only if the warrantor had "knowledge" that the drawer's signature was unauthorized. UCC §§3-417(a)(3), 4-208(a)(3). The analogous transfer warranty (the warranty available to parties other than the payor bank) includes an absolute avowal of the authenticity of the drawer's signature. UCC §§3-416(a)(2), 4-207(a)(2). Step 2 (the limitation of the payor bank's recovery to presentment warranties) appears in the rule that the parties that can pursue transfer warranties must be parties to whom an instrument has been transferred. UCC §§3-416(a), 4-207(a). Because an instrument is presented to the payor bank, not transferred to it, the payor bank cannot pursue the broader transfer warranties. It is typical of the archaic style of Articles 3 and 4 that a rule so central to operating practice is stated so indirectly.

As with indorser liability, the presenting bank would have a number of potential defendants. Indeed, each party that transferred the check for consideration would be liable for a breach of warranty. But in the end, liability flows back to the earliest solvent party in the chain because any party that is liable to the presenting bank on its transfer warranty is entitled to sue earlier transferors on their transfer warranties.

One twist on the warranty rules is the interaction between Articles 3 and 4. The Article 4 transfer warranties provide liability only against banks and their customers (the parties that deposit the bogus checks). Accordingly, a party seeking to pass liability to a party that handled the check before it got to a bank (a party that transferred it, for example, to a check-casher) would have to rely on the Article 3 transfer warranties (set forth in UCC §3-416); those warranties are substantively identical to the Article 4 transfer warranties. The only significant difference is the rule in UCC §3-416(a) that Article 3 transfer warranties can be enforced by remote transferees only against entities that indorsed the check.

(iii)   The Special Case of Telephone Checks.   The problems that make it difficult for the payor bank to identify forged checks have led to considerable discussion of the possibility of overruling Price v. Neal and allowing payor banks generally to shift losses from forged checks up the chain to depositary banks (and, in turn, to their depositors). Revisions to Articles 3 and 4 have taken that position for a narrow class of items described by the statute as "remotely-created consumer check[s]," but colloquially referred to as "telephone checks."

The situation arises when a payee obtains consent for a transaction completed over the telephone. If the payee wants to use a telephone check to obtain payment, it will induce the customer (the drawer of the check) to recite (from the bottom of one of the customer's conventional checks) the routing number for the customer's bank and the account number of the customer. The payee (typically a bill collection service or a telemarketer) then will use that information (together with software readily available on the Internet) to print a check drawn on the customer's account. The check, of course, will not include a manual signature by the customer but will suggest in some way that a signature is not required (for example, by a stamp that might say "AUTHORIZED BY DRAWER" or (with less sincerity) "SIGNATURE ON FILE").

Under applicable FTC regulations, the payee must retain a "verifiable authorization" of the transaction for 24 months. 16 C.F.R. §310.5(a)(5). That authorization could be in writing, or it could be a tape recording of an oral authorization. 16 C.F.R. §310.3(a)(3). Given the purpose of the system — to allow payees to obtain payment without waiting for the payor to transmit a written check — it is not surprising that the companies that have designed telephone-check software recommend that their customers rely on oral authorizations.

As the existence of the FTC regulation suggests, some of the businesses that use telephone checks have come under fire for processing checks that have not been authorized by their customers (or, in some cases, checks in amounts larger than the amounts authorized by their customers). Responding to that problem, amendments to UCC Articles 3 and 4 altered the warranty rules for such items. Those amendments add a new subsection to each of the warranty provisions under which each transferor makes a transfer warranty and a presentment warranty that the purported drawer has authorized the item in the amount in which the item has been issued. See UCC §§3-416(a)(6), 3-417(a)(4), 4-207(a)(6), 4-208(a)(4). When adoption of those provisions by the separate states went slowly, the Federal

Reserve then stepped in to adopt a similar provision as part of Regulation CC, 12 C.F.R. §229.34(b).

The premise of those provisions is that in that context at least the possibility of fraud is better policed by action on the part of the depositary bank. For example, depositary banks that accept deposits of telephone checks might be induced to monitor the activities of those customers or require them to provide financial assurances of the authenticity of the items, lest the depositary bank be left holding the bag on warranty claims for unauthorized items. It is too early to say whether those revisions will be an isolated change or the first step toward an eventual eradication of Price v. Neal.

(b) Forged Indorsements. The second type of forgery is a forged indorsement: The drawer actually signs the check in the first instance, but some other party subsequently forges an indorsement on the check. For example, an employee's paycheck might be stolen and cashed after the thief forged the employee's name to the check. The rules that apply in that situation are much more favorable to the payor bank than the rules related to forged drawers' signatures. Generally, they allow the payor bank — even if it mistakenly honors the check — to pass the loss back to the earliest solvent person in the chain after the forgery.

(i) What If the Payor Bank Dishonors the Check Because of the Forged Indorsement? The situation is simple if the payor bank dishonors the check. In that case, the system works much the same as it does with a forged drawer's signature. The presenting bank is left with the dishonored check but can recover its loss by pursuing transfer warranties. Because neither the forger nor any party after the forger in the process of collection is a person entitled to enforce the instrument, and because the indorsement itself is forged, each of those parties has breached its transfer warranty, either under UCC §4-207(a)(1) & (2) or under UCC §3-416(a)(1) & (2).

(ii) What If the Payor Bank Pays the Check Despite the Forged Indorsement? The worst case for the payor bank is the case in which the payor bank fails to notice the forged indorsement and thus pays the check. Unfortunately for the payor bank, it is no more proper to charge the drawer's account in that case than in the case of a forged drawer's signature. Because the check was presented at the instance of the forger, rather than by somebody claiming under the payee, it was not proper for the payor bank to pay the check. Accordingly, the payor bank is not entitled to charge the drawer's account. UCC §4-401(a) & comment 1. Also, for the reasons discussed above, the payor bank cannot recover under UCC §3-418 (payment by mistake) from the parties earlier in the chain of collection if those parties took the instrument "in good faith and for value," as they will have done in the typical case.

The payor bank, however, can recover for a breach of presentment warranty. Under UCC §4-208(a)(1), the presenting bank (and each of the earlier transferors of the check) warrants that it is "a person entitled to enforce the draft" or is collecting the check on behalf of a person entitled to enforce the draft. If the depositary bank took the check from someone that had forged the payee's indorsement of the check (or from someone that took it from the forger), then the depositary bank was not a person entitled to enforce the draft. That is true because, absent a valid indorsement by the payee (or some other legitimate transfer of the check), nobody other than the payee can become a person entitled to enforce a check. UCC §3-301. Accordingly, a presenting bank that took a check from a forger would have breached its presentment warranty to the payor bank.

Thus, the payor bank would be entitled to recover its loss from the presenting bank. If the presenting bank did not deal directly with the forger, the presenting bank, in turn, would be entitled to pass the loss to parties earlier in the chain of collection because those earlier parties would have breached the analogous transfer warranty set forth in UCC §4-207(a)(1) & (2). In the end, the loss generally should pass to the earliest solvent person after the forger (or the forger itself in the odd case in which the forger is solvent and available).

It is not an accident that the payor bank that mistakenly honors a check can recover its loss if the problem is a forged indorsement, although (as discussed above) the payor bank normally cannot recover its loss if the problem is a forged drawers' signature. As explained above, the payor bank's account relationship with the customer gives it the capability to develop systems for detecting forged drawers' signatures. There is not, however, any systematic reason to believe that the payor bank is better placed than anybody else to detect forged payees' signatures. Indeed, absent some special circumstances, the party best placed to detect a forged indorsement is the person that accepts the indorsement (ordinarily a depositary bank). For example, in response to persistent losses to check fraud, many banks have begun to institute biometric identification programs to deter fraud by their customers. The most common (and controversial) plan is a program that requires parties cashing checks to allow the bank to retain an electronic image of the check-casher's fingerprint. Although the program was vilified in the popular press when first adopted, it apparently reduces depositary bank losses from check fraud by 40 to 60 percent. As with the rules discussed above for forged drawers' signatures, the efforts of banks to develop mechanisms for limiting fraud suggest that the incentives that come from allocating losses can motivate financial institutions to expend the resources necessary to make the system function more safely.

(iii) Conversion. A final problem to be dealt with in the forged-indorsement situation involves the rights of the party from whom the check has been stolen (ordinarily the payee). The rules discussed above are likely to lead to a situation in which the drawer's account has not been charged for the check and in which the payee has not been paid. Because the payee of a stolen instrument is barred from enforcing the underlying obligation under UCC §3-310(b)(4), the payee's loss of the check often deprives it of the ability to obtain the funds to which it was entitled. That leaves the payee looking for some recourse for the theft of the check.

The obvious remedy is that the payee/victim has a common-law right to pursue the thief for conversion. Recognizing that a right to pursue the thief might not provide a great deal of comfort, UCC §3-420(a) also grants the victim a statutory action for conversion against parties that purchase the check from the thief. Under that provision, the victim can pursue a bank that cashes the check for the thief (the depositary bank) or a payor bank that honors the check over the forged indorsement. UCC §3-420(a). A suit under UCC §3-420(a) is limited somewhat by the prohibition in UCC §3-420(c) on any action against nondepositary "representatives" in the collection process. Although the text of the statute is obscure, the comment explains that the statute is designed to bar a suit against an intermediary bank that does nothing but process the check for collection as a representative of the depositary bank's customer. UCC §3-420(c) & comment 3.

The payee's right to pursue a payor bank for conversion is in tension with the drawer's right to prevent the payor bank from deducting the funds from its account on the theory that the check was not properly payable. Exercise of both of those rights as to the same check would result in an unfair burden on the payor bank: The payor bank would pay the payee under UCC §3-420(a), but would not be able to charge the drawer's account under UCC §4-401(a). Indeed, the payor bank would have paid twice — once on the forged check and once to the payee — with no obvious recourse for either payment. In that case, however, the payor bank is protected by the subrogation provisions in UCC §4-407(2), which allow the payor bank that pays the payee under UCC §3-420(a) to charge the drawer's account just as if the item had been properly payable. In that case, the funds from the drawer's account compensate the payor bank for its payment to the payee in the conversion action. The payor bank can recover the funds that it paid on the check during the initial process of collection — that is, the funds that went to the thief — by suing down the chain for a breach of presentment warranty.

If the payee sues the depositary bank directly and recovers, a similar result would follow. If the payor bank already has used presentment warranties to pass the loss down to the depositary bank (based on the depositary bank's error in accepting the check with the forged indorsement), then the depositary bank should be able to recover the amount that it has paid through equitable (that is, nonstatutory) subrogation to the payor bank's right against the drawer. See UCC §1-103. Otherwise, the drawer would have a windfall, keeping whatever it purchased from the payee without having any obligation to pay for it.

3. Alteration

The last major type of misconduct with respect to a check is an unauthorized alteration of the check. The UCC recognizes two main types of alterations: a change in some relevant aspect of the check as originally written and an addition to an instrument that was incomplete when written.

Generally, UCC treatment of the first type of alteration is the same as for a forged indorsement. Thus, if the payor bank honors a check that has been altered to increase its amount, it cannot charge the drawer's account for the amount that it paid out on the check. Rather, it can enforce the check only "according to [the] original terms" of the check." UCC §3-407(c). The payor bank, however, can recover any loss by pursuing earlier parties in the chain of collection for a breach of a presentment warranty that the check had not been altered. UCC §4-208(a)(2). Any party against whom the payor bank recovers is entitled, in turn, to pursue earlier parties based on a breach of a similar transfer warranty. UCC §§4-207(a)(3), 3-416(a)(3). Thus, as with a forged indorsement, the loss, at least in the ordinary case, will rest with the earliest solvent party to handle the check after the alteration.

The rules are different if the alteration is the completion of a check that was incomplete at the time it was signed by the drawer. In that case, the payor bank can enforce the instrument as completed, even if "the instrument was stolen from the issuer and completed after the theft." UCC §3-407 comment 2. Thus, the bank is entitled to charge the drawer for such an item. UCC §4-401(d)(2). That rule reflects the notion that a party that signs an incomplete instrument bears a large portion of the responsibility for any loss that ensues when the instrument is completed fraudulently.

B.   Special Rules

The framework outlined in the preceding section operates at a high level of generality, under rules that rest on generalized assumptions about the ability of the individual parties to prevent the losses in question. In many contexts, however, it is easy to see that one party might have prevented the loss much more easily than the party that would bear the liability under the general framework outlined above. Recognizing the variety of problems that can arise in different contexts, the UCC does not stick to a rigid "one-rule-fits-all" approach. Instead, it mitigates the force of the broad framework outlined above by including four more specific rules that enhance the general framework by shifting the risks in particular situations from the parties that normally bear them to other parties that more easily could have prevented losses in particular cases. The sections that follow discuss the first three of those rules; the next assignment discusses the last one.

1.   Negligence

Negligence is the basic theme of all the special provisions. If one of the innocent parties was negligent in a way that contributed substantially to the loss, it makes more sense to place the loss on that party than on an innocent party that was not negligent. As discussed above, a depositary bank that disburses funds to a customer that has forged an indorsement on the check ordinarily bears that loss if all of the other parties are innocent. But the UCC shifts that loss to the drawer if the drawer's negligence substantially contributes to the forgery. See UCC §3-406(a) (precluding a party "whose failure to exercise ordinary care substantially contributes to . . . the making of a forged signature . . . from asserting the . . . forgery against a person who, in good faith, pays the instrument"). For a typical example of how such a claim can be made, consider the following case.

Thompson v. First BancoAmericano

518 F.3d 128 (2d Cir. 2007)

Before: McLaughlin, Cabranes, and Sack, Circuit Judges.

José A. Cabranes, Circuit Judge:

This appeal involves the allocation of liability for altered checks outlined in Articles 3 and 4 of the Uniform Commercial Code ("U.C.C.") and the operation of the check collection system. . . . Plaintiff-appellee J. Walter Thompson ("JWT") is the drawer of the check. Bank of America ("BoA") is the payor bank and the drawee of the check. The Federal Reserve Bank of Atlanta ("Atlanta Fed") is a collecting bank and a presenting bank. First BancoAmericano ("FBA") is the depositary bank, a collecting bank, and a presenting bank.

We are asked to determine (1) whether JWT acted negligently in failing to take certain preventive measures upon learning of prior fraud on its checking account with BoA and, if so, whether that negligence "substantially contributed" to the check fraud, thereby barring JWT from obtaining a recovery pursuant to U.C.C. §3-406(a); (2) whether BoA acted in good faith in paying the altered check and, if BoA did not, whether the lack-of-good-faith exception to the presentment warranty, *see* U.C.C. §4-208, bars its claims for breach of the presentment warranty against the two presenting and collecting banks; and (3) whether a district court may grant summary judgment to a payor bank for losses associated with a presenting bank's breach of the presentment warranty before the payor bank has reimbursed the drawer for the amount of the altered check.

BACKGROUND

. . .

On October 31, 2001, plaintiff-appellant JWT, an advertising agency, issued a check in the amount of $382,210.15 ("Check") payable to one of its vendors, Outdoor Life Network. The Check was issued from JWT's checking account ("Account") at BoA. At an unknown date, an unknown person altered the payee on the Check to "Diversified Business Enterpises [sic], Inc" and deposited the Check into an account maintained by Diversified Business Enterprises at First BankAmericano. FBA then presented the Check to the Federal Reserve Bank of New York, which, in turn, presented it to the Federal Reserve Bank of Atlanta. The Atlanta Fed then presented it to Bank of America via BoA's check processing facility in Georgia. BoA debited $382,210.15 from the Account of JWT and transmitted the payment back "upstream" through the bank collection system to FBA, which, presumably, deposited the funds into the account held by Diversified Business Enterprises. Later, JWT discovered that the payee of the Check had been altered, notified BoA the same day of the alteration and the fact that BoA had made a payment on the altered Check, and sought to have its Account credited for the amount of the Check. BoA did not credit the Account but, instead, demanded that FBA remit the proceeds of the Check to BoA. FBA refused to do so.

At the time of the events at issue, BoA had a program in place to identify potentially fraudulent checks (the "Positive Pay Program" or "Positive Pay"), and JWT subscribed to this service during the relevant time period. Positive Pay permitted BoA to match check numbers, dates, and amounts on the checks that were presented to BoA with a list provided by JWT prior to payment of a check. If the Positive Pay Program identified a discrepancy in any of this information, BoA would not make payment on the check. At the time of the instant fraud, Positive Pay did not have the capability of matching payee names ("payee matching"), a capability that arguably would have detected the fraud here.

Prior to the payment of the Check, ten other instances of check fraud or attempted check fraud occurred on checks issued from JWT's Account. At least one of these instances involved the simple alteration of a payee name. BoA credited the Account for the amount of that altered check, so JWT did not suffer a loss associated with that earlier payee alteration. Another of the instances involved both the alteration of a payee name along with the alteration of the amount of the check. BoA's Positive Pay system detected this particular fraud and JWT's account was not charged. The loss suffered by JWT associated with the remaining prior instances of fraud was less than $9,000.

D. Procedural History

After JWT discovered the fraud at issue here and BoA refused to credit its Account for the amount of the Check, JWT brought this action against BoA. JWT alleged that BoA was negligent and that BoA had violated its duties under U.C.C. §§4-103 and 4-401 (the provision governing when items are "properly payable"). BoA, in turn, filed a third-party complaint against FBA and the Atlanta Fed for violations of [the transfer and presentment warranties].

After the completion of discovery, JWT moved for summary judgment against BoA, and BoA moved for summary judgment against FBA and the Atlanta Fed. FBA opposed JWT's motion on the merits but BoA did not. The District Court granted both motions, concluding that BoA was strictly liable to JWT for charging JWT's Account for an item not "properly payable," U.C.C. §4-401(a). [The court rejected the contentions of FBA and the Atlanta Fed that JWT acted negligently in a way that substantially contributed to the alterations.] The Court also concluded that FBA and the Atlanta Fed had breached the presentment warranties they had extended to BoA under U.C.C. §4-208.

. . .

DISCUSSION

. . .

We conclude that JWT's alleged failures do not constitute negligence within the meaning of U.C.C. §3-406, and that JWT's alleged post-alteration negligence could not have substantially contributed to the check alteration, as required to preclude recovery under U.C.C. §3-406. We also hold that the standard of "good faith" for a drawee/payor bank under the U.C.C. is one that commands a "duty of fair dealing" and not a "duty of care." In light of the applicable standard, we conclude that BoA did not violate its duty of fair dealing and therefore did not act in bad faith. Finally, we hold that a drawee/payor bank is not required to reimburse the drawer before proceeding against the collecting banks for breach of warranty.

A.   WHETHER ALLEGATIONS OF BoA'S AND JWT'S NEGLIGENCE ARE SUFFICIENT TO DEFEAT SUMMARY JUDGMENT

The presentment scheme outlined in the U.C.C. shifts losses up the collection stream to presenting and depositary banks. Accordingly, the drawee/payor bank that pays an altered check in good faith may bring an action for damages against the presenting banks for breaching the presentment warranty. *See* U.C.C. §4-208(b). In a case such as this, in which a check has been altered, the usual result will be that the presenting banks are strictly liable to the drawer and the drawee/payor bank for breaching the presentment warranty. The exceptions to this result arise when either the drawee/payor bank lacked good faith in paying the draft, *see id.* §4-208(a), or when the drawer failed to exercise ordinary care which "substantially contribute[d]" to the alteration of the check, *id.* §3-406(a). Because neither of these exceptions apply in this case, we affirm the District Court's summary judgment in favor of JWT and BoA.

(1)   Drawer's Alleged Negligence Pursuant to U.C.C. §3-406(a)

The primary issue on this appeal is whether JWT's failure to take certain preventive measures after learning of previous fraud on the Account constituted negligence which "substantially contribute[d]," *id.* §3-406(a), to the alteration of the Check. FBA and Atlanta Fed contend that, upon learning of the prior instances of fraud, JWT should have (1) closed the Account and (2) instituted a payee matching system to detect future fraud. They argue that JWT's failure to take these steps constituted negligence that substantially contributed to the alteration of the check and JWT should, therefore, be estopped from asserting the alteration against BoA.

. . .

. . . Based on the facts before us, however, we conclude that ordinary care did not compel JWT to adopt either of these measures. As the District Court observed, the previous incidents of altered checks resulted in *de minimis* losses compared to the significant costs which JWT would have incurred by closing the Account. In addition, FBA came forward with no evidence showing that had JWT closed the Account and drawn checks on a different account, the new account would have been less susceptible to check theft, thereby averting the theft giving rise to this litigation. Under these circumstances, closing the Account would not have been a reasonable, much less a necessary, exercise of ordinary care. With respect to FBA's suggestion that JWT should have implemented payee matching, the record shows that payee matching was not available to JWT and BoA at the time of the presentment of the Check. JWT reasonably relied on BoA's Positive Pay fraud detection service with the technological limitations that existed at the time. JWT's failure to *utilize* an unavailable technology can hardly be said to constitute a "failure to exercise ordinary care" pursuant to U.C.C. §3-406.

We further hold that a defense based on a drawer's alleged post-alteration negligence is foreclosed by the plain language of U.C.C. §3-406. When a drawer's own negligence "substantially contributes" to the alteration of a check, the drawer is "precluded from asserting the alteration" against a collecting or presenting bank, such as FBA, that processes the check in good faith. *Id.* §3-406(a). The Official Comments to Section 3-406 define "substantial contribution" as an action which is "a contributing cause of the alteration . . . and a substantial factor in bringing it about." U.C.C. §3-406 cmt. 2. The Comments also provide certain examples of negligent conduct that would satisfy this test, including: (a) a drawer who writes the amount of the check in a manner that makes it easy to alter the amount and (b) a drawer who mails the check to the wrong payee. *Id.* §3-406 cmt. 3. Accordingly, "while the principal cause of the alteration may be the act of a [third-party wrong-doer], things that make the [wrong-doer's] job easier" may constitute negligence that "substantially contributes" to the alteration of a check and therefore preclude a claim based on the alteration.[13.] White & Summers, *ante*, at 571.

The lack of payee matching cannot, as a matter of logic, have "substantially contributed" to the alteration at issue in this litigation. A payee matching mechanism identifies check fraud when an altered check is presented to the drawee/payor bank for payment, in other words, after the alteration has already occurred. Because this technology detects alterations after the fact, but does not prevent them in the first instance, JWT's alleged failure to adopt payee matching cannot have "contributed" or "set the stage" for the alteration. We therefore conclude that JWT's alleged failures to take certain preventive measures suggested by FBA here did not constitute negligence which substantially contributed to the alteration of the Check.

(2)   Drawee/Payor Bank's Alleged Lack of Good Faith Pursuant to U.C.C. §4-208(a)

U.C.C. §4-208(a) outlines the presentment warranty owed to a drawee/payor bank that pays an altered check in good faith. Good faith, in turn, is defined as

---

13. It should be noted, however, that the substantial-contribution rule does not conform to the principle that the party who can best prevent the loss bears the burden for the loss. . . . The substantial contribution rule means that a drawer will never bear the brunt of its own failure to take certain preventive measures or to adopt state-of-the-art warning techniques for check alterations. The substantial-contribution rule rests on the notion that alteration can best be detected by the bank which first takes the check from the wrong-doer, *see ante* note 2 and accompanying text. In some instances, such as the alteration of the payee name, it may be that the payor bank or drawee would be best suited to detect the fraud. *See* [Wachovia Bank, N.A. v. Foster Bancshares, Inc., 457 F.3d 619, 622-623 (7th Cir. 2006), excerpted below in Assignment 10] (noting that "modern copying technology" may render the distinction between forgery and alteration, and its loss allocation rules, obsolete). Although the substantial-contribution rule may not reflect comparative advantage in preventing losses associated with altered checks, it is the role of the U.C.C. drafters, not this Court, to determine whether the rule should be reconsidered in light of the changing technological landscape.

"honesty in fact and the observance of reasonable commercial standards of fair dealing." U.C.C. §3-103[a](4). Therefore, if a drawee/payor bank pays an altered check in good faith, it receives the benefit of the presentment warranty and shifts the loss to the presenting banks.

The good faith requirement incorporates standards of honesty and fair dealing but not of negligence. In other words, the good faith requirement does not impose a standard of care but, rather, a standard of *fair dealing*. Because FBA has not alleged that BoA acted unfairly or dishonestly, this distinction is fatal to FBA's argument that BoA did not act in good faith.

FBA and the Atlanta Fed point to no action or inaction that would suggest, much less establish, that BoA did not act with "honesty in fact." Instead, they suggest that BoA acted negligently because it should have closed the Account of its own accord or employed more advanced fraud detection capabilities, such as payee matching. While these alleged failures, if proven, might arguably establish negligence, they do not demonstrate a lack of "honesty in fact" or a failure to "observ[e] . . . reasonable commercial standards of fair dealing." U.C.C. §3-103[a](4). Indeed, the Fourth Circuit has held that a payor bank's reliance on a Positive Pay system, instead of on other methods of fraud detection, precluded a finding of a lack of good faith. We conclude, therefore, that BoA acted in good faith within the meaning of Section 4-207 and can properly claim the benefit of the presentment warranty.

In sum, the District Court properly granted summary judgment to JWT and BoA. FBA and the Atlanta Fed have pointed to no material disputes of fact on the issue of JWT's alleged negligence or BoA's lack of good faith.

B.   WHETHER THE DISTRICT COURT PREMATURELY GRANTED SUMMARY JUDGMENT IN FAVOR OF BoA BEFORE BoA REIMBURSED JWT FOR THE ALTERED CHECK

FBA and the Atlanta Fed contend that the District Court erroneously granted summary judgment to BoA. They question whether BoA has, in fact, incurred a loss associated from the Check in light of BoA's decision to delay crediting JWT's Account for the amount of the loss.

We find no requirement in the text of U.C.C. §4-208 suggesting that a drawee/payor bank must first credit the drawer's account with the amount of the loss before it can bring a presentment warranty action against the presenting banks to recover that loss. Section 4-208(b) states that "[i]f the drawee accepts the draft (i) breach of warranty is a defense to the obligation of the acceptor, and (ii) if the acceptor makes payment with respect to the draft, the acceptor is entitled to recover from a warrantor for breach of warranty the amounts stated in this subsection." Those amounts include both damages "equal to the amount paid by the drawee less the amount the drawee received or is entitled to receive from the drawer because of the payment" as well as "compensation for expenses and loss of interest resulting from the breach." U.C.C. §4-208(b).

Courts have routinely granted summary judgment in favor of a payor bank that had not yet reimbursed the drawer. [Citations omitted.] The facts of this litigation do not compel a different result. Judgment has been entered against BoA in favor of JWT; accordingly, there is nothing premature in finding FBA and the Atlanta

Fed liable, in due course, to BoA. The District Court's grant of summary judgment was proper.

CONCLUSION

For the reasons stated above, we conclude that (1) JWT's alleged failures do not constitute negligence within the meaning of U.C.C. §3-406; (2) JWT's alleged post-alteration negligence could not have substantially contributed to the check alteration; (3) BoA acted in good faith and, accordingly, was entitled to pursue a claim for breach of the presentment warranty; and (4) the District Court did not err in granting summary judgment to BoA before BoA reimbursed JWT for the loss arising from the alteration of the Check.

The judgment of the District Court is AFFIRMED.

[An Appendix to the official version of the opinion includes a useful chart illustrating the flow of warranties among the parties.]

———

As *Thompson* makes clear, Section 3-406 does not provide a general right to challenge negligence. It provides a defense only when the negligence leads to the forgery. *Thompson* also illustrates the point that the UCC's imposition of a duty of ordinary care is not limited to customers. The UCC imposes a general duty on banks to exercise "ordinary care" in processing and paying checks. See, e.g., UCC §§4-103(a) (barring enforcement of agreements that waive a bank's responsibility for failure to exercise ordinary care), 4-202(a) (imposing a duty on collecting banks to "exercise ordinary care"), 4-406(e) (imposing liability on payor bank if "the bank failed to exercise ordinary care in [deciding to] pa[y an] item [if] the failure substantially contributed to loss").

The key question for the rules imposing a duty of ordinary care on banks is what constitutes "ordinary care." On that point, the UCC is remarkably deferential to general banking usage. Specifically, the bank establishes a prima facie case that it has exercised ordinary care if it can establish that its activities conform to "general banking usage." UCC §4-103(c); see also UCC §§3-103(a)(7) (defining ordinary care for businesses as the "observance of reasonable commercial standards, prevailing in the area in which the person is located"), 4-104(c) (incorporating the "ordinary care" definition from UCC §3-103(a)(7) into Article 4), 4-103 comment 4 (discussing a court's limited power to conclude that conduct conforming to general banking usage can fail to constitute ordinary care).

As *Thompson* suggests, establishing standards to govern bank conduct is a tricky issue. The comments to UCC §4-103 explain that the decision to govern banking operations with such an indeterminate standard rests on a concern that "it would be unwise to freeze present methods of operation by mandatory statutory rules." UCC §4-103 comment 1. Thus, the adoption of an indeterminate standard allows the banking industry to adopt new procedures that might prevent losses more effectively at lower costs for the system. On the other hand, the provisions that tie determinations regarding "ordinary care" to general banking usage limit the incentive of individual banks to experiment with new procedures to prevent losses, even when the procedures are likely to be cost effective. If a bank can show that most banks have not yet adopted a new procedure that would have prevented a loss, then the bank's potential liability if it keeps the old procedure is relatively small. Conversely, adoption of a new procedure that departs from general banking usage actually might enhance the likelihood that the bank would be held liable for any losses that ensue.

The bottom line, though, is that the UCC generally does not address such questions, trusting the market eventually to force banks to develop cost-effective procedures for preventing loss. Whether the market is forceful enough to serve that function is an empirical question that turns on considerations about which it is difficult to generalize. The size of the industry's losses from fraud and the industry's continuing experimentation with more and more sophisticated systems for the detection and prevention of fraud do suggest, however, that the market provides a considerable incentive for banks to attend to the problem.

Finally, the framework specifically contemplates the possibility of negligence by both the customer and one of the relevant banks. To cover that circumstance, the modern UCC includes a regime of comparative negligence, under which each party should bear the portion of the loss attributable to its failure to exercise ordinary care. UCC §3-406(b).

2.   Theft by Employees

The remaining three rules deal with specific types of losses that the drawer (or in some cases the payee) could have prevented. I defer discussion of the most general (the bank-statement rule of UCC §4-406) to the last assignment of the chapter, but discuss the other two here. The first of those deals with defalcation by employees, and specifically with an employee's forgery of a signature on a check related to its employer's business. The most common case for applying that rule occurs when an employee forges the employer's indorsement on a check payable to the employer. In many cases, either the general negligence rule or the bank-statement rule places such a loss on the employer. But when the loss is caused by a responsible employee, the UCC (specifically UCC §3-405) places the loss on the employer even if those more general rules do not apply. One complicating factor in such cases is that they often involve two counterarguments that the drawer/employer might use to shift the loss back to a bank: not only the comparative negligence argument discussed above (codified in this context in UCC §3-405(b)), but also claims that a bank's willingness to allow an employee to obtain funds from the employer's account amounts to participation in the employee's breach of fiduciary duty (the topic of UCC §3-307).

Often in cases that involve employee fraud, the employer will have no substantial claim against the payor bank because the checks will not appear sufficiently unusual on their face to warrant a claim that the payor bank was negligent in paying the items. Thus, the question frequently arises whether the employer can pursue a claim directly against the depositary bank for losses that the employer sustained from the scheme; often it will appear reasonable to suggest that the depositary bank could have stopped the fraud if it had followed customary banking practices. Because the UCC does not resolve that question directly, courts have struggled in deciding whether to permit such suits.

Halifax Corp. v. Wachovia Bank
604 S.E.2d 403 (Va. 2004)

Opinion by Senior Justice Harry L. Carrico.

INTRODUCTION

In the period from August 1995 to February 1999, Mary K. Adams embezzled approximately $15.4 million while serving as comptroller for companies that are now known as Halifax Corporation (Halifax). Adams accomplished the embezzlement by writing more than 300 checks on Halifax's account with Signet Bank and its successor, First Union National Bank (collectively, First Union). Adams used a stamp bearing the facsimile signature of Halifax's president and, in her own handwriting, made the checks payable to herself, to companies she had formed, or to cash. She deposited the checks in several accounts she maintained with Central Fidelity Bank and its successor, Wachovia Bank (collectively, Wachovia), receiving cash from some of the checks.

PROCEDURAL BACKGROUND

Upon discovery of the embezzlement, Halifax brought an action against First Union as the drawee bank and Wachovia as the depositary bank. (*Halifax I.*) The trial court [dismissed the complaint and Halifax appealed]. We affirmed . . ., holding that Halifax's claim was barred pursuant to [UCC §4-406(f)] for Halifax's failure to notify First Union of the unauthorized signatures within one year after the bank's statement covering the checks in question was made available to Halifax.

While the appeal to this Court was pending, Halifax filed in the court below a three-count motion for judgment asserting that Wachovia and First Union were liable to Halifax for the amounts embezzled by Adams. (*Halifax II.*) Count I alleged negligence, gross negligence, and bad faith on the part of Wachovia in violation of UCC §§3-404, -405, and -406. Count II alleged common law conversion by Wachovia and First Union. Count III alleged that Wachovia and First Union aided and abetted Adams' breach of fiduciary duty. . . .

[The trial court granted summary judgment for Wachovia on all counts and Halifax appealed again.]

FACTUAL BACKGROUND

. . . Mary Adams, also known as Mary Collins, became comptroller at Halifax's Richmond office in August 1995 and continued in that position until March 1999. She maintained four personal and two commercial accounts with Wachovia. One of the commercial accounts was styled "Collins Racing, Inc." and the other "Collins Ostrich Ranch."

When Adams first began embezzling money from Halifax in August 1995, she deposited in her personal accounts with Wachovia several checks each month for over $5,000.00. The amounts of the checks soon increased to between $10,000.00 and $15,000.00 each and before long to amounts ranging from $50,000.00 to $150,000.00 each, and deposits were made multiple times a day or week. For example, in July 1997, Adams deposited on July 9 a check for $95,550.00, on July 14, one check for $55,000.00 and another for $99,300.00, on July 16, a check for $93,500.00, on July 21, a check for $80,600.00, and, on July 30, a check for $149,305.00, totaling $573,255.00. In all, Adams drew 328 checks totaling $15,429,665.42 on Halifax's account with First Union.

Adams was "one of the best and largest individual customers" of Wachovia's branch where she did business. Managers and tellers saw Adams "'a lot,' and she stood out because of her large checks and banking activity." The entire branch was curious about her "because of her large checks," the likes of which "none of the tellers had ever seen . . . before." Some tellers claimed "to have believed or assumed that Adams 'was at least part owner' of the corporate drawer."

Wachovia "repeatedly accepted such huge handwritten checks drawn on the account of Adams' employer despite the gross disparity with [Adams'] payroll amount [of about $1,000.00 per pay period] shown on each teller and manager screen." The tellers "had concerns about individual checks or the check activity, or both." Bank officials knew Adams was Halifax's comptroller and understood that "such transactions by a financial officer, or even a part owner, present[ed] a serious potential for fraud." Yet, branch "[m]anagers and supervisors told the tellers to do whatever Adams wanted."

DISCUSSION

NEGLIGENCE, GROSS NEGLIGENCE, AND BAD FAITH

Halifax contends that [UCC §3-406], when read in light of [UCC §§3-404 and -405], gives rise to an affirmative cause of action for the negligence of a depositary bank with respect to the alteration of an instrument or the making of a forged signature. . . .

In support of its contention that [UCC §3-406] creates an affirmative cause of action, Halifax cites our decision in Gina Chin & Assoc., Inc. v. First Union Bank, 500 S.E.2d 516 (1998). That case involved both forged signatures of the drawer and forged indorsements of the payee. The drawer sought recovery from the depositary bank. The latter claimed it was liable under [UCC §§3-404 and -405] only for forged indorsements and not where both the payee's indorsements and the drawer's signatures are forged.

We disagreed. We stated that the depositary bank was erroneous in "its conclusion that [UCC §§3-404 and -405] cannot be utilized by a drawer against the depositary bank in a double forgery situation," and that the drawer "was not precluded from asserting a cause of action against [the depositary bank] pursuant to [UCC §§3-404 and -405]." . . .

It is plain, however, that the language quoted from *Gina Chin* has reference solely to [UCC §§3-404 and -405]. Indeed, the sentence immediately preceding the quotation states that "[t]he revisions to [UCC §§3-404 and -405] changed the previous law by allowing 'the person bearing the loss' to seek recovery for a loss caused by the negligence of any person paying the instrument or taking it for value based on comparative negligence principles." *Gina Chin*, 500 S.E.2d at 517. [UCC §3-406] simply was not an issue in the case in any manner. *Gina Chin*, therefore, does not serve as authority for Halifax's contention that [UCC §3-406] creates an affirmative cause of action. . . .

We conclude that the trial court did not err in its holding that [UCC §3-406] does not create an affirmative cause of action and in awarding summary judgment to Wachovia with respect to that claim.

---

3.   Impostors

The last of the UCC's special loss-allocation rules deals with checks procured by impostors or payable to fictitious persons. The general idea (reflected in UCC §3-404(a)) is that the loss should be allocated to the person that was victimized by the fraud. Although that might seem a little harsh to the victim of the trick, the idea is that it is better to place the loss on that party than on other parties that might have had no real opportunity to prevent the loss. The following case is atypical in that it involves cashier's checks rather than conventional checks, but it does aptly illustrate both how UCC §3-404 applies and how a malefactor might construct a successful scheme to steal money through the use of a fictitious person.

State Security Check Cashing, Inc. v.
American General Financial Services (DE)
972 A.2d 882 (Md. 2009)

Opinion by HARRELL, J.

In this case we are asked to determine which party, as between the issuer of a check and the check cashing business that cashed it, is liable under [UCC §3-404] for the face amount of the check, when an imposter, posing successfully as another individual in securing a loan (the proceeds of which were represented by the check) from the issuer, subsequently negotiated the check at the check cashing business. We shall hold that, under the circumstances presented in this case, the issuer of the check is liable for the amount of the check.

I. FACTUAL AND PROCEDURAL BACKGROUND

On 20 June 2007, American General Financial Services, Inc. ("American General") was contacted by telephone by a man, later revealed to be an imposter posing as Ronald E. Wilder (we shall refer to this person as the "imposter," though he was not known to be so at most relevant times in this case). The imposter sought a $20,000.00 loan. Based on the information supplied by him over the telephone, American General ran a credit check on Ronald E. Wilder, finding his credit to be excellent. American General informed the imposter that it would need personal tax returns for the prior two years, and asked him what he intended to do with the proceeds of the desired loan. The imposter sent by electronic facsimile to American General the requested tax returns of Mr. Wilder and explained that he wanted the loan to renovate a property he owned. On Friday, 22 June 2007, American General's District Manager received the completed loan application and tax returns, performed a cash flow analysis, and obtained approval from senior management for an $18,000.00 loan.

On that same morning, American General informed the imposter that the loan was approved. The imposter appeared at noon at American General's Security Boulevard office in Baltimore County. He proffered an apparent Maryland driver's license bearing Mr. Wilder's personal information and the imposter's photograph. He remained in the loan office for approximately thirty minutes, meeting with the branch manager and a customer account specialist during the loan closing. After all the loan documents were signed, American General issued to the imposter a loan check for $18,000.00, drawn on Wachovia Bank, N.A., and payable to Ronald E. Wilder.

Later that afternoon, the imposter presented the check to State Security Check Cashing, Inc. ("State Security"), a check cashing business. At the time the imposter appeared in State Security's office, also on Security Boulevard in Baltimore County, only one employee was on duty, Wanda Decker. Decker considered the same driver's license that the imposter presented to American General, and reviewed the American General loan documents related to the check. She also compared the check to other checks issued by American General which had been cashed previously by State Security. Deeming the amount of the check relatively "large," Decker called Joel Deutsch, State Security's compliance officer, to confirm that she had taken the proper steps in verifying the check. Deutsch directed Decker to verify the date of the check, the name of the payee on the check, the address of the licensee, the supporting loan paperwork, and whether the check matched other checks in State Security's system from the issuer. Decker confirmed the results of all of these steps, and, upon Deutsch's approval, cashed the check, on behalf of State Security, for the imposter for a fee of 3–5% of the face value of the check.

On Monday, 25 June, the next business day after the imposter negotiated the check at State Security, the real Ronald E. Wilder appeared at the offices of American General indicating that he had been notified by the U.S. Secret Service that a person applied for a loan in his name. At that time, the true Ronald E. Wilder completed an Affidavit of Forgery. As a result of the Affidavit, Thurman Toland, the Branch Manager of American General's Security Boulevard branch, called Wachovia Bank to determine whether the $18,000.00 check had been presented for payment. Learning that the check had not been presented yet, Toland placed a "stop payment" on the check.

State Security filed a civil claim in the District Court of Maryland, sitting in Baltimore County, against American General for the face value of the check, plus interest, asserting that it was a holder in due course of American General's check, that it received the check in good faith, without knowledge of fraud, and that it gave value for the check. On 3 December 2007, the District Court conducted a bench trial. During the trial, the testimonies of Deutsch and Toland revealed three additional, potentially important points: (a) had State Security personnel called American General on 22 June 2007 to verify that American General issued a check to Ronald E. Wilder for $18,000.00, Toland would have confirmed that to be the case; (b) State Security employed a thumb print identification system for its check-cashing business, but, at the time the imposter cashed the check, it was unclear whether it was functional; and (c) although, as part of the loan application process, American General obtained names and telephone numbers of personal references from the imposter, it did not call any of the references before delivering the check.

On 19 December 2007, the District Court held in favor of American General, [holding that State Security failed to exercise ordinary care and that its failure substantially contributed to the loss. The Circuit Court affirmed and the State's highest court, the Maryland Court of Appeals, granted discretionary review.]

II.   DISCUSSION

In the District Court and the Circuit Court, State Security argued that, under [UCC] §3-302, it was a holder in due course of the check issued by American General. Neither the District Court nor the Circuit Court, however, resolved that claim in reaching their respective judgments. In order to resolve the rights of the parties, it is necessary to address State Security's §3-302 claim.

A.   [UCC] §3-302

. . . [The court summarizes the requirements for status as a holder in due course, including the requirement that the party took the check in good faith.]

American General argues that, because of the "suspicious circumstances" under which the imposter negotiated the check with State Security, State Security failed to satisfy the [Article] 3 requirement of good faith. In support of this position, American General advances five points, which, the company argues, when considered together, should defeat State Security's claim:

(1) State Security's failure to develop any special procedures to validate the authenticity of large checks being presented at its check cashing business, as confirmed by the testimony of Decker and Deutsch that all checks are treated the same, regardless of amount, and that when Decker called Deutsch for assistance, Deutsch merely re-traced the steps Decker already had taken;

(2) State Security "should have known that no competent businessman uses a check-cashing facility for an $18,000 check unless a stop payment order is likely." In support of this contention, American General states:

> State Security was much better positioned to detect the fraud because reasonable businessmen, while they commonly use finance companies to obtain $18,000 loans to develop property, rarely, if ever, use check-cashing services that immediately slice 3–5% off their investment to process their loans. . . .

Appellee American General, a finance company, had no reason to suspect a customer who had two years of tax returns showing he was self-employed, a high credit score, and a valid Maryland driver's license was perpetrating a crime when seeking an $18,000 loan purportedly to develop a property he owned. Appellant State Security, however, a fee-charging check cashing service, had every reason to suspect wrongdoing when someone walked in off the street with an out-of-state $18,000 loan check and agreed to share several hundred dollars of it with State Security. Yet, seeing a hefty transaction fee, State Security turned a blind eye to these suspicious circumstances.

   . . .

(3) Wilder had not been a customer of State Security previously and was not a member of State Security's business. (See Md. Code, Fin. Inst. Art. §12-120(b) (capping check cashing service membership fees at a one-time fee of $5));

(4) State Security's failure to use its thumbprint identification system, even though the system may not have been functioning at the time of the transaction, was critical because "[h]ad State Security told the impostor that it would not complete the transaction without his thumbprint, he likely would not have proceeded and looked instead for a more careless victim"; and

(5) the imposter presented the check to State Security on a Friday afternoon, "just hours before most banks and businesses closed for the weekend."

State Security retorts that, under the circumstances of this case, its actions were sufficient to satisfy the good faith statutory requirement. State Security argues:

> It cannot be seriously argued that State Security did not act in good faith. There was no evidence that it had any idea that the person presenting the check was not Ronald E. Wilder. To the contrary, all the evidence points to State Security having made all commercially reasonable efforts to verify that the person presenting the check was the person who was intended to have the check. By matching the signatures on the loan documents with the signature of the person who presented the check, and by verifying that against the driver's license, State Security did all that could be expected of it.

The definition of "good faith," for the purposes of [UCC Article 3], [requires] "honesty in fact and the observance of reasonable commercial standards of fair dealing." [UCC] §3-103. Official Comment 4 to §3-103 expounds further regarding the intended meaning of "good faith" [explaining, among other things, that "fair dealing . . . is concerned with the fairness of conduct rather than the care with which an act is performed."]

Professors White and Summers explain this definition of "good faith," and the commentary provided in Comment 4, as follows:

> What does all of that mean? And what evidence is likely to be introduced to prove lack of reasonable commercial standards? Note that under section 3-308(b) a plaintiff confronted with defenses or claims has the burden of proving "rights of a holder in due course," and thus the burden will be on the creditor plaintiff to show good faith.
>
> Where might this arise? One can imagine many variations on this basic theme: a depositary bank takes a check, only to have other banks say they would not have taken such a check and that to do so violated commercial standards. For example, would it violate commercial standards for a bank to take a $100,000 check to open an account and later to allow the depositor to withdraw the funds? If not, the bank could be a holder in due course who might take free of a drawer's claim to that instrument even though the person with whom it dealt was a thief, not so? For reasons stated below we think the bank here would be in good faith. Can a payee violate commercial standards by demanding payment on a "demand note" where there has been no default in the underlying obligation?
>
> Similar arguments might well arise at the closing of a kite, where one of the banks seeks to defend itself against a restitution claim by arguing it gave value in good faith and is protected by 3-418. That bank might be met with the argument that it was not a good faith holder of the checks passing through its hands because by observing reasonable commercial standards it should have understood the checks to be part of a kite. As we indicate elsewhere, we hope that few people are successful in asserting restitution causes of action after kites, but we anticipate that those arguments will be made.
>
> Before one concludes that the banks described in the preceding paragraphs are not in good faith, return to the definition. A bank that fails to follow commercial standards is not in good faith only if it deviates from commercial standards of "fair dealing." Deviating from such standards on the side of generosity and gullibility rather than venality does not render one's act in bad faith. So beware, good faith does not require general conformity to "reasonable commercial standards," but only to "reasonable commercial standards of fair dealing." The issue is one of "unfairness" not of "negligence." If the Code is tilting back toward an objective standard, it is going only so far. We are clear on that point, but the courts are divided. As we see below, some courts insist on confusing negligence with unfairness. Some also find a duty for a depositary bank to consider the interests of all parties involved, including the drafter of the note with whom the banks has [sic] never had dealings.

2 [White & Summers, Uniform Commercial Code] §17-6, at 191-92 (5th ed. 2008).

. . .

Arguing that . . . the need for speed in cashing a large business check "is consistent with a drawer who, for whatever reason, might stop payment," American General contends that the ersatz Wilder's negotiation of the $18,000 check for a 3–5% fee at a check cashing store should have put State Security on "inquiry notice that some confirmation or explanation should be obtained," and that because State Security applied the same level of scrutiny to checks presented, regardless of their amounts, State Security "makes itself a magnet for impostors," thereby shedding its ability to claim "good faith." . . .

. . . [N]ot surprisingly, State Security reasons that the relevant inquiry in the present case is whether it took adequate steps before cashing the check to ensure that the $18,000 check issued by American General was valid. State Security posits that " . . . State Security cannot be legally obligated to determine that American General should not have wanted to issue the check it issued." It points here to the testimony of Toland, American General's Branch Manager, who stated that, had State Security called him, he would have verified that the check represented the proceeds of a loan transaction American General had closed with someone it believed to be Wilder. Based on this distinction, State Security argues [for] a finding of good faith here because had State Security contacted American General regarding the validity of the check presented by the imposter, it would have learned only that the check was valid.

Professors White and Summers express some skepticism at how many courts have viewed check cashing businesses with regard to the good faith requirement for a holder in due course:

> Check cashing companies appear to be the pariahs of holder in due course law. In Buckeye Check Cashing, Inc. v. Camp, [825 N.E.2d 644 (Ohio Ct. App. 2005),] a check cashing company sued drawer for payment after drawer contacted his bank and ordered the bank to stop payment. Drawer of check had negotiated with a contractor for services to be completed over the next three days and drawer drafted a post-dated check as payment. (The check bore the date of the projected date of completion of the services.) Contractor immediately cashed check with plaintiff, who submitted the check for payment. The drawer, fearing services would not be completed, contacted his bank the same day and ordered it to stop payment. The court held that the future date on the check should have put the check cashing company on notice that the check might not be good. The court also held that the company failed to act in a commercially reasonable manner, and did not take the check in "good faith," when it did not attempt to verify the check. We are less certain than the court is about the commercial practice with respect to postdated checks. In some circumstances it might be commercially unreasonable to take a postdated check over-the-counter without some explanation from the customer, but that surely would not be true of a check presented to an ATM.
>
> In Any Kind Checks Cashed, Inc. v. Talcott, a court held that the check cashing service did not act in good faith and should have verified a $10,000 check drawn on a 93 year-old's account when presented for cashing by a financial broker. "[The] procedures followed were not reasonably related to achieve fair dealing, . . . taking into consideration all of the participants in the transaction." The court held that the financial broker was not the typical customer of a check cashing outlet because small businessmen rarely use a check cashing service that charges a 5% fee instead of a traditional bank. The business check is not the welfare or payroll check usually cashed at such an establishment. The court held that the need for speed in cashing a large business check is consistent with a drawer who might stop payment and fair dealing requires that the $10,000 check be approached with caution. "The concept of 'fair dealing' includes not being an easy, safe harbor for the dishonest."
>
> Both the *Buckeye Check-Cashing* case and the *Any Kind Checks Cashed* case show courts that are quick to deny holder in due course status to check cashing facilities. We wonder how these courts would have handled these cases had the plaintiffs been banks and not check cashing facilities. In effect the courts are asking check cashers to adhere to a higher standard than might be required of a bank. Given the clientele of check cashing facilities, the courts' skepticism might be justified, but we would

like to see a little more evidence that check-cashing facilities are a home for persons engaged in fraudulent behavior before we would subject them to higher standards than might be applied to a bank.

White & Summers, supra, §17-6, at 197-98.

Under §3-308(b), the burden is on a plaintiff to prove "rights of a holder in due course," including situations such as the present, where the defense is that the plaintiff did not take the instrument in good faith. [See UCC] §3-308 cmt. 2 ("Subsection (b) means only that if the plaintiff claims the rights of a holder in due course against the defense or claim in recoupment, the plaintiff has the burden of proof on that issue."). We conclude here that State Security is entitled to enforce the check because it has met its burden of proving that it took the check in good faith.

The core of the dispute between banking institutions over the good faith requirement most often distills to one banking institution taking a check, only to have another banking institution charge that, under the circumstances, it would not have taken that check, and that taking the check was a violation of commercial standards. See White & Summers, supra, §17-6, at 191 ("Where might th[e good faith issue] arise? One can imagine many variations on this basic theme: a depositary bank takes a check, only to have other banks say they would not have taken such a check and that to do so violated commercial standards."). This is the dispute presented in the present case, albeit not between two banks.

Here, . . . State Security took a check, issued by American General to the imposter in person, and relied on much of the same documentation and/or identification that American General had relied on in giving the imposter the loan proceeds check in the first place. That the check presented in this case was a check drawn by American General, a financial institution, is . . . significant . . . for two reasons: the check itself was more likely to be valid, including the drawer's signature, as confirmed by State Security's comparing it to prior American General checks it had cashed; and the payee of the check was more likely to have been subjected to an examination of her or his personal identification, creditworthiness, and purpose for taking out the loan, as confirmed by State Security's review of the driver's license presented and the loan documents before cashing the check.

American General's position that State Security did not take the check in good faith seems anomalous when State Security relied on the same document for personal identification, as well as the loan documents that American General generated in issuing the check to the imposter, when cashing the check. Because the check was issued by American General as the proceeds of a loan, a transaction verified by State Security, adoption of American General's position would require us to hold State Security, a check cashing business, to a higher commercial standard than American General, simply because the financial institution was duped into issuing the check to an imposter.

American General's desire that we hold the check cashing company here to a higher standard shall not carry the day. First, although it may be unusual for a person in the imposter's situation to use a check cashing business, instead of a traditional bank, whatever inhering "unusualness" does not inexorably negate good faith on State Security's part. [Citation and quotation marks omitted.] State Security examined the same document of identification of the imposter (the forged driver's license), as well as the accompanying loan documents American General had prepared, to verify that the check presented by the imposter was the proceeds of a loan issued validly by American General, with the imposter as the intended payee, before cashing the check.

The other four points of concern advanced by American General are too speculative to alter our analysis. The fact that State Security "has no special procedures to validate large checks" is irrelevant for two reasons: a) the procedures State Security did utilize were quite similar to that of American General; and b) American General presented no evidence of any procedure State Security was "lacking" when it cashed the imposter's check that, if present, should have persuaded State Security to proceed other than as it did. Second, the fact that Ronald E. Wilder had not been a customer of State Security previously is irrelevant because of the verification steps State Security took before cashing the check, and because it does not appear from the record that American General itself was familiar with Wilder before the transactions in question. Third, we find American General's assertion that, had State Security asked the imposter to submit a thumbprint, the imposter likely would not have proceeded, to be the most speculative argument of all. The testimony in the record reveals that State Security's thumbprint machine may not have been working at the time and, in any event, because the machine was not connected to any centralized database, the thumbprint could be effective only in identifying the imposter after the fact or for future transactions at State Security. Without any supporting evidence, we do not accept American General's bald assertion that this imposter, who obtained and utilized two years of tax returns and other personal identification information for Mr. Wilder, would have been dissuaded from accomplishing the final step of an identity theft by being asked for his thumbprint. And fourth, the fact that the imposter presented the check at State Security on a Friday afternoon is equally likely to be coincidental, in light of the substantial identity theft actions undertaken, with the timing of his receipt of the check from American General — that same Friday afternoon — than with the conclusion that the timing was premeditated because the weekend was near. . . . Although being asked for a thumbprint may serve as a powerful deterrent to those attempting to pass bad checks, we cannot accept American General's position here, without more support, that an imposter, who already went to the lengths of securing two years of Mr. Wilder's tax returns and much of his personal information for the forged driver's license and credit applications, likely would have stopped short of completing this theft by being asked for his thumbprint.

We conclude therefore that State Security overcame American General's defense of a lack of good faith, as required under §3-308(b), and, thus, that State Security took the check from the imposter in "good faith," defined as "honesty in fact and the observance of reasonable commercial standards of fair dealing." As State Security indicates, there was no evidence at the time the check was presented that the person presenting the check was not the true Ronald E. Wilder, and State Security, as we have concluded, took commercially reasonable efforts to verify that the person presenting the check was the person who was intended to have the check as the proceeds of a valid loan issued by American General. Because we conclude that State Security took the check in "good faith," and American General does not dispute any of the other requirements for State Security to be considered a holder in due course of the check, we resolve that State Security was a holder in due course of the check cashed by the imposter.

B.   [UCC] §3-404

[UCC] §3-404 addresses the circumstances, among other situations, of imposters. Regarding our imposter in the present case, the District Court ruled, under §3-404(d), that State Security did not exercise ordinary care in paying the check presented by him, and that the failure to exercise such care contributed substantially to the loss. The Circuit Court, in affirming that judgment, concluded that there was substantial evidence to support the District Court's finding, and therefore the District Court's finding was not clearly erroneous. . . .

The District Court determined initially and correctly that the imposter rule applies in this case because all of the pertinent requirements of [UCC] §3-404(a) were present. . . . Although "imposter" is not defined in the [UCC], . . . [Maryland courts have] concluded that "imposter" [includes] one who poses as another to obtain benefits under a negotiable instrument. [Brackets, citations, and quotation marks omitted.] There is no doubt that, by appearing in person at both American General and State Security to conduct transactions, which included the presentation of a forged driver's license with the imposter's picture, but the name and personal identification information of Ronald E. Wilder, the individual in this case was a person who posed as another to obtain the benefits of the check issued by American General. There also is no doubt that, by posing as Mr. Wilder, the imposter induced American General to issue the check to him. When the imposter negotiated the check at State Security, he indorsed the check in the name of the check's payee, Ronald E. Wilder. As we have concluded already, *supra*, State Security took the instrument in good faith. Thus, our reversal of the judgments below turns on the interpretation of the remaining pertinent subsection, [UCC §3-404(d).]

. . . Official Comment 3 to §3-404 addresses expressly the default allocation of loss in circumstances such as the present one. . . . As Official Comment 3 indicates, the default loss in cases involving imposters lies with the drawer because the drawer is the party that dealt directly with the imposter and thus was in the best position to detect the fraud. In certain situations, a drawer may reduce its loss by recovering damages from a person who failed to exercise ordinary care in paying the instrument or taking it for value or collection, if that failure contributed substantially to loss resulting from payment of the instrument, to the extent the failure to exercise care contributed to the loss.

The District Court's ruling in favor of American General erred in two respects: a) the ruling is not in accord with the statutory definition of "ordinary care," in light of the uncontradicted testimony of Deutsch, State Security's compliance officer, and b) the ruling erred by shifting the default burden of loss in an imposter case to the subsequent holder, State Security, rather than the party who was in the best position to detect the fraud, the drawer, American General.

With regard to the interpretation of "ordinary care," the statutory definition of "ordinary care" contains three elements: 1) observance of reasonable commercial standards, 2) which prevail in the area in which the person is located, 3) with respect to the business in which the person is engaged. [UCC] §3-103(a)(7). In the proceedings before the District Court, the testimony of Deutsch, the manager who "run[s] State Security Check Cashing," bore directly upon State Security's conduct on the day in question and, more generally, upon State Security's general business procedures in the check cashing business. Deutsch testified that he has been involved in the check cashing business for twenty-two years and that he had occasion to cash "large" checks in the past. American General did not challenge Deutsch's testimony on cross-examination, nor did American General offer any countervailing testimony reflecting upon State Security's conduct in light of its business practices or the location of its branch office. The only testimony American General elicited on point was through cross-examination of Wanda Decker, State Security's clerk, who testified that State Security, before disbursing, does not hold a check (regardless of the amount) to ascertain whether the funds are available. That testimony alone, however, does not diminish State Security's conduct in the matter in question. Thus, American General did not present sufficient evidence at trial to establish that State Security's conduct lacked "ordinary care" under the statutory definition.

With regard to the burden of loss, the District Court imagined that the one action either party could have taken to prevent the loss was for State Security to have withheld payment until American General's check cleared. The trial court concluded that State Security chose not to delay the payment because it earned a fee from cashing the check, and that in so doing, it ran the risk that the check may be dishonored.

Simply put, the conclusion the trial court reached does not comport with sustainable "ordinary care" analysis. That a business charges a fee for the utilization of its services, albeit here a check cashing business, for cashing the check, is not determinative of whether the conduct of that business on the occasion in question lacked "ordinary care." Under the circumstances of this case, the trial court's reasoning seems directed more towards the "good faith," rather than the "ordinary care," requirement. As Judge Easterbrook stated succinctly in State Bank of the Lakes v. Kansas Bankers Surety Co., 328 F.3d 906 (7th Cir. 2003): "[G]ood faith" is in a different phylum from "due care." . . . Article 3 of the UCC, which contains a definition of "good faith[,]" . . . links commercial reasonableness to "fair dealing." Avoidance of advantage-taking, which this section is getting at, differs from due care. Id. at 909. The trial court seemed persuaded that by cashing the check for a percentage fee, State Security took unfair advantage of the situation. We have already rejected, however, American General's claim that State Security's taking the check from the imposter in the circumstances noted above lacked "good faith."

More significantly, the trial court's ruling in favor of American General is contrary to the position emphasized in Official Comment 3 of §3-404 that "[i]f a check payable to an impostor . . . is paid, the effect of subsections (a) and (b) is to place the loss on the drawer of the check rather than on the drawee or the Depositary Bank that took the check for collection." This is due to the recognition that the "drawer is in the best position to avoid the fraud and thus should take the loss." [UCC] §3-404 cmt. 3. We found no evidence in the record of this case to suggest the application of this default rule would be inappropriate. Of either party involved here, American General had the best means available by which to protect itself against the fraud, the least of which included contacting the personal references the imposter listed on the credit application, which may have helped protect American General against the fraud. We reject American General's attempt to shift the burden of the loss here to State Security on so tenuous a basis as State Security's failure to ask the imposter for his thumbprint before cashing the check, where State Security examined the same driver's license and the loan documents American General created and found satisfactory in issuing the check.

Problem Set 9

9.1. Late one afternoon you get a call from Cliff Janeway, your book-dealer friend. He tells you that he is in Seattle and that yesterday he received a $200,000 check as a finder's fee for locating some rare books and manuscripts for an eccentric collector. He just got off the plane and has realized that he left the check on the seat of the airplane.

a. Does he have anything to fear if a third party takes the check, forges his indorsement, and cashes it? UCC §§3-301, 3-310(b), 3-406, 3-420.
b. Assume that the thief deposited the check into an account, and that the bank of first deposit forwarded the check for collection through the Federal Reserve. Assuming that the thief is financially irresponsible, who would end up bearing the loss? Does it matter if the check bounces or if it clears?

9.2. A new client named Integrity Bank calls this afternoon about a large check returned to it as uncollected. The check was drawn on the account of Sunnyside School, apparently written by the school's receptionist to one of the school's book suppliers. The receptionist forged the signature of the school principal's name and the name of the supplier and then cashed the check at Checks2Cash. After Checks2Cash deposited the check in an account it has at Darrow Bank, Darrow forwarded the check for collection through its correspondent Integrity Bank. Pinnacle Bank (the payor bank) dishonored the check and returned it to Integrity Bank. Integrity wants you to assess its rights.

a. Pursuing the receptionist is probably fruitless; the check was bounced because Pinnacle discovered yesterday that the receptionist has been doing this kind of thing for years, cashing some checks at various check cashers, often depositing them in her own account at Pinnacle, or even cashing them at Pinnacle from time to time. It is possible, though, that the receptionist will be ordered to pay some restitution as part of her criminal sentence and that a small recovery might be available from her as well. Integrity wants to know if it can recover from the receptionist, Darrow, or Sunnyside. See UCC §§3-405, 3-406, 3-414, 3-415, 4-207, 4-214.

b. Suppose that Pinnacle Bank had honored the check, but recredited the school's account when it discovered the fraud. Against whom might it have rights? UCC §§3-405, 3-406, 3-415, 3-418, 4-207, 4-208.

c. Suppose that the depositary bank included the following legend as part of its indorsement: "Without Recourse and Without Any Warranty Whatsoever." How might that change your answers to a and b?

d. Now suppose you instead were dealing with a check the receptionist had written to herself, indorsed in her own name, and deposited at Darrow. How might that change your answers to a, b, and c?

e. Finally, suppose the thief is an employee in the school's accounting department rather than a receptionist, considering alternatively the possibilities that the employee is either authorized to issue checks on behalf of the school or authorized to indorse checks on behalf of the school.

9.3.   Ben Darrow calls you with a new problem. Reviewing her statements this week, Carol Long noticed a check that she recalled writing to one of her suppliers for $10,000. At some point in the collection process, the check was altered to indicate an amount of $100,000. Darrow's bank FSB did not notice the skillful alteration and honored the check for the full amount. Darrow tells you that he assumes that he can't charge Carol for anything but the $10,000 for which she wrote the check. What he wants to know is whether he can recover the extra $90,000 from anybody. What is your advice? UCC §§3-407(c), 4-208(a)(2), 4-401(d)(1).

9.4.   Dorothea Brooke receives a telephone call from a marketer selling encyclopedias. At first, she is quite attracted to the idea of buying a new encyclopedia. The marketer asks her for her checking-account number so that he can collect payment. Dorothea then gives him the number. After further discussion, however, she decides not to go through with the transaction until she receives further details in the mail. To her surprise, the next month she finds that the telemarketer (EncarPedia.com) has created and processed a check charging her $1,800 for the encyclopedias. The check was deposited at Bulstrode Bank and paid by her bank, Wessex Bank. Assuming that EncarPedia.com is insolvent, who will bear the loss? UCC §§3-416, 3-417, 4-207, 4-208; 12 C.F.R. §229.34(d).

9.5.   A law-reform committee of your state bar's commercial law section has proposed the addition of a new subsection (d) to UCC §3-406, modeled on the last sentence of UCC §3-405(b). The specific proposal follows:

> (d) If the person paying the instrument or taking it for value or for collection fails to exercise ordinary care in paying or taking the instrument and that failure substantially contributes to loss resulting from the fraud, the person bearing the loss may recover from the person failing to exercise ordinary care to the extent the failure to exercise ordinary care contributed to the loss.

Would you support the proposal? Why?

Assignment 10:   Collection of Checks

Once the payee receives a check from the drawer, the payee is left — like any party that takes a noncash payment — with the task of converting the payment into cash or some other form of readily available funds. That task raises two separate questions, one legal and one practical. The legal question is whether the payee has a legal right to force the payor bank to pay the check. But whatever the answer to that question, a second, more practical question remains: How does the payee obtain payment?

A.   The Payor Bank's Obligation to the Payee

The checking system's approach to the payee's rights against the payor bank is simple. The UCC characterizes the payee (or any bank that acquires the check from the payee) as a "person entitled to enforce" an instrument. UCC §3-301. That designation is central to the rules about negotiability discussed in Chapter 7, but it says nothing about the payee's rights to collect from the payor bank. On the contrary, in an ordinary check transaction, the payee has no rights whatsoever against the payor bank. First, for the reasons discussed in Assignment 8, even the drawer cannot complain if a payor bank dishonors a check because the account has insufficient funds to cover it. UCC §4-402(a). Perhaps more surprisingly, the payee cannot force the bank to pay even if the account does have sufficient funds. As explained in UCC §3-408, the check "does not of itself operate as an assignment of funds . . . available for its payment, and the drawee is not liable on the instrument until the drawee accepts it." Thus, although the payor bank might be liable to the drawer for wrongful dishonor, the payee itself ordinarily can do nothing to force the payor bank to pay the check.

This rule does not impose any undue risk on the payee. If a payee is concerned about the possibility that the payor bank will decline to pay, it can protect itself in several ways. Most obviously, the payee could refuse to accept an ordinary check. The prudent payee instead might ask for a special check that offers an assurance that the payor bank will pay the check when presented. For example, the payee can require the drawer to obtain the payor bank's agreement to pay before the payee accepts the check; that "pre-accepted" check is called a certified check. UCC §3-409(d). Similarly, the payee can ask for a check drawn on a bank itself. That type of check would be a "cashier's check" or a "teller's check," depending on whether the drawer and drawee banks were the same or different institutions. UCC §3-104(g), (h). In the existing milieu, certified checks, cashier's checks, and teller's checks are not a large component of the system as a whole, mainly because of the inconvenience they require: a special trip to the financial institution to produce the check. They are used most frequently to complete consumer transactions where certainty of payment is particularly important, such as purchases of automobiles or homes.

B. The Traditional Process of Collection

Even though the payor bank is not legally obligated to pay the check, the practical reality is that payor banks pay more than 99 percent of the checks that are presented to them. Nevertheless, because the payee starts out not knowing whether any particular check will be paid, the collection process must complete two distinct functions: (1) the payee has to find out whether payment will be forthcoming, and (2) the payee has to obtain payment. You will recall from the first chapter that in the modern payment-card systems, the payee can find out if the financial institution will make payment before completing the transaction (the so-called authorization transaction). Absent the use of certified or cashier's checks, the payee accepting a check has no similar protection. Rather, it takes the riskier step of completing the transaction (parting with whatever it is selling) and then attempting to convert the check to readily available funds.

The payee has two different ways to pursue collection. The payee can go directly to the payor bank and obtain payment (a relatively unusual course of action); or the payee can obtain payment indirectly by transferring the check to an intermediary (depositing the check in a bank), and the intermediary, in turn (if all goes well), gives the payee funds in return for the check and then obtains payment from the payor bank itself. The complexities of that process occupy the remainder of this chapter.

1. Obtaining Payment Directly

The payee can obtain payment from the payor bank in two ways. The simplest is to cash the check, which the payee does by presenting the check "for immediate payment over the counter," in the phrasing of UCC §4-301(a). When the payor bank makes such a payment, the payment is final. UCC §§4-215(a)(2), 4-215 comment 4 (paragraph 5). Thus, if Archie cashed Cliff's check "over the counter" at Rocky Mountain Bank, Rocky Mountain could not recover the money from Archie even if Cliff's account did not have enough money to cover the check. That problem is not particularly significant, however, because the payor bank normally would refuse to cash the check if the drawer's account did not contain funds sufficient to cover the check.

The second way for the payee to obtain direct payment happens almost as a matter of coincidence, when the payee has an account at the same bank as the drawer. In that case, the payee gets the check to the payor bank when the payee deposits the check in its own account. From the perspective of the payor/depositary bank, that produces an "on-us" item: an item drawn "on us." Ordinarily, the payor bank gives the depositor credit (a "provisional settlement") for the item on the day that it receives the item. As long as the payor bank provides that provisional settlement on the day that it receives the item, the payor bank has until its "midnight deadline" — midnight of the next banking day, UCC §4-104(a)(10) — to decide whether it wishes to honor the check. UCC §4-301(a), (b).

If the payor bank honors the check, it credits (increases) the payee's account by the amount of the check and deducts a corresponding sum from the drawer's account. For example, if Archie deposits Cliff's $1,000 check in Archie's account at Rocky Mountain Bank, the bank removes $1,000 from Cliff's account and adds the same amount to Archie's account. Because of the offsetting entries, the transaction has no net effect on Rocky Mountain Bank. Alternatively, if the payor bank decides not to honor the check, it sends a notice of dishonor to the payee/customer. Finally, if the payor bank does nothing — if it fails to send a notice of dishonor by the midnight deadline — it loses the right to dishonor the check. UCC §§4-214(c), 4-301(b). Here, as elsewhere, the system generally operates on the empirically reasonable assumption that each check will be honored. Thus, although payor banks do not start out with any obligation to pay checks drawn on them, the system imposes such an obligation if the payor bank fails to move swiftly to dishonor a check that comes to it.

If the bank properly dishonors an on-us item, then it can "charge back" (that is, remove) the credit that it gave the payee's account when the payee deposited the check. Thus, if Rocky Mountain dishonored Cliff's check for lack of funds, Rocky Mountain would be entitled to take the $1,000 back out of Archie's account, which would leave the bank back where it started. If Archie already has withdrawn the money from his account, the payor/depositary bank can sue him to recover the money. UCC §§4-214(c), 4-301(b). In that event, the check-collection part of the transaction has been completely nullified, without providing payment. At that point, as discussed in previous assignments, the payee is left under UCC §3-310 with the check itself and the right to attempt to obtain payment from the purchaser on the underlying obligation. Finally, if Rocky Mountain is unable to recover from Archie, it should be able to recover from Cliff by pursuing him either as the drawer of the check under UCC §3-414(b) (discussed in Chapter 7) or under a general common-law restitutionary theory, see UCC §1-103.

2.   Obtaining Payment Through Intermediaries

As we all know, in most cases it is not convenient for the payee to cash the check at the payor bank or to deposit the check into an account at the payor bank. Rather, the payee deposits the check into the payee's own account at its chosen depositary bank. The need to move the check from the depositary bank to the payor bank makes the process considerably more complicated. The simplest way to discuss the process is to break it down into two separate steps: what happens when the check goes from the payee to the depositary bank and what happens when the check goes from the depositary bank to the payor bank.

(a) Payee/Customer to Depositary Bank.   When the customer deposits a check into its account, two things happen. The first is a legal artifact — the creation of an agency relationship between the customer and the bank. Under UCC §4-201(a), the bank where the customer has deposited the check (the depositary bank) accepts a responsibility to act as the customer's agent in the process of obtaining payment from the payor bank. See UCC §4-201(a) (characterizing the depositary and intermediary banks as "agent[s]" of the customer). Charged with that responsibility, the depositary bank becomes a "collecting bank" in the UCC's terminology, see UCC §4-105(5), a status that carries with it a statutory duty to exercise ordinary care, UCC §4-202(a).

The second is a more practical point: While it is attempting to obtain payment, the depositary bank ordinarily gives the customer a "provisional settlement" for the item. The settlement is a credit (addition) to the customer's account for the amount of the check. The settlement is called "provisional" because (as discussed above) the depositary bank retains the so-called chargeback right. That right allows the depositary bank to revoke the settlement and remove the funds from the customer's account if the payor bank does not honor the check. UCC §4-214.

(b) Depositary Bank to Payor Bank.   Once the depositary bank has the check, the depositary bank is free to choose how it will go about attempting to collect from the payor bank, subject only to its obligation of ordinary care under UCC §4-202. See UCC §4-204 (giving collecting banks broad discretion about method of collection). Of course, the funds-availability rules discussed earlier in the chapter give the depositary bank an incentive to move as quickly as possible to find out if the payor bank will honor the check. As you should recall, the depositary bank will have to make the funds represented by the deposited item available to the depositor in just a few days, even if the depositary bank has not yet learned what the payor bank will do when it receives the check. Thus, banks have a considerable incentive to develop and use expeditious procedures for collection of checks they receive for deposit.

During the twentieth century, procedures for check collection focused on the physical object: the piece of paper written by the drawer and delivered to the payee. Thus, in those days, the depositary bank physically transmitted the check to the payor bank. As systems for image-based processing have developed, transmission of paper has become increasingly uncommon. (The next section discusses the legal framework under which the images "count" as the paper item.) In any event, whether the payor bank receives the paper check or an image, it decides whether it wishes to honor the check or return it, generally applying the doctrines discussed above.

In deciding how to transmit the check to the payor bank, the depositary bank chooses from among several different methods of transmission based on the relative cost and speed of the options available for each check. One of the most prominent options — clearance through the Federal Reserve process — is operated by the federal government. The other principal options — multilateral clearinghouses, bilateral correspondents, and direct-send arrangements — are established by private contracts among the banks involved. Most banks use some combination of all of those options, depending on the circumstances of each check.

When checks come into the bank (through either personal deposits to a teller or deposits at an ATM), the twentieth-century bank typically transported the checks to an operations center that served all of the bank's branches in the area. At the operations center, the checks were placed in assembly-line feeders that carried each individual check to a keyboard operator, who imprinted a string of magnetic-ink characters normally referred to as a MICR (pronounced "miker," rhyming with "biker") line, indicating the amount of the check at the bottom right-hand corner. The machines then routed the checks to the appropriate "end point," relying on the first string of characters on the bottom of the check, which provided the standard routing number assigned to the payor bank by the American Bankers Association (ABA).

Now, it is substantially more likely (almost certain) that the depositary bank will convert the check to an image, send the physical check to storage (in the unlikely event it is needed in the future), and send the electronic image to the payor bank. The next section discusses that process. If the depositary bank does not convert the check to an image, it has several options for getting the check to the payor bank.

- If the check is drawn on a bank with which the depositary bank has a bilateral clearing arrangement, the depositary bank would bundle the check with others going to the same bank and send a package to that bank (typically once each day). In that case, the parties can settle for the checks with debits or credits to accounts at the two banks; ordinarily the settlement is made for the full amount of each package (based on a so-called cash letter that summarizes the items included in the package).
- If the check is drawn on a bank that is a member of a local clearinghouse, the depositary bank would send it to the clearinghouse (in a package with other similarly situated checks), where it would be sorted and delivered to the bank on which it is drawn. In that case, the clearinghouse ordinarily settles for the checks by making net debits or credits to the account of each member bank at the local Federal Reserve bank, based on the net inflow (or outflow) of checks to that bank.
- If neither of those options is available, the depositary bank ordinarily sends it to its Federal Reserve bank. Like the clearinghouse, the Federal Reserve settles with each of its member banks daily, based on the net inflow and outflow of checks, with a debit or credit to the bank's account with the Federal Reserve.

The process of getting the check to the payor bank is simple, because it involves little risk and no discretion or decision making beyond identifying the appropriate way to transmit the check. But the arrival of the check at the payor bank is a moment of legal significance, which starts the clock on a variety of things, all centered around the ability of the payor bank to refuse to pay ("dishonor") the check. As you will recall from the previous assignment, the check is "transferred" at each of the earlier stages — so that the party in possession technically owns the item. But the final transmission to the payor bank is not a "transfer" of the item; it is rather a "presentation" of the item. See UCC §3-501(a).

(c)   Dishonor and Return.   Once the item is presented, the bank can dishonor only if it acts by the appropriate time. If it fails to do so, then the right to dishonor lapses, the item is finally paid, and the obligation for which the check was given is discharged. See UCC §§4-215(a)(3), 3-310(b). The required notice is simple: The payor bank must "return" the check, which can be as simple as depositing the check in the mail or as expeditious as sending it by overnight courier. See UCC §§1-201(b)(36) (defining "send" to include depositing in the mail), 4-301(d)(2) (explaining that the "return" requirement is satisfied if the check is "sent *or* delivered"). Even that requirement might seem redundant in this electronic age, but as we shall see in the material below, banks frequently (almost always) have the option under applicable agreements to return the check electronically, by sending an image. That is superior for all involved, at least in part because it gets notice back to the depositary bank much more quickly, which often might help the depositary bank retain any funds it might have made available based on the now-dishonored item.

The flow of money in the return process works exactly the same as it did in the discussion above of the "forward" collection process. The check is included in the next package of checks going to the appropriate collection (usually, though not always, the place from which the payor bank received the check). It is itemized on the cash letter, so that funds for the returned check flow back to the payor bank just as funds for the check flowed out to the depositary bank a few days earlier when the check initially was processed. When the check finally gets back to the depositor, it is left in much the same place as it was before depositing the check: holding a check that might or might not be collectible. The big difference is that, because the payor bank has dishonored the check, the holder now can pursue the person that wrote the check. UCC §3-414(b).

What is not nearly so simple is understanding how quickly the payor bank has to act. The reason is that the bank faces several different deadlines. The first set of rules come from Article 4 of the UCC, not surprisingly. The second come from subpart C of Regulation CC, starting at 12 C.F.R. §229.30, the regulation adopted by the Federal Reserve to implement the Expedited Funds Availability Act. If that is not enough, there also is the likelihood (hinted at above) is that the bank also faces self-imposed deadlines, either from contracts for bilateral clearance arrangements or from the rules of local clearinghouses. The following sections discuss the UCC and Regulation CC deadlines.

(i)   The UCC's "Midnight" Deadline.   The UCC deadline is the venerable "midnight deadline": midnight at the close of the first banking day *after* the banking day on which the payor bank receives the "item" (Article 4's ubiquitous term for a check). See UCC §§4-104(a)(10), 4-215(a)(3), 4-301(a). You might have some trouble getting that idea from the statute, because §4-301(a) limits that deadline to cases in which the bank "settles for the item

. . . presented otherwise than for immediate payment over the counter before midnight of the banking day of receipt." You will recall from the discussion above that the ordinary collection processes universally involve a flow of funds simultaneous with the transmission of the check; that means that the payor bank will have settled more or less immediately (and certainly on the day it receives) any check that comes through that process. The reference to "immediate payment over the counter" (the exception to the exception in the drafting of the statute) simply means that the bank cannot dishonor a check that it cashes over the counter: Payment "over the counter" is final when made. So collectively, what that means is that the payor bank can spend the entire day *after* the banking day on which it receives the check making up its mind, but it has to act by midnight of that day.

Just to make matters a little more complicated, Regulation CC includes two extensions of the UCC's midnight deadline (which alter the UCC in the same way federal law always preempts inconsistent state law). The first extension waives the midnight deadline as long as the payor bank delivers the check to its transferor (in this case, its Federal Reserve bank) by the first banking day after the deadline. For example, even if the Article 4 midnight deadline calls for action before the end of Wednesday, the payor bank acts properly if it sends the check to its Federal Reserve bank by messenger early Thursday morning (a process that is much more expeditious than depositing the check in the mail on Wednesday evening). The second extension waives the midnight deadline when the payor bank uses a "highly expeditious means of transportation, even if that means of transportation ordinarily would result in delivery after the receiving bank's next banking day." Regulation CC, §229.30(c)(1). Thus, assume now that because of the size of its operations in Southern California, a payor bank in New York deals directly with the Los Angeles Federal Reserve Bank and that the payor bank has decided to dishonor a check that it received directly from the Los Angeles Federal Reserve Bank. In that case (again assuming that the Article 4 midnight deadline calls for action by the end of Wednesday), Regulation CC permits the payor bank to forgo using the Wednesday night mail, wait until Thursday, and then send the check to the Los Angeles Federal Reserve Bank by an overnight delivery service for delivery Friday morning.

(ii)   The Regulation CC Expeditious Return Rule.   Unlike the UCC return obligation — which focuses only on the date that the payor bank puts the check in the mail — the Regulation CC deadline is more functional: It focuses on the speed with which the depositary bank actually receives the dishonored check. Specifically, it imposes a requirement of "expeditious" return, a so-called "two-day" rule that obligates the payor bank to send the check so "that the check would normally be received by the depositary bank not later than 2:00 p.m." on the second business day. Regulation CC, §229.31(b)(1). (The "four-day" part of the rule no longer has practical application — it established a longer deadline for nonlocal checks.)

(iii)   Regulation CC and the UCC's Midnight Deadline.   It is important to distinguish between the effects of failure to meet the midnight deadline

(as modified by Regulation CC, §229.31(g)(1)) and failure to satisfy the Regulation CC obligation to make an expeditious return. Failure to meet the midnight deadline is the "magical" act that directly affects the settlement chain: The payor bank becomes "accountable" for the item under UCC §4-302, payment becomes final under UCC §4-215, and the depositary bank loses any right of charge-back under UCC §4-214. Failure to satisfy the Regulation CC requirements has much less dramatic consequences, generally limited to damages under Regulation CC, §229.38. To put it another way, a payor bank that meets the midnight deadline avoids responsibility for the item under the UCC even if it fails to satisfy its return obligation under Regulation CC.

The following cases illustrate how those provisions operate in practice. As you read them, consider the extent to which the use of electronic processing tends to exacerbate or mitigate the kinds of practical mishaps that led to the disputes in question.

Troy Bank & Trust Co. v. The Citizens Bank

2014 WL 4851511 (Ala. Sept. 30, 2014)

PARKER, Justice.

Troy Bank and Trust Company ("Troy Bank") appeals a summary judgment entered in favor of The Citizens Bank ("Citizens Bank"). We reverse the circuit court's judgment and remand the cause.

FACTS AND PROCEDURAL HISTORY

[Gilley wrote a check for $100,000 to Cile. Cile deposited the check at Citizens Bank on December 16. Citizens Bank made an error encoding the check, and processed it for $1,000 instead of $100,000. The check was sent through the Federal Reserve to Troy Bank (Gilley's Bank) and paid in the ordinary course (at a time when Gilley's account held enough funds to cover the full $100,000). On January 22, Citizens Bank discovered the mistake and sent an adjustment notice using standard Federal Reserve forms, seeking to recover the additional $99,000. Troy Bank honored the notice and sent back the funds, although Gilley's account no longer had funds to cover the item.

Troy Bank sued Citizens Bank on its encoding warranty, UCC §4-209(a). Citizens argued that Troy Bank lost the right to proceed under the warranty because it neither dishonored the item before its midnight deadline, nor presented a claim for the underencoding within the 20 days the Federal Reserve administrative procedures permit for such a claim. The trial court agreed with Citizens.]

DISCUSSION

This case involves Alabama's check-encoding warranty ("the encoding warranty") . . . . Troy Bank argues that the encoding warranty "makes clear that *any* party that encodes a check warrants the correctness of that information and is liable for *any* loss due to an encoding error."

Initially, we must address the issue of which law applies in this case. In its brief, Citizens Bank agrees that it breached the encoding warranty, but it argues that "binding federal banking regulations and operating circulars" prevent Troy Bank from recovering under the encoding warranty and, contrary to the encoding warranty, shift liability to Troy Bank. Specifically, Citizens Bank argues that Regulation CC, 12 C.F.R. [Part] 229 et seq., and Operating Circular No. 3 set forth a claim procedure ("the claim procedure") that Troy Bank failed to follow. Citizens Bank argues that Troy Bank's failure to follow the claim procedure rendered Troy Bank strictly liable for any loss it suffered in relation to Citizens Bank's encoding error. Citizens Bank does not argue that the encoding warranty in this case is preempted by the claim procedure; rather, it argues that the claim procedure complements the encoding warranty and, thus, must be followed to recover damages under the encoding warranty. We disagree.

[I]n drafting the form to be used to initiate the claim procedure, the Federal Reserve Bank clearly stated that the claim procedure was not the exclusive recovery method for a bank that had suffered a loss due to an encoding error made by another bank but expressly recognized that recovery could be pursued by the bank that had suffered the loss outside the claim procedure by dealing directly with the misencoding bank. In fact, as Troy Bank notes, Operating Circular No. 3 states in subsection 20.1 that "[a] bank may need to pursue other kinds of claims directly with another bank *or by making a legal claim rather than, or in addition to, an adjustment request.*" (Emphasis added.) As Troy Bank argues on appeal, it was not required to use the claim procedure but, instead, chose to pursue recovery under the encoding warranty.

. . .

However, before we turn our attention to the issue whether the encoding warranty shifts liability for the encoding error from Troy Bank to Citizens Bank, we first consider Troy Bank's liability for the full $100,000 amount of the check. It is important to note that the parties agree that Troy Bank became liable for the full $100,000 amount of the check; the parties disagree, however, as to *when* Troy Bank became liable for the full amount of the check. The circuit court — apparently applying the "final-payment" and "midnight-deadline" rules set forth in [§§]4-215 and [4]-301 respectively . . . — determined that Troy Bank became liable for the full amount of the check when the adjustment notice was paid and Troy Bank failed to "return the [adjustment notice] or send written notice of dishonor before the midnight deadline [running from receipt of the adjustment notice]. [Ed.: Note that the adjustment notice was paid more than a month after the initial processing of the check.] Citizens Bank agrees with the circuit court's conclusion. Troy Bank argues that it became liable for the full amount of the check at the time the check was presented to Troy Bank, and it paid the underencoded amount and did not dishonor the check by its midnight deadline. For the reasons set forth below, we agree with Troy Bank.

. . .

The final-payment rule and the midnight-deadline rule operated to make Troy Bank, the payor bank, liable for the full face amount of the check when it paid the underencoded amount of the check pursuant to [§]4-215 (setting forth the final-payment rule) and did not dishonor the check within the time prescribed in [§]4-301 (setting forth the midnight-deadline rule).

This is in accord with the Official Comment to [§]4-209, which states, in pertinent part:

> If a drawer wrote a check for $25,000 and the depositary bank encoded $2,500, *the payor bank becomes liable for the full amount of the check.* The payor bank's rights against the depositary bank depend on whether the payor bank has suffered a loss. Since the payor bank can debit the drawer's account for $25,000, the payor bank has a loss only to the extent that the drawer's account is less than the full amount of the check. There is no requirement that the payor bank pursue collection against the drawer beyond the amount in the drawer's account as a condition to the payor bank's action against the depositary bank for breach of warranty.

[S]*ee also* White & Summers, *Uniform Commercial Code* §20-6c. ("The comment and [§4-209] seem to adopt the proposition that a payor who pays an underencoded amount has made final payment on the check or has liability for the full face amount to other parties. However, the payor can recover or set off any difference that it cannot get from its customer from the encoding depositary bank. Thus, the payor would first have to attempt to charge its depositor's account for the amount of the check and if it could not — either because the account had been closed or there was a stop payment — it would have a warranty claim against the depositary bank.")

. . .

In the present case, Ronnie Gilley Properties, LLC ("Gilley"), the drawer, issued a $100,000 check to Cile Way Properties, LLC ("Cile"). Cile deposited the check in its account at Citizens Bank, the depositary bank. Citizens Bank encoded the check in order to collect the funds from Gilley's bank — Troy Bank, the payor bank. However, Citizens Bank incorrectly encoded the check for $1,000 instead of $100,000; Citizens Bank underencoded the check by $99,000. Therefore, when Troy Bank was presented with the check, it was encoded for $1,000, and Troy Bank paid Citizens Bank $1,000. Troy Bank paid the check and at no time sought to dishonor the check. Therefore, . . . at the time Troy Bank paid the underencoded amount of $1,000, it became liable for the *full* amount of the check — $100,000 — because it made payment on the check and did not dishonor the check within the midnight deadline.

Having concluded that Troy Bank became liable for the full amount of the check when it paid the underencoded amount of the check and did not revoke its settlement of the check by the midnight deadline, we now turn to whether the encoding warranty shifts liability from Troy Bank to Citizens Bank. Based on the principles set forth above, we conclude that the encoding warranty shifts liability to Citizens Bank.

Citizens Bank discovered its encoding error after Troy Bank had honored the check and had paid the underencoded amount. Citizens Bank then submitted to the Federal Reserve Bank the adjustment notice requesting that $99,000 be transferred from Troy Bank to Citizens Bank to cover the full amount of the check. At the time the Federal Reserve Bank transferred $99,000 from Troy Bank's Federal Reserve Bank account to Citizens Bank's Federal Reserve Bank account, Gilley's account no longer had sufficient funds to pay the full amount of the check. After receiving notice that the Federal Reserve Bank had paid Citizens Bank's adjustment notice, Troy Bank discovered that Gilley's account no longer had sufficient funds to cover the full amount of the check and realized damage in the alleged amount of $98,436.43.

It is important to note that had Citizens Bank properly encoded the check there would have been no damage. As set forth above, Gilley's account had sufficient funds to cover the full amount of the check when Troy Bank was presented with the check. However, Gilley all but emptied the checking account after the underencoded amount of $1,000 was withdrawn from its account so that, when Citizens Bank realized its error and sent the adjustment notice, there were no longer sufficient funds in Gilley's account to cover the full amount of the check. Citizens Bank's encoding error caused Troy Bank to incur damage.

. . .

CONCLUSION

Based on the foregoing, we conclude that the circuit court erred in its application of the law to the undisputed facts of this case. Citizens Bank's initiation of the claim procedure did not deprive Troy Bank of its statutory right to seek damages under the encoding warranty. Under the encoding warranty, Citizens Bank is liable for the alleged damage to Troy Bank. Accordingly, we reverse the circuit court's summary judgment and remand the cause for the circuit court to enter a summary judgment in favor of Troy Bank in the amount of damages supported by the substantial evidence.

REVERSED AND REMANDED.

NBT Bank v. First National Community Bank

393 F.3d 404 (3d Cir. 2004)

Before RENDELL, FUENTES and SMITH, Circuit Judges.

SMITH, Circuit Judge.

This is an appeal from an order of the District Court denying the motion of Appellant NBT Bank, N.A. ("NBT") for summary judgment, and granting summary judgment in favor of Appellee First National Community Bank ("FNCB"). At issue is a claim by NBT under Article 4 of Pennsylvania's Uniform Commercial Code ("UCC"), seeking to recover the face value of a $706,000 check (the "Disputed Check") that was drawn on an FNCB account and deposited at NBT by a participant in a check-kiting scheme.

In accordance with its established practice, NBT forwarded the Disputed Check to the Federal Reserve Bank of Philadelphia ("Reserve Bank"), which serves as a clearinghouse or transferor for checking transactions involving a number of banks, including both NBT and FNCB. When the Disputed Check was presented by the Reserve Bank to FNCB for payment, FNCB recognized that the drawer had overdrawn its account. Thus, FNCB sought to dishonor the Disputed Check and to return it to the Reserve Bank. Under the UCC, FNCB was required to return the Disputed Check to the Reserve Bank prior to the "midnight deadline," defined as midnight of the following banking day after the day the check was first presented to FNCB.

The parties agree that the Disputed Check was physically delivered to the Reserve Bank prior to the midnight deadline. The parties also agree that FNCB prepared the Disputed Check as a "qualified return check," meaning it was to be encoded with a magnetic strip containing information that would facilitate automated processing by the Reserve Bank. However, FNCB erroneously encoded the magnetic strip with the routing number for PNC Bank (which otherwise has no connection to this appeal), rather than NBT. The parties agree that NBT did not suffer damages as a result of this encoding error. Nonetheless, NBT seeks to hold FNCB accountable for the full amount of the Disputed Check, pursuant to the strict accountability provisions of [UCC §§4-301 and 4-302]. The key issue in this appeal is whether FNCB's violation of a Federal Reserve regulation requiring proper encoding provides a basis for imposing strict accountability on FNCB under §4-302 of the UCC, despite the fact that NBT incurred no actual loss as a result of FNCB's error.

Because we believe the District Court correctly concluded that NBT may not recover on the facts presented here, we will affirm the District Court's order granting summary judgment in favor of FNCB.

FACTUAL BACKGROUND

A.   THE DISPUTED CHECK

. . . The dispute arises out of a check-kiting scheme under which a small group of Pennsylvania business entities arranged to write checks on one account, drawing on non-existent funds, and then cover these overdrafts with checks drawn on another account that also lacked sufficient funds. In this manner, the perpetrators of the scheme sought to obtain funds to which they were not entitled. The scheme collapsed when three checks initially deposited at NBT, and subsequently presented for payment to FNCB, were discovered by FNCB to have been drawn on an FNCB account that lacked sufficient funds. There is no dispute between the parties that two of these three checks were properly returned by FNCB to the Reserve Bank prior to the applicable midnight deadline.

The Disputed Check (i.e., the third check, for $706,000), was drawn on an FNCB account and drafted by an entity called Human Services Consultants, Inc. On March 8, 2001, the Disputed Check was proffered for deposit at NBT by an entity called Human Services Consultants Management, Inc., d/b/a "PA Health." Thus, in relation to the Disputed Check, NBT was the "depositary bank" (the first to receive the item), and FNCB was the "payor bank," meaning that the Disputed Check was drawn on an FNCB account held by a participant in the check-kiting scheme.

B.   The Provisional Settlement

After the Disputed Check was presented for deposit at NBT, the bank gave provisional credit to the depositor, PA Health, for the amount of the Disputed Check. NBT also transmitted the Disputed Check to the Reserve Bank for presentment to FNCB. Upon transmission to the Reserve Bank, NBT was given a provisional credit from FNCB's Reserve Bank account for the face amount of the Disputed Check. The Reserve Bank then forwarded the Disputed Check to FNCB, and FNCB received it on March 12, 2001. Under the UCC, if FNCB wished to refuse payment on the Disputed Check, FNCB was obligated to revoke the provisional settlement granted to NBT by 11:59 p.m. on March 13, 2001.

C.   FNCB's Efforts to Return the Disputed Check

On March 13, 2001, FNCB determined it would not pay the Disputed Check because of the absence of sufficient funds in the account on which the check was drawn. That same day, FNCB sought to return the Disputed Check to NBT through the Reserve Bank. The parties agree that the Disputed Check was physically delivered to the Reserve Bank prior to 11:59 p.m. on March 13. In addition to sending the Disputed Check back to the Reserve Bank on March 13, FNCB also sent a notice of dishonor to NBT via the FedLine [a proprietary Federal Reserve communications system], in which FNCB indicated that it did not intend to pay the Disputed Check. NBT received this notice prior to the close of business on March 13. In addition, on the morning of March 14, 2001, FNCB executives telephoned NBT officials and telefaxed a letter to NBT, advising NBT that FNCB had decided to dishonor the Disputed Check.

D.   FNCB's Encoding Error

When FNCB sent the Disputed Check to the Reserve Bank on March 13, 2001, FNCB included a letter designating it as a "Qualified Return Check" prepared for high speed processing. In so doing FNCB communicated to the Reserve Bank that it had attached to the Disputed Check a strip of paper encoded with magnetic ink that would permit the check to be processed through the Reserve Bank's automated processing system. However, FNCB erroneously encoded the strip with the routing number for PNC Bank instead of the routing number for NBT.

In sum, the Reserve Bank physically received the Disputed Check complete with the wrongly encoded strip prior to 11:59 p.m. on March 13, 2001. Because the Disputed Check was improperly encoded, NBT did not receive it back from the Reserve Bank until March 16, 2001. With proper encoding the Disputed Check likely would have been received on March 14, 2001. The parties have stipulated, however, that NBT suffered no damages or actual loss as a result of the encoding error, inasmuch as NBT had actual notice from FNCB on March 13 that the Disputed Check had been dishonored.

II.   THE DISTRICT COURT PROCEEDINGS

NBT instituted this action against FNCB on May 25, 2001. The only claim before the District Court was a claim under the Pennsylvania UCC. NBT claimed that FNCB's encoding error meant FNCB had failed to return the Disputed Check prior to the midnight deadline as required by the UCC, and that FNCB was therefore accountable to NBT for the full amount of the Disputed Check. The parties stipulated to the facts and filed cross-motions for summary judgment.

The District Court granted FNCB's motion and denied NBT's motion. . . . NBT appeals.

III.   DISCUSSION

. . .

B.   Pennsylvania UCC Provisions Governing Check-Return Procedures

Article 4 of the UCC as adopted by Pennsylvania defines the rights between parties with respect to bank deposits and collections involving banks located in Pennsylvania. To the extent not preempted or superseded by federal law, Article 4 governs the process by which banks present checks for payment, settle on checks, and, if necessary, dishonor and return checks. NBT notes three inter-related UCC provisions that establish the circumstances under which a bank may return a dishonored check [UCC §§4-301(a) (defining the midnight deadline), 4-301(d) (defining the required act of return), and 4-215 (defining final payment)].

C.   Regulation CC, Reserve Bank Operating Circulars, and Variation by Agreement

The Pennsylvania UCC provisions governing check-return procedures do not operate in a vacuum. Federal law forms part of the legal framework within which check-processing activities take place. Of particular relevance to this appeal are the 1988 regulations adopted by the Federal Reserve implementing the Expedited Funds Availability Act, 12 U.S.C. §§4001-4010. See 12 C.F.R. Pt. 229. These regulations, referred to collectively as "Regulation CC," complement but do not necessarily replace the requirements of Article 4 of the UCC. See 12 C.F.R. §229.41.

. . . Regarding encoding, subpart C provides:

> A paying bank may convert a check to a qualified return check. A qualified returned check must be encoded in magnetic ink with the routing number of the depositary bank, the amount of the returned check, and a "2" in position 44 of the MICR [Magnetic Ink Character Recognition] line as a return identifier.

12 C.F.R. §229.30(a)(2)(iii) [currently §229.31(a)(3)].

Subpart C of Regulation CC also contains its own liability standard and its own remedy provision for a failure to comply with its requirements:

> A bank shall exercise ordinary care and act in good faith in complying with the requirements of this subpart[, which includes the encoding requirements referenced above]. A bank that fails to exercise ordinary care or act in good faith under this subpart may be liable to the depositary bank, the depositary bank's customer, the owner of a check, or another party to the check. The measure of damages for failure to exercise ordinary care is the amount of the loss incurred, up to the amount of the check, reduced by the amount of the loss that party would have incurred even if the bank had exercised ordinary care.

12 C.F.R. §229.38(a).

Along with Regulation CC, the Federal Reserve has adopted Operating Circulars utilized by Reserve Banks in connection with their check-processing services. Both Regulation CC and Federal Reserve Operating Circular No. 3 (which contains provisions relevant to this appeal), "apply to the handling of all cash items that [Reserve Banks] accept for collection and all returned checks that [Reserve Banks] accept for return."

Operating Circular No. 3 is not the original source of the encoding requirement at the center of this appeal, which instead is set forth in subpart C of Regulation CC, as noted above. However, Operating Circular No. 3 emphasizes that in handling a "qualified return check" the Reserve Bank may rely on the accuracy of "the identification of the depositary bank by routing number in magnetic ink." Circular No. 3 further provides that the payor bank will indemnify the Reserve Bank for any loss or expense incurred by the Reserve Bank arising from an encoding error by the payor bank. Circular No. 3 also notes that if for any reason a returned check is mistakenly forwarded by the Reserve Bank to the wrong depositary bank, the recipient should either send the returned check directly to the proper depositary bank or promptly return it to the Reserve Bank.

The Pennsylvania UCC also addresses the applicability of the federal regulatory provisions contained in Regulation CC and Operating Circular No. 3. Section [4-103(a)] of the UCC directs that the terms of the UCC may be varied by agreement, although parties cannot disclaim the duty to act in good faith and exercise ordinary care or limit the measure of damages for a failure to exercise ordinary care. Section [4-103(b)] states that "Federal Reserve regulations and operating circulars, clearinghouse rules and the like have the effect of agreements under subsection (a), whether or not specifically assented to by all parties interested in items handled." Section [4-103(c)] notes that a bank's compliance with Federal Reserve regulations and operating circulars constitutes prima facie evidence of the exercise of ordinary care.

In sum, under the UCC, the provisions of Regulation CC function as a binding agreement between the parties with respect to check-return transactions. This agreement supersedes any inconsistent provisions of the UCC itself, but only to the extent of the inconsistency. Similarly, the provisions of Operating Circular No. 3 are also binding on the parties in connection with the check-return activities at issue here. The rights and obligations granted and imposed by Operating Circular No. 3 overlap to a certain extent with the parties' rights and obligations under the UCC's statutory provisions and under Regulation CC. The provisions of Operating

Circular No. 3 take precedence over any inconsistent portions of Regulation CC, but only to the extent of the inconsistency.

D. Construing the UCC's Check-Return Provisions

NBT's claim raises a number of difficult questions of statutory construction under the UCC. An understanding of these issues aids in assessing the underlying theory of NBT's claim. [FNCB argues that it returned the item because it "delivered [it] to the clearinghouse" (§4-301(d)(1)), but NBT argues the item was not returned because the defective encoding prevented the delivery from occurring "in accordance with clearinghouse rules" (§4-301(d)(1). The court notes the strong textual support for the first reading, but assumes for the purposes of the decision that the return was improper and thus that the item finally was paid under §4-215.] In the end, however, such assumptions do not change the result, because, as set forth in part III.E below, the UCC's check-return provisions do not operate in a vacuum. Even if NBT's interpretation of the UCC's check-return provisions is correct, Regulation CC and Operating Circular No. 3 preclude NBT from holding FNCB strictly accountable for the Disputed Check where NBT suffered no actual loss as a result of FNCB's encoding error.

E. The Damage Limitations Included in Regulation CC and Incorporated in Operating Circular No. 3 Preclude NBT from Recovering on Its UCC Claim

NBT argues that under §[4-301(d)] of the UCC, FNCB's encoding error effectively nullifies FNCB's efforts to "return" the Disputed Check. NBT contends that Regulation CC's encoding requirement for qualified return checks is a clearinghouse rule or transferor instruction concerning the manner in which the Disputed Check was to be returned. NBT argues that FNCB's failure properly to comply with such a rule or instruction means that (1) FNCB did not revoke its provisional settlement in the "manner permitted by statute, clearinghouse rule or agreement[,]" as required by §[4-215]; and (2) the Disputed Check was not returned prior to the midnight deadline as required under §[4-301]. Thus, according to NBT, FNCB is strictly accountable for the full amount of the Disputed Check pursuant to §[4-302].

FNCB counters that, because *all* of Regulation CC is binding on the parties (pursuant to both Regulation CC's own terms, and as an "agreement" under §[4-103] of the UCC), NBT may not rely on FNCB's encoding error as a basis for recovering the amount of the Disputed Check. FNCB notes that Regulation CC specifies that damages for a bank's failure to exercise ordinary care in fulfilling its obligations under Regulation CC must be calculated based upon the actual loss caused by such failure. Implicit in FNCB's position is the concession that it failed to exercise ordinary care in encoding the Disputed Check. FNCB argues that, even if NBT's reading of the UCC is correct (a proposition FNCB disputes), Regulation CC has effectively amended §§[4-215], [4-301], and [4-302] of the UCC to preclude strict accountability where a payor bank's failure to return an item by the midnight deadline is based solely on the payor bank's noncompliance with an obligation imposed by Regulation CC. Instead, according to FNCB, where a payor bank's violation of a clearinghouse rule or transferor instruction arises solely from its failure to exercise ordinary care in executing its obligations under Regulation CC, Regulation CC's clause tying the measure of damages to a claimant's actual loss is incorporated into the UCC by operation of section [4-103]. FNCB contends this analysis precludes imposition of strict accountability in situations where, as here, the claimant seeking recovery concedes it suffered no loss as a result of the payor bank's actions.

We believe the District Court's analysis of this issue, which is largely consistent with FNCB's position, is correct. Regulation CC indisputably binds the parties, pursuant to both its own terms, see 12 C.F.R. §229.1(b)(3), as well as §[4-103] of the UCC, which indicates that "Federal Reserve regulations" are to be treated as agreements that may vary the terms of the UCC, see UCC §[4-103](a)-(b). Such agreements are binding "whether or not specifically assented to by all parties interested in items handled." UCC §[4-103](b). . . .

Because Regulation CC *as a whole* is binding on the parties, and because Regulation CC is the source of the encoding requirement invoked by NBT, the extent of FNCB's liability for its encoding error must be measured by the standards set forth in Regulation CC. Regulation CC states that a bank that fails to exercise ordinary care in complying with the provisions of subpart C of Regulation CC (which includes the encoding requirement referenced above) "may be liable" to the depositary bank. Then, in broad, unrestricted language, Regulation CC states:

> The measure of damages for failure to exercise ordinary care is the amount of the loss incurred, up to the amount of the check, reduced by the amount of the loss that the [plaintiff bank] would have incurred even if the [defendant] bank had exercised ordinary care.

12 C.F.R. §229.38(a). This provision does not provide an exception to this standard for measuring damages in instances where noncompliance with Regulation CC is alleged to have resulted in noncompliance with the UCC's midnight deadline rule. Here, the parties have stipulated that NBT suffered no loss as a result of FNCB's encoding error. Thus, under the plain language of Regulation CC, NBT may not recover from FNCB for the amount of the Disputed Check.

This analysis is reinforced by Appendix E to Regulation CC, which contains the Federal Reserve Board's commentary interpreting the provisions of Regulation CC and providing examples "to aid in understanding how a particular requirement is to work." 12 C.F.R. Part 229, App. E, §I, A, 1. Appendix E states:

> Generally, under the standard of care imposed by §229.38, a paying or returning bank would be liable for *any damages incurred due to miscoding of the routing number,* the amount of the check, or return identifier on a qualified return check. . . . A qualified return check that contains an encoding error would still be a qualified return check for purposes of the regulation.

This Reserve Board commentary is significant, because as noted above, both Regulation CC and the UCC indicate that Regulation CC's provisions are binding on the parties, and that Regulation CC's provisions supersede any inconsistent provisions of the UCC. The fact that Appendix E specifically contemplates the possibility that a payor bank could encode a returned check with the wrong routing number, and yet states that the remedy for such an error is to be calculated based upon the damages caused by the error, strongly indicates that encoding errors do not give rise to strict accountability for a payor bank.

Notably, Appendix E also states that a wrongly encoded check is still considered a qualified return check. This statement illustrates that there is a distinction between whether a check has been properly encoded and whether a check has been properly returned. NBT's attempt to incorporate the proper encoding of a routing number as an essential element in determining whether a check has been "returned" under §[4-301] of the UCC is contrary to the approach required under Regulation CC. Thus, FNCB's encoding error, while constituting a violation of Regulation CC's encoding requirements, does not provide an adequate basis for imposing strict accountability on FNCB pursuant to the UCC's midnight deadline provisions.

NBT offers two reasons why it believes it should recover the full amount of the Disputed Check notwithstanding the measure of damages specified in Regulation CC. We find that these arguments lack merit. NBT's primary argument challenges the applicability of the Regulation CC provision concerning calculation of damages based upon actual loss. NBT believes this provision has no relevance because NBT's claim is brought under the UCC rather than under Regulation CC. NBT states, "[w]hether or not [FNCB] would have been liable on a claim under Regulation CC is wholly irrelevant to the issue presented here. The issue here is whether [FNCB] is accountable under the UCC[.]"

There are several problems with NBT's attempt to draw a sharp distinction between a claim "under the UCC" and a claim covered by Regulation CC. It is obvious that NBT's UCC claim is at least partially dependent on Regulation CC, in that Regulation CC is the source of the encoding requirement that directs a payor bank to include the routing number of the depositary bank in magnetic ink on all qualified return checks. Indeed, to the extent the UCC itself addresses encoding, it specifically provides that the measure of damages for an encoding error is the actual loss incurred by the claimant. See UCC §[4-209(a), (c)]. NBT's position also overlooks the fact that, pursuant to §[4-103] of the UCC, *all* of Regulation CC is binding on the parties. Moreover, to the extent there is a conflict between Regulation CC's broadly worded "actual loss" remedy and the provisions of the UCC that create a strict accountability regime with respect to the midnight deadline rule, such a conflict must be resolved in favor of Regulation CC. Support for this result flows from subpart C of Regulation CC itself, which states that "the provisions of this subpart supersede any inconsistent provisions of the UCC as adopted in any state. . . . " See 12 C.F.R. §229.41. This result is also supported by §[4-103] of the UCC, which, as set forth above, indicates that Federal Reserve regulations are binding on all parties operating under the UCC and that such regulations are considered "agreements" that may vary the effect of the UCC's provisions. In sum, where NBT's claim is dependent upon FNCB's noncompliance with the encoding requirements imposed by Regulation CC, NBT cannot render the Regulation CC damages clause inapplicable merely by characterizing its claim as an effort to hold FNCB accountable under the UCC.

NBT offers a second argument in support of its view that Regulation CC's ordinary care liability standard and "actual loss" remedy provision do not alter the UCC's regime of strict accountability for noncompliance with the midnight deadline rule in the circumstances presented here. NBT asserts that §[4-301](d) of the UCC requires a payor bank to comply with clearinghouse rules or transferor instructions in order effectively to return an item prior to the midnight deadline. NBT points out that the rules or instructions governing the Reserve Bank's check- processing services are contained in Federal Reserve Operating Circular No. 3. NBT argues that Operating Circular No. 3's references to encoding requirements, when read in conjunction with §[4-301] of the UCC, create an independent obligation on the part of FNCB to encode the Disputed Check with the correct routing number, and that FNCB's failure to do so means that the Disputed Check was not "returned" within the meaning of the midnight deadline rule.

While NBT correctly states that Operating Circular No. 3 binds the parties, NBT incorrectly asserts that the Circular's references to encoding requirements somehow negate Regulation CC's requirement that damages be measured with reference to actual loss. Operating Circular No. 3 does not contain an independent encoding requirement. Instead, it incorporates subpart C of Regulation CC *in its entirety*, including both the encoding requirement as well as ordinary care liability standard and the remedy provision stating that the measure of damages for failure to comply with subpart C of Regulation CC is to be measured by the claimant's actual loss. While Operating Circular No. 3 does state that its own provisions supersede any inconsistent provisions of the UCC and Regulation CC, nothing in Operating Circular No. 3 contradicts or is inconsistent with the Regulation CC provision calling for measurement of damages based upon actual loss. Nor does Operating Circular No. 3 impose an encoding requirement separate or apart from its incorporation of the encoding provisions of Regulation CC. The Circular's references to encoding simply emphasize that Reserve Banks retain the right to rely on the routing number encoded on a qualified return check, while stating that a payor bank that erroneously encodes a routing number agrees to indemnify the Reserve Bank for any loss suffered as a result of the error.

These encoding references in Operating Circular No. 3 do not impose a separate encoding obligation apart from the encoding requirement imposed by Regulation CC, and they in no way alter or conflict with Operating Circular No. 3's incorporation of the Regulation CC provision requiring that damages resulting from noncompliance be measured with reference to the claimant's actual loss. Thus, to the extent Regulation CC's encoding requirement is deemed a "clearinghouse rule" or "transferor instruction" by virtue of its incorporation into Operating Circular No. 3, it is a rule or instruction with a specific remedy attached. Moreover, to the extent that this remedy (damages based upon actual loss) conflicts with the strict accountability remedy available under the UCC's check-return provisions, the conflict must be resolved in favor of the former. As discussed above, this result is dictated by Operating Circular No. 3, which states that the Circular's provisions supersede any inconsistent provisions of the UCC. This result is also supported by the UCC itself, which provides that clearinghouse rules are binding on the parties involved in a checking transaction, and that such a binding agreement may vary the UCC so long as it does not purport to disclaim a bank's obligation to act in good faith and exercise ordinary care. See 13 Pa. Cons. Stat. Ann. §[4-103](a)-(b).

IV.   CONCLUSION

NBT has consistently emphasized that it seeks recovery pursuant to §§[4-215], [4-301], and [4-302] of the UCC. The UCC itself directs that its provisions, including those that create a strict accountability regime in connection with the midnight deadline rule, may be altered by agreement. The UCC also provides that Federal Reserve regulations and operating circulars are by operation of law deemed binding agreements governing all parties subject to Article 4 of the UCC. The encoding requirements invoked by NBT are found in subpart C of Regulation CC. Subpart C indicates that compliance with its provisions is to be measured by a standard of ordinary care. Subpart C also states that the measure of damages for a failure to exercise ordinary care in complying with its requirements is the actual loss a claimant suffers as a result of such failure.

In the present case, the parties stipulated that NBT did not suffer any actual damages as a result of FNCB's encoding error. The parties are bound by Regulation CC in its entirety, including its remedy provision, which supersedes any inconsistent provisions of the UCC. NBT thus may not invoke §§[4-215], [4-301], and [4-302] of the UCC to require that FNCB be held strictly accountable for the Disputed Check based upon FNCB's failure to comply with Regulation CC's encoding requirement.

The fact that the parties are also bound by Federal Reserve Operating Circular No. 3 does not change the result. To the extent Operating Circular No. 3 incorporates the encoding requirement of Regulation CC, it also incorporates Regulation CC's liability standard and remedy provision. As with Regulation CC, the provisions of Operating Circular No. 3 by operation of law form an agreement that binds the parties and that varies any inconsistent UCC provisions. NBT's attempt to invoke UCC provisions that create strict accountability in connection with the midnight deadline rule fails to acknowledge that, in this case, these provisions have been effectively amended by Operating Circular No. 3's incorporation of Regulation CC's "actual loss" remedy provision.

Accordingly, because the facts are not in dispute, and because NBT's claim fails as a matter of law, we affirm the order of the District Court granting summary judgment in favor of FNCB.

C.   Truncation and Check 21

From the perspective of the banking industry, the process described above — transporting and sorting checks and delivering them to their customers each month — was a wasteful expenditure of resources. Thus, the banking industry for decades tried to develop procedures that limit its need to transport checks and return them to those who wrote them. Those procedures generally are referred to as check truncation, because they "truncate" the check-transportation process.

1. Payor-Bank Truncation

The simplest way in which truncation can occur is at the payor bank: When the checks reach the payor bank, the bank does not sort the checks and return them to its customers. Instead, it retains the checks (or destroys them) and provides the customer a statement that either includes images of the items or describes the items in some detail. The UCC formally authorizes that practice in UCC §4-406(a):

> [The] bank . . . shall either return or make available to the customer the items paid or provide information in the statement of account sufficient to allow the customer reasonably to identify the items paid. The statement of account provides sufficient information if the item is described by item number, amount, and date of payment.

The content of the statement is important because the statement triggers the final of the four major exceptions to the basic loss rules for checks established by the warranty and indorsement provisions: the bank-statement rule in UCC §4-406. Working much like the rules you have seen before in the payment-card systems, the bank-statement rule bars customers from complaining about improperly paid items if they wait too long to examine their statements.

2. Depositary-Bank Truncation

A more significant step toward truncation is the effort to develop systems for truncating check processing at the depositary bank.

The biggest problem in getting check-truncation systems into place is this country's highly dispersed check-collection system. If our country had a single entity on which all checks were drawn, electronic processing could be implemented easily enough, whenever that bank chose to accept electronic information in lieu of the paper checks. As it happens, however, checks are drawn on literally thousands of banks. No single payor bank can implement a full system for electronic processing of checks that its customers deposit until each and every one of the thousands of payor banks is in a position to accept and process electronic information.

Another complicating factor is the reality that there are situations in which it is useful to examine the original check, where an image is not a satisfactory substitute. For example, in a dispute about the authenticity of a check, examination of the original might provide information about the signature (the traces of the actual physical impression made at the time of signing) that currently is not included in the image or the substitute check. For an excellent example of how that problem arises, consider Judge Posner's discussion in the case that follows.

Wachovia Bank, N.A. v. Foster Bancshares, Inc.

457 F.3d 619 (7th Cir. 2006)

POSNER, Circuit Judge.

This diversity suit pits two banks . . . against each other in a quarrel over liability for a forged or altered check.

A customer of Foster Bank named Choi deposited in her account a check for $133,026 that listed her as the payee. The check had been drawn on Wachovia Bank by a company called MediaEdge that had an account with that bank. Foster presented the check to Wachovia for payment. Wachovia paid Foster and debited MediaEdge's account. Now as it happened the actual payee of the check as originally issued had not been Choi; it had been a company called CMP Media. When CMP Media told MediaEdge that it had not received the check, an investigation ensued and revealed that Choi had somehow gotten her name substituted for CMP Media on the check she'd deposited with Foster. By the time this was discovered, Choi had withdrawn the money from her account and vanished, while Wachovia had destroyed the paper check that Foster had presented to it for payment. It had done this pursuant to its normal practice, the lawfulness of which is not questioned. It had retained a computer image of the check, but whether the image is of the original check drawn on Wachovia, with an alteration, or a forged check, cannot be determined.

MediaEdge sued Wachovia in New York for the amount of the check. That suit has been stayed pending the outcome of the present suit, in which Wachovia seeks a declaratory judgment that Foster must indemnify it in the event that MediaEdge obtains a favorable judgment in the New York suit. Wachovia's suit is based on the Uniform Commercial Code's "presentment warranty": when a depositary bank, Foster in this case, presents a check for payment by the bank that issued the check, it warrants that the check "has not been altered." UCC §§3-417(a)1-2, 4-208(a)1-2. The district court granted summary judgment for Wachovia. Foster had impleaded Choi as a third-party defendant but could not serve her because of her disappearance, so the district court dismissed the third- party claim. Foster does not challenge that ruling. . . .

. . . The bank argues that Wachovia, because it cannot produce the paper check, cannot prove that the check was altered. For all we know, rather than the check being "altered" in the usual sense, Choi used sophisticated copying technology to produce a copy that was identical in every respect to the original check (including the authorized signature by MediaEdge's chief financial officer) except for an undetectable change of the payee's name. Had the original paper check not been destroyed, it could be examined and the examination might reveal whether the check had been forged as just described or the payee's name had been changed by chemical washing of the check or by some other method that utilized rather than replaced the original check.

The bank on which a check is drawn (Wachovia in this case) [accepts responsibility for the risk] that the check is [not] genuine, hence not forged, while as we know the presenting bank warrants that the check hasn't been altered since its issuance. When checks were inspected by hand, when copying technology was primitive, and when cancelled checks were stored rather than digitized copies alone retained, this allocation of liability was consistent with the sensible economic principle that the duty to avoid a loss should be placed on the party that can prevent the loss at lower cost. Having no dealings with MediaEdge, Foster could not determine at reasonable cost whether, for example, the drawer's signature had been forged. Wachovia might be able to determine this by comparing the signature on the check presented to it for payment with the authorized signature in its files. But Wachovia would have no idea who the intended payee was, while Foster might have reason to suspect that the person who deposited the check with it was not the intended payee. And it would be in as good a position as Wachovia to spot an alteration on the check.

But this last point assumes that a payee's name would be altered in the old-fashioned way, by whiting out or otherwise physically effacing the name on the paper check. If Choi created a new check, there would be no physical alteration to alert Foster when she deposited the check with the bank. That is why Foster complains that Wachovia's failure to retain the paper check prevents determining how the "alteration" was effected — more precisely, whether it is a case of alteration or of forgery. The fact that MediaEdge acknowledges having issued a check to CMP Media is not conclusive on the question because Choi might have destroyed that check, rather than altering it, and substituted a copy that seemed perfectly genuine, with her name in place of CMP Media.

So the case comes down to whether, in cases of doubt, forgery should be assumed or alteration should be assumed. If the former, Foster wins, and if the latter, Wachovia. It seems to us that the tie should go to the drawe[e] bank, Wachovia. Changing the payee's name is the classic alteration. It can with modern technology be effected by forging a check rather than by altering an original check, but since this *is* a novel method, the presenting bank must do more than merely assert the possibility of it. Granted, it is the duty of the drawee bank to take reasonable measures to prevent the forging of its checks, as by marking them in a way that a forger could not discover and therefore duplicate. But Foster has made no effort to show that retention of mountains of paper checks — which would be necessary to determine whether the original check had such a marking — would be a reasonable method of determining whether the drawee bank or the presenting bank should be liable for the loss.

Nor did Foster make any effort to show — as it might have been able to do — that duplication of the entire check (that is, forgery of the check deposited with the presenting bank), rather than just physical alteration of the payee's name on the original check, has become a common method of bank fraud. Nor did it try to show that banks have, as they are allowed to do, been contracting around the provisions of the UCC relating to the warranties of drawee and presenting banks in cases such as this. Nor did it try to show what Choi's *modus operandi* was, assuming that she had stolen money in this way on other occasions, though such evidence may of course have been unobtainable.

Even if Foster had shown that forgery of the entire check has become a routine method of altering the payee's name, we would not adopt the rule for which it contends, which is that the drawee bank cannot enforce the presentment warranty unless it retains the paper check. The question of which bank was, in the language of economic analysis of law, the "cheaper cost avoider" would still be open. (Maybe neither bank is — which would hardly be a persuasive ground for changing a long-settled rule of law.) A depositary bank can sometimes discover

an alteration of the payee's name even when there is no physical alteration in the check presented to the bank for deposit. The size of the check may be a warning flag that induces the bank to delay making funds deposited by the check available for withdrawal. The check that Choi deposited with Foster was for a hefty $133,000, and there is no evidence that Choi had previously deposited large checks. We do not suggest that Foster was careless in deciding to make the money available for withdrawal when it did. But the uncertainties that the bank has made no effort to dispel counsel against adopting the legal change that it urges. Reform if needed in the light of modern copying technology should be left to the Uniform State Commissioners [sic] rather than engineered by a federal court in a diversity case. The judgment for Wachovia is therefore
    AFFIRMED.

----

3.   *Check 21*

Frustrated as the long-standing hostility to check truncation stymied efforts to update check law at the state-law UCC level, the Federal Reserve eventually stepped in to address the problem at the federal level, with what ultimately was enacted as the Check Clearing for the 21st Century Act of 2003 (commonly known as Check 21), 12 U.S.C. §§5001-5018. Given the discussion below about the sea change the statute has wrought in check processing, the most important thing to understand about Check 21 is its limited formal scope. The purpose of the statute is to make a "substitute check" the legal equivalent of the original check. Check 21 does not authorize electronic check processing: A bank can collect or present an electronic check only by means of a contractual agreement with the bank to which the check is being transferred or presented. Similarly, because Check 21 does not require banks to accept electronic images, it imposes no obligations on those that create them. Nor does Check 21 even alter whatever rights customers currently have to the return of their original checks.

    All of the provisions of Check 21 relate to the intermediate practical questions described above: facilitating truncation by depositary banks through the creation of reliable mechanisms for making an acceptable substitute of the original check in the few cases in which a substitute is necessary. Thus, the process contemplated by Check 21 is that banks will agree among themselves to present and accept electronic images of checks; the statute will facilitate the reconversion of those images to paper documents.

    The centerpiece of the statute is the concept of the substitute check, defined in §3(16) (and 12 C.F.R. §229.2) as follows:

The term "substitute check" means a paper reproduction of the original check that —

    (A) contains an image of the front and back of the original check;
    (B) bears a MICR line containing all the information appearing on the MICR line of the original check, except as provided under generally applicable industry standards for substitute checks to facilitate the processing of substitute checks;

(C) conforms, in paper stock, dimension, and otherwise, with generally applicable industry standards for substitute checks; and

(D) is suitable for automated processing in the same manner as the original check.

To give that definition some content, consider the image below illustrating the typical format.

To help foster public acceptance, the statute requires that banks provide customers with a plain-English statement — evident in the image below — that states: "This is a legal copy of your check. You can use it the same way you would use the original check." The most important substantive provision of the statute provides that a substitute check that includes that legend and accurately represents the information on the original check is the legal equivalent of the check for all purposes. Check 21 §4(b); see 12 C.F.R. §229.51(a). Similarly, although the statute does nothing directly to authorize the processing of electronic checks, it does provide that a person can deposit, present, or send a substitute check without consent of the party to whom it is sent. Check 21 §4(a).

The advantage of this system is that it fosters electronic processing for a portion of a check transaction even in cases in which one party in the processing chain will not accept the image. Thus, the system no longer requires end-to-end electronics. Instead, any party can convert to electronics as long as its immediate transferee will accept electronic transmission. Because the Federal Reserve accepts electronics, this makes electronics an option on all items for all depository banks. For example, assume that a depository bank receives a check for deposit in Los Angeles, drawn on a payor bank in New York that does not accept electronic images (because it still provides original checks to its customers). The depository bank can truncate the check and send a Check 21 qualifying image to the Federal Reserve Bank in San Francisco. The San Francisco Fed can transmit that image to the Philadelphia Fed, which will create a substitute check for presentment to the payor bank. Although the paper check remains with the depository bank (if it has not already been destroyed), the substitute check created at the Federal Reserve Bank in Philadelphia is the legal equivalent of the original check.

The Check 21 regime has been quite successful. Since its adoption, the share of checks that travel in their original form through the entire collection process has fallen dramatically. More than 99 percent of all checks are now processed entirely on images from the depository bank to the payor bank.

Indeed, many checks (about one in six) are now converted to electronics by the payee, and sent electronically to the bank of first deposit (through a process known as remote deposit capture). The rate of paper-based processing has declined so rapidly that as of 2010 the Federal Reserve has only a single processing center for paper checks, whereas it had dozens as recently as the mid-1980s. That processing center (in Atlanta) now processes about 25 million checks a day. Of those, only 5,000 or so are sent on paper (almost always because of problems that make it difficult to create adequate images); the center reconverts only about 10,000 checks a day: Paper is now only a small fraction of a percent of the processing.

Figure 10.1
Form Substitute Check

Original Scanned Front

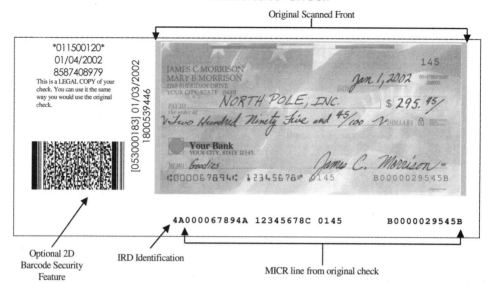

Optional 2D
Barcode Security
Feature

IRD Identification

MICR line from original check

Original Scanned Back

Subsequent endorsements
overlay printed on Original

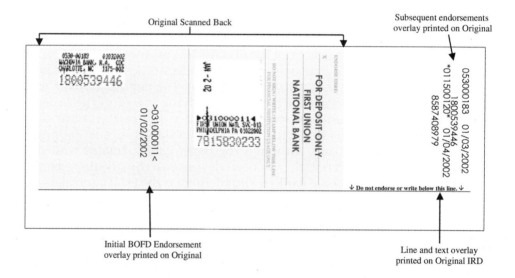

Initial BOFD Endorsement
overlay printed on Original

Line and text overlay
printed on Original IRD

This also has changed the speed of processing. Now, a check sent to Atlanta in the morning normally will be received by the payor bank on the same day; in some cases, dishonor by the payor bank could have the item returned to the depositary bank on the same day as the deposit!

To implement those rules, Check 21 creates a new series of warranties and indemnities. Those rules generally deal with three problems. The first is the problem that the image might not accurately reflect the original check. On that point, Section 5(1) obligates the reconverting bank to warrant that the substitute check meets the requirements for legal equivalence in Section

4(b) — which means, among other things, that the reconverting bank must warrant that the substitute check (made from an image that the reconverting bank has received from the converting bank) accurately represents the check still in the possession of the converting bank.

The second is the problem that despite the presentment of a check electronically the original paper check somehow might find its way into the check-collection process and be presented for payment in the future. To avoid losses from that scenario, the reconverting bank must warrant that no party will be called upon to pay either the original item or a subsequent substitute check made from that item. Check 21 §5(2); see 12 C.F.R. §229.52(a)(2).

The third problem (the topic of *Wachovia*) is that the substitute check in some way might be an inadequate substitute for the original check. On that point, Section 6 obligates the reconverting bank and subsequent banks that process the substitute check to indemnify parties that suffer a loss because of the receipt of a substitute check instead of the original. If the substitute check complied with the statute, the indemnity is limited to the amount of the check, plus interest and expenses. Check 21 §6(b); see 12 C.F.R. §229.53(b). If the check did *not* comply with the statute, the reconverting bank is liable for the entire loss proximately caused by the breach. Check 21 §6(b); see 12 C.F.R. §229.53(b). To make it clear that banks can protect themselves by providing the original when it is necessary, liability on that indemnity is limited to losses that are incurred before the original check (or a copy that remedies a defect in the substitute check) is provided. Check 21 §6(d); see 12 C.F.R. §229.53(b)(3).

Finally, the most controversial provision of the statute is an expedited recredit right for consumers, set forth in Check 21 §7; see 12 C.F.R. §229.54. Under that provision, a consumer can claim a recredit if the consumer asserts that an item is not properly payable or that there has been a breach of one of the warranties in Section 5. Check 21 §7(a)(1); see 12 C.F.R. §229.54(a). The consumer must make the claim within 40 days of the date that the bank has delivered to the customer the substitute check and the relevant bank statement. Check 21 §7(a)(2); see 12 C.F.R. §229.54(b)(1). The bank then must provide the recredit if it cannot "demonstrate[e] to the consumer that the substitute check was properly charged to the consumer account." Check 21 §7(c)(1); see 12 C.F.R. §229.54(c)(2) & (e)(2). The recredit must be made no later than the end of the business day following the business day on which the bank determines the claim is valid. Check 21 §7(c)(2); see 12 C.F.R. §229.54(c)(3). Pending investigation, the recredit must be made before the end of the tenth business day after the submission of the claim. (If the item is for more than $2,500, the bank can delay recrediting the excess over $2,500 until the forty-fifth calendar day after the claim.) To protect the payor bank responding to such a claim, Section 8 includes a parallel expedited recredit right that permits the payor bank to recover funds from the bank from which it received the item in question. My inquiries to banking professionals suggest that the provision, designed to palliate consumers, has rarely (if ever?) come into play.

Problem Set 10

10.1. Late one Thursday afternoon Ben Darrow (your friend from so many earlier problems) calls you frantically and wants to know what he should do about a bad check his bank (FSB) received this morning. Bud Lassen came in first thing this morning and deposited a $10,000 check written by Carol Long. When Bud deposited the check, Carol's account contained only $100. Accordingly, the check was sent to Darrow for action. Darrow promptly placed a hold on the funds in Bud's account and placed a telephone call to Carol to see whether Carol would deposit funds to cover the check.

    a. Later in the morning, Bud came back down to the bank and attempted to cash a check for the total balance in his account ($12,000, including the funds from Carol's check). Because Darrow had placed a hold on the funds, the teller refused to cash the check. Early in the afternoon, Darrow learned that Carol had left town indefinitely to work on a construction project several hundred miles away. Accordingly, Darrow doubts that he will be able to get funds from Carol to cover the check. What should Darrow do? UCC §§4-214(c), 4-215(a), 4-301(a) & (b).

    b. Assume instead that the bank allowed Bud to cash Carol's check when he first presented that check in the morning. Where would that leave the bank? UCC §§4-215(a)(1), 4-301(a).

    c. Finally, assume that Darrow neglected to place a hold on the funds, perhaps because he thought that the bank's computerized check-processing system would do that automatically. As a result, the teller readily cashed Bud's check when Bud returned late in the morning. Now what is the bank's situation? UCC §§4-214(c), 4-301(a) & (b), 4-301 comment 4.

10.2. Consider the facts of the well-known check-kiting case First National Bank v. Colonial Bank, 898 F. Supp. 1220 (N.D. Ill. 1995) (excerpted in several earlier editions of this book, when check kiting was more common): Shelly is running a check-kiting scheme through First National Bank (FNB) and Colonial Bank. On Tuesday, February 11, First National presents $1.5 million of checks to Colonial for payment. The checks had been deposited at FNB and drawn on one of the accounts of a Shelly entity at Colonial. Although Colonial is concerned about the possibility that something is amiss, Colonial does not dishonor the checks on Tuesday or Wednesday, largely because an officer at Shelly's company assures the Colonial loan officer that everything is fine. Thursday morning, however, Colonial discovers the seriousness of Shelly's misconduct and attempts to dishonor the checks at that time.

    Colonial lost the case because it had delayed its return of the checks past midnight Wednesday. If you had been called in by Colonial early Thursday morning, could you have suggested anything that might have helped its chances? UCC §§4-104(a)(10), 4-215(a)(3), 4-301(a), 4-302(a); Regulation CC, §229.31(g)(1).

10.3. Having dealt with all of Ben Darrow's problems, you come back in the office on Friday morning to find an urgent phone message from Jodi Kay at CountryBank. When you call her back, Jodi tells you that she has a large problem with a long-time customer named Carl Eben. Carl wrote a check for $10.37 to purchase some materials at Deuce Hardware. Deuce's sales terminal mistakenly imprinted a MICR line indicating that the check was for $1,037,000.00. When Deuce deposited the check in its account at Hunt Bank, Hunt did not examine the check manually, but instead blindly deposited the million dollars to Deuce's account and forwarded the check to CountryBank. Because Jodi had authorized complete overdraft protection for Carl's account, CountryBank paid the million dollars to Hunt Bank and charged Carl's account; the computer generated and mailed an overdraft notice to Carl. Carl called Jodi to object this morning when he got the notice. When Jodi called Hunt to complain, Hunt pointed out that the mistake was made by Deuce, not Hunt. Jodi asks you what she should do. UCC §4-209(a), (c); Regulation CC, §229.34(c)(3).

10.4.   The next morning your Carl Eben comes to see you again. He has just discovered that a thief has been stealing money from him for several months. The thief has been stealing from Carl's mailbox on a regular basis and managed to steal an incoming package with some blank checks as well as several outgoing envelopes with payments to Carl's suppliers. The thief then wrote several checks payable to himself, which he cashed. On the checks to Carl's suppliers, he forged the name of the suppliers and in some cases altered the check to change the name of the payee to his own name. He then cashed the checks at a local bank (not the bank on which the checks were drawn).

When you asked Carl why he did not notice this on his bank statement, he admitted that he has been very busy lately and has simply failed to reconcile his bank statement for the last six months. Carl's bank admits that Carl ordinarily would not be responsible for any of the checks cashed by the thief. (Carl says that the officer said something about the checks not being "properly payable" under UCC §4-401.) The bank has, however, told Carl that Carl is liable for all of the unauthorized checks because of his failure to notify the bank about the problems when they sent him statements showing the charges for the forged checks. Carl has brought the statements with him. They are summary statements that show only the item number, amount, and date of payment. Is the bank right? UCC §4-406(a), (c), (d), and comment 1.

10.5.   Jodi Kay wants to discuss another problem that CountryBank faces. Carl Eben (Jodi's long-time customer) has just been victimized by a lengthy forgery scheme by his accounts-payable clerk. The clerk forged checks on the account for 18 months before being caught, stealing a total of about $1,350,000. Because Carl never noticed any of the forgeries on his statement, Jodi is guessing (but is not sure) that the bank has no obligation to return the funds to Carl's account. Because of its long-standing (and highly profitable) relationship with Carl, however, the bank has decided that it is better to return the funds without getting into any messy arguments about who is responsible.

Jodi wants to know what the bank can do in the future to mitigate these problems. She wants to mitigate both the bank's exposure to legal liability and the possibility that the losses will occur in the first place. But she has to be conscious of costs: "You can't ask me to do anything crazy like recommend that we actually look at the checks to identify forged signatures." Is the bank liable for losses such as this? If so, what can Jodi do to limit that liability and the likelihood of future losses? UCC §§3-103(a)(7), 4-104(c), 4-208(b), 4-406.

10.6. When Bertie Wooster reviews his bank statement, he observes a $5,000 charge corresponding to a $1,000 check that he wrote. When he complains to JPMorgan Chase (his bank), JPMorgan Chase promptly credits his account. After investigation, JPMorgan Chase discovers that it honored the check based on a substitute check provided to it by the Federal Reserve Bank of New York. The Federal Reserve had received an electronic image from Wells Fargo. Based on the image, it appears that a thief altered the amount of the check to increase it from $1,000 to $5,000. What is not clear, however, is whether the thief altered the original item (by erasing and replacing the amount) or instead took a picture of the image and altered the image on a desktop computer. The only way to tell would be to examine the line beneath the drawer's signature, which includes a microprinting security feature that is apparent on the original item but not discernible on the Check 21 image. JPMorgan Chase cares because it would be responsible for the item if it were forged, but it would have a warranty claim under UCC §4-208(a)(2) if the item has been altered.

    a.   What rights does JPMorgan Chase have under Check 21? Check 21 §§5, 6, 7; 12 C.F.R. §§229.52, 229.53, 229.54.

    b.   Would your answer change if the Federal Reserve had presented an electronic image to JPMorgan Chase? ECCHO Rule XIX(L).

10.7. Thursday morning you come into the office to find your old friend from college Mike McLaughlin waiting for you. Mike operates a computer services business. He wants to talk to you about a check for $20,000 that he recently received from one of his customers in payment of an invoice. When he deposited the check, it bounced. His bank did not, however, return the original check to him. Instead, it returned the image. He wants to know if this will hinder him in trying to collect the funds from the customer. (You should assume for purposes of the question that Mike would have been a person entitled to enforce the check if the check had been returned to him. The issue on which you should focus is whether he will be hindered by having an image of the check instead of the original.)

    a.   What if the image is a simple photocopy? UCC §§3-309, 3-310(b)(1), 3-414(b).

    b.   What if the image is a substitute check that complies with Check 21? Check 21 §4(b); 12 C.F.R. §229.51(a).

10.8. Mike's next problem relates to a $10,000 check he wrote to a supplier. He sees that this check was charged against his account twice. When he inquires, it appears that the supplier transformed the check into an image, which was sent through remote deposit capture to the supplier's depositary bank and processed from there, presenting a substitute check to Mike's bank. Several months later, the supplier also took the original check to a different bank, where he deposited it. Because Mike's bank had deleted the data about the earlier image from its "duplication" database by the time the original item came through, it paid it without noticing the duplication. Discuss the legal remedies available to Mike and his bank. Consider how your answers would differ if Mike (or his bank) had received an electronic image instead of a substitute check in the first instance. ECCHO Rule XIX(L).

Chapter 4.   Wire Transfers

Assignment 11:   The Wire-Transfer System

Measured by dollar volume alone, wire transfers are the dominant payment system in our country. Every day about $5 trillion are transferred in the United States by wire. Although financial institutions make many of those transfers to settle transactions originally made by other payment systems, the use of wire transfers as a mechanism for payment in the first instance has increased considerably in recent decades, especially since the promulgation of UCC Article 4A.

A.   Introduction

Wire-transfer payments are attractive to businesses because they offer almost instantaneous payment at the time of the transaction. When a payee receives a payment by wire transfer, the payment normally reaches the payee in the form of immediately available funds in the payee's bank account. Immediate funds are much more satisfying to the payee than payment by check or credit card. When a payee accepts a check or credit card, the payee must deposit the check or credit-card slip with its own bank and hope that the stakeholder (the payor bank or the issuing bank, as the case may be) honors the transaction and remains solvent long enough to forward payment to the payee. In contrast, a payment received by wire transfer is much more like a payment by debit card, final for all practical purposes at the moment of receipt by the payee. The largest risk that the payee faces is that its own bank will become insolvent before the payee withdraws the funds.

Most wire-transfer transactions are made through networks of participating institutions. The three largest networks used by American banks are Fedwire, CHIPS, and SWIFT. Fedwire is a government institution operated by the Federal Reserve, which provides the predominant method for making domestic interbank wire transfers. CHIPS (the Clearing House Interbank Payment System) is a privately operated facility of the New York Clearing House (a group of Manhattan financial institutions). CHIPS is predominantly used to clear international transfers in dollars; it settles those transactions by transferring amounts in the accounts of participants at the Federal Reserve Bank of New York. SWIFT (the Society for Worldwide Interbank Financial Telecommunications) is an automated international system for sending funds-transfer messages that is the predominant method for completing international transfers that are not denominated in dollars. SWIFT transactions are settled by debits and credits on the books of the participating institutions.

The principal body of American law applicable to wire transfers is Article 4A of the Uniform Commercial Code. Article 4A applies only to "credit" transfers (transfers initiated by the entity making payment). UCC §§4A-102, 4A-104 comment 4. A typical example would be a direction by Riverfront Tools, Inc. (RFT) to its bank to transfer $1,000,000 from RFT's account into a designated account of California Pneumatic Tools. Because the Federal Reserve's Regulation J, 12 C.F.R. Part 210, adopts Article 4A as the governing law for all transfers by Fedwire, Article 4A governs Fedwire transfers as a matter of federal law. Regulation J, §210.25(b). Article 4A does not, however, apply to debit transfers (transfers initiated by the entity being paid). UCC §4A-104 comment 4. For example, Article 4A would not apply to the monthly transfers that would occur if RFT authorized its mortgage lender to obtain RFT's monthly loan payment by means of an automatic debit from RFT's checking account. A simple way to put it is to think of Article 4A as applying to transfers that "push" money to another party, but not to transfers that "pull" money from the other party.

Another major exclusion from Article 4A governs transfers such as the ACH or debit-card transfers described in preceding assignments. See UCC §4A-108 (excluding transfers covered by the EFTA); EFTA §903(6)(B) (limiting "electronic fund transfer[s]" covered by the EFTA to funds transfers made on systems "designed primarily to transfer funds on behalf of a [natural person]"). Although those exclusions from Article 4A are defined by consumer use, they do not reflect a desire to allow special rules to protect consumers in the other systems. Rather, the exclusions reflect a functional distinction between the types of systems used for consumer transfers and the highly developed and specialized systems that banks use for wire transfers. The purpose of Article 4A is to provide a consistent body of law for credit transfers made by businesses; it would make little sense to apply it to the wide variety of other systems for electronic funds transfers.

B.   How Does It Work?

1.   Initiating the Wire Transfer: From the Originator to the Originator's Bank

The process of initiating payment by wire transfer is not complicated. The party that wants to make the payment simply asks its bank to make the transfer. The request could be made in person (if the customer is at the bank), by telecopy, by telex, by electronic mail, or even by telephone. In the terms of Article 4A, the customer is the "originator" of a "funds transfer," to be implemented by the "originator's bank," sent to the "beneficiary's bank," and there credited to the "beneficiary." See UCC §4A-105. In Article 4A's terminology, each step from the originator to the beneficiary's bank constitutes a separate "payment order"; the parties to each payment order are called a "sender" and a "receiving bank." UCC §§4A-103, 4A-104. The strange lack of parallelism—you would expect the statute to refer to a "sender" and a "receiver"—arises from the statute's definition in UCC §4A-103(a) of a payment order as an instruction to a bank to pay funds to a third party. That definition means that the receiving party always will be a bank (and thus can be called the receiving bank), although the sending party need not be a bank (and thus could not be called the sending bank).

As the last part of this assignment explains, the originator's bank has no significant opportunity to avoid payment once it sends a payment order into the system. Accordingly, the originator's bank ordinarily obtains payment from the originator before taking action. The originator's bank typically obtains that payment by removing funds from the originator's account or, in some cases, by placing a hold on the funds (but leaving them in the account until the transfer is completed). If the originator's bank cannot obtain payment at the time of the transfer and is unwilling to rely on its ability to collect payment at a later time, it can reject the originator's payment order under UCC §4A-210(a).

Regardless of whether the originator's bank has obtained funds from the originator before sending the funds transfer, Article 4A (in its convoluted way) grants the originator's bank (as the receiving bank of the customer's payment order) a right to collect payment from the originator (as sender of that payment order) if the originator's bank executes the payment order as directed by the originator. See UCC §§4A-402(c) (receiving bank entitled to payment upon "acceptance" of the order), 4A-209(a) (receiving bank accepts an order when it "executes" it), 4A-301(a) (receiving bank "execute[s]" a payment order when it issues a new payment order carrying out the payment order that it received).

Trustmark Insurance Co. v. Bank One
48 P.3d 485 (Ariz. 2002)

GEMMILL, Judge.

If a banking customer sends a bank a letter of instructions requesting wire transfers of funds upon future occurrences of a specified balance condition in the customer's account, does the letter of instructions constitute a "payment order" under Article 4A of Arizona's Uniform Commercial Code ("UCC")? We address this question . . . in this decision.

Bank One, Arizona, NA ("Bank One") appeals from a jury verdict for Trustmark Insurance Company ("Trustmark") on Trustmark's claim under Article 4A of the UCC and from the trial court's award of attorneys' fees to Trustmark. . . . We reverse the judgment on the UCC claim. . . .

FACTUAL AND PROCEDURAL BACKGROUND

This case involves a commercial dispute between Bank One and Trustmark over a wire transfer arrangement. In February 1995, Trustmark set up a deposit account ("Account One") at Bank One governed by Bank One's deposit account rules. At the same time, Trustmark executed a wire transfer agreement with Bank One.

In May 1995, Trustmark sent Bank One a letter (the "Letter of Instructions") regarding a second deposit account ("Account Two"). Account Two was subject to the same deposit account rules and wire transfer agreement as Account

One. In the Letter of Instructions, Trustmark instructed Bank One to (1) retain a daily balance of $10,000 in Account Two and (2) transfer funds in Account Two automatically to a Trustmark account at the Harris Bank ("Harris Account") whenever Account Two reached a balance of $110,000 or more. In September 1995, Trustmark's Arizona agent began depositing funds into Account Two. Bank One began transferring funds to the Harris Account whenever the Account Two balance rose above $110,000.

In August 1996, Bank One automated its wire transfer functions and consolidated its local departments into a central wire transfer department. Under the automated process, each account from which wire transfers were anticipated needed a new wire transfer agreement. In preparation, Bank One sent all of its wire transfer customers, including Trustmark, a letter dated July 1, 1996 informing the customers that Bank One required a new funds transfer agreement for each account from which wire transfers were anticipated. The letter stated that if a new funds transfer agreement was not in place by July 19, 1996, Bank One could not ensure uninterrupted wire transfer service from accounts lacking such agreements. Trustmark denies ever receiving this letter and never sent Bank One a new funds transfer agreement for Account Two.

In September 1996, the Account Two balance rose above $110,000 for the first time since the July 19, 1996 deadline. Bank One did not transfer funds from Account Two into the Harris Account. Bank One sent regular account statements to Trustmark showing the balances in Account Two, but received no further instructions from Trustmark. The Account Two balance continued to grow until December 1997, when Bank One brought the balance to the specific attention of Trustmark's Arizona agent, who contacted Trustmark's management. Bank One transferred $19,220,099.80 to the Harris Account, leaving $10,000 in Account Two. In early 1998, Trustmark instructed Bank One to transfer Account Two's remaining funds to the Harris Account and thereafter closed Account Two.

Trustmark then filed this action against Bank One, alleging a claim under Article 4A of the UCC, as well as claims for unjust enrichment and negligence. Trustmark alleged that Bank One failed to complete wire transfers from Trustmark's non-interest bearing account at Bank One (Account Two) to Trustmark's investment account at Harris Bank (Harris Account), contrary to the Letter of Instructions. Trustmark asserted a loss of more than $500,000 in interest on its funds as a result of Bank One's inaction, and that Bank One reaped a corresponding windfall profit through interest Bank One earned on Trustmark's money. Trustmark did not assert a breach of contract claim. According to Bank One, the contractual documents eliminated recovery or significantly limited the amount recoverable for breach of contract. However, Article 4A—if applicable—restricts the right of a bank to limit its liability regarding funds transfers. See [UCC §4A-305(f).]

Bank One filed motions to dismiss and for summary judgment on the UCC claim, arguing that the wire transfers at issue were not subject to Article 4A because the Letter of Instructions was not a "payment order" under Article 4A. The trial court denied Bank One's motions, and the case proceeded to a jury trial. At the close of evidence, the court granted Bank One's motion for judgment as a matter of law on the unjust enrichment claim, but continued to reject Bank One's argument that Article 4A of the UCC was not applicable. The court submitted Trustmark's UCC claim and its negligence claim to the jury.

The jury returned a verdict for Trustmark on the UCC claim and found damages of $573,197.02. . . . The trial court entered judgment for Trustmark with damages of $573,197.02, as well as pre-judgment interest, attorneys' fees, and taxable costs.

ISSUES ON APPEAL AND CROSS APPEAL

Bank One argues on appeal that Trustmark's judgment should be reversed as a matter of law because Article 4A of the UCC is not applicable. According to Bank One, the Letter of Instructions was not a "payment order" under Article 4A, and the trial court should not have sent this UCC claim to the jury.

BANK ONE'S APPEAL

. . . Whether the Letter of Instructions is a "payment order" is initially a question of law that we independently review.

As a Matter of Law, the UCC Does Not Apply Because the Letter of Instructions Was Not a "Payment Order" Under Article 4A

We begin our analysis of the applicability of Article 4A by noting its recent origin and its purpose. In 1989 the National Conference of Commissioners on Uniform State Laws and the American Law Institute promulgated Article 4A of the UCC, addressing funds transfers. Over the next several years, all fifty states and the District of Columbia enacted Article 4A as part of their existing UCC statutes. Arizona enacted Article 4A in 1991.

Technological developments in recent decades have enabled banks to transfer funds electronically, without physical delivery of paper instruments. Before Article 4A, no comprehensive body of law had defined the rights and obligations that arise from wire transfers. Article 4A was intended to provide a new and controlling body of law for those wire transfers within its scope. . . .

Because there are very few reported decisions—and none from Arizona— interpreting and applying the provisions of Article 4A defining its scope, we have considered primarily the language of the pertinent statutes, the purpose of Article 4A, and the comments of its drafters. In the Prefatory Note to Article 4A, the drafters discussed the funds transfers intended to be covered and several factors considered in the drafting process:

> There are a number of characteristics of funds transfers covered by Article 4A that have influenced the drafting of the statute. The typical funds transfer involves a large amount of money. Multimillion dollar transactions are commonplace. The originator of the transfer and the beneficiary are typically sophisticated business or financial organizations. High speed is another predominant characteristic. Most funds transfers are completed on the same day, even in complex transactions in which there are several intermediary banks in the transmission chain. A funds transfer is a highly efficient substitute for payments made by the delivery of paper instruments. Another characteristic is extremely low cost. A transfer that involves many millions of dollars can be

made for a price of a few dollars. Price does not normally vary very much or at all with the amount of the transfer. This system of pricing may not be feasible if the bank is exposed to very large liabilities in connection with the transaction.

Article 4A applies only to "funds transfers" as defined in the statute. [UCC §4A-102.] A "funds transfer" is "the series of transactions, beginning with the originator's *payment order*, made for the purpose of making payment to the beneficiary of the order." [UCC §4A-104(1) (emphasis added by court).] Accordingly, to fall within the scope of Article 4A, a transaction must begin with a "payment order."

A "payment order" is defined by the UCC, in pertinent part, as:

> [A]n instruction of a sender to a receiving bank, transmitted orally, electronically, or in writing, to pay, or to cause another bank to pay, a *fixed or determinable amount of money* to a beneficiary if:

> [i]   The instruction does not state a condition to payment to the beneficiary other than time of payment.

[UCC §4A-103(a)(1) (emphasis added by court).]

Bank One argues that the Letter of Instructions was not a payment order, because the Letter was not for a "fixed or determinable amount of money" and imposed two conditions other than time of payment: that the account balance always remain $10,000 ("balance condition") and that transfers not occur until subsequent deposits have raised the balance to $110,000 or more ("deposit condition"). Trustmark argues that the conditions at issue were merely conditions regarding the time of payment—that the balance and deposit conditions essentially determined when transfers were to be made. Trustmark asserts that time of payment need not be set by a specific date, but may be set by events such as the bank's receipt of an incoming wire or deposit. However, the amounts to be transferred did not relate to incoming wires for the same amounts or even wires received on the same day of each month. Rather, Trustmark's agent made deposits sporadically and in varying amounts. Therefore, the conditions in the Letter of Instructions required Bank One to continuously monitor Trustmark's account balance to determine whether sufficient deposits had been made to enable the bank to make a transfer that satisfied both the deposit and balance conditions.

Neither party has cited, nor has our own research revealed, any reported decision addressing the precise issue presented: whether a letter of instructions from an account holder to its bank, requesting automatic wire transfers of funds in excess of a minimum balance whenever the total balance equals or exceeds a specified amount, constitutes a "payment order" governed by UCC Article 4A. We conclude that the Letter of Instructions was not a "payment order," because the Letter subjected Bank One to a condition to payment other than the time of payment.

Article 4A applies to discrete, mechanical transfers of funds. Comment 3 to UCC §4A-104 provides:

> The function of banks in a funds transfer under Article 4A is comparable to their role in the collection and payment of checks in that it is essentially mechanical in nature. The low price and high speed that characterize funds transfers reflect this fact.

Conditions to payment . . . other than time of payment impose responsibilities on [the] bank that go beyond those in Article 4A funds transfers.

Bank One's obligation to make an ongoing inquiry as to Account Two's balance status removes the Letter of Instructions from the Article 4A definition of a "payment order." Conditions other than time of payment are anathema to Article 4A, which facilitates the low price, high speed, and mechanical nature of funds transfers. [Quotation marks, brackets, and citation omitted.] In their treatise on the UCC, James J. White and Robert S. Summers further explain:

A payment order must not "state a condition to payment of the beneficiary other than time of payment." Few transactions will include such conditions. The exception for "time of payment" means that a payment order need not order immediate payment, though most do. For example, a payment order may specify that a certain amount of money must be paid on a certain date to a particular beneficiary.

3 James J. White & Robert S. Summers, *Uniform Commercial Code* §22-2 (4th ed. 1995) (citation omitted). White and Summers then quoted the same language from Comment 3 that we quote [above] to explain that "the drafters did not wish to involve banks in [inquiries] into whether other conditions have occurred." *Id.*

Based on the language defining "payment order," the purpose of Article 4A, and the drafters' intent that payment orders be virtually unconditional, we conclude that requiring the bank to continually examine the account balance is a condition to payment other than time of payment under [UCC §4A-103(a)(1)(i).] We perceive a qualitative difference between a condition requiring daily monitoring of the account balance and an instruction to wire funds on a specific day.

Trustmark also argues that the balance and deposit conditions were permissible conditions observed by Bank One in the past, and therefore Bank One cannot now argue that the conditions were impermissible under Article 4A. The fact that Bank One provided these services to Trustmark under the wire transfer agreement and the Letter of Instructions does not alter our analysis and is irrelevant to whether the Letter of Instructions falls within the definition of a "payment order." Bank One does not argue that such conditions are impermissible *per se*; Bank One simply argues that the Letter's conditions are beyond the permissible conditions for an Article 4A "payment order." Although parties may appropriately and legitimately make such a long-term arrangement for transfers to and from various accounts, their agreement does not automatically transform the arrangement into an Article 4A funds transfer . . . .

We conclude, as a matter of law, that Trustmark does not have a claim under UCC Article 4A, because the Letter of Instructions is not an Article 4A "payment order." Therefore, we reverse the judgment against Bank One on Trustmark's UCC claim.

———————

As suggested above, one of the focal points of Article 4A is the decision of a bank to accept a payment order. As the following case illustrates, the first principle of acceptance is that no bank other than the beneficiary's bank has any obligation to do anything when it receives a payment order.

Receivers of Sabena SA v. Deutsche Bank A.G.

90 U.C.C. Rep. Serv. 2d 19 (N.Y. App. Div. 2016)

FRIEDMAN, J.

This appeal concerns an electronic funds transfer (EFT), governed by Article 4-A of the Uniform Commercial Code (UCC), that was frozen for more than a decade at a New York intermediary bank pursuant to a federal executive order. The question to be answered is whether, upon the federal government's issuance of a license permitting the release of the funds, the intermediary bank had an obligation, enforceable by the beneficiary, to complete the EFT by issuing an order to the beneficiary's bank to pay the beneficiary. We hold that the intermediary bank had no such obligation.

As more fully discussed below, Article 4-A of the UCC furnishes "the exclusive means of determining the rights, duties and liabilities of the affected parties in any situation [it] cover[s]" (UCC 4-A-102, Official Comment), and "[a] bank owes no duty to any party to the funds transfer except as provided in . . . Article [4-A] or by express agreement" (UCC 4-A-212). Article 4-A plainly provides that, in the absence of an express agreement, an intermediary bank receiving a payment order as part of an intended EFT, even in the absence of any outside interference, has no obligation to complete the EFT (UCC 4-A-212). In this case, the EFT was canceled by operation of law when it was not completed within five business days (UCC 4-A-211[4]). That cancellation cut off the intermediary bank's option to accept the payment order it had received from the originator's bank (UCC 4-A-211[5]) and triggered the right of the originator's bank to a refund from the intermediary bank to the extent the originator's bank had already paid the intermediary bank with respect to the transaction (UCC 4-A-402[3], [4]). Thus, the beneficiary of the EFT did not hold title to the funds—which were in fact just a credit in a bank account—in the figurative possession of the intermediary bank while in transit. Further, because the intermediary bank's return of the funds to the originator's bank fully complied with the requirements of Article 4-A, no common-law claim for conversion may be predicated on that conduct. Nor does the federal license that permitted the release of the funds give rise to any cause of action against the intermediary bank on the part of the beneficiary. We therefore reverse the order appealed from and grant the defendant intermediary bank's motion to dismiss the complaint filed by the receivers of the beneficiary, who are the plaintiffs in this action.

. . .

. . . The beneficiary of the EFT at issue in this action, and the predecessor-in-interest of plaintiffs in this action, was Sabena SA, the former national airline of Belgium. Part of Sabena's business was providing aircraft repair and maintenance services to other airlines. Among Sabena's customers for repair and maintenance services was Sudan Airways Ltd., which is not a party to this action.

On November 4, 1997, Sudan Airways originated an EFT to Sabena, as beneficiary, in the amount of $360,500, to pay for technical services that Sabena had contracted to provide for two Sudan Airways aircraft. The EFT was wired from the National Bank of Abu Dhabi (NBAD), as the originator's bank, to Bankers Trust in New York, as intermediary bank, for further transmission to Generale Bank in Brussels, as the beneficiary's bank, where Sabena maintained accounts. Bankers Trust's successor-in-interest is defendant Deutsche Bank Trust Company

Americas (DBTCA), a New York corporation with its principal place of business in New York City.

Although, as noted, the EFT had been intended to reach its terminus at the beneficiary's bank in Belgium, it came to a halt at DBTCA, the intermediary bank in New York. This was due to an executive order that had been issued by the President of the United States the day before Sudan Airways initiated the EFT. Specifically, on November 3, 1997, President Clinton, pursuant to his authority under the International Emergency Economic Powers Act (50 U.S.C. §1701 *et seq.*) and the National Emergencies Act (50 U.S.C. §1601 *et seq.*), and based on a finding that the Government of Sudan posed a threat to the national security of the United States, issued an executive order providing, in pertinent part, that "all property and interests in property of the Government of Sudan that are in the United States, that hereafter come within the United States, or that hereafter come within the possession or control of United States persons . . . are blocked" (Exec Order No 13067, 62 Fed Reg 59989 [1997]) (Executive Order 13067). Executive Order 13067 defines the term "Government of Sudan" to include, inter alia, that government's "agencies, instrumentalities and controlled entities."

On July 1, 1998, the Office of Foreign Asset Control (OFAC) of the United States Department of the Treasury issued detailed regulations to carry out the purposes of Executive Order 13067 (31 C.F.R. part 538). The regulations provide that "no property or interests in property of the Government of Sudan, that are in the United States, that hereafter come within the United States, or that are or hereafter come within the possession of or control of U.S. persons . . . may be transferred, paid, exported, withdrawn or otherwise dealt in" (31 C.F.R. 538.201[a]). It is undisputed that Sudan Airways falls within the regulatory definition of the term "Government of Sudan" (31 C.F.R. 538.305).

On November 4, 1997, upon receiving NBAD's payment order for Sudan Airways' EFT to Sabena, DBTCA immediately blocked the order pursuant to Executive Order 13067, which, by its terms, had gone into effect at 12:01 a.m. that day. Accordingly, instead of accepting the payment order by executing it — i.e., by sending its own payment order to Generale Bank, the beneficiary's bank, for the benefit of Sabena (*see* UCC 4-A-209[1], 4-A-301[1], quoted in pertinent part at footnote 2, *supra*) — DBTCA credited the funds to a segregated, interest-bearing account.[9] For the next 14 years and four months, the credit representing the EFT remained frozen.

In 2009, Sabena, through counsel, applied to OFAC for a license, pursuant to subpart E of 31 C.F.R. part 538, authorizing DBTCA to release the funds. In 2012, OFAC issued such a license. The license, dated March 5, 2012, is addressed to DBTCA, and states:

> [DBTCA] blocked this transfer pursuant to U.S. sanctions administered by [OFAC]. OFAC has carefully reviewed the information presented and otherwise available to it

---

9. We note that which party held title to the EFT in the hands of the intermediary bank under state banking law is an entirely different question from whether Sudan Airways is deemed to have had an "interest []" (31 C.F.R. 538.201[a]) in the EFT for purposes of the federal sanctions regime. It is undisputed that Executive Order 13067 and the implementing regulations required DBTCA to block the EFT even though, as more fully discussed below, Sudan Airways did not hold title to the EFT under state law while it was in the possession of the intermediary bank.

in connection with this transfer and, based on the assertions made in the incoming application from Nankin & Verma PLLC [Sabena's counsel], has determined that [DBTCA] is authorized to release these funds.

After the license was issued, Sabena's counsel contacted DBTCA to discuss the anticipated release of the EFT. After receiving Sabena's instructions for directing the funds to its account, DBTCA allegedly asked Sabena's counsel if it could "obtain a release from Sudan Airways and its bank, NBAD, 'as they may have claim to an interrupted wire transfer under the UCC.'" Sabena's counsel allegedly responded by "immediately ask[ing] if [DBTCA] was 'imposing a requirement that releases be provided before it transfers the funds to my client?'" According to the complaint, "[t]hat same day [DBTCA's] counsel advised that his client had released the funds to NBAD."

Based on the foregoing allegations, Sabena commenced this action against DBTCA in October 2012. Sabena's complaint asserts four causes of action, three of which (the first, second and fourth) are at issue on this appeal. The first cause of action is for DBTCA's "fail[ure] to remit the funds [upon OFAC's issuance of the license] to Sabena, the intended beneficiary under the wire transfer, as required by UCC Article 4A [sic]," on the theory that a federal block of an EFT is "a mere interruption in the wire transfer, and upon its removal, the previously restrained intermediary bank should proceed with the funds transfer by carrying it onward for payment to the intended beneficiary." The second cause of action alleges that, "[b]y sending the funds back to Sudan Airways via its bank, [DBTCA] violated . . . the License" by which OFAC had released the block of the EFT. Finally, the fourth cause of action asserts the theory that DBTCA's transfer of the funds back to NBAD upon the issuance of the license was "a distinct act of domain [sic] wrongfully exerted of [sic] [Sabena's] personal property in denial of or inconsistent with its rights therein and constitutes conversion."

DBTCA responded to the complaint by moving to dismiss it for legal insufficiency . . . . As it does on appeal, DBTCA argued that the complaint failed to state any cause of action because: (1) Sabena, as the beneficiary, had no property interest in the EFT while it was midstream; (2) DBTCA, as an intermediary bank, owed no duty to Sabena, the beneficiary, with respect to the EFT; and (3) upon the release of the federal block, the UCC's "money-back guarantee" provision obligated DBTCA to refund to the originator's bank any payment the latter had made for the unexecuted payment order. [The Supreme Court denied the motion to dismiss.] . . . As noted at the opening of this writing, upon DBTCA's appeal . . . we reverse and grant the motion to dismiss.

We begin our analysis by reiterating that, as the Court of Appeals recognized shortly after Article 4-A went into effect in this state, that article—which has been enacted by all 50 states and the District of Columbia, and has been adopted by the Board of Governors of the Federal Reserve System to govern the wire transfer service of the Federal Reserve Banks (*see* 12 C.F.R. part 210, subpart B, appendix B)—was enacted to remedy the previous lack of "'[a] comprehensive body of law that defines the rights and obligations that arise from wire transfers'" (Banque Worms v. BankAmerica Intl., 570 N.E.2d 189, quoting National Conference of Commissioners on Uniform State Laws and American Law Institute, Prefatory Note to UCC Article 4-A [Prefatory Note]). Accordingly, the drafters of Article 4-A

"undertook to develop a body of unique principles of law that would address every aspect of the electronic funds transfer process and define the rights and liabilities of all parties involved in such transfers" (*Banque Worms*, 570 N.E.2d 189, citing Prefatory Note) to further the policy goals of "[n]ational uniformity in the treatment of electronic funds transfers . . ., speed, efficiency, certainty . . ., and finality" (*Banque Worms*, 570 N.E.2d 189). In this regard, the drafters of Article 4-A explained:

> A deliberate decision was . . . made [in drafting the article] to use precise and detailed rules to assign responsibility, define behavioral norms, allocate risks and establish limits on liability, rather than to rely on broadly stated, flexible principles. In the drafting of these rules, a critical consideration was that the various parties to funds transfers need to be able to predict risk with certainty, to insure against risk, to adjust operational and security procedures, and to price funds transfer services appropriately. This consideration is particularly important, given the very large amounts of money that are involved in funds transfers.
>
> Funds transfers involve competing interests—those of the banks that provide funds transfer services and the commercial and financial organizations that use the services, as well as the public interest. These competing interests were represented in the drafting process and they were thoroughly considered. The rules that emerged represent a careful and delicate balancing of those interests and *are intended to be the exclusive means of determining the rights, duties and liabilities of the affected parties in any situation covered by particular provisions of the Article.* Consequently, resort to principles of law or equity outside of Article [4-A] is not appropriate to create rights, duties and liabilities inconsistent with those stated in this Article" (UCC 4-A-102, Official Comment [emphasis of *Sabena* Court]).

Consistent with the intention to make Article 4-A "the exclusive means of determining the rights, duties and liabilities" arising from an EFT, the statute expressly limits the obligations and potential liability of a "receiving bank"—i.e., a bank, like DBTCA in this case, to which a payment order is addressed (UCC 4-A-103[1][d])—with respect to the payment order. UCC 4-A-212 provides:

> If a receiving bank fails to accept a payment order that it is obliged by express agreement to accept, the bank is liable for breach of the agreement to the extent provided in the agreement or in this Article, *but does not otherwise have any duty to accept a payment order or, before acceptance, to take any action, or refrain from taking action, with respect to the order except as provided in this Article or by express agreement.* Liability based on acceptance arises only when acceptance occurs as stated in Section 4-A-209 [i.e., in the case of a receiving bank other than the beneficiary's bank, when the bank executes the order (UCC 4-A-209[1]) by issuing its own payment order to the next bank in the chain (UCC 4-A-301(1)]), and liability is limited to that provided in this Article. A receiving bank is not the agent of the sender or beneficiary of the payment order it accepts, or of any other party to the funds transfer, and *the bank owes no duty to any party to the funds transfer except as provided in this Article or by express agreement*" [emphasis of *Sabena* Court].

Thus, even if Executive Order 13067 had never intervened, DBTCA, as intermediary bank, would not have had any obligation under Article 4-A to accept the payment order it received from NBAD, the originator's bank, by sending a further payment order to Generale Bank, the beneficiary's bank. Indeed, even if DBTCA had sent a further payment order to the beneficiary's bank (which it never did), DBTCA would have incurred an obligation to the beneficiary's bank only, not to the beneficiary—Sabena—itself. From the above-quoted statutory definition of a "funds transfer" as comprising a "series of transactions" (UCC 4-A-104[1]), it is evident that "Article 4-A treats a funds transfer as a series of individual transactions, each of which involve[s] two parties dealing directly with each other," or, stated otherwise, "as a series of transactions each of which involves only the parties to the individual payment order." [Citation omitted.]

Here, the failed EFT from Sudan Airways to Sabena comprised two payment orders, the first from Sudan Airways to NBAD, the second from NBAD to DBTCA. Sabena, the intended beneficiary of the EFT, was not a party to the payment order addressed to DBTCA, the intermediary bank, and Sabena therefore has no rights under that payment order (*see* PEB Commentary No. 16 at 2 ["The intermediary bank has no contractual obligation to the originator or to the beneficiary, and neither the originator nor the beneficiary has any contractual obligation to or rights flowing from the intermediary bank"]; *id.* at 3 [in the event an EFT is not completed, "(t)he beneficiary . . . has no claim to any payment from the intermediary bank"]).

. . .

Not only did DBTCA never have any legal obligation to Sabena with respect to the subject EFT, the delay of more than five business days imposed by the federal blocking order resulted, under UCC 4-A-211(4), in the cancellation, by operation of law, of the payment order DBTCA had received from the originator's bank. The cancellation of the payment order excused the obligation of the originator's bank to pay DBTCA, the intermediary bank, for that payment order (UCC 4-A-402[3]). By the same token, the cancellation of the originator's bank's payment order obligated DBTCA, upon the lifting of the federal block, to refund to the originator's bank any payment the latter had already made for that payment order, pursuant to the "money-back guarantee" provision of UCC 4-A-402(4) (*see* UCC 4-A-402, Official Comment 2). Specifically, in language that leaves little room for interpretation, UCC 4-A-402(4) provides: "If the sender of a payment order pays the order and was not obligated to pay all or part of the amount paid, *the bank receiving payment is obliged to refund payment to the extent the sender was not obliged to pay*" (emphasis added) (*see* PEB Commentary No. 16 at 3 [in the event an EFT is not completed, "the only party with a claim against the intermediary bank is the sender to that bank, which is typically the originator's bank" and "(t)he intermediary bank owes its refund obligation to its sender, the originator's bank"]).

. . .

In the present case, to reiterate, based on the allegations of Sabena's complaint, NBAD, the originator's bank—rather than Sabena, the intended beneficiary of the failed EFT—was plainly the entity that passed the EFT on to DBTCA, the bank where it rested until the federal block was released. It follows that NBAD was the only entity with a property interest in the stopped EFT at DBTCA and that, upon the release of the block, DBTCA properly refunded NBAD's payment for the EFT pursuant to UCC 4-A-402(4), given that the EFT had long since been cancelled by operation of law under UCC 4-A-211(4). It also follows that, pursuant to UCC 4-A-212, Sabena has no claim against DBTCA with respect to this transaction. DBTCA owed nothing to Sabena as the beneficiary since an intermediary bank has no legal obligation to the beneficiary and, perforce, Sabena never had title to the funds. [Brackets, citation, ellipses, and quotation marks omitted throughout the preceding paragraph.]

. . .

Sabena suggests in its brief that whether the originator of an EFT is "innocent" should affect the obligations of an intermediary bank. This suggestion flies in the face of Article 4-A's concern to keep the funds transfer system running smoothly by setting forth "precise and detailed rules" for banks and their customers to follow (UCC 4-A-102, Official Comment) and by limiting each party's risks to those arising from the other parties with which it has chosen to deal directly. In this case, DBTCA, as an intermediary bank in privity with neither Sabena nor Sudan Airways, was entitled, when the funds were unblocked, to look to the express provisions of Article 4-A to determine its obligations, without worrying about whether the character of the originator might vary those obligations and, if a court later disagreed with DBTCA's assessment, result in the bank's incurring double liability. It is Sabena, not DBTCA, that chose to do business with Sudan Airways, and it is Sabena that should bear the risk of loss from that choice.

The foregoing, we believe, establishes that Sabena has not stated a legal cause of action against DBTCA under Article 4-A of the UCC. Neither has Sabena stated any viable cause of action against DBTCA under the license OFAC issued, releasing the previous federal block on the funds. As previously noted, the license was issued pursuant to subpart E of 31 C.F.R. part 538, and simply provided that DBTCA was "authorized to release these funds," without specifying to which party the funds should be released. Nonetheless, Sabena claims that DBTCA violated the license by remitting the funds back to NBAD, pointing to a regulation (31 C.F.R. 538.403[b]) that Sabena construes (without citing supporting authority) to mean that a license unblocking property does not permit the property to be transferred toward Sudan (as opposed to away from it) unless the license specifically so provides.

Even if Sabena's construction of 31 C.F.R. 538.403 might be correct, we find that Sabena's attempt to state a cause of action under the license fails by reason of 31 C.F.R. 538.501(c), which provides in pertinent part: "Unless [a] regulation, ruling, instruction, or license [issued under part 538 to authorize an otherwise prohibited transaction] otherwise specifies, *such an authorization does not create any right, duty, obligation, claim or interest in, or with respect to, any property which would not otherwise exist under ordinary principles of law*" [emphasis of *Sabena* Court]. Thus, even if the license did not permit DBTCA to send the funds back to Sudan Airways' bank—which would be a matter to be addressed by the federal authorities—the license did not confer upon Sabena any rights or claims with respect to the funds that Sabena would not otherwise have had "under ordinary principles of law"— here, Article 4-A of the New York UCC. Stated otherwise, the OFAC license, whatever its proper construction, did not turn Sabena into the owner of a bank credit not otherwise owed to it under New York law.

Finally, because Article 4-A of the UCC governs this matter exclusively and, assuming the truth of the allegations of the complaint, it is plain, as previously discussed, that DBTCA acted properly with respect to the subject EFT, in which Sabena had no ownership or possessory interest, Sabena's cause of action for conversion, which seeks to impose liability inconsistent with the rights and liabilities expressly created by Article 4-A, is legally insufficient.

---

2. Executing the Transfer: From the Originator's Bank to the Beneficiary's Bank

As suggested above, the originator's bank has several choices in determining how to execute a funds transfer for its customer. In the absence of an instruction from the customer, the originator's bank ordinarily is free to "use any funds-transfer system [that it wishes] if use of that system is reasonable in the circumstances." UCC §4A-302(b)(i). The UCC's deference to the originator's bank allows the originator's bank to ignore its originator's instruction as to the method of sending the transfer if the bank, "in good faith, determines that it is not feasible to follow the instruction or that following the instruction would unduly delay completion of the funds transfer." UCC §4A-302(b).

In some cases, the originator's bank can complete the transfer by crediting an account of the beneficiary on its own books. See UCC §4A-104 comment 1 (Case #1). In most cases, however, wire transfers are used to transfer funds from one bank to another. To execute such a payment order, the originator's bank must find a way to do two things: notify the beneficiary's bank of the transfer and forward payment to the beneficiary's bank to cover the payment to the beneficiary. The following sections describe three systems for accomplishing those things, in increasing order of complexity.

(a) Bilateral Systems (Including SWIFT). The most direct process is a simple bilateral arrangement: The originator's bank sends a message directly to the beneficiary's bank, asking the beneficiary's bank to complete the transfer. Theoretically, a bank could send such a message by telephone, telecopy, or even regular mail; in most cases, however, banks use more secure methods of transmission. In international transactions, banks frequently send such messages through the SWIFT system, which transmits a mind-boggling 30 million messages each day for the more than 10,000 institutions that it serves.

Devising a secure method for sending a payment order is insufficient without some method for sending payment from the sender/originator's bank to the receiving/beneficiary's bank. If the sender and receiving bank have substantial relations between themselves, that can be done by arranging for orders to be paid by debits from accounts of the sender at the receiving bank. To continue with the example from above, First Bank could use SWIFT to execute RFT's requests by sending a payment order to Wells Fargo under an agreement that Wells Fargo would obtain payment by debiting First Bank's account at Wells Fargo. Under UCC §4A-403(a)(3), First Bank's obligation to pay Wells Fargo for the payment order would be satisfied by such a debit. See UCC §4A-403 comment 3.

A common enhancement of that process would provide for daily "netting" of the obligations of the parties. Because that arrangement is between only two parties, it is called bilateral netting. Under that arrangement, Wells Fargo and First Bank would not debit each other's accounts for each individual payment order sent between them each day. Instead, at the end of each day, they would add up all of the transfers sent between them that day, produce a single net figure for all of the transfers, and then "settle" for those transfers with a single debit covering that net figure. For example, assume that all of the payment orders First Bank sent to Wells Fargo on the date of RFT's order totaled $75,000,000 and that Wells Fargo sent $70,000,000 of payment orders to First Bank on the same day. Under a bilateral netting arrangement, the parties could pay for those orders by agreeing that Wells Fargo would make a single $5,000,000 debit from First Bank's account at Wells Fargo (or that First Bank would make a single $5,000,000 credit to Wells Fargo's account at First Bank).

Under UCC §4A-403(c), that single debit would satisfy both banks' obligations as senders of payment orders on that day. See UCC §4A-403 comment 4. Thus, once Wells Fargo made the $5,000,000 debit, the offset reflected in the bilateral netting arrangement would satisfy First Bank's obligation under UCC §4A-402 to pay Wells Fargo for its payment orders. The obligations would be satisfied even though First Bank would not have forwarded any funds to Wells Fargo for that day's payment orders.

(b) CHIPS. Bilateral systems can be costly and inconvenient because they require each bank to establish, maintain, and administer separate relations with each bank to which it sends wire transfers. Thus, it would be much cheaper for a bank to use a system that allows a large number of participants to send all messages through a central clearinghouse that can aggregate and net out all of the transfers for all participants at the end of each day. That process is described as multilateral netting.

The largest such system is CHIPS (the Clearinghouse Interbank Payment System) in New York City. (A similar system called CHAPS operates in London.) CHIPS clears transactions for about 50 entities, settling more than 400,000 transfers a day and totaling almost $1.5 trillion a day. CHIPS uses a complicated array of netting mechanisms to transfer value as quickly as possible during the course of each day. At the beginning of each day, each participant funds a special CHIPS account at the Federal Reserve Bank of New York. As the day progresses, that participant's account decreases (to account for outgoing transfers charged to that participant) and increases (to account for incoming transfers charged to that participant). Because the overwhelming majority of CHIPS transfers are relatively small, 95 percent of all CHIPS transfers (amounting to about 30 percent of the value of all CHIPS transfers) can be settled immediately by deductions from those prefunded accounts; for those transactions, the receiving participant effectively receives final payment at that time.

In cases where adequate funds are not in the prefunded accounts of the originator's banks of the relevant parties, the transactions are settled either by bilateral netting or by multilateral netting. Bilateral netting occurs when the CHIPS computer identifies transactions going in opposite directions between two financial institutions; the computer can settle the smaller of those transactions immediately. About 5 percent of CHIPS transfers are settled by bilateral netting (amounting to 15–20 percent of the value of all CHIPS transfers).

Finally, in cases where bilateral netting is not adequate, the parties rely on the CHIPS (patented) multilateral netting algorithm, in which transfers from three (or more) institutions are netted. For example, assume that Bank A, with $3M available in its account, needs to send $25M to Bank B; that Bank B, with $2.5M available in its account, needs to send $26M to Bank C; and that Bank C, with $2.6M available in its account, needs to send $22.5M to Bank A and $3M to Bank B. The CHIPS server would resolve those transactions by reducing Bank A's account to $.5M, increasing Bank B's account to $4.5M, and increasing Bank C's account to $3.1M. Multilateral netting occurs in very large transfers: only about 1 percent of CHIPS transfers by number, but more than half of the value of all transactions.

(c) Fedwire. Notwithstanding the advantages of CHIPS, the Federal Reserve banks' Fedwire system remains the dominant system for transfers between U.S. banks: Fedwire completes about 600,000 transfers a day worth more than $3.5 trillion each day. One reason for Fedwire's domination is its ability to provide immediate settlement at the time of payment. Another reason is the inclusiveness of the Fedwire system: Fedwire serves more than 10,000 financial institutions. The cost of participating is remarkably modest: a monthly fee (depending on the type of connection the bank uses) of several hundred dollars, plus a per-transfer fee of about 50 cents. In addition to the fees, a bank that wants to use Fedwire must maintain an account at the Federal Reserve bank for its location. Although Fedwire does permit "offline" transfers, almost all banks in the system also maintain an electronic communication link with their Federal Reserve bank (functionally equivalent to an e-mail system) over which Fedwire transactions proceed.

To initiate a transfer by Fedwire, the originating bank sends a funds-transfer message to its local Federal Reserve bank. In addition to a variety of technical details, that message must identify the beneficiary and the beneficiary's bank so that the Federal Reserve bank can determine how to carry out the request. To facilitate automated message processing, all messages must conform to a rigidly standardized format, which consists of a series of fields of information that occur in a specified sequence. The message appears in the form of a standard identifier (field tag) for each of the given fields. After the message is typed into a terminal at the originating bank, software provided by the Federal Reserve encrypts the message and transmits it to the local Federal Reserve bank.

When the originator's bank sends a payment order to the Federal Reserve, it hopes that the Federal Reserve as receiving bank will execute the payment order it has received by sending a second payment order moving the funds toward the beneficiary. As sender of that second payment order, the Federal Reserve ordinarily will not have a later opportunity to avoid payment. Rather, when the receiving bank accepts the Federal Reserve's payment order, the Federal Reserve becomes directly obligated to pay that order, even if the bank that initially sent the message to the Federal Reserve fails to pay the Federal Reserve for its payment order. UCC §4A-402(b) & (c).

Accordingly, the first step a Federal Reserve bank takes when it receives an incoming Fedwire payment order is to determine whether the sender (for convenience assume that it is the originator's bank) has sufficient funds to cover the payment order. The Federal Reserve bank makes that determination by referring to a working balance that it maintains for each bank during the course of each business day. For example, First Bank's working balance starts with the balance in First Bank's Federal Reserve account at the beginning of the day, increases when First Bank receives incoming wire transfers or other credits, and decreases when First Bank executes outgoing wire transfers or when its account otherwise is debited. Because of the huge volume of transfers made by wire each day, it is common for a bank's working balance to go below zero. When that happens, the bank is said to have incurred a "daylight overdraft." Although it is common for banks to incur daylight overdrafts, Regulation J requires banks to cover those overdrafts by the end of each day. See Regulation J, §210.28(b)(1)(i) (requiring sender to cover overdrafts by the close of the day).

Modest daylight overdrafts cause no concern; they often result from the fact that most of a bank's outgoing wires on a given day are transmitted before the bulk of its incoming wires are received. The Federal Reserve, however, regulates the level of overdrafts closely, hoping to prevent any bank from getting so far out of balance during the course of a day that the bank will not be able to cover the overdrafts at the end of the day. The Federal Reserve's regulation takes two forms. First, since 1994, the Federal Reserve has discouraged daylight overdrafts by exacting a substantial fee for tolerating those overdrafts (currently 0.50 percent of the amount of the overdraft). That fee apparently caused a significant flow of business away from Fedwire to CHIPS, although the loss of Fedwire business to date appears to have been less than the Federal Reserve expected when it first imposed the fee.

Second, the Federal Reserve limits overdrafts more directly by placing a bank-by-bank cap on daylight overdrafts. The Federal Reserve has a detailed (and frequently revised framework) that permits small *de minimis* overdrafts without requiring payment of the fee. For example, if the institution is sufficiently serious about making regular overdrafts to file with the Federal Reserve a resolution of its board of directors authorizing such transactions, the Federal Reserve will tolerate as *de minimis* daylight overdrafts of up to 40 percent of an institution's capital. Overdrafts that do not exceed the lesser of 20 percent or $10 million do not even require the board of directors resolution for *de minimis* treatment.

Most banks also internally manage the level of their daylight overdrafts, both as a matter of prudence and to avoid the daylight overdraft fee. Thus, a bank might establish a general policy that it will not incur a daylight overdraft exceeding $60 million, even if its Federal Reserve cap is $80 million. In that event, a central wire-transfer control office at the bank holds any outgoing wire-transfer requests that would cause the working balance to pass that level. If one of the bank's officers requested a $10 million transfer at a time when the bank's working balance was $55 million below zero, the central wire-transfer office would wait for an incoming transfer to offset the outgoing wire request. If a $5 million wire came in a few minutes later (increasing the bank's working balance to $50 million below zero), the bank then could release the $10 million outgoing wire without passing the $60 million internal overdraft limit. That practice is the reason transactional lawyers so frequently sit around at closings waiting for the "wire to go through" hours after the bank officer has authorized transmission of the wire. It is not the wire-transfer system that takes so long; it is the bank's internal funding priorities that slow completion of the transaction.

If the payment order will cause the working balance of the originator's bank to sink below its permitted overdraft level, the transfer does not occur. Conversely, if the payment order is consistent with the permitted overdraft level, the Federal Reserve bank obtains payment under UCC §4A-402(c) by removing the amount of the transfer from the working balance of the account of the originator's bank. See Regulation J, §210.28(a) (authorizing Federal Reserve to debit account of sender). The Federal Reserve bank then executes the originator's bank's payment order by sending a second payment order to the beneficiary's bank. If the beneficiary's bank has an account with that Federal Reserve bank, the Federal Reserve bank sends a message directly to the beneficiary's bank's Fedwire connection and simultaneously credits the account of the beneficiary's bank for the amount of the order. See Regulation J, §210.29(a) (authorizing Federal Reserve to execute payment orders by crediting the account of the receiving bank).

If the beneficiary's bank is located in a different Federal Reserve district, the originator's bank's Federal Reserve bank sends the message on to the beneficiary's bank's Federal Reserve bank, using an internal Federal Reserve encrypted e-mail system. See Regulation J, §210.30(b) (authorizing Federal Reserve to send Fedwire orders to the Federal Reserve bank of the beneficiary's bank). The beneficiary's bank's Federal Reserve bank then debits the account of the originator's bank's Federal Reserve bank on its books and credits the account of the beneficiary's bank. Finally, the beneficiary's bank's Federal Reserve bank sends the funds transfer message to the beneficiary's bank in the form of an encrypted signal to that bank's Fedwire connection.

3. Completing the Funds Transfer: From the Beneficiary's Bank to the Beneficiary

When a beneficiary's bank receives a payment order, it technically has a right to reject the payment order. UCC §§4A-210, 4A-209 comment 8. As discussed above, UCC §4A-210 grants that right of rejection to protect the receiving bank from the risk that the sender will not pay for the sender's payment order even if the receiving bank properly executes that order. That right is particularly important to the beneficiary's bank because a beneficiary's bank that accepts a payment order becomes obligated to pay the beneficiary even if the beneficiary's bank never obtains payment from the sender. UCC §4A-404(a).

As a practical matter, however, it is quite uncommon for a beneficiary's bank to reject a payment order because of a concern that the sender will not pay. In most (although certainly not all) cases, there is no doubt about payment because the parties have a regular arrangement that removes any concern of the receiving bank. Thus, just as the checking system operates on the assumption that checks will be honored unless the payor bank sends a prompt notice of dishonor, the wire-transfer system provides that the beneficiary's bank accepts a payment order if it does not act promptly to reject it. Generally, assuming that the receiving bank has been paid for the order or has access to adequate funds in the sender's account with the receiving bank, acceptance occurs at the beginning of the next business day after the date that the beneficiary's bank receives the order unless the receiving bank rejects the payment order within the first hour of that business day. UCC §4A-209(b)(3) (deemed acceptance on the day after the payment date); see UCC §4A-401 (absent special instructions, the payment date is the date that the order is received). Hence, when the receiving bank has funds on hand that it could take as payment for the order, the passage of the deadline automatically results in the beneficiary's bank's acceptance of the order, the beneficiary's entitlement to payment from the beneficiary's bank, and the beneficiary's bank's entitlement to payment from the sender. UCC §§4A-402(b), 4A-404(a). In the odd case where acceptance does not occur under that rule — usually because the sender has not paid for the order — the order is rejected by operation of law on the fifth business day after receipt at the receiving bank. UCC §4A-211(d); see UCC §4A-211 comment 7.

The rules related to rights of acceptance and rejection have no significance for payments transmitted by Fedwire. As explained above, Fedwire simultaneously provides final payment to the beneficiary's bank and transmission of the message to that bank by means of a credit to the Federal Reserve account of the beneficiary's bank. Thus, there is no reason to wait for the beneficiary's bank to decide whether to accept the order; the acceptance of the beneficiary's bank is implied at the instant that it receives a Fedwire message. UCC §§4A-209(b)(2), 4A-209 comment 6. As a result, the beneficiary's bank becomes directly obligated to pay the beneficiary the moment that it receives the Fedwire transfer. UCC §4A-404(a); Regulation J, §210.31(a) (bank receiving Fedwire payment is deemed paid when it receives the Fedwire message). In commercial payment transactions, the bank normally notifies the beneficiary in a matter of minutes, either by telephone or by some pre-arranged form of electronic communication. See also UCC §4A-404(b) (requiring notice by end of next day).

The rules treating Fedwire orders as automatically and immediately final reflect the willingness of the Federal Reserve to accept the risk that institutions using Fedwire will become insolvent during the course of the day. The Federal Reserve does its best to monitor that risk and to obtain compensation for it (through the daylight overdraft fees it assesses). But if it agrees to send the wire, it guarantees the beneficiary immediately available funds, backing that guarantee with the credit of our nation's central bank. The Federal Reserve's willingness to provide reliably immediate funds gives an important boost to the finalization of large commercial transactions. It is much easier to complete a transaction when irrevocable receipt of the appropriate sum can be verified at the closing table than it would be if the parties had to wait until banks settled their accounts after the close of business at the end of the day.

C. Discharge of the Originator's Underlying Obligation

In most cases, the purpose of a wire-transfer payment is for the originator to discharge some underlying obligation that the originator owes to the beneficiary. Under UCC §4A-406(a), a payment made by wire transfer generally satisfies the underlying obligation of the originator as of the moment that the beneficiary's bank accepts a payment order for the benefit of the beneficiary. That rule reflects the perspective that in common contemplation an obligation is paid when the payor causes a bank to make a binding commitment to the payee. The same perspective underlies the rule in UCC §3-310(a), which discharges a payment obligation when the payee takes a cashier's check, even though acceptance of an ordinary check would only suspend the obligation under UCC §3-310(b)(1).

The cashier's check rule in UCC §3-310(a), however, is not absolute. It discharges the obligation only if the payee accepts the cashier's check for the obligation. Similarly, a wire transfer does not discharge the underlying obligation if the wire transfer is made in a manner that violates the underlying contract specifying the obligation to the beneficiary. UCC §4A-406(b). Of course, the beneficiary suffers no damages if the funds transfer is completed without incident. The point of UCC §4A-406(b), however, is the same as the point of UCC §3-310(a): to ensure that a payee cannot lose an underlying obligation through the failure of a bank to complete a payment transaction if the payee does not accept the bank's commitment to pay as satisfaction of the underlying obligation.

Another interesting problem in the use of wire transfers to satisfy obligations arises when one or more of the receiving banks in the course of a funds transfer deducts charges from the amount of the payment order before sending the order forward. If that occurs, the payment received by the beneficiary will be slightly less than the original amount of the originator's payment order. Given the trivial size of the typical charges in the system (in the tens of dollars) compared to the size of the typical transfer (in the millions of dollars), deductions for those charges are not likely to pose a significant problem for the beneficiary. An opportunistic beneficiary, however, might seize on the slight deficiency in the amount credited to its account as an excuse for claiming that the originator had failed to make payment in a timely manner. The UCC prevents that opportunistic response by providing that the original payment is deemed to discharge the entire obligation, even if deductions for bank charges reduce the actual payment slightly below the amount of the obligation, as long as the originator promptly forwards payment to the beneficiary for the charges. UCC §4A-406(c).

D. Finality of Payment

One feature of wire-transfer payment that makes it attractive to the beneficiary is the extremely limited right of the payor/originator to stop payment. Unlike the checking and credit-card systems, where the payor has days to change its mind, in most cases the time for the payor to cancel a payment authorized by wire transfer is measured in hours or even minutes.

Aleo International, Ltd. v. CitiBank, N.A.

612 N.Y.S.2d 540 (Sup. Ct. N.Y. County 1994)

HERMAN CAHN, Justice.

Plaintiff Aleo International, Ltd. ("Aleo") is a domestic corporation. On October 13, 1992, one of Aleo's vice-presidents, Vera Eyzerovich ("Ms. Eyzerovich"), entered her local CitiBank branch and instructed CitiBank to make an electronic transfer of $284,563 US dollars to the Dresdner Bank in Berlin, Germany, to the account of an individual named Behzad Hermatjou ("Hermatjou"). The documentary evidence submitted shows that at 5:27 p.m. on October 13, 1992, CitiBank sent the payment order to the Dresdner Bank by electronic message. Dresdner Bank later sent CitiBank an electronic message: "Regarding your payment for USD 284.563,00 DD 13.10.92 [indecipherable] f/o Behzad Hermatjou, Pls be advised that we have credited A.M. beneficiary DD 14.10.92 val 16.10.92 with the net amount of USD 284.136,16." This information was confirmed by the Dresdner Bank by fax to CitiBank on July 29, 1993: "Please be advised that on 14.10.92 at 09:59 o'clock Berlin time Dresdner Bank credited the account of Behzad Hermatjou with USD 284.136,16 (USD 284.563,00 less our charges)." It is undisputed that Berlin time is six hours ahead of New York time, and that 9:59 a.m. Berlin time would be 3:59 a.m. New York time. At approximately 9 a.m. on October 14, 1992, Ms. Eyzerovich instructed CitiBank to stop the transfer. When CitiBank did not, this action ensued.

Article 4-A of the Uniform Commercial Code ("UCC") governs electronic "funds transfers." The Official Comment to UCC 4-A-102 states that the provisions of Article 4-A

> are intended to be the exclusive means of determining the rights, duties and liabilities of the affected parties in any situation covered by particular provisions of the Article. Consequently, resort to principles of law or equity outside of Article 4A is not appropriate to create rights, duties and liabilities inconsistent with those stated in this Article.

Article 4-A does not include any provision for a cause of action in negligence. Thus, unless CitiBank's failure to cancel Ms. Eyzerovich's transfer order was not in conformity with Article 4-A, plaintiff Aleo has failed to state a cause of action, and this action must be dismissed.

UCC 4-A-211(2), which governs the cancellation and amendment of payment orders, provides that

> [a] communication by the sender cancelling or amending a payment order is effective to cancel or amend the order if notice of the communication is received at a time and in a manner affording the receiving bank a reasonable opportunity to act on the communication before the bank accepts the payment order.

"Acceptance of Payment Order" is defined by UCC 4-A-209(2), which provides that[]

> a beneficiary's bank accepts a payment order at the earliest of the following times: (a) when the bank (i) pays the beneficiary . . . or (ii) notifies the beneficiary of receipt of the order or that the account of the beneficiary has been credited with respect to the order. . . .

The documentary evidence shows that Hermatjou's account was credited on October 14, 1992 at 9:59 a.m. Berlin time. Thus, as of 3:59 a.m. New York time, the Dresdner Bank "paid the beneficiary" and thereby accepted the payment order. Because this payment and acceptance occurred prior to Ms. Eyzerovich's stop transfer order at 9 a.m. on that day, according to UCC 4-A-211(2), Ms. Eyzerovich's attempt to cancel the payment order was ineffective, and CitiBank may not be held liable for failing to honor it.

In a conversation with the author, counsel for Aleo explained that Ms. Eyzerovich tried to cancel the wire because she discovered that she had described the account incorrectly: The funds were sent to some random account holder at the Berlin bank. As discussed in the next assignment, she theoretically should have been able to recover the money from the account holder, but that would have required a suit in the German courts, an expensive undertaking. The final-payment rule does not always lead to a "correct" result, but the certainty it provides is a benefit to commercial transactions that depend on irrevocable payments.

Problem Set 11

11.1. Your first appointment this week is with Nicholas Nickleby, who tells you he has a problem related to a payment from Walter Bray. Bray owed Nickleby $1,000,000 on a promissory note; the entire sum was due to Nickleby on April 1. Accordingly, on Monday March 30, Bray asked his bank (Gride National Bank) to send a wire transfer to Nickleby's account at Cheeryble State Bank. Gride sent a telex to Cheeryble executing Bray's request on the morning of Tuesday March 31, calling for payment to Nickleby on April 1. Pursuant to a preexisting agreement between Gride and Cheeryble, Cheeryble was entitled to obtain payment for that order from Gride's account at Cheeryble. At the time, that account contained more than enough funds to cover the Nickleby order.

Unfortunately, the Nickleby order was misplaced on the desk of the Cheeryble clerk (Timothy Linkinwater). Accordingly, Cheeryble did not accept or reject the order and did not notify Nickleby that the payment from Bray had come in by wire. On Friday April 3, the Comptroller of the Currency closed Gride and appointed the Federal Deposit Insurance Corporation receiver to supervise the winding up of Gride's affairs. Because Gride had withdrawn all of its funds late Thursday afternoon, no funds remained in the Gride account at Cheeryble.

  a. Nicholas is frustrated that he has not yet been paid. Given the fact that it is now April 6, five days late, can he pursue Bray for the $1,000,000? Alternatively, if he cannot sue Bray for the money, Nickleby wants to know if he is entitled to payment from Cheeryble. UCC §§4A-209(b), 4A-401, 4A-404(a), 4A-406.

b. How would your answers to Nickleby differ if Linkinwater had rejected the order immediately after Cheeryble received it? (You should assume that Linkinwater's rejection of the Nickleby order was not a breach of Cheeryble's agreement with Gride.) UCC §4A-210(a).

c. How would your answers to Nickleby differ if the payment to Cheeryble had been made by Fedwire instead of through an agreement that Cheeryble debit Gride's account with Cheeryble? UCC §§4A-209(b)(2), 4A-209 comment 6, 4A-403(a)(1); Regulation J, §210.29(a).

11.2.   As you walk back into your office after your meeting with Nicholas Nickleby, your secretary tells you that Ben Darrow is holding on the telephone. When you pick up the telephone, he tells you that he is handling the bank's wire-transfer desk today while another officer is on vacation. Because he has had only outgoing wires during the past hour, FSB's working balance at the Federal Reserve has been declining constantly. As Ben is speaking to you, the computer terminal that shows that balance indicates that the current balance is down to $3 million. The reason for Ben's call to you is that Ben has just received a request from another officer to send out a wire for $5 million. When Ben told the officer that FSB did not have enough money to send the wire right now, the officer told Ben that the bank regularly sends wires out for up to $20 million more than it has on deposit at the Federal Reserve. Ben is calling you because he wants to know how FSB possibly could send out a wire paying money that it does not yet have. Can the other officer be correct? Why would the Federal Reserve let FSB do this?

11.3.   Consider the facts of *Aleo*. You will recall that one of Aleo's vice presidents (Ms. Eyzerovich) sent a payment order on October 13 to an account in Dresdner Bank in Germany, that CitiBank (Aleo's bank) transmitted the request to the Dresdner Bank at 5:27 p.m. on October 13, that Dresdner Bank sent a fax confirming acceptance of the order at 3:59 a.m. New York time (9:59 a.m. Dresdner time), and that Ms. Eyzerovich returned to CitiBank to cancel the request at 9 a.m. New York time on the 14th. Would anything have been different if Ms. Eyzerovich had contacted CitiBank's wire-transfer personnel at 9 p.m. on the 13th? You should assume that CitiBank's wire-transfer personnel operate 24 hours a day, 7 days a week, and that they would immediately forward any appropriate notice to the Dresdner Bank.

a. Would Aleo's action cancel the requested funds transfer? UCC §§4A-209, 4A-211, 4A-301.

b. Whatever your answer to question (a), would CitiBank be in a position to cancel the payment order that it sent to Dresdner Bank? UCC §§4A-209, 4A-211.

c. Would your answers change if, in order to get funds to Dresdner Bank, CitiBank had made a transfer through Fedwire to Deutsche Bank, and that it was Deutsche Bank that sent the 5:27 p.m. payment order to Dresdner Bank?

d. Would it matter if Deutsche Bank by 9 p.m. had received the Fedwire transfer but had not yet sent the payment order to Dresdner Bank?

11.4.   At the end of the day, Ben Darrow calls you back to ask your advice about two other mistakes that he fears he made during the course of the day. The first relates to a wire-transfer request that Carol Long submitted, asking the bank to transfer $7.5 million from her checking account. She explained to Ben that she was transferring the funds out of her account at FSB (which does not bear interest) to an account at Wells Fargo that bears interest at 8 percent per annum. Although she submitted the request in time for it to be executed today and although the funds were in her account at the time, Ben nevertheless neglected to send out the wire. As he calls, it is too late to send the wire out until tomorrow morning. He is getting ready to call Carol and apologize, but before he calls her, he wants to know what damages she can seek from the bank. In particular, he wants to know if Carol's damages will be likely to exceed the interest that Ben's bank can earn by investing the funds until the time that it transfers them as Carol requested. Assuming that the bank's agreement with Carol does not address the issue of damages, what do you tell Ben? UCC §§4A-210(b), 4A-506(b), 4A-506 comment 2.

11.5.   Ben Darrow's last problem relates to a payment order that he received by electronic mail this morning (April 6) from Matacora Realtors, an account holder at his bank. The message asked FSB to make a $500,000 payment to a designated account of Jasmine Ball that also is at FSB. Priding himself on his efficiency, Darrow immediately sent back a message accepting the order, deducted the funds from Matacora Realtors' account, and called Jasmine to tell Jasmine that the funds were available. Jasmine promptly came down to FSB and had the funds wired to an account in her name at a bank in Mexico. Darrow became worried a few minutes ago when he received a second message from Matacora Realtors, canceling the Ball payment order; the client apparently had just learned that Ball was going out of business. On reviewing the file, Darrow noticed that the payment order that he received this morning stated at the top: "Transmission date: April 6; Payment date: April 8." Darrow is concerned because he is not sure that he can recover the funds from Ball. Does Darrow have to return the funds to the account of Matacora Realtors? UCC §§4A-209(b) & (d), 4A-211(b), 4A-401, 4A-402(b), (d). (You can leave for the next assignment the question whether Darrow can recover the funds from Ball.)

11.6.   Same facts as Problem 11.5, but now assume that Jasmine Ball's account is at Wessex Bank. UCC §§4A-209, 4A-211, 4A-301, 4A-401, 4A-402.

11.7.   Your last call of the day is from Carl Eben at Riverfront Tools, Inc. (RFT). His problem arises out of a contract with California Pneumatic Tools (CPT). RFT sold CPT $450,000 worth of tools. The contract called for CPT to pay for the tools with a wire transfer to an account at JPMorgan Chase. Notwithstanding that provision in the contract, CPT instead attempted to wire funds to an account of RFT at Texas American Bank (TAB). RFT had accepted payment by transfers into that account in several earlier contracts, but has not been using that account for several months because of Carl's decision to phase out RFT's relationship with TAB.

In any event, Wells Fargo (CPT's bank) accepted CPT's payment order, debited CPT's account, failed to notice the change to JPMorgan Chase, and executed the transfer to TAB. TAB, in turn, notified Carl that it had received the funds for RFT. Carl immediately called CPT to complain, but later that afternoon (before CPT could respond), the Comptroller of the Currency closed TAB and appointed the Federal Deposit Insurance Corporation receiver to supervise the winding up of TAB's affairs. The receiver informed Carl this morning that RFT probably would obtain very little from the account and certainly would be unable to obtain the entire $450,000. Carl wants to know if RFT still has a claim against CPT. What do you tell him? If he does have a claim against CPT, does CPT have any remedy? UCC §§4A-209(b)(1), 4A-402(c) & (d), 4A-404(a), 4A-406(b).

Assignment 12:   Error in Wire-Transfer Transactions

Because wire transfers are the most common choice for large transfers of funds, losses on wire-transfer systems are particularly serious. Thus, wire-transfer systems exhibit some of the most sophisticated mechanisms for limiting losses. This assignment introduces that topic with discussion of nonfraudulent errors. The following assignment continues with a discussion of some more complex loss issues about fraud and system failure.

As the *Aleo* case in the previous assignment suggests, the wire-transfer system is just as vulnerable to mistaken payments as any other payment system. The mistake common to the wire-transfer system is a transfer that delivers funds to a beneficiary contrary to the subjective intent of the originator. Even without any fraudulent intent, that can happen for two general reasons: because of a mistaken description of the order by the originator or because of an inadvertent alteration of the order by the originator's bank or one of the other parties sending that order through the system. Whenever such an error occurs, the originator will want to recover the funds that it paid to the originator's bank. To see how the system responds to the originator's desire to recover those funds, it is useful to distinguish between claims against parties in the system (the originator's bank, some intermediary bank, or the beneficiary's bank) and claims against the party that received the funds (the de facto beneficiary).

A.   Recovering from Parties in the System

The wire-transfer system is not for the fainthearted or careless. For the most part, it assigns responsibility for errors based on the simple and unforgiving principle that each party bears responsibility for its own errors. That principle might seem common, but wire-transfer systems apply it more vigorously than most analogous areas of the law. Most important, in the wire-transfer system, that principle carries with it a strong corollary: Parties that participate in a transaction after the error have no obligation to discover or correct an error that one party made earlier in the transaction.

Thus, a party that makes a mistake in a payment order has little or no recourse against later parties in the system that faithfully execute the mistaken order. That is true however easy it might have been for them to detect the mistake, however obvious the mistake might have been. Instead, Article 4A obligates the sender to pay any payment order that the receiving bank executes as instructed. UCC §4A-402(b), (c). To understand how unusual that rule is, consider the wide variety of contributory negligence rules in the checking system that give a bank potential exposure for failing to notice errors by a check writer. See, e.g., UCC §§3-404(d), 3-405(b), 3-406(b), 4-406(e). If the wire-transfer rule sounds harsh, it is worth recalling that Article 4A has no application to systems designed primarily for use by natural persons. UCC §4A-108; EFTA §§903(5), 903(6)(B).

1. Errors by the Originator

As the foregoing discussion suggests, wire-transfer systems generally hold an originator responsible for any mistakes that it makes in describing its order to the originator's bank. That rule applies even if the error is made not by the originator itself, but by some third-party communications network, on the theory that (at least as between the originator and the originator's bank) the originator is responsible for the communications network that it uses. UCC §4A-206(a).

The system's firm commitment to hold originators to a high standard of care is not limited to rules that protect parties that comply with the literal terms of erroneous orders. In some cases, the originator also is burdened with losses that arise through execution of ambiguous orders. For example, a common payment-order error (apparently the problem in the *Aleo* case) is to identify a beneficiary by name, but (because of an inadvertent typographical error) to call for payment to an account of some other (random) party. Ordinary rules of interpretation would give preference to the name of the payee over the numerical designation of the account. See, e.g., UCC §3-114 ("If an instrument contains contradictory terms, . . . words prevail over numbers."). The wire-transfer system, by contrast, allows the beneficiary's bank to rely on the number indicated in the order and deposit the money into that account, even if the identified beneficiary does not own the designated account. UCC §4A-207(b), (c); Regulation J, §210.27(b). The same rule applies to errors that the originator makes in describing the beneficiary's bank. See UCC §4A-208(b) (authorizing receiving bank to rely on routing number to identify beneficiary's bank, even if order also identifies beneficiary's bank by name); Regulation J, §210.27(a) (same rule for Federal Reserve).

Indeed, the case that follows suggests that the system affirmatively discourages any efforts to find such errors by people in the latter phase of wire-transfer transactions.

Phil & Kathy's Inc. v. Safra National Bank

595 F. Supp. 2d 330 (S.D.N.Y. 2009)

SAND, Chief Judge.

Plaintiff Phil & Kathy's, Inc. filed this suit seeking to recover $1,500,000 it claims was erroneously deposited into an account and disbursed to a third party by defendant Safra National Bank. Defendant's motion to dismiss . . . calls on this Court to determine whether upon a bank's receipt of a payment order to a non-identifiable or nonexistent customer the order is void by operation of law or whether the recipient bank is entitled to act pursuant to an amendment of the order. The Court finds New York's Uniform Commercial Code (UCC) §4-A-211(4) dispositive because it allows a recipient bank to await and act upon a timely amendment of a payment order, and accordingly dismisses the complaint.

JURISDICTION AND FACTUAL BACKGROUND

Plaintiff is an Illinois corporation in the business of repackaging and selling prescription drugs. Defendant is a national banking association with its main office in New York City, with no branches in Illinois. . . .

On July 2, 2003, plaintiff's authorized agent, Phil Giannino, went to the bank maintaining plaintiff's account in Illinois, Harris Trust and Savings Bank. Giannino asked Harris Bank to wire $1,500,000 from plaintiff's account to defendant, who was to put the money into a designated beneficiary account. The payment order requested by Giannino identified the beneficiary account's owner as "Banco Do Brasil SA/Proteknika Do Brasil." Harris processed the request for the payment order that same day. The beneficiary account was misidentified, making payment to the beneficiary impossible. Plaintiff was made aware of this on July 3, 2003. Banco do Brasil advised plaintiff to change the name on the payment order to "Blue Vale" in order to have the payment order properly processed. Giannino returned to Harris on July 3 and made a second $1,500,000 payment order, this time to Blue Vale. After Giannino left Harris Bank on July 3 an agent for Harris Bank sent the first of three urgent wires to defendant asking it to amend the original payment order so that Blue Vale would receive the payment.

Defendant received the second payment order, and processed it on the next business day, which was July 7, 2003 due to the Independence Day holiday. The second order was successfully credited to Blue Vale's account by defendant.

On July 9, 2003, [within] five business days [of] the placement of the initial payment order on July 2, defendant credited Blue Vale with the $1,500,000 as specified by the wire orders amending the initial payment order. On June 26, 2006, plaintiff instituted suit in the Southern District of New York to recover from defendant the excess $1,500,000 in addition to costs and interest. Plaintiff contends that, because no beneficiary was identifiable by defendant on July 2, the payment order was cancelled by operation of law. Defendant argues that UCC §4-A-211(4) gives banks a five business day window to allow amendments to payment orders, and that the payments only become void by operation of law after the end of five days.

. . . The laws of the location of the recipient bank govern in wire transfer cases; in this case New York law applies. N.Y.U.C.C. §4-A-507(1)(a) ("The rights and obligations between the sender of a payment order and the receiving bank are governed by the law of the jurisdiction in which the receiving bank is located.").

DISCUSSION

Though plaintiff states no specific statutory or common law basis for the suit, it is clear that the facts of this case fall within the provisions of Article 4A of the

UCC. UCC Article 4A is a comprehensive scheme enacted to govern electronic wire transfers of the sort engaged in here. See official comment to N.Y.U.C.C. §4-A-101. Additionally, "parties whose conflict arises out of a funds transfer should look first and foremost to Article 4-A for guidance in bringing and resolving their claims." Sheerbonnet, Ltd. v. Am. Express Bank, Ltd., 951 F. Supp. 403, 407 (S.D.N.Y. 1995). Accordingly this Court will view the facts of this case in light of the UCC.

The processing scheme for an ordinary payment order is set forth in Article 4-A. The statute is triggered by placement of a "payment order" with the receiving bank, in this case defendant Safra National Bank. See N.Y.U.C.C. §4-A-104(1). A "payment order" is an order to the recipient bank to pay a fixed amount of money to a beneficiary. See N.Y.U.C.C. §4-A-103(1)(a). The payment order is given to the recipient bank by "the sender," here, Harris Bank. See N.Y.U.C.C. §4-A-103(1)(e). A recipient bank is unable to accept payment "if the beneficiary of the payment order does not have an account with the receiving bank. . . ." N.Y.U.C.C. §4-A-209(3). It follows that if the beneficiary's "name, bank account number or other identification of the beneficiary refers to a nonexistent or unidentifiable person or account, no person has rights as a beneficiary of the order and acceptance of the order cannot occur." N.Y.U.C.C. §4-A-207(1). But this does not mean that a payment order's unidentifiable beneficiary serves to eradicate the order itself, as the order can be freely amended or cancelled. N.Y.U.C.C. §4-A-211(2) ("[A] communication by the sender canceling or amending a payment order is effective to cancel or amend the order if notice of the communication is received at a time and in a manner affording the receiving bank a reasonable opportunity to act on the communication" before acceptance.). Additionally, "[a]n unaccepted payment order is cancelled by operation of law at the close of the fifth funds-transfer business day of the receiving bank after the execution date or payment date of the order." N.Y.U.C.C. §4-A-211(4).

Applying the UCC to the facts of this case, it is clear that defendant dealt with the two payment orders correctly. The second payment order followed the usual course of acceptance and dis[bu]rsal, and is not in contest. As for the first payment order it is clear that defendant was in receipt of it on July 2 but that the order had an unidentifiable beneficiary. Accordingly defendant could not accept the payment order of July 2 and pay out the fixed sum. However plaintiff is incorrect in asserting that because there was no identifiable beneficiary the payment order of July 2 became a nullity. The UCC clearly states that a sender may amend or cancel a payment order prior to acceptance. See N.Y.U.C.C. §4-A-211(2). Acting as the sender, Harris Bank wired defendant three separate times asking it to amend the payment order of July 2, which it did. Harris Bank could have cancelled the first payment order or allowed the five day period to lapse. Instead Harris chose to amend the order. Once the order was amended to include an identifiable beneficiary, Blue Vale, defendant could accept the payment order and credit Blue Vale with the fixed amount of money plaintiff desired to give it. The UCC gives banks five business days to accept a payment order. See N.Y.U.C.C. §4-A-211(4). Defendant complied with the UCC by accepting the first payment order on July 9, which was [within] five business days [of] July 2. Similarly, defendant acted properly under the UCC when it accepted the second payment order of July 3 and credited Blue Vale with the additional $1,500,000.

Plaintiff's claim that the first payment order was a nullity ignores the language and structure of the UCC which deals logically and chronologically with what may occur when an initial payment order improperly sets forth the identity of the beneficiaries and when these events may take place. The claim that the first order is an unamendable nullity simply ignores the language of N.Y.U.C.C. §4-A-211(2) and its obvious purpose. Equally unavailing is plaintiff's claim that it suffered prejudice because the defendant did not immediately apprise it of the original error. Defendant had no duty to alert plaintiff of the error, as the UCC[-]provided sequence for amendment or cancellation does not require the recipient bank to act. In fact plaintiff was apprised of the error the day after the original order was sent when Blue Vale notified it that the money had yet to be dis[bu]rsed. At this point a distinct second payment order was placed, but this had no effect on the initial unaccepted payment order which plaintiff remained free to cancel or amend at any point prior to the expiration of the five day window provided for by the UCC. Plaintiff paid out $1,500,000 more than it wanted to when its initial payment order was amended by Harris Bank and plaintiff issued a second $1,500,000 payment order, but this excess outlay is not the result of defendant's conduct, which comported entirely with the UCC.

CONCLUSION

Because the facts as alleged in the complaint show that defendant complied with all applicable provisions of the UCC, plaintiff is unable to prove any set of facts that would entitle it to relief. Therefore, defendant's motion to dismiss for failure to state a claim is granted.

The error might be simple, but the case makes an important point. In general, the simple per se rules that obviate any need for the receiving bank to exercise judgment in interpreting a poorly or erroneously crafted payment order do more than shift losses back to the originator. They also improve the efficiency of the system in two ways. First, they give originators (and the banks that want their business) a strong incentive to develop systems that eradicate errors before funds-transfer orders enter the wire-transfer system. Second, they limit the costs that a receiving bank needs to expend to operate a wire-transfer system. A system that does not require the exercise of judgment, but only rote mechanical responses, makes it safe for banks to hire employees (and program machines) that respond mechanically. Ideally, such a system would lower the level of negligence by originators and their banks, which bear the losses of the errors they make.

Article 4A does contain one exception to the rule absolving later parties in the system from noticing and correcting errors that an originator makes in formulating and transmitting payment orders. That exception, however, applies only when a bank has agreed that it will take specified steps to identify errors. UCC §4A-205 covers the common situation in which an originator and originator's bank have agreed on a security procedure for the detection of errors. When a bank has made such an agreement, UCC §4A-205 alters the standard "your error, your loss" rule in any case in which the bank fails to comply with the required procedure, if compliance with the procedure would have revealed the error. UCC §4A-205(a)(1). Indeed, at first glance, paragraphs (2) and (3) of UCC §4A-205(a) suggest that the originator is excused from paying all erroneous orders. The second paragraph of comment 1 makes it clear, however, that UCC §4A-205 provides an excuse for the originator only if the parties have agreed on an error-detection procedure and only if the bank's compliance with that procedure would have detected the error. UCC §4A-205 comment 1.

To get a sense for how that works in practice, consider the common procedure usually referred to as a "four-party callback." That procedure requires the involvement of four individuals: (1) the originator's employee that places a payment order; (2) the bank employee that receives the payment order from the originator's employee; (3) another bank employee, who places a call back to the originator, seeking an employee different from the one that placed the order in the first instance; and (4) that second employee of the originator. If the originator can show that such a telephone call would have caught the mistake—because the second originator employee would have noticed the error in the order—UCC §4A-205 shifts any loss from the originator to the receiving bank.

2.   *Errors in the System*

Originators are not the only parties that make mistakes in wire-transfer systems. On the contrary, several of the leading cases involve errors by banks that failed to comply with the instructions they received from the originator. As you should expect by this point, Article 4A generally imposes the losses from those errors on the party that makes the error. But establishing rules to govern those errors is considerably more difficult than establishing rules for originator-error cases because providing a remedy requires at least partial reversal of the wire-transfer transaction. The emphasis on finality in the wire-transfer system complicates any effort to reverse transactions.

To understand how UCC Article 4A responds to those errors, it is useful to divide the potential errors into two classes: those that send the beneficiary excessive funds and those that send the beneficiary funds that are inadequate or untimely.

(a)   Sending Excessive Funds.   A bank could send excessive funds in a variety of ways. The most obvious is a simple mistake in the amount of the transfer; the bank could send the money at the correct time to the correct place, but set the amount of the transfer too high. The same problem, however, could arise for at least two other reasons. In one situation, the bank could respond to a payment order from its customer by sending two or more wires, thus sending two (or more) times the appropriate amount of money. Finally, the bank could respond to a payment order from its customer by sending the money to the wrong party.

The remedy for that type of error has two parts. First, because the originator's obligation under UCC §4A-402 is limited to the payment order that it sends, the originator is obligated to the originator's bank only for the correct amount of its order that the originator's bank has executed. UCC §4A-402(b), (c). Thus, in the excessive-amount and duplicate-order cases, the originator is obligated only for the amount designated in its payment order. UCC §4A-303(a). In the incorrect beneficiary case, the originator is obligated for nothing because it sent no payment order calling for payment to that beneficiary. UCC §4A-303(c).

The second part of the remedy recognizes the reality that the originator frequently (almost always) will pay for the payment order before the originator's bank executes it, through mechanisms that authorize the originator's bank to remove funds from the originator's account to pay for payment orders that the originator's bank sends on behalf of the originator. Accordingly, to remedy an excessive transfer, the system must require the originator's bank to refund to the originator the money that the originator's bank took as compensation for the order. UCC §4A-402(d) imposes that obligation on the originator's bank. As part of that obligation, the originator's bank also must pay interest on the funds from the date on which it initially paid the funds. UCC §4A-402(d); see UCC §4A-506 (describing rate at which interest accrues for purposes of UCC Article 4A). Finally, in some cases, the originator's bank might be able to recover its loss from the party to which it incorrectly sent the funds. The last section of this assignment addresses that topic.

(b) Sending Inadequate Funds. The converse problem occurs when the bank fails to send adequate funds to the beneficiary. Again, that problem could arise for several reasons, starting from a simple error in setting the amount of the payment order sent to the beneficiary. An inadequate-funds error also would occur in the incorrect-beneficiary scenario mentioned above. For example, if the bank mistakenly sends funds to Cliff Janeway when it was supposed to send them to Archie Moon, then it has the problem of an excessive transfer to Cliff at the same time that it has the problem of an inadequate transfer to Archie. Finally, the bank's error could be nothing more than delay: The bank sends the correct order, but fails to send it in a timely manner.

The response to inadequate-funds errors is analogous to the response to excessive-funds errors. First, the originator is obligated only for the amount of the transfer that the bank actually sends. Thus, even though UCC §4A-202 generally obligates an originator to pay the originator's bank the entire amount of its payment order, the originator is not obligated to the originator's bank beyond the amount that the originator's bank transmits. UCC §4A-303(b). The UCC does, however, permit the originator's bank to correct the error by sending a second wire that makes up the deficiency in the original wire. If the originator's bank sends a wire adequately supplementing the deficient wire, the originator remains obligated for the entire amount of its original order. UCC §4A-303(b).

As a corollary to the rule limiting the originator's obligation to funds actually sent by its bank, the originator's bank must return to the originator any funds that the originator's bank collected to reimburse itself for the payment order beyond the amount that it actually sent. UCC §4A-402(d). As with excessive-funds transfers, the originator's bank must pay interest on any funds that it improperly collected. UCC §4A-402(d).

One final problem, unique to the inadequate-funds error, arises from the originator's underlying obligation to the beneficiary. An error by the originator's bank that sends excessive funds to the beneficiary causes no difficulty for the originator as against the beneficiary because the excessive-funds transfer satisfies the obligation that motivated the originator to send the payment order. When the originator's bank sends funds that are too little or too late, however, the bank's error often will cause further damage to the originator. That damage can occur either because the bank has retained funds of the originator's longer than it should have or because the failure of the originator to make the payment to the beneficiary causes a default on the originator's obligation to the beneficiary.

The UCC includes three separate rules to deal with those damages. First, if the only problem is that the bank sent the funds later than it should have, then the bank must pay interest to compensate for its retention of the funds beyond the period during which it should have held them. UCC §4A-305(a). Second, if the bank fails to correct the error — the bank never completes the originator's payment order — then the bank must compensate the originator not only for interest losses, but also for the originator's expenses in the transaction. UCC §4A-305(b), (d).

The last rule deals with consequential damages, the most common of which would be the damages that the originator suffered from a default on its obligation to the beneficiary caused by a mistake of the originator's bank. For obvious reasons, the consequential damages for failure to make a wiretransfer payment in a timely manner could be quite large. Accordingly, they present a crucial issue for parties using wire-transfer systems. It is important for originators to protect themselves from the losses from mistakes by their bank. Conversely, it is important for banks to protect themselves from large and unforeseeable damage awards. Indeed, one of the principal motivations for the drafting of Article 4A was the decision in Evra Corp. v. Swiss Bank Corp., 673 F.2d 951 (7th Cir. 1982) (per Posner, J.), suggesting the possibility of such damages. The UCC adopts a default rule that bars consequential damages in the absence of an express written agreement. UCC §4A-305(c). Given the unforeseeable nature of possible damages, standard agreements ordinarily do not allow originators an unqualified right to consequential damages. Rather, they either bar such damages entirely or limit recoveries to some specified and foreseeable damage amount (such as the late charges imposed by the intended beneficiary).

(c) Bank-Statement Rule. The last important part of the rules governing the originator's recovery for errors in the transmission of its orders is a bank-statement rule analogous to the rules in EFTA §909 (for debit cards) and UCC §4-406 (for checks). The wire-transfer bank-statement rule operates in two tiers. First, UCC §4A-304 generally imposes on the originator a duty of ordinary care to review statements regarding wire-transfer transactions. If the originator fails to use ordinary care to review those statements, then it cannot recover

interest on any amounts that the bank is obligated to refund to it under UCC
§4A-402(d). The UCC does not give the originator a specific amount of time
within which it can act to preserve its rights. Instead, it gives the bank a safe
harbor by stating that any originator challenge more than 90 days after receipt
of the statement is too late. UCC §4A-304. Moreover, comment 2 to UCC
§4A-204 makes it clear that a customer can lose its entitlement to interest earlier than 90 days if the circumstances indicate that the originator would have
discovered the error sooner if it had reviewed the bank statements with ordinary care. Finally, for payment orders transmitted to Federal Reserve banks,
the Federal Reserve has issued a regulation establishing 30 calendar days as a
reasonable time. Regulation J, §210.28(c).

The second tier of the rule precludes the originator from challenging any
debit from its account for a wire-transfer order unless the originator challenges
the transaction within one year of the date that the originator received notice
of the transaction from the originator's bank. UCC §4A-505. That rule is much
more onerous than the 90-day rule discussed in the preceding paragraph
because it bars the originator's claim to recover the principal amount of the
transfer, a much more serious consequence than a bar on recovering interest
losses. In one of the most important decisions under Article 4A, the New York
Court of Appeals held in the opinion that follows that banks cannot (as they
theretofore had done with great regularity) shorten that one-year period by
contract with their customer.

Regatos v. North Fork Bank
5 N.Y.3d 395 (2005)

ROSENBLATT, J.

The United States Court of Appeals for the Second Circuit, by certified questions,
asks us whether a commercial bank customer can recover funds that the bank
improperly transferred out of his account, even though he did not notify the bank
of the unauthorized transfer until well after the time limit stated in his account
agreement. This issue requires us to decide whether the one-year period of repose
in our Uniform Commercial Code §4-A-505 may be modified by agreement. We
also resolve whether UCC 4-A-204(1) requires the bank actually to send the customer notice of an unauthorized transfer in order to trigger the running of a "reasonable time" within the meaning of that section, or whether a private agreement
to hold a customer's mail can allow constructive notice to start that period. These
are questions of first impression in this Court, and apparently in every other court
of last resort in states that have adopted the relevant statutes.

In accord with the United States District Court for the Southern District of
New York, we hold for the customer on both questions. The one-year period of
repose in UCC 4-A-505, governing the customer's time in which to notify the bank
of the unauthorized transfer, may not be modified by contract. Furthermore, both
the one-year statute of repose and the "reasonable time" referred to in section
4-A-204(1), which determines the customer's ability to recover interest on the
misallocated money, begin to run when the customer receives actual notice of the
improper transfer.

I.

Tomáz Mendes Regatos held a commercial account with Commercial Bank of New York, the predecessor to North Fork Bank. His agreement with the bank required him to notify the bank of any irregularity regarding his account within 15 days after the bank statement and items were first mailed or made available to him. The agreement did not provide for notice to him of electronic funds transfers, except to the extent those transfers appeared on his monthly statements. The bank adopted a practice of holding Regatos's bank statements rather than mailing them to him, and expected him to request the statements when he wanted to see them.

On March 23, 2001, the bank received a funds transfer order from someone it believed to be Regatos, but failed to follow agreed security procedures to confirm the order. Without authorization, the bank then transferred $450,000 out of his account. On April 6, 2001, the bank received another transfer order, again failed to follow its security procedures and without authorization transferred an additional $150,000 out of his account. Together, these transfers represented most of the value of the account.

Regatos did not learn of the unauthorized transfers until he checked his accumulated account statements on August 9, 2001. The transfers were reflected on statements issued on March 23, 2001 and April 25, 2001, but the bank held these statements until he asked for them, following its standard practice in relation to him. He informed the bank of the unauthorized transfers on the day he learned of them, August 9, 2001.

When the bank refused to reimburse Regatos for the lost funds, he sued in the United States District Court for the Southern District of New York. In a comprehensive, well-reasoned opinion, District Judge Shira Scheindlin denied the bank's motion for summary judgment . . . .

A federal jury found in favor of Regatos. Following UCC 4-A-204, the court awarded him both the principal ($600,000) and the interest from the date the bank improperly transferred the funds.

The bank appealed, and the United States Court of Appeals for the Second Circuit determined that the legal issues necessary to dispose of the case were novel, important questions of New York law. The Second Circuit certified to this Court, and we accepted, the following questions:

> [1] Can the one-year statute of repose established by New York U.C.C. 4-A-505 be varied by agreement? If so, are there any minimum limits on the variation thereof (such as "reasonable time") that estop [the bank] from denying Regatos recovery in this case? . . .

> [2] In the absence of agreement, does New York U.C.C. Article 4-A require actual notice, rather than merely constructive notice? If so, can this requirement be altered by agreement of the parties and was such achieved here?

We answer the first part of the first question "no," rendering the second part academic. We answer the first part of the second question "yes" and the second part of the second question "no."

II.

UCC 4-A-204 establishes a bank's basic obligation to make good on unauthorized and ineffective transfers and, with one exception, forbids any variation of that obligation by agreement. . . .

   . . .
. . . UCC 4-A-505 provides that

> [i]f a receiving bank has received payment from its customer with respect to a payment order issued in the name of the customer as sender and accepted by the bank, and the customer received notification reasonably identifying the order, the customer is precluded from asserting that the bank is not entitled to retain the payment unless the customer notifies the bank of the customer's objection to the payment within one year after the notification was received by the customer.

Regatos argues that the one-year statutory period is an integral part of the bank's "obligation . . . to refund payment" under UCC 4-A-204(1) and so, pursuant to UCC 4-A-204(2), "may not . . . be varied by agreement." The bank and its supporting amici point out that the notice provision is in section 4-A-505, not section 4-A-204(1), and rely on UCC 4-A-501(1), which declares that "[e]xcept as otherwise provided . . . the rights and obligations of a party to a funds transfer may be varied by agreement of the affected party." The bank maintains that the customer's duty to notify the bank of the error before recovering misallocated funds is an "obligation" separate from that created by section 4-A-204(1) and therefore modifiable.

We agree with Regatos's reading of the statutes. In context, the policy behind article 4-A encourages banks to adopt appropriate security procedures. Only when a commercially reasonable security procedure is in place (or has been offered to the customer) may the bank disclaim its liability for unauthorized transfers (UCC 4-A-202). Permitting banks to vary the notice period by agreement would reduce the effectiveness of the statute's one-year period of repose as an incentive for banks to create and follow security procedures.

While the issue is close, we cannot accept the bank's argument that the customer's responsibility to notify the bank of its error is modifiable. UCC 4-A-204(1) states that "[t]he bank is not entitled to any recovery from the customer on account of a failure by the customer to give notification as stated in this section." Accordingly, a bank has an obligation to refund the principal regardless of notice, provided such notice is given within one year in accordance with UCC 4-A-505 (see 3 James J. White and Robert S. Summers, Uniform Commercial Code §22-4 [4th ed.]). Moreover, as the District Court pointed out, section 4-A-505 (the one-year notice period) appears in the "Miscellaneous Provisions" part of the article, not the parts touching upon substantive rights and obligations. The period of repose in section 4-A-505 is essentially a jurisdictional attribute of the "rights and obligations" contained in UCC 4-A-204(1). To vary the period of repose would, in effect, impair the customer's section 4-A-204(1) right to a refund, a modification that section 4-A-204(2) forbids.

Article 4-A was intended, in significant part, to promote finality of banking operations and to give the bank relief from unknown liabilities of potentially indefinite duration (see Banque Worms v. BankAmerica Intl., 77 N.Y.2d 362, 371 [1991]). This legislative purpose does not suggest that those interests alter (or should alter) the statute's fine-tuned balance between the customer and the bank as to who should bear the burden of unauthorized transfers.

Therefore, we hold that the one-year repose period in section 4-A-505 cannot be modified by agreement. By notifying the bank on August 9, 2001, the day he received actual notice, and four or five months after the statements were available, Regatos acted either way within the year-long period of repose. This clearly satisfied the statutory requirement and he is entitled to recover at least his $600,000 principal.

III.

The Second Circuit next asks whether actual notice is required under article 4-A (or whether mere constructive notice will do) and, consequently, whether Regatos is also entitled to recover interest on the misdirected funds.

The bank made Regatos's monthly account statements available for his review, but waited for him to request them rather than send them to him. According to its agreed security procedures, the bank was to reach him by telephone immediately after it received a funds transfer order, to confirm that he had actually authorized the transfer. Other than that call, which the jury found was never made, the only notice available to him would come from his own perusal of the account statements.

In his earlier dealings with the bank, Regatos tended to check his statements regularly. By 2001, however, he reviewed the bank's statements only intermittently. In that year, he asked to see his statements some time before the unauthorized transfer on March 23, 2001 and did not ask again until August 9, 2001, after the bank had generated statements on March 23, 2001 and April 25, 2001. These two statements revealed the unauthorized transfers, but the bank continued to hold the statements until Regatos asked for them. As discussed, he immediately notified the bank of its error when he discovered it on August 9, 2001.

The bank argues that Regatos obtained constructive notice of the transfers on March 23, 2001 and April 25, 2001, when the statements disclosing them were first generated. UCC 4-A-204 requires a customer seeking to recover interest on funds lost due to an unauthorized transfer "to notify the bank of the relevant facts within a reasonable time not exceeding ninety days after the date the customer received notification from the bank that the order was accepted." We agree with Regatos that this requirement may not be waived.

Under the bank's reading of the statute, an agreed 15-day notice period could run before a bank statement was even available for the customer's review. If the burden of checking whether the bank has wrongfully transferred funds out of the customer's account were to fall on the customer, as it would under a constructive notice interpretation, the customer's duty to check would presumably arise as soon as the data became available for review. In electronic funds transfers, the bank would be able to inform an inquiring customer of the transfer well before the formal monthly statement is compiled. Conceivably, the crucial information could be sitting in the bank's possession for weeks, awaiting discovery by the customer. If the customer did not inquire, and the agreement's 15-day period ran, the customer would lose the transferred funds even though the error was entirely the bank's. This seems to us both the logical consequence of a constructive notice system and an unreasonable view of actual banking relationships. Because interpretation of the UCC is always conducted with an eye toward business realities and the predictable consequences of legal rules, we reject a statutory interpretation that conflicts with reasonable business practices.

Policy arguments support an actual notice requirement. An invariable statutory rule provides a bright line for banks and their customers, bringing reliability and certainty to these dealings. Constructive notice is far less exact, leaving too much room for varying interpretation and disorder. If the bank had complied with its security procedures, it would have called Regatos the same day it received each purported transfer order, thereby providing him with actual notice of the events.

Even where customers enter "hold mail" agreements with their banks, the actual notice rule still applies. Just as the one-year notice limitation is an inherent aspect of the customer's right to recover unauthorized payments, the actual notice requirement provides the bedrock for the exercise of that right. Permitting banks to enforce "agreements" to accept constructive notice would defeat article 4-A's guarantee of recovery for unauthorized payments.

In response to the second certified question, we answer that article 4-A requires actual notice, and that this requirement cannot be varied by a "hold mail" agreement, neither to begin the statute of repose, nor to begin "reasonable time" under the account agreement. Regatos notified the bank of his loss within an indisputably reasonable time after receiving actual notice, and is therefore entitled to recover the interest on his lost principal (UCC 4-A-204).

Accordingly, the first part of certified question 1 should be answered in the negative and the second part not answered as unnecessary, and the first part of certified question 2 should be answered in the affirmative and the second part in the negative.

---

3.   Circuity of Recovery

Grain Traders, Inc. v. CitiBank, N.A.

160 F.3d 97 (2d Cir. 1998)

JOHN M. WALKER, JR., Circuit Judge.

Plaintiff Grain Traders, Inc., ("Grain Traders") appeals from the April 16, 1997, judgment granting summary judgment for defendant CitiBank, N.A., ("CitiBank") and dismissing Grain Traders's diversity action brought under Article 4-A of New York's Uniform Commercial Code ("Article 4-A") and principles of common law seeking a refund from CitiBank for an alleged uncompleted electronic funds transfer.

BACKGROUND

Grain Traders, in order to make a payment of $310,000 to Claudio Goidanich Kraemer ("Kraemer"), initiated a funds transfer on December 22, 1994, by issuing a payment order to its bank, Banco de Credito Nacional ("BCN"), that stated[:]

> WE HEREBY AUTHORIZE YOU DEBIT OUR ACCOUNT NR.509364 FOR THE AMOUNT OF US $310,000.00 AND TRANSFER TO:
>
> BANQUE DU CREDIT ET INVESTISSEMENT LTD. ACCOUNT 36013997 AT CITIBANK NEW YORK IN FAVOUR OF BANCO EXTRADER S.A. ACCOUNT NR. 30114—BENEFICIARY CLAUDIO GOIDANICH KRAEMER—UNDER FAX ADVISE TO BANCO EXTRADER NR. 00541-318 0057/318-0184 AT. DISTEFANO/M. FLIGUEIRA.

Thus the transfer, as instructed by Grain Traders, required BCN to debit Grain Traders's account at BCN in the amount of $310,000, and then to issue a payment order to CitiBank. That payment order, in turn, was to require CitiBank to debit $310,000 from BCN's account at CitiBank and to credit that amount to the account that Banque du Credit et Investissement Ltd. ("BCIL") maintained at Citi-Bank. CitiBank, in turn, was to issue a payment order to BCIL instructing it to transfer, by unspecified means, $310,000 to Banco Extrader, S.A. ("Extrader"). Extrader was then to credit the $310,000 to the account maintained at Extrader by Kraemer.

BCN duly carried out Grain Traders's instructions. CitiBank, in turn, executed BCN's payment order by debiting $310,000 from BCN's account at CitiBank, crediting that amount to BCIL's account at CitiBank, and issuing a payment order to BCIL concerning the further transfers.

Both BCIL and Extrader suspended payments at some point after CitiBank executed the payment order. BCIL apparently began closing its offices on December 31, 1994, and its banking license was revoked in July of 1995. Similarly, Extrader became insolvent sometime in late December of 1994 or early January of 1995. On December 28, 1994, apparently at Grain Traders's request, BCN contacted CitiBank and requested cancellation of its payment order and return of the amount of the payment order. The message sent by BCN stated:

> REGARDING OUR PAYMENT ORDER FROM 12/22/94 FOR USD 310,000 TO BANCO EXTRADER S.A. ACCT. NO. 30114 F/O BANQUE DE CREDIT ET INVESTISSEMENT LTD. ACCT NO. 36013997 F/C TO CLAUDIO GOLDANICH [SIC] KRAEMER. PLEASE NOTE THAT WE ARE REQUESTING FUNDS BACK AS SOON AS POSSIBLE.
>
> YOUR IMMEDIATE ATTENTION TO THIS MATTER IS APPRECIATED.

CitiBank sought authorization from BCIL to debit the amount that had been credited to its account on December 22, 1994, and, after several unsuccessful attempts to contact BCIL, received a message on January 3, 1995, from BCIL that purportedly authorized the debit. CitiBank asserts that it was at this juncture that it determined that BCIL had exceeded its credit limitations and placed the account on a "debit no-post" status, meaning no further debits would be posted to the account. CitiBank refused BCN's request to cancel the payment order, stating:

> RE: YOUR PAYMENT [ORDER] . . . WE ARE UNABLE TO RETURN FUNDS AS BNF [SIC] BANK HAS AN INSUFFICIENT BALANCE IN THEIR ACCOUNT. FOR FURTHER INFORMATION WE SUGGEST THAT YOU CONTACT THEM DIRECTLY. WE CLOSE OUR FILE.

In November of 1995, Grain Traders filed this action seeking a refund from CitiBank pursuant to U.C.C. §§4-A-402(4), 4-A-209, 4-A-301, 4-A-305, and [1-304], as well as common law theories of conversion and money had and received. Grain Traders alleges that the transfer was never completed—i.e., Extrader never credited Kraemer's account for the $310,000. Grain Traders further claims that the reason the transfer was not completed was because CitiBank had already placed BCIL's account on a "hold for funds" status before it credited the $310,000 intended for Kraemer to BCIL's account. By making the credit to BCIL's allegedly frozen account, Grain Traders contends, CitiBank improperly used the funds to offset BCIL's indebtedness to it and prevented BCIL from withdrawing the funds to complete the transfer.

Grain Traders moved for summary judgment on its Article 4-A claim. CitiBank cross-moved for summary judgment on the grounds that Grain Traders had failed to state a claim under Article 4-A, could not establish its common law claims, and that its common law claims were, in any event, pre-empted by Article 4-A. The district court denied summary judgment to Grain Traders and granted summary judgment in favor of CitiBank. Grain Traders now appeals.

DISCUSSION

In its opinion, the district court held that . . . Section 402 of Article 4-A established a cause of action only by a sender against its receiving bank, thus Grain Traders, who was a sender only with respect to BCN, had sued the wrong bank . . . . On appeal, Grain Traders argues that the district court erred in dismissing its claim under U.C.C. §4-A-402 . . . . For the following reasons, we affirm the district court's judgment. . . .

Article 4-A of the U.C.C. governs the procedures, rights, and liabilities arising out of commercial electronic funds transfers. . . .

[A]s noted by the district court, "funds are 'transferred' through a series of debits and credits to a series of bank accounts." A "sender" is defined as "the person giving the instruction [directly] to the receiving bank," and a "receiving bank" is defined as "the bank to which the sender's instruction is addressed." There are other defined roles in a given funds transfer for the senders, receiving banks, or other participants, including the "originator" of the funds transfer (here Grain Traders), the "originator's bank" (here BCN), the "beneficiary" (here Kraemer) and the "beneficiary's bank" (here Extrader). For any given funds transfer, there can be only one originator, originator's bank, beneficiary, and beneficiary's bank, but there can be several senders and receiving banks, one of each for every payment order required to complete the funds transfer. See N.Y.U.C.C. §4-A-103.

A.   GRAIN TRADERS'S REFUND CLAIM UNDER §4-A-402

Section 4-A-402 ("Section 402") covers the obligation of a sender of a payment order to make payment to the receiving bank after the order has been accepted as well as the obligation of a receiving bank to refund payment in the event the transfer is not completed. . . . [U]nder Section 402(3), the sender's obligation to pay the receiving bank is excused in the event that the transfer is not completed. If payment has already been made, a sender can seek a refund from the bank it paid under Section 402(4). It was this so-called "money-back guarantee" provision that Grain Traders invoked to obtain a refund from CitiBank.

The district court held that Grain Traders's refund action against CitiBank, an intermediary bank for the purposes of Grain Traders's funds transfer, was barred because a Section 402 refund action could only be maintained by a "sender" against the receiving bank to whom the sender had issued a payment order and whom the sender had paid. Thus, because Grain Traders was a "sender" only with respect to the payment order it issued to BCN, Grain Traders could look only to BCN, the receiving bank, for a refund.

In reaching its conclusion, the district court relied on the plain language of Section 402(4) as well as other provisions of Article 4-A. It found that the language of Section 402(4) establishes a right of refund only between a sender and the receiving bank it paid. BCN, not Grain Traders, was the sender that issued the payment order to CitiBank and paid CitiBank by having its account debited in the amount of $310,000. Grain Traders argues that the fact that Section 402(4) does not use the words "receiving bank" but instead refers to "the bank receiving payment" means that the sender can sue any bank in the chain that received payment. We agree with CitiBank that because the words "receiving bank" are defined as the bank that receives a payment order, Section 402(4)'s use of the words "bank receiving payment" simply clarifies that the right to a refund arises only after the sender has satisfied its obligation to pay the receiving bank.

The Official Comment to §4-A-402 supports this interpretation. It states, in relevant part:

> The money-back guarantee [of §4-A-402(4)] is particularly important to Originator if noncompletion of the funds transfer is due to the fault of an intermediary bank rather than Bank A [the Originator's bank]. *In that case Bank A must refund payment to Originator, and Bank A has the burden of obtaining refund from the intermediary bank that it paid.*

§4-A-402, cmt. 2 (emphasis added [by court]). We think this comment makes plain the intent of the Article 4-A drafters to effect an orderly unraveling of a funds transfer in the event that the transfer was not completed, and accomplished this by incorporating a "privity" requirement into the "money back guarantee" provision so that it applies only between the parties to a particular payment order and not to the parties to the funds transfer as a whole.

The district court also relied on the express right of subrogation created by Section 402(5), which applies when one of the receiving banks is unable to issue a refund because it has suspended payments. Section 402(5) provides that:

> If a funds transfer is not completed as stated in subsection (3) and an intermediary bank is obliged to refund payment as stated in subsection (4) but is unable to do so because not permitted by applicable law or because the bank suspends payments, a sender in the funds transfer that executed a payment order in compliance with

an instruction, as stated in [§4-A-302(1)(a)] to route the funds transfer through that intermediary bank is entitled to receive or retain payment from the sender of the payment order that it accepted. The first sender in the funds transfer that issued an instruction requiring routing through that intermediary bank is subrogated to the right of the bank that paid the intermediary bank to refund as stated in subsection (4).

Where a right to refund has been triggered because a transfer was not completed, but one of the banks that received payment is unable to issue a refund because it has suspended payments, the orderly unraveling of the transfer is prevented and the risk of loss will be borne by some party to the transfer. Article 4-A allocates that risk of loss to the party that first designated the failed bank to be used in the transfer. See N.Y.U.C.C. §4-A-402, cmt. 2 (where "Bank A [the sender] was required to issue its payment order to Bank C [the insolvent bank] because Bank C was designated as an intermediary bank by Originator[,] . . . Originator takes the risk of insolvency of Bank C"). Under Section 402(5), all intervening senders are entitled to receive and retain payment and the party that designated the failed bank bears the burden of recovery by being subrogated to the right of the sender that paid the failed bank. We agree with the district court that

> the subrogation language of §4-A-402(5) demonstrates that the originator does not, as a general matter, have a right to sue all the parties to a funds transfer . . . [and] makes clear . . . that under §4-A-402(4) no right to a refund otherwise exists between the originator and an intermediary bank. This is evident because there would be no need for the subrogation language of subsection (5) if the originator (as the first sender) already had a right to assert a refund claim directly against all intermediary banks.

In sum, we agree with the district court's thoughtful analysis and conclude that §4-A-402 allows each sender of a payment order to seek refund only from the receiving bank it paid. Not only do the provisions of Article 4-A support the district court's interpretation, there are sound policy reasons for limiting the right to seek a refund to the sender who directly paid the receiving bank. One of Article 4-A's primary goals is to promote certainty and finality so that "the various parties to funds transfers [will] be able to predict risk with certainty, to insure against risk, to adjust operational and security procedures, and to price funds transfer services appropriately." N.Y.U.C.C. §4-A-102, cmt. To allow a party to, in effect, skip over the bank with which it dealt directly, and go to the next bank in the chain would result in uncertainty as to rights and liabilities, would create a risk of multiple or inconsistent liabilities, and would require intermediary banks to investigate the financial circumstances and various legal relations of the other parties to the transfer. These are matters as to which an intermediary bank ordinarily should not have to be concerned and, if it were otherwise, would impede the use of rapid electronic funds transfers in commerce by causing delays and driving up costs. Accordingly, we affirm the district court's dismissal of Grain Traders's refund claim under Section 402(4).

B. Recovering from the Mistaken Recipient

Most erroneous wire transfers, like the transfer at issue in the *Aleo* case, result in a transfer of money to a party that has no right to receive it. Although Article 4A limits the right of the party that makes the error to pass that loss on to other parties in the system, it does contemplate a recovery of the money from the unintended recipient under common-law principles of restitution. Thus, if the originator commits the error, the originator can pursue a restitution action against the incorrect beneficiary. See, e.g., UCC §§4A-207(d) (error in describing beneficiary), 4A-209(d) (error in date of execution), 4A-211(c)(2) (erroneous order canceled after acceptance by beneficiary). Similarly, when a bank makes a mistake that causes it to send excessive funds, the bank can pursue a restitution action against the party that received the funds. See, e.g., UCC §§4A-303(a), (c) (excessive-funds errors); Regulation J, §210.32(c) (error by Federal Reserve bank). Thus, although the originator in *Aleo* failed to recover her funds from the banks operating the wire-transfer system, Article 4A would permit her to pursue the party that received the unintended transmissions. Unfortunately, the boundaries of those rights to restitution are quite murky because the UCC does nothing to describe the circumstances in which restitution is available. Instead, in each case Article 4A simply states that the originators and receiving banks responsible for an error are "entitled to recover from the beneficiary of the erroneous order the excess payment received to the extent allowed by the law governing mistake and restitution." E.g., UCC §4A-303(a).

For reasons that are difficult to understand, the rules governing the availability of restitution from an incorrect beneficiary have been one of the most fertile grounds for high-stakes wire-transfer litigation. The most difficult issues have been raised in a series of cases in which the mistaken recipient of the transfer happened to have an independent right to payment from the originator. That situation is not nearly so farfetched as it sounds: It produced two of the most celebrated wire-transfer cases of the 1990s, both of which involved mistakes by banks in processing transfer requests. In the first case, an Australian company named Spedley asked Security Pacific to wire about $2 million into an account at BankAmerica in the name of Banque Worms (a French bank to which Spedley owed money). Spedley canceled the wire-transfer request a few hours later, before Security Pacific made the transfer. Security Pacific nevertheless mistakenly proceeded with the transfer. Cf. UCC §4A-211(b) (cancellation of payment order is valid if received when the receiving bank has "a reasonable opportunity to act on the communication"). After protracted litigation, the New York Court of Appeals held that Banque Worms was entitled to retain the money because Banque Worms had applied the money to discharge a debt that Spedley owed to it (the debt that had been the basis for Spedley's original payment order). Banque Worms v. BankAmerica Int'l, 570 N.E.2d 189 (N.Y. 1991).

The second case involved an attempt by a company named Duchow's Marine to defraud General Electric Capital Corporation (GECC). GECC financed Duchow's inventory of boats under an arrangement that required all proceeds from the sale of boats to be transferred into a special "blocked" account. The dispute arose when Duchow (wrongfully) instructed one of its customers to wire its payment into Duchow's regular (unrestricted) account. One of the banks processing the transfer, however, mistakenly dropped the number of the unrestricted account from the payment order. When the transfer reached Duchow's bank, that bank placed the funds in the blocked account. Showing considerable pluck, Duchow challenged the mistake and convinced its bank to reverse the transfer and move the funds into Duchow's unrestricted account (from which the funds promptly vanished). Writing for the United States Court of Appeals for the Seventh Circuit, Judge Easterbrook held that the beneficiary's bank erred when it corrected the mistake. Relying on *Banque Worms*, the court reasoned that GECC's entitlement to the funds placed in the blocked account in accordance with the original payment order was enough to defeat the (admittedly inequitable) claim of the intended recipient. General Elec. Capital Corp. v. Central Bank, 49 F.3d 280 (7th Cir. 1995).

It is easy to quarrel with the results of *Banque Worms* and *GECC*. First, those decisions interpret the bank's right of restitution more narrowly than traditional common-law principles, which would not allow a creditor in the position of Banque Worms or GECC to retain those funds unless the creditor could prove that it had detrimentally relied on the payment by changing its position toward the debtor. Nothing in Article 4A justifies a narrowing of the common-law restitution remedy in the wire-transfer context. Indeed, as explained above, the text of Article 4A is avowedly agnostic about the limits of that remedy.

Moreover, especially in the context of *GECC*, a rule protecting the improper transferee seems to forgive the transferee's failure to protect itself. As Professor Andrew Kull explains, Judge Easterbrook's decision in *GECC* effectively protects the secured creditor from the consequences of its own lax monitoring of its borrower:

> Denial of restitution shifts (to one of the banks) the consequences of a risk that GECC had agreed to bear: namely, the risk of the debtor's misconduct. GECC was paid to accept this risk; GECC negotiated the terms on which it would manage it (in its security agreement with the debtor); GECC was the only party in a position to police the debtor's behavior. The secured credit agreement, not the wire transfer, was the transaction that went seriously wrong in this case, yet to this transaction the banks were total strangers. Requiring them to bear a loss they could not control offends not only equity and good conscience but ordinary precepts of risk-spreading as well.

Andrew Kull, *Rationalizing Restitution*, 83 Cal. L. Rev. 1191, 1241 n.143 (1995).

Problem Set 12

12.1. Consider yet again the facts of Aleo v. CitiBank, in which Aleo's payment order apparently described an account of Behzad Hermatjou (the intended recipient) by an incorrect account number, resulting in a transfer into the account of an individual unknown to Aleo.

    a.   Why shouldn't the presence of the correct name ("Hermatjou") in the payment order be enough to alert the banks to the problem, and allow Aleo to recover from CitiBank? Do you need to know anything further to answer the question? UCC §4A-207(c) & comment 2.

    b.   If Aleo cannot recover from CitiBank, does it have any way to recover the money? UCC §4A-207(d).

    c.   How would your answer change if you discovered that Dresdner Bank recognized the discrepancy before it accepted the payment order from CitiBank? UCC §§4A-207, 4A-402. If you conclude that Aleo now could recover the funds from CitiBank, do you think that CitiBank could recover from Dresdner? Dresdner, from the unknown account holder?

    12.2.   Ben Darrow from FSB calls you to discuss a problem with a recent wire transfer the bank sent for one of Darrow's customers. Jasmine Ball sent FSB an e-mail message requesting a wire transfer for $100,000 to an account of Carol Long at the Second National Bank (SNB) of Muleshoe. The request was processed by a novice clerk at FSB, who accidentally duplicated the transaction and sent two identical $100,000 transfers, rather than one. FSB's processing system automatically deducted funds from Ball's account to cover both orders. Ball called to complain later that day when she happened to notice the unusually low balance in her account. As soon as Darrow discovered the problem, he called SNB. SNB told him that it had received the funds and notified Ms. Long, but that she had not yet removed the excess money. Darrow has several questions.

    a.   First, can Darrow force SNB to send the extra $100,000 back to FSB? UCC §§4A-209(b), 4A-209 comments 4 & 5, 4A-211(c), 4A-211 comments 3 & 4, 4A-402(b), 4A-404(a).

    b.   If not, can FSB recover the excess funds from Long? Do you need to know anything else about the relation between Ball and Long? What if Ball in fact owes Long $1,000,000? UCC §4A-303(a) & comment 3.

    c.   If FSB has no right to recover the excess funds from SNB or Long, can FSB retain all of the funds that it debited from Ball's account to pay for the orders? UCC §§4A-303(a), 4A-303 comments 2 & 3, 4A-402(c), (d).

    d.   How would your answer change if the error was made by Jasmine herself rather than by the clerk at FSB?

    e.   What if SNB voluntarily agrees to cancel the order? UCC §4A-211(c), (e), & (f) & comment 4.

    12.3.   When you see Jeeves walking across the room toward you just as you start to enjoy your weekly lunch at the Drones Club, you groan inwardly at the prospect of facing another one of Bertie Wooster's problems. Thus, you are not the least bit surprised when Jeeves asks for a moment of your time to discuss a problem of Wooster's. The problem arises out of a wire transfer in the amount of $500,000 that was made from Wooster's account 13 months ago. Wooster's bank dutifully mailed a bank statement to Wooster reflecting that transfer the day after the transfer. Unfortunately, the notification was lost in the mail and received by Wooster only yesterday. When Jeeves looked at the notification for Wooster, Jeeves remembered immediately that Wooster had authorized a transfer for $50,000, not $500,000. Because the transfer had been shown on the lost statement, none of the intervening months' statements showed anything about the transfer.

If Jeeves is correct in his recollection (and he always is), can Wooster force the bank to recredit the funds from the transfer? If so, is Wooster entitled to interest as well? UCC §§4A-304, 4A-402(d), 4A-505.

12.4. Consider the facts of *Grain Traders*.

a. What would have happened if Grain Traders instead had sued its own bank instead of CitiBank? Who would have ended up bearing the loss? Where would the money be? UCC §§4A-402(d), (e).

b. Now assume that it was BCN, not Grain Traders, that directed the transmission through BCIL. How would the liabilities change?

Assignment 13: Fraud and System Failure in Wire-Transfer Systems

This assignment turns to problems in the system — losses that stem from fraud and system failure.

A. Fraud

Wire transfers are particularly attractive as a target for fraud both because they readily carry huge sums of money and because they are largely automated. Banks have responded by implementing a variety of security procedures to enhance the difficulty of theft from the system. Those procedures take a variety of more or less sophisticated forms. For example, online Fedwire transactions require an identification code and a confidential password to access the system, as well as encryption of the payment order during the transmission process. By contrast, offline Fedwire transfers are confirmed through the more antiquated "four-party call-back" process described in the previous assignment. Many banks use a similar four-party procedure to confirm wire transfers requested by their customers. Some banks, however, use much less cautious procedures, such as a "listen-back" requirement, under which a second employee listens to a tape recording of the initial request. That procedure may limit the opportunity for theft by bank employees, but it does little or nothing to limit theft by outsiders.

Another common mechanism that indirectly limits fraud is a contractual overdraft limit. The bank and the customer commonly agree that the bank is *not* authorized to send any wire transfer that would create an overdraft in the customer's account (an agreement directly contrary to the overdraft protection a large customer generally would have on its checking account). See UCC §4A-203 comment 3. Then, if the bank receives a large wire-transfer order that exceeds the balance in the customer's account, the bank will not accept the payment order. Given the significant chance that the wire-transfer thief will not be sure exactly what the customer's balance is at any time, a wire-transfer thief frequently might try to send orders that would cause an overdraft. The agreement between the customer and the bank would keep such orders from being executed even if the thief managed to satisfy the security procedure. That approach would not catch a few small, incidental thefts, but it does limit the possibility of a really large theft in one transaction.

Because customers ordinarily are liable only for orders that they authorize, UCC §4A-202(a), the significant possibility of unauthorized orders gives banks a strong incentive to develop security procedures that prevent unauthorized orders. Article 4A buttresses that incentive with an unusual provision that rewards the bank for implementing security procedures by deeming customers to have authorized all orders made in conformity with pre-approved security procedures even if the customers in fact did not authorize the orders. UCC §4A-202(b). For example, if a thief with illicit access to the customer's computer uses the passwords from that computer to place unauthorized orders, the customer is fully responsible for those orders (subject only to a right to pursue restitution from the wrongdoer).

The statute imposes three significant restrictions on the bank's ability to use the security-procedure rule to charge its customer for orders that the customer in fact did not authorize. First, the security procedure must be commercially reasonable. UCC §4A-202(b)(i). That rule allows a customer charged for an unauthorized order to contend that the security procedure to which it agreed was so defective that it would be unreasonable to hold the customer to unauthorized orders sent pursuant to that procedure. Although the vagueness of that rule does limit the bank's ability to be sure that it is protected from responsibility for unauthorized orders, it does enhance even further the bank's incentive to develop the most sophisticated practicable procedures for preventing unauthorized wire-transfer orders. See UCC §4A-203 comment 4 (discussing the factors that determine the commercial reasonability of a security procedure). As the case below demonstrates, advances in information technology will require constant vigilance for a bank to ensure that its security procedures are commercially reasonable at any given time.

Patco Construction Co. v. People's United Bank
684 F.3d 197 (1st Cir. 2012)

Before Lynch, Chief Judge, Lipez and Howard, Circuit Judges.
Lynch, Chief Judge.
Over seven days in May 2009, Ocean Bank, a southern Maine community bank, authorized six apparently fraudulent withdrawals, totaling $588,851.26, from an account held by Patco Construction Company, after the perpetrators correctly supplied Patco's customized answers to security questions. Although the bank's security system flagged each of these transactions as unusually "high-risk" because they were inconsistent with the timing, value, and geographic location of Patco's regular payment orders, the bank's security system did not notify its commercial customers of this information and allowed the payments to go through. Ocean Bank was able to block or recover $243,406.83, leaving a residual loss to Patco of $345,444.43.

Patco brought suit, setting forth six counts against People's United Bank, a regional bank which had acquired Ocean Bank. The suit alleged, inter alia, that the bank should bear the loss because its security system was not commercially reasonable under Article 4A of the Uniform Commercial Code ("UCC"), . . . and that Patco had not consented to the procedures.

. . . [T]he district court held that the bank's security system was commercially reasonable and on that basis entered judgment in favor of the bank . . . .

We reverse the district court's grant of summary judgment in favor of the bank and affirm its denial of Patco's motion for summary judgment on the first count. In particular, we leave open the question of what, if any, obligations or responsibilities Article 4A imposes on Patco.

I.

. . .

A.   THE PARTIES

Patco is a small property development and contractor business located in Sanford, Maine. Patco began banking with Ocean Bank in 1985. Ocean Bank was acquired by the Chittenden family of banks, which was later acquired by People's United Bank, a regional bank based in Bridgeport, Connecticut. People's United Bank operates other local Maine banks such as Maine Bank & Trust, where Patco also had an account in May 2009. Ocean Bank was a division of People's United at the time of the fraudulent withdrawals at issue in this case.

In September 2003, Patco added internet banking—also known as "eBanking"—to its commercial checking account at Ocean Bank. Ocean Bank allows its eBanking commercial customers to make electronic funds transfers through Ocean Bank via the Automated Clearing House ("ACH") network, a system used by banks to transfer funds electronically between accounts. Patco used eBanking primarily to make regular weekly payroll payments. These regular payroll payments had certain repeated characteristics: they were always made on Fridays; they were always initiated from one of the computers housed at Patco's offices in Sanford, Maine; they originated from a single static Internet Protocol ("IP") address; and they were accompanied by weekly withdrawals for federal and state tax withholding as well as 401(k) contributions. The highest payroll payment Patco ever made using eBanking was $36,634.74. Until October of 2008, Patco also used eBanking to transfer money from the accounts of Patco and related entities at Maine Bank & Trust, which maintains a branch in Sanford, Maine, into its Ocean Bank checking account.

In September 2003, when it added eBanking services, Patco entered into several agreements with Ocean Bank. Most significantly, Patco entered into the eBanking for Business Agreement. The eBanking agreement stated that "use of the *Ocean National Bank's eBanking for Business* password constitutes authentication of all transactions performed by you or on your behalf." The eBanking agreement stated that Ocean Bank did not "assume[] any responsibilities" with respect to Patco's use of eBanking, that "electronic transmission of confidential business and sensitive personal information" was at Patco's risk, and that Ocean Bank was liable only for its gross negligence, limited to six months of fees. The eBanking agreement also provided that:

> [U]se of *Ocean National Bank's eBanking for Business* by any one owner of a joint account or by an authorized signor on an account, shall be deemed an authorized

transaction on an account unless you provide us with written notice that the use of *Ocean National Bank's eBanking for Business* is terminated or that the joint account owner or authorized signor has been validly removed form [sic] the account.

The agreement provided that Patco had to contact the bank immediately upon discovery of an unauthorized transaction.

The bank also reserved the right to modify the terms and conditions of the eBanking agreement at any time, effective upon publication. The bank claims that at some point before May 2009, it modified the eBanking agreement to state:

If you choose to receive ACH debit transactions on your commercial accounts, you assume all liability and responsibility to monitor those commercial accounts on a daily basis. In the event that you object to any ACH debit, you agree to notify us of your objection on the same day the debit occurs.

The bank claims that it published this modified eBanking agreement on its website before May 2009. Patco disputes that this agreement was modified and/ or published on the bank's website before May 2009, and argues that the modified agreement was therefore not effective as between the parties.

B. OCEAN BANK'S SECURITY MEASURES

In 2004, Ocean Bank began using Jack Henry & Associates to provide its core online banking platform, known as "NetTeller." Jack Henry provides the NetTeller product to approximately 1,300 of its 1,500 bank customers.

In October 2005, the agencies of the Federal Financial Institutions Examination Council[4] ("FFIEC"), responding to increased online banking fraud, issued guidance titled "Authentication in an Internet Banking Environment." *See* Fed. Fin. Insts. Examination Council, Authentication in an Internet Banking Environment (Aug. 8, 2001), *available at* http://www.ffiec. gov/pdf/authentication_guidance.pdf [hereinafter "FFIEC Guidance"]. The Guidance was intended to aid financial institutions in "evaluating and implementing authentication systems and practices whether they are provided internally or by a service provider." The Guidance provides that "financial institutions should periodically . . . [a]djust, as appropriate, their information security program in light of any relevant changes in technology, the sensitivity of its customer information, and internal or external threats to information."

The Guidance explains that existing authentication methodologies involve three basic "factors": (1) something the user knows (e.g., password, personal identification number); (2) something the user has (e.g., ATM card, smart card); and (3) something the user is (e.g., biometric characteristic, such as a fingerprint). It states:

---

4. The FFIEC is an interagency body created by statute and charged with "establish[ing] uniform principles and standards and report forms for the examination of financial institutions which shall be applied by the Federal financial institutions regulatory agencies." 12 U.S.C. §3305(a). [Ed.: It includes the Board of Governors of the Federal Reserve, the FDIC, the National Credit Union Administration, the Office of the Comptroller of the Currency, the Consumer Financial Protection Bureau, and also representatives from the Conference of State Bank Supervisors, the American Council of State Savings Supervisors, and the National Association of State Credit Union Supervisors.]

Authentication methods that depend on more than one factor are more difficult to compromise than single-factor methods. Accordingly, properly designed and implemented multifactor authentication methods are more reliable and stronger fraud deterrents. For example, the use of a logon ID/password is single-factor authentication (i.e., something the user knows); whereas, an ATM transaction requires multifactor authentication: something the user possesses (i.e., the card) combined with something the user knows (i.e., PIN). A multifactor authentication methodology may also include "out-of-band" controls for risk mitigation.

The Guidance also states:

The agencies consider single-factor authentication, as the only control mechanism, to be inadequate for high-risk transactions involving access to customer information or the movement of funds to other parties . . . . Account fraud and identity theft are frequently the result of single-factor (e.g., ID/password) authentication exploitation. Where risk assessments indicate that the use of single-factor authentication is inadequate, financial institutions should implement multifactor authentication, layered security, or other controls reasonably calculated to mitigate those risks.

Following publication of the FFIEC Guidance, Ocean Bank worked with Jack Henry to conduct a risk assessment and institute appropriate authentication protocols to comply with the Guidance. The bank determined that its eBanking product was a "high risk" system that required enhanced security, and in particular, multifactor authentication.

Jack Henry entered into a re-seller agreement with Cyota, Inc., an RSA Security Company ("RSA/Cyota"), for a multifactor authentication system to integrate into its NetTeller product so that it could offer security solutions compliant with the FFIEC Guidance. Through collaboration with RSA/Cyota, Jack Henry made two multifactor authentication products available to its customers to meet the FFIEC Guidance: the "Basic" package and the "Premium" package.

Ocean Bank selected the Jack Henry "Premium" package, which it implemented by January 2007. The system, as implemented by Ocean Bank, had six key features:

1. *User IDs and Passwords:* The system required each authorized Patco employee to use both a company ID and password and a user-specific ID and password to access online banking.

2. *Invisible Device Authentication:* The system placed a "device cookie" onto customers' computers to identify particular computers used to access online banking. The device cookie would be used to help establish a secure communication session with the NetTeller environment and to contribute to the component risk score. Whenever the cookie was changed or was new, that impacted the risk score and potentially triggered challenge questions.

3. *Risk Profiling:* The system entailed the building of a risk profile for each customer by RSA/Cyota based on a number of different factors, including the location from which a user logged in, when/how often a user logged in, what a user did while on the system, and the size, type, and frequency of payment orders normally issued by the customer to the bank. The Premium Product noted the IP address that the customer typically used to log into online banking and added it to the customer profile.

RSA/Cyota's adaptive monitoring provided a risk score to the bank for every log-in attempt and transaction based on a multitude of data, including but not limited to IP address, device cookie ID, Geo location, and transaction activity. If a user's transaction differed from its normal profile, RSA/Cyota reported to the bank an elevated risk score for that transaction. RSA/Cyota considered transactions generating risk scores in excess of 750, on a scale from 0 to 1,000, to be high-risk transactions. "Challenge questions," described below, were prompted any time the risk score for a transaction exceeded 750.

4. *Challenge Questions:* The system required users, during initial log-in, to select three challenge questions and responses. The challenge questions might be prompted for various reasons. For example, if the risk score associated with a particular transaction exceeded 750, the challenge questions would be triggered. If the challenge question responses entered by the user did not match the ones originally provided, the customer would receive an error message. If the customer was unable to answer the challenge questions in three attempts, the customer was blocked from online banking and would be required to contact the bank.

5. *Dollar Amount Rule:* The system permitted financial institutions to set a dollar threshold amount above which a transaction would automatically trigger the challenge questions even if the user ID, password, and device cookie were all valid. In August 2007, Ocean Bank set the dollar amount rule to $100,000. On June 6, 2008, Ocean Bank lowered the dollar amount rule from $100,000 to $1. After the Bank lowered the threshold to $1, Patco was prompted to answer challenge questions every time it initiated a transaction. In May 2009, when the fraud at issue in this case occurred, the dollar amount rule threshold remained at $1.

6. *Subscription to the eFraud Network:* The Jack Henry Premium Product provided Ocean Bank with a subscription to the eFraud Network, which compared characteristics of the transaction (such as the IP address of the user seeking access to the Bank's system) with those of known instances of fraud. The eFraud Network allowed financial institutions to report IP addresses or other discrete identifying characteristics identified with instances of fraud. An attempt to access a customer's NetTeller account initiated by someone with that characteristic would then be automatically blocked. The individual would not even be prompted for challenge questions.

Ocean Bank asserts that on December 1, 2006, as it began to implement the Jack Henry system, it also began to offer the option of e-mail alerts to its eBanking customers. If the customer chose to receive such alerts, the bank would send the customer e-mails regarding incoming/outgoing transactions, changes to the customer's balance, the clearing of checks, and/or alerts on certain customer-specified dates. Patco claims it did not receive notice that e-mail alerts were available and this is a disputed issue of fact. It appears that notice of the availability of e-mail alerts was not readily visible. To set up alerts through the eBanking system, a user would have to first click the "Preferences" tab on the eBanking webpage, then click on a second tab labeled "Alerts," and then follow several additional steps to activate individual alerts. Patco claims it never saw anything on the website indicating that e-mail alerts were available, and it therefore never set up e-mail alerts.

C. Security Measures Available Which Ocean Bank Chose Not to Implement

There were several additional security measures that were available to Ocean Bank but that the bank chose not to implement:

1. *Out-of-Band Authentication:* Jack Henry offered Ocean Bank a version of the NetTeller system that included an out-of-band authentication option. Out-of-band authentication "generally refers to additional steps or actions taken beyond the technology boundaries of a typical transaction." Examples of out-of-band authentication include notification to the customer, callback (voice) verification, e-mail approval from the customer, and cell phone based challenge/response processes. The FFIEC Guidance identifies out-of-band authentication as a useful method of risk mitigation.

2. *User-Selected Picture:* Ocean Bank's security procedures did not include the user-selected picture function that was available through Jack Henry's Premium option. Ocean Bank states that it did not utilize the user-selected picture function because it already utilized other anti-phishing controls.

3. *Tokens:* Tokens are physical devices (something the person has), such as a USB token device, a smart card, or a password-generating token. The FFIEC Guidance identifies tokens as a useful part of a multifactor authentication scheme. Tokens were not available from Jack Henry when Ocean Bank implemented its system in 2007, but were readily available to financial institutions at that time through other sources. Although People's United Bank has used tokens since at least January of 2008, Ocean Bank did not do so until after the fraud in this case occurred.

4. *Monitoring of Risk-Scoring Reports:* In May 2009, bank personnel did not monitor the risk-scoring reports received as part of the Premium Product package, nor did the bank conduct any other regular review of transactions that generated high risk scores. In May 2009, the bank had the capability to conduct manual review of high-risk transactions through its transaction-profiling and risk-scoring system, but did not do so. The bank also had the ability to call a customer if it detected fraudulent activity, but did not do so. The bank began conducting manual reviews of high-risk transactions in late 2009, after the fraud in this case occurred. Since then, the bank has instituted a policy of calling the customer in the case of uncharacteristic transactions to inquire if the customer did indeed initiate the transaction.

D. The Fraudulent Transfers

Beginning on May 7, 2009, a series of withdrawals were made on Patco's account over the course of several days.

On May 7, unknown third parties initiated a $56,594 ACH withdrawal from Patco's account. The perpetrators supplied the proper credentials of one of Patco's employees, including her ID, password, and answers to her challenge questions. The payment on this withdrawal was directed to go to the accounts of numerous individuals, none of whom had previously been sent money by Patco. The perpetrators logged in from a device unrecognized by Ocean Bank's system, and from an IP address that Patco had never before used. The risk-scoring engine generated a risk score of 790 for the transaction, a significant departure from Patco's usual risk scores, which generally ranged from 10 to 214. There is no evidence that Patco's risk scores prior to the fraudulent transfers in this case ever exceeded 214. The risk-scoring engine reported the following contributors to the risk score for that transaction: (1) "Very high risk non-authenticated device"; (2) "High risk transaction amount"; (3) "IP anomaly"; and (4) "Risk score distributor per cookie age." An RSA manual describing risk score contributors states that any transaction triggering the contributor "Very high risk non-authenticated device" is "a very high-risk transaction." Despite this high risk score, Patco was not notified. Moreover, it appears no one at the bank monitored these high-risk transactions. Bank personnel did not manually review the May 7, 2009 transaction. The bank batched and processed the transaction as usual, and it was paid the next day.

The activities of May 7 having successfully resulted in payment, on Friday, May 8, 2009, unknown third parties again successfully initiated an ACH payment order from Patco's account, this time for $115,620.26. As before, the perpetrators wired money to multiple individual accounts to which Patco had never before sent funds. The perpetrators again used a device that was not recognized by Ocean Bank's system. The payment order originated from the same IP address as the day before. The transaction was larger by several magnitudes than any ACH transfer Patco had ever made to third parties. Despite these unusual characteristics, the bank again took no steps to notify Patco and batched and processed the transaction as usual, which was paid by the bank on Monday, May 11, 2009.

On May 11, 12, and 13, unknown third parties initiated further withdrawals from Patco's account in the amounts of $99,068, $91,959, and $113,647, respectively. Like the prior fraudulent transactions, these transactions were uncharacteristic in that they sent money to numerous individuals to whom Patco had never before sent funds, were for greater amounts than Patco's ordinary third-party transactions, were sent from computers that were not recognized by Ocean Bank's system, and originated from IP addresses that were not recognized as valid IP addresses of Patco. As a result of these unusual characteristics, the transactions continued to generate higher than normal risk scores. The May 11 transaction generated a risk score of 720, the May 12 transaction triggered a risk score of 563, and the transaction on May 13 generated a risk score of 785. The Bank did not manually review any of these transactions to determine their legitimacy or notify Patco.

Portions of the transfers, beginning with the first transfer initiated on May 7, 2009, were automatically returned to the bank because certain of the account numbers to which the money was slated to be transferred were invalid. As a result, the bank sent limited "return" notices to the home of Mark Patterson, one of Patco's principals, via U.S. mail. Patterson received the first such notice after work on the evening of May 13, six days after the allegedly fraudulent withdrawals began.

The next morning, on May 14, 2009, Patco called the bank to inform it that Patco had not authorized the transactions. Also on the morning of May 14, another alleged fraudulent transaction was initiated from Patco's account in the amount of $111,963. Despite the information from Patco, the bank initially processed this payment order on May 15, 2009. However, because of the alert from Patco of the ongoing fraud, the bank then took steps to block completion of a portion of this transaction and recovered a portion of the transferred funds shortly thereafter.

At the end of the string of thefts, the amount of money fraudulently withdrawn from Patco's account totaled $588,851.26, of which $243,406.83 was automatically returned or blocked and recovered.

According to Ocean Bank, on May 14, 2009, immediately after the allegedly fraudulent withdrawals occurred, the bank gave instructions to Patco. It instructed Patco to disconnect the computers it used for electronic banking from its network; to stop using these computers for work purposes; to leave the computers turned on; and to bring in a third-party forensic professional or law enforcement to create a forensic image of the computers to determine whether a security breach had occurred. Ocean Bank claims, and Patco disputes, that Patco did not isolate its computers or forensically preserve the hard drives; and that Patco employees continued to use their computers during the week following the alleged fraud. In another dispute of fact, Patco states that Ocean Bank recommended only that Patco check its system for a security breach using a third-party forensic professional, which Patco did.

Shortly after the fraudulent transfers, Patco hired an IT consultant, who ran anti-malware scans on the computers. A remnant of a Zeus/Zbot malware was found. However, the Zeus/Zbot malware, which contained the encryption key for the Zeus/Zbot configuration file, was quarantined and then deleted by the anti-malware scan. Without the encryption key, it is impossible to decrypt the configuration file and identify what information, if any, the Zeus/Zbot malware would have captured, if in fact it was of a type that would have intercepted authentication credentials.

II.

On September 18, 2009, Patco filed suit against People's United in Maine Superior Court, York County. The complaint included [counts for, among other things,] liability under Article 4A of the Uniform Commercial Code ("UCC") . . . . On October 9, 2009, People's United removed the case to the United States District Court for the District of Maine.

On August 27, 2010, Patco moved for summary judgment on . . . its claim under Article 4A of the UCC. That same day, the bank moved for summary judgment on all six counts. [The district court granted summary judgment for the bank.]

III.

A.   Article 4A of the UCC

The claim under Count I is governed by Article 4A of the UCC, which was meant to govern the rights, duties, and liabilities of banks and their commercial customers with respect to electronic funds transfers. *See* [UCC §4A-102 cmt.] Article 4A was enacted in toto by Maine in 1991, well before the transfers at issue in this case.

Article 4A was developed to address wholesale wire transfers and commercial ACH transfers, generally between businesses and their financial institutions. Before

Article 4A was drafted, "there was no comprehensive body of law—statutory or judicial—that defined the juridical nature of a [commercial] funds transfer or the rights and obligations flowing from payment orders." Instead, judges relied on general principles of common law, sought guidance from other provisions of the UCC, or analogized to laws applicable to other payment methods. The drafters of Article 4A sought to deliver clarity to this area of law by "us[ing] precise and detailed rules to assign responsibility, define behavioral norms, allocate risks and establish limits on liability" in order to allow parties to predict and insure against risk with greater certainty, given the very large amounts of money involved in commercial funds transfers.

. . .

Under Article 4A, a bank receiving a payment order ordinarily bears the risk of loss of any unauthorized funds transfer. [§4A-]204. The bank may shift the risk of loss to the customer in one of two ways, one of which involves the commercial reasonableness of security procedures and one of which does not. First, the bank may show that the "payment order received . . . is the authorized order of the person identified as sender if that person authorized the order or is otherwise bound by it under the law of agency." [§4A-]202(1). But, as the Article 4A commentary explains, "[i]n a very large percentage of cases covered by Article 4A, . . . [c]ommon law concepts of authority of agent to bind principal are not helpful" because the payment order is transmitted electronically and the bank "may be required to act on the basis of a message that appears on a computer screen." [§4A-]203 cmt. 1.

If the sender of the payment order had no authority to act for the customer, and there are no additional facts on which estoppel might be found, the "Customer is not liable to pay the order and [the] Bank takes the loss." *Id.* cmt. 2. In such cases, "these legal principles [of agency] give the receiving bank very little protection . . . . The only remedy of [the] Bank is to seek recovery from the person who received payment as beneficiary of the fraudulent order." *Id.* cmts. 1, 2.

Accordingly, the drafters provided a second way by which a bank may shift the risk of loss and protect itself whether or not the payment order is authorized. This, in turn, has several components:

> If a bank and its customer have agreed that the authenticity of payment orders issued to the bank in the name of the customer as sender will be verified pursuant to a security procedure, a payment order received by the receiving bank is effective as the order of the customer, whether or not authorized, if:
>
> (a) The security procedure is a commercially reasonable method of providing security against unauthorized payment orders; and
> (b) The bank proves that it accepted the payment order in good faith and in compliance with the security procedure and any written agreement or instruction of the customer restricting acceptance of payment orders issued in the name of the customer. The bank is not required to follow an instruction that violates a written agreement with the customer or notice of which is not received at a time and in a manner affording the bank a reasonable opportunity to act on it before the payment order is accepted.

[§4A-]202(2).

In turn, Article 4A defines a security procedure as:

[A] procedure established by agreement of a customer and a receiving bank for the purpose of: (1) Verifying that a payment order or communication amending or cancelling a payment order is that of the customer; or (2) Detecting error in the transmission or the content of the payment order or communication.

[§4A-]201. One question raised in this appeal is the scope of any agreement reached.

The UCC explains that the "[c]ommercial reasonableness of a security procedure is a question of law" to be determined by the court. [§4A-]202(3). There are two ways by which a security procedure may be shown to be commercially reasonable. First is by reference to:

[T]he wishes of the customer expressed to the bank, the circumstances of the customer known to the bank, including the size, type and frequency of payment orders normally issued by the customer to the bank, alternative security procedures offered to the customer and security procedures in general use by customers and receiving banks similarly situated.

[§4A-]202(3). The Article is explicit that "[t]he standard is not whether the security procedure is the best available. Rather it is whether the procedure is reasonable for the particular customer and the particular bank . . . ." [§4A-]203 cmt. 4. The UCC explains that "[t]he burden of making available commercially reasonable security procedures is imposed on receiving banks because they generally determine what security procedures can be used and are in the best position to evaluate the efficacy of procedures offered to customers to combat fraud." *Id.* cmt. 3.

. . .

If the bank shows both that its security procedure was commercially reasonable and that it accepted the payment order "in good faith and in compliance with the security procedure," the payment order is effective as an authorized order of the customer. [§§4A-]202(2)(b), -203(1). In such a case, the bank may, "[b]y express written agreement, . . . limit the extent to which it is entitled to enforce or retain payment of the payment order." [§4A-]203(1)(a).

Once the bank has shown commercial reasonableness, the customer may shift the risk of loss back to the bank if the customer proves that the order was not "caused, either directly or indirectly, by a person":

(i) Entrusted at any time with duties to act for the customer with respect to payment orders or the security procedure or who obtained access to transmitting facilities of the customer; or
(ii) Who obtained from a source controlled by the customer and without authority of the receiving bank information facilitating breach of the security procedure, regardless of how the information was obtained or whether the customer was at fault. Information includes any access device, computer software or the like.

[§4A-]203(1)(b). As the commentary explains, this section of the UCC places a burden on the customer, when the security procedure is commercially reasonable, "to supervise its employees to assure compliance with the security procedure and to safeguard confidential security information and access to transmitting facilities so that the security procedure cannot be breached." [§4A-]203 cmt. 3.

If the bank does not make its showing of commercial reasonableness, then the analysis goes back to the question of agency under [§4A-]202(a), described above. If the court determines, under any of these provisions, that the bank bears the risk of loss, "the bank shall refund any payment of the payment order received from the customer to the extent the bank is not entitled to enforce payment and shall pay interest on the refundable amount calculated from the date the bank received payment to the date of the refund." [§4A-]204(1).

B.   OCEAN BANK'S MOTION FOR SUMMARY JUDGMENT

Ocean Bank argues that because Patco agreed to the security system in use, and because the security system was commercially reasonable, it is entitled to summary judgment.

Patco counters that the bank's security system was not commercially reasonable, that it did not agree to all of the procedures, and that the bank did not comply with its own procedures.

As to commercial reasonableness, Patco argues the bank's decision to lower the dollar amount rule to $1 increased the risk of compromised security, and that the bank's failure in light of this increased risk to monitor and immediately notify customers of abnormal transactions which met high-risk criteria was not commercially reasonable. Patco also argues that it was not offered and it did not decline an e-mail notice system for transactions.

Essentially, Patco argues that when Ocean Bank decided in June of 2008 to trigger challenge questions for any transaction over $1, the bank increased the frequency with which a user was required to enter the answers to his or her challenge questions. Indeed, at a $1 threshold, the frequency as to Patco became 100%, covering every transaction. For customers like Patco who made regular ACH transfers, the risks were even greater than for customers who rarely made such transfers. This, in turn, also increased the risk that such answers would be compromised by keyloggers[8] or other malware that would capture that information for unauthorized uses. By thus increasing the risk of fraud through unauthorized use of compromised security answers, Patco argues, Ocean Bank's security system failed to be commercially reasonable because it did not incorporate additional security measures, at the very least monitoring of high risk score transactions, use of e-mail alerts and inquiries, or other immediate notice to customers of high-risk transactions.

In our view, Ocean Bank did substantially increase the risk of fraud by asking for security answers for every $1 transaction, particularly for customers like Patco which had frequent, regular, and high dollar transfers. Then, when it had warning

---

8. A "keylogger" is a form of computer malware, or malicious code, capable of infecting a user's system, secretly monitoring the user's Internet activity, recognizing when the user has browsed to the website of a financial institution, and recording the user's key strokes on that website. In this way, the keylogger is able to capture a user's authentication credentials, which the keylogger then transmits to a cyber thief.

that such fraud was likely occurring in a given transaction, Ocean Bank neither monitored that transaction nor provided notice to customers before allowing the transaction to be completed. Because it had the capacity to do all of those things, yet failed to do so, we cannot conclude that its security system was commercially reasonable. We emphasize that it was these collective failures taken as a whole, rather than any single failure, which rendered Ocean Bank's security system commercially unreasonable.

The Jack Henry Premium Product was designed to harness the power of the risk-scoring system and included a device identification system to trigger an additional layer of authentication—challenge questions—whenever the bank's system detected unusual or suspicious transactions. In May of 2009, bank personnel did not monitor the risk-scoring reports, nor did the bank conduct any other regular review of transactions that generated high-risk scores. Thus, the only result of a high-risk score or an unidentified device was that a customer would be prompted to answer his or her challenge questions.

When Ocean Bank lowered the dollar amount rule from $100,000 to $1, it essentially deprived the complex Jack Henry risk-scoring system of its core functionality. The $1 dollar amount rule guaranteed that challenge questions would be triggered on every transaction unless caught by a separate eFraud network, which depended on the use of known fraudulent IP addresses. The eFraud network was of no use if the address and like information were not already known to law enforcement. Accordingly, cyber criminals equipped with keyloggers had the much more frequent opportunity to capture all information necessary to compromise an account every time the customer initiated an ACH transaction. In Patco's case, ACH transactions were initiated at least weekly, and often several times per week. In the event a customer's computer became infected with a keylogger, it was likely that the customer would be prompted to answer its challenge questions before the malware was discovered and removed from the customer's computer.

Patco's argument is supported both by evidence and by common sense. Patco's expert testified that at the times in question, keylogging malware was a persistent problem throughout the financial industry. It was foreseeable, against this background, that triggering the use of the same challenge questions for high-risk transactions as were used for ordinary transactions, was ineffective as a stand-alone backstop to password/ID entry. Indeed, it was well known that setting challenge questions to be asked on every transaction greatly increases the risk that a fraudster equipped with a keylogger would be able to access the answers to a customer's challenge questions because it increases the frequency with which such information is entered through a user's keyboard.

As early as 2005, RSA/Cyota cautioned against the regular and frequent use of challenge questions as a stand-alone backstop to the exclusion of further controls, stating that challenge questions were "quicker and simpler to adopt" but were "less secure," and should be used only "in the short term, as the first phase of a full project." According to RSA/Cyota, challenge questions should be triggered only selectively, when unusual or suspicious activity is detected, so that they are less likely to be asked after a keylogger is installed on a customer's computer and before it can be removed. When asked frequently, they should not be used as the only line of defense beyond a password/ID, since a password/ID and answers to challenge questions could all be simultaneously captured by a keylogger.

Ocean Bank's decision to set the dollar amount rule at $1 for all of its customers also ignored Article 4A's mandate that security procedures take into account "the circumstances of the customer" known to the bank. [§4A-]202(3). Article 4A directs banks to consider such circumstances as "the size, type and frequency of payment orders normally issued by the customer to the bank." *Id.* In Patco's case, these characteristics were regular and predictable. Patco used eBanking primarily to make payroll payments to employees. These payments were made weekly, generally on Fridays; they originated from a single static IP address; and they were always made from the same set of computers at Patco's offices in Sanford, Maine. The highest such payment Patco ever made was $36,634.74, well below the former $100,000 threshold. The bank does not assert that it ever offered to adjust the threshold amount for particular customers. Instead, the bank adopted a "one-size-fits-all" dollar amount rule of $1 for its customers.

Ocean Bank argues that it did take Patco's circumstances into account by building a risk profile based on Patco's eBanking habits, such that the security system could compare the characteristics of each transaction against those in Patco's profile. This argument misses the mark because, in fact, the risk profile information played no role. It triggered no additional authentication requirements, and the bank did nothing with the information generated by comparing the fraudulent transactions against Patco's profile.

Ocean Bank also argues that it was commercially reasonable for it to universally lower the dollar amount rule to $1 in order to target low-dollar fraud. Whether or not that is true for certain customers, it is beside the point. Here, the increase in risk to the consumer who engaged in regular high dollar transfers, such as Patco, was sufficiently serious to require a corollary increase in security measures for a security system to remain commercially reasonable. The bank's generic "one-size-fits-all" approach to customers violates Article 4A's instruction to take the customer's circumstances into account. Further, the reduction of the dollar amount rule to $1 was for commercial customers, who are quite unlikely to have transfers of less than $1.

Ocean Bank introduced no additional security measures in tandem with its decision to lower the dollar amount rule, despite the fact that several such security measures were not uncommon in the industry and were relatively easy to implement. Patco's expert testified that all of her other banking clients using the same Jack Henry Premium Product employed manual reviews or some other additional security measure to protect against the type of fraud that occurred in this case.

For example, by May 2009, internet banking security had largely moved to hardware-based tokens and other means of generating "one-time" passwords.[10.] As of then, People's United Bank (which had acquired Ocean Bank), several national banks, and many New England community banks were using tokens for commercial accounts. Of those banks that did not use tokens in May 2009, New England

---

10. Although tokens can be compromised, bypassing them requires greater sophistication than is needed to obtain challenge questions. The perpetrator must use the information within seconds of acquiring it, before the system generates a new password to replace the old. The answers to challenge questions, by contrast, may be used at the perpetrator's leisure, particularly when, as was the case at Ocean Bank, the answers are static. Even if a token had been used and compromised in this case, the magnitude of the resulting fraud would have been greatly reduced because the captured password could not have been used after the initial transaction.

community banks commonly used some form of manual review or customer verification to authenticate uncharacteristic or suspicious transactions. Such security procedures self-evidently would not have been difficult to implement.

This failure to implement additional procedures was especially unreasonable in light of the bank's knowledge of ongoing fraud. As early as 2008, Ocean Bank had received notification of substantial increases in internet fraud involving keylogging malware. By May 2009, Ocean Bank had itself experienced at least two incidents of fraud on the bank's system which it attributed to either keylogging malware or internal fraud. In both instances, the perpetrators had acquired and successfully applied the customer's passwords, IDs, and answers to challenge questions.

Thus, by May 2009, when the fraud in this case occurred, it was commercially unreasonable for Ocean Bank's security system to trigger nothing more than what was triggered in the event of a perfectly ordinary transaction in response to the high risk scores that were generated by the withdrawals from Patco's account. The payment orders at issue were entirely uncharacteristic of Patco's ordinary transactions: they were directed to accounts to which Patco had never before transferred money; they originated from computers Patco had never before used; they originated from an IP address that Patco had never before used; and they specified payment amounts significantly higher than the payments Patco ordinarily made to third parties. As a result, the security system flagged these transactions as uncharacteristic, highly suspicious, and potentially fraudulent from a "very high risk non-authenticated device." The transactions generated unprecedentedly high risk scores ranging from 563 to 790, well above Patco's regular risk scores which ranged from 10 to 214.

These collective failures, taken as a whole, rendered Ocean Bank's security procedures commercially unreasonable. We reverse the district court's grant of summary judgment as to Count I.

That does not, however, end the matter, even as to Count I. The issues briefed to us on appeal have largely involved commercial reasonableness. Our conclusion that the security procedures were not commercially reasonable does not end the analysis of the Article 4A issues. Our conclusion as to Count I and commercial reasonableness does, though, also lead us to vacate the district court's grant of summary judgment on the two claims—Count V (unjust enrichment) and Count VI (conversion)—which the district court considered to be dependent on the success of Count I.

C. PATCO'S MOTION FOR SUMMARY JUDGMENT

We affirm the district court's decision to deny Patco's motion for summary judgment. There remain several genuine and disputed issues of fact which may be material to the question of whether Patco has satisfied its obligations and responsibilities under Article 4A, or at least to the question of damages. The district court did not reach, and the parties have not briefed, the question of what, if any, obligations or responsibilities Article 4A imposes on a commercial customer even where a bank's security system is commercially unreasonable. We leave these questions open on remand so that the district court may, after briefing, assess whether such obligations exist, either for liability purposes or for mitigation of damages.

As to the genuine and disputed issues of fact, the parties dispute the facts surrounding Patco's lack of e-mail alerts. Patco alleges that it requested e-mail alerts from the bank, but that the bank ignored these requests and never notified Patco when e-mail alerts became available to bank customers. The bank counters with its own allegation that it sent out a general e-mail to customers that it would make e-mail alerts available. Patco states that it received no such e-mail, and that instead, a customer would have had to follow a complicated series of steps to find an "Alerts" tab on the bank's website in order to learn that such e-mail alerts had become available. Moreover, Patco alleges that its account was not even set up with an "Alerts" tab; that the account only features a "Preferences" tab. While one of Patco's employees did successfully navigate to the "Preferences" tab, she alleges she never saw an "Alerts" tab. Additionally, neither party has submitted into the record an example of such an e-mail alert or specified when such an e-mail alert would have been sent, such that it is unclear what Patco would have learned from such an e-mail alert and whether and when such an e-mail would have placed Patco on notice of the fraudulent transfer.

The parties also disagree as to whether the fraud in this case was caused by malware and keylogging in the first place, or whether Patco shares some responsibility. Ocean Bank argues that because Patco irreparably altered the evidence on its hard drives by using and scanning its computers before making forensic copies, it is unclear whether keylogging malware existed on Patco's computers and enabled the alleged fraud. These disputed issues of fact may be material.

Article 4A does not appear to be a one-way street. Commercial customers have obligations and responsibilities as well, under at least [§4A-]204. . . . Section [4A-]204, entitled "Refund of payment and duty of customer to report with respect to unauthorized payment order," provides:

> The customer is not entitled to interest from the bank on the amount to be refunded if the customer fails to exercise ordinary care to determine that the order was not authorized by the customer and to notify the bank of the relevant facts within a reasonable time not exceeding 90 days after the date the customer received notification from the bank that the order was accepted or that the customer's account was debited with respect to the order.

It is unclear, however, what, if any, obligations a commercial customer has when a bank's security system is found to be commercially unreasonable.

In short, we leave open for the parties to brief on remand the question of what, if any, obligations or responsibilities are imposed on a commercial customer under Article 4A even where a bank's security system is commercially unreasonable. The record requires further development on these issues, precluding summary judgment at this stage.

. . .

IV.

We reverse the district court's grant of summary judgment in favor of the bank, and affirm the district court's denial of Patco's motion for summary judgment. We remand for further proceedings in accordance with this opinion. On remand the parties may wish to consider whether it would be wiser to invest their resources in resolving this matter by agreement.

———————

One problem with imposing responsibility on the bank for unauthorized orders that go undiscovered by lax security procedures is the possibility that the customer will prefer a lax procedure because of the expense and inconvenience of more secure procedures. The statute deals with that problem by absolving the bank for responsibility for the customer's use of an unreasonably lax procedure if the bank previously offered the customer an appropriate procedure, but the customer selected the unreasonable procedure anyway. UCC §4A-202(c); see UCC §4A-203 comment 4. Consider how that approach differs from the approach in the checking system, where a bank's attempt to disclaim responsibility for negligence in response to a customer's decision not to employ the bank's preferred security procedures would violate UCC § 4-103(a). See Majestic Bldg. Maintenance v. Huntington Bancshares, 864 F.3d 455 (6th Cir. 2017).

The second restriction requires the bank to show that it processed the order in accordance with the agreement of the victimized customer. UCC §4A-202(b)(ii). Accordingly, the bank cannot charge its customer for an unauthorized order issued pursuant to a security procedure — even if the procedure is reasonable — if the bank failed to comply with the procedure or if the order violated some other provision of the bank's agreement with its customer (such as an overdraft limit). See UCC §4A-203 comment 3.

The third exception permits the customer to pass the liability back to the bank if the customer can identify the breach of the security procedure and demonstrate that the information that allowed the fraud was not obtained "from a source controlled by the customer." UCC §4A-203(a). Thus, where it is clear that the thief operated by compromising the bank's own computer system, the bank must accept responsibility for the unauthorized transactions. Notwithstanding the apparent generosity of that provision, two problems with the details of the provision make it likely that customers occasionally will bear responsibility for fraud committed by persons that do not obtain information from the customer.

First, the exception applies only in cases in which the customer can discover how the fraud was committed. See UCC §§4A-203(a)(2) (relief available only to customers that "prov[e]" that the malefactor did not obtain access through the customer), 4A-105(a)(7) (defining "[p]rove" to mean "meet the burden of establishing the fact"). If the customer cannot determine who committed the fraud or how it was done, the customer will remain responsible. The drafters of Article 4A apparently found that turn of events improbable; UCC §4A-203 comment 5 states that appropriate investigation ordinarily will discover the source of the fraud. The facts of *Patco* indicate that that optimism might have been unwarranted.

Second, the statute's use of "contro[l] by the customer" as the key for allocating responsibility introduces substantial ambiguity into the system. For example, it is not clear how that test would treat one of the most likely types of theft: a man-in-the-middle attack that operates by interception of messages between the customer and the bank. Does the customer "contro[l]" the line over which it sends a message to its bank? A sensible rule would place that loss on the bank — without regard to abstract concepts of "control" of the line — because the bank is the only party realistically able to upgrade the security of the transmission. But UCC §4A-206 suggests that Article 4A would view the communications system as an agent of the customer and thus hold the customer liable for any malfeasance.

The last issue of the fraud topic is what happens when the system executes a fraudulent wire-transfer order. The rules closely resemble the rules for erroneous orders discussed in the preceding assignment. The simplest possibility is that the order is treated as authorized under the security procedure rules. In that case, the customer is treated as the sender of the order under UCC §4A-202(d) and accordingly is obligated to pay the order under UCC §4A-402(c). The customer's remedy is limited to a suit for conversion against the defrauder.

If the order cannot be treated as an authorized order under UCC §4A-202, then the bank must refund any sums that the customer already paid with respect to the order, with interest. UCC §4A-204(a). As with interest compensation for erroneous orders, the customer can lose its right to interest if it fails to complain within a reasonable time (not to exceed 90 days) of the time that the customer was notified of the unauthorized order. UCC §4A-204(a). For payment orders sent to Federal Reserve banks, the Federal Reserve has issued a regulation stating that 30 calendar days from the date that the sender receives notice is a reasonable time. Regulation J, §210.28(c).

B.   System Failure

The last significant risk involved in wire-transfer payments is the risk of system failure. As discussed early in this chapter, the wire-transfer system as currently structured accepts a considerable amount of credit risk in the form of daylight overdrafts. To get an idea of the difficulty of redesigning the system to avoid those overdrafts, consider the fact that a financial institution active in the area might turn over its assets about 1.5 times every day. If a significant bank failed to satisfy its obligations at the end of the day, the resulting losses would place severe stress on the financial system. Policymakers have focused on that problem since the 1974 failure of the German bank Herstatt made it clear how serious a problem bank failure would be for the multilateral clearing systems that are common in modern wire-transfer practice.

Concerns about that risk have produced considerable attention to system design, as banks strive to provide "real-time gross settlement" services — immediate payment in full on an order-by-order basis, without exposing the participants to substantial systemic settlement risk. Trying to provide a backstop for that risk, Section 4A-405(e) (and comment 4) establishes a process for unwinding if such a disaster should occur. In reality, though, the major systems in use at this date have developed designs that come quite close to providing both real-time payment and limited systemic settlement risk.

Because the SWIFT system provides for bilateral settlement, system failure is not a significant problem. Each bank accepts transfers from other banks only when it has determined that it is satisfied with the ability of the sending bank to pay that particular transfer. Thus, the worst thing that a SWIFT-participating bank could suffer upon the failure of another SWIFT user would be that the surviving bank would lose the funds for transfers that it chose to complete without obtaining prior payment. Banks can address that risk directly by treating their exposure under those bilateral agreements as an extension of credit to the counterparty, an extension that presumably could be terminated (or adjusted) on a day-to-day (or even hour-to-hour) basis.

The risk is similarly minimal for Fedwire participants because those participants incur no cognizable credit risk. The Federal Reserve, as operator of the Fedwire system, has undertaken to accept all of the risk that a Fedwire participant will fail. Thus, there is no provision in the UCC or Regulation J that would allow for the unraveling of a completed Fedwire transaction. Those transfers truly become final just a few moments after execution. The only systemic risk is the failure of a participant of a size that would destabilize the Federal Reserve itself. That risk, in turn, is limited to the pervasive attention by the Federal Reserve to daylight overdrafts as an extension of credit.

The system-failure problem is only slightly more serious for CHIPS and its participants. Where Fedwire operates its system through the Federal Reserve and thus has the credit of our central banking system to support its settlements, CHIPS is a private institution that has no similar source of financial backing for the trillions of dollars that it transfers each day. As explained above, CHIPS has developed a complicated procedure for bilateral and multilateral netting that allows it to settle the overwhelming majority of its transactions during the course of the business day. Although, at an earlier time, CHIPS participants were forced to accept the risk each day that the system would be unable to settle at the end of the day (the possibility discussed in UCC §4A-405(e) and comment 4), the modern CHIPS process eliminates that risk. The cost is the inability to provide absolutely immediate gross settlement, but in practice, except for very large transfers, the multilateral netting system produces reliably swift settlement.

Problem Set 13

13.1. Your client Ben Darrow (the banker from FSB) calls you to discuss a funds-transfer services agreement that he is negotiating with his customer Carol Long. FSB currently is marketing to its customers a newly developed AccuWire system that uses sophisticated encryption and multiple passwords to provide a high degree of security in wire transfers. When Ben started to describe the system to Carol, she said she was not interested (right after he told her that it would cost her "only" $35,000 to have the system installed). She says that she trusts her employees completely, believes that her workplace is totally secure, and has no interest in spending money on some expensive security procedure developed by an out-of-state bank that recently acquired FSB.

Carol tells Ben to draw up an agreement stating that FSB is authorized to act on any written instruction that it receives from the customer's designated e-mail account. Ben wants your help drafting the agreement. Does the agreement that Carol has proposed expose Ben or FSB to any significant risks? UCC §§4A-201, 4A-202, 4A-203, 4A-501(a).

13.2. Bertrand Oswald comes to you, hoping to cancel a wire transfer that he sent to purchase an antique silver cow creamer. Bertie tells you that Threepwood (the seller of the creamer) defrauded Bertie in the underlying sales transaction. The fraud is in claiming that the cow creamer is "antique." Jeeves has discovered through examination of a smith's mark on the creamer that the creamer was manufactured less than ten years ago. By the time Bertie approaches you with this question, the beneficiary's bank has notified Threepwood, the beneficiary, of the incoming transfer, but Threepwood has not yet withdrawn the funds.

a. Assuming that Bertie could persuade the banks of the fraud, would Threepwood's fraud enable Bertie to keep the beneficiary's bank from paying the funds to Threepwood? UCC §§4A-209(b)(1)(ii), 4A-211(c), (e) & comment 4, 4A-404 comment 3.

b. Would your answer be any different if the transfer was wholly fraudulent—sent from Bertie's computer without his involvement in any way? UCC §4A-211(c) comment 4. If it did change your answer, would Threepwood's bank be able to recover the funds from Threepwood?

13.3. Roderick Spode comes to see you with a problem about unauthorized wire transfers. Although his bank's security software is supposed to prevent transfers of more than $1 million in any single transfer, a glitch last week permitted an unintended transfer of $2 million, which should have been only $200,000, to an account in the Netherlands Antilles from which the funds cannot be recovered. Does Spode have a claim against his bank? UCC §§4A-202, 4A-203, 4A-205. If so, can the two banks retrieve the money from the recipient?

13.4. First on your schedule this week is a closing, at which Bill Robertson is selling one of his grocery stores to a consortium of Canadian investors put together by Rick Compo. Conforming to his usual habit, Bill peppers you with questions at the closing, trying to make sure that you have thought of everything bad that could happen to him. Just before he signs the papers, he asks about the security of the payment coming to him by wire transfer: "I've never thought about it before. I've just assumed it was safe. Am I absolutely safe if I go ahead and convey the property based on my bank's advising me that it has received the purchase price by wire?" What do you tell him? UCC §§4A-209(b), 4A-404(a), 4A-405(d) & (e), 4A-405 comment 3. Would your answer change if the payment was being made in pounds sterling?

Assignment 14. The Nature of the Wire Transfer

One of the most contested wire-transfer issues in recent years has related to the fundamental nature of the transfer. In a series of high-profile cases, litigants with claims against parties to funds transfers have sought to pull funds back out of the wire-transfer system. Although UCC Article 4A is drafted to prevent those challenges in many cases, courts have been occasionally receptive. The cases that follow illustrate the tortuous path those issues have followed.

Shipping Corp. of India, Ltd. v. Jaldhi Overseas Pte Ltd.
585 F.3d 58 (2d Cir. 2009)

Before: FEINBERG, WINTER, and CABRANES, Circuit Judges.

This case is based on a dispute between a company incorporated in India and a company incorporated in Singapore over an accident that occurred in India while one company was shipping products to China; the dispute was to be arbitrated in England. Because the parties' banks had accounts in New York banks, electronic fund transfers ("EFTs") between one party involved in the dispute and third parties passed through New York electronically for an instant. Under Winter Storm Shipping, Ltd. v. TPI, 310 F.3d 263, 278 (2d Cir. 2002), this momentary passage was sufficient to vest jurisdiction in the United States District Court of the Southern District of New York.

We are now presented with the question of whether the rule of *Winter Storm* should be reconsidered and, upon reconsideration, overruled. Specifically, this appeal raises the issue of whether EFTs of which defendants are the beneficiary are attachable property of the defendant pursuant to Rule B of the Supplemental Rules for Admiralty or Maritime Claims and Asset Forfeiture Actions of the Federal Rules of Civil Procedure ("Rule B" of "the Admiralty Rules"). . . . We now conclude, with the consent of all of the judges of the Court in active service, that *Winter Storm* was erroneously decided and therefore should no longer be binding precedent in our Circuit.

Our decision in *Winter Storm* produced a substantial body of critical commentary. . . . See, e.g., Permanent Editorial Bd. for the Uniform Commercial Code, PEB Commentary No. 16: Sections 4A-502(d) and 4A-503, at 5 n.4 (July 1, 2009) ("PEB Commentary") ("[T]he *Winter Storm* approach is proving to be practically unworkable."). And some have even suggested that *Winter Storm* has threatened the usefulness of the dollar in international transactions. See generally id. ("[T]his explosion of writs creates an additional threat to the U.S. dollar as the world's primary reserve currency and New York's standing as a center of international banking and finance."); see also Lawrence W. Newman & David Zaslowsky, *Is There Finally a*

Backlash Against Rule B Attachments?, 241 N.Y. L.J. 3 (2009) ("[W]hen lawyers are advising their clients that the best way to avoid Rule B attachments is to conduct maritime and perhaps other transactions in a currency other than U.S. dollars, there are emerging risks of a significant reduction in the use of the dollar as the dominant currency of international commerce.").

The unforeseen consequences of *Winter Storm* have been significant. According to *amicus curiae* The Clearing House Association L.L.C. — whose members [include ABN AMRO, Bank of America, Bank of New York Mellon, CitiBank, Deutsche Bank, HSBC, JPMorgan Chase, US Bank, and Wells Fargo]—from October 1, 2008 to January 31, 2009 alone "maritime plaintiffs filed 962 lawsuits seeking to attach a total of $1.35 billion. These lawsuits constituted 33% of all lawsuits filed in the Southern District, and the resulting maritime writs only add to the burden of 800 to 900 writs already served daily on the District's banks." Amicus Br. 3-4. . . .

BACKGROUND

In this action, plaintiff The Shipping Corporation of India, Ltd. ("SCI" or "plaintiff") appeals from a June 27, 2008 order of the United States District Court for the Southern District of New York (Jed S. Rakoff, Judge) insofar as it vacated portions of an order of maritime attachment and garnishment (the "attachment") entered by the District Court on May 7, 2008, pursuant to Rule B. Specifically, the June 2008 order vacated the attachment of EFTs sent from third parties not involved in this litigation to defendant Jaldhi Overseas Pte Ltd. ("Jaldhi" or "defendant") in the amount of $3,533,522. . . .

The relevant factual and procedural history is as follows. In March 2008, SCI chartered its vessel M/V Rishikesh (the "vessel") to defendant to transport iron ore from India to China. Specifically, the charter provided that SCI was to deliver the vessel to Jaldhi on March 29, 2008, "with hull, machinery, and equipment in a thoroughly efficient state." The vessel was delivered to Jaldhi on March 29, 2008, in compliance with the terms of the charter. While in port in Kolkata, India the next day, a crane on board the vessel collapsed, killing the crane operator, halting cargo operations, and causing Jaldhi to place the vessel "off hire," i.e., to suspend the charter.

On May 2, 2008, SCI issued an invoice to Jaldhi seeking payment of Jaldhi's unpaid balance of $3,608,445. After not receiving payment, SCI filed a complaint in the District Court seeking an ex parte maritime attachment pursuant to Rule B of the Admiralty Rules on May 7, 2008 for the balance, interest, and attorneys' fees for a total of $4,816,218. According to SCI, the vessel came back "on hire" on April 13, 2008, when its cranes passed safety inspections, and therefore Jaldhi owes payments under the charter from that date forward. On May 8, 2008, the District Court entered an ex parte order of Maritime Attachment and Garnishment in the amount of $4,816,218 and noted in its order that the attachment applied against all tangible or intangible property belonging to, claimed by or being held for the Defendant by any garnishees within this District, including but not limited to electronic fund transfers originated by, payable to, or otherwise for the benefit of Defendant. . . .

. . . SCI successfully attached EFTs in the amount of $4,873,404.90. EFTs where defendant was the beneficiary comprised $4,590,678.60 of the total amount attached, with the remainder consisting of EFTs where defendant was the originator.

[The District Court subsequently vacated the attachment based on its limiting construction of *Winter Storm* and certified the question for immediate appeal pursuant to 28 U.S.C. §1292(b).]

DISCUSSION

Rule B of the Admiralty Rules permits attachment of "the defendant's tangible or intangible personal property." Fed. R. Civ. P. Supp. R. B(1)(a). From a plain reading of the text, it is clear that to attach an EFT under Rule B, the EFT must both (1) be "tangible or intangible property" and (2) be the "defendant's."

Before we can reach the question presented squarely in this appeal—whether an EFT is defendant's property when defendant is the beneficiary of that EFT—we must first consider the threshold issue of whether EFTs are indeed "defendant's" property subject at all to attachment under the Admiralty Rules. We first held that EFTs were in fact attachable property under Rule B seven years ago in *Winter Storm*. Although we have subsequently applied *Winter Storm* in numerous cases, we now conclude, as noted earlier, that *Winter Storm* was erroneously decided and should no longer be binding precedent in this Circuit.

We readily acknowledge that a panel of our Court is "bound by the decisions of prior panels until such time as they are overruled either by an *en banc* panel of our Court or by the Supreme Court," United States v. Wilkerson, 361 F.3d 717, and thus that it would ordinarily be neither appropriate nor possible for us to reverse an existing Circuit precedent. In this case, however, we have circulated this opinion to all active members of this Court prior to filing and have received no objection. See, e.g., United States v. Crosby, 397 F.3d 103; Jacobson v. Fireman's Fund Ins. Co., 111 F.3d 261.

Our reasons for reversing a relatively recent case are twofold. First, and most importantly, we conclude that the holding in *Winter Storm* erroneously relied on United States v. Daccarett, 6 F.3d 37, to conclude that EFTs are attachable property. *Winter Storm*, 310 F.3d at 276-78. Second, as noted above, the effects of *Winter Storm* on the federal courts and international banks in New York are too significant to let this error go uncorrected simply to avoid overturning a recent precedent. . . .

Upon further consideration, we find *Winter Storm*'s reasons unpersuasive and its consequences untenable. Most importantly, we find that *Winter Storm*'s reliance on *Daccarett* was misplaced. *Daccarett* did not decide that the originator or beneficiary of an EFT had a property interest in the EFT; it held only that funds traceable to an illegal activity were subject to forfeiture under 21 U.S.C. §881. Under the forfeiture laws, funds can be seized even if they do not constitute property of the defendant because "no property right shall exist in . . . [all] moneys . . . traceable to [a violation of Title 21, Chapter 13, Subchapter I of the United States Code]." 21 U.S.C. §881(a). To be eligible for forfeiture, the EFTs needed only to be traceable to the illegal activities, and thus the court in *Daccarett* was required only to assess whether the EFTs in that case were in fact traceable to illegal activities. No further inquiry into the identity of the owner of the EFTs was necessary—indeed, that question was wholly irrelevant.

For maritime attachments under Rule B, however, the question of ownership is critical. As a remedy *quasi in rem*, the validity of a Rule B attachment depends entirely on the determination that the *res* at issue is the property of the defendant at the moment the *res* is attached. Because a requirement of Rule B attachments is that the defendant is not "found within the district," the *res* is the only means by which a court can obtain jurisdiction over the defendant. If the *res* is not the property of the defendant, then the court lacks jurisdiction. In contrast, civil forfeiture is a remedy *in rem*. *In rem* jurisdiction is based on the well-established theory that the "thing is itself treated as the offender and made the defendant by name or description." California v. Deep Sea Research, Inc., 523 U.S. 491 (1998). Thus, for *in rem* remedies such as forfeitures, ownership of the *res* is irrelevant, as the court has personal jurisdiction regardless of who owns the *res* at issue. Although not considered by the *Winter Storm* panel, this distinction provides, in our view, a principled basis for allowing EFTs to be subject to forfeiture but not attachment. In sum, *Daccarett* provides no persuasive guidance on the validity of Rule B attachments of EFTs and should not serve as the foundation for a rule that allows the attachment of EFTs under Rule B.

Without the support of *Daccarett*, we are unpersuaded that either the text of Rule B or our past maritime holdings relating to defendants' bank accounts compel us to conclude as a matter of federal law that an EFT is "*defendant's . . . personal property*." Fed. R. Civ. P. Supp. R. B(1)(a) (emphasis added). Moreover, we are unaware of any historical rationale that justifies the extension of federal maritime common law to support the Rule B practices that have taken place under the rule of *Winter Storm*. One of the primary grounds for the historical development of Rule B attachments was that "[a] ship may be here today and gone tomorrow." Polar Shipping Ltd. v. Oriental Shipping Corp., 680 F.2d 627, 637 (9th Cir. 1982); see also Schiffahartsgesellschaft Leonhardt & Co. v. A. Bottacchi S.A. De Navegacion, 732 F.2d 154 (noting that a "relevant commercial . . . consideration[]" relating to Rule B practices is that "a ship's ability to dock, unload cargo, and fill its hold with goods intended for another destination — all within twenty four hours — imposes tremendous pressure on creditors desiring to attach a vessel or property located aboard"). EFTs, like ships in a port, are transitory. Streamlined Rule B practices, however, developed out of the concern that ships might set sail quickly, not because the courts intended to arm maritime plaintiffs with writs of attachment prior to the arrival of the ship in port. Under *Winter Storm*, however, maritime plaintiffs now seek writs of attachment pursuant to Rule B long before the defendant's property enters the relevant district, often based solely on the speculative hope or expectation that the defendant will engage in a dollar-denominated transaction that involves an EFT during the period the attachment order is in effect. Such practices, which have increased dramatically since *Winter Storm*, bear little, if any, relation to the text of Rule B or to our jurisprudence relating to the bank accounts of maritime defendants.

When there is no federal maritime law to guide our decision, we generally look to state law to determine property rights. Accordingly, we now look to state law to determine whether EFTs can be considered a "defendant's" property for purposes of attachment under Rule B.

New York State does not permit attachment of EFTs that are in the possession of an intermediary bank. Specifically, New York law states that "a court may restrain . . . the beneficiary's bank from releasing funds to the beneficiary or the beneficiary from withdrawing the funds." N.Y. U.C.C. §4-A-503; see also id. §4-A-503 cmt. 1 ("After the funds transfer is completed by acceptance of a payment order by the beneficiary's bank, [the beneficiary's] bank can be enjoined from releasing funds to the beneficiary or the beneficiary can be enjoined from withdrawing funds.").

As for those interested in obtaining the originator's funds, New York law is also clear. Specifically, "a court may restrain . . . an originator's bank from executing the payment order of the originator." Id. §4-A-503; see also id. §4-A-502 cmt. 4 ("A creditor of the *originator* can levy on the account of the originator in the originator's bank *before the funds transfer is initiated. . . .* The creditor of the orig-inator *cannot reach any other funds because no property of the originator is being transferred.*" (emphases added)). Apart from these injunctions, "[a] court may not otherwise restrain [any activity] with respect to a funds transfer." Id. §4-A-503; see also European Am. Bank v. Bank of N.S., 12 A.D.3d 189 (Sup. Ct. 2009) (noting that attachments served on intermediary banks cannot be enforced); N.Y. U.C.C. §4-A-503 cmt. 1 ("*No other injunction is permitted.* In particular, *intermediary banks are protected. . . .*" (emphases added)).

Finally, an authoritative comment accompanying the New York Uniform Commercial Code states that a beneficiary has no property interest in an EFT because "until the funds transfer is completed by acceptance by the beneficiary's bank of a payment order for the benefit of the beneficiary, *the beneficiary has no property interest in the funds transfer* which the beneficiary's creditor can reach." N. Y. U.C.C. §4-A-502 cmt. 4 (emphasis added); cf. Sigmoil Res., N.V. v. Pan Ocean Oil Corp. (Nigeria), 234 A.D.2d 103 (S. Ct. 1996) ("Neither the originator who initiates payment nor the beneficiary who receives it holds title to the funds in the account at the correspondent bank."). Taken together, these provisions of New York law establish that EFTs are neither the property of the originator nor the beneficiary while briefly in the possession of an intermediary bank.

Because EFTs in the temporary possession of an intermediary bank are not prop-erty of either the originator or the beneficiary under New York law, they cannot be subject to attachment under Rule B. As stated earlier, *Rule B* allows attachment only of "*defendant's* . . . property." Fed. R. Civ. P. Supp. R. B(1)(a) (emphasis added). If the EFTs are not the property of either the originator or the beneficiary, then they cannot be "defendant's . . . property" and therefore are not subject to Rule B attachment.

In sum, because there is no governing federal law on the issue and New York law clearly prohibits attachment of EFTs, we conclude that EFTs being processed by an intermediary bank in New York are not subject to Rule B attachment. Accordingly, we conclude that the District Court did not err in vacating the portions of the order in this action affecting EFTs of which defendant was the beneficiary. We remand the cause to the District Court with directions to consider whether there are grounds for not vacating the remaining portions of the attachment order affecting EFTs of which defendant was the originator.

Export-Import Bank of the United States v. Asia Pulp & Paper Co.

609 F.3d 111 (2d Cir. 2010)

Before STRAUB and WESLEY, Circuit Judges, Gardephe, District Judge.
Straub, Circuit Judge:

Plaintiff Export-Import Bank of the United States ("ExIm") appeals from a May 27, 2009 order of the United States District Court for the Southern District of New York . . . quashing two writs of garnishment in connection with ExIm's efforts to collect a $144 million judgment against defendants pursuant to the Federal Debt Collection Procedures Act [sic] ("FDCPA"), 28 U.S.C. §3205 *et seq.* The District Court quashed the writs of garnishment to the extent they restrained electronic fund transfer ("EFT") credits at intermediary banks. For the reasons set forth below, we affirm the District Court's order and hold that an EFT temporarily in the possession of an intermediary bank in New York may not be garnished under the FDCPA to satisfy judgment debts owed by the originator or intended beneficiary of that EFT.

BACKGROUND

I.   The Parties

ExIm, a government corporation organized and existing under federal law as the official export credit agency of the United States, 12 U.S.C. §635 *et seq.*, is the holder of over $100 million of debt owed by defendants. ExIm is an agency of the United States and has a mandate to maintain and increase U.S. employment and to promote the export of domestic products by providing financial support for export sales to overseas buyers. 12 U.S.C. §635. In carrying out its mandate, ExIm offers direct loans, loan guarantees, working capital guarantees, and insurance. When ExIm guarantees a loan and the borrower defaults on payment obligations, ExIm pays the lender an amount up to the outstanding principal and interest on the loan. In return, ExIm is assigned the lender's rights to the debt and any associated security interests.

Defendants together form one of the largest paper manufacturers in the world. Defendant Asia Pulp & Paper Company, Ltd. ("APP") is the former parent company of the three other defendants in this case: PT Indah Kiat Pulp and Paper TBK; PT Pabrik Kertas Tjiwi Kimia TBK ("Tjiwi Kimia"); and PT Pindo Deli Pulp & Paper Mills ("Pindo Deli") (collectively known as the Principal Indonesian Operating Companies ("PIOCs")). The PIOCs are Indonesian companies, while APP is based in Singapore.

II.   LOAN DEFAULT

The PIOCs borrowed over $100 million via thirteen different loans issued through ExIm's direct loan and loan guarantee programs. Of these thirteen loans, twelve were private loans that ExIm guaranteed and one was issued directly to defendants by ExIm. Three of the thirteen notes also included a separate guarantee signed by APP that obligated APP as guarantor to repay the loans.

In March 2001, defendants announced a worldwide "standstill" on the repayment of over $7 billion of debt, including the thirteen loans relevant to this appeal. Upon defendants' default, ExIm fully paid the private lenders on the twelve private loans and, in return, the private lenders assigned ExIm their respective rights, title, and interest in the loans.

III.   THE DISTRICT COURT PROCEEDINGS

Following defendants' default, ExIm sued for breach of contract, breach of promissory notes, and breach of guarantee and sought relief pursuant to the FDCPA. On February 6, 2008, the District Court granted ExIm's motion for summary judgment, finding that there was no dispute that defendants had defaulted on their loans and that defendants had failed to raise an issue of fact about whether their default should be excused. On May 28, 2008, the District Court entered a judgment in excess of $144 million in favor of ExIm against defendants, which we subsequently affirmed.

On February 3, 2009, seeking to collect on the judgment, ExIm applied pursuant to the FDCPA for the issuance of writs of garnishment to retain property in which several defendants purportedly had a nonexempt interest. The following day, the District Court granted ExIm's applications, and ExIm promptly served the writs on Deutsche Bank Trust Company Americas ("Deutsche Bank") and Bank of New York Mellon Corporation ("BONY"), directing them to withhold all property in their possession, custody or control in which defendants Tjiwi Kimia and Pindo Deli, respectively, had a "substantial nonexempt interest."

On March 6, 2009, Deutsche Bank answered the writ of garnishment it had received, noting that Tjiwi Kimia did not maintain any accounts at Deutsche Bank, but that Deutsche Bank nevertheless had in its "custody, possession and control" seven EFTs "belonging to or in the name of Tjiwi Kimia," which Deutsche Bank had "intercepted and restrained" as an intermediary bank. The seven EFTs intercepted and restrained by Deutsche Bank, totaling $160,337.97, include three transfers for which Tjiwi Kimia is listed as "Originator" and four transfers for which Tjiwi Kimia is listed as "Beneficiary."

On March 27, 2009, BONY answered the writ of garnishment that it had received, stating that the only property it possessed in which Pindo Deli "may have a property interest" consisted of EFTs for which BONY "was the intermediary bank." Specifically, between February 10, 2009, and March 19, 2009, BONY received thirty-two EFT payment orders either to or from Pindo Deli. In total, BONY had in its possession $1,174,889.91 in bank credits for Pindo Deli-related EFTs.

Defendants Tjiwi Kimia and Pindo Deli objected to the answers of Deutsche Bank and BONY, respectively, arguing that (1) New York law prohibits the restraint of EFTs at intermediary banks and (2) as originator or intended beneficiary of the EFTs, neither Tjiwi Kimia nor Pindo Deli had any property interest in the EFTs restrained by Deutsche Bank and BONY. On April 17, 2009, the District Court quashed the writs of garnishment "insofar as they may have been interpreted to permit garnishment of EFTs between intermediary banks."

DISCUSSION

The present appeal requires us to determine whether an EFT temporarily in the possession of an intermediary bank in New York — *i.e.*, a midstream EFT —may be garnished under the FDCPA to satisfy judgment debts owed by either the originator or the intended beneficiary of the EFT. To answer this question we first look to New York law to determine the scope and contours of the relationship between the midstream EFT and the originator or intended beneficiary; in other words, we look to New York law to determine the interests and rights, if any, that an originator or intended beneficiary has with regard to an EFT temporarily in the possession of an intermediary bank. We then must determine as a matter of federal law whether those state-delineated interests and rights, if any, are sufficient to trigger application of the FDCPA, a federal statute that authorizes the garnishment of property in which a debtor has a "substantial . . . interest." 28 U.S.C. §3205(a). . . .

I.   THE ATTACHMENT OF MIDSTREAM EFTS UNDER VARIOUS FEDERAL STATUTES

In addressing whether EFTs may be subject to garnishment or attachment in various contexts, we consider both the nature of EFTs and the legal provisions that regulate them. [The court summarizes the reasoning and holding of *Jaldhi*.]

In sum, *Jaldhi* instructs that whether or not midstream EFTs may be attached or seized depends upon the nature and wording of the statute pursuant to which attachment or seizure is sought.

Here, ExIm sought writs of garnishment pursuant to the FDCPA. In line with *Jaldhi*, we therefore look to the FDCPA's language to determine whether the District Court properly quashed ExIm's writs of garnishment to the extent those writs restrained EFTs at intermediary banks.

II.   THE FDCPA

The FDCPA "provides the exclusive civil procedures for the United States to recover a judgment on a debt." 28 U.S.C. §3001(a)(1). The statute was enacted "to create a comprehensive statutory framework for the collection of debts owed to the United States government" and "to improve the efficiency and speed in collecting those debts." N.L.R.B. v. E.D.P. Med. Computer Sys., Inc., 6 F.3d 951, 954 (2d Cir. 1993). In contrast to Rule B, which requires that funds be the "defendant's . . . property" in order to be attached, the FDCPA authorizes the issuance of writs of garnishment to any person in "possession, custody or control" of property "in which the debtor has a *substantial nonexempt interest*." 28 U.S.C. §3205(a) (emphasis added). Subject to several exceptions not relevant here, the FDCPA broadly defines "property" to "include[] any present or future interest, whether legal or equitable, in real, personal (including choses in action), or mixed property, tangible or intangible, vested or contingent, wherever located and however held . . . ." *Id.* §3002(12).

Although the FDCPA specifically defines the types of "property" potentially subject to garnishment, the FDCPA does not identify who has a right or interest in that property. This is unsurprising: the FDCPA — the Federal Debt Collection *Procedures* Act — is a procedural statute enacted "to give the Justice Department *uniform Federal procedures* . . . to collect debts owed the United States nation-wide." H.R. Rep. No. 103-883, at 81 (1995) (emphasis added) (explaining change from pre-FDCPA scheme of reliance on diverse state procedural rules); *see also* H.R. Rep. No. 101-736 (1990) (noting that "the purported goal of creating federal legislation regarding debt collection is simply to establish uniform procedural standards"). There is no evidence, either from the statute's language or legislative history, that the FDCPA *creates* any interests or rights in property. In the absence of a superseding federal statute or regulation, state law generally governs the nature of any interests in or rights to property that an entity may have. E.g., Barnhill v. Johnson, 503 U.S. 393, 398 (1992). Accordingly, although the FDCPA expressly "preempt[s] State Law to the extent such law is inconsistent with a provision of [the FDCPA]," 28 U.S.C. §3003(d), there appears to be no inconsistency between the FDCPA's procedural framework and New York state laws that govern the scope and contours of an entity's interests and rights in property. This results because the FDCPA "itself 'creates no property rights but merely attaches consequences, federally defined, to rights created under state law.'" United States v. Craft, 535 U.S. 274, 278 (2002) (quoting United States v. Bess, 357 U.S. 51, 55 (1958)) (in reference to federal tax lien statute, 26 U.S.C. §6321).

Our analysis here — much like the analysis of the federal tax lien statute, 26 U.S.C. §6321, another federal statute that, like the FDCPA, "creates no property rights but merely attaches consequences, federally defined, to rights created under state law," *id.* — therefore proceeds in two steps. First, we look initially to state law to determine what rights the judgment debtor has in the property the Government seeks to reach. [Brackets, citation, and quotation marks omitted.] Second, we then look to federal law to determine whether the judgment debtor's state-delineated rights constitute a "substantial . . . interest" in property sufficient to trigger application of the FDCPA. [Brackets, citation, and quotation marks omitted.] Although the answer to this federal question largely depends upon state law, it is ultimately a question of federal law whether or not the FDCPA applies and authorizes garnishment of the judgment debtor's state-delineated property rights and interests. [Brackets, citation, ellipses, and quotation marks omitted.] Drawing upon the well known "bundle of sticks" analogy to describe property rights, state law determines only what sticks are in a person's bundle; federal law then dictates what may be done with that state-given bundle. [Brackets, citation, and quotation marks omitted.]

It is important to highlight that the two steps of this analysis, although related, are distinct. In looking to state law, we must be careful to consider the substance of the rights state law provides, not merely the labels the State gives these rights or the conclusions it draws from them. Such state law labels are irrelevant to the federal question of which bundles of rights amount to a substantial interest so as to be attachable under the FDCPA. [Citation and quotation marks omitted.] Our initial inquiry in this case is thus whether and to what extent an originator or an intended beneficiary has any interest in or right to a midstream EFT under New York law, *not* whether New York shields any such interest or right from garnishment. If at step one of our analysis we determine that an interest or right exists under state law, and if at step two we determine that interest or right to be a "substantial . . . interest" in property under the FDCPA, state law would be impotent to shield that interest or right from garnishment under the FDCPA. The FDCPA preempts state law "to the extent such law is inconsistent with a provision of this chapter," 28 U.S.C. §3003(d), and a state law provision that shields a state-created interest or right from collection would be inconsistent with the FDCPA provisions that authorize garnishment of property in which the defendant has a "substantial . . . interest," 28 U.S.C. §3205(a).

III.   WHETHER AN ORIGINATOR OR INTENDED BENEFICIARY HAS A
"SUBSTANTIAL . . . INTEREST" IN A MIDSTREAM EFT UNDER THE FDCPA

Applying the two-step framework outlined above, we conclude that whatever interest or right an originator or intended beneficiary has in a midstream EFT under New York law, if any, it is insufficient to constitute a "substantial . . . interest" under the FDCPA.

Article 4-A of New York's Uniform Commercial Code ("Article 4-A") governs EFTs, N.Y. U.C.C. §4-A-102, and was enacted to provide a "comprehensive body of law that defines the rights and obligations that arise from wire transfers," *Banque Worms v. BankAmerica Int'l, 77 N.Y.2d 362, 369 (1991)*. The system Article 4-A establishes is not intuitive. As various provisions of Article 4-A make clear, wire transfers, which include EFTs, are a unique type of transaction to which ordinary rules do not necessarily apply. *See, e.g.,* N.Y. U.C.C. §4-A-102 cmt. (stating that the provisions of Article 4-A "are intended to be the exclusive means of determining the rights, duties and liabilities of the affected parties" to covered EFT transactions); *Banque Worms,* 77 N.Y.2d at 369 (noting that "attempts to define rights and obligations in funds transfers by general principles or by analogy to rights and obligations in [other more traditional areas of law] have not been satisfactory").

Pursuant to Article 4-A, "[a] receiving bank is not the agent of the sender or beneficiary of the payment order it accepts, or of any other party to the funds transfer, and the bank owes no duty to any other party to the funds transfer except as provided in this article or by express agreement." N.Y. U.C.C. §4-A-212. An authoritative comment accompanying Article 4-A further states that a creditor of an originator may serve process on an originator's bank *before* a funds transfer is initiated, but not afterwards, because "no property of the originator is being transferred" during the funds transfer process. N.Y. U.C.C. §4-A-502 cmt. 4; *see Jaldhi, 585 F.3d at 71* (describing the above comment as "authoritative"). Likewise, "until the funds transfer is completed by acceptance by the beneficiary's bank of a payment order for the benefit of the beneficiary, the beneficiary has no property interest in the funds transfer which the beneficiary's creditor can reach." N.Y. U.C.C. §4-A-502 cmt. 4.

Recent commentary of the Permanent Editorial Board for the Uniform Commercial Code ("PEB"), which drafted the U.C.C., notes:

> Under Article 4A . . . the originator does not have any claim against the intermediary bank for return of the value in the event the funds transfer is not completed. Rather, the only party with a claim against the intermediary bank is the sender to that bank, which is typically the originator's bank . . . . The originator's bank must refund to the originator even if it cannot recover from the intermediary bank. The beneficiary likewise has no claim to any payment from the intermediary bank.

PEB Commentary No. 16, §§4A-502(d) and 4A-503, at 3 (2009). According to the PEB, this is so because

> [t]he intermediary bank has no contractual obligation to the originator or to the beneficiary, and neither the originator nor the beneficiary has any contractual obligation to or rights flowing from the intermediary bank. Thus, credits in an intermediary bank are credits in favor of the originator's bank, and are not property of either the originator or the beneficiary.

All of this is just to say that, according to the PEB,

> under the Article 4A structure, the issuance and acceptance of payment orders creates rights and obligations only as between the sender of the payment order and its receiving bank (e.g., between originator and originator's bank as to the originator's payment order), between the originator's bank and an intermediary bank as to the originator's bank's payment order, between the intermediary bank and the beneficiary bank as to the intermediary bank's payment order, and finally, as between the beneficiary bank that has accepted a payment order and that beneficiary.

We have readily determined that these various provisions and commentary "establish that EFTs are neither the property of the originator nor the beneficiary while briefly in the possession of an intermediary bank." [*Jaldhi*, 585 F.3d at 71.] Resolution of the "ownership" issue, however, does not definitively answer our threshold question concerning the existence and scope of an originator or intended beneficiary's right or interest, if any, in a midstream EFT. An "interest" in property is not necessarily synonymous with "title to" or "ownership of" property. *See, e.g.,* Black's Law Dictionary 149 (7th ed. 1999) (defining a "beneficial interest" as "[a] right or expectancy in something . . ., as opposed to legal title in that thing"). Indeed, we have recognized that it would be reasonable for a court to hold that an individual has an interest in property, even when he does not own that property, so long as the property benefitted him as if he had received the property directly.

Noting that "[t]he terms 'interest' and 'title' are clearly not synonymous," the Appellate Division of the New York Supreme Court has stated that, although Article 4-A establishes that neither an originator nor a beneficiary owns or has title to a midstream EFT, Article 4-A does *not* address the separate issue of who has an "*interest*" in an EFT. Bank of N.Y. v. Nickel, 14 A.D.3d 140, 145-47 (1st Dep't 2004). The *Nickel* court found no conflict between Article 4-A — which, it says, governs only passage of "title" — and a different federal statute that authorized the blocking or freezing of certain entities' "interests" in property. *Id.* at 147.

According to the *Nickel* court, Article 4-A and the federal statute that authorized the freezing of certain entities' EFTs "simply addressed different issues."[9.]

Even though, according to *Nickel*, Article 4-A does not directly or explicitly address whether an originator or intended beneficiary has an "interest" in a midstream EFT, Article 4-A undoubtedly addresses some related issues and imposes significant limitations on the rights and expected benefits associated with such EFTs. First, as already noted, an intermediary bank is the legal agent of neither the originator nor the intended beneficiary. N.Y. U.C.C. §4-A-212. Second, an originator and intended beneficiary have no legal claim or contractual rights against an intermediary bank in the event that a funds transfer is not completed. *See* Grain Traders, Inc. v. Citibank, N.A., 160 F.3d 97, 101-02 (2d Cir. 1998); PEB Commentary No. 16, §§4A-502(d) and 4A-503, at 3. Finally, although an originator or intended beneficiary's lack of "ownership" is not dispositive of whether they have an interest in a midstream EFT, it nevertheless suggests that whatever interests or rights exist, if any, are limited.

Based on these limitations, we conclude that whatever interest or right an originator or intended beneficiary has in a midstream EFT under New York law, it is insufficient to constitute a "substantial . . . interest" under the FDCPA. Because neither the statutory language nor the legislative history of the FDCPA defines the phrase "substantial . . . interest," we look to the common, ordinary definition of the words. Some of the common definitions of "substantial" include "essential," "material," "firmly or solidly established," and "weighty." 17 Oxford English Dictionary 67 (2d ed. 1989). Our analysis of whether a right or interest in property constitutes a "substantial . . . interest" is further guided by how "direct and tangible" an originator or beneficiary's benefit from the property appears.

Although originators and intended beneficiaries presumably derive some benefit from midstream EFTs — as EFTs are frequently used and destined to satisfy debts owed by the originator to the intended beneficiary — this benefit is insufficient to qualify as a "substantial . . . interest" under the FDCPA. We have recognized that it would be reasonable for a court to hold that a judgment debtor has an interest in funds, even though he never acquired physical possession of those funds, if the funds benefitted him as if he had received the money directly. [Citation and quotation marks omitted.] While an EFT is temporarily in the possession of an intermediary bank, however, that EFT clearly does not benefit the originator or intended beneficiary in the same way as if they had received the money directly. As noted earlier, neither an originator nor an intended beneficiary own an EFT while it is temporarily in the possession of an intermediary bank; they cannot seek a refund from the intermediary bank if the funds transfer is not completed; and an intermediary bank is not the agent of either the originator or the intended beneficiary. For these reasons, we conclude that an originator or intended beneficiary's interests

9. We pause to reiterate that we look to state law only to determine whether and to what extent an entity has an interest or a right in a midstream EFT and that we look to federal law to determine whether that state-delineated interest or right, if any, constitutes a "substantial . . . interest" under the FDCPA. To the extent the *Nickel* court was simply stating that Article 4-A does not address the federal law issue of whether an entity has an "interest" in property, as that term is defined by a federal statute, we understand the *Nickel* court to be addressing a different issue from our present inquiry. Our threshold inquiry is not whether Article 4-A addresses the federal law issue of whether an originator or beneficiary has a "substantial . . . interest" in a midstream EFT under the FDCPA; our threshold inquiry

and rights in a midstream EFT, if any, are not sufficiently "essential," "material," "firmly or solidly established," "weighty," or "direct and tangible," to constitute a "substantial . . . interest" under the FDCPA. Accordingly, we hold that an EFT temporarily in the possession of an intermediary bank may not be garnished under the FDCPA to satisfy judgment debts owed by the beneficiary or originator of that EFT.

CONCLUSION

For the reasons stated above, the order of the District Court is AFFIRMED.

———————

Regions Bank v. The Provident Bank, Inc.

345 F.3d 1267 (11th Cir. 2003)

Before BARKETT, MARCUS and ALARCON, Circuit Judges. Honorable ARTHUR L. ALARCON, United States Circuit Judge for the Ninth Circuit, sitting by designation.

Alarcon, Circuit Judge:

Regions Bank ("Regions") appeals from the final order and judgment of the district court dismissing this action. . . . Regions seeks reversal on the ground that the district court erred in ruling that Regions's state law claims were preempted by Article 4A of the Uniform Commercial Code ("U.C.C.") and that genuine issues of material fact exist regarding whether Provident knew or should have known that funds it received from Morningstar Mortgage Bankers, Inc. ("Morningstar"), by means of a wire transfer, had been fraudulently obtained.

We affirm because we conclude that Regions failed to demonstrate that Provident knew or should have known that funds transferred from Fleet Bank were fraudulently obtained by Morningstar.

I

Regions and Provident are commercial banks that act as "warehouse lenders" for the residential real estate market. Provident and Regions advance money to independent mortgage lenders, known as originators, who fund loans to home buyers.

---

is whether an originator or intended beneficiary has any interest or right in a midstream EFT under *state* law.

In addition, we express no opinion about whether the International Emergency Economic Powers Act ("IEEPA"), 50 U.S.C. §1701 *et seq.,* and its accompanying regulations — the statute and regulations at issue in *Nickel* — supersede state law governing substantive property rights. The IEEPA empowers the President to block the property and interests in property of nationals of countries that are involved in "any unusual and extraordinary threat . . . to the national security, foreign policy, or economy of the United States." 50 U.S.C. §§1701(a), 1702(a)(1)(B). Regulations that accompany the IEEPA often specifically define the terms "property" and "interest" in property, *see, e.g.,* 31 CFR §§585.303, 585.304, and the IEEPA's purpose differs considerably from the procedural nature and purpose of the FDCPA.

Under the typical warehouse loan agreement, the warehouse lender wires the funds requested by the originator to a closing agent or attorney who is instructed to disburse the funds to the home buyer. The original note signed by the home buyer serves as collateral for the loan, and the warehouse lender maintains a security interest in the property purchased with the loan. In order to pay off its debt with the warehouse lender, the originator sells the loan to a third party investor at a premium.

On August 25, 1998, Provident entered into a warehouse loan agreement with Morningstar [hereinafter Provident Warehouse Line]. Morningstar agreed to use the money lent to it by Provident to make mortgage loans to home buyers. Morningstar promised to use the proceeds from sales of the individual mortgage loans to third party investors to pay off its debt to Provident. If Morningstar failed to locate an investor to purchase its loans, and Provident's funds remained outstanding for more than the time period specified by Schedule A of the particular loan agreement, Morningstar agreed to repay Provident or purchase the loans itself.

Provident twice suspended Morningstar's warehouse line of credit, in January 1999, and March 2000, in response to its failure to make prompt payments on the loans or to sell them to third party investors. On April 4, 2000, John Haag Jiras, a closing attorney, informed Provident that his signature had been forged on closing documents pertaining to the Closing Agent Agreement and Errors and Omissions insurance policy that had been submitted to Provident by Morningstar, and that the FBI was investigating his allegations. Shortly thereafter, an FBI agent contacted Provident's in-house counsel regarding the investigation instigated by Mr. Jiras.

On April 5, 2000, Provident sent a letter to Angela Daidone, president and CEO of Morningstar, demanding repayment of all outstanding loans within ten days. Ms. Daidone informed Provident that she owned ten acres of land in Long Island, New York that she would liquidate, and that she would wire the funds into the demand deposit account ("DDA") that Morningstar maintained at Provident Bank. Morningstar had previously reimbursed Provident from monies deposited in this account.

On April 6, 2000, Provident discovered that First Union Mortgage Corporation ("First Union") possessed the original note for one of Provident's outstanding home loans. On March 29, 2000, First Union had forwarded the funds to pay for the loan to Chase Manhattan Bank ("Chase"), for deposit into Morningstar's Paine Webber account.

Meanwhile, on April 4, 2000, Morningstar entered into a warehouse loan agreement with Regions [hereinafter Regions Warehouse Line]. Pursuant to this agreement, Morningstar requested that Regions transmit funds by wire to the escrow account of closing attorneys Weider & Mastroianni ("W&M") at Fleet Bank. On April 10, 2000, Morningstar requested $171,720 from Regions to fund a loan for Ever T. Aguado. Regions wired the requested funds to Fleet Bank. Regions instructed W&M that the funds were to be used to pay for the loan to Mr. Aguado.

On April 11, 2000, Morningstar [asked Regions for] $465,000 in order to fund a loan for Marjorie Crawford. Regions wired this amount to the W&M escrow account at Fleet Bank on April 11, 2000, with instructions that the funds were for a loan for Ms. Crawford. On the same date, Peter Mastroianni of W&M contacted

Ms. Daidone at Morningstar for further instructions regarding how the funds in the escrow account should be put towards the loans for Mr. Aguado and Ms. Crawford. Ms. Daidone told Mr. Mastroianni that Regions had transferred funds to W&M's escrow account in error. She asserted that she was the intended recipient of the funds. Ms. Daidone requested that W&M instruct Fleet Bank to wire $171,720 of the funds in W&M's escrow account to Morningstar's DDA at Provident. On April 11, 2000, Fleet Bank wired the $171,720 to Morningstar's DDA at Provident. The payment order from Provident to Fleet Bank listed Morningstar's account number at Provident Bank and stated that "Orig to BNF info: Re: Aguado-Morningstar Mortgage Bankers, Inc."

After Fleet Bank transferred $171,720 to Morningstar's DDA at Provident, Ms. Daidone informed Provident that funds were available in Morningstar's DDA to settle an outstanding loan on the Provident Warehouse Line. On April 12, 2000, Provident debited Morningstar's account by the $171,720 and credited the Provident Warehouse Line. On April 12, 2000, at Morningstar's request, Regions wired $162,000 to the W&M escrow account, with instructions to fund a loan for Mario Graziosi.

On April 11 or 12, 2000, FBI agents informed the internal security department at Regions that it had been monitoring the wire transfers from Regions to W&M. Thomas J. Holland, Senior Vice-President of Regions Mortgage, testified at his deposition that the FBI agents stated that the FBI "had monitored Ms. Daidone and that they felt there was a major problem with her, and they were going to try to arrest her almost immediately." The FBI also informed Regions that it should attempt to retrieve monies that Regions had wired for the closing of particular loans immediately.

On April 13, 2000, Ms. Daidone instructed Fleet Bank to wire $627,000 that Regions had wired to the W&M escrow account on April 11 and 12, 2000 to Morningstar's DDA at Provident. The payment order to Provident from Fleet Bank listed Morningstar's account number and stated that "Orig to BNF info: Re Graziosi $162,000 Crawford $465,000." The same day, Ms. Daidone advised Provident that it could apply the funds wire-transferred by Fleet Bank, against Morningstar's outstanding debt.

At 5:42 p.m. on April 13, 2000, Jaime Robison of Fleet Bank placed a call to a suburban Cincinnati branch of Provident Bank. Ms. Robison spoke with an unidentified Provident employee. The Provident employee informed Ms. Robison that the DDA belonged to Morningstar and that the funds were still in that account. Ms. Robison informed the Provident employee that "it was possible that the funds had been sent to the wrong institution."

Immediately after speaking with the Provident employee, Ms. Robison called an employee in the funds transfer department of Fleet Bank to initiate the process of recalling the wire transfer. Ms. Robison was informed that she would need to draft a supporting memo requesting the recall and specifying the beneficiary information and dollar amounts of the transfers. Ms. Robison drafted the memo on April 13, 2000 and sent it to Fleet Bank's funds transfer department. Fleet Bank did not contact Provident on April 13, 2000.

On April 13, Regions's attorney, John G. Aldridge, contacted Peter Mastroianni at W&M and asked him to attempt to reverse the wire transfers that had been sent to Morningstar's DDA at Provident. Mr. Aldridge testified at his deposition that it was his understanding on April 14, 2000, that Mr. Mastroianni "had discussed the situation with his bank and this bank was taking the appropriate steps to reverse the wire transfer." There is no indication in the record that Mr. Mastroianni contacted Provident directly in an effort to reverse the wire transfers. Regions also asked the FBI to attempt to locate and seize the funds. Regions did not contact Provident regarding the funds in Morningstar's DDA until April 17, 2000.

On April 14, 2000, around 10:00 a.m., Provident applied the $627,000 in Morningstar's DDA, that Fleet Bank had wired to the account the previous day, against four outstanding loans in the Provident Warehouse Line. Later that day, around 4:30 p.m., Provident received a copy of an *in rem* foreclosure complaint from the FBI detailing Morningstar's fraud against Provident and Regions. That same afternoon, Provident also received a two-page fax from Fleet Bank regarding the wire transfers for $171,720 and $627,000 to Morningstar's DDA which stated "pls note possible fraud pls rtn as sent in error no indemnity. . . . Possible fraud."

On April 17, 2000, Mr. Aldridge telephoned Provident to request the return of the funds that were wired into Morningstar's DDA by Fleet Bank. On April 21, 2000, Mr. Aldridge also sent a formal written demand for repayment of the funds to Provident's in-house counsel. On May 15, 2000, counsel for Provident responded by letter to Regions's demand and refused to return the funds.

Regions filed a complaint in the District Court for the Northern District of Georgia on June 30, 2000, asserting state law claims against Provident for conversion, unjust enrichment, receipt of stolen property, wrongful set-off and violations of Georgia and federal racketeering statutes. . . .

. . . [T]he district court granted Provident's motion for summary judgment, holding that each of Regions's state law claims was preempted by Article 4A of the U.C.C. ("Article 4A"). The court also found that "because [W&M's] possible fraud notifications arrived after Provident accepted the payment orders, they were ineffective to cancel them." . . .

II

Regions asserts that the district court erred in holding that Regions's state law claims were preempted by Article 4A. Regions argues that "nothing in Article 4A suggest that the drafters intended it to insulate a wrongdoer from liability in connection with funds transfers that were effectuated as intended." Regions asserts that its claims were not preempted because Provident accepted the funds when it knew or should have known that the funds were fraudulently obtained . . . .

. . . Regions's claims are based on Morningstar's direction to Fleet Bank to transfer funds, illegally obtained from Regions, to Morningstar's DDA at Provident. Because the wire transfers at issue here occurred via the Federal Reserve Wire Transfer Network, or "Fedwire," which is owned and operated by the Federal Reserve Banks, Subpart B of Federal Reserve Regulation J ("Regulation J"), 12 C.F.R. §§210.25-210.32, applies. Moreover, Regulation J "incorporates the provisions of Article 4A" of the U.C.C. as set forth in the Regulation, id. §210.25(b)(1), and "governs the rights and obligations of," inter alia, "parties to a funds transfer any part of which is carried out through Fedwire. . . . " Id. §210.25(b)(2)(v). . . .

The rules that emerged during the drafting of the U.C.C. "are intended to be the exclusive means of determining the rights, duties and liabilities of the affected parties *in any situation covered by particular provisions of the Article.*" U.C.C. §4A-102 cmt. (emphasis added). However, Article 4A is not the "exclusive means by which a plaintiff can seek to redress an alleged harm arising from a funds transfer." [Sheerbonnet, Ltd. v. American Express Bank, 951 F. Supp. 403, 409 (S.D.N.Y. 1995).] "The Article itself is replete with references to common law remedies." *Sheerbonnet*, 951 F. Supp. at 408. "The Drafting Committee intended that Article 4A would be supplemented, enhanced, and in some places, super[s]eded by other bodies of law . . . the Article is intended to synergize with other legal doctrines." T. C. Baxter & R. Bhala, *The Interrelationship of Article 4A with Other Law*, 45 Business Lawyer 1485, 1485 (1990) [Ed.: Tom Baxter is a senior official at the Federal Reserve Bank of New York and was an influential adviser to the drafting committee for UCC Article 4A.] "The legislative intent reflected here is that carefully drafted provisions . . . are not to be side-stepped when convenient by reference to other sources of law. But where the provisions do not venture, the claimant need not turn back; he or she may seek other guides, statutory or judicial." *Sheerbonnet*, 951 F. Supp. at 408. Therefore, the only restraint on a plaintiff is that "resort to principles of law or equity outside of Article 4A is not appropriate to create rights, duties and liabilities *inconsistent* with those stated in this Article." U.C.C. §4A-102 cmt. (emphasis added).

The parties do not dispute that Provident complied with the relevant provisions of the U.C.C. in accepting the transfer and setting off the funds to credit the debt owed to Provident by Morningstar. [Ed.: The rules for setoff appear in UCC §4A-502.] Regions argues that the "provisions of Article 4A deal with allocation of risk and responsibility" with regards to claims based on mistake and error and that " . . . the drafters intended it to insulate a wrongdoer from liability in connection with funds transfers that were effectuated as intended." Provident asserts that the text of Article 4A and the official commentary do not suggest that Article 4A is limited to claims based on mistake and errors.

Article 4A is silent with regard to claims based on the theory that the beneficiary bank accepted funds when it knew or should have known that the funds were fraudulently obtained. Therefore, a provision of state law that requires a receiving or beneficiary bank to disgorge funds that it knew or should have known were obtained illegally when it accepted a wire transfer is not inconsistent with the goals or provisions of Article 4A. The U.C.C. supports this conclusion. Article 4A defines good faith as "honesty in fact and the observance of reasonable commercial standards of fair dealing." U.C.C. §4A-105(a)(6). The U.C.C. also provides that "every contract or duty within [the U.C.C.] imposes an obligation of good faith in its performance or enforcement." *Id.* §[1-304]. Furthermore, we are mindful that the Supreme Court has repeatedly held that "if possible, [a court] should avoid construing [a] statute in a way that produces absurd results." Dewsnup v. Timm, 502 U.S. 410, 427 (1992). Interpreting Article 4A in a manner that would allow a beneficiary bank to accept funds when it knows or should know that they were fraudulently obtained, would allow banks to use Article 4A as a shield for fraudulent activity. It could hardly have been the intent of the drafters to enable a party to succeed in engaging in fraudulent activity, so long as it complied with the provisions of Article 4A.

Regions argues that it presented sufficient facts to demonstrate that there is a genuine issue of fact in dispute regarding whether Provident knew or should have known that the funds it received by Morningstar were obtained by fraud. Regions bases its state law claims on the fundamental principle of property law that "no one can obtain title to stolen property, however innocent a buyer may have been in the purchase; public policy forbids the acquisition of title through the thief." [Brackets, citations, ellipses, and quotation marks omitted.] . . . Had Provident known or had reason to know that the funds it received from Morningstar were obtained by fraud, it could not have obtained title to the funds upon acceptance of the wire transfer from Fleet Bank because it would have acted in bad faith . . . .

A beneficiary bank accepts a payment order when the "bank receives payment of the entire amount of the sender's order." U.C.C. §4A-209(b)(2). Provident accepted payment orders from Fleet Bank and deposited the funds into the DDA held by Morningstar at Provident, on April 11 and 13, 2000. Title to funds in a wire transfer passes to the beneficiary bank upon acceptance of a payment order; Official Comment of U.C.C. §4A-102 (explaining that in the drafting of Article 4A, substantial consideration was given to policy goals of assigning responsibility, allocating risks, and predicting risk with certainty in electronic fund wire transactions). If Provident received the payment order without "knowing or having reasonable cause to believe that the property [had] been obtained through commission of a theft offense," Ohio Rev. Code Ann. §2913.51, title to the funds lawfully passed to Provident on April 11 and 13, 2000, upon its acceptance of the payment orders on behalf of Morningstar's DDA.

Regions conceded during oral argument that the phone call from Ms. Robison of Fleet Bank on April 13, 2000 at 5:42 p.m. to an employee at a suburban Cincinnati branch of Provident Bank, "was indeed the first direct statement from someone to Provident Bank that the particular wires at issue were potentially fraudulent or the product of criminal activity." However, this phone call occurred *after* both payment orders were received by Provident on behalf of Morningstar's DDA. To state a valid claim requiring disgorgement of the funds wired to Provident, Regions was required to demonstrate that Provident knew or had reasonable cause to believe that it was receiving fraudulently obtained funds *before* it received the wire transfers and acquired title to the funds.

Regions contends that there were a number of "red flags" raised by Morningstar's conduct before 5:42 p.m. on April 13, 2000, which gave notice to Provident that the funds coming into Morningstar's account were the product of fraudulent or criminal activity. Regions notes that Provident knew that Morningstar failed to make prompt payments on the loans from the Provident Warehouse Line or to sell the outstanding loans to investors within the time periods required by the loan agreements. The fact that Morningstar frequently missed the deadlines imposed by Provident shows that Morningstar engaged in poor business or accounting practices, but not fraud. Provident's awareness that the FBI was investigating whether Morningstar had forged Mr. Jiras's signature on loan closing documents submitted to Provident does not demonstrate that the money subsequently paid by Morningstar to Provident to repay the loans was obtained by fraud.

The record shows that Provident knew that Morningstar used the same collateral to obtain funding from both Provident and First Union. This knowledge was not sufficient to put Provident on notice that the money it received was obtained by fraud. These so-called "red flags" were sufficient to demonstrate to Provident that Morningstar was an inept business entity with questionable ethical standards which prompted Provident to demand payment of all outstanding loans made to Morningstar. None of these facts is evidence that the wire transfers transmitted by Fleet Bank were obtained by fraud.

The record shows that Morningstar informed Provident that it planned to liquidate certain of its assets in order to pay off its debt. Regions has not demonstrated that Provident knew or should have known that Morningstar did not possess sufficient assets to cover its business losses. . . .

Because the "red flags" identified by Regions are insufficient as a matter of law to prove that Provident "[knew] or [had] reasonable cause to believe that the [funds had] been obtained through commission of a theft offense," Ohio Rev. Code Ann. §2913.51, Provident would not be liable for receiving stolen property under Ohio law.

Regions also asserted claims of conversion, unjust enrichment, and unlawful setoff against Provident. Since one acting in good faith may obtain title to money from a thief, Provident obtained legal title to the funds when it accepted the wire transfers from Fleet Bank on April 11 and 13, 2000. Following Provident's acceptance of the funds transferred by Fleet Bank, Regions no longer had title to those funds. When Provident debited Morningstar's account and credited the warehouse line on April 12 and 14, 2000, Provident's possessory interest in the funds was superior to Regions's. Because Regions has not demonstrated that Provident acted in bad faith, Regions has failed to prove an essential element of each of its state law claims.

CONCLUSION

We agree with Regions's assertion that Article 4A does not preempt a state law claim if money is transferred by wire to a party that knows or should have known that the funds were obtained illegally. Nonetheless, we are persuaded from our independent review of the record that Regions has failed to present evidence demonstrating that there is a genuine issue of fact regarding whether Provident knew or should have known that the funds it received from Morningstar had been fraudulently obtained. Such proof was necessary to support a judgment on each of Regions's state law claims. The district court's decision to grant Provident's motion for summary judgment is AFFIRMED.

Problem Set 14

14.1.   You get a call this afternoon from Jodi. She calls to report that she has just received a payment order from her customer, asking her to send all the funds in the account to an account at a bank in the Bahamas. As it happens, it took her some time to identify the best way to send the funds to the Bahamas; before she took any action to send the funds, she received a writ of garnishment against the customer. Jodi wants to understand her options. Can she act on the payment order at this time? UCC §§4A-209, 4A-502(b).

14.2.   Calling again the next day, Jodi reports that her bank has just received notice of a large incoming transfer, sent by SWIFT for one of the bank's customers. The transfer, if accepted, would be settled under a bilateral arrangement, with a withdrawal from an account in the name of the sender and a corresponding deposit into the account of the customer. When the transfer came in, it triggered an alert because the bank recently was served with a writ of garnishment against the customer. Jodi wants to understand her options. UCC §4A-502(c) & comment 2.

   a.   Can she allow her customer to withdraw the funds without advising the creditor of the transfer?
   b.   If her customer presently is overdrawn, can she take the money for herself instead of sending it to the creditor, by offsetting the incoming funds against the debt the customer owes to her?
   c.   Can she simply reject the transfer, protecting her customer by returning the funds to the originator rather than turning them over to the creditor?
   d.   Would your answers change if she had made the transfer of funds from the account of the originator's bank to the account of the beneficiary, but had not yet notified the beneficiary? UCC §§4A-209(b), 4A-403(a), 4A-405(a).

14.3.   Consider a transaction precisely the same as *Jaldhi Overseas*, except that the funds were sent by Fedwire and the case is before the United States Court of Appeals for the Ninth Circuit (which is not bound by the Second Circuit's decision in *Jaldhi Overseas*).

14.4.   You work on an organized-crime task force in the office of the United States Attorney for the Southern District of New York. You have been asked for advice on the question whether *Daccarett* remains good law. What do you say? UCC §§4A-502, 4A-503.

14.5.   Consider a transaction precisely the same as *Regions Bank* except that the FBI sent its *in rem* foreclosure complaint to Provident Bank at 9 a.m. on April 14 (after Provident accepted the payment order but before it set off the funds). UCC §4A-502.

14.6.   In the mid-1990s, Argentina defaulted on a large bond issuance. It persuaded most of the holders to accept substantially smaller payments (about 10 cents on the dollar). It then resumed making the diminished payments to those that agreed to accept them; it made no payments to the holdouts that refused to accept the smaller payments. Years later, the holdouts persuaded a trial judge that the payments to those accepting the deal violated the terms of the bonds. The trial judge ordered Argentina to make no further payments to the compliant bondholders until it brought the holdouts current. When Argentina refused to comply, the district court issued an order enjoining any party from participating in making a forbidden payment, including, specifically, (i) the Argentina national bank, through which Argentina sent funds to the bond's "indenture trustee" in the United States, (ii) the indenture trustee, a bank in the United States that maintains records of the individual bondholders, and (iii) any bank receiving a payment on behalf of a beneficiary. On appeal, Argentina and the indenture trustee argue that the injunction violates Article 4A. What do you think?

Part Two
Credit Enhancement and Letters of Credit

Chapter 5.   Credit Enhancement

Assignment 15:   Credit Enhancement by Guaranty

A.   The Role of Guaranties

When the parties to a transaction decide that payment will be deferred, the risk that the party that promises to pay (the borrower) will not pay as promised is a key factor in determining how much compensation is necessary to make deferred payment acceptable to the party to whom payment is due (the lender). If the lender thinks that the borrower is financially unsound, the lender might insist on a great deal of compensation for deferral to offset the possibility that the borrower ultimately will not pay the debt.

Alternatively (and probably more commonly), a lender might be altogether unwilling to enter into a transaction unless the borrower can convince the lender that the borrower is sufficiently creditworthy to satisfy the lender's concerns. In that event, the borrower might go to another type of lender to obtain the money that it wishes to borrow. For example, if a bank refuses to provide the desired funding, perhaps an asset financier or some other lender that specializes in more risky projects might be willing to provide the necessary financing (albeit at interest rates significantly higher than those ordinarily charged by banks). If those avenues fail as well, the business may be unable to obtain the money that it wants.

Organizational structure is one of the main reasons that many small businesses have particularly questionable credit. It is common for a small business to be organized as a separate entity (often a corporation or limited liability company) distinct from the entrepreneur or family that owns and operates the business. Although courts in some cases look through the entity to the individual or company behind the corporation — pierce the corporate veil, to use the common phrase — the organization of a separate corporation creates a strong presumption that the individual behind the corporation is not liable for the debts of the corporation. Accordingly, if the corporation borrows money and fails to repay it, ordinarily the creditor cannot pursue the owner of the corporation to obtain repayment. To overturn the presumption that the owner is not liable, a plaintiff must establish some substantial wrongdoing or misuse of the corporate entity. The mere existence of unpaid corporate creditors is not an adequate justification for allowing recourse against the owner.

That common organizational structure suggests an easy way to satisfy some of a lender's concerns about the creditworthiness of the small business. The business can offer a guaranty from its owner that allows the lender to pursue not only the business entity, but also the individual owner (who may have assets other than the business). For example, suppose that a wealthy individual

named Carl Eben is the founder, president, and sole owner of a small industrial tooling company named Riverfront Tools, Inc. (RFT). RFT needs about
$500,000 to finance its development of some new tool designs. If RFT is a rela-
tively small company or does not have a lengthy track record in its industry, a
lender advancing the $500,000 to RFT would worry that RFT might fail to repay
the loan. The risks to the lender are easy to see: RFT might have a poor business
plan that produces insufficient operating revenue to repay its creditors, RFT
might be subjected to a large tort judgment if one of its tools fails to work properly, or (sorry to say) Carl might abscond with RFT's funds. In many (if not
most) cases, those risks would convince institutional lenders that it would not
be profitable to make a loan to RFT standing alone. Instead, an institutional
lender ordinarily would insist on a guaranty from Carl Eben personally.

By executing a guaranty, Carl would provide a backup source of payment
for the lender, from which the lender could obtain payment even if RFT was
unable (or unwilling) to repay its debt voluntarily. In legal parlance, Carl
would become a guarantor, a surety, or (more formally) a secondary obligor.
The party that owes the money directly (RFT) would be known as the principal
obligor or just as the principal. Finally, the party to whom the money is owed
(the lender) would be referred to as the creditor or the obligee (the person to
whom the obligor is obliged).

One of the most important considerations to a lender in evaluating a guaranty
is the creditworthiness of the guarantor. The general idea is that a guaranty from
a strong and creditworthy guarantor provides a firm enhancement of the credit
of the borrower because of the strong likelihood that the guarantor will repay
the loan even if the borrower fails to do so. Conversely, a guarantor of undistin-
guished financial strength provides little or no assurance of payment beyond the
assurance that would come from the borrower's direct promise to pay.

Creditworthiness is a relatively subjective concept. For starters, the fact that
a company has valuable assets or significant operating revenues says little about
its creditworthiness. An airline with a troubled operating history that recently
went through bankruptcy would not generally be considered creditworthy
even if the company had a large fleet of valuable airplanes and a relatively
small level of existing debt. Conversely, a single individual with a lengthy and
impeccable business record might be considered an excellent credit risk even if
his tangible assets were relatively modest. The size of the guaranteed debt also
is crucial to the concept of creditworthiness: Carl might be considered creditworthy in the context of providing a guaranty for a $500,000 loan, but not in
the context of a $50 million transaction.

Another significant factor in evaluating the usefulness of a proposed guaranty is the relation of the guarantor to the borrower. In many cases (especially
those that involve small businesses), the status of the guarantor is just as important as (or even more important than) the creditworthiness of the guarantor
standing alone. To continue with our example, Carl's relation to RFT would
make a lender considering a loan to RFT particularly interested in obtaining a
guaranty from Carl. When the lender obtains a guaranty from Carl, the lender
forces Carl to commit his personal assets to repaying the loan and thus ties Carl
to the company. If Carl does not guarantee the loan, he always has the option

of walking away from the company, letting it fail, and using his resources to start another company. Alternatively, he might engage in conduct that harms the business more subtly. For example, Carl might lose interest in RFT and devote his interests to a new project. A guaranty mitigates the lender's concern about those problems. When Carl has guaranteed the loan, he has a direct interest in RFT's success because RFT's success is necessary to Carl's ability to protect Carl's personal assets from the lender. That interest gives Carl's guaranty a unique value that the lender could not obtain from another source, even if the alternate source has a balance sheet more impressive than Carl's.

The guaranty relationship occurs (under a number of different names) in a wide variety of contexts. For example, in a simple lending transaction like a car loan, a lender might ask a relative of the borrower to be a cosigner on the note. Although the status would depend on the terms of the note, the relative ordinarily would become a guarantor (rather than a primary obligor). Similarly, Article 3 of the Uniform Commercial Code (which deals with negotiable instruments) creates a set of implied guaranty obligations to deal with the rights of accommodation parties and accommodated parties. An accommodation party is any party that signs a negotiable instrument for the purpose of incurring liability without directly benefiting from the value that the creditor gives for the instrument. UCC §3-419(a). The accommodated party is the party for whose benefit the value was given, generally the principal borrower or issuer of the instrument. Under Article 3, an accommodation party is treated as a guarantor; the accommodated party is treated as the primary obligor. UCC §§3-419, 3-605.

Moving further afield, the surety and insurance industries are founded on such transactions. If an insurance company issued an insurance policy for RFT, the insurance company would be the surety, RFT would be the principal, and the party with a claim against RFT (hoping to be paid by the insurer) would be the creditor or obligee. Similarly, if RFT obtained a bond to back up its performance on a construction contract, the issuer of the bond would be a surety, RFT would be the principal, and the beneficiary of the bond would be the obligee or creditor.

There is no universal form for a guaranty, and insurance policies and surety bonds obviously have provisions called for by particularities of the industries in which they are used. Most forms for guaranty transactions, however, contain relatively similar terms. I reprint at the end of this chapter a standard form for a guaranty that would be used in a relatively simple commercial lending transaction. (Later references to this document describe it as the Guaranty Agreement.)

To make any sense out of a guaranty transaction, it is necessary to understand the legal relations that arise when a party executes a guaranty. The rules establishing those relations are usually referred to as the law of suretyship, because surety bonds are one of the oldest and most important areas in which those rules apply. The remainder of this assignment focuses on the first set of relations: the rights of the creditor against the guarantor. The next assignment continues that discussion by examining the rights of the guarantor against the principal and the creditor.

B.   Rights of the Creditor Against the Guarantor

Although the guarantor or surety is called a "secondary" obligor, there is little that is secondary about the guarantor's obligation to the creditor. In the absence of some special language in the guaranty, the guarantor is liable to pay the obligation in question immediately upon the default of the principal. Restatement of Suretyship §15(a). Thus, the lender can sue Carl the instant that RFT defaults. The lender does not have to seek payment first from RFT, and the lender certainly does not have to sue RFT or otherwise consider whether it would be able to force RFT to pay. Rather, the lender is free to proceed as it deems appropriate: suing the principal first or suing the guarantor first.

Although it may seem surprising to allow the lender to proceed directly against the *secondary* obligor without first trying to extract payment from the *principal* obligor, a little thought shows the sense of the rule. A contrary rule would limit the value of a guaranty considerably because in many cases it would obligate a lender to pursue recovery against an insolvent principal, even though the lender might be able to recover the money immediately by suing the guarantor directly. Almost invariably the reason that a principal has failed to pay as promised is that the principal is unable to pay. In those cases, it is pointless to construct a legal rule that requires the lender to sue the principal before proceeding to collect from the solvent guarantor.

That is not to say that the parties cannot create an arrangement in which the creditor has to pursue the principal first and can sue the guarantor only after its efforts to collect from the principal are unsuccessful. Such an arrangement is called a guaranty of collection. To create that arrangement, the parties should describe Carl in the guaranty as a "guarantor of collection" or title the document a "guaranty of collection," in order to overcome the default presumption in favor of a conventional guaranty. If the parties use those terms, then the lender ordinarily cannot pursue the guarantor unless (1) it is unable to locate and serve the principal, (2) the principal is insolvent, or (3) the lender is unsuccessful in obtaining payment even after it obtains a judgment against the principal. UCC §3-419(d); Restatement of Suretyship §15(b).

Given the impracticality of forcing a lender to satisfy those requirements before obtaining payment, it is not surprising that the guaranty of collection is relatively rare. Indeed, the lender's desire to avoid any obligation to sue the principal ordinarily is underscored by a lengthy and explicit statement in the guaranty in which the lender requires the guarantor to acknowledge with considerable repetitiveness that the document creates a conventional guaranty obligation rather than a guaranty of collection. See, e.g., Guaranty Agreement §§2, 4.

Although guaranties of collection are rare, the bankruptcy process provides another mechanism by which a guarantor that controls its principal can prevent a creditor from collecting on a guaranty. However clear the law regarding the independence of the guarantor's obligation to the creditor and however clear the terms of a particular guaranty, it is not unusual for bankruptcy courts faced with a bankruptcy by the principal to enjoin the creditor from attempting to collect from the surety. The standards for issuing such an injunction are flexible, but in recent years they have become more common. Judge Posner's discussion in the case below gives some sense of when courts are likely to issue, or refuse to issue, such an order.

In re Caesars Entertainment Operating Co.
(Caesars Entertainment Operating Co. v. BOKF, N.A.)

808 F.3d 1186 (7th Cir. 2015)

Before POSNER, MANION, and SYKES, Circuit Judges.

POSNER, Circuit Judge.

This is an immense, and immensely complicated, bankruptcy proceeding, but the issue presented by the appeal is straightforward, enabling us to spare the reader a mountain of details. For both the bankruptcy judge, and the district judge to whom the bankruptcy judge's ruling was unsuccessfully appealed, based their decisions on a question of statutory interpretation. We must decide simply whether their interpretation was correct.

Caesars Entertainment Operating Company, which the parties call CEOC, owns and operates a chain of casinos and is the leading debtor in a Chapter 11 bankruptcy proceeding. It is the only debtor we need discuss because the others are subsidiaries of CEOC. (In other words, to simplify our opinion we pretend that CEOC is the sole debtor.) CEOC used to be wholly owned by Caesars Entertainment Corp. (CEC), which remains its principal owner. Beginning in the mid–2000s and continuing in recent years, CEOC borrowed billions of dollars to finance its operations, issuing notes to the lenders that were guaranteed by CEC. As CEOC's financial position worsened, CEC tried to eliminate its guaranty obligations by selling assets of CEOC to other parties and terminating the guaranties that it had issued. Creditors of CEOC who had received the guaranties challenged CEC's repudiation of them by filing suits in state and federal courts against CEC. The suits sought damages *in toto* of approximately $12 billion. Further complicating the picture, CEOC in its bankruptcy proceeding has asserted claims against CEC alleging that CEC caused CEOC to transfer highly valuable assets to CEC at less than fair value, leaving CEOC saddled with billions of dollars of debt; the transfers had therefore allegedly been fraudulent transfers—part of a scheme by CEC to snatch CEOC's most valuable assets while ensuring that the guaranty plaintiffs could not recover on their notes.

CEOC fears that those guaranty suits will "thwart[ ] [CEOC's] multi-billion-dollar restructuring effort, which depends on a substantial contribution from CEC in settlement of [CEOC's] claims against it," and thus will "let [the guaranty plaintiffs] jump the line in front of other creditors, including more senior ones," of the bankrupt estate. CEOC therefore asked the bankruptcy judge to enjoin the guaranty suits until 60 days after a bankruptcy examiner, appointed by the judge to make an independent assessment of the bankruptcy claims, completes his report. The hope was that the report might help the parties negotiate a reorganization of the bankrupt estate. The bankruptcy judge, seconded by the district judge, to whom CEOC appealed the first judge's ruling, refused to issue the injunction. The bankruptcy judge . . . thought he lacked statutory authority to enter an injunction under the relevant provision of the Bankruptcy Code, section 105(a), which provides, so far as relates to this case, that "the [bankruptcy] court may issue *any* order, process, or judgment that is necessary or appropriate to carry out the provisions of this title." 11 U.S.C. §105(a) (emphasis added). Despite this broad grant of power, the bankruptcy judge thought that for litigation against a non-debtor to be enjoinable it must arise out of the "same acts" of the non-debtor that gave rise to disputes in the bankruptcy proceeding. The disputes in CEOC's bankruptcy arise out of CEC's alleged fraudulent transfers, while the claims being pressed against CEC in the lawsuits that CEOC is endeavoring to enjoin arise from CEC's alleged repudiation of the guaranties that it issued to the firms that lent money to CEOC. They are not the same claims. (The guaranty plaintiffs also have claims against CEOC, but those claims are automatically stayed pursuant to 11 U.S.C. §362(a).)

But nothing in 11 U.S.C. §105(a) authorizes the limitation on the powers of a bankruptcy judge that CEC's creditors (the guaranty plaintiffs) successfully urged on the judges below. Though section 105(a) does not give the bankruptcy court carte blanche—the court cannot, for example, take an action prohibited by another provision of the Bankruptcy Code, Law v. Siegel, 134 S. Ct. 1188 (2014); In re Kmart Corp., 359 F.3d 866, 871 (7th Cir. 2004)—it grants the extensive equitable powers that bankruptcy courts need in order to be able to perform their statutory duties.

The question that the bankruptcy judge and the district judge failed to address because of their cramped interpretation of section 105(a) is whether the injunction sought by CEOC is likely to enhance the prospects for a successful resolution of the disputes attending its bankruptcy. If it is, and its denial will thus endanger the success of the bankruptcy proceedings, the grant of the injunction would, in the language of section 105(a), be "appropriate to carry out the provisions" of the Bankruptcy Code, since successful resolution of disputes arising in bankruptcy proceedings is one of the Code's central objectives. If before CEOC's bankruptcy is wound up CEC is drained of capital by the lenders' suits to enforce the guaranties that CEC had given them, there will be that much less money for CEOC's creditors to recover in the bankruptcy proceeding. CEOC seeks on behalf of the creditors to recover from CEC assets that CEC caused to be fraudulently transferred to it from CEOC, and to use the recovered assets to pay the creditors. The less capital CEC has for CEOC to recapture through prosecution or settlement of its fraudulent-transfer claims, the less money its creditors will receive in the bankruptcy proceeding. Those creditors, and CEOC as their debtor, thus have a direct and substantial interest in the litigation between CEC and the firms to which it has issued guaranties. That interest would be furthered by a temporary injunction staying the lenders' lawsuits against CEC.

One can envision a situation in which CEC, having both obligations on the guaranties it issued to CEOC's lenders, and obligations to CEOC arising from the latter's fraudulent-transfer claims, would lack the money to satisfy all its obligees, and would thus become the badminton birdie in a contest between the two groups of claimants. CEOC contends that if the guaranty litigation against CEC can be frozen for a time by an order issued by the bankruptcy judge, the bankruptcy examiner's report analyzing the disputed transactions will provide the parties with information they need to have a clear shot at negotiating an overall settlement of what amounts to a three-cornered battle among CEC, its direct creditors via CEC's guaranties to them, and CEOC's creditors, some of whom are also CEC's creditors by virtue of CEC's guaranteeing CEOC's debts.

If this analysis is correct, there is nothing in section 105(a) to bar the order sought by CEOC; for the statute, to repeat, authorizes "any order . . . that is . . . appropriate to carry out the provisions of" the Bankruptcy Code. Whether the temporary injunction sought by CEOC is such an "appropriate" order is a factual issue that remains to be determined.

Earlier we questioned the "same acts" limitation that the bankruptcy judge and the district judge placed on section 105(a). But the guaranty plaintiffs (CEC's creditors) argue that two decisions by this court have endorsed that limitation: Fisher v. Apostolou, 155 F.3d 876 (7th Cir. 1998), and In re Teknek, LLC, 563 F.3d 639 (7th Cir. 2009). The issue in *Fisher* was "whether claims that the defrauded investors have against the accomplices [of the fraudster, whose corporation was in bankruptcy] and against the futures commission merchant through which they conducted much of their business may be stayed for the duration of the [corporation's] bankruptcy proceeding." 155 F.3d at 877. The bankruptcy court stayed (i.e., enjoined) the investors' suits under 11 U.S.C. §105(a). *Id.* at 878. We approved, saying that

> while the [investor] Plaintiffs' claims are not "property of" the estate [and so were not subject to an automatic stay under 11 U.S.C. §362], it is difficult to imagine how those claims could be more closely "related to" it [under 28 U.S.C. §1334(b)]. They are claims to the same limited pool of money, in the possession of the same defendants, as a result of the same acts, performed by the same individuals, as part of the same conspiracy. We can think of no hypothetical change to this case which would bring it closer to a "property of" case without converting it into one.

That was a more clear-cut case for relief under section 105(a) than this one, given that "both parties were pursuing the same dollars from the same defendants to redress the same harms." But it doesn't follow that a less clear-cut case is necessarily beyond the reach of section 105(a). In both *Fisher* and the present case the issuance of a temporary injunction against a class of creditors could well facilitate a prompt and orderly wind-up of the bankruptcy.

Teknek approves *Fisher*, remarking that in that case "even though the investor-creditors' fraud claims were personal and distinct from claims that could be brought by other creditors, they were so related to the bankruptcy proceeding that, if not temporarily enjoined, they would have derailed those proceedings' efforts to recover for the class of creditors as a whole." But *Teknek* in contrast was a case involving "separate acts, which caused separate injuries to two separate companies, only one of which is in bankruptcy." The plaintiff had won a patent-infringement case against two companies—one of which later filed for bankruptcy—and subsequently obtained an enlargement of the judgment to reach shareholders (called "alter egos") of the defendants. The plaintiff claimed that the alter egos had looted the two companies by moving the companies' assets into a holding company in order to avoid having to pay the judgment. The bankruptcy trustee sought to enjoin the plaintiff from enforcing its judgment against the shareholders, arguing that they and the holding company had indeed looted the bankrupt entity; thus the trustee was seeking recovery from the same pool of money as the patent plaintiff. We ruled that the patent claims were not sufficiently related to the debtor's bankruptcy to allow such an injunction to be issued. The patent holder's suit had been against both Teknek (the bankrupt company) and a firm called Electronics (the non-bankrupt company). We noted that the "alter egos [had] looted both Teknek and Electronics[,] . . . [which were] separate acts, *which caused separate injuries to two separate companies, only one of which is in bankruptcy.*" Because the entire judgment could be collected from the non-bankrupt entity, Electronics, there was no reason to allow Teknek to obtain an injunction that would prevent the patent holder from going after Electronics. In the present case, in contrast, the misconduct alleged in the third-party litigation (misconduct by CEC) directly harms the debtor, and concerns transactions that are closely related to, and sometimes overlapping with, those challenged in the bankruptcy.

Furthermore, the patent holder was Teknek's only major creditor, so allowing the third-party action of that creditor to proceed would not affect a larger group of creditors in the bankruptcy. (Indeed we were puzzled why the case was even in bankruptcy, given what was effectively a creditor class consisting of only one creditor. The usual purpose of bankruptcy is to allocate the distribution of the bankrupt's assets among creditors.) In our case the potential injuries to the numerous creditors in the bankruptcy (whose prospects depend on CEOC's assets), and to the guaranty plaintiffs (whose loans CEC has guaranteed), are not readily separable. Both injuries, according to CEOC, stem from CEC's broad scheme to transfer CEOC's assets to itself. Indeed, some of the same creditors have claims against both CEOC and CEC for repayment of the same loans, and so their ability to recover from CEC (the guarantor) may depend on the amount they can recover directly from CEOC, their borrower. And were guarantor liability to be imposed on CEC, CEC's ability to satisfy CEOC's fraudulent-conveyance claims against it—and thus pay other creditors—would be impaired.

We don't say that the stay sought by CEOC must be granted—that's an issue for the bankruptcy judge to resolve in the first instance—but only that both he and the district judge erred in thinking that section 105(a) as interpreted in *Fisher* and *Teknek* foreclosed such a procedure. That was a misreading of the statute and our cases. The denial of the injunction sought by CEOC is therefore vacated and the case remanded for further proceedings consistent with this opinion.

———

The inquiry into whether a debtor's bankruptcy presents sufficiently unusual circumstances to justify an injunction preventing a lender from pursuing a guarantor is so imprecise that a guarantor will rarely be confident that initiating a bankruptcy proceeding for its principal will allow it to defer payment. Thus, the guarantor cannot use bankruptcy as a reliable mechanism for holding off the lender. But the converse is just as true: The vagueness of the legal rule means that a lender rarely can be sure that it will be able to enforce the guaranty against a guarantor if (as is frequently the case) the guarantor is one of the prime movers of the borrower. Accordingly, the threat of a bankruptcy filing by the borrower makes the lender concerned about the possibility that the borrower's bankruptcy will defer the lender's ability to pursue the nonbankrupt guarantor.

Problem Set 15

15.1. Your friend Terry Lydgate comes by this morning to discuss his latest round of financial difficulties. He says that he has found one bright spot in one of his transactions and wants to tell you about it. Lydgate is the guarantor of a large loan from Bulstrode Bank to Middlemarch Medical Clinics, Inc. (MMC). MMC has just closed its doors after protracted litigation with Bulstrode. Lydgate tells you that although he is depressed that MMC has no remaining assets to pay Bulstrode or any of its other creditors, he is satisfied that he has an ironclad defense to the Bank's action to collect the debt—the underlying transaction was usurious. Assuming Lydgate is correct, how does that affect Bulstrode's ability to collect from Lydgate? Consider the result under the default rules in the Restatement of Suretyship and also under the terms of the Guaranty Agreement. Restatement of Suretyship §§15, 21.

15.2. Jude Fawley (a wealthy stonemason friend of yours) comes to consult you about some serious problems with his business, Obscure Wessex Headstones (OWH). Several years ago you organized Jude's business as a corporation, with Jude as the sole shareholder. Jude has guaranteed OWH's $1.2 million line of credit with Wessex Bank. Over the last six months, OWH's net monthly income has decreased from $20,000 to only $2,000. At the same time, operating expenses have caused OWH to draw down its entire line of credit, so that it now owes Wessex the entire $1.2 million. OWH has only $10,000 cash on hand right now. Its current obligations include a $10,000 monthly payment due to Wessex on the first of the month and $8,000 in overdue bills from suppliers.

Jude tells you that he would feel terrible if he did not pay his suppliers, many of whom have been doing business with him for decades, but that he doesn't want to do anything that would worsen his personal financial situation. He also tells you that he doesn't mind all that much if he loses the stonemason business as long as he can keep the rest of his assets (which include a multimillion-dollar business syndicating walking tours of rural Britain).

   a. If it comes to litigation, will Wessex need to sue OWH first or can it come directly against Fawley?
   b. Consider the result under the default rules in the Restatement of Suretyship and also under the terms of the Guaranty Agreement. Restatement of Suretyship §15.
   c. As a planning matter, which bills would you recommend that Fawley pay first?

15.3. Ben Darrow (your friend from First State Bank of Matacora) calls you in distress. He read in the paper this morning that one of his borrowers, Matacora Pipelines, Inc., was hit yesterday with a $1 million tort judgment. The judgment resulted from a tragic accident in which a Matacora employee working on the construction of a new pipeline was killed by an exploding dynamite charge. Ben knows that Matacora does not have enough assets to pay the judgment and is worried about his bank's $250,000 loan to Matacora (for which Ben has no collateral). On further questioning, Ben tells you that he has a personal guaranty from Bud Lassen, the independently wealthy owner and operator of Matacora. Ben also tells you that he believes the entry of the tort judgment is a default on the loan to Matacora because it constitutes a "material adverse change" in Matacora's financial condition. What are Ben's rights against Matacora? What are his rights against Lassen? Will the situation change if Matacora files for bankruptcy?

15.4.   Impressed with your work on the Jude Fawley matter (in Problem 15.2), Wessex Bank retains you to handle a proposed restructuring of one of its loans. For several years, Wessex has been lending to a growing chain of specialty stores called We-R-Red, which specialize in bright red clothing and accessories. Until now the business has been operated as a sole proprietorship owned by Diggory Venn. Because of Venn's considerable wealth, Wessex traditionally has considered the relationship a safe one even though the loan is unsecured.

Venn recently learned that the Environmental Protection Agency has decided to list as a toxic substance the chemical that Venn uses to makes his products (reddelic acid). Venn believes that the resultant dye (ordinary "reddle") is completely safe, but is worried about the possibility of some accident that would result in environmental liability that would wipe out all of his assets. Federal policy states that, in the case of such a violation, the EPA can sue the corporation but cannot collect from its shareholders. In response, Venn has decided to incorporate the business under the name of We-R-Red, Inc. Venn will remain the controlling shareholder and chief executive officer. Venn would like to transfer the loan to the new entity, but is willing to issue a guaranty of the loan himself. The loan officer at Wessex, Eustacia ("Stacy") Vye, wants to know what you think about Venn's proposal and whether this new structure will be more or less favorable to the lender. What do you say?

Assignment 16: Protections for Guarantors

A. Rights of the Guarantor Against the Principal

As the preceding assignment suggests, in most cases a guarantor is closely affiliated with the principal whose debt it guarantees. Accordingly, it is relatively uncommon for a guarantor and a principal to execute a written agreement memorializing the terms of their relationship. As a result, their relations generally are governed by a set of obligations that are implied as a matter of common law (supplemented in some contexts by statute). Specifically, the law grants the guarantor three major rights against the principal: the rights of performance, reimbursement, and subrogation (see Figure 16.1). Although those rights overlap in many circumstances, it is useful to analyze the substance of each of them separately.

1. Performance

The right of performance (or exoneration) allows the guarantor to sue the principal in order to force the principal to perform the guaranteed obligation. Restatement of Suretyship §21. The idea behind the right of performance is that the guarantor should not have to go to the trouble of performing and then seeking reimbursement from the principal when the principal is able to perform. The right of performance rarely is significant because in most cases the principal would be performing if it could. Thus, an injunction formally commanding performance ordinarily does not alter the difficulties that keep the principal from performing in the first place. Moreover, in the typical case where the guarantor is a controlling officer or owner of the principal, a guarantor usually will have more direct ways to induce the principal to render any possible performance than filing a lawsuit seeking an injunction.

2. Reimbursement

The right of reimbursement entitles the guarantor to recover from the principal any sums that the guarantor pays to the creditor under the guaranty. Again, it exists entirely apart from any specific contractual agreement, and is implied as a matter of law. Restatement of Suretyship §22; UCC §3-419(e) (applying that rule to payments by an accommodation party to a negotiable instrument).

3.   Subrogation

The third of the guarantor's rights, subrogation, is the most difficult to understand. Generally, subrogation allows a guarantor forced to pay on its guaranty to recover that payment by stepping into the shoes of the creditor and asserting against the principal all of the rights that the creditor could have asserted against the principal. Restatement of Suretyship §§27-28. As a practical matter, subrogation ordinarily works as if the rights of the creditor had been assigned to the guarantor in return for the guarantor's payment on the underlying debt. For that reason, older decisions describe subrogation as "equitable assignment" or "assignment by operation of law." For example, if Carl paid the lender $500,000 on Carl's guaranty of a debt owed by RFT, Carl would be subrogated to the lender's rights against RFT. Thus, Carl could sue RFT to collect that $500,000 just as the lender could have sued RFT on the note for the $500,000.

In a simple transaction where the lender's only right against RFT is to sue RFT to collect the debt, the right of subrogation has no independent significance because it duplicates Carl's right of reimbursement. But in more complex transactions the lender will have rights beyond a simple right to sue, such as a lien or security interest, or perhaps an Article 2 right of reclamation (see UCC §2-702). The guarantor's ability to obtain those rights makes subrogation an important tool for the guarantor.

To see how that might occur, suppose that OmniBank loaned RFT $500,000, taking back both a lien on RFT's factory (RFT's only significant asset) and a guaranty from Carl. Now suppose that one of RFT's tools causes a catastrophic accident, resulting in a $2 million judgment lien against RFT's factory. When RFT fails to pay OmniBank in a timely manner, RFT's lender calls on Carl's guaranty. If Carl has substantial assets outside of his interest in RFT, he might proceed to pay OmniBank on the guaranty. Carl's right of reimbursement would provide Carl little solace in this situation. Carl's claim

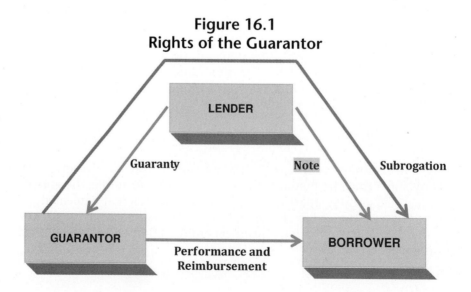

Figure 16.1
Rights of the Guarantor

for reimbursement would be an unsecured claim, which would go nowhere in the face of the judgment lien covering RFT's factory. The judgment lienholder would be entitled to be paid out of the assets against which it had a lien; Carl would be entitled to payment on his claim for reimbursement only after the judgment lienholder had been satisfied.

Carl's right of subrogation, however, would protect him in that situation. Subrogation would allow Carl to step into the shoes of OmniBank and take advantage of OmniBank's lien. Because OmniBank's lien ordinarily would be superior to the lien of the judgment lienholder (because OmniBank's lien came first in time), Carl's right of subrogation would give Carl a first claim against the assets. That claim would be far more valuable than anything that Carl could obtain by exercising his right of reimbursement. The following case shows how important that right can be.

Chemical Bank v. Meltzer
712 N.E.2d 656 (N.Y. 1999)

WESLEY, J.

This appeal highlights the innovative and complex financing strategies used by local government officials to attract corporations to their municipalities and to stimulate economic development. We are asked to dust off the venerable law of suretyship, guaranty and subrogation and to reexamine these principles within the context of a multifaceted, contemporary business transaction which involves several parties, sophisticated financing arrangements and a variety of legal obligations.

In 1984 Major Building Products Wholesalers, Inc. sought to acquire land to construct a new facility for its business. In an effort to assist Major Building with this venture and to encourage the company to construct the facility within the Town of Brookhaven, the Town's Industrial Development Agency (IDA) offered the company favorable financing arrangements and tax incentives. The IDA issued a nonrecourse Industrial Development Revenue Bond in the amount of $1.1 million in December 1984. Pursuant to the terms of the bond purchase agreement, the IDA sold the bond to Manufacturers Hanover Trust Company, which subsequently merged with plaintiff Chemical Bank (Bank). As security for payment of all sums due the Bank under the bond purchase agreement, the IDA granted the Bank a first mortgage on the property and facility.

At the time the bond was issued, the IDA took title to the facility in its own name, and a lease between Major Building (as tenant) and the IDA (as landlord) was executed. The IDA then pledged and assigned the lease to the Bank as additional security on the bond. According to the terms of the lease Major Building was entitled to occupy the facility for a term of 15 years. Additionally, the bond proceeds were to be used to acquire equipment and/or renovate the facility. Major Building also agreed to remit rent directly to the Bank, rather than to the IDA, in amounts equal to the monthly debt service on the bond. Thus, under the terms of the entire transaction, Major Building's rent payments were to be used to make the installment payments of principal and interest under the bond until fully paid, at which time Major Building would purchase the facility for $1.

A guaranty also was executed by Major Building, its principal (General Building Products Corporation) and defendant Meltzer, president of Major Building. The guarantors jointly and severally agreed to guarantee payment of the bond in the event of an IDA default. The guaranty states that "upon any default . . . in the payment when due, of the principal of, any premium on, or interest on the Bond or of any sum payable . . . under the Bond Purchase Agreement, the Mortgage or the Assignment, [Meltzer] will promptly pay the same" and that he and the other signatories of the guaranty were "jointly and severally, absolutely, irrevocably and unconditionally" liable to the Bank for all payments due under this financing arrangement, "each as a primary obligor and not merely as a surety."

On April 16, 1991 the Bank extended additional credit to Major Building via the IDA and took a $2 million second mortgage on the property in order to settle a debt Major Building owed to another bank. This mortgage recited that it was "subject and subordinate to the lien of an existing first mortgage dated December 1, 1984 made by the [IDA] to the [Bank] in the original principal sum of $1,100,000.00." The second mortgage was executed by the IDA as mortgagor, accepted by the Bank as mortgagee, and approved by Major Building as "the lessee of the [mortgaged] premises." Meltzer did not guarantee payment under the second loan in any capacity. He did not sign any other writing in connection with the second mortgage, nor did he participate in this transaction.

Between January 1985 and January 1993, Major Building paid all sums due under the 1984 IDA financing scheme. In 1993, however, the company defaulted on its lease payments to the IDA. Given that these payments were specifically earmarked to service the debt on the bond, the IDA subsequently defaulted on the bond. The Bank then sought to enforce the guaranty to secure payment. General Building defaulted on the guaranty by seeking bankruptcy protection, leaving Major Building and Meltzer as the only collection possibilities under the guaranty.

After the Bank unsuccessfully demanded payment from Meltzer and Major Building it filed a motion against them on the guaranty for summary judgment in lieu of complaint pursuant to CPLR 3213. The Bank sought $337,756 in principal, $59,698.37 in interest through July 29, 1995, interest computed at prime rate from July 29, 1995 to entry of judgment, and attorneys' fees.

Meltzer then offered to tender the full amount due under the bond, on the condition that he be subrogated to the Bank's rights as a creditor under the 1984 bond purchase agreement. He asked that the first mortgage, given as security for the 1984 loan, be assigned to him. The Bank refused, but indicated that it would instead supply a satisfaction of the mortgage pursuant to Real Property Law §275. Meltzer declined the proposal and cross-moved to compel the Bank to honor his common-law right as subrogee by assigning the bond and first mortgage to him conditioned upon his payment of all sums due. Major Building did not appear.

[The] Supreme Court . . . concluded that Meltzer was a guarantor and not a surety and therefore was not entitled to assignment of the Bank's mortgage rights. The court also noted that assignment of the first mortgage would be inequitable, as it would defeat the purpose of the guaranty and would impair the Bank's second mortgage if Meltzer foreclosed. . . . [Ed.: The distinction that the court draws between a "guaranty" and a "surety" is an artifact of local law, under which "surety" describes a relationship that includes subrogation, while "guarantor" describes a relationship that does not include subrogation.]

The Appellate Division, with one Justice dissenting, affirmed. . . .

Presiding Justice Murphy dissented. . . . We granted leave to appeal and agree with Justice Murphy. The Appellate Division order therefore should be reversed.

A suretyship arrangement is, at its core, the confluence of three distinct, yet interrelated, obligations. These obligations are embodied in the tripartite relationship of principal obligor and obligee; obligee and secondary obligor; and secondary obligor and principal obligor. When a secondary obligor is bound to pay for the debt or answer for the default of the principal obligor to the obligee, the secondary obligor is said to have suretyship status. In other words, in transactions giving rise to suretyship status, the secondary obligor is answerable to the obligee in some way with respect to a duty, the cost of which, as between the principal obligor and the secondary obligor, ought to be borne by the principal obligor (Restatement [Third] of Suretyship and Guaranty §1, comment b). While commercial transactions have evolved over the years, these principles remain at the core of suretyship doctrine.

In order to determine Meltzer's status, we must first look to the substance of the entire transaction, rather than its form (Restatement [Third] of Suretyship and Guaranty §1[3][a]). As this Court stated half a century ago, "a contract of suretyship *does not depend upon the use of technical words* but upon a clear intent that one party as surety is bound to the second party as creditor to pay a debt contracted by a third party, either immediately upon default of the third party or after attempts to effect collection from the third party have failed." [Brackets and citation omitted; emphasis of *Chemical Bank* court.] The existence of suretyship status depends upon the respective roles of the parties and the nature of the underlying transaction.

When the guaranty is read in conjunction with the bond purchase agreement, lease, assignment and mortgage—each is incorporated into the guaranty by specific reference—it is clear that Meltzer has suretyship status. Viewing the entire transaction as an integrated business deal, Major Building's lease payments were the conduit for financing the nonrecourse bond. The lease provisions provide that Major Building was obligated to make its payments directly to the Bank. Additionally, Major Building agreed to make all late payment penalties and interest charges on the bond. Moreover, the company unconditionally obligated itself to make these payments notwithstanding any defenses or claims it might have against the IDA. Thus, given the way in which this transaction was structured, any default by Major Building on its lease payments directly translated into an IDA default on the bond.

Here, as the primary obligor to Chemical Bank, Major Building bore the responsibilities for the bond payments and also reaped the lion's share of the benefits. Notably, Meltzer was not a party to the lease and it did not impose any responsibilities on him. He was never called upon to pay anything on the bond until Major Building defaulted, nor did he receive any direct benefit from the transaction. He was required to pay the debt only after Major Building's default—the hallmark of a suretyship arrangement. Meltzer therefore bore the risks associated with a classic surety (Restatement [Third] of Suretyship and Guaranty §1[3]).

In reaching the conclusion that Meltzer was not a surety, the lower courts erroneously relied on the contradictory language of one instrument—the guaranty. While it is true that a court may not rewrite clear and unambiguous contracts, the guaranty here is replete with inconsistencies. The express language of the guaranty does identify the guarantors as "primary obligors" to the Bank on the bond, and "not merely sureties." The document itself, however, is a guaranty, and those bound by the instrument are referred to as "guarantors." These references are confounded by the fact that both guarantors and sureties can be afforded suretyship status as long as the fundamental nature of this status is present and the core criteria of a suretyship are fulfilled (Restatement [Third] of Suretyship and Guaranty §1, comment c).

Moreover, contrary to the lower courts' focus on a few words of a single instrument, this transaction must be analyzed as an integrated whole. To adopt the approach employed by the lower courts would elevate form over substance, obfuscate the nature of Meltzer's legal obligations and gloss over the essential character of this transaction.

As a surety, Meltzer is entitled to the rights that accompany his standing, including the right of subrogation. Rooted in equity, the purpose of the subrogation doctrine is to afford a person who pays a debt that is owed primarily by someone else every opportunity to be reimbursed in full. Ordinarily, in situations involving a party with suretyship status, "the surety upon payment of the debt is entitled, not only to an assignment or effectual transfer of all such additional collaterals taken and held by the creditor, but also to an assignment or effectual transfer of the debt and of the bond or other instrument evidencing the debt" (citation omitted; see also, Restatement [Third] of Suretyship and Guaranty §§18, 27-31). A surety's right of subrogation attaches at the time the surety pledges its obligation to the creditor, and the surety is entitled to insist upon priority to the proceeds of the collateral.

Pursuant to these traditional common-law principles, Meltzer has the right to be subrogated to the Bank under the bond and mortgage; this right attached upon his execution of the guaranty. The fact that Meltzer was not a party to the transaction giving rise to the second mortgage in no way deprives him of his subrogation rights with regard to the first transaction.

Here, Chemical Bank negotiated a second loan and mortgage on the same premises six years after the first transaction. The second transaction had nothing to do with the lease for which Meltzer stands as surety; he was not a party to it. When it entered into the second transaction, the Bank, a sophisticated creditor, was well aware of the nature of Meltzer's guaranty and thus was aware of Meltzer's already established priority right of subrogation. If the Bank saw fit to place itself in that position, then it must be bound by the legal effects of that decision. Meltzer is entitled to his full subrogation rights. To rule otherwise would place the Bank in a better position vis-a-vis Meltzer despite its failure to consolidate the second loan into the first mortgage or to obtain Meltzer's guaranty of the later debt.

. . .

The Bank also argues the *Restatement* supports the position of the lower courts that allowing Meltzer the right of subrogation on the first mortgage would inequitably impair the Bank's position on the second mortgage. Contrary to the Bank's misleading arguments, this case does not involve a single mortgage securing two separate debts, with Meltzer having surety status with regard to only one of the obligations (see, Restatement of Security §141, illustration 10).[3]

3. This illustration relied upon by the Bank states: "P owes C $3000 and $2000. S is surety for only the $3000 obligation. P has given C a mortgage securing both debts. P defaults, and S pays C $3000. S is not subrogated to the mortgage until C has realized $2000 out of it."

Meltzer's surety status, and its concomitant rights of subrogation, is not being used to defeat the superior position of a second debt not covered by Meltzer's surety obligation.

In sum, we know of no case in which (and can think of no reason why) the essential nature of this commercial transaction must be altered and a liability enforced against Meltzer without giving him the benefit of his suretyship status. To rule otherwise would conflict with the spirit of the contract, violate the manifest intention of the parties and mask the true nature of the obligations and relationships that form the basis of this transaction.

Accordingly, the order of the Appellate Division, insofar as appealed from, should be reversed, with costs, and defendant Meltzer's cross motion to compel assignment of the subject bond and mortgage should be granted.

The most important limitation on the right of subrogation is that the guarantor normally has no right of subrogation until the entire guaranteed debt has been paid. Restatement of Suretyship §27(1). Allowing a guarantor to acquire a right of subrogation by repaying only a portion of the debt would have a number of odd consequences. For example, as one court explained:

> [I]f the surety upon making a partial payment became entitled to subrogation pro tanto, . . . it would operate to place such surety upon a footing of equality with the holders of the unpaid part of the debt, and, in case the property was insufficient to pay the remainder of the debt for which the guarantor was bound, the loss would logically fall proportionately upon the creditor and upon the surety. Such a result would be grossly inequitable.

Jessee v. First Nat'l Bank, 267 S.E.2d 803, 805 (Ga. App. 1979).

Perhaps more serious is the possibility that the guarantor's "pro tanto" right of subrogation might hinder the creditor's attempt to collect from the borrower. If pro tanto subrogation were available, a borrower in difficulty could derail its creditor's collection efforts by causing its guarantor to make a partial payment of the debt. Asserting its rights of subrogation, the guarantor then could argue that its pro tanto share of the claim against the borrower entitled it to participate in the litigation pursuing the borrower. The guarantor's ability to impair the creditor's pursuit of the principal usually would not be catastrophic, however, because the creditor would retain the ability to go directly against the guarantor for debt unpaid by the principal. Moreover, the right of subrogation would not be the only way that the guarantor could obtain a right to sue the borrower; even the right of reimbursement would give the guarantor a right to sue the borrower (albeit not a right to pursue the creditor's collateral) without repaying the debt in full. The parties can contract around these default rules: The guarantor and lender might agree to allow pro tanto subrogation (unlikely), or the guarantor may waive its right to subrogation altogether (much more likely).

Stahl v. Simon (In re Adamson Apparel, Inc.)

785 F.3d 1285 (9th Cir. 2015)

RONALD LEE GILMAN, SUSAN P. GRABER, and CONSUELO M. CALLAHAN, Circuit Judges.
GILMAN, Circuit Judge:

This case presents an unresolved issue of bankruptcy law. The question is whether a corporate insider who personally guaranteed his corporation's loan is absolved of any preference liability to which he might otherwise have been subjected, where he had previously waived his indemnification rights against the corporation, he had a bona fide basis for doing so, and he took no subsequent actions to negate the economic impact of that waiver. Bankruptcy courts have split on this issue, and neither party has been able to cite to any district- or appellate-court decision addressing the question.

Both the bankruptcy court and the district court below ruled in favor of the corporate insider. For the reasons set forth below, we AFFIRM the judgment of the district court.

I.   BACKGROUND

A.   The loan, pledges, and guaranties

Adamson Apparel, Inc. (Adamson) manufactures and sells clothing and accessories. On April 18, 2002, Adamson took out a multimillion-dollar loan from CIT Group Commercial Services, Inc. (CIT). To secure the loan, Adamson granted CIT a lien on its inventory and accounts receivable. Arnold H. Simon, Adamson's president and CEO, subsequently entered into two separate agreements with CIT to guarantee the loan: a Cash Collateral Pledge Agreement (the Pledge) and a Limited Guaranty (the Guaranty). In these agreements, Simon took responsibility for Adamson's debt in the event that Adamson was unable to fully repay the loan. Simon would ordinarily have been entitled to have Adamson reimburse him for any amount that he was obligated to pay on the corporation's behalf to settle the loan with CIT, but the agreements waived that right to indemnification. (As used throughout this opinion, Simon's right to "indemnification" encompasses his rights to subrogation, reimbursement, or any other form of repayment.)

Over the next 18 months, the Pledge and the Guaranty were revised several times. Both agreements were initially signed on November 12, 2002. The Guaranty was updated on February 11, 2003, then "amended and restated" on April 9, 2003. Both documents were further "amended and restated" on April 25, 2003, then updated again on August 5, 2003. A letter dated December 2, 2003 increased the amount that had been guaranteed in the August 5, 2003 update of the Pledge.

Toward the end of 2003, an entity known as BP Clothing L.L.C. purchased a large amount of merchandise from Adamson. On December 18, 2003, Adamson instructed BP Clothing to transfer the purchase price (specifically, $4,989,934.65) to CIT in partial satisfaction of the debt owed by Adamson to CIT, this being the very debt guaranteed by Simon. Adamson filed for bankruptcy under Chapter 11 of the Bankruptcy Code nine months later. On or about March 31, 2004, Simon paid the balance of the loan, totaling over $3.5 million, from his personal funds.

B.   Lower-court proceedings

After Adamson filed for Chapter 11 bankruptcy in September 2004, the Committee of Unsecured Creditors (the Committee) was appointed to represent the interests of Adamson's unsecured creditors. The Committee filed this adversary action against Simon under a preference-liability theory. Preference liability is "a mechanism that allows [a] debtor or trustee to recover from creditors who received payments in the weeks or months prior to the bankruptcy so that they can be distributed to all bankruptcy estate creditors in accordance with their priority." [Citation omitted.] The Committee sought to recover from Simon the $4,989,934.65 paid by BP Clothing to CIT in December 2003, arguing that Simon was a corporate insider who received a preference because he had guaranteed the loan from CIT. Any reduction in that debt was therefore to his benefit.

In June 2007, Simon filed a motion for summary judgment, contending that because he had waived his right to claim indemnification from Adamson, he was not a creditor and therefore not subject to preference liability. The bankruptcy court granted that motion the following month. It held that Simon had fully waived his right to indemnification, which eliminated his status as a creditor for preference-liability purposes. The Committee appealed to the district court.

The district court reversed the grant of summary judgment and remanded the case to the bankruptcy court for further factual development. It pointed out that an ambiguity existed between the Pledge and the Guaranty as to whether Simon had fully and irrevocably waived his right to indemnification. The case was remanded to the bankruptcy court for a resolution of this issue.

A bench trial in bankruptcy court took place in September 2010. At trial, Simon testified that he understood at all times that he would never have any right to seek indemnification from Adamson for any funds that he expended to settle its debt to CIT. He told the court that CIT had required him to include the indemnification waiver in the Pledge and the Guaranty, although his own preference would have been to retain the right to seek reimbursement. Simon also pointed out that he had never filed a proof of claim in Adamson's bankruptcy case.

. . . The court . . . held that the Committee had failed to carry its burden of establishing Simon's "creditor" status under 11 U.S.C. §§101(10) & 547(b). Simon's testimony as to his understanding of his rights under the Pledge and the Guaranty, together with his failure to file a proof of claim in Adamson's bankruptcy case, defeated the Committee's arguments based on the ambiguous wording of the documents. The bankruptcy court subsequently entered judgment in favor of Simon, holding that he was exempt from preference liability because he was not a creditor of Adamson.

The Committee again appealed to the district court, which affirmed the judgment of the bankruptcy court . . . . This timely appeal followed . . . .

II.   ANALYSIS

. . .

B.   Simon's status as an alleged creditor of Adamson

Title 11 U.S.C. §547(b)(1) requires that the transfer of assets in question must be "to or for the benefit of a creditor" in order for preference liability to attach. In relevant part, a creditor is defined in §101(10) of the Bankruptcy Code as an "entity that has a claim against the debtor that arose at the time of or before the order for relief concerning the debtor." 11 U.S.C. §101(10). A claim is further defined as a "right to payment" or a "right to an equitable remedy for breach of performance if such breach gives rise to a right to payment." 11 U.S.C. §101(5). The Trustee bears the burden of establishing that Simon meets this definition, as well as satisfying each of the other preference-liability requirements, in order to prevail on its claim against him.

[The court concludes that the contract documents taken as a whole were ambiguous as to whether Simon's waiver of indemnification was unconditional, but affirms the bankruptcy court's determination that the waiver should be regarded as unconditional.]

> 3.   *Having fully waived his right of indemnification and taken no subsequent actions that would negate the economic impact of that waiver, Simon has no claim against Adamson and thus cannot be considered a creditor.*

The Trustee offers no additional theory regarding any claim that Simon might have against Adamson that would cause Simon to meet the definition of a creditor as set forth in the Bankruptcy Code. Instead, it urges this court to join several bankruptcy courts in stepping away from the plain text of the Code and subjecting an insider guarantor to preference liability where a transfer works to his benefit, even if he has unconditionally waived all claims against the debtor.

The above line of cases relied upon by the Trustee stems from the Seventh Circuit's decision in Levit v. Ingersoll Rand Fin. Corp. (In re Deprizio), 874 F.2d 1186, 1194 (7th Cir.1989), and Congress's subsequent response to *Deprizio* in 1994. In principle, the Bankruptcy Code seeks to effect an equitable distribution of a debtor's assets to the debtor's various creditors through the Code's statutory provisions and the use of a bankruptcy trustee. A simple way to achieve that goal in many situations is to collect all of a debtor's assets at the time of bankruptcy and apportion those assets ratably to the creditors according to their priority. But Congress has recognized that such a simple scheme would not be equitable if creditors who sensed financial difficulty could demand payment and have their demands fully satisfied in the period leading up to the filing of a bankruptcy petition, leaving the remaining creditors with a shortfall.

To remedy that concern, Congress empowered the trustee to set aside any transactions benefiting a creditor in the 90 days before the filing of a bankruptcy petition. *See* 11 U.S.C. §547(b). Congress apparently decided that 90 days is an adequate time for reasonably alert creditors to notice potential preferential treatment and force a debtor to either pay up or face an involuntary bankruptcy petition.

But, as courts have noted and Congress has recognized, "[i]nsiders pose special problems." In re Deprizio, 874 F.2d at 1195. The Bankruptcy Code defines insiders of a corporation as any director, officer, general partner, or person in control of the corporation, as well as any of their relatives. *See* 11 U.S.C. §101(31)(B). The court in *Deprizio* highlighted the particular complications that they cause as follows:

> Insiders will be the first to recognize that the firm is in a downward spiral. If insiders and outsiders had the same preference-recovery period, insiders who lent money to the firm could use their knowledge to advantage by paying their own loans preferentially, then putting off filing the petition in bankruptcy until the preference period had passed.

In re Deprizio, 874 F.2d at 1195.

Congress responded to that concern by extending the preference-recovery period to *one year* for transactions that benefit insiders, where the insider is a creditor. The Bankruptcy Code implements this policy through 11 U.S.C. §547(b):

> Except [for certain exceptions not relevant here], the trustee may avoid any transfer of an interest of the debtor in property (1) to or for the benefit of a creditor; [and] . . . (4) made (A) on or within 90 days before the date of the filing of the petition; or (B) between ninety days and one year before the date of the filing of the petition, if such creditor at the time of such transfer was an insider[.]

For ordinary transactions, that provision is straightforward. But what happens when a lender makes a loan to the debtor and, as part of the loan, an insider personally guarantees the loan? May the trustee avoid payments made to the lender during the extended preference-recovery period? The Seventh Circuit in *Deprizio* held that, by the plain text of the Bankruptcy Code, the answer is "yes"—the longer preference-recovery period applies to those payments.

In so holding, the Seventh Circuit reasoned that "[a] guarantor has a contingent right to payment from the debtor: if Lender collects from Guarantor, Guarantor succeeds to Lender's entitlements and can collect from Firm. So Guarantor is a 'creditor' in Firm's bankruptcy." *Id.* at 1190. Accordingly, the requirements of §547(b) are met and the longer preference-recovery period of one year applies to payments on loans guaranteed by insiders. Other circuit courts, including this one, soon adopted the Seventh Circuit's analysis in *Deprizio.*

Congress remedied the perceived inequity to innocent lenders ensnared by *Deprizio* and its progeny in a 1994 amendment to the Bankruptcy Code. Under that amendment, which is still in effect, the extended recovery period applies to payments made on loans guaranteed by insiders, but the trustee may seek recovery only from the insider and not from the lender. 11 U.S.C. §550(c).

Two separate lines of cases developed in *Deprizio*'s wake; one is relied upon by the Trustee and the other by Simon. The caselaw favorable to Simon developed first, after *Deprizio* was handed down but before the 1994 amendment to the Bankruptcy Code. Those cases conclude that bona fide indemnification waivers are valid and excuse an insider guarantor from preference liability. They "apply the letter of the statute to the facts before [them]" rather than focusing on broader concerns of public policy. [Citations omitted.] Because a guarantor has no legally cognizable claim against the borrower's estate once he has waived his right to indemnification, these courts concluded that insider guarantors who had done so in good faith were not "creditors" under the Bankruptcy Code and therefore were not subject to preference liability.

The cases relied upon by the Trustee, on the other hand, conclude that such waivers are simply not valid. As explained by [one of those] court[s]:

> such a waiver has no economic impact—if the principal debtor pays the note, the insider guarantor would escape preference liability, but if the principal debtor does not pay the note, the insider could still obtain a claim against the debtor, simply by purchasing the lender's note rather than paying on the guarantee. Thus, the "Deprizio waiver" could only be seen as an effort to eliminate, by contract, a provision of the Bankruptcy Code. The attempted waiver of subordination rights was thus held to be a sham provision, unenforceable as a matter of public policy.

[Telesphere Liquidating Tr. v. Galesi (In re Telesphere Commc'ns), 229 B.R. 173, 176 n.3 (Bankr. N.D. Ill. 1999).] [S]ubsequent cases adopted *Telesphere*'s reasoning. Despite this split of authority in the bankruptcy courts, no district or circuit court has yet weighed in on the validity of these so-called "*Deprizio* waivers."

We begin our assessment by noting that the latter cases' concern about the possibility of "sham" waivers is a valid one. A savvy insider guarantor might well agree to waive his right to indemnification from the corporate debtor, but then simply purchase the debt from the lender rather than pay it off if the debtor is later unable to meet its obligations. Such maneuvering would transform the original guarantor into the lender directly rather than by way of subrogation and, in that capacity, he would clearly have a claim against the debtor's bankruptcy estate without the burden of the one-year preference period for insider guarantors.

But the mere possibility of such avoidance does not mean that it will routinely occur. The post–1994 bankruptcy courts that have considered this question, as well as our dissenting colleague, would establish a bright-line rule based on a fear of what *could* happen. We believe the sounder approach is to consider what actually *has* happened. Rather than negating every *Deprizio* waiver based on a hypothetical scenario, the courts should instead examine the totality of the facts before them for evidence of "sham" conduct in the circumstances presented. In the present case, all evidence in the record indicates that the waiver at issue was not a sham.

First, CIT held a lien on Adamson's inventory and accounts receivable to secure the loan. This lien gave CIT a priority claim against these assets of Adamson in the event of bankruptcy. CIT's claim would therefore have been satisfied to the extent of the remaining inventory and accounts receivable even in the absence of Simon's guarantee.

Second, Simon never filed a proof of claim in the bankruptcy case. Counsel for both sides acknowledged at oral argument that the funds at issue here were not sufficient to cover Adamson's entire debt to CIT, and that Simon personally paid CIT over $3.5 million to clear Adamson's debt without ever seeking reimbursement. If the concern raised by the post–1994 bankruptcy cases were at play here,

Simon would have simply purchased the balance of the CIT note and then filed a claim as the successor to CIT in the bankruptcy case. Instead, he personally paid the debt without ever filing a claim against the estate.

. . .

A third factor indicating that the waiver here was not a sham is the fact that Simon had no unilateral right to purchase the note from CIT if Adamson defaulted. Although he could have pursued that possibility, CIT was also free to refuse to sell him the note and instead insist on payment. This factor might explain why Simon did not, in fact, purchase the note rather than pay it off when called upon to do so. If Simon had had a contractual right to purchase the note from CIT, then we would be more concerned about the waiver being a sham.

Finally, the Trustee presented no evidence that the debt in question was the only debt that Simon guaranteed on Adamson's behalf. Adamson is a closely held corporation, and Simon is its president and CEO. There is no reason to assume that he did not personally guarantee additional Adamson debts that he has been called upon to satisfy. Under such circumstances, Simon would have received no benefit by satisfying CIT's debt first rather than any other debts of equivalent magnitude that he might have personally guaranteed. The Trustee's failure (or inability) to establish that the CIT loan was the only one personally guaranteed by Simon further lessens our concern about the bona fide nature of the waiver.

All of these factors lead us to the conclusion that the waiver at issue in this case was not a sham. The concern of the *Telesphere* line of bankruptcy cases is simply not present where Simon's waiver prevented him from filing a claim to recover the amount that he personally paid to satisfy the balance of Adamson's debt to CIT. We cannot say that a waiver totally eliminating Simon's right to recover over $3.5 million has no economic substance. Given that the waiver is valid, Simon does not have a claim against the Adamson estate and thus does not meet the definition of a creditor under the Bankruptcy Code.

Moreover, when faced with a clearly drafted statute, we are not at liberty to deviate from the text in favor of a generalized notion of public policy. The Supreme Court decided in Norwest Bank Worthington v. Ahlers, 485 U.S. 197, 206 (1988), that "whatever equitable powers remain in the bankruptcy courts must and can only be exercised within the confines of the Bankruptcy Code." In order to be subject to preference liability, a person or an entity must be a creditor. 11 U.S.C. §547(b). A person is a creditor only if he has a right to payment from the debtor. 11 U.S.C. §101(10). Here, Simon waived any such right at the insistence of CIT. Nothing in the Bankruptcy Code prevented him from doing so, nor does any portion of the Code subject Simon to preference liability simply because he received a benefit—and a contingent one at that—from the payment by BP Clothing to CIT. *See* In re Deprizio, 874 F.2d at 1190–92 (holding that corporate insiders were not "creditors" subject to a preference claim when the corporation paid the Internal Revenue Service for delinquent wage withholding taxes, despite the benefit that they received by being relieved of personal liability for the taxes).

The public-policy concern raised by the Trustee in this case is far from frivolous, but that concern is more properly addressed to Congress, which has the ability to amend the Bankruptcy Code. This court's equitable powers are limited by the text of the Code as presently worded. Accordingly, we hold that when an insider guarantor has a bona fide basis to waive his indemnification rights against the debtor in bankruptcy and takes no subsequent actions that would negate the economic impact of that waiver, he is absolved of any preference liability to which he might otherwise have been subjected.

III.   CONCLUSION

For all the reasons set forth above, we AFFIRM the judgment of the district court.

GRABER, Circuit Judge, dissenting:
I respectfully dissent. . . . I would follow every bankruptcy court to have decided the issue and hold that insider-guarantors such as Simon are "creditors." The majority errs by looking to extraneous facts to decide whether the waiver is valid. . . .

A.   Insiders and the Right to Indemnity

As its president and CEO, Simon is an insider of Adamson Apparel, Inc. Adamson took out a loan from CIT Group Commercial Services, Inc. Simon personally guaranteed the loan. Adamson made a partial payment of about $5 million on the loan in December 2003. In September 2004, Adamson filed for bankruptcy.

Title 11 U.S.C. § 547(b) authorizes the bankruptcy trustee to avoid certain pre-filing transfers: all transfers made in the 90-day period before filing and all transfers made for the benefit of a "creditor" in the one-year period before filing. Because the December 2003 partial payment occurred less than a year before filing but more than 90 days before filing, the trustee's ability to avoid the transfer turns on whether Simon was a "creditor" of Adamson in December 2003.

Every bankruptcy court to have addressed this issue since the important 1994 amendments to the Bankruptcy Code have agreed: insider-guarantors such as Simon are "creditors" for purposes of the Code even if they nominally have waived their right to indemnity. . . . The majority opinion generally agrees with the . . . analysis [it quotes from *Telesphere*]. But the majority opinion then goes a step further — looking at additional facts in an open-ended inquiry into whether the waiver was a "sham." I disagree with that approach, which is not supported by precedent or by the logic of what Congress tried to accomplish. The waivers are invalid for purposes of the Bankruptcy Code because they attempt to defeat the one-year look-back period via contract, even though the waivers have no real-world economic impact. The majority opinion searches for clues as to whether Simon actually planned to purchase the note, but that inquiry is irrelevant. Because Simon easily *could have* purchased the note as of December 2003, the waiver had no real-world effect other than to defeat the Bankruptcy Code's longer look-back period for insiders. Therefore, Simon was a creditor.

I would follow the unanimous view of the bankruptcy courts that have ruled on this issue and would hold that an insider-guarantor is a "creditor" for purposes of the Bankruptcy Code.

. . .

I would reverse the bankruptcy court's holding that Simon was not a "creditor" and would remand for further proceedings. Accordingly, I dissent.

B.   Rights of the Guarantor Against the Creditor

1.   Suretyship Defenses

The preceding assignment explained that the guarantor's "secondary" status does not ordinarily limit the creditor's right to proceed directly against the guarantor in response to a default by the principal obligor. That is not to say, however, that the secondary nature of the guarantor's obligation has no effect on the rights of the creditor. To the contrary, the secondary nature of the obligation drives a series of rules that release the guarantor from its obligation. Those rules serve as a remedy for creditor misconduct that might harm the guarantor by increasing the likelihood or amount that the guarantor will have to pay on the guaranty.

The simplest rule relates to impairment of collateral. Recall the hypothetical in which Carl Eben guaranteed a loan that OmniBank has made to RFT. Suppose now that RFT's obligation to repay OmniBank is secured by a perfected security interest in RFT's accounts receivable, equipment, and inventory. OmniBank's security interest becomes unperfected, however, because OmniBank fails to make the filings required by Article 9 of the Uniform Commercial Code. Because that mistake would "impair" OmniBank's interest in the collateral it took from RFT, it usually is referred to as impairment of collateral.

If RFT becomes insolvent and OmniBank is unable to collect from RFT because of OmniBank's failure to maintain perfection of its security interest, OmniBank then would look to the guarantor, Carl, for payment. As between RFT and OmniBank, RFT certainly could not complain about OmniBank's failure to maintain perfection. Rather, RFT is directly liable on the debt whether or not OmniBank takes care to protect OmniBank's interest in the assets that RFT offered as collateral. Carl, however, would have some justification for a complaint because OmniBank's actions lessened OmniBank's ability to recover from RFT, thus increasing the probability that OmniBank would collect from Carl as guarantor. In fact (absent some contrary agreement), Carl would have a defense to a suit on his guaranty to the extent that OmniBank's mistake harmed Carl. The harm would be the amount that OmniBank would have recovered from RFT if OmniBank had maintained perfection, reduced by the amount that OmniBank actually recovered from RFT notwithstanding OmniBank's mistake. Restatement of Suretyship §42(1), (2)(a); UCC §3-605(d).

Impairing collateral is not the only thing a creditor can do that might increase the exposure of the guarantor. Another common possibility is for the creditor to grant the principal an extension of time to pay. Suppose that RFT's loan from OmniBank is due on July 1, 1999. On the due date, RFT is still solvent, but experiencing financial difficulties. OmniBank does not force RFT to pay at that time, but instead grants a one-year extension. By the time the extension expires, RFT is insolvent. OmniBank collects nothing and sues Carl on his guaranty. In that event, Carl would argue that OmniBank's grant of an extension to RFT caused Carl a loss by decreasing the amount that OmniBank was able to recover from RFT. The merits of that claim, however, are not as clear as those of the impairment-of-collateral claim because there is no obvious reason why the extension would be more likely to harm Carl than to help him. From the point of view of the creditor at the time that it grants the extension, it is hard to predict whether it would be better to pursue RFT vigorously on the original due date or instead to grant the extension. A premature suit might destroy RFT unnecessarily, but an extension might defer collection efforts until all of RFT's assets have been dissipated. Notwithstanding the dilemma that the creditor faces, the law generally offers Carl a discharge on his guaranty to the extent that he can prove that the extension decreased OmniBank's ability to recover from RFT. Restatement of Suretyship §40(b); UCC §3-605(c).

A third common situation occurs when the creditor grants some modification of the indebtedness other than an extension of the due date. For example, suppose that RFT defaults on its loan and the creditor chooses not to enforce its remedies against RFT immediately; instead, the creditor allows RFT to reinstate the loan, conditioned on an increase in the interest rate of 11 percent per annum. If RFT eventually fails to repay the loan and OmniBank pursues Carl, Carl could defend against OmniBank's claim by arguing that the amendment of the loan increased Carl's exposure on the guaranty. For example, Carl might try to prove that OmniBank would have been paid in full if it had exercised its rights against RFT on the first default or that the outstanding balance would have been smaller if OmniBank and RFT had not raised the interest rate. If a court found either of those things to be true, Carl would have at least a partial defense to OmniBank's claim. Restatement of Suretyship §41(b); UCC §3-605(c).

A more extreme situation occurs when the creditor completely releases the principal from liability and then proceeds to sue the guarantor. The intuitive response to this situation would be that a complete release of the principal should clearly justify release of the guarantor, because a complete release of the principal is the most serious possible modification of the principal obligation. The law has not, however, taken that course.

Instead, the traditional approach to a release of the principal obligor focuses on whether the creditor intended for its release of the principal to also release the guarantor. If the terms of the release indicate that the creditor intended to retain its right to pursue the guarantor (usually referred to as a "reservation of rights"), then the creditor retains its right to pursue the guarantor. A typical provision would state: "Nothing in this Release shall be construed to release any right of Lender to recover the Debt from Guarantor or any party other than Borrower that is primarily or secondarily liable for all or any portion of the debt."

The law justifies the rule allowing the creditor to pursue the guarantor after granting a release to the principal by also allowing the guarantor to retain its right to pursue the principal (via reimbursement or subrogation), even though the creditor has released the principal. Restatement of Suretyship §39; UCC §3-605(a). From the borrower's perspective, however, that result is highly counterintuitive. The borrower, having negotiated a release of its liability to the creditor in return for a partial payment, discovers that the release granted by the creditor is meaningless because the guarantor still can pursue the borrower for any amount of the debt that the borrower failed to pay. UCC §3-605(a)(2).

2. *Waiver of Suretyship Defenses*

The complicated rules discussed above rest on a desire to protect the guarantor from the corrosive prejudice of agreements between the principal and the creditor. Those rules take on a surreal aspect in a world in which the majority of guaranties are issued by guarantors that are closely related to the principals. Because those rules threaten the lender with a loss of its rights against the guarantor as a result of the lender's dealings with the principal, they severely limit the lender's ability to respond flexibly to a default by its borrower. Moreover, it is unreasonable to release Carl from liability because of OmniBank's willingness to accommodate the company that Carl owns and operates.

Fortunately, the legal system provides a solution to that problem, permitting the guarantor to waive the suretyship defenses. Both common-law rules and the UCC treat those waivers as enforceable. Restatement of Suretyship §48(1); UCC §3-605(f). As a result, it is rare for a commercial guaranty to omit a thorough waiver of suretyship defenses. See Guaranty Agreement §9.

Courts reviewing clauses waiving suretyship defenses traditionally construed those clauses quite narrowly, often to the point of ignoring their plain intent. These courts usually referred to the antiquated principle of *strictissimi juris*, under which creditors must conform their dealings with guarantors to standards of the "utmost equity." Not surprisingly, guarantors have not been above invoking that doctrine to seek a release of their liability even when it is absolutely clear that the guarantor controlled the borrower and participated directly in the lender's decision to grant the accommodation on which the guarantor bases its claim for a release. As the following case shows, recent decisions have been less sympathetic to such claims, reflecting a growing willingness to enforce the plain intent of provisions waiving suretyship defenses.

Data Sales Co. v. Diamond Z Manufacturing

74 P.3d 268 (Ariz. Ct. App. 2003)

IRVINE, Judge.

Diamond Z Manufacturing appeals from the trial court's order denying its request to set aside the judgment finding Diamond Z liable under a guaranty agreement. We find that surety defenses can be expressly or implicitly waived within the guaranty contract. Therefore, we affirm the judgment.

FACTS AND PROCEDURAL HISTORY

Diamond Z is an Idaho corporation that manufactures recycling equipment known as tub grinders. Tub grinders are large industrial machines designed to grind solid materials such as tires, stumps, logs, and railroad ties, into small pieces one inch or less in size. In 1993, Zehr Wood & Tire Grinding, Inc. ("Zehr Wood") purchased a Model 1463T tub grinder, the largest model manufactured by Diamond Z. Vernon and Rodney Zehr, father and son, owned and operated Zehr Wood. Vernon and Rodney are the uncle and cousin, respectively, of Marty Zehr, an owner of Diamond Z. At the time Zehr Wood purchased the tub grinder, Diamond Z neither received nor requested anything in writing from Zehr Wood and Zehr Wood made no written commitment to make scheduled payments for the grinder. The approximate purchase price of the tub grinder was $425,000. As of December 1996, Zehr Wood still owed a balance of $375,000 on the grinder's purchase price.

Data Sales Company, Inc. finances and leases equipment. Equipment Leasing Corporation ("ELC") often brokers these transactions. ELC finds a proposed lessee or buyer and then submits the deal to Data Sales for financing. If Data Sales approves the deal, the buyer or lessee signs the appropriate documents with ELC, and the documents are then assigned to Data Sales, which funds the transaction. Data Sales and ELC have done several financing transactions with Diamond Z, its affiliates, and Zehr family members.

On December 5, 1996, Zehr Wood and ELC entered into a purchase/leaseback transaction in which Zehr Wood sold the grinder to ELC for the outstanding balance due to Diamond Z ($375,000), and ELC leased the tub grinder back to Zehr Wood. The terms and conditions of the purchase/leaseback transaction were set forth in a Master Lease Agreement for Equipment ("the lease"). The lease required 42 monthly payments of $11,844, with total payments over the life of the lease of $497,448. As part of the transaction, ELC required Diamond Z to execute a Continuing Corporate Guaranty ("the guaranty") guaranteeing Zehr Wood's payment obligations under the lease. Diamond Z's general counsel Alan Malone reviewed the guaranty. On December 5, 1996, Diamond Z executed the guaranty in the form ELC requested. Under the guaranty, Diamond Z agreed that it was fully conversant with the financial status and situation of Zehr Wood at the time it signed the guaranty. Diamond Z also agreed that Data Sales had no duty to disclose to Diamond Z any facts or information it may acquire about Zehr Wood.

Data Sales provided the funding for the transaction and transferred the funds directly to Diamond Z. On December 6, 1996, ELC, as lessor, assigned all of its interest in the lease with Zehr Wood to Data Sales. ELC and Data Sales also required Rodney Zehr to personally guarantee the debt.

Within weeks after signing the lease, Rodney and Vernon Zehr informed Data Sales that they wanted out of the grinding business. Marty Zehr was also aware of Rodney's and Vernon's desire to leave the grinding business. In October 1996, prior to signing the lease, Rodney had contacted Global Intermark ("Global"), an equipment broker in Missouri. On December 3, 1996, Zehr Wood entered into a marketing contract with Global, wherein Global agreed to find a party interested in acquiring the tub grinder. Shortly thereafter, Global located a party who was interested in acquiring the grinder, Breaux Bridge Resources, Inc. ("Breaux Bridge"), located in Shreveport, Louisiana.

In January 1997, Data Sales, Zehr Wood, and Breaux Bridge executed an assignment of the lease. Zehr Wood remained obligated for the full amount of the lease. At that time, Zehr Wood had already made the January lease payment. Zehr Wood was not in default under the lease at the time of the assignment.

Breaux Bridge made only three lease payments to Data Sales, all of which were late. On May 21, 1997, Data Sales sent a formal default notice to Breaux Bridge. Data Sales did not copy Diamond Z on this notice, nor did Data Sales ever contact Diamond Z with regard to Breaux Bridge's default at the time. Data Sales initially sought payment from Breaux Bridge. Breaux Bridge filed for bankruptcy on October 2, 1997. Data Sales was not able to collect from Rodney Zehr because he filed for bankruptcy.

In February 1999, Data Sales brought suit against Diamond Z, Zehr Wood, and Rodney Zehr. Zehr Wood and Rodney Zehr never answered or appeared, and were ultimately dismissed from this case. [After a jury trial, the trial court rejected Diamond Z's challenges to the enforceability of the guaranty.]

. . .

DISCUSSION

Diamond Z claims that the trial court erred in denying its motion for summary judgment because under Restatement §48 it could not consent in advance to material modifications of the lease. Therefore, when Zehr Wood assigned its rights to Breaux Bridge, Diamond Z was discharged of its obligations under the guaranty contract. . . .

The common law recognized that the rights of a guarantor could be changed by actions of the primary parties to the debt transactions. The doctrines collectively known as "suretyship defenses" have developed to prevent the creditor ("obligee") from destroying the guarantor's ("secondary obligor") rights or diminishing its practical ability to enforce them. *See* Neil B. Cohen, *Striking the Balance: The Evolving Nature of Suretyship Defenses*, 34 Wm. & Mary L. Rev. 1025, 1033 (1993). At the same time, suretyship law has also deferred to freedom of contract and allowed the waiver of suretyship defenses.

Arizona law is well settled that surety rights can be waived by contract. The issue raised by Diamond Z, however, is one of first impression. There is no Arizona case law on point nor is there an Arizona case that addresses the applicable provisions of the Restatement (Third) of Suretyship & Guaranty (1996). Accordingly, we look to the Restatement and other jurisdictions for guidance.

Diamond Z claims that Restatement §48 creates an inference that the suretyship defense regarding modification of the underlying obligation found in Restatement §41(b)(i) cannot be waived or consented to in the guaranty agreement, because §48 excluded the defense from its list of waivable defenses. Diamond Z does not cite any legal authority that reaches such a conclusion. Indeed, without addressing the §48 argument raised by Diamond Z, several jurisdictions have found that a guarantor that assents, either expressly or impliedly, to a modification of the underlying obligation is not discharged from its obligations under the guaranty. . . .

Diamond Z argues, however, that the general rule that a suretyship defense can be waived in advance has been modified by the new language of Restatement

§48(1). That section specifies that a guarantor may waive the discharge of its liability pursuant to sections 39(c)(ii)-(iii), 40(b), 41(b)(ii), 42(1), 43, and 44. Because the modification defense contained in §41(b)(i) is not among those listed, Diamond Z concludes that the Restatement must be read as precluding its waiver in advance. As further support, Diamond Z points out that Tentative Draft No. 2 of the Restatement provided that all suretyship defenses could be waived. See Restatement (Third) of Suretyship §42 cmt. a (Tentative Draft No. 2, 1993). The final Restatement ultimately revised what became §48 and listed only certain sections and subsections.

It is not clear to us why Restatement §48 excludes some of the surety defenses in its list of those that can be waived by consent. Neither party has provided us with the rationale of the drafters of the Restatement. Nor have they articulated any relevant differences between the defenses listed and not listed in §48 that would allow only some to be waived.

We do not find the failure to include certain surety defenses in §48 sufficient to overcome the general principle that the parties to commercial transactions may generally structure their agreements as they see fit. Section 6 of the Restatement plainly states that "[e]ach rule in this Restatement stating the effect of suretyship status may be varied by contract between the parties subject to it." Indeed, comment a to Restatement §6 plainly allows waivers to be included in the guaranty contract, i.e., in advance:

> Suretyship law provides rules governing the relationship between various combinations of parties to a suretyship arrangement. If those parties prefer to order their relationship in a different way, suretyship law defers to that private ordering. Indeed, agreements to do so are quite common . . . . Agreements between the secondary obligor and the obligee as to the availability and scope of suretyship defenses are typically incorporated into the contract creating the secondary obligation.

Other Restatement provisions also reflect a general policy allowing waivers. Comment d to Restatement §48 states that a guarantor can forego its suretyship defenses, "by agreement or waiver," and it can forego "the benefit of the rules in §§39-44 that might otherwise result in such discharges." This comment suggests that parties to a guaranty contract may waive *any* of the suretyship defenses found in Restatement §§39-44. Section 37 of the Restatement generally describes all the suretyship defenses, including the modification contained in §41(b)(i) and all the defenses listed in §48. Comment e to §37 specifically provides that the suretyship defenses listed in §37 may be foregone by the guarantor. No attempt is made to distinguish between the different defenses.

Section 48 lists only some of the suretyship defenses as being waivable. It does not, however, go further and plainly preclude waiver of any others. Given the general policy that parties may contractually waive defenses, and absent any persuasive reason to treat the modification defense differently, we hold that Diamond Z could waive its suretyship defenses in advance.

This does not mean, however, that all rights may be waived. According to the Restatement, a party's freedom to contract to be a guarantor is still limited by principles of contract law such as unconscionability, good faith and fair dealing, and the statute of frauds. See Restatement §6 cmt. b, §48 cmt. a. None of these principles is controlling here.

Diamond Z argues that it is against public policy and unconscionable to allow the suretyship defense like the one described in §41(b)(i) to be waived in advance. Diamond Z fails to explain why waiver of this particular defense would be against public policy or provide evidence that enforcing the waiver would be unconscionable. First, Diamond Z freely entered into the contract and it received an immediate payment of $375,000. Second, Diamond Z's legal counsel negotiated the contract. Although the terms of the guaranty contract favor Data Sales, this is not unreasonable under the circumstances, especially in light of the direct benefit Diamond Z received when it was paid the balance due on the tub grinder. Data Sales would only fund the purchase/leaseback transaction if Diamond Z agreed to sign a "bulletproof" guaranty. Requiring Diamond Z to consent in advance to certain modifications of the lease provided additional assurances that the terms would be satisfied. In a case such as this, where the guarantor received a direct business benefit and the guaranty was well-documented, we can find no public policy that would preclude enforcing the terms of the guaranty, including the consent and waiver provisions.

The language of the guaranty in section 1.3(b) expressly allows the lease to be amended without notice to Diamond Z and without its consent. Section 2.2 of the guaranty allows Data Sales to make several modifications to the lease, including acquiring or releasing collateral as well as substituting or releasing parties to the lease. The guaranty contract's language is unambiguous and we agree with the trial court that the contract gave Data Sales the authority to allow Zehr Wood to assign its rights and interests in the lease to Breaux Bridge without notice to or consent from Diamond Z.

Moreover, nothing in the language of the guaranty limits Data Sales' authority to exercise its rights under sections 1.3 and 2.2 to times when Zehr Wood was in default. Diamond Z correctly points out that its obligation was only triggered by the default of the principal obligor, but this fact does not help its arguments because Data Sales did not turn to Diamond Z until after Zehr Wood was in default. Data Sales' right to modify the lease could be exercised at any time after Diamond Z gave its consent, i.e., signed the guarantee.

To summarize, we agree with the trial court's interpretation of Restatement §48 and hold that pursuant to Arizona law, surety defenses, including the defense found at Restatement §41(b)(i), can be expressly or impliedly waived within the guaranty contract. Our ruling is consistent with Arizona case law . . . holding that most surety rights can be waived by contract. Accordingly, the trial court did not err by denying Diamond Z's motion for summary judgment.

Waivers of suretyship defenses may be quite common, but they are still problematic. The biggest difficulty with those provisions is the difficulty that they can cause the guarantor if the guarantor loses control of the principal. For example, suppose that Carl sold RFT to Rick Compo at a time when RFT's obligation to OmniBank remained outstanding, still guaranteed by Carl. Suppose then that OmniBank and Compo subsequently agreed to a sale of RFT's assets at a price of $250,000 when Carl believed that a fair price would be $500,000. If Carl had signed a guaranty in a customary form (like the form at the end of the chapter), Carl's rights to challenge the sale would be quite limited. OmniBank could collect the proceeds of the sale and then sue Carl for the amount that remained unpaid on RFT's obligation. If Carl complained that OmniBank's actions had harmed Carl by impairing the collateral, OmniBank could point to the provisions in the guaranty in which Carl released the bank from responsibility for "any impairment of any collateral" and "the failure to sell any collateral in a commercially reasonable manner or as otherwise required by law." Guaranty Agreement §8. If a court enforced those provisions as written, Carl would have no defense to the suit by OmniBank, even if OmniBank's action in agreeing to the sale did cause harm to Carl.

The most common way for commercial parties to resolve that dilemma is to include in the guaranty a "defeasance" provision, which gives the guarantor an absolute right to terminate its liability under the guaranty by purchasing the debt from the creditor. A typical, relatively simple provision might read as follows:

> Notwithstanding anything to the contrary elsewhere in this Guaranty, Guarantor's liability on the Debt shall terminate entirely upon Guarantor's payment to Lender of the entire amount of principal and interest due on the Debt. Upon payment by Guarantor of that amount, the Debt and all of Lender's rights related to the Debt shall be assigned to Guarantor, and Lender agrees to execute an instrument in a form satisfactory to Lender reflecting that assignment. Lender also agrees to provide Guarantor a written statement of that amount (including a method for calculating daily accruals of interest) on five (5) business days' notice; Lender shall warrant to Guarantor the accuracy of that statement. If Guarantor in good faith disagrees with Lender as to the amount due, Guarantor shall be entitled to terminate its liability on the Debt by (a) paying to Lender unconditionally the amount that Guarantor acknowledges to be due; and (b) depositing into the registry of a court of competent jurisdiction the additional amount claimed by Lender, the deposited funds to be disbursed by the court in accordance with the court's resolution of the disagreement. In connection with any such purchase, Guarantor must provide Lender with a release by Borrower of all claims Borrower might have against Lender arising out of or related to the Debt or Lender's administration of it.

A defeasance provision solves the concerns that make the creditor wary of suretyship defenses: The creditor retains free discretion to deal with the borrower until the creditor has received full payment. Conversely, it mitigates the guarantor's concerns about inappropriate leniency by the creditor by allowing the guarantor to take over the creditor's position and deal with the principal as the guarantor wishes.

Of course, a defeasance provision does little for the guarantor that is not in a position to pay off the underlying obligation. But the guarantor's risk is considerably diminished when the guarantor's own financial status is precarious. If the guarantor's ability to perform is in doubt, the creditor is unlikely to behave recklessly in its dealings with the principal. For example, in the hypothetical sale to Rick Compo discussed above, OmniBank would be much less inclined to agree to a fire-sale price for RFT's assets if it knew that the guarantor would be unable to pay any balance of the debt that remained after the sale. The cases where the guarantor is most worried about the creditor behaving recklessly are the opposite cases, in which the creditor does not care what it gets from the principal because it knows that it easily can obtain full payment from the guarantor. If OmniBank is sure that it can collect its debt from Carl, then it has little reason to quibble with Compo about anything.

C. Bankruptcy of the Guarantor

The last topic here is the effect of the bankruptcy of the guarantor. The normal expectation might be that such cases would be rare: If the guarantor was selected to enhance the credit of the principal, we should not expect to see the guarantor failing nearly so often as the principal. In any event, when a guarantor does become bankrupt, that bankruptcy can have the same effect as the bankruptcy of a principal (discussed in the preceding assignment). Thus, where the courts in that context delay the creditor's right to proceed against the guarantor, the following case delays the creditor's right to proceed against the principal.

Trimec, Inc. v. Zale Corporation
150 B.R. 685 (N.D. Ill. 1993)

ANN CLAIRE WILLIAMS, District Judge.

In June 1984, Aeroplex O'Hare, a joint venture between Aeroplex Stores, Inc. ("Aeroplex")[1] and Trimec, Inc. ("Trimec"), contracted with the City of Chicago (the "City") to operate three drug store concessions at O'Hare International Airport. The agreement required Aeroplex O'Hare to operate the concessions for five years and pay the City a license fee of approximately $14 million during that time. Zale guaranteed Aeroplex O'Hare's obligations under the contract and Aeroplex O'Hare also posted a $1 million performance bond guaranteed by the Federal Insurance Company (FIC). The concessions were not successful and, after approximately two years and with several million dollars of rent past due, Aeroplex O'Hare abandoned its operations at O'Hare International Airport.

In 1986, Trimec brought suit against Aeroplex and Zale to recover its lost capitalization funds and profits. Aeroplex and Zale then filed a third-party complaint against the City and three former officials of the City's Department of Aviation, alleging [various causes of action not relevant to this opinion]. The City filed a counterclaim against Aeroplex O'Hare, Trimec, Aeroplex, Zale in its capacity as guarantor of Aeroplex O'Hare, and FIC as the surety of Aeroplex O'Hare's performance bond. Trimec has settled its lawsuit with Aeroplex and Zale. The litigation involving the City remains.

In January 1992, Zale went into bankruptcy and the automatic stay provision of the Bankruptcy Code, 11 U.S.C. §362, stayed all further proceedings against Zale,

---

1. At the time, Aeroplex was a wholly-owned subsidiary of Zale Corporation ("Zale"). In June 1986, Zale sold all of its interest in Aeroplex.

including those in this case. On November 3, 1992, the City moved to have the automatic stay lifted to permit this case to proceed. Zale objected to this motion and moved to extend the stay to cover all parties to this action. . . .

THE MOTION TO STAY THE CASE

Zale, Aeroplex, and Trimec (the "parties") move to stay this proceeding pending resolution of the claim submitted by the City in Zale's bankruptcy case. The parties argue that proceeding in this case without Zale would be inequitable because Zale would be bound by a judgment in favor of the City since it is Aeroplex O'Hare's guarantor under the contract and has agreed to indemnify the other defendants. . . .

The City counters that it is inappropriate to stay this proceeding merely because one party has filed for bankruptcy. According to the City, a stay which protects solvent parties is inconsistent with the statutory scheme established in the federal bankruptcy code which limits the protection of the automatic stay to bankrupt parties. Moreover, the City argues that discovery has been completed and this case is ready to go to trial. The City claims that staying the proceeding at this late date would deny the City its right to vigorously pursue its action against the solvent defendants.

As the City suggests, the automatic stay is generally only available to the debtor, and not related third-party defendants or solvent co-defendants. However, there is a limited exception to this rule in "unusual circumstances" where the relief sought against the third party would result in harm to the debtor. As the Fourth Circuit explained in [A.H. Robins Co. Inc. v. Piccinin, 788 F.2d 994, 999 (4th Cir. 1986)], a stay is appropriate where "there is such identity between the debtor and the third-party defendant that the debtor may be said to be the real party defendant and that the judgment against the third-party defendant will in effect be a judgment or finding against the debtor."

This court finds that a judgment in favor of the City in the instant action would serve as a judgment against Zale, thus improperly defeating the purpose of the automatic stay invoked in Zale's bankruptcy proceeding. As explained above, Zale would be bound by a judgment in this case regardless of whether it was involved in the litigation because Zale is Aeroplex O'Hare's guarantor under the contract and agreed to indemnify the other defendants. Permitting such a judgment to be entered against Zale would be inequitable since Zale would not have had the opportunity to defend itself and a judgment in favor of the City could have a significant impact on Zale's estate in its bankruptcy proceeding. Given the identity of the parties and the effect of this proceeding on the debtor's estate, an extension of the stay to the solvent parties in this action is clearly warranted as the parties suggest.

. . .

It is difficult to see anything unusual about the circumstances of the *Trimec* guaranty. Thus, *Trimec* presents a strategic opportunity for the borrower with a related guarantor that has significant financial problems. At the same time, it poses a corresponding strategic hazard to the lender considering whether to take a guaranty from a party of questionable financial strength. Of course, the lender ordinarily could solve the problem by waiving its rights against the guarantor. In *Trimec*, however, and probably in other large-firm bankruptcies as well, the likelihood that the guarantor would emerge from bankruptcy with significant assets makes that alternative unpalatable.

Problem Set 16

16.1. Jude Fawley is back to see you again, following up on the issues that you discussed with him in Problem 15.2. Shortly after the events at issue in that problem, Jude managed to sell his company OWH to a new investor (a Canadian named Rick Compo), who planned to put up the additional funds necessary to keep the business running. Unfortunately, the headstone business was not as profitable as Compo anticipated. Compo called Jude this morning to advise him that OWH will not make a loan payment that is due from OWH to Wessex next week. OWH is primarily obligated on that loan, with a guaranty by Jude individually. Jude thinks that OWH's assets still have considerable value and thus has determined that the best approach is make the payment out of his personal assets and then try to recover from the business. Would your answers change if Jude decided that he would limit his intervention, for now at least, to making the single payment that is now due?

    a. Consider the result under the default rules in the Restatement of Suretyship and also under the terms of the Guaranty Agreement. Restatement of Suretyship §§22, 27.

    b. Can you recommend a better approach that Jude's lawyers could have taken?

16.2. Your regular client Jodi Kay from CountryBank has a question about a guaranty that she is negotiating. She sent the potential guarantor her standard-form guaranty. The guarantor responded by asking her to delete a provision that currently states:

> Guarantors shall have no right of subrogation, and waive any right to enforce any remedy that Lender now has or may hereafter have against Borrower, and waive any benefit of, and any right of reimbursement, indemnity, or contribution or to participate in any security now or hereafter held by Lender.

The guarantor proposes replacing it with the following: "Guarantors shall be entitled to rights of reimbursement and subrogation, but only to the extent of payments actually made to Lender under this Guaranty." Jodi wants to know how you would respond to the request. What do you say? Please consider the differences among the existing and proposed provisions, the default rules in the Restatement of Suretyship, and the parallel provision in the Guaranty Agreement.

Consider the advice guarantor's counsel has provided. Do you believe that the advice is appropriate? 11 U.S.C. §547(b).

16.3.   Consider the facts of *Chemical Bank*.

a.   What was the purpose of the guaranty's description of Meltzer as a "primary obligor"?
b.   Is the decision allowing pro tanto subrogation consistent with Restatement of Suretyship §27 Illustrations 2, 3, & 4? If so, what should the lender have done to protect itself from pro tanto subrogation?

16.4.   Cynthia Sharples has been referred to you by a friend of yours who practices family law. It appears that Cynthia and her former husband, Ernest, owned a framing business as partners, for which they obtained a loan. In their divorce last year, Cynthia transferred her interest in the business to Ernest, along with full responsibility for the loan (the balance of which at the time was about $2,200,000). (You should assume that the transaction leaves Cynthia secondarily liable for that obligation under Restatement of Suretyship §2(f).)

Cynthia knew that the business was not doing well, but she learned yesterday that it had gotten worse than she had known. Specifically, Cynthia received a letter from the lender advising her that the lender graciously has accepted her ex-husband's request to modify the terms of the loan to increase the stated interest rate from 8 percent to a floating rate of prime plus eight percent (prime currently is two percent). In return, the lender also has agreed to forgo taking action in response to Ernest's failure to make a number of past-due payments that total about $320,000; the lender proposes to add those payments to the current principal balance, together with fees for this transaction. At the end of the day, the total principal balance would be about $2,565,000.

The lender is seeking Cynthia's consent and a reaffirmation that she will remain obligated on the loan as modified. The letter is courteous, but it closes by expressing an intention to pursue its remedies as aggressively as possible if Cynthia does not agree to the proposal by the end of the week. Should she consent to the modification? What are the lender's options if she does not?

16.5.   A few months after your conversations with Cynthia, she returns to tell you that she has learned that the lender has agreed to settle with Ernest for a one-time payment of $1,600,000. She understands that Ernest's payment would leave a remaining balance due on the loan of $1,000,000 and that the lender plans to pursue Cynthia to recover that sum. She is very upset because she thinks Ernest could pay the entire amount if pressed. Is she right to be concerned about a suit from the lender? If so, will she be able to recover from Ernest anything she has to pay to the lender? Consider three possibilities:

a.   The settlement agreement between Ernest and the lender does not include any terms that address the effect of the settlement and release of Ernest on the rights of the lender against Cynthia or Cynthia's rights against Ernest. Restatement of Suretyship §§38, 39.
b.   The settlement agreement states that the lender reserves the right to pursue Cynthia for the remaining balance. Restatement of Suretyship §§38, 39.

c. The settlement agreement states that the lender retains the right to pursue Cynthia for the remaining balance and that Cynthia in turn retains her rights to recover from Ernest. Restatement of Suretyship §§38, 39.

GUARANTY AGREEMENT

THIS GUARANTY AGREEMENT (this "*Guaranty*") is executed as of January __, 2015, by SUBSIDIARY, INC., a Delaware corporation, and its permitted assigns ("*Guarantor*"), whose address for notice purposes is [Address], for the benefit of LENDER, INC., a Delaware corporation ("*Lender*"), and its Affiliates (Lender and its Affiliates, together with their successors and assigns, herein sometimes collectively called "*Beneficiaries*"). Unless otherwise defined herein, all capitalized terms have the meanings given to such terms in the Note.

INTRODUCTORY PROVISIONS:

A. Borrower and Lender executed that certain Promissory Note dated as of January __, 2015 (the "Note").
B. Borrower, Guarantor, and Lender acknowledge and agree that the execution by Guarantor of this Guaranty is required as a condition to Lender's execution of the Note.
C. Guarantor is an Affiliate of Borrower and the execution of the Note and the extension of credit to Borrower under the Note is a substantial and direct benefit to Guarantor.

NOW, THEREFORE, for valuable consideration, the receipt and adequacy of which are hereby acknowledged, Guarantor hereby guarantees to Beneficiaries the prompt payment and performance of the Guaranteed Obligations, this Guaranty being upon the following terms and conditions:

1. Definitions. As used in this Guaranty, the following terms have the following meanings:

"*Affiliates*" when used with respect to any Person, any other Person that, directly or indirectly, controls or is controlled by or is under common control with such Person. For purposes of this definition "control" (including with correlative meanings, the terms "controlled by" and under "common control with"), with respect to any Person, means possession directly or indirectly of the power to direct or cause the direction of the management and policies of such Person, whether through the ownership of voting securities, by contract or otherwise.

"*Borrower*" shall mean Borrower, Inc., a Delaware corporation, and without limitation Borrower's successors and assigns (regardless of whether such successor or assign is formed by or results from any merger, consolidation, conversion, sale or transfer of assets, reorganization, or otherwise).

"*Debtor Relief Laws*" shall mean Title 11 of the United States Code, as now or hereafter in effect, or any other applicable law, domestic or foreign, as now or hereafter in effect, relating to bankruptcy, insolvency, liquidation, receivership, reorganization, arrangement or composition, extension or adjustment of debts, or similar laws affecting the rights of creditors.

"*Dispute*" shall mean any action, dispute, claim or controversy of any kind, whether in contract or tort, statutory or common law, legal or equitable, now existing or hereafter arising under or in connection with, or in any way pertaining to, this Guaranty and each other document, contract and instrument required hereby or now or hereafter delivered to Lender in connection herewith, or any past, present or future extensions of credit and other activities, transactions or obligations of any kind related directly or indirectly to any of the foregoing documents, including without limitation any of the foregoing arising in connection with the exercise of any self-help, ancillary or other remedies pursuant to any of the foregoing documents.

"*Guaranteed Indebtedness*" shall mean all (a) "Obligation," as defined in the Loan Documents, including without limitation any and all pre- and post-maturity interest thereon, including without limitation post-petition interest and expenses (including attorneys' fees), if the Borrower is the debtor in a bankruptcy proceeding under the Debtor Relief Laws, whether or not allowed under any Debtor Relief Law, (b) indebtedness, obligations and liabilities of Borrower to Beneficiaries, or any or some of them, of any kind or character, now existing or hereafter arising, whether direct, indirect, related, unrelated, fixed, contingent, liquidated, unliquidated, joint, several or joint and several, and regardless of whether such indebtedness, obligations and liabilities may, prior to their acquisitions by Beneficiaries, or any or some of them, be or have been payable to or in favor of a third-party and subsequently acquired by Beneficiaries, or any or some of them (it being contemplated that Beneficiaries, or any or some of them, may make such acquisitions from third-parties), including without limitation all indebtedness, obligations and liabilities of Borrower to Beneficiaries, or any or some of them, now existing or hereafter arising by note, draft, acceptance, guaranty, endorsement, letter of credit, assignment, purchase, overdraft, discount, indemnity agreement or otherwise, (c) obligations of Borrower to any Beneficiary under any documents evidencing, securing, governing and/or pertaining to all or any part of the indebtedness described in (a) and (b) above, (d) costs and expenses incurred by any Beneficiary in connection with the collection and administration of all or any part of the indebtedness and obligations described in (a), (b) and (c) above or the protection or preservation of, or realization upon, the collateral securing all or any part of such indebtedness and obligations, including without limitation all reasonable attorneys' fees, and (e) renewals, extensions, modifications and rearrangements of the indebtedness and obligations described in (a), (b), (c) and (d) above.

"*Guaranteed Obligations*" shall mean the Guaranteed Indebtedness and the Guaranteed Performance Obligations.

"*Guaranteed Performance Obligations*" shall mean all of the obligations of Borrower and any Guarantor under the Loan Documents other than an obligation to pay money.

"*Note*" shall mean that certain Promissory Note dated as of January __, 2015, by and between Borrower and Lender, as renewed, extended, restated, amended, or replaced from time to time.

"*Person*" shall mean any individual, corporation, partnership, joint venture, limited liability company or partnership (general or limited) association, trust, unincorporated association, joint stock company, government, municipality, political subdivision or agency, or other entity.

2. Payment. Guarantor hereby unconditionally and irrevocably guarantees to Beneficiaries the punctual payment when due, whether by lapse of time, by acceleration of maturity, or otherwise, and at all times thereafter, of the Guaranteed Indebtedness. This Guaranty covers the Guaranteed Indebtedness, whether presently outstanding or arising subsequent to the date hereof, including all amounts advanced by any Beneficiary in stages or installments. The guaranty of Guarantor as set forth in this Section 2 is a continuing guaranty of payment and not a guaranty of collection. Guarantor acknowledges and agrees that Guarantor may be required to pay and perform the Guaranteed Indebtedness in full without assistance or support from Borrower or any other party. Guarantor agrees that if all or any part of the Guaranteed Indebtedness shall not be punctually paid when due, whether on the scheduled payment date, by lapse of time, by acceleration of maturity or otherwise, Guarantor shall, immediately upon demand by a Beneficiary, pay the amount due on the Guaranteed Indebtedness to such Beneficiary at Beneficiary's address as set forth herein. Such demand(s) may be made at any time coincident with or after the time for payment of all or part of the Guaranteed Indebtedness, and may be made from time to time with respect to the same or different items of Guaranteed Indebtedness. Such demand shall be made, given and received in accordance with the notice provisions hereof.

3. Performance. Guarantor hereby unconditionally and irrevocably guarantees to Beneficiaries the timely performance of the Guaranteed Performance Obligations. If any of the Guaranteed Performance Obligations of Borrower are not satisfied or complied with in any respect whatsoever, and without the necessity of any notice from a Beneficiary to Guarantor, Guarantor agrees to indemnify and hold Beneficiaries harmless from any and all loss, cost, liability or expense that Beneficiaries may suffer by any reason of any such non-performance or non-compliance. The obligations and liability of Guarantor under this Section 3 shall not be limited or restricted by the existence of, or any terms of, the guaranty of payment under Section 2 of this Guaranty.

4. Primary Liability of Guarantor.

(a) This Guaranty is an absolute, irrevocable and unconditional guaranty of payment and performance. Guarantor is and shall be jointly and severally liable for the payment and performance of the Guaranteed Obligations, as set forth in this Guaranty, as a primary obligor.

(b) In the event of default in payment or performance of the Guaranteed Obligations, or any part thereof, when such Guaranteed Obligations become due, whether by its terms, by acceleration, or otherwise, Guarantor shall promptly pay the amount due thereon to Beneficiaries without notice or demand, of any kind or nature, in lawful money of the United States of America or perform the obligations to be performed hereunder, and it shall not be necessary for any Beneficiary in order to enforce such payment and performance by Guarantor first, or contemporaneously, to institute suit or exhaust remedies against Borrower or others liable on the Guaranteed Obligations, or to enforce any rights, remedies, powers, privileges or benefits of any Beneficiary against any Collateral, or any other security or collateral which shall ever have been given to secure the Guaranteed Obligations.

(c) Suit may be brought or demand may be made against all parties who have signed this Guaranty or any other guaranty in favor of Beneficiaries covering all or any part of the Guaranteed Obligations, or against any one or more of them, separately or together, without impairing the rights of any Beneficiary against any party hereto. Any time that a Beneficiary is entitled to exercise its rights or remedies hereunder, such Beneficiary may in its discretion elect to demand payment and/or performance. If a Beneficiary elects to demand performance, it shall at all times thereafter have the right to demand payment until all of the Guaranteed Obligations have been paid and performed in full. If a Beneficiary elects to demand payment, it shall at all times thereafter have the right to demand performance until all of the Guaranteed Obligations have been paid and performed in full.

5. Other Guaranteed Debt. If Guarantor becomes liable for any indebtedness owing by Borrower to Beneficiaries, or any or some of them, by endorsement or otherwise, other than under this Guaranty, such liability shall not be in any manner impaired or affected hereby, and the rights and remedies hereunder shall be cumulative of any and all other rights and remedies that Beneficiaries may ever have against Guarantor. The exercise by Beneficiary of any right or remedy hereunder or under any other instrument, or at law or in equity, shall not preclude the concurrent or subsequent exercise of any other right or remedy by such Beneficiary or any other Beneficiary.

6. Subrogation. Until the Guaranteed Obligations have been paid, in full, Guarantor hereby covenants and agrees that it shall not assert, enforce, or otherwise exercise (a) any right of subrogation to any of the rights, remedies or liens of Beneficiaries or any other beneficiary against Borrower or its Affiliates or any other guarantor of the Guaranteed Obligations or any collateral or other security, or (b) unless such rights are expressly made subordinate to the Guaranteed Obligations (in form and upon terms acceptable to Lender) and the rights or remedies of Beneficiaries under this Guaranty and the Loan Documents, any right of recourse, reimbursement, contribution, indemnification, or similar right against Borrower or its Affiliates or any other guarantor of all or any part of the Guaranteed Obligations.

7. Subordinated Debt. All principal of and interest on all indebtedness, liabilities, and obligations of Borrower or its Affiliates to Guarantor (the "*Subordinated Debt*") now or hereafter existing, due or to become due to Guarantor, or held or to be held by Guarantor, whether created directly or acquired by assignment or otherwise, and whether evidenced by written instrument or not, shall be expressly subordinated to the Guaranteed Obligations. Until such time as the Guaranteed Obligations is paid and performed in full and all commitments to lend under the Loan Documents have terminated, Guarantor agrees not to receive or accept any payment from Borrower with respect to the Subordinated Debt at any time an Event of Default has occurred and is continuing; and, in the event Guarantor receives any payment on the Subordinated Debt in violation of the foregoing, Guarantor will hold any such payment in trust for Beneficiaries and forthwith turn it over to Beneficiaries in the form received, to be applied to the Guaranteed Obligations.

8. Obligations Not to Be Diminished. Guarantor hereby agrees that its obligations under this Guaranty shall not be released, discharged, diminished, impaired, reduced, or affected for any reason or by the occurrence of any event, including, without limitation, one or more of the following events, whether or not with notice to or the consent of Guarantor: (a) the taking or accepting of collateral as security for any or all of the Guaranteed Obligations or the release, surrender, exchange, or subordination of any collateral now or hereafter securing any or all of the Guaranteed Obligations; (b) any partial release of the liability of Borrower or Guarantor hereunder, or the full or partial release of any other guarantor or obligor from liability for any or all of the Guaranteed Obligations; (c) any disability of Borrower or the dissolution, insolvency, or bankruptcy of Borrower or any other guarantor or any other party at any time liable for the payment of any or all of the Guaranteed Obligations; (d) any renewal, extension, modification, waiver, amendment, or rearrangement of any or all of the Guaranteed Obligations or any instrument, document, or agreement evidencing, securing, or otherwise relating to any or all of the Guaranteed Obligations; (e) any adjustment, indulgence, forbearance, waiver, or compromise that may be granted or given by any Beneficiary to Borrower, Guarantor, or any other party ever liable for any or all of the Guaranteed Obligations; (f) any neglect, delay, omission, failure, or refusal of any Beneficiary to take or prosecute any action for the collection of any of the Guaranteed Obligations or to foreclose or take or prosecute any action in connection with any instrument, document, or agreement evidencing, securing, or otherwise relating to any or all of the Guaranteed Obligations; (g) the unenforceability or invalidity of any or all of the Guaranteed Obligations or of any instrument, document, or agreement evidencing, securing, or otherwise relating to any or all of the Guaranteed Obligations; (h) any payment by Borrower or any other party to any Beneficiary is held to constitute a preference under applicable bankruptcy or insolvency law or if for any other reason any Beneficiary is required to refund any payment or pay the amount thereof to someone else; (i) the settlement or compromise of any of the Guaranteed Obligations; (j) the non-perfection of any security interest or lien securing any or all of the Guaranteed Obligations; (k) any impairment of any collateral securing any or all of the Guaranteed Obligations; (l) the failure of any Beneficiary to sell any collateral securing any or all of the Guaranteed Obligations in a commercially reasonable manner or as otherwise required by law; (m) any change in the corporate existence, structure, or ownership of Borrower; or (n) any other circumstance which might otherwise constitute a defense available to, or discharge of, Borrower or Guarantor.

9. Waivers. Guarantor waives (a) any right to revoke this Guaranty with respect to future indebtedness; (b) any right to require any Beneficiary to do any of the following before Guarantor is obligated to pay the Guaranteed Obligations or before any Beneficiary may proceed against Guarantor: (i) sue or exhaust remedies against Borrower and other guarantors or obligors, (ii) sue on an accrued right of action in respect of any of the Guaranteed Obligations or bring any other action, exercise any other right, or exhaust all other remedies, or (iii) enforce rights against Borrower's assets or the collateral pledged by Borrower to secure the Guaranteed Obligations; (c) any right relating to the timing, manner, or conduct of such Beneficiary's enforcement of rights against Borrower's assets or the collateral pledged by Borrower to secure the Guaranteed Obligations; (d) if Guarantor and Borrower (or a third party) have each pledged assets to secure the Guaranteed Obligations, any right to require any Beneficiary to proceed first against the other collateral before proceeding against collateral pledged by Guarantor; (e) except as expressly required hereby, promptness, diligence, notice of any default under the

Guaranteed Obligations, notice of acceleration or intent to accelerate, demand for payment, notice of acceptance of this Guaranty, presentment, notice of protest, notice of dishonor, notice of the incurring by Borrower of additional indebtedness, notice of any suit or other action by any Beneficiary against Borrower or any other Person, any notice to any party liable for the obligation which is the subject of the suit or action, and all other notices and demands with respect to the Guaranteed Obligations and this Guaranty; (f) each of the foregoing rights or defenses regardless whether they arise under (i) Section 34.01 et seq. of the Texas Business and Commerce Code, as amended, (ii) Section 17.001 of the Texas Civil Practice and Remedies Code, as amended, (iii) Rule 31 of the Texas Rules of Civil Procedure, as amended, (iv) common law, in equity, under contract, by statute, or otherwise; and (g) any and all rights under Sections 51.003, 51.004 and 51.005 of the Texas Property Code, as amended.

10. Insolvency. Should Guarantor become insolvent, or fail to pay Guarantor's debts generally as they become due, or voluntarily seek, consent to, or acquiesce in the benefit or benefits of any Debtor Relief Law, or become a party to (or be made the subject of) any proceeding provided for by any Debtor Relief Law (other than as a creditor or claimant) that could suspend or otherwise adversely affect the rights and remedies of Beneficiaries granted hereunder, then, in any such event, the Guaranteed Obligations shall be, as between Guarantor and Beneficiaries, a fully matured, due, and payable obligation of Guarantor to Beneficiaries (without regard to whether Borrower is then in default under the Note or whether the Obligation, or any part thereof is then due and owing by Borrower to Beneficiaries), payable in full by Guarantor to Beneficiaries upon demand, which shall be the estimated amount owing in respect of the contingent claim created hereunder.

11. Termination. Guarantor's obligations hereunder shall remain in full force and effect until all commitments to lend under the Loan Documents have terminated, and the Guaranteed Obligations have been paid in full. If at any time any payment of the principal of or interest or any other amount payable by Borrower under the Loan Documents is rescinded or must be otherwise restored or returned upon the insolvency, bankruptcy, or reorganization of Borrower or otherwise, Guarantor's obligations hereunder with respect to such payment shall be reinstated as though such payment had been due but not made at such time.

12. Representations and Warranties. Guarantor represents and warrants as follows:

(a) Guarantor has the power and authority and legal right to execute, deliver, and perform its obligations under this Guaranty and this Guaranty constitutes the legal, valid, and binding obligation of Guarantor, enforceable against Guarantor in accordance with its terms, except as limited by bankruptcy, insolvency, or other laws of general application relating to the enforcement of creditor's rights.

(b) The execution, delivery, and performance by Guarantor of this Guaranty do not and will not violate or conflict with any law, rule, or regulation or any order, writ, injunction, or decree of any court, governmental authority or agency, or arbitrator and do not and will not conflict with, result in a breach of, or constitute a default under, or result in the imposition of any lien upon any assets of Guarantor pursuant to the provisions of any indenture, mortgage, deed of trust, security agreement, franchise, permit, license, or other instrument or agreement to which Guarantor or its properties are bound.

(c) No authorization, approval, or consent of, and no filing or registration with, any court, governmental authority, or third party is necessary for the execution, delivery, or performance by Guarantor of this Guaranty or the validity or enforceability thereof.

(d) Guarantor has, independently and without reliance upon any Beneficiary and based upon such documents and information as Guarantor has deemed appropriate, made its own analysis and decision to enter into this Guaranty, and Guarantor has adequate means to obtain from Borrower on a continuing basis information concerning the financial condition and assets of Borrower, and Guarantor is not relying upon any Beneficiary to provide (and no Beneficiary shall have duty to provide) any such information to Guarantor either now or in the future.

(e) The value of the consideration received and to be received by Guarantor is reasonably worth at least as much as the liability and obligation of Guarantor hereunder, and such liability and obligation may reasonably be expected to benefit Guarantor directly or indirectly.

13. Covenants. So long as this Guaranty remains in full force and effect, Guarantor shall, unless Beneficiaries shall otherwise consent in writing:

(a) Furnish to Beneficiaries such financial information of Guarantor as required pursuant to Section 5 of the Note.

(b) Furnish to Beneficiaries written notice of the occurrence of any Potential Default or Event of Default promptly upon obtaining knowledge thereof.

(c) Furnish to Beneficiaries such additional information concerning Guarantor, Borrower or any other Person under the control of Guarantor as Beneficiaries may request.

(d) Obtain at any time and from time to time all authorizations, licenses, consents or approvals as shall now or hereafter be necessary or desirable under all applicable laws or regulations or otherwise in connection with the execution, delivery and performance of this Guaranty and will promptly furnish copies thereof to Beneficiaries.

14. No Fraudulent Transfer. It is the intention of Guarantor and Beneficiaries that the amount of the Guaranteed Obligations guaranteed by Guarantor by this Guaranty shall be in, but not in excess of, the maximum amount permitted by fraudulent conveyance, fraudulent transfer, or similar laws applicable to Guarantor. Accordingly, notwithstanding anything to the contrary contained in this Guaranty or any other agreement or instrument executed in connection with the payment of any of the Guaranteed Obligations, the amount of the Guaranteed Obligations guaranteed by Guarantor by this Guaranty shall be limited to that amount which after giving effect thereto would not (a) render Guarantor insolvent, (b) result in the fair saleable value of the assets of Guarantor being less than the amount required to pay its debts and other liabilities (including contingent liabilities) as they mature, or (c) leave Guarantor with unreasonably small capital to carry out its business as now conducted and as proposed to be conducted, including its capital needs, as such concepts described in clauses (a), (b) and (c) of this **Section 14** are determined under applicable law, if the obligations of Guarantor hereunder would otherwise be set aside, terminated, annulled or avoided for such reason by a court of competent jurisdiction in a proceeding actually pending before such court. For purposes of this Guaranty, the term **"applicable law"** means as to Guarantor each statute, law, ordinance, regulation, order, judgment, injunction or decree of the United States or any state or commonwealth, any municipality, any foreign country, or any territory, possession or tribunal applicable to Guarantor.

15. Successors and Assigns. This Guaranty is for the benefit of Beneficiaries and their successors and assigns, and, in the event of an assignment of the Guaranteed Obligations in accordance with the provisions of the Note, or any part thereof, the rights and remedies hereunder, to the extent applicable to the indebtedness so assigned, may be transferred with such indebtedness. This Guaranty is binding on Guarantor, and its successors and permitted assigns; provided that, Guarantor may not assign its obligations under this Guaranty without obtaining the prior written consent of Beneficiaries, and any assignment purported to be made without the prior written consent of Beneficiaries shall be null and void.

16. Note. The Note, and all of the terms thereof, is incorporated herein by reference, the same as if stated verbatim herein, and Guarantor agrees that Beneficiaries may exercise any and all rights granted to it under the Note and the other Loan Documents without affecting the validity or enforceability of this Guaranty.

17. Amendments. No amendment or waiver of any provision herein nor consent to any departure therefrom by Guarantor shall be effective unless the same shall be in writing and signed by Beneficiaries, and then such amendment, waiver, or consent shall be effective only in the specific instance and for the specific purpose for which given.

18. Setoff Rights. Beneficiaries shall have the right to set off and apply against this Guaranty or the Guaranteed Obligations or both, at any time and without notice to Guarantor, any and all deposits (general or special, time or demand, provisional or final) or other sums at any time credited by or owing from any Beneficiary to Guarantor whether or not the Guaranteed Obligations are then due and irrespective of whether or not such Beneficiary shall have made any demand under this Guaranty. As security for this Guaranty and the Guaranteed Obligations, Guarantor hereby grants Beneficiaries a security interest in all money, instruments, certificates of deposit, and other property of Guarantor now or hereafter held by Beneficiaries, including, without limitation, property held in safekeeping. In addition to Beneficiaries' right of setoff and as further security for this Guaranty and the Guaranteed Obligations, Guarantor hereby grants Beneficiaries a security interest in all deposits (general or special, time or demand, provisional or final) and all other accounts of Guarantor now or hereafter on deposit with or held by Beneficiaries or any or some of them and all other sums at any time credited by or owing from each Beneficiary to Guarantor. The rights and remedies of Beneficiaries hereunder are in addition to other rights and remedies (including, without limitation, other rights of setoff) which Beneficiaries may have.

19. Time of Essence. Time shall be of the essence in this Guaranty Agreement with respect to all of Guarantor's obligations hereunder.

20. Governing Law. This Guaranty is executed and delivered as an incident to a lending transaction negotiated and consummated in Harris County, Texas, and shall be governed by and construed in accordance with the laws of the State of Texas. Guarantor, for itself and its successors and assigns, hereby irrevocably (a) submits to the nonexclusive jurisdiction of the state and federal courts in Texas, (b) waives, to the fullest extent permitted by law, any objection that it may now or in the future have to the laying of venue of any litigation arising out of or in connection with any Loan Document brought in the District Court of Harris County, Texas, or in the United States District Court for the Southern District of Texas, Houston Division, (c) waives any objection it may now or hereafter have as to the venue of any such action or proceeding brought in such court or that such court is an inconvenient forum, and (d) agrees that any legal proceeding against any party to this Guaranty arising out of or in connection with this Guaranty may be brought in one of the foregoing courts. Guarantor agrees that service of process upon it may be made by certified or registered mail, return receipt requested, at its address specified herein. Nothing herein shall affect the right of Beneficiaries to serve process in any other manner permitted by law or shall limit the right of Beneficiaries to bring any action or proceeding against Guarantor or with respect to any of Guarantor's property in courts in other jurisdictions. The scope of each of the foregoing waivers is intended to be all encompassing of any and all disputes that may be filed in any court and that relate to the subject matter of this transaction, including, without limitation, contract claims, tort claims, breach of duty claims, and all other common law and statutory claims. Guarantor acknowledges that these waivers are a material inducement to Lender's agreement to enter into agreements and obligations evidenced by the Note, that Lender and each other Beneficiary has already relied on these waivers and will continue to rely on each of these waivers in related future dealings. The waivers in this section are irrevocable, meaning that they may not be modified either orally or in writing, and these waivers apply to any future renewals, extensions, amendments, modifications, or replacements in respect of the documents related in any manner to the transactions evidenced by the Note. In connection with any litigation, this Guaranty may be filed as a written consent to a trial by the court.

21. Counterparts. This Guaranty may be executed in multiple counterparts, each of which, for all purposes, shall be deemed an original, and all of which taken together shall constitute but one and the same instrument.

22. Waiver of Right to Trial by Jury. GUARANTOR HEREBY IRREVOCABLY AND UNCONDITIONALLY WAIVES ALL RIGHT TO TRIAL BY JURY IN ANY ACTION, SUIT, PROCEEDING, OR COUNTERCLAIM THAT RELATES TO OR ARISES OUT OF THIS GUARANTY OR ANY OF THE LOAN DOCUMENTS OR THE ACTS OR FAILURE TO ACT OF OR BY ANY BENEFICIARY IN THE ENFORCEMENT OF ANY OF THE TERMS OR PROVISIONS OF THIS GUARANTY OR THE OTHER LOAN DOCUMENTS.

23. Arbitration. All claims and disputes arising out of or related to this Guaranty (other than disputes with respect to the enforcement by Lender of its rights and remedies under this Guaranty where Guarantor seeks equitable relief in the form of a restraining order or injunction) shall be settled by arbitration in accordance with the rules of the American Arbitration Association then in effect. The award rendered by the arbitrators in any such proceeding shall be final, and judgment may be entered upon such award in any court having jurisdiction thereof. In the event of any dispute under this Guaranty which is not resolved satisfactorily to both parties within ten days after notice of such dispute is delivered by either party to the other party, then either party concerned in such dispute shall have the right at any time thereafter to refer resolution of the dispute to arbitration and all parties agree to cooperate in obtaining such arbitration. Each arbitration shall be held in the City of Houston, Texas, and the number of arbitrators appointed shall be selected by Lender. Guarantor shall pay all expenses of arbitration, including without limitation, any reasonable attorneys' fees of Lender.

24. No Oral Agreements. THIS GUARANTY REPRESENTS THE FINAL AGREEMENT BETWEEN THE PARTIES AND MAY NOT BE CONTRADICTED BY EVIDENCE OF PRIOR, CONTEMPORANEOUS, OR SUBSEQUENT ORAL AGREEMENTS BY THE PARTIES. THERE ARE NO UNWRITTEN ORAL AGREEMENTS BETWEEN THE PARTIES.

25. Lender Acts for Beneficiaries. Lender shall (absent written notification by a Beneficiary to the contrary) act for all Beneficiaries for the purposes of making demands hereunder, obtaining information, amending or waiving provisions hereof and otherwise taking action on behalf of the Beneficiaries, and (absent written notice to the contrary) Guarantor shall be entitled to rely on the authority of Lender to act for all Beneficiaries without further investigation.

26. Joint and Several. If any Person makes any guaranty of any of the Obligations guaranteed hereby or gives any security for them. Guarantor's obligations hereunder shall be joint and several with the obligations of such other Person pursuant to such agreements or other papers making the guaranty or giving the security.

EXECUTED as of the first date herein set forth.

_____

GUARANTOR

Chapter 6. Letters of Credit

Assignment 17: Letters of Credit — The Basics

In form, the letter of credit is nothing more than a letter from a financial institution promising to pay a stated sum of money upon the receipt of specified documents. The basic concept is that the prospective payor goes to a bank and asks it to issue a letter of credit to the prospective payee.

As you will see later in this assignment, the letter of credit is attractive to the payee because issuance of a letter of credit provides an assurance of payment that has two particularly favorable aspects: The stakeholder (almost always a bank or similar financial institution) provides an advance commitment that it will make payment when the actual date for payment arrives, and the transaction payor has no right to cancel payment at any point after the institution makes that commitment. Thus, a payee that receives a letter of credit before performing faces a relatively small risk of nonpayment after it performs. Those features distinguish letters of credit from all the payment systems discussed in the previous assignments of this book because none of those payment systems provides an advance assurance of payment as firm as a letter of credit.

Although letters of credit have been common for centuries, the growth of other modern payment systems has limited the types of transactions in which they are useful. They continue to be widely used, however, to provide payment in international transactions for the sale of goods, a usage that has important implications for the continuing development of the applicable legal rules. The only major domestic context involves the "standby" letter of credit. Because standby letters of credit serve a credit function quite different from the function that letters of credit serve as a payment system, discussion of standby letters of credit is deferred to the end of the chapter. Hence, this assignment and the next are devoted exclusively to the "commercial" letter of credit, a letter of credit used as a payment mechanism in sale-of-goods transactions.

Among other things, the increasingly international use of letters of credit has enhanced the importance of reliably uniform international legal principles. For decades, banks have responded to that concern by providing in most of their letters of credit for the application of the rules set forth in the Uniform Customs and Practice for Documentary Credits, a publication of the International Chamber of Commerce commonly referred to as the UCP. The current version is ICC Publication No. 600 (2007). Unfortunately, the rules established for letters of credit in the original version of Article 5 of the Uniform Commercial Code were not entirely consistent with the UCP. In response to that concern (among others), in 1995 the American Law Institute and the National Conference of Commissioners on Uniform State Laws adopted a revised version of Article 5 of the UCC, designed to bring American law into closer conformity with the UCP. See, e.g., UCC §5-116(c) (stating a general rule that in the event of a conflict between the UCP and Article 5, a letter of credit that incorporates the UCP should be interpreted in accordance with the UCP). Thus, widespread adoption of the new Article 5 has brought international uniformity considerably closer than it had been.

A.   The Underlying Transaction

To understand the letter of credit as a payment system, it is necessary to examine it in the context of the transaction in which it commonly is used. For illustrative purposes, assume that a company in Missouri (the Toy Importing Company) has contracted to buy certain toys from a company in Hong Kong (the Toy Manufacturing Company) for a price of $250,000. The task of providing payment presents something of a "chicken-and-egg" problem. The Hong Kong company is reluctant to ship the goods overseas until it has been paid, but the American company is reluctant to send money to Hong Kong until it has received the goods. The letter of credit provides a compromise solution that addresses the concerns of both of the companies. The American company (as "applicant," see UCC §5-102(a)(2)) can ask its bank (Boatmen's National Bank of St. Louis, the "issuer," see UCC §5-102(a)(9)) to issue a letter of credit in favor of the Hong Kong company (as "beneficiary," see UCC §5-102(a)(3)), in which the issuing bank commits to pay $250,000 upon proof that the goods have been shipped. The charges for letters of credit vary considerably in different markets, but the major fees for issuing and providing payment on a typical letter of credit ordinarily come to about one quarter of 1 percent of the amount of the letter of credit ($625 in this case); for particularly good customers, the fees might drop by as much as 50 percent.

One problem with that arrangement is that the Hong Kong company may have neither a close relationship with Boatmen's in St. Louis nor a desire to travel to Missouri to obtain payment or resolve any disputes about its entitlement to payment. To solve that problem, Boatmen's can nominate a bank — a "nominated person" for purposes of UCC §5-102(a)(11) — with an office at the location of the beneficiary to process payment for the beneficiary. The nominated person proceeds on the implicit understanding that Boatmen's will reimburse the nominated person if it makes a payment under the letter of credit. Similarly, Boatmen's also might use a bank in the beneficiary's location to provide more expeditious notification of Boatmen's issuance of the letter of credit. A bank that plays the latter role — advising the beneficiary of the terms of the letter of credit that Boatmen's has issued — is known as an adviser or advising bank. UCC §5-102(a)(1). As you will see, the nature of a bank's role is important because Article 5 and the UCP impose different types of liability on nominated persons, advising banks, and issuers of letters of credit.

The most common practice in the transaction described above would be for Boatmen's to send the letter of credit to a Hong Kong bank (Hang Seng Bank in our example) that would assist the beneficiary at both stages of the transaction, as an adviser (when the credit is issued) and as a nominated person (when the beneficiary seeks payment). Thus, Hang Seng Bank would deliver the letter of credit to the Toy Manufacturing Company in Hong Kong and formally "advise" the Toy Manufacturing Company that the credit has been issued. The use of the adviser expedites the notification of the issuance of the letter of credit because Boatmen's usually can send the letter of credit to Hang Seng in Hong Kong by a secure electronic transmission that would be much faster and more secure than conventional delivery services. See UCP art.

11(a) (permitting issuance of a credit by "authorized teletransmission"); UCC §5-104 comment 3. Unlike the checking system, Article 5 can accommodate fully electronic letters of credit because it requires only a "record" of the letter of credit (see UCC §§5-102(a)(14), 5-104) not the writing required by UCC §3-104(a) for items in the checking system.

When Hang Seng receives that transmission, it prints out a hard copy of the letter of credit and authenticates a single original for delivery to the Toy Manufacturing Company (the beneficiary). Different banks have different ways of authenticating original letters of credit. Most use some combination of special secure paper (paper that is not easily photocopied) or a special colored-ink stamp, together with a manual signature by a responsible officer of the bank. I set out a typical form for a commercial letter of credit at the end of this assignment.

B.   Advising and Confirming Banks

If the Hang Seng Bank does nothing more than advise of the issuance of the credit and agree to serve as a nominated person to process payment, the Hang Seng Bank has no independent liability on the letter of credit. Accordingly, it normally would charge only a nominal fee (such as $75) for that service. Neither status—as an adviser or as a nominated person—creates any obligation to honor requests for payment under the letter of credit. UCC §5-107(b), (c); UCP art. 9(a). Rather, those roles are purely procedural: providing the original credit, on the one hand, and receiving and forwarding requests for payment, on the other.

In most transactions involving imports into the United States, the foreign seller is satisfied with the credit of the American bank issuing the credit and thus is satisfied to obtain the procedural assistance from its local advising bank that is described above. Hence, in the letter of credit reproduced in Figure 17.1, the beneficiary was content with advice from Hang Seng Bank. By contrast, in a significant number of transactions involving exports from the United States, the American beneficiary is not satisfied with the credit of the foreign bank (something that might be rendered doubtful by, among other things, concerns about the stability of the country in which the foreign bank is located). To protect itself from the risk of relying on the foreign bank's credit, the American beneficiary frequently seeks a direct commitment of payment from its local bank. If the nominated person wishes to accommodate that concern, it will not stop at advising the credit, but will proceed to "confirm" the credit as well. If Hang Seng Bank confirmed the credit, it implicitly would have accepted direct liability on the credit, just as if it had issued the credit itself. UCC §5-107(a); UCP art. 8(c). The fees for that service vary considerably based on the stability of the country in which the underlying letter of credit is issued and the reputation of the bank that issues it. Generally, though, an American bank confirming a letter issued in a solid country by a bank of ordinary reputation would charge something in the range of one-twentieth to one-tenth of a percent per calendar quarter that the confirmation was outstanding. In our example of a $250,000 letter of credit, those fees would range from $125 to $250 if the confirmation was outstanding less than one quarter.

C.   The Terms of the Credit

As the opening paragraphs of this assignment explained, the principal reason that a seller seeks a letter of credit is to obtain a particularly firm assurance that payment will be forthcoming if the seller in fact ships the goods called for by the seller's contract with the purchaser. For the letter of credit to give the seller a satisfactory assurance of payment, the conditions on the obligation of the issuer need to be as objective as possible. Thus, payment ordinarily is not directly conditioned on the seller's satisfaction of the terms of the contract (a condition that frequently would be subject to good-faith dispute), but is conditioned instead on the seller's presentation of a request for payment (usually called a "draft"), together with specified documents that ordinarily would be available only if the seller in fact had satisfied the contract. See UCP art. 5 ("In Credit operations all parties deal with documents, and not with goods, services and/or other performances to which the documents may relate.").

For example, the letter of credit set forth in Figure 17.1 on page 378 requires the seller to present five documents to obtain payment: an invoice and a packing list (items that the seller itself can prepare), a certificate of origin (satisfying customs regulations), a certificate of inspection (evidence of the quality of the goods that would be readily available at the point of shipment), and a set of bills of lading (evidencing receipt of the goods by a common carrier). If the seller actually has shipped the goods as required by the contract, it should be easy for the seller to provide those documents. Conversely, if the seller in fact has failed to ship the goods, it will be unable to obtain those documents (at least in the absence of some relatively bald-faced fraud). Thus, the letter of credit gives the seller satisfactory assurance of payment because the seller can determine in advance, when it receives the letter of credit, that it will be easy to satisfy the conditions on the issuer's obligation to pay. At the same time, because the seller's ability to obtain payment is conditioned on the seller's having obtained documents that evidence a proper shipment, the credit does not expose the buyer to an undue risk that it will be forced to pay without receiving performance from the seller.

By conditioning payment on the presentation of documents, rather than actual performance by the seller, the letter of credit limits the obligation of the issuer to determine whether the seller actually has complied with the contract. That limit might seem a bit unreasonable (especially to an applicant/purchaser whose bank pays on a letter of credit when the beneficiary/seller actually has breached the underlying sales contract), but it is essential to the letter-of-credit system. If a purchaser could prevent its bank from honoring a letter of credit by demonstrating that the seller had failed to conform to the terms of the underlying sales contract, then banks could not decide whether to honor a draft on a letter of credit without inquiring into all of the factual issues that would be relevant in a suit for breach of contract between the beneficiary/seller and the applicant/purchaser.

For the letter of credit to provide a reliable assurance of payment, it must create an entirely independent obligation between the issuer and the beneficiary so that the issuer is obligated to pay upon satisfaction of the specified documentary conditions, regardless of whether the beneficiary has complied with the beneficiary's underlying contract with the applicant. As the UCC puts it: "Rights and obligations of an issuer to a beneficiary . . . under a letter of credit are independent of the existence, performance, or nonperformance of a contract or arrangement out of which the letter of credit arises . . ., including contracts or arrangements between the . . . applicant and the beneficiary." UCC §5-103(d). Article 4(a) of the UCP sets out the same principle in more emphatic terms:

> A credit by its nature is a separate transaction from the sales or other contract(s) on which it may be based. Banks are in no way concerned with or bound by such contract, even if any reference whatsoever to it is included in the credit. Consequently, the undertaking of a bank to honour, to negotiate or to fulfil any other obligation under the credit is not subject to claims or defences by the Applicant resulting from his relationships with the issuing bank or the beneficiary.

As you will see in the next assignment, the UCC does recognize a narrow exception to the independence principle, but it applies only in cases of egregious fraud by the beneficiary; it requires misconduct much more serious than a garden-variety contract dispute. Moreover, even the most egregious fraud does not undermine the issuer's *right* to honor the letter of credit in good faith.

That separation of the issuer's obligation on the letter of credit from the applicant's obligation on the underlying contract — often called the "independence" principle — has important implications for the solidity of the assurance of payment provided by the letter of credit. To pick one of the most common implications, the independence principle means that a bank is obligated to honor a proper draft on a letter of credit even if the applicant has gone into bankruptcy. Thus, although bankruptcy's automatic stay generally bars actions to collect debts of the applicant (11 U.S.C. §362(a)), the issuer's obligation to honor a letter of credit should continue in full force even during the applicant's bankruptcy.

The UCP includes a wide variety of rules designed to enhance the objectivity of the requirements that the parties set forth in a letter of credit. Those provisions not only provide guidance as to how issuers should draft letters of credit to limit ambiguity, but also frequently provide rules of interpretation that produce a meaning much more objective than the literal terms of the credit. For example, the UCP urges issuers to refrain from using vague "[t]erms such as 'first class,' 'well known,' 'qualified,' 'independent,' 'official,' 'competent,' 'local' and the like" to describe the parties issuing documents to be presented under a letter of credit. UCP art. 3. But if an issuer ignores that advice — for example, by issuing a letter of credit calling for a bill of lading issued by a "first-class" shipping company — the UCP directs the issuer to ignore that term in determining whether to honor a request for payment under the credit. Specifically, Article 3(7) calls for the issuer to honor a request for payment if the document in question comes from any party but the beneficiary.

Similarly, as discussed above, Articles 4 and 5 of the UCP state that the parties to credits should deal only with documents, not with the underlying contract. If an issuer ignores that advice and issues a credit that contains conditions that cannot be satisfied by the presentation of documents, the UCP provides that the nondocumentary conditions should be ignored: "If a credit contains a condition without stipulating the document to indicate compliance with the condition, banks will deem such condition as not stated and will disregard it." UCP art. 14(h); see UCC §5-108(g) (adopting the same rule).

The UCP's focus on objectivity also manifests itself in a number of interpretive rules that provide uniform answers to questions that frequently arise in the course of administration of letters of credit. By providing that definitional background, the UCP obviates the need for the parties to address those questions in the terms of each individual letter of credit. Article 30 of the UCP provides a good example, a three-tiered rule to address variations in price and quantity. First, if a letter of credit describes a quantity or price term as "about," "approximately," or "circa" some numerical figure, the UCP provides that the credit permits a 10 percent variance. UCP art. 30(a). Second, if the credit calls for shipment of a quantity of goods without any qualification, the UCP permits a 5 percent variance from the stated quantity. UCP art. 30(b). Finally, the credit requires precise adherence to a stated quantity term if the credit "stipulates that the quantity of the goods specified must not be exceeded or reduced" or if the credit "stipulates the quantity in terms of a stated number of packing units or individual items." UCP art. 30(b).

D. Drawing on the Credit

Once the seller/beneficiary has performed its obligations on the underlying contract, obtaining payment under the credit is a simple process. The seller collects the documents called for by the credit and then prepares a "draft" under the credit. The "draft" is in form little more than a letter written to the issuer, from the beneficiary, identifying the credit and seeking to "draw" on the credit.

When the issuer receives the draft and the accompanying documents, the issuer compares the draft and the documents with the letter of credit to determine whether the draft satisfies the letter of credit. The goal of the system is for that task of comparison to be as ministerial as possible: If the documents themselves conform to the terms of the letter of credit, the issuer should honor the draft and pay the sum called for by the letter of credit; if they do not, the issuer should dishonor the draft and refuse to pay. To emphasize the ministerial nature of the task, the UCC adopts a "strict compliance" standard and rejects the "substantial compliance" standard that had been adopted in some earlier American cases: "[A]n issuer shall honor a presentation that . . . appears on its face strictly to comply with the terms and conditions of the letter of credit." UCC §5-108(a); see UCC §5-108 comment 1 (discussing rejection of "substantial compliance" standard).

The ministerial task envisioned by the strict compliance standard is closely related to the independence principle discussed above. By requiring strict compliance with the terms of the letter of credit and ignoring circumstances not evident from the face of the documents submitted with the draft, the system helps to insulate the issuer's obligation on the letter of credit from disputes about the quality of the beneficiary's performance on the underlying contract.

As the following case suggests, the strict compliance rule is designed to facilitate an almost shamelessly literal interpretation of letters of credit. It is only a slight exaggeration to state that the issuer must dishonor a presentation that is inconsistent with the terms of the letter of credit, no matter how clear it might be that the beneficiary is entitled to payment under the beneficiary's underlying contract with the applicant. A right to payment on the underlying contract is a matter for resolution under ordinary contract principles in litigation between the parties to that contract. It is completely independent from the issuer's obligation, which depends entirely on the terms of the letter of credit itself.

Gilday v. Suffolk County National Bank

954 N.Y.S.2d 109 (App. Div. 2012)

In an action to recover payment pursuant to a letter of credit, the plaintiffs appeal from an order of the Supreme Court [that] denied their motion for summary judgment on the complaint.

[T]he order is reversed . . . and the plaintiffs' motion for summary judgment on the complaint is granted.

The Electrical Industry Board of Nassau and Suffolk Counties, New York (hereinafter the EIB), administers employee benefit funds for members of the plaintiff Local 25, the International Brotherhood of Electrical Workers, AFL-CIO (hereinafter Local 25). As employers of Local 25 members, Elemco Testing Company, Inc., Elemco Electrical Construction Co., Inc., and Elemco Industries, Inc. (hereinafter collectively the Elemco parties), agreed to be bound by a collective bargaining agreement that required them to make weekly and monthly contributions to the EIB to fund various employee benefits, and to maintain a surety bond to secure such contributions. In November 2008, the Elemco parties filed a chapter 11 bankruptcy petition in the United States District Court for the Eastern District of New York (hereinafter the Bankruptcy Court). At the time the bankruptcy petition was filed, the Elemco parties were allegedly in default of accrued but unpaid employee contributions in excess of $400,000, which included contributions to 401(k) retirement plans that they deducted from employee salaries.

During the course of the Bankruptcy Court proceeding, in June 2009 the Elemco parties' primary lender, the defendant Suffolk County National Bank (hereinafter the Bank), agreed to issue a $50,000 letter of credit in favor of the plaintiffs, as beneficiaries, to substitute for the surety bond which the Elemco parties were required to maintain to secure payment of their employee benefit contributions.

In accordance with the agreement, on June 15, 2009, the Bankruptcy Court issued an interim order which authorized the Elemco parties to borrow $50,000 pursuant to a letter of credit for the benefit of the plaintiffs, to terminate either upon a sale of the Elemco parties' assets, the Elemco parties obtaining a surety bond, or December 31, 2009.

More than two months later, on September 4, 2009, the Bank issued a letter of credit in favor of the plaintiffs, which provided for payment of the sum of $50,000 upon presentation of the instrument together with a sight draft and "a final Order of the United States Bankruptcy Court certifying that Elemco Testing Company, Inc. has failed to satisfactorily remit funds due." By its stated terms, the letter of credit was to expire on September 4, 2010, one year after its issuance.

On September 1, 2010, three days before the stated expiration date of the letter of credit, the plaintiff John Gilday, the EIB's executive director, presented the instrument to the Bank, accompanied by a signed sight draft and a final order of the Bankruptcy Court, dated August 10, 2010, which found that Elemco Testing Company, Inc., had "failed to satisfactorily remit funds due to EIB." The Bank refused to make payment, taking the position that under the terms of the agreement reached in the Bankruptcy Court proceeding prior to the issuance of the letter of credit, as set forth in the Bankruptcy Court order dated June 15, 2009, the letter of credit had actually terminated on May 13, 2010, when the Bankruptcy Court authorized the Elemco parties to close on a sale of their assets. The plaintiffs then commenced this action seeking to recover payment pursuant to the letter of credit. After joinder of issue, the plaintiffs moved for summary judgment on the complaint. The Supreme Court denied the motion, concluding that there was an issue of fact as to whether the letter of credit had actually expired upon the sale of the Elemco parties' assets. The plaintiffs appeal, and we reverse.

Letters of credit are commercial instruments that provide a beneficiary with a guaranteed means of payment from a creditworthy third party (the issuer) in lieu of relying solely on the financial status of a buyer or borrower (the applicant). Under a letter of credit, the issuer must honor a draft or demand for payment from the beneficiary so long as the documents presented conform to the terms of the letter of credit. (*see* UCC 5-108(a)). The issuer's obligation to honor a properly presented draft is independent of any underlying contractual arrangement between the account party (i.e., its customer) and the beneficiary. This independence principle is codified in UCC 5-103(d), which provides that the rights of a beneficiary under a letter of credit "are independent of the existence, performance, or nonperformance of a contract or arrangement out of which the letter of credit arises or which underlies it, including contracts or arrangements between the issuer and the applicant."

Furthermore, New York has long adhered to the principle that letters of credit must be strictly construed and performed in compliance with their stated terms. The reason for this rule is rooted in the very purpose of a letter of credit: by conditioning payment solely upon the terms set forth in the letter of credit, the justifications for an issuing bank's refusal to honor the credit are severely restricted, thereby assuring the reliability of letters of credit as a payment mechanism.

Applying these principles here, the plaintiffs made a prima facie showing of their entitlement to judgment as a matter of law on the complaint by demonstrating that they presented the letter of credit to the Bank for payment prior to the expiration date set forth on the face of the instrument, and that their presentment conformed to the letter of credit by including a sight draft and a final order of the Bankruptcy Court certifying that Elemco Testing Company, Inc., "has failed to satisfactorily remit funds due to EIB" (*see* UCC 5-108(a)).

In opposition to the plaintiffs' prima facie showing that they timely presented the letter of credit for payment together with the documents required by the terms of the instrument, the Bank failed to raise a triable issue of fact. The Bank opposed the motion by offering evidence that the Bankruptcy Court order authorizing the Elemco parties to borrow $50,000 pursuant to a letter of credit provided, inter alia, for termination of the letter of credit upon the sale of the Elemco parties' assets, which occurred in or around May 2010. However, the letter of credit created a distinct contractual relationship between the plaintiffs as beneficiaries and the Bank as issuer, which was independent of the Bankruptcy Court order authorizing the Elemco parties to obtain the letter of credit to provide security for the Elemco parties' obligations under the collective bargaining agreement (*see* UCC 5-103[d]).

Thus, the fact that the Bankruptcy Court order set forth a termination date for the letter of credit that was at variance with the stated terms of the instrument itself is not a defense to the Bank's refusal to make payment in accordance with its obligation to the plaintiffs. Accordingly, the plaintiffs' motion for summary judgment on the complaint should have been granted.

———————

An unfortunate side effect of the strict-compliance rule is its potential to allow issuers to seize on obviously irrelevant mistakes as a pretext for dishonoring drafts drawn on their letters of credit. The UCC and UCP respond to that problem in two ways. First, they provide that even the strict compliance standard can accept some minimal defects that would be condemned under an absolute compliance standard. Thus, the UCC calls for the question of strict compliance to be determined in accordance with "standard practice of financial institutions that regularly issue letters of credit" and makes it clear that "oppressive perfectionism" and "slavish conformity" to the literal terms of the credit are neither required nor appropriate. UCC §5-108(e) & comment 1. The UCP adopts a similar standard, calling for compliance to be determined in accordance with "the applicable provisions of these rules and international standard banking practice." UCP art. 2.

Comment 1 to UCC §5-108 walks a fine line, trying to confirm the vigor of the strict compliance standard and, at the same time, to give a sense for the types of drafts that should be honored despite some type of noncompliance. Not surprisingly, the examples all involve cases of trivial and plainly nonsubstantive typographical errors. For example, in one case, a letter of credit called for "drafts Drawn under Bank of Clarksville Letter of Credit Number 105," but the draft referred to "Bank of Clarksville, Clarksville, Tennessee letter of Credit No. 105." Comment 1 states that the draft should have been honored even though it failed to conform to the letter of credit in three respects: the superfluous reference to Clarksville, Tennessee; the lower-case "l" in the word "Letter"; and the abbreviation of the word "Number." UCC §5-108 comment 1. Similarly, an authoritative interpretation of the UCP (from the ICC) holds that a bank should ignore an obvious typographical error, even if the error prevents the submitted documents from complying precisely with the requirements of the letter of credit. The interpretation offers the example of an address that refers to a location in an "Industrial Parl" rather than an "Industrial Park." ICC Opinions, Response No. 209. For a good example of mistakes that a court might forgive as adequately strict compliance, consider the case that follows.

Carter Petroleum Products, Inc. v. Brotherhood Bank & Trust Co.

97 P.3d 505 (Kan. Ct. App. 2004)

Green, P.J.

This action involves a bank's wrongful refusal to honor a letter of credit. Carter Petroleum Products, Inc. (Carter) sued Brotherhood Bank & Trust Company (Bank) for its failure to honor a letter of credit. The Bank appeals from a judgment of the trial court granting summary judgment in favor of Carter on the letter of credit. On appeal, the Bank contends that the untimely presentment of the letter of credit and the noncompliance of the submitted documents with the letter of credit relieved the Bank of its duty to honor the letter of credit. We disagree and affirm.

Carter is in the petroleum business and sells fuel products to Highway 210, LLC (Highway 210), which operates a gas station. Highway 210 is also a customer of the Bank. On October 19, 2001, the Bank issued a letter of credit, No. 2001-270, in the aggregate amount of $175,000, for the benefit of Carter on the account of Highway 210.

By its terms, the letter of credit authorized Carter to draw on the Bank on the account of Highway 210, to the aggregate amount of $175,000 available by Carter's draft at sight accompanied by the following document: "STATEMENT SIGNED BY CARTER PETROLEUM PRODUCTS STATING THAT HIGHWAY 210, LLC HAS FAILED TO PAY OUTSTANDING INVOICES IN ACCORDANCE WITH TERMS OF PAYMENT."

The letter of credit further provided that "[e]ach draft must state that it is 'Drawn under Brotherhood Bank & Trust Company's Letter of Credit #2001-270 dated July 26, 2001.' This credit must accompany the draft(s)." The date of "July 26, 2001" in the aforementioned quotation was a typographical error because the letter of credit at issue was dated October 19, 2001. This letter of credit was a renewal of one of a series of previous letters of credit which were referenced in the lower margin of the letter of credit. The October letter of credit replaced the letter of credit dated July 26, 2001, in the amount of $125,000.

Additionally, the letter of credit stated "that all draft(s) drawn under and in compliance with the terms of this credit will be duly honored on delivery of documents as specified if presented at this office in Shawnee, KS no later than June 26, 2002." The letter of credit was also subject to the Uniform Customs and Practice for Documentary Credits, International Chamber of Commerce Publication No. 500 (1993 Revision) (UCP).

Hal O'Donnell, Carter's credit manager, delivered a draft request to the Bank for payment on June 26, 2002. Carter's draft request contained the following statement:

Pursuant to the terms stated in the Letter of Credit #2001-270 dated October 19, 2001 (copy attached), Carter Petroleum Products, Inc., hereby exercises its option to draw against said Brotherhood Bank and Trust Company's Letter of Credit in the amount of $175,000 due to non-payment of invoices in accordance with terms of payment (copies also attached).

The account name listed on the draft request was Highway 210 Texaco Travel Plaza, LLC, not Highway 210, LLC, as listed on the letter of credit. In addition, the draft request contained a statement that Highway 210 had failed to pay outstanding invoices and contained a statement that Carter was exercising its rights under the letter of credit. Carter's draft request was accompanied by the letter of credit and copies of Carter's outstanding invoices to Highway 210.

O'Donnell arrived at the Bank at approximately 5 P.M. on June 26, 2002, to present the draft request. When O'Donnell arrived at the Bank, the lobby doors were locked, but after O'Donnell knocked on the door, an employee of the Bank admitted O'Donnell into the lobby. O'Donnell indicated he was there to see Ward Kerby, the assistant vice president of the Bank. Upon meeting Kerby, O'Donnell handed him the draft request accompanied by the letter of credit and unpaid Carter invoices of Highway 210. The draft request was then stamped received on June 26, 2002, and was signed by Kerby with a notation that it was received at 5:05 P.M.

When O'Donnell delivered Carter's draft request to the Bank, the drive-through window was still open for business. O'Donnell maintained that had the employee of the Bank not opened the lobby, he would have delivered the draft request along with the attachments to the drive-through window attendant.

June 26, 2002, was a Wednesday. There is no dispute that the lobby of the Bank closed at 5 P.M. on Wednesdays. Similarly, there is no dispute that the drive-through lane at the Bank was open until 7 P.M. on Wednesdays. Additionally, inside the Bank there were several signs which alerted customers that any transactions occurring after 2 P.M. would be posted on the next business day.

The Bank dishonored Carter's draft request on the letter of credit on June 28, 2002. The Bank's dishonor notice stated two reasons: (1) The draft request was presented to the Bank after regular banking hours of the Bank on the date the letter of credit expired, and (2) the request failed to contain the specific language required by the letter of credit: "Drawn under Brotherhood Bank & Trust Company's Letter of Credit #2001-270 dated July 26, 2001."

Carter sued the Bank for its failure to honor the letter of credit. Both parties moved for summary judgment. The trial court ruled in favor of Carter and granted its motion for summary judgment. The Bank requested time to conduct further discovery concerning Highway 210's current debt to Carter. Carter furnished the Bank's counsel with copies of documents including an acknowledgment by Highway 210 that its debt to Carter exceeded the $175,000 face amount of the letter of credit. Later, the trial court entered its judgment in favor of Carter in the amount of $175,000, plus interest, costs, and attorney fees. . . .

On appeal, the Bank relies on two theories. First, the Bank contends that the attempted presentment of the draft request was untimely. The Bank makes two separate arguments. It argues that the presentment was untimely either because it occurred past 2 P.M. and, thus, should be considered on the next day's business or because the presentment occurred past 5 P.M., after the regular banking hours of the Bank. Second, the Bank argues that the draft request did not strictly comply with the terms of the letter of credit. . . .

Turning first to the issue of timeliness, we notice that there is no dispute that the letter of credit was subject to the UCP. Both parties agree that Article 45 of the UCP provides that "[b]anks are under no obligation to accept presentation of documents outside their banking hours." . . .

The letter of credit first stated that $175,000 was available by Carter's draft at "sight" accompanied by certain documents. It then stated that the letter of credit would be honored "if presented at this office in Shawnee, KS no later than June 26, 2002." The only office referred to in the letter of credit is the Bank's office at 7499 Quivira, Shawnee, Kansas.

O'Donnell arrived at the Bank just after 5 P.M., and the lobby was closed. The drive-through window at the Bank, located at 7499 Quivira, was still open. The letter of credit made no reference that the sight draft must be presented before the lobby closed on June 26, 2002. Similarly, it did not state that the draft needed to be presented before 2 P.M. or before 5 P.M. The letter of credit did not state that the draft needed to be presented to a loan officer, a vice president, or any particular person. The letter of credit simply stated that the money was available by draft at "sight" and would be honored "if presented at this office in Shawnee, KS no later than June 26, 2002."

Under the rules of construction, the presentment of the draft did comply with the requirements set forth for the time and place of presentment. The draft was presented at the Bank on June 26, 2002, at a time when the Bank was still open for business. Although the lobby was closed, by the terms of the letter of credit, anyone working at the Bank was authorized and could have accepted the draft, including the drive-through teller who was open for business.

Although the Bank may have intended to limit the presentment of a sight draft to either before 2 P.M. or 5 P.M. on June 26, 2002, the Bank did not specify in the letter of credit that presentment was to be conducted in this way. This was the source of the confusion; other than the date, no specific time of day was mentioned as to when it must be presented. For example, the letter of credit could have stated that it must be presented "no later than 5 P.M., June 26, 2002, at which date and time the letter of credit expires." The letter of credit failed to contain such language or any similar language to that effect. "Any ambiguity in a letter of credit must be resolved against the party drafting it." East Girard Sav. Ass'n v. Citizens Nat. Bank & Trust Co. of Baytown, 593 F.2d 598, 602 (5th Cir. 1979). The Bank was the sole drafter of the letter of credit. Accordingly, if the Bank wanted more specificity as to when and where Carter had to make presentment, the Bank could have included such provisions in its letter of credit. The ambiguities or lack of explicitness in the letter of credit stemmed from the Bank's own pen. As a result, the Bank's argument fails.

Next, we must consider whether the draft request strictly complied with the terms of the letter of credit. When do documents comply with the terms of the letter of credit so that a bank is forced to pay the draft is a difficult legal question. The UCC furnishes no easy answer to this question. . . .

On appeal, the Bank contends that the demand was not in strict compliance because (1) the draft request stated the account name as "Highway 210 Texaco Travel Plaza, LLC," not "Highway 210, LLC," and (2) the draft request did not contain the exact language from the letter of credit. . . .

In the instant case, although the draft request submitted by Carter was not in complete conformity with the letter of credit issued by the Bank, it did contain all the necessary information requested by the letter of credit. Moreover, the Bank could not have been misled by the nonconformity.

Although the draft request listed the account name as "Highway 210 Texaco Travel Plaza, LLC," not "Highway 210, LLC" as requested in the letter of credit, the draw request was accompanied by the letter of credit which properly named the account. Obviously, there was no confusion caused by the different name referred to in the draft request because the Bank did not rely on this ground in rejecting the letter of credit. Moreover, the Bank failed to raise this particular argument before the trial court. Issues not raised before the trial court cannot be raised on appeal.

The draft request also contained all of the other pertinent information requested in the letter of credit. The letter of credit accompanied the draft, the draft stated it was drawn under Brotherhood Bank and Trust Company's letter of credit, and the draft contained the correct letter of credit number: #2001-270. Additionally, as required by the letter of credit, the draft stated that Carter was exercising its option to draw against the Bank due to nonpayment of invoices in accordance with the terms of payment.

The draft request differed from the requirements stated in the letter of credit in that the letter of credit mistakenly referred to the letter of credit dated July 26, 2001. In its draft request, Carter properly referred to the letter of credit dated October 19, 2001. Had Carter referred to the incorrect date as specified in the letter of credit, it would have been likely to cause confusion on the part of the Bank because the October 19, 2001, letter of credit was for a different amount and superceded the July 26, 2001, letter of credit. As a result, the Bank's argument fails.

———————

The second response is more interesting: rules that require banks to give prompt notice of defects they perceive in drafts. A bank is precluded from justifying a decision to dishonor a draft by reference to any defect of which the bank did not promptly advise the beneficiary. UCP art. 16(f); UCC §§5-108(c), 5-108 comment 3. The idea is that if a defect is substantial enough to justify a dishonor, the bank will notice the defect when the bank first examines the draft and supporting documents. It would undermine the reliability of letters of credit to permit issuers to dishonor for illegitimate reasons (such as the bank's desire to accommodate the applicant or the bank's inability to obtain reimbursement from the applicant) and then prevail in subsequent litigation by identifying a defect that the bank failed to notice at the time of the dishonor and first noticed only in the harsh light of litigation. You will perhaps observe that the *Carter* court dismissed out of hand one of the defects the bank proffered in litigation that had not been mentioned at the time of dishonor; the court well might have mentioned that the UCP and UCC provisions cited above precluded the bank from relying on that defect.

The pretextual-dishonor problem is complicated by the fact that most drafts on commercial letters of credit do not satisfy the strict compliance standard. Although the rate of compliance surely differs from place to place, empirical research in the files of American issuers suggests that less than 25 percent of the drafts presented against commercial letters of credit comply with the letters of credit. The normal course of events is for the issuer to seek a waiver from the applicant of the identifiable defects. See UCP art. 16(b) (allowing issuer to seek such a waiver); UCC §5-108(a) (permitting an issuer to honor a nonconforming presentation when it has "agreed with the applicant" to do so). In the overwhelming majority of cases, the applicant grants the waiver because waiving the defect ordinarily is the simplest way for the applicant to provide payment to the beneficiary and thus to fulfill the applicant's obligation under its contract with the beneficiary. If the applicant declines to grant the waiver, the issuer sends a notice to the beneficiary specifying the defects identified by the issuer. That notice gives the beneficiary an opportunity to cure the defects. As the following case illustrates, it is less clear that letter of credit law comfortably accommodates efforts to seek the views of the applicant.

LaBarge Pipe & Steel Co. v. First Bank

550 F.3d 442 (5th Cir. 2008)

Before JONES, Chief Judge, GARWOOD, and JOLLY, Circuit Judges.

Plaintiff-appellant, LaBarge Pipe & Steel Co. (LaBarge), appeals the district court's grant of summary judgment for defendants-appellees, First Bank and Allen David. LaBarge sued defendants asserting claims relating to the Irrevocable Standby Letter of Credit No. 180 that First Bank issued to LaBarge, including claims for wrongful dishonor, breach of a letter of credit, detrimental reliance, breach of a good faith obligation, and negligent misrepresentation. For the reasons stated below, we affirm in part and reverse and remand in part to the district court.

FACTS AND PROCEEDINGS BELOW

LaBarge, a Missouri company, sells industrial pipe across the United States. PVF USA, LLC (PVF), a Louisiana company, sold industrial pipe, valves, and fittings from its office in Port Allen, Louisiana. On November 19, 2002, PVF requested and received a quote for the purchase of steel pipe from LaBarge. On November 25, 2002, PVF ordered 3,800 feet of thirty-inch pipe from LaBarge for a total price of $143,613.40. Matthew Mannhard, a LaBarge salesman, reviewed PVF's credit history, and informed PVF that LaBarge would not sell the requested pipe on open credit terms. Therefore, he gave PVF the following payment options: sending a cashiers check via overnight mail, wire transferring the funds, or obtaining a letter of credit. PVF chose to obtain a letter of credit.

PVF then contacted First Bank, a commercial bank in Baton Rouge, Louisiana, to arrange for First Bank to issue the letter of credit. Acting as LaBarge's representative in the arrangement, Mannhard worked with Allen David, a First Bank employee, to arrange for First Bank to issue a standby letter of credit in the amount of

$144,000.00 for the benefit of LaBarge. David and Mannhard discussed and final-ized the letter of credit. On November 25, 2002, David faxed a copy of the letter of credit to LaBarge. The facsimile cover sheet stated: "Here is the letter of credit you requested. Please let me know if you need any additional information." After reviewing the facsimile copy of the letter of credit, Mannhard requested a change in the language of the letter of credit, which First Bank made. On November 26, 2002, David faxed a copy of the thus amended letter of credit to LaBarge. The fac-simile cover sheet, which contained David's signature, stated: "Here is the revision to the letter of credit you requested. Please let me know if you need any additional information."

The letter of credit issued by First Bank is dated November 25, 2002. It reflects that "LaBarge Pipe & Steel, Co." is "BENEFICIARY" and that "PVF USA, L.L.C." is "APPLICANT." It is addressed to LaBarge and states "We hereby establish our Irrevocable Standby Letter of Credit No. 180 in your favor for the account of PVF USA available by your drafts on us payable at sight for any sum of money not to exceed a total of $144,000 . . . when accompanied by this Irrevocable Letter of Credit" and by LaBarge's statement certifying that invoices to PVF "remain unpaid 30 days or more after invoice date" and by copies of the invoices. It also states that: "the original Irrevocable Letter of Credit must be presented with any drawing so that drawings can be endorsed on the reverse thereof." Furthermore, it states that "Except so far as otherwise expressly stated, this irrevocable Letter of Credit is subject to the 'Uniform Customs and Practice for Documentary Credits (1983 Revision) International Chamber of Commerce Brochure No. 400'" (the UCP 400). Finally, the letter of credit states that it "shall be valid until February 23, 2003." It bears the handwritten signatures of David and a First Bank Vice President.

LaBarge claims that in a phone conversation on November 26, 2002, Mannhard asked David at what point LaBarge would be protected by the letter of credit so that it could safely ship the pipe to PVF. At this point, Mannhard allegedly informed David that LaBarge did not want to ship the pipe to PVF until the pur-chase price was fully secured by the letter of credit. According to LaBarge, David told Mannhard that the letter of credit was issued, that First Bank was obligated to pay if PVF defaulted on its obligations, and that LaBarge could now safely ship the pipe. In their brief, First Bank and David do not explicitly affirm or deny that David made these representations to Mannhard. However, in his deposition, David testified that he did not recall speaking with Mannhard on November 25 or 26, 2002 regarding whether LaBarge was secure under the letter of credit at that time.

After these alleged conversations occurred, LaBarge shipped pipe invoiced at $95,216.60 to PVF on November 26, 2002. It sent an additional shipment of pipe (invoiced at $48,396.80) to PVF on December 4, 2002. The total amount of pipe shipped was invoiced at $143,613.40. PVF did not make any payment for any of the pipe, and filed bankruptcy on January 9, 2003.

David never told Mannhard or any other LaBarge representative what he planned to do with the original signed version of the letter of credit. It is unclear what happened to the original November 25, 2002 letter of the credit as LaBarge, First Bank, and PVF have not been able to locate it. In David's deposition, he testified that he kept the letter of credit after faxing a copy of it to LaBarge on November 26, 2002, and called PVF officials multiple times to encourage them to collect the letter of credit from his office. He testified that on December 2, 2002,

PVF official, Scott Kirby, took the letter of credit when he came to First Bank to make a deposit. However, in his deposition, Kirby denies ever having received the original letter of credit. Furthermore, in its original complaint, LaBarge asserted that on December 10, 2002, First Bank informed LaBarge that it had given the original of the letter of credit to PVF. Then, from January 15 to 20, 2003, LaBarge attempted to locate the original letter of credit from PVF and First Bank without success.

In the latter part of January and early February of 2003, LaBarge and First Bank representatives twice talked on the telephone to discuss the documentation that LaBarge needed to present in order to draw on the letter of credit. During these two telephone conversations, LaBarge employees informed First Bank's executive vice president, Andrew Adler, that they could not locate the original letter of credit and only had the facsimile copy that they received from First Bank on November 26, 2002. Adler informed LaBarge representatives that First Bank would not honor a presentation without the original credit. After these conversations, Harold Burroughs, counsel for LaBarge, called for Adler to discuss payment under the letter of credit. James Lackie, First Bank's counsel, returned the call on February 6, 2003. In that phone call, Burroughs informed Lackie that LaBarge could not locate the original letter of credit. Burroughs again so informed Lackie in a letter dated February 11, 2003.

In February 2003, LaBarge attempted to draw on the letter of credit in the amount of $143,613.40, the total price of all pipe it had shipped to PVF. It mailed the letter of credit facsimile it had received on November 26, 2002, along with the relevant unpaid invoice copies and its certificate that they remained unpaid for thirty days or more after their dates, to First Bank on February 14, 2003. First Bank received these documents on the morning of Monday, February 17, 2003. Also included with LaBarge's February 14, letter was an Affidavit of Beneficiary of Irrevocable Letter of Credit and Indemnification of Issuer signed by Michael Brand, CFO, Secretary, and Treasurer of LaBarge, which stated that the "original letter of credit" could not be produced because it was not delivered to LaBarge and was lost or destroyed. This document also essentially provided that LaBarge would reimburse First Bank if someone were to present the original letter of credit and were able to successfully draw on that document. First Bank, on the day it received LaBarge's presentation, Monday, February 17, 2003, mailed to LaBarge a letter dishonoring its draw. LaBarge received this letter on Friday, February 21, 2003. The letter, which was written by First Bank's attorney, did not advise that First Bank was holding LaBarge's documents at its disposal, or that First Bank would return the documents to LaBarge. While LaBarge was waiting for a response from First Bank, Brand called First Bank officials two times on Wednesday, February 19, 2003. Brand received no response to his inquiries concerning the draw on the letter of credit until Adler returned Brand's call during the afternoon of Thursday, February 20, 2003, and informed Brand that First Bank would not honor the letter of credit because LaBarge did not include the original letter of credit in its presentation.

On April 11, 2003, LaBarge filed suit against First Bank, asserting claims for wrongful dishonor, breach of the letter of credit, detrimental reliance, and breach of a good faith obligation. [The district court ruled for First Bank and LaBarge appealed.]

DISCUSSION

We limit our discussion to the issues raised by the parties on appeal: whether LaBarge presented the "original" letter of credit with its request to draw; [and] whether UCP 400, Article 16(e) precludes First Bank from asserting that the documents LaBarge presented are not in accordance with the terms and conditions of the letter of credit. For the reasons stated below, we reverse the district court's judgment denying LaBarge's recovery from First Bank on the letter of credit. . . .

A.   Letters of Credit

Letters of credit, or "credits," are commercial devices generally used to relieve the tension between merchants and buyers when the merchant is hesitant to lose possession of its goods before being paid, but the buyer would like to have the goods before parting with its money. Letters of credit come in two forms, "commercial" and "standby." The credit at issue in this case is a standby letter of credit.

In a typical standby letter of credit arrangement, a financial institution, the "issuer," serves as something like a guarantor of an amount of money in a transaction between a buyer, the "customer" or "applicant," and a seller, the "beneficiary" of the letter of credit. If the applicant breaches the underlying agreement with the beneficiary, the beneficiary seeks payment from the issuer by presenting to the issuer a request for payment and certain documents specified in the letter of credit, such as documents of title, transport, insurance, and commercial invoices. There is generally a reimbursement contract (also called an "application agreement") between the issuer and the applicant that requires the applicant to reimburse the issuer for payments made under the letter of credit.

A standby letter of credit is similar to a guaranty in that it acts as a protection against default by a customer in a purchase agreement. However, a guaranty differs from a standby letter of credit in that under a standby letter of credit, the beneficiary has bargained for the right to be paid upon presentation of specific documents, even if the beneficiary defaults on the underlying contract with the applicant. The issuer of a letter of credit may not raise the defenses that the applicant may assert against payment to the beneficiary. The issuer's liability generally turns solely on whether the beneficiary presents the documents specified in the credit.

The obligation of the issuer to pay the beneficiary is independent of any obligation of the applicant to the issuer. Thus, if the applicant enters bankruptcy after the letter has been issued, but before it has been drawn upon, despite the fact that the applicant may not be able to pay the issuer, the issuer must pay the beneficiary on a properly presented draw on the letter of credit.

In this case, LaBarge and PVF had an underlying contract for the sale of pipe. First Bank acted as the "issuer" of the letter of credit, while LaBarge was the "beneficiary," and PVF was the "applicant." The letter of credit is an "undertaking" (as opposed to a contract) between the First Bank and LaBarge in which First Bank promised to pay LaBarge if PVF did not pay before thirty days after the date of LaBarge's invoices for the sale of pipe and if LaBarge presented to First Bank specified documents in its timely request to draw on the credit.

B.   UCP 400 AND THE UCC

The letter of credit in this case is governed by both Article Five of the Uniform Commercial Code as adopted by Louisiana (the UCC or Article Five) and the UCP 400. The Uniform Customs and Practice (UCP) is a compilation of the usage of the trade for letters of credit. Many revisions of the UCP have been issued since the International Chamber of Commerce issued the first version in 1930. The latest version of the UCP is the UCP 600, which became effective on July 1, 2007. The letter of credit at issue in this case explicitly incorporates the rules of the UCP 400, the 1983 version of the UCP. See La. Rev. Stat. Ann. §10:5-116(c) ("Except as otherwise provided in this Subsection, the liability of an issuer . . . is governed by any rules of custom or practice, such as the Uniform Customs and Practice for Documentary Credits, to which the letter of credit . . . is expressly made subject."). Thus, in deciding this case, this court must follow the terms of the UCP 400.

However, Article 5 indicates that "letters of credit that incorporate the UCP or similar practice will still be subject to Article 5 in certain respects." Id. at §10:5-116(c) cmt. 3. Thus, the incorporation of UCP 400 into the letter of credit does not render Article 5 completely inapplicable in this case. Instead, "where there is no conflict between Article 5 and the relevant provision of the UCP . . . both apply." Id. However, the UCP 400 governs where there is a conflict between its provisions and those of Article 5. La. Rev. Stat. Ann. §10:5-116(c). . . .

C.   THE "ORIGINAL" LETTER OF CREDIT

The letter of credit at issue in this case states that "The original Irrevocable Letter of Credit must be presented with any drawing so that drawings can be endorsed on the reverse thereof." First Bank refused to honor LaBarge's request to draw on the letter of credit because it presented the facsimile version of the credit that it received from First Bank on November 26, 2002 instead of the original credit. The district court held that "it is undisputed that LaBarge did not submit the original letter of credit to First Bank when LaBarge attempted to draw on the letter of credit." However, LaBarge contends that the facsimile letter of credit that it presented to First Bank qualifies as the original letter of credit. We disagree.

The UCP 400 and Louisiana law provide guidance as to what form of a letter of credit a beneficiary can present to an issuer. Note three of the UCC comments to La. Rev. Stat. Ann. §10:5-104 indicates that letters of credit may be issued electronically instead of as hard copies (at least when marked by the relevant bank as "original"). This suggests that a letter of credit transmitted to a beneficiary via fax machine could be successfully presented to an issuer. Furthermore, UCP 400, Article 12 states:

> a. When an issuing bank instructs a bank (advising bank) by any teletransmission to advise a credit . . . and intends the mail confirmation to be the operative credit instrument . . . the teletransmission must state "full details to follow" (or words of similar effect), or that the mail confirmation will be the operative credit instrument. . . . The issuing bank must forward the operative credit instrument . . . to such advising bank without delay.

> b. The teletransmission will be deemed to be the operative credit instrument . . . and no mail confirmation should be sent, unless the teletransmission states "full details to follow" (or words of similar effect), or states that the mail confirmation is to be the operative credit instrument.

This language suggests that the facsimile sent to LaBarge by First Bank might be considered the "operative credit instrument" because it does not state "full details to follow" or similar language, and does not state that a mail confirmation will be the operative letter of credit.

This language addresses what "documents" should be considered originals. This Article only appears to apply to the authenticity of supporting documents, not to letters of credit themselves because it indicates that the instructions regarding the documents it describes should be contained in the letter of credit. Furthermore, as Article 12 specifically addresses what should be considered an "operative credit instrument," and contains different requirements than those found in Article 22 for original "documents," the two articles would conflict if they both applied to the letters of credit themselves. Moreover, the facsimile in question is not "marked as [an] original[]." However, because the letter of credit at issue in this case specifically requires the "original" credit to be presented for a successful draw, and we hold that the language of the credit, not any provisions of UCP 400, govern this issue, we need not now address this issue.

Nonetheless, these provisions do not apply in this case because the letter of credit specifically provides that LaBarge must present the "original" to successfully draw. The term "original" is not defined in the credit, Article Five, or the UCP 400. Article 12 of UCP 400 discusses what should be considered the "operative credit instrument," but does not use the term "original." However, the plain meaning of the term is clear. In its definition of "original," a leading legal dictionary states that "[a]s applied to documents, the original is the first copy or archetype; that from which another instrument is transcribed, copied, or imitated." Black's Law Dictionary 1099 (6th ed. 1990). Thus, it is clear that the term "original" in the instant letter of credit referred to the actual first copy of the document. Though a facsimile copy may in certain circumstances qualify as an "operative credit instrument" under UCP 400, Article 12, it is not necessarily the "original" letter of credit. Because the letter of credit expressly required LaBarge to present the "original" of the credit, LaBarge could not present anything other than the document from which the facsimile copy was made in order to successfully draw.

Furthermore, First Bank's actions do not alter the plain meaning of the term "original" in the letter of credit. LaBarge suggests that the words that First Bank wrote on the cover sheets to the facsimile copies of the credit that it sent to LaBarge on November 25 and 26, 2002 indicate that the facsimile copy is the original letter of credit. On the facsimile cover sheet sent November 25, 2002, David wrote "Here is the letter of credit you requested." On the cover sheet sent with the facsimile on November 26, 2002, he wrote, "Here is the revision to the letter of credit you requested." LaBarge suggests that by referring on November 25 to the facsimile version as "the" letter of credit, and by making an arguably somewhat similar reference on November 26, First Bank indicated that the facsimiles were the original copies of the credit. This argument is without merit. The language on the cover sheets merely indicates that the facsimile is a copy of the original credit.

It does not alter the plain meaning of the term "original" as it is used in the text of the credit.

Moreover, LaBarge suggests that the facsimile copy of the credit is the original because First Bank represented to LaBarge that LaBarge had everything necessary to secure payment under the credit when it only had the facsimile copy. However, these alleged representations only demonstrate that First Bank gave faulty information, not that the facsimile copy should be considered the original.

The language of the letter of credit is clear. Therefore, we hold that the district court properly concluded that LaBarge did not present the "original" letter of credit to First Bank when it presented the November 26, 2003 facsimile copy of the credit to First Bank in its attempt to draw in February of 2003 and that LaBarge's only attempted draw on the letter of credit was hence invalid.

D.   UCP 400, ARTICLE 16(E) PRECLUSION

LaBarge argues that First Bank should have to honor the letter of credit because it did not comply with the terms of the UCP 400 when dishonoring LaBarge's request to draw. Under UCP 400, Article 16(c) and (d), an issuing bank must take specific steps when dishonoring a request to draw on a letter of credit. First, the issuing bank has a "reasonable time" to examine the documents and decide whether to pay or dishonor the request to draw. UCP 400, Article 16(c). Next, if the bank decides to dishonor, it then "must give notice to that effect without delay by telecommunication or, if that is not possible, by other expeditious means . . . to the beneficiary," and must state the discrepancies on which it bases its decision to dishonor. UCP 400, Article 16(d). Finally, it must state whether it will hold the documents or return them to the beneficiary. If a bank does not comply with these steps when dishonoring a request to draw, it "shall be precluded from claiming that the documents are not in accordance with the terms and conditions of the credit." UCP 400, Article 16(e). LaBarge contends, and this court agrees, that First Bank did not comply with Article 16(d) when dishonoring LaBarge's request to draw because once First Bank decided not to honor the draw it did not then provide notice of dishonor "without delay," and it did not "without delay" state the discrepancies in respect of which it refused to honor or inform LaBarge of the disposition of the documents it presented. . . .

1.   Strict Compliance

Under the doctrine of strict compliance, which applies to this transaction under Louisiana law, the documentation that the beneficiary of a letter of credit presents to the issuer in order to draw on a credit must comply exactly with the requirements of the credit or the issuer is entitled to refuse payment. La. Rev. Stat. Ann. §10:5-108(a). Thus, an issuer properly dishonors a request to draw if the documents presented do not strictly comply with the credit's requirements and it timely and sufficiently notifies the beneficiary of its intent to dishonor.

The facts regarding the documents presented to First Bank by LaBarge are not disputed. In its request to draw, LaBarge presented the facsimile copy of the letter of credit that it received from First Bank on November 26, 2002. However, the letter of credit required that "the original Irrevocable Letter of Credit must be presented with any drawing so that drawings can be endorsed on the reverse thereof." Because the facsimile version of the letter of credit was not "the original," LaBarge did not strictly comply with the terms of the letter of credit in making its request to draw. If First Bank had timely and properly dishonored LaBarge's presentation, it would have properly denied LaBarge's request because LaBarge did not strictly comply with the terms of the letter of credit. However, this case is complicated by the fact that First Bank did not follow the proper procedures when dishonoring LaBarge's request to draw on the letter of credit.

2.   Timeliness and Sufficiency of Notice of Dishonor

First Bank failed to comply with the requirements of UCP 400, Article 16(d), when dishonoring LaBarge's presentation under the letter of credit. First, First Bank failed to give notice of its decision (and of the document discrepancies in respect to which it refused) "without delay by telecommunication," and second, when it did notify LaBarge that it would dishonor the presentation, it failed to state whether it was going to hold LaBarge's documents or return them to LaBarge. Article 16(e) of UCP 400 provides that when the issuing bank does not follow one of these required steps when dishonoring a draw, it "shall be precluded from claiming that the documents are not in accordance with the terms and conditions of the credit."

a.   Timeliness of Notice

LaBarge contends that First Bank did not give timely notice under UCP 400, Article 16(d), which requires that "[i]f the issuing bank decides to refuse the documents [in a presentation], it must give notice [to the beneficiary] to that effect without delay by telecommunication or, if that is not possible, by other expeditious means . . . " and that notice also "must state the discrepancies in respect of which the issuing bank refuses the documents and must also state whether it is holding the documents at the disposal of, or is returning them to the presentor." LaBarge contends that First Bank did not give notice by telecommunication and did not give notice "without delay."

The district court held that First Bank timely notified LaBarge that it would not honor the presentation. It noted that the UCP 400 did not define "without delay," but that Article 5 provides that "[a]n issuer has a reasonable time after presentation, of at least three days, but not beyond the end of the seventh business day of the issuer after the day of its receipt of documents . . . to honor . . . [or] to give notice to the presenter of discrepancies in the presentation." La. Rev. Stat. Ann. §10:5-108(b). Thus, the court concluded that First Bank complied with the requirements of Louisiana law by giving notice by telecommunication three days after the presentation. It held that the letter, which LaBarge received on February 21, 2003 (four days after First Bank received and decided to deny LaBarge's requested draw), and the phone call from Adler on February 20, 2003 (three days after First Bank received and decided to deny the request) were timely notice of dishonor. We disagree.

The district court erred in concluding that La. Rev. Stat. Ann. §10:5-108(b) provided the relevant time for giving notice in this case. UCP 400 does not define or explain the meaning of "without delay." However, the lack of an explicit definition of the time period that constitutes notice "without delay" does not indicate that section 10:5-108(b) applies in place of or in addition to UCP 400, Article 16(d). The terms of UCP 400 (requiring notice "without delay" after "issuing bank decides to refuse the documents") are clear and unambiguous, and they conflict with the terms of section 10:5-108(b) to the extent that the latter provides that notice of dishonor and of discrepancies in the presentation is always timely if given within three business days of presentment. Thus, this court should apply only the terms of the UCP 400 to this case. See La. Rev. Stat. Ann. §10:5-116(c) (indicating that in most cases when a letter of credit incorporates the UCP, and the terms of the UCP conflict with the terms of the UCC, the terms of the UCP govern).

Furthermore, the term is defined as "[i]nstantly; at once," or "[w]ithin the time reasonably allowed by law." Black's Law Dictionary 1632 (8th ed. 2004). As UCP 400, Article 16(d) does not otherwise define "without delay" under this provision, that phrase must at least mean in the shortest time period reasonably possible. Thus, Article 16(d)'s requirement that an issuer give notice "without delay" commands that it give notice as quickly as reasonably possible after it has decided to dishonor a draw. Because the language of the UCP 400, Article 16(d) is clear, although other sources of law or other articulations of customary practices may provide specific time periods during which an issuer's notice of dishonor will always be timely, such sources are not controlling in this case. As the UCP 400 does not provide a specific time during which an issuer's notice of dishonor will always be timely, none should be inferred into its provisions. . . .

Under the common meaning of the term, First Bank clearly did not notify LaBarge "without delay by telecommunication" (or otherwise) that it would not honor the presentation (or of any discrepancy in the documents presented). After First Bank received LaBarge's presentation on Monday, February 17, 2003, it waited until February 20, 2003 to call LaBarge to inform the company that it would not honor the draw. However, First Bank determined not to honor LaBarge's request to draw on February 17, 2003, the day it received the presentation, and First Bank wrote a letter to LaBarge on that date informing LaBarge of its decision. Nonetheless, First Bank waited over three days, from the morning of Thursday, February 17, 2003 until the afternoon of February 20, 2003, to inform LaBarge by telephone that it would not honor the presentation. Furthermore, when First Bank did call LaBarge, it was only in response to LaBarge's two February 19 phone calls. The letter dated February 17, 2003 (which is not notice "by telecommunication") arrived at LaBarge on February 21, 2003, four days after First Bank had received the presentation. These communications cannot be considered notice "without delay" as they were by no means within the shortest reasonably possible interval. First Bank could have easily replied to LaBarge virtually immediately, or at least in fewer than three days, by simply picking up the telephone and calling the company or faxing the February 17 letter to it. It did not even attempt to do so. Therefore, we hold that as a matter of law, under UCP 400, Article 16(d), First Bank did not notify LaBarge "without delay" that it would not honor its presentation.

b. Disposition of Documents

LaBarge also argues that First Bank must pay on the letter of credit because it failed to address the disposition of LaBarge's documents in any of the notices of dishonor that it did give, in violation of UCP 400, Article 16(d). Article 16(d) provides that when notifying a beneficiary of dishonor, the issuer must state "whether [it] is holding the documents at the disposal of, or is returning them to the [beneficiary]." First Bank does not dispute that it failed to provide LaBarge with this information when it notified LaBarge that it would not honor the presentation.

3. Possible Exceptions to Preclusion Under UCP 400, Article 16(e)

Because First Bank failed to comply with the requirements of UCP 400, Article 16(d) when dishonoring LaBarge's presentation, UCP 400, Article 16(e) provides that it "shall be precluded from claiming that the documents are not in accordance with the terms and conditions of the credit." However, pertinent case law suggests two possible exceptions to this preclusion requirement.

a. Presentation of Documents with Known Defects

LaBarge did not and apparently could not strictly comply with the terms of the letter of credit when presenting it because it did not have the original credit. Furthermore, it had previously been told by First Bank that the presentation would not be honored absent this essential document. Thus, LaBarge may have knowingly presented discrepant documents to First Bank. The district court held that because LaBarge knowingly presented an improper document when making its presentation to First Bank, the preclusion provision of Article 16(e) should not be enforced in this case.

The district court's decision was guided by [Philadelphia Gear Corp. v. Central Bank, 717 F.2d 230 (5th Cir. 1983)], a Fifth Circuit case in which Louisiana law applied, as it does here. In that case, the beneficiary knowingly presented discrepant documents in an attempt to draft on a letter of credit. The issuing bank timely notified the beneficiary that the documents did not comply with the terms of the credit, but did not specify the defects on which it based the dishonor. The issuer also did not return the documents to the beneficiary or inform the beneficiary that it would hold the documents on file for inspection. On appeal, this court held that with respect to the drafts that the beneficiary knew to be defective, the issuer's notice was not deficient. It held that because a beneficiary knowingly presented defective documents, the issuer was not required by the UCP to notify the beneficiary of the precise reasons it would not accept the nonconforming documents when it dishonored the beneficiary's request to draw. We there stated that "[i]t would be a strange rule indeed under which a party could tender drafts containing defects of which it knew and yet attain recovery on the ground that it was not advised of them."

[The court rejected the application of *Philadelphia Gear*, largely because of changes between UCP 290 and UCP 400 that had led other courts of appeals to reject it.]

For the reasons stated, we decline to apply *Philadelphia Gear* to this case by holding that a beneficiary cannot knowingly present defective documents and obtain recovery based on untimely and insufficient notice of dishonor by the issuer under UCP 400, Article 16(e).

b.   The Incurable Defect Exception

First Bank relies on LeaseAmerica Corp. v. Norwest Bank Duluth, 940 F.2d 345 (8th Cir. 1991). In *LeaseAmerica,* as in this case, when dishonoring a request to draw, the issuing bank did not notify the beneficiary whether it was holding or returning the presented documents to the beneficiary. The Eighth Circuit held that the failure of the bank to comply with that UCP 400, Article 16(d) requirement did not preclude it from dishonoring the draw because the defects in the beneficiary's presentation were not curable. It explained that the language of UCP 400, Article 16(e) is meant to provide a beneficiary with the opportunity to cure defects in its presentation, so if the defects cannot be cured, the preclusion rule should not be enforced.

This court made a similar statement in dicta in Heritage Bank v. Redcom Laboratories, Inc., 250 F.3d 319, (5th Cir. 2001), a case applying Texas law. In *Heritage Bank,* the issuing bank dishonored a letter of credit, but did not notify the beneficiary of the deficiencies in the presentation, which violated the preclusion rule of the UCP 500. This court held that the issuing bank waived all discrepancies related to the presentation because it did not notify the beneficiary of the deficiencies, the defects could have been cured, and the beneficiary would suffer prejudice if it were not notified of the defects. In dicta, the court suggested, citing a Texas case, that it may have applied the incurable defect exception to the UCP 500 preclusion rule had the defect at issue in the presentation been incurable. *Id.* ("If the presentment were untimely, no cure would be possible, and the bank had no duty to notify Redcom of the defect."). But the court concluded that Redcom's presentment was timely, so Redcom could have cured any defects.

However, other courts have rejected the incurable defect exception to the preclusion rule and have held that the preclusion rule should be strictly enforced. [Citations omitted.]

We decline to apply the *LeaseAmerica* incurable defect approach here. . . .

[W]e conclude that the Louisiana courts would not adopt the incurable defect exception. While we realize that what is ultimately controlling here, by virtue of La. Rev. Stat. Ann. §10:5-116(c), is UCP 400 Article 16(d) and (e), nevertheless the post *LeaseAmerica* revision of UCC Article 5 reflected in La. Rev. Stat. Ann. 10:5-108, made effective January 1, 2000, plainly indicates the legislative intent to apply a rule of strict preclusion, rather than prejudice to the beneficiary, in respect of the issuer's failure to timely give notice of dishonor and defects in the presentation. R.S. 10:5-108(c) provides:

> (c) Except as otherwise provided in Subsection (d) [relating to fraud, forgery and expiration of the letter before presentation], an issuer is precluded from asserting as a basis for dishonor any discrepancy if timely notice is not given, or any discrepancy not stated in the notice if timely notice is given.

The UCC comment to this amendment of Article 5 includes the following:

> 3. The requirement that the issuer send notice of the discrepancies or be precluded from asserting discrepancies is new to Article 5. It is taken from the similar provision in the UCP and is intended to promote certainty and finality.

The section thus substitutes a strict preclusion principle for the doctrines of waiver and estoppel that might otherwise apply under Section 1-103. It rejects the reasoning in Flagship Cruises, Ltd. v. New England Merchants Nat. Bank, 569 F.2d 699 (1st Cir. 1978), and Wing on Bank Ltd. v. American Nat. Bank & Trust Co., 457 F.2d 328 (5th Cir. 1972), where the issuer was held to be estopped only if the beneficiary relied on the issuer's failure to give notice.

Assume, for example, that the beneficiary presented documents to the issuer shortly before the letter of credit expired, in circumstances in which the beneficiary could not have cured any discrepancy before expiration. Under the reasoning of *Flagship* and *Wing On*, the beneficiary's inability to cure, even if it had received notice, would absolve the issuer of its failure to give notice. The virtue of the preclusion obligation adopted in this section is that it forecloses litigation about reliance and detriment.

As the language of UCP 400 Article 16(d) and (e) does not on its face suggest an incurable defect exception and the jurisprudence is divided, we believe that the Louisiana courts would not apply such an exception. . . .

First Bank is strictly precluded by UCP 400 Article 16(e) from raising the defects in LaBarge's presentation. The district court's judgment in favor of First Bank on LaBarge's claim against it under the letter of credit is reversed and the case is remanded for the district court to enter judgment in favor of LaBarge on that claim. The court should award LaBarge the amount of its draw on the letter of credit, namely $143,613.40, plus any appropriate legal interest under Louisiana law, less any payments made by PVF to LaBarge for the purchase of the pipe. The district court should also award LaBarge its attorney's fees and other litigation expenses on its letter of credit claim (but not its other claims) under La. Rev. Stat. Ann. §10:5-111(e).

E.   Reimbursement

If the beneficiary makes an appropriate draft on the letter of credit and the confirming bank honors the draft and pays, the confirming bank has a statutory right to immediate reimbursement from the issuing bank. UCP art. 8(c); UCC §§5-107(a), 5-108(i)(1). The confirming bank ordinarily obtains that reimbursement by forwarding to the issuing bank the documents on which the confirming bank paid. If the issuing bank agrees that the draft was proper, the issuing bank reimburses the confirming bank. The issuing bank then has a right to reimbursement from the applicant. UCC §5-108(i)(1). In most cases, though, that right to reimbursement is not significant because the issuer ordinarily will have obtained payment from the applicant in advance or, at a minimum, will have required the applicant to maintain a deposit account balance with the issuer adequate to cover the amount of the credit. Although some courts have quibbled on this point, the premise of the system is that the issuing bank is obligated to reimburse the confirming bank even if the issuing bank might have had a defense to payment. Because the issuing bank's customer is the applicant that will be disappointed if payment is made, it is not surprising for the issuer to have a greater willingness to refuse payment.

The case that follows illustrates how that problem can lead to serious disputes.

Banco Nacional De Mexico v. Societe Generale

820 N.Y.S.2d 588 (N.Y. Sup. Ct. 2006)

Before NARDELLI, J.P., WILLIAMS, McGUIRE and MALONE, JJ., concur. Opinion by CATTERSON, J.

Plaintiff Banco Nacional De Mexico, S.A., Integrante Del Grupo Financiero Banamex (hereinafter referred to as Banco Nacional) commenced this action seeking reimbursement for payments made to the beneficiary of a letter of credit. The letter of credit (hereinafter referred to as the Letter) was issued on December 10, 2002, in connection with the construction of a power plant in Mexico. It was issued at the request of nonparties Alstom Power and Rosarito Power (hereinafter referred to as Alstom and Rosarito) in favor of the Commission Federal de Electricidad (hereinafter referred to as CFE) up to an amount of $36,812,687.68. The issuing bank was Societe Generale (hereinafter referred to as SG), a French bank doing business in New York, which subsequently requested Banco Nacional to be the confirming bank.

The parties to the Letter agreed that it was to be governed by the UCP. Further, despite the fact that the agreement was executed in Mexico and involved Mexican parties, they agreed that where there was no contradiction with the UCP, the Letter was to be governed and interpreted under New York law. The Letter additionally provided that "any dispute arising herefrom shall be resolved exclusively before the courts of the United States of America with seat in Manhattan, New York City, State of New York."

The Letter also provided that CFE had the right to demand from the issuing bank, SG, partial payments or full payment "upon presentation of a signed written request . . . specifying the amount of the request for payment and . . . that at that time the commission [CFE] has a right to receive such payment from the companies [Alstom and Rosarito] pursuant to the provisions of the agreement." The Letter further provided that if a request for payment did not comply with its terms and conditions, SG must immediately notify CFE in writing.

On September 1, 2004, CFE hand-delivered a signed written request for payment to plaintiff Banco Nacional pursuant to the terms of the Letter. The request demanded the full amount obligated under the Letter. The payment demand strictly conformed to the terms of the Letter.

Subsequently, Banco Nacional informed defendant SG of CFE's conforming payment demand and provided supporting documentation and a reimbursement request indicating the complete amount to be paid to Banco Nacional.

On September 3, 2004, SG informed Banco Nacional that Alstom and Rosarito had questioned CFE's right to payment on the grounds that no final arbitration award had been rendered against them. Within days, Alstom and Rosarito commenced an action against CFE in two Mexican courts and obtained ex parte

Mexican orders purporting to stay payment on the Letter pursuant to the application of Mexican law. The first order was a provisional order to stay, which specifically stated that the stay was not based on the merits. The second order was also a provisional order to stay, which subsequently was revoked on appeal. Based on the two Mexican court orders, Alstom and Rosarito maintained that CFE was not entitled to payment under the agreement.

Banco Nacional responded that pursuant to the law governing the Letter, the UCP and the laws of the State of New York, disputes between parties to the agreement are irrelevant to the bank payment obligations under the Letter.

On September 8, 2004, Banco Nacional paid CFE the full amount obligated under the Letter, and immediately requested reimbursement from defendant. SG refused to reimburse plaintiff on the grounds that the Mexican orders excused it from payment.

Banco Nacional commenced this action seeking reimbursement plus interest. SG asserted that the Mexican injunctions prevented it from paying any party under the Letter. Subsequently, plaintiff moved for summary judgment on the grounds that payment was required under the terms of the Letter and that the orders of the Mexican courts did not constitute a proper basis for refusal of payment. SG opposed, arguing that plaintiff was aware that CFE had no right to demand payment and therefore the payment was fraudulent.

The motion court rejected SG's claim of fraud, and held that SG would have had to comply with the Letter and would have been required to reimburse Banco Nacional if not for the doctrine of comity which required the court to honor the injunctions of the Mexican courts since the place of performance of the Letter was Mexico. The court thus denied plaintiff's motion for summary judgment. For the reasons set forth below, we reverse, and grant summary judgment to plaintiff, and order defendant to reimburse plaintiff with interest.

1. The motion court erred in invoking the doctrine of comity. It is true that under certain circumstances, the doctrine of comity requires New York courts to honor foreign judgments. However, there is no such requirement in the instant case.

At the heart of this action lies a commercial letter of credit transaction. The transaction in the instant case involves, as do all letter of credit transactions, three separate contractual relationships . . .: the underlying contract for the purchase and sale of goods or services; the agreement between the issuer, usually a bank, and its customer, the applicant for the letter of credit; and the letter of credit itself in which the issuer/bank undertakes to honor drafts presented by the beneficiary upon compliance with the terms and conditions specified in the letter of credit.

The fundamental principle governing letters of credit, as reflected in the UCP, and long-recognized by New York courts, is the doctrine of independent contracts. The Court of Appeals has explained the doctrine thus:

> [T]he issuing bank's obligation to honor drafts drawn on a letter of credit by the beneficiary is separate and independent from any obligation of its customer to the beneficiary under the sale of goods contract and separate as well from any obligation of the issuer to its customer under their agreement. (First Commercial Bank v. Gotham Originals, 475 N.E.2d 1255, 1259 [1985].)

In November 2000, this independence principle was codified in a general revision of article 5 ("Letters of Credit") of the Uniform Commercial Code. UCC 5-103(d) now provides that:

> [r]ights and obligations of an issuer to a beneficiary or a nominated person under a letter of credit are independent of the existence, performance, or nonperformance of a contract or arrangement out of which the letter of credit arises or which underlies it, including contracts or arrangements between the issuer and the applicant and between the applicant and the beneficiary.

In other words, the "letter of credit" prong of any commercial transaction concerns the documents themselves and is not dependent on the resolution of disputes or questions of fact concerning the underlying transaction.

In the instant case, the contractual relationships are comprised as follows: the underlying contract was made between Alstom/Rosarito and CFE; the issuer of the Letter was SG, whose customers are Alstom/Rosarito; and the letter of credit is an undertaking by SG to honor any drafts presented by CFE according to the terms of the Letter. Further, the dispute here is between banks. SG is the bank which issued the Letter, and Banco Nacional confirmed it, which created a relationship separate and independent of the underlying transaction in Mexico between CFE, the beneficiary, and Alstom and Rosarito, the applicants for SG's letter of credit.

Consequently, based on the doctrine of independent contract, SG's obligation to honor Banco Nacional's presentation to SG is dependent only on the validity of the presentation which the Letter subjects exclusively to New York law and the New York forum. . . .

2. However, even while acknowledging that the Letter contained the exclusive choice of New York law and forum clauses, the court conducted a "place of performance" analysis and erroneously determined that, in this case, the doctrine of comity supersedes that of independent contract. The court reasoned that because the performance of the Letter, that is, "presenting the demand and then Request, the issuance of the Confirmation, [and] the Notice by SG," all took place in Mexico City, the doctrine of comity applied and therefore the injunctions of the Mexican courts staying payment on the Letter "must" be recognized. This was error.

The motion court ignored the provision of revised UCC 5-116(a) that states that "[t]he jurisdiction whose law is chosen [to govern the letter of credit] need not bear any relation to the transaction." This provision requires application of New York substantive letter of credit law when the parties choose it, regardless of any relationship or lack thereof with New York State.

Section 5-116 became effective when article 5 was revised in 2000, so that it conformed to international trade practice. The section replaced former UCC 1-105(1) which required a "reasonable relation" between New York and the letter of credit for New York law to apply. A "contacts" and "place of performance" analysis, therefore, is neither necessary nor permissible under UCC 5-116. Thus, even though the Mexican courts may have jurisdiction of the underlying transaction under the "contacts" and the "place of performance" analysis, their injunctions have no bearing on the letter of credit.

On appeal, SG argues, nevertheless, that the change in the law resulting from the enactment of UCC 5-116(a) did not alter the principles of comity or preclude New York courts from recognizing foreign orders in the letter of credit context.

SG relies on [a case permitting the holder of a note to choose the law and forum of either New York or Argentina]. Here, by contrast, there was an explicit choice of law clause that established New York law as the exclusive governing law and forum. Moreover, as plaintiff correctly asserts, public policy considerations favor enforcing explicit choice of New York law clauses in letter of credit agreements. As a primary financial center and a clearinghouse of international transactions, the State of New York has a strong interest in maintaining its preeminent financial position and in protecting the justifiable expectation of the parties who choose New York law as the governing law of a letter of credit. The doctrine of independent contract, as codified in UCC article 5, allows the letter of credit to provide a quick, economic and trustworthy means of financing transactions for parties not willing to deal on open accounts. [Citation and quotation marks omitted.] Indeed, the utility of the letter of credit rests heavily on strict adherence to the agreed terms and the doctrine of independent contract. . . .

3. On its cross appeal, defendant further argues that the motion court erred in failing to find the existence of a triable issue of fact relating to Banco National's good faith in paying on the Letter. However, SG cannot merely assert a lack of "good faith" as a collateral attack on reimbursement of a confirming bank. Good faith is relevant only after an issuing bank has established a valid claim of fraud.

UCC 5-109(a) provides in relevant part that[]

> [i]f a presentation is made that appears on its face strictly to comply with the terms and conditions of the letter of credit, but a required document is forged or materially fraudulent, or honor of the presentation would facilitate a material fraud by the beneficiary on the issuer or applicant:
>
> (1) The issuer shall honor the presentation, if honor is demanded by . . . (ii) a confirmer who has honored its confirmation in good faith.

Thus, an issuing bank must first establish that a presentation is fraudulent and only then does the burden shift to the confirming or negotiating bank to show that it paid in good faith.

In the instant case, defendant raised the question of Banco Nacional's good faith but did not allege, let alone raise an issue of fact as to a fraud-in-the-transaction defense.

Problem Set 17

17.1.   Jodi Kay at CountryBank calls first thing this morning to ask you about a minor letter-of-credit problem. Her problem arises from a letter of credit that her bank has issued, which states that it will provide payment for goods shipped "during the first half of February 2017." She received a draft this morning including an invoice for goods shipped on February 15, 2017. She tells you that the letter of credit incorporates the UCP by reference. Can it be possible that the draft complies? UCP art. 3.

17.2.   Right after you get off the phone with Jodi, your assistant tells you that you have a call holding from Cliff Janeway (your book-dealer friend).

Cliff is frustrated because he is having trouble collecting on a letter of credit for a large shipment of books that he just sent overseas. When he submitted a draft on the letter of credit, the confirming bank (SecondBank) told him that it was not obligated to pay Cliff because the issuing bank (FirstBank) had closed. Thus, the officer explained to Cliff, SecondBank would not be able to obtain any reimbursement if it paid Cliff. Accordingly, the officer argued, SecondBank's confirmation of Cliff's letter of credit was unenforceable for lack of consideration. Cliff wants to know what he can do to obtain payment. UCC §§5-105 & comment, 5-107, 5-108; UCP art. 8(a)(i).

17.3. Ben Darrow (your banker client from FSB) has an appointment this morning to discuss two letter-of-credit problems with you. The first arises from a situation where FSB misfiled a draft presented on a letter of credit and thus failed to respond to it. In the case in question, the beneficiary presented a draft on January 5, 2008. Ben's bank did absolutely nothing until the beneficiary wrote in early February and repeated its demand for payment. Upon review of the letter of credit, Ben saw that the letter of credit called for payment based on documents covering a shipment of 100 cases of Llano Estacado wine at a price of "approximately $140 per case." The draft seeks payment of $120 per case. Ben wants to know if he is obligated to pay on the credit. What do you say? UCP arts. 14, 16, 30; UCC §§5-108(c), 5-108 comment 3.

17.4. You return from lunch to an appointment with Jane Halley from Boatmen's Bank. She has a customer, Toy Importing Company (TIC), for whom she has issued a letter of credit in the form set forth in Figure 17.1. The letter of credit was to pay for a shipment of toys from Toy Manufacturing Company (TMC) in Hong Kong. Because TIC is dissatisfied with the toys, TIC wants Boatmen's to reject the draft that has been presented to Boatmen's under the letter of credit. Jane wants to be as accommodating as possible, but does not want the bank to dishonor a proper draft.

Acting under that letter of credit, TMC on September 21, 2016, submitted a draft with the appropriate documents to its main bank, Nanyang Commercial Bank. Nanyang Commercial Bank processed those documents, paid TMC on the letter of credit, and submitted the draft to Boatmen's on September 24, 2016. Jane wants to know if she can reject the draft because it was presented to her after the letter of credit had expired. She says she could understand if she was obligated to accept a draft presented to Hang Seng Bank (the advising bank) in a timely manner, but how can she possibly be obligated to respect a draft presented to some bank with which she has not had any prior dealings? What do you tell her? UCC §§5-102(a)(11), 5-102 comment 7, 5-108 comment 1; UCP arts. 2, 7(c), 12.

17.5. Before Jane leaves your office, she raises one other situation with you. One of her department's largest customers is the April Company, a department store that has a large volume of imported shipments. As part of a master letter-of-credit agreement with Boatmen's, the April Company and Boatmen's established special procedures for drafts submitted under letters of credit issued to some of April's regular suppliers. April and Boatmen's agreed that Boatmen's would provide same-day service on drafts for less than $25,000 submitted on designated "Express Draft" letters of credit. As part of that arrangement, April agreed that Boatmen's would not be obligated to review any of the documents submitted with such drafts, and Boatmen's agreed to reduce its normal processing fees by 50 percent for those drafts.

Jane's problem comes from a $20,000 draft submitted last week on one of the "Express Draft" letters of credit. Following its normal practice, Jane's department honored the draft in a few hours, without even looking at the underlying documents. When the documents got to April, April noticed that the documents did not include the bill of lading called for by the letter of credit. On further inquiry, April has discovered that the supplier/beneficiary (a small Indonesian company) in fact did not ship the goods in question; indeed, that company has become insolvent and stopped operations. April's shipping clerk called Jane yesterday and said that under the circumstances April did not want to reimburse Boatmen's for that draft. Jane tells you that she is not sure she wants to make an issue of the matter, but she wants to know whether she has a right to payment from April. What do you say? UCC §§4-103(a), 5-103(c), 5-103 comment 2, 5-108(a) & (i)(1), 5-108 comment 1 paragraph 6.

Figure 17.1
COMMERCIAL LETTER OF CREDIT FORM

DATE: _____

IRREVOCABLE LETTER OF CREDIT NO. _____

ADVISING BANK: APPLICANT:
HANG SENG BANK   TOY IMPORTING COMPANY
(ADDRESS)   (ADDRESS)

BENEFICIARY:
TOY MANUFACTURING COMPANY
(ADDRESS)

AMOUNT: $250,000.00

WE HEREBY ESTABLISH OUR IRREVOCABLE DOCUMENTARY LETTER OF CREDIT
IN YOUR FAVOR.

DATE AND PLACE OF EXPIRY: SEPTEMBER 22, 2016 IN THE COUNTRY OF THE
BENEFICIARY

CREDIT AVAILABLE WITH: ANY BANK

BY: NEGOTIATION OF YOUR DRAFT(S) AT SIGHT DRAWN ON THE BOATMEN'S
NATIONAL BANK OF ST. LOUIS BEARING THE CLAUSE "DRAWN UNDER THE
BOATMEN'S NATIONAL BANK OF ST. LOUIS LETTER OF CREDIT NO. _____
_" ACCOMPANIED BY THE DOCUMENTS INDICATED HEREIN:

1. COMMERCIAL INVOICE IN TRIPLICATE
2. PACKING LIST IN TRIPLICATE
3. CERTIFICATE OF ORIGIN IN TRIPLICATE
4. CERTIFICATE OF INSPECTION IN TRIPLICATE
5. FULL SET OF CLEAN ON BOARD OCEAN BILLS OF LADING CONSIGNED
    TO APPLICANT (AS SHOWN ABOVE) MARKED NOTIFY APPLICANT (AS
    SHOWN ABOVE) AND "BROKER" AND FREIGHT COLLECT

MERCHANDISE DESCRIPTION — MUST BE DESCRIBED IN INVOICE AS: TOYS
PER P.O. 1234

SHIPPING TERM: FOB HONG KONG

SHIPMENT FROM: HONG KONG TO ANY U.S. PORT

LATEST SHIPMENT DATE: SEPTEMBER 1, 2016

PARTIAL SHIPMENTS PERMITTED

TRANSSHIPMENTS PERMITTED

INSURANCE IS COVERED BY APPLICANT

DOCUMENTS MUST BE PRESENTED WITHIN 21 DAYS AFTER DATE OF SHIPMENT BUT WITHIN THE VALIDITY OF THE CREDIT.

NEGOTIATING BANK IS REQUESTED TO FORWARD ONE SET OF ORIGINAL DOCUMENTS BY COURIER TO (BROKER) AND THEIR STATEMENT TO THIS EFFECT MUST ACCOMPANY THE REMAINING DOCUMENTS WHICH ARE TO BE SENT TO US. ALL BANKING CHARGES, EXCEPT THOSE OF THE ISSUING BANK, ARE FOR THE ACCOUNT OF THE BENEFICIARY.

UPON RECEIVING DOCUMENTS IN COMPLIANCE, WE WILL REMIT THE PROCEEDS AS PER THE NEGOTIATING BANK'S INSTRUCTIONS.

THE AMOUNT OF EACH DRAFT MUST BE ENDORSED ON THE REVERSE OF THIS CREDIT BY THE NEGOTIATING BANK. WE HEREBY ENGAGE WITH DRAWERS AND/OR BONA FIDE HOLDERS THAT DRAFTS DRAWN AND NEGOTIATED IN CONFORMITY WITH THE TERMS OF THIS CREDIT WILL BE DULY HONORED ON PRESENTATION AND THAT DRAFTS ACCEPTED WITHIN THE TERMS OF THIS CREDIT WILL BE DULY HONORED AT MATURITY. DRAFTS MUST BE MARKED AS DRAWN UNDER THIS CREDIT.

THIS CREDIT IS SUBJECT TO THE UNIFORM CUSTOMS AND PRACTICE FOR DOCUMENTARY CREDITS (2007 REVISION) INTERNATIONAL CHAMBER OF COMMERCE PUBLICATION 600.

AUTHORIZED SIGNATURE

Assignment 18:   Letters of Credit—Advanced Topics

Letter-of-credit transactions are not always as simple as the picture set out in the preceding assignment. This assignment discusses three of the most significant complicating problems: error and fraud, assignment by the beneficiary of its rights under the letter of credit, and choice-of-law problems in transnational transactions.

A.   Error and Fraud in Letter-of-Credit Transactions

Assuming that a letter of credit has been issued and delivered to the beneficiary without incident, the transaction can go awry in four major ways. First, the beneficiary can fail to perform, and the issuer can rely on that failure to justify its refusal to pay. That problem poses no difficulty for the payment system because it matches nonperformance by the beneficiary with nonpayment by the applicant. The other three problems, however, are more tricky: wrongful honor (the issuer honors a draft on the letter of credit despite the beneficiary's failure to present the required documents), wrongful dishonor (the issuer dishonors a draft on the letter of credit even though the beneficiary presented the required documents), and fraud (the beneficiary presents fraudulent documents that comply with the letter of credit even though the beneficiary did not in fact perform its underlying obligations to the applicant). The following sections discuss those three topics.

1.   Wrongful Honor

A wrongful honor occurs if a bank honors a letter of credit even though the beneficiary fails to present the appropriate documents. The rules for responding to that problem are straightforward, much like the rules applicable to a bank's decision to honor a check that is not properly payable. First, because the honor was not a proper use of the applicant's funds, the issuer has no right to reimbursement. Interestingly, like the rule in UCC §4-401(a) that a bank cannot charge a checking account for a check that is not properly payable, the no-reimbursement rule does not appear explicitly in the statute. Instead, it must be implied from the direct statement that a bank is entitled to reimbursement when it honors a presentation "as permitted or required by [Article 5]." UCC §5-108(i).

The same analysis applies when a confirming bank honors a letter of credit improperly and seeks reimbursement from the issuer. As the preceding assignment notes, the confirming bank's right to seek reimbursement from the issuer for a proper honor derives from the statement in UCC §5-107(a) that a confirmer "has rights against . . . the issuer as if the issuer were an applicant and the confirmer had issued the letter of credit": The confirming bank (a quasi-issuer) seeks reimbursement from the issuer (a quasi-applicant) under the same rule that the issuer would use to seek reimbursement from the applicant. UCC §5-108(i)(1). Thus, the confirming bank's right to reimbursement from the issuer, like the issuer's right to seek reimbursement from the applicant, is implicitly limited to cases of proper honor. See also UCP art. 7(c) (obligating issuer to reimburse confirming bank that pays "against documents which appear on their face to be in compliance with the terms and conditions of the Credit").

It is rare for an applicant successfully to sue an issuer for wrongful honor, mostly because it is relatively uncommon for a bank to honor a draft that has significant defects without first obtaining a waiver from the applicant of any defects in the draft. That is true for several reasons. First, the bank is the party skilled in evaluating drafts; the bank is much more likely to find trivial defects that would justify dishonor (and much less likely to miss them) than the applicant. Second, by the nature of the transaction, the issuer is much more likely to have ongoing relations with the applicant than with the beneficiary. Accordingly, if anything, the issuer is more likely to err on the side of dishonoring a questionable presentation than honoring it.

It is easy to make too much of the last point because the issuer that decides to dishonor a draft on a letter of credit must consider not only the reaction of the applicant, but also the adverse effects on the issuer's reputation that flow from an insufficient readiness to honor its letters of credit. Financial institutions prize the solidity of letters of credit, and they prize their reputations as solid issuers of them. They do not lightly dishonor letters of credit just to accommodate their customer/applicants that become involved in commercial disputes with beneficiaries.

In the rare event that an applicant successfully establishes that the issuer has acted wrongfully in honoring a draft on a letter of credit, Article 5 limits the applicant's right to recover its funds from the issuer in just the same way that Article 4 limits the rights of the bank customer to recover funds from the payor bank that honors a check that was not properly payable. Specifically, UCC §5-117(a) recognizes a right of subrogation that permits the issuer to assert whatever rights the beneficiary has against the applicant on the underlying transaction. For example, suppose that an issuer honored a draft on a letter of credit even though the draft was not accompanied by the invoice required by the terms of the letter of credit. If the omission of the invoice was an inadvertent mistake and if the beneficiary in fact had performed all of its obligations to the applicant, the applicant would remain obligated to the beneficiary on the underlying sales contract even if it was improper for the issuer to honor the draft on the letter of credit. In that event, the issuer's right of subrogation under UCC §5-117(a) to the beneficiary's right to seek payment from the applicant would bar the applicant from any recovery from the issuer for the wrongful honor. That right of subrogation is particularly important in the standby letter-of-credit context, discussed in the next assignment.

The same perspective informs the UCC's rules regarding damages for wrongful honor. Under UCC §5-111(c), an issuer that wrongfully honors a draft on a letter of credit is responsible to the applicant for "damages resulting from the breach, including incidental but not consequential damages, less any amount saved as a result of the breach." Comment 2 explains that when the beneficiary properly performs the underlying contract, the applicant frequently will suffer no harm because the issuer's breach will not affect the applicant's obligation on that underlying contract. Essentially, the funds paid out in the wrongful honor by the issuer are "a[n] amount saved as a result of the breach" for purposes of UCC §5-111(c) in the sense that the applicant would have been forced to pay the beneficiary for the properly delivered goods even if the issuer had dishonored the improper draft on the letter of credit.

The remedies for wrongful honor by a confirming bank operate in precisely the same way. First, the confirming bank is subrogated to the rights of the beneficiary against the applicant in the same way that the original issuer would be. UCC §5-117(c)(2). Second, the confirming bank's responsibility for damages for wrongful honor is limited in the same way as the responsibility of the issuer is limited under UCC §5-111(c). See UCC §5-111(c) ("To the extent of the confirmation, a confirmer has the liability of an issuer specified in this subsection.").

2. Wrongful Dishonor

Wrongful dishonor is the opposite problem from wrongful honor: A beneficiary presents documents that in fact comply, but the issuer nevertheless refuses to pay. Two features of the letter-of-credit system suggest that a generous measure of damages is appropriate here. The first, mentioned above, is the possibility that the issuer's relation with the applicant will influence the issuer's evaluation of a draft on the letter of credit; the issuer might try to curry favor with its customer (the applicant) by dishonoring a proper draft. The second is more fundamental: the emphasis that the letter-of-credit system places on certainty of payment. Unlike any of the payment systems discussed in the preceding assignments, the letter-of-credit system is designed to provide an up-front commitment that the issuer will pay. That commitment is designed to induce the seller to part with value by performing its obligations (shipping its goods) even before it receives payment from the purchaser—the shipment comes *before* payment, not at the same time as the payment. As part of that arrangement, it is important that the applicant have no right to stop payment. Thus, as discussed below, the only thing that can justify an issuer's refusal to pay a proper draft is egregious fraud.

For that system to work, the issuer must have a significant incentive to honor a proper draft. Given the importance of reputation in the commercial banking industry, the reputational harms from wrongful dishonor probably provide a more significant remedy than anything that the legal system can impose. But that is no reason for the legal system to refrain from providing relief. And so it is no surprise that Article 5 includes a strong remedial framework for the beneficiary faced with wrongful dishonor by the issuer.

The most important rule limits the excuses that the issuer can use to justify its decision to dishonor. Under the independence principle, the only proper justification for dishonor is a failure of the documents to comply with the terms and conditions of the letter of credit. Failure of the beneficiary to comply with the underlying contract with the applicant is not relevant (except for occasions of egregious fraud, discussed below). In this context, the UCC relies on this principle to bar the issuer from defending its decision to dishonor by reference to the beneficiary's failure to perform on the underlying contract. Thus, although UCC §5-117 generally grants the issuer broad rights of subrogation (frequently broader than those recognized under prior law), UCC §5-117(d) specifically bars the assertion of subrogation by an issuer that does not honor a letter of credit. Thus, the issuer that dishonors generally cannot rely on defects in the beneficiary's performance on the contract to offset the issuer's obligation to the beneficiary on the letter of credit. See UCC §5-117 comment 2 ("[A]n issuer may not dishonor and then defend its dishonor or assert a setoff on the ground that it is subrogated to another person's rights.").

Article 5 also provides a relatively generous remedy for wrongful dishonor. First, the beneficiary can sue the issuer for specific performance and also recover any incidental damages that result from the breach, together with a mandatory award of attorney's fees and other litigation expenses. UCC §5-111(a), (d), (e). Furthermore, recognizing the likelihood that a delayed payment will cause significant harm, Article 5 includes an express right to interest as compensation for the delay. UCC §5-111(d). Moreover, in a departure from the general trend in modern commercial transactions, Article 5 provides that the beneficiary has no obligation to mitigate damages. As comment 1 to UCC §5-111 explains, the drafters of the revised Article 5 concluded that it would not be sufficiently painful for the issuer to dishonor if the issuer could rely on the beneficiary to mitigate any losses flowing from the issuer's wrongful refusal to honor.

Nevertheless, the UCC stops short of allowing the beneficiary to receive fully compensatory damages. In particular, the UCC expressly bars the beneficiary from recovering consequential damages. UCC §5-111(a). As comment 4 to UCC §5-111 explains, that rule rests on "the fear that imposing consequential damages on issuers would raise the cost of the letter of credit to a level that might render it uneconomic." That rationale is difficult to evaluate because it depends on assumptions about the extent to which the system otherwise provides issuers an adequate motivation to honor proper drafts. Several considerations, however, suggest that the issuer is adequately motivated even without potential liability for consequential damages. First, by including liability for incidental damages, costs of litigation, and attorney's fees, the UCC remedy for wrongful dishonor already exposes the bank to damages that easily could exceed the amount of the letter of credit. Additional motivation is generated by the reputational harm discussed above, the problems a bank would suffer if it became known as a bank that was willing to bow to improper influence from its customer and dishonor proper drafts on its letters of credit. In context, it is implausible to suggest that issuers take lightly their obligation to honor proper drafts on their letters of credit.

3.   Fraud

As with all payment systems, the most difficult problems are not those that
arise from simple mistakes by the parties in the system, but those that arise
from fraud. In the letter-of-credit system, two kinds of fraud warrant discussion: forged drafts on letters of credit submitted by a party other than the beneficiary and drafts that the beneficiary submits even though the beneficiary
knows that it is not entitled to payment on the underlying contract.

(a) Forged Drafts.   One type of fraud that can disrupt a letter-of-credit
transaction occurs if an interloper—a party not acting on behalf of the beneficiary—submits a draft on the letter of credit. If the interloper deceives the
issuer into honoring the forged draft, the issuer then will have expended the
funds it was obligated to expend on the letter of credit, but will not yet have
paid the beneficiary. That occurrence would pose a significant problem if the
beneficiary subsequently submitted an authentic draft on the letter of credit.

UCC §5-108(i)(5) addresses that situation by stating that the issuer's obligation to honor a draft on a letter of credit is not discharged if it honors a presentation that bears a forged signature of the beneficiary. Thus, when the beneficiary submits an authentic presentation after a forged presentation that the
issuer previously has honored, the issuer still must pay the beneficiary even
though the issuer already has paid the forger. See UCC §5-108 comment 13 ("If
the issuer pays against documents on which a required signature of the beneficiary is forged, it remains liable to the true beneficiary.").

Provided it did not know that the draft included a forgery, the issuer that
honors a forged draft is entitled to reimbursement from the applicant. UCC
§5-109(a) states that an "issuer, acting in good faith, may honor or dishonor" a
presentation in which "a required document is forged." UCC §5-108 comment
12 states, in turn, that "[a]n issuer is entitled to reimbursement from the applicant after honor of a forged . . . drawing if honor was permitted under Section
5-109(a)." See also UCP art. 7(c) (issuer's obligation to reimburse confirming
bank extends to presentations in which "documents . . . appear on their face to
be in compliance with the terms and conditions of the Credit").

At first glance, a rule permitting the issuer to obtain reimbursement when it
honors a forged draft appears difficult to reconcile with the principles discussed in
the earlier payment systems. After all, a rule casting those losses on the issuer (like
the analogous rules in the checking and credit-card systems) would enhance the
issuer's incentive to scrutinize presentations carefully for authenticity and would
motivate the issuer to develop mechanisms for issuing and designing letters of
credit that make it more difficult for forgers to submit forged drafts. As it happens,
however, the absence of any legal responsibility by issuers in those cases does not
appear to be a significant problem. The relative rarity of such schemes—I am not
aware of any case involving such a draft—suggests that issuers have not been
unduly lax in examining presentations for forged signatures.

(b) Fraudulent Submissions by the Beneficiary.   The hardest case for the
letter-of-credit system involves not a forged draft submitted by a stranger to
the transaction, but a draft submitted by the beneficiary itself. The problem

arises when the beneficiary does not perform its underlying obligations, but nevertheless presents documents that comply on their face with the terms of the credit. The focus of the letter-of-credit system on the documents that actually are presented to the issuer makes that case particularly difficult. A rule that broadly permitted issuers to dishonor based on uncertainty about the beneficiary's performance in the underlying transaction would remove the reliability that is the most attractive feature of the system. On the other hand, courts and legislators have been unwilling to accept a rule that unequivocally requires the issuer to honor the draft in that situation: That rule would leave beneficiaries an opportunity for fraud that almost everybody finds unacceptable.

In response to those directly conflicting concerns, the current version of the UCC articulates a compromise solution to that situation. The heart of that solution is a rule — the same rule that protects the issuer that honors a forged draft — that gives broad discretion to the issuer to decide whether it wishes to honor or dishonor the presentation. If the issuer is skeptical of the applicant's claim of fraud, the issuer is almost completely free to ignore the claim and honor the presentation. UCC §5-109 comment 2. The sole limitation on the issuer's right to honor is that the issuer act in good faith. UCC §5-109(a)(2). Because good faith in Article 5 requires nothing more than "honesty in fact," UCC §5-102(a)(7), the issuer ordinarily would be safe to reject any claim of fraud unless the applicant actually could convince the issuer that the claim was true.

The rule does not, however, *require* the issuer to honor fraudulent presentations solely because they are facially compliant. Rather, the rule gives the issuer latitude to dishonor a facially compliant presentation based on a claim of fraud, but only if the fraud satisfies the rigorous standard set forth in the opening clause of UCC §5-109(a): "[A] required document is forged or materially fraudulent, or honor of the presentation would facilitate a material fraud by the beneficiary on the issuer or applicant." As comment 1 to UCC §5-109 emphasizes, the drafters intended the "material fraud" standard to be a rigorous one. Even a willful default by the beneficiary on the underlying contract is likely to fall far short of material fraud. To justify dishonor, the fraud must be so severe that "the beneficiary has *no* colorable right to expect honor" and "there is *no* basis in fact to support . . . a right to honor." UCC §5-109 comment 1 (emphasis added).

The drafters of the UCC expected that issuers faced with the foregoing rules generally would reject claims of fraud and proceed to honor drafts on letters of credit even when applicants presented plausible arguments that beneficiaries had committed the kind of material fraud that would permit dishonor under UCC §5-109. The drafters went further in cases where the issuer receives a draft from a confirming bank or other party that properly has honored a draft in good faith. In that case, the issuer *must* honor the draft, even if the issuer believes that the draft is materially fraudulent. UCC §5-109(a)(1). In either case, honor would be proper under Article 5. Hence, the applicant would be obligated to reimburse the issuer even if the presentation had been totally fraudulent. The applicant then would be entitled to sue the beneficiary for making the fraudulent presentation. UCC §5-110(a)(2).

That framework presents a serious problem for the applicant in situations in which the applicant has no effective remedy against the beneficiary. For example, the beneficiary might be judgment-proof or otherwise inaccessible (in a foreign country, for instance). One response, of course, is that the applicant should have thought about the responsibility and trustworthiness of the beneficiary before obtaining a letter of credit in the beneficiary's favor, and the statutory framework certainly rests in part on that sentiment. But Article 5 does provide one narrow mechanism by which the applicant can protect itself. Specifically, UCC §5-109(b) authorizes the applicant to obtain an injunction against honor if it can convince a court that the presentation satisfies the material fraud standard set forth in UCC §5-109. That rule does not impose undue uncertainty on the issuer because Article 5 authorizes the issuer to dishonor a draft in response to a judicial injunction issued under UCC §5-109(b). Thus, the issuer safely can obey that injunction with no risk that it will be held liable to the beneficiary for wrongful dishonor.

B. Assigning Letters of Credit

Letter-of-credit practice traditionally has been hostile to efforts by beneficiaries to transfer letters of credit after they have been issued. The most common justification for that hostility is the implicit trust that a letter of credit requires an applicant to bestow on its beneficiary. As the discussion of fraud in the previous section should make clear, a purchaser/applicant's willingness to obtain a letter of credit in favor of a seller/beneficiary with whom it is doing business leaves the applicant exposed to a considerable risk of loss if the beneficiary is not trustworthy. Article 5 follows the UCP's lead on that point by adopting a default rule that letters of credit are not transferable. UCC §5-112(a); UCP art. 38(a); see UCC §5-112 comment 1. Thus, a beneficiary that plans to transfer a letter of credit before performance needs to obtain a letter of credit that states expressly that it is transferable.

Article 5 articulates two significant exceptions to that rule. First, UCC §5-113 provides rules for transfers by operation of law. Those transfers occur in the context of corporate mergers, as well as on the occasion of the appointment of a receiver or trustee to deal with insolvency. When such a transaction occurs, the issuer must recognize the successor as the beneficiary of the letter of credit and thus must honor a presentation from the successor. The only limitation is that the successor must comply with reasonable requirements imposed by the issuer to ensure that the successor is authentic. UCC §5-113(b).

Given the limited likelihood that a party will submit a presentation fraudulently claiming to be the successor of the beneficiary, the UCC absolves the issuer of any obligation to "determine whether a purported successor is a successor of a beneficiary or whether the signature of a purported successor is genuine or authorized." UCC §5-113(c). Instead, the UCC states that payment of a presentation submitted in support of such a scheme—a presentation that purports to be from a successor, but, in fact, is from a fraudulent interloper — is treated as a proper payment under UCC §5-108(i). UCC §5-113(d). The forged documents are treated under the standard fraud rule in UCC §5-109, so that the issuer is entitled to honor the draft from the purported successor so long as the issuer proceeds in good faith. UCC §5-113(d).

The second exception to the default rule against transferability draws a distinction between an assignment of the letter of credit per se and an assignment of the beneficiary's right to receive proceeds under the letter of credit. Although hostile to the former, both the UCC and the UCP permit the latter. See UCC §5-114(b) (permitting such an assignment); UCP art. 39 (same). That type of transfer does not raise the concerns that motivate the general rule against an assignment by a beneficiary of a letter of credit because it continues to condition the issuer's obligation to pay on performance by the original stated beneficiary. The only thing that is assigned is the beneficiary's right to receive proceeds in the event that the beneficiary performs. Thus, if the beneficiary in fact performs after such an assignment, the issuer will pay the funds from the transaction to the assignee, not the named beneficiary. If the beneficiary fails to perform, the issuer will not be obligated to disburse funds under the letter of credit, even if the assignee attempts to perform.

Perhaps the most common use of an assignment of a beneficiary's right to receive proceeds of a letter of credit is to enhance the ability of the beneficiary to obtain funds to finance the beneficiary's purchase or production of the goods that it is selling. For example, in the typical letter-of-credit transaction in which the beneficiary is a seller of goods, the beneficiary might have an arrangement with a lender under which the lender advances funds to the beneficiary that the beneficiary uses to support its manufacturing operations or to purchase inventory from some other party that manufactures the goods in question. In either case, the lender funding the beneficiary's operations will want its loan (or at least the relevant portion of the loan) to be repaid when the beneficiary sells the goods in question. If the beneficiary is being paid by means of a letter of credit, the lender commonly will prefer for the proceeds of the letter of credit to be paid directly to the lender because direct payment to the lender will limit the ability of the beneficiary to abscond with the funds instead of repaying the loan.

As the preceding paragraph suggests, it is not enough from the perspective of the lender/assignee for the statute to make an assignment of the right to receive proceeds from a letter of credit effective as against the beneficiary. The assignee wants more than a right to force the beneficiary to pay; the loan agreement undoubtedly already contains that right. What the assignee really wants is a way to force the issuer to pay the letter-of-credit proceeds directly to the assignee. The issuer, however, would be reluctant to accept that arrangement unless it could be sure that it could avoid the risk of duplicate presentations under the letter of credit: The issuer wants to know at all times the identity of a single party to whom it is obligated to make payments under its letter. To accommodate that concern, the UCC states that an issuer generally has no obligation to recognize an assignment of proceeds of a letter of credit. UCC §5-114(c). Thus, absent some action by the issuer, the assignee will not be able to force the issuer to pay the proceeds directly to it.

The assignee can solve that problem, however, by taking a few simple steps to limit the possibility of duplicate presentations. Specifically, if the letter of credit requires presentation of the original letter as a condition to honor and if the assignee obtains that original from the beneficiary, then the assignee can satisfy the issuer that only the assignee will be in a position to present proper drafts under the letter of credit. See UCC §5-114 comment 3 (stating that "the risk to the issuer . . . of having to pay twice is minimized" in those circumstances). In that case, the UCC states that the issuer cannot unreasonably withhold its consent to the assignment. UCC §5-114(d). The drafters obviously expect issuers to consent to an assignment that involves those characteristics. After such a consent, the assignee is protected because "the issuer . . . becomes bound . . . to pay to the assignee the assigned letter of credit proceeds that the issuer or nominated person otherwise would pay to the beneficiary." UCC §5-114 comment 3.

C.   Choice-of-Law Rules

At first glance, the frequently transnational character of letter-of-credit transactions suggests that choice-of-law rules would be crucial to letter-of-credit transactions because of the need to determine what body of law specifies the rights and obligations of each party to such a transaction. Responding to that likelihood, Article 5 includes a choice-of-law provision (UCC §5-116) much like the wire-transfer provision in UCC §4A-507. The first and last subsections of UCC §5-116 set out a broad and absolute deference to choice-of-law and choice-of-forum clauses, including a statement that the chosen jurisdiction "need not bear any relation to the transaction." UCC §5-116(a), (e). If the letter of credit does not include a choice-of-law clause, the liability of a party obligated on the letter of credit is governed by the law where that party is located. UCC §5-116(b). Article 5 does not include a choice-of-law rule governing the liability of the applicant, apparently because of a perception that there is no need for such a rule. See UCC §5-116 comment 1.

Choice-of-law rules have practical significance only in cases in which different legal systems resolve the same dispute in different ways. As the drafters of Article 5 recognized, that is not likely to occur frequently in the letter-of-credit system. Indeed, even before the revised version of Article 5 was adopted, the general consistency of letter-of-credit law in different nations made such disputes uncommon. See UCC §5-116 comment 2. And the revised version of Article 5 should make those disputes even less common, both because Article 5 now adopts rules that follow as closely as practicable the rules articulated in the UCP, UCC §5-101 comment, and because Article 5 generally allows application of the UCP in cases where those rules conflict with rules set out in Article 5, see UCC §5-116(c). Thus, substantial choice-of-law conflicts should be relatively rare in transactions involving letters of credit. See UCC §5-116 comment 2. Their most common occurrence (as *Banco Nacional* from the previous assignment suggests) is an attempt by a party opposing payment to seek relief in a court other than the one specified in the letter of credit and related documents.

Problem Set 18

18.1.   Consider anew the facts of Problem 17.3, in which FSB failed to make a timely response to a draft on a $120,000 letter of credit issued by FSB. As the facts of that problem indicate, the draft did not comply with the requirements of the letter of credit.

   a.   Assume that FSB received a $120,000 deposit from the applicant at the time that FSB issued the letter of credit. If FSB is forced to pay $120,000 to the beneficiary, can FSB keep the $120,000 to reimburse itself? UCC §§4-407, 5-108(i)(1), 5-117(a), 5-117 comment 1.

   b.   Same facts as question a, but FSB did not take a deposit from the applicant. Can FSB recover the $120,000 from the applicant? UCC §5-117(a).

18.2.   Jane Halley from Boatmen's Bank (introduced in Problem Set 17) calls first thing one morning with another letter-of-credit problem for you. This one involves a letter of credit that Boatmen's issued for $1 million to Riverfront Tools (RFT). Early last week (ten days ago) she received a draft on the letter of credit, which appeared to contain all of the requisite documents. For reasons that are not clear, her office failed to process the draft in a timely manner. When she found out about the problem this morning, she immediately contacted the applicant to tell it that she had found the draft and was about to process it. The applicant told her that the draft must be forged because the applicant had talked that morning to Carl Eben (the president of RFT), who had told the applicant that RFT would be submitting a draft tomorrow. Given Jane's delay, must Boatmen's honor the draft? UCC §5-108(b), (c), (d); UCP arts. 14, 16.

18.3.   At a meeting with Jodi Kay, Jodi asks your advice about some of the risks she faces in letter-of-credit transactions. Specifically, she wants to know what her responsibility will be if she receives a presentation drawing on one of her letters of credit that is totally forged, fails to understand that the presentation is forged, and consequently honors it. Specifically, she wants to know if she will be able to obtain reimbursement from her customer and if she will still be obligated to honor a later legitimate draft. (She wants to know whether she can be forced to pay twice.) What do you tell her? UCC §§5-108(a), 5-108(i)(1), 5-108(i)(5), 5-108 comment 12, 5-109(a)(2).

18.4.   Same facts as Problem 18.3, but now assume that the beneficiary sends two drafts, one directly to the issuer and a second subsequent one through a confirming bank that pays it with no notice that it is a duplicate.

18.5.   As you get ready to leave the office for the weekend, you get a desperate call from Archie Moon. He tells you that he has just received a shipment from Malay Ink Company of what should have been four barrels of expensive indigo ink. Unfortunately, the barrels appear to contain ordinary black printer's ink, which has only one-fourth the value of the ink that he ordered.

Archie is concerned because he obtained a $75,000 letter of credit to pay the shipper and is worried that his bank will proceed to pay a draft on the letter of credit; apparently the beneficiary prepared a fraudulent bill of lading that incorrectly described the goods. Archie called his bank this morning. The banker told Archie that she had received a draft on the letter of credit and that the draft appeared to be in order. The banker declined to defer her consideration of the draft and told Archie that in the ordinary course of business the bank would honor the draft Monday morning. What do you advise? UCC §§2-601, 2-711, 5-108(a) & (i)(1), 5-109(b), 5-109 comment 1, 5-111.

18.6.   Same facts as Problem 18.5, but assume now that the draft and supporting documents were presented to the issuer by the Bank of Hong Kong, that the Bank of Hong Kong already paid the beneficiary based on those documents, and that nobody at that bank had any reason to doubt the legitimacy of those documents or the underlying transaction. Does your answer change? UCC §§5-108(i)(1), 5-109(a)(2), 5-109(b)(2). Would it matter if the issuer received evidence that it regarded as incontrovertible establishing that the bill of lading was fraudulent?

18.7.   When Jane Halley comes in at the end of the day to finish up some paperwork associated with Problem 18.2, she mentions another problem related to a letter of credit that she has issued with Toy Manufacturing Company as the beneficiary. The letter of credit is in the form set forth in Figure 17.1. Today she received a draft drawn on that letter of credit by Hong Kong Toys. The draft included all the documents specified by the letter of credit. Attached to the draft was the original letter of credit, to which a single piece of paper was stapled. The piece of paper appears to be signed by Sun Yat Toy as president of Toy Manufacturing Company and reads as follows: "The undersigned Toy Manufacturing Company hereby transfers the attached letter of credit and all rights under that letter of credit to Hong Kong Toys."

   a. Is Jane obligated to honor the draft? Should she honor the draft? UCC §§5-112(a), 5-114(d).
   b. Would your answer change if the draft also included a cover letter explaining that Hong Kong Toys had acquired the letter of credit in connection with a transaction in which it merged with Toy Manufacturing Company? UCC §5-113.

Assignment 19:   Third-Party Credit Enhancement — Standby Letters of Credit

A.   The Standby Letter-of-Credit Transaction

Many borrowers cannot solve their credit problems with the kind of related party guaranty discussed in the preceding chapter. In some cases, no party related to the borrower has enough financial strength to satisfy the creditor's concerns. In other cases, even if some party related to the borrower has considerable wealth, the potential creditor has doubts about the reputation or the credibility of the related party that undermine the creditor's willingness to rely on a commitment by the related party to back up the obligation in question. In still other cases (particularly international transactions), the parties are so geographically separated that the creditor prefers a right to proceed against a party located nearby (at least in the creditor's home country).

The most common way to solve those problems is for the borrower to obtain a backup promise from a third party with financial strength, credibility, and location that are satisfactory to the creditor. In this country, that promise usually comes from a bank. Although such a transaction closely resembles a guaranty in substance, historical concerns cause U.S. banks to provide that service with a document styled "letter of credit," rather than "guaranty." To distinguish it from the letter of credit used in a simple payment transaction (the subject of the preceding assignments), this type of letter of credit is called a "standby" letter of credit. Antiquated limitations on the power of state and national banks in this country often prohibit those institutions from doing business as a "guarantor" or a "surety." Because overseas banks commonly engage in that business — through the issuance of what are called "bank guaranties" or "demand guaranties" — competitive pressures have driven U.S. banks to use the standby letter of credit to provide a similar service. Thus, although the standby letter-of-credit transaction has something of the substance of a conventional guaranty, the common use of the practice has motivated federal regulatory authorities to confirm the legitimacy of the standby letter of credit. Accordingly, however much the standby letter of credit looks like a guaranty, it is now well settled that domestic banks can issue standby letters of credit even if they cannot issue ordinary guaranties. See, e.g., Citizens State Bank v. FDIC, 946 F.2d 408, 414 (5th Cir. 1991) (discussing Federal Reserve regulations governing standby letters of credit issued by national banks); American Ins.

Ass'n v. Clarke, 865 F.2d 278, 281-282 (D.C. Cir. 1988) (discussing regulations issued by the Comptroller of the Currency governing standby letters of credit issued by national banks).

Like the conventional letters of credit discussed in the preceding assignments, the standby letter of credit (or demand guaranty) is frequently used in international business transactions. The last few decades have seen several efforts to standardize the law in that area. One project by the United Nations Commission on International Trade Law produced the UNCITRAL Convention on Independent Guarantees and Stand-by Letters of Credit. That document, however, has not yet been adopted by any of the important commercial countries. A more successful project is the International Standby Practices promulgated by the International Chamber of Commerce in 1998 (ISP98). Like the Uniform Customs and Practice for Documentary Credits, banks frequently incorporate ISP98 by reference into international letters of credit to which it would be relevant. Because ISP98 is similar to the rules that American courts apply under Article 5 of the Uniform Commercial Code, the result is a substantially uniform body of law that applies regardless of the location of the parties to the standby letter-of-credit transaction.

To see how parties would use a standby letter of credit, consider again the transaction between RFT and OmniBank, used as an example in the preceding chapter on guaranties. Suppose that OmniBank is unwilling to provide a $4 million loan that RFT needs to fund construction of a new factory even if Carl guarantees the loan. OmniBank might be willing to make the loan, however, if RFT provides a $500,000 letter of credit from CountryBank. That letter of credit would provide that OmniBank could draw $500,000 from CountryBank upon any default by RFT under the construction loan. The letter of credit thus would reduce considerably the risk that OmniBank's construction loan would go unpaid: OmniBank would have the letter of credit from CountryBank, *in addition to* its normal rights to pursue RFT, Carl (if Carl guarantees the loan), and any collateral that OmniBank might obtain from RFT or Carl. Moreover, CountryBank's obligation on the letter of credit (unlike Carl's obligation on the guaranty) would be unconditional; because of the independence principle, CountryBank would not be entitled to assert defenses to RFT's underlying obligation that might allow Carl as a guarantor to withhold payment. ISP98 Rule 1.06(c). CountryBank, in turn, should be willing to issue that letter of credit only if it is confident that it could obtain reimbursement from Carl (or RFT) if CountryBank were called on to pay on the standby letter of credit.

Relational considerations are almost as important in the standby letter-of-credit transaction as they are in the standard guaranty transaction. In the abstract, it might seem puzzling that Carl and RFT can persuade CountryBank to issue a letter of credit that exposes CountryBank to the same risk of nonpayment that makes OmniBank unwilling to accept Carl and RFT's credit in the same transaction. But CountryBank's willingness to accept that risk does not necessarily suggest that CountryBank is less prudent than OmniBank. On the contrary, it probably indicates that CountryBank is more familiar than OmniBank with the credit and reputation of Carl and RFT. The ordinary practice would be for Carl and RFT to obtain a standby letter of credit from the institution with which Carl and RFT do their regular business banking. For example, if CountryBank has a long business relationship with Carl and RFT, CountryBank should be more comfortable with the financial strength and commitment of Carl and RFT than a lender engaged in a first-time transaction with Carl and RFT; in many cases, it might help that CountryBank has a lien on substantially all of the assets of Carl and RFT. From that perspective, the standby letter of credit provides a relatively inexpensive and effective mechanism by which Carl and RFT can convince third parties of the reliability that Carl and RFT already have demonstrated to their principal lender. For that service, CountryBank typically would charge Carl a fee equal to the return over its cost of funds that CountryBank would expect on a typical loan to Carl. For a typical customer, that fee might be 1 percent per annum; for a high-quality customer, the fee might drop as low as one-tenth of that amount.

The resulting transaction is functionally similar to a conventional guaranty transaction, but has the issuing bank playing the role of the guarantor, the applicant as the borrower or principal obligor, and the beneficiary as the creditor. When the creditor believes that the applicant/borrower has committed a default on the underlying obligation, it simply submits a draft on the letter of credit to the issuer. At that point, the issuer is obligated to pay the creditor much as a conventional guarantor would be. The only difference is that the rules governing that obligation are the (somewhat different) rules in Article 5 of the Uniform Commercial Code, rather than the common-law rules of traditional guaranties.

The dynamics of the standby letter-of-credit transaction differ in important respects from those of the conventional letter-of-credit transaction discussed in the preceding assignments. The letter of credit issued in that conventional transaction normally is referred to as a "payment" or "commercial" letter of credit. In the commercial letter-of-credit transaction, where the letter of credit is a simple payment device, the parties anticipate a draw on the letter of credit in the ordinary course of business. The key condition for payment is the beneficiary's production of documents suggesting that the beneficiary has complied with the obligations imposed on it by its contract with the applicant. In a standby letter-of-credit transaction, by contrast, a draft on the letter of credit is the unusual, unhoped-for event. It should occur only if the applicant defaults. Thus, a typical banker would receive drafts on only 5–10 percent of its standby letters of credit, where it would receive drafts on almost all of the commercial letters of credit that it issues.

The following case is a good example of the transactions that give rise to standby letters of credit.

Nobel Insurance Co. v. First National Bank

821 So. 2d 210 (Ala. 2001)

Harwood, Justice.

Nobel Insurance Company (hereinafter referred to as "Nobel") appeals the summary judgment for The First National Bank of Brundidge (hereinafter referred to as "the Bank"), J.T. Ramage III, Henry T. Strother, Jr., William F. Hamrick, and Palomar Insurance Corporation (hereinafter referred to as "Palomar"). . . . We reverse and remand.

Nobel first sued the Bank in the United States District Court for the Middle District of Alabama to enforce certain letters of credit issued by the Bank. The letters of credit were issued by order of the Bank's customers, Strother and Hamrick, both of whom were insurance brokers for Palomar. The letters of credit were signed by Ramage, the Bank's president, and issued in favor of Western American Specialized Transportation Service, Inc. (hereinafter referred to as "Western American"), one of Hamrick's clients who sought insurance coverage from Nobel. . . .

[Nobel issued various insurance policies to Western American, which had large deductible amounts. The policies required that Nobel hold collateral to secure the obligation of Western American to pay those amounts. Western American satisfied that requirement by causing the Bank to issue the three letters of credit in issue. When Western American became indebted to Nobel for uncollected deductibles, Nobel drew on the letters of credit, but the Bank refused to pay.

[The district court ruled in favor of the Bank, relying on general principles of suretyship law, including an Alabama statute that provides]:

> A surety upon any contract for the payment of money or for the delivery or payment of personal property may require the creditor or anyone having the beneficial interest in the contract, by notice in writing, to bring an action thereon against the principal debtor or against any cosurety to such contract.
>
> (b) If an action is not brought thereon in three months after the receipt of such notice and prosecuted with diligence according to the ordinary course of law, the surety giving such notice is discharged from all liability as surety or his aliquot proportion of the debt, as the case may be.
>
> (c) One surety may give notice in behalf of his cosureties.

[Ala. Code §8-3-13.]

[The court noted that the applicants for the letters of credit sent such a notice and that Nobel did not dispute the receipt or the sufficiency of the notice.] . . .

Nobel argues that the trial court erred in applying suretyship law to the transaction underlying this lawsuit because, it argues, letters of credit are subject to a separate body of law. Under the law governing letters of credit, Nobel argues, the letters of credit in this case cannot be extinguished by application of §8-3-13 even though they were arguably posted as collateral by Strother and Hamrick, as sureties, to answer for the debt of Western American.

The letters of credit at issue all state, in pertinent part:

> We hereby agree with the drawers, endorsers and bona fide holders of drafts drawn under and in compliance with the terms of this credit that such drafts will be duly honored upon presentation to the drawee. *The obligation of The First National Bank of Brundidge, under this Letter of Credit is the individual obligation of The First National Bank of Brundidge and is in no way contingent upon reimbursement with respect thereto.*
>
> Except as otherwise stated herein, this credit is subject to the Uniform Customs and Practice for Commercial Documentary Credits (1983 Revision) I.C.C. Publication No. 400. Notwithstanding Article 19 of said publication, if this credit expires during an interruption of business as described in Article 19, we agree to effect payment if the credit is drawn against within thirty (30) days after resumption of business.

(Emphasis added [by court].) . . .

[The court relied heavily on its explanation of the function of standby letters of credit in an earlier decision:]

> Parties that enter into a credit arrangement do so to avail themselves of the benefits of that arrangement. Shifting litigation costs is one of the functions of a standby credit. In this situation, the parties negotiate their relationship while bearing in mind that litigation may occur. This cost-shifting function gives one party the benefit of the money in hand pending the outcome of any litigation. It is important to understand the functions of letters of credit in order to fully understand the consequences the fraud exception has on this commercial device. A demand for payment made upon a standby credit usually indicates that something has gone wrong in the contract. Indeed, this is the nature of the standby letter of credit. In contrast to the commercial credit, nonperformance that triggers payment in a standby credit situation usually indicates some form of financial weakness by the applicant. For this reason, parties choose this security arrangement over another so that they may have the benefit of prompt payment before any litigation occurs. We recognize that, as a general rule, letters of credit cannot exist without independence from the underlying transaction. Thus, when courts begin delving into the underlying contract, they are impeding the swift completion of the credit transaction. The certainty of payment is the most important aspect of a letter of credit transaction, and this certainty encourages hesitant parties to enter into transactions, by providing them with a secure source of credit. [Citations and quotation marks omitted.]
>
> The extensive use of the fraud exception may operate to transform the credit transaction into a surety contract. A standby credit is essentially equivalent to a loan made by the issuing bank to the applicant. *Like a surety contract, the standby credit ensures against the applicant's nonperformance of an obligation. Unlike a surety contract, however, the beneficiary of the standby credit may receive its money first, regardless of pending litigation with the applicant.* The applicant may then sue the beneficiary for breach of contract or breach of warranty, or may sue in tort, but without the money. *Parties to standby credit transactions have bargained for a distinct and less expensive kind of credit transaction.* [Emphasis in original.]

In light of the analysis [above], we agree that the letters of credit issued by the Bank to Nobel are properly characterized as "standby" letters of credit. Because we also conclude that the letters of credit are properly viewed as distinct from the parties' surety arrangements, we must also conclude that the trial court erred in applying the law of suretyship to extinguish the Bank's responsibility to honor the letters of credit. The letters of credit are independent of the underlying transaction between Nobel and Western American.

[W]e reverse the trial court's summary judgment in favor of the Bank, Ramage, Strother, Hamrick, and Palomar, and we remand the cause for further proceedings consistent with this opinion.

The documentary conditions for a draw on a standby letter of credit normally focus on establishing that the applicant has defaulted, rather than establishing that the beneficiary has performed. For example, Figure 19.1 sets forth a standard form for a standby letter of credit promulgated by the leading industry trade association. It differs from the typical commercial letter of credit (like the one in Assignment 17) in that it does not require the beneficiary to provide nearly the level of detailed objective proof that the beneficiary has complied with its obligations (such as a bill of lading or some type of transport document). The result is that it tends to be much easier for the beneficiary to comply with the requirements of the letter of credit; the form includes a typical compliant form of a demand for payment. As Assignment 18 explained, bankers report that most presentations on commercial letters of credit do not comply with the letter of credit; the same bankers report that the overwhelming majority of presentations on standby letters of credit do comply and thus are honored by the issuing bank.

<h3 style="text-align:center">Figure 19.1
Form Standby Letter of Credit (ISP98 Form 1)</h3>

[name and address of beneficiary]   [date of issuance]

Issuance. At the request and for the account of **[name and address of applicant]** ("Applicant"), we **[name and address of issuer at place of issuance]** ("Issuer") issue this irrevocable standby letter of credit number **[reference number]** ("Standby") in favour of **[name and address of beneficiary]** ("Beneficiary") in the maximum aggregate amount of **[currency/amount]**.

Undertaking. Issuer undertakes to Beneficiary to pay Beneficiary's demand for payment in the currency and for an amount available under this Standby and in the form of the Annexed Payment Demand completed as indicated and presented to Issuer at the following place for presentation: **[address of place for presentation]**, on or before the expiration date.

Expiration. The expiration date of this Standby is **[date]**.

[Payment. Payment against a complying presentation shall be made within 3 business days after presentation at the place for presentation or by wire transfer to a duly requested account of Beneficiary. An advice of such payment shall be sent to Beneficiary's above-stated address.]

[Drawing. Partial and multiple drawings are permitted.]

[Reduction. Any payment made under this Standby shall reduce the amount available under it.]

ISP98. This Standby is issued subject to the International Standby Practices 1998 (ISP98) (International Chamber of Commerce Publication No. 590).
[Communications. Communications other than demands may be made to Issuer by telephone, telefax, or SWIFT message, to the following: **[numbers/addresses]**. Beneficiary requests for amendment of this Standby, including

amendment to reflect a change in Beneficiary's address, should be made to Applicant, who may then request Issuer *to issue the desired amendment.*]

[Issuer's name]

[signature]_____

Authorized Signature

* * *

Annexed Payment Demand

[INSERT <u>DATE</u>]

[name and address of Issuer or other addressee at place of presentation as stated in standby]

Re: Standby Letter of Credit No. **[reference number]**, dated **[date]**, issued by **[Issuer's name]** ("Standby")

The undersigned Beneficiary demands payment of [INSERT <u>CURRENCY/AMOUNT</u>] under the Standby.

Beneficiary states that Applicant is obligated to pay to Beneficiary the amount demanded[, *which amount is due and unpaid*] under [*or in connection with*] the agreement between Beneficiary and Applicant titled **[agreement title]** and dated **[date]**.

[Beneficiary further states that the proceeds from this demand will be used to satisfy the above-identified obligations and that Beneficiary will account to Applicant for any proceeds that are not so used.]

Beneficiary requests that payment be made by wire transfer to an account of Beneficiary as follows: [insert <u>name, address, and routing number of beneficiary's bank, and name and number of beneficiary's account</u>].

[Beneficiary's name and address]

By its authorized officer:

[insert original signature]

[insert typed/printed name and title]

[Before the standby is issued, all text in **[bold]** should be completed, and optional text in [*italics*] should be included or deleted (or redrafted). Text in the annexed demand form preceded by "INSERT" (or other ALL CAPITALS guidance) and in [ALL CAPITALS UNDERLINED] is to be completed as indicated when the beneficiary prepares and presents a demand.]

Because the standby letter-of-credit transaction contemplates that the beneficiary will draw on the letter of credit only if the applicant defaults on its
contract with the beneficiary, the conditions on the beneficiary's right to draw
on the letter of credit are crucial to the success of the beneficiary in obtaining
payment. A failure by the beneficiary to comply with the conditions of a commercial letter of credit normally has little consequence because the applicant
has received the goods and thus has to pay for them if it wishes to keep them.
In that context, insistence by the applicant on strict compliance with the letter
of credit only increases the procedural obstacles to payment, and thus the cost
of payment; it does not avoid payment. By contrast, a beneficiary will not present a draft on a standby letter of credit until a serious dispute arises. In that
context, the beneficiary frequently will be unable to obtain payment through
any avenue other than the letter of credit. Thus, failure of the beneficiary to
comply with the requirements for a draft on a standby letter of credit normally
is a much more serious problem.

The key point of demarcation in the conditions under which a beneficiary can draw on a standby letter of credit is whether the letter of credit is
"clean."

If the letter of credit is clean, the beneficiary need present nothing more than
a draft demanding payment (and perhaps the letter of credit itself); no additional documentation is necessary. Thus, for example, the form set forth in
Figure 19.1 is not technically a clean standby letter of credit because it requires
the beneficiary to include a signed statement that some specified invoice is
due, but unpaid. The difference between a clean and an "unclean" standby
letter of credit may be unimportant in cases where the applicant's default is
clear, but the following case shows how certification requirements like those
required in Figure 19.1 can make the difference between a successful and an
unsuccessful attempt to draw on the letter of credit.

Wood v. State Bank

609 N.Y.S.2d 665 (App. Div. 1994)

Before Thompson, J.P., and Pizzuto, Santucci and Goldstein, JJ.

. . .

On January 29, 1987, the plaintiffs and Jacklyn Construction Corp. (hereinafter
Jacklyn) entered into a contract for Jacklyn to buy the plaintiffs' real property.
Under clauses 5 and 6 of the rider to the contract of sale, the parties agreed that
certain moneys "shall be a non-refundable payment to the [plaintiffs] for allowing
[Jacklyn] to obtain the zoning approvals and for agreeing to sell said property and
making said property subject to the change of zone." As part of the contemplated
payment, Jacklyn caused the State Bank of Long Island (hereinafter the State Bank)
to open a clean irrevocable letter of credit in favor of "Thomas F. Wood Esq., as
attorney for [the plaintiffs]." The letter of credit provided for payment on or before
the close of business on January 16, 1988, against a sight draft making reference to
credit number 1147 and a sworn statement by the plaintiffs' attorney "certifying
that: Jacklyn . . . or its assigns, has willfully failed to close title in accordance with
the provisions of a certain contract, dated on or about January 29, 1987 between

[the plaintiffs] and Jacklyn." On or about January 12, 1988, State Bank received a sight draft that made no reference to State Bank's credit number and an affidavit of the plaintiffs' attorney that mentioned the credit number and read: "1. That he is the attorney for [the plaintiffs], and makes this affidavit pursuant to the terms and conditions of a Letter of Credit No. 1147. . . . 2. That pursuant to a contract dated January 29, 1987 . . . the sum of FORTY THOUSAND ($40,000.00) DOLLARS was to be deposited with him on or before January 1, 1988. 3. That pursuant to said contract of sale, your affiant makes demand upon the State Bank of Long Island for the sum of FORTY THOUSAND ($40,000.00) DOLLARS pursuant to Letter of Credit No. 1147."

The Supreme Court found that the plaintiffs complied in all respects with the letter of credit and granted summary judgment in their favor. We disagree.

New York requires strict compliance with the terms of a letter of credit, rather than the more relaxed standard of substantial compliance. The documents presented against the letter of credit must comply precisely with the requirements of the letter of credit. The New York Court of Appeals thus stated the rule: "We have heretofore held that these letters of credit are to be strictly complied with, which means that the papers, documents and shipping descriptions must be followed as stated in the letter. There is no discretion in the bank or trust company to waive any of these requirements" (Anglo-South American Trust Co. v. Uhe, 261 N.Y. 150, 156-157). The letter of credit is not tied to or dependent upon the underlying commercial transaction.

In the case at bar, the plaintiffs' counsel was required under the terms of the letter of credit to present a sight draft mentioning credit number 1147, accompanied by a certification that Jacklyn "has willfully failed to close title in accordance with the provisions of [the contract]." He failed to comply precisely with the terms of the letter of credit. Therefore, State Bank properly refused to honor the letter of credit. Accordingly, we deny the plaintiffs' motion for summary judgment and grant summary judgment in State Bank's favor.

Although the court could describe the letter of credit in this case as clean in the sense that it did not require any ancillary documentation regarding the beneficiary's performance, it was not entirely clean because it did require a certification that the applicant "willfully failed" to perform. In considering the transaction that led to the litigation, consider whether it is more likely that the attorney's failure to present a draft that complied was an unfortunate oversight or instead reflected a conscious unwillingness to provide the appropriate certification. Is it really plausible that the attorney could have been so incompetent as to fail to understand how to prepare a proper draft? It is more likely (although admittedly impossible to tell from the published opinion) that the attorney acted with full knowledge of the detailed certification called for by the letter of credit but was unwilling to provide it.

When a letter of credit is completely clean, a beneficiary can draw on the letter of credit without any significant difficulty even when the beneficiary has no right to the money. And the high standard for fraud set forth in UCC §5-109 (discussed in the preceding assignment) will make it quite difficult for the issuer to avoid payment even if the beneficiary has no right to the money. The beneficiary might submit such a draft because of frustration over unrelated disagreements with the applicant or even because of completely unrelated financial difficulties. But even the simplest certification requirements can make it considerably more hazardous for a beneficiary to present an unjustified draft on a letter of credit. Among other things, a draft that includes a false statement of fact would expose the party signing the draft to a federal felony conviction under 18 U.S.C. §1344 (criminalizing any knowing scheme to obtain moneys of a federally insured financial institution by means of false representations). Thus, a requirement that a beneficiary describe the basis for the draft with some particularity (like the requirement in *Wood*) might deter beneficiaries from submitting false drafts.

It is worth noting that the form of draft submitted in *Wood* could have been factually accurate even if the beneficiary was not entitled to draw on the letter of credit. The fact that the draft was found inadequate rested entirely on the "unclean" aspects of the letter of credit. Absent those departures from "cleanness," the beneficiary in *Wood* could have succeeded in obtaining funds from the bank even if the beneficiary's draft was completely unjustified. The following case shows some of the risks of allowing the issuance of a clean letter of credit.

3M Co. v. HSBC Bank USA, N.A.
95 U.C.C. Rep. Serv. 2d 896 (S.D.N.Y. 2018)

Paul G. Gardephe, United States District Judge
In this action, Plaintiff 3M Company ("3M") seeks an injunction prohibiting Defendant HSBC Bank USA, N.A. ("HSBC") from making payment on a letter of credit (the "Amended HSBC Letter of Credit") issued in favor of Turkiye Cumhuriyeti Ziraat Bankasi ("Ziraat Bank"). 3M obtained the Amended HSBC Letter of Credit to guarantee its performance as a subcontractor on a government project in Turkey. Ziraat Bank has attempted to draw on the Amended HSBC Letter of Credit. 3M claims that the attempted draw on the Amended HSBC Letter of Credit is fraudulent and that it is entitled to injunctive relief, because payment on the Amended HSBC Letter of Credit would facilitate the alleged fraud and cause irreparable harm to 3M. [*See* UCC §5-109.]

3M has moved for a preliminary injunction to prohibit HSBC from making payment on the Amended HSBC Letter of Credit. For the reasons stated below, 3M's motion will be denied.

BACKGROUND

I.   FACTS

A.   3M's Involvement as Subcontractor in Turkey

3M is a technology company that develops, manufactures, and sells electronics. In 2012, 3M began working in a subcontracting role on a project for Posta Telgraf

Teskilati Genel Mudurlugu ("PTT"), which is a subdivision of the Turkish government. The project was for the development of the Electronic Toll Collection System
(referred to as the "HGS Project").

PTT's prime contractor on the HGS project was Vendeka Bilgi Teknolojileri Ticaret
Ltd. ("Vendeka"), a private Turkish company. PTT contracted with Vendeka for the
provision and installation of certain components to be used in the HGS Project.
Vendeka, in turn, subcontracted part of the work to Federal Signal Technologies
Group ("Federal"). In a May 23, 2011 agreement with Vendeka (the "Service
Agreement"), Federal agreed to provide certain computer hardware and software
to be used in the HGS Project.

On June 20, 2012, 3M entered into an asset purchase agreement with Federal.
As part of the transaction, Federal assigned the Service Agreement to 3M. Federal
notified Vendeka of the proposed assignment on July 9, 2012, and Vendeka subsequently agreed to the assignment. 3M worked with Vendeka on the HGS Project
from June 2012 until October 2015, when PTT removed Vendeka as primary contractor and replaced it with Tetra HGS Elektronic Sistemleri A.S. ("Tetra"). 3M then
continued to work with Tetra in a subcontracting role.

B.   HSBC Letter of Credit

1.   3M's Application for a Letter of Credit

Under the Service Agreement that 3M assumed as a result of its acquisition of
Federal, 3M was obligated to post a letter of credit in favor of Vendeka as a performance guarantee for its work on the HGS Project. Under the terms of its agreement
with PTT, Vendeka was likewise obligated to post a performance guarantee in favor
of PTT.

Section 4.2 of the Service Agreement provides:

> [Federal] will provide a performance guarantee to VENDEKA in the form of a letter
> of credit. The value of the letter of credit will be $ 1,000,000 (one million) USD. The
> letter of credit must be accepted by the banks in Turkey and valid through the war-
> ranty as outlined in [other provisions of the agreement].

The conditions for Vendeka to draw on the letter of credit are as follows:

> Subject to Article 4.11, VENDEKA is entitled to payment pursuant to the letter of
> credit issued by [Federal] only under the following circumstances:
>> i. PTT declares in writing that VENDEKA is in default in an amount certain
>> under any letter of credit, performance bond or other performance guarantee
>> that VENDEKA has issued to PTT related to the HGS Project;
>> ii. Said default of VENDEKA [rests on an event defined as a default in the
>> Agreement between VENDEKA and PTT]; and,
>> iii. Said event of default of VENDEKA . . . is in turn caused by [Federal's]
>> failure to perform one or more of its obligations as set forth in this Agreement.
>> iv. The LOC shall reference 4.2 above.

On August 29, 2012, 3M submitted an application to HSBC for a $1 million
standby letter of credit "on account of Aktif Yatirim Bankasi A.S. as advising bank

for [Vendeka] and in favor of [PTT]." 3M's application explains that the letter of credit will serve as a guarantee for Vendeka's performance under its contract with PTT, and requests that the letter of credit include as a condition for drawing on the letter of credit that "[s]uch demand . . . be supported by [a] written statement certifying that [the party demanding payment has] received a demand for payment . . . in accordance with [the] terms [of the letter of credit] and that such demand is due to Federal Signal Technologies['] responsibilities under Section 4.2 of the Service Agreement dated 23 June 2011."

3M's application further requests that another Turkish bank—Ziraat Bank, Vakifbank, or T. Halk Bankasi—serve as the counterparty for the HSBC Letter of Credit to be issued in favor of Aktif Yatirim Bankasi ("Aktif Bank"). In other words, there would be a three-bank structure. The HSBC Letter of Credit would run in favor of one of the three Turkish banks listed above, and that bank would issue a letter of credit in favor of Aktif Bank.

From the list of three Turkish banks listed in 3M's application, HSBC selected Ziraat Bank — an instrumentality of the Turkish government — as a counterparty to issue a counter standby letter of credit to Aktif.

Before finalizing the HSBC Letter of Credit, however, HSBC sought clarification from 3M as to the roles that the Turkish banks would play in the transaction:

> Please clarify the following on your Standby request to Turkey (USD 1,000,000.00) What is the role of [Ziraat] Bankasi and, Aktif Bankasi
>
> 1) HSBC Bank USA is issuing their Standby LC in favor of [Ziraat] Bankasi to issue their local guarantee to Aktif Yatirim Bankasi who will issue their local guarantee to [PTT]
>
> or
>
> 2) [Ziraat] Bankasi is just merely an advising bank.
>
> or
>
> 3) Aktif Bankasi is the advising bank (as mentioned [in] the application) or the local issuer?
>
> Please advise to revise the format.

3M responded that "the beneficiary [PTT] wanted to use Aktif Bankasi so it should be option 1." As discussed below, HSBC used the three-bank structure in issuing its letter of credit to Ziraat Bank.

2. Issuance and Amendment of the HSBC Letter of Credit

On October 30, 2012, HSBC issued the standby letter of credit that 3M had requested. The HSBC Letter of Credit is in favor of Ziraat Bank in the amount of $1 million. The HSBC Letter of Credit further provides that Ziraat Bank will issue a "guarantee" to Aktif Bank in the amount of $1 million, and that Ziraat Bank will request that Aktif Bank "issue their local guarantee in favor of [PTT] for an amount of USD1,000,000.00 (USD One Million)[.]" The HSBC Letter of Credit recites that its purpose is to guarantee Vendeka's "delivery of the toll road equipment and systems specified in Section 4.2 of the draft [S]ervice [A]greement dated 23 June 2011."

Under the terms of the HSBC Letter of Credit, Ziraat Bank could only draw upon the HSBC Letter of Credit if it made a demand

> supported by [a] written statement certifying that [it had] received a demand for payment . . . in accordance with [the] terms [of the letter of credit it had issued to

Aktif Bank] and that such demand is due to Federal Signal Technologies['] responsibilities under Section 4.2 of the Service Agreement. . . .

The HSBC Letter of Credit specifies that it will be governed and construed in accordance with the International Standby Practices (1998), International Chamber of Commerce Publications No. 590 ("ISP98"). For matters not addressed by ISP98, the HSBC Letter of Credit provides that New York law will govern.

On November 2, 2012 — three days after the HSBC Letter of Credit was issued — Ziraat Bank requested that the HSBC Letter of Credit be amended. Ziraat Bank informed HSBC that certain changes in the HSBC Letter of Credit were required before Aktif Bank would issue its local guarantee to PTT.

Ziraat Bank requested that the existing drawing conditions in the HSBC Letter of Credit be replaced with a statement that Ziraat Bank would be entitled to payment

upon receipt by [HSBC of Ziraat Bank's] first written demand via authenticated SWIFT. Such demand shall be supported by [Ziraat Bank's] written statement certifying that [Ziraat Bank] ha[s] received a demand for payment under [the letter of credit Ziraat Bank issued in favor of Aktif Bank] in accordance with [that letter of credit's] terms.

The revised drawing conditions requested by Ziraat Bank and Aktif Bank removed any reference to the conditions set forth in Section 4.2 of the Service Agreement.

On November 5, 2012, 3M approved Ziraat Bank's proposed amendment to the HSBC Letter of Credit. HSBC issued the Amended HSBC Letter of Credit that same day. The Amended HSBC Letter of Credit provides that payment to Ziraat Bank would be due once HSBC received Ziraat Bank's "written demand via authenticated SWIFT," such demand being supported by a "written statement [from Ziraat Bank] certifying that [Ziraat Bank] ha[s] received a demand for payment under [the letter of credit Ziraat Bank issued in favor of Aktif Bank] in accordance with [that letter of credit's] terms." . . .

C.   Demand on the Amended HSBC Letter of Credit

On July 18, 2016, PTT made a demand on the letter of credit posted by Aktif Bank as a performance guarantee for Vendeka. The drawdown occurred on the day Aktif Bank's letter of credit in favor of PTT was due to expire. As of July 18, 2016, Vendeka had not performed work on the HGS Project for approximately nine months, having been replaced by Tetra as the primary contractor. Moreover, Tetra had provided PTT with a substitute performance guarantee to replace the guarantee covering Vendeka. Vendeka sought the return of its performance guarantee in the months after it was removed as primary contractor.

The parties here dispute the reason for the drawdown on the Aktif Bank letter of credit: as discussed below, 3M contends that PTT's demand for payment on the Aktif Bank letter of credit is fraudulent, while HSBC contends that PTT had a legitimate basis for its demand.

According to 3M, Aktif Bank satisfied PTT's demand for payment on the Aktif Bank letter of credit, and PTT deposited the $1 million it obtained from Aktif Bank into an account it controls at Ziraat Bank. Thereafter, PTT instructed Ziraat Bank to transfer the $1 million to an account controlled by Vendeka. 3M alleges that once the money was transferred to Vendeka's account, it was "promptly seized by the creditors of Vendeka."

PTT's demand on the Aktif Bank letter of credit triggered demands on the two remaining standby letters of credit. Aktif Bank demanded payment on the letter of credit issued by Ziraat Bank, and Ziraat Bank in turn made a demand on the Amended HSBC Letter of Credit. On July 18, 2016—the same day PTT drew down on the Aktif Bank letter of credit—HSBC received a communication from Ziraat Bank requesting that its account at Bank of New York Mellon be credited in the full amount of the Amended HSBC Letter of Credit. Ziraat Bank stated that it had "received a valid demand for payment for USD 1,000,000[] from [] Aktif Yatirim Bankasi under our stan[d]by letter of credit in accordance with its terms."

HSBC contends that Ziraat Bank's demand constitutes a conforming draw on the Amended HSBC Letter of Credit issued in favor of Ziraat Bank and seeks to make payment to Ziraat Bank. 3M argues that HSBC should be enjoined from making payment due to fraud in the transaction. According to 3M, Vendeka did not default in performing its contract with PTT; 3M did not default in performing its obligations under the Service Agreement; PTT has offered conflicting explanations as to why it drew down on the Aktif Bank letter of credit, and ultimately admitted that it was not entitled to do so; and Vendeka has admitted that it had no right to the $1 million that PTT had transferred to its account. 3M also alleges that Ziraat Bank is a direct participant in the alleged fraud, because—in addition to demanding payment on the Amended HSBC Letter of Credit—it has "refused to provide to HSBC the documentation for its letter of credit in favor of Aktif Bank or the documentation of Aktif Bank's demand for payment to Ziraat Bank, all of which ha[s] been requested by 3M from HSBC."

II. PROCEDURAL HISTORY

3M commenced this action on July 27, 2016 and moved for a temporary restraining order and an order to show cause for a preliminary injunction. After a hearing held on July 27, 2016, this Court issued a temporary restraining order enjoining HSBC from making any payment on the Amended HSBC Letter of Credit . . . .

DISCUSSION

. . .

II. ANALYSIS

A. Irreparable Harm

. . .

Here, 3M has demonstrated that it will likely suffer irreparable harm if the preliminary injunction is not granted. To the extent 3M seeks to pursue its claims against Vendeka, those claims are unlikely to succeed due to Vendeka's financial condition. . . . Vendeka's creditors have frozen its bank accounts and claimed its assets, including the $1 million at issue. Accordingly, in the event that HSBC releases the $1 million that is the subject of the HSBC Letter of Credit, it appears unlikely that 3M could recover these funds from Vendeka.

It also appears unlikely that 3M could recover the $1 million from PTT and Ziraat Bank. PTT and Ziraat Bank are instrumentalities of the Turkish state. An action against either entity in the United States is likely barred by the Foreign Sovereign Immunities Act ("FSIA"). 3M further argues that political uncertainty following a failed coup attempt in Turkey in July 2016 limits the availability of judicial relief in Turkey. Political upheaval may support a showing of irreparable harm. Political turmoil in Turkey continues, along with animosity between the governments of Turkey and the United States. Accordingly, it is uncertain whether any judicial remedy would be available to 3M in Turkey, particularly as against instrumentalities of the Turkish state.

. . .

B.   Likelihood of Success on the Merits

To obtain a preliminary injunction, 3M also must demonstrate a likelihood of success on the merits. . . .

1.   Applicable Law

a.   *Letters of Credit*

"Letters of credit are commercial instruments that provide a [beneficiary] with a guaranteed means of payment from a creditworthy third party (the issuer) in lieu of relying solely on the financial status of [the applicant]." Nissho Iwai Europe v. Korea First Bank, 99 N.Y.2d 115, 119 (2002). . . .

. . . "[T]he issuing bank's obligation to honor drafts drawn on a letter of credit by the beneficiary is separate and independent from any obligation of its customer to the beneficiary under the sale of goods contract and separate as well from any obligation of the issuer to its customer under their agreement." 3Com Corp. v. Banco do Brasil, S.A., 171 F.3d 739, 741 (2d Cir. 1999) [citation and internal quotation marks omitted; alteration by court].

This independence principle is predicated upon the fundamental policy that a letter of credit would lose its commercial vitality if before honoring drafts the issuer could look beyond the terms of the credit to the underlying contractual controversy or performance between its customer and the beneficiary. [Citation and quotation marks omitted.] . . .

The "independence principle" is embodied in Article 5 of the New York Uniform Commercial Code. *See* N.Y. U.C.C. Law §5-103(d) ("Rights and obligations of an issuer to a beneficiary . . . under a letter of credit are independent of the existence, performance, or nonperformance of a contract or arrangement out of which the letter of credit arises or which underlies it, including contracts or arrangements between the issuer and the applicant and between the applicant and the beneficiary.").

In sum, when the beneficiary of a letter of credit makes a demand that conforms to the terms of that letter, the issuing bank must pay the amount due. [Citation and quotation marks omitted.] This duty to pay is absolute . . . .

b. The Fraud Exception

Fraud provides a well-established exception to the rule that banks must pay a beneficiary under a letter of credit when documents conforming on their face to the terms of the letter of credit are presented. [Citation and quotation marks omitted.] The HSBC Letter of Credit at issue here is governed by ISP98 and, for matters not addressed by ISP98, by New York law. While ISP98 makes no provision for a fraud exception, *see* ISP98 §1.05(c), such an exception has been codified under the New York Uniform Commercial Code.

Section 5-109(a) of the Code provides:

> If a presentation is made that appears on its face strictly to comply with the terms and conditions of the letter of credit, but a required document is forged or materially fraudulent, or honor of the presentation would facilitate a material fraud by the beneficiary on the issuer or applicant[,] . . . [t]he issuer, acting in good faith, may honor or dishonor the presentation. . . .

N.Y. U.C.C. Law §5-109(a)(2).

The fraud exception is limited in scope. . . .

Commentary to the New York Uniform Commercial Code explains that, in order for the fraud exception to apply, the following conditions must be met: (1) "fraud must be found either in the documents or must have been committed by the beneficiary on the issuer or applicant"; and (2) the "fraud must be 'material.'" N.Y. U.C.C. §5-109, Official Comment 1. Moreover, "[m]aterial fraud by the beneficiary occurs only when the beneficiary has no colorable right to expect honor and where there is no basis in fact to support such a right to honor." The commentary further explains that a court may enjoin payment on a letter of credit on the basis of "material fraud" where the circumstances *plainly* show that the underlying contract forbids the beneficiary to call a letter of credit; where they show that the contract deprives the beneficiary of even a *colorable* right to do so; where the contract and circumstances reveal that the beneficiary's demand for payment has absolutely no basis in fact; or where the beneficiary's conduct has so vitiated the entire transaction that the legitimate purposes of the independence of the issuer's obligation would no longer be served. N.Y. U.C.C. §5-109, Official Comment 1 [brackets, citation, and quotation marks omitted].

The Second Circuit has reiterated that the fraud defense "authorizes dishonor only where a drawdown would amount to an outright fraudulent practice by the beneficiary." *3Com Corp.*, 171 F.3d at 747 [citation and internal quotation marks omitted]. . . .

Where, as here, a bank has issued a "clean" letter of credit—that is, "one calling only for a draft and no other documents"—the commentary to the New York Uniform Commercial Code cautions that courts should be particularly "skeptical" of fraud claims. *See* N.Y. U.C.C. §5-109, Official Comment 3 ("The courts should be skeptical of claims of fraud by one who has signed a 'suicide' or clean credit and thus granted a beneficiary the right to draw by mere presentation of a draft.").

2.   Analysis

In support of its motion for a preliminary injunction, 3M argues that Ziraat Bank has committed fraud or, alternatively, PTT as the ultimate beneficiary has committed fraud that may be imputed to Ziraat Bank.

a.   *Fraud by Ziraat Bank*

As discussed above, the commentary to the New York Uniform Commercial Code makes clear that—in order for the fraud exception to apply—"fraud must be found either in the documents or must have been committed by the beneficiary on the issuer or applicant." N.Y. U.C.C. §5-109, Official Comment 1. . . . Accordingly, this Court must determine whether 3M has demonstrated a likelihood of success on its claim that Ziraat Bank's demand was fraudulent.

As an initial matter, 3M does not contend that Ziraat Bank knew that the HSBC Letter of Credit—either in its original or amended form—was fraudulent *ab initio*. While Ziraat Bank requested that the original conditions premised on Section 4.2 of the Service Agreement be deleted—representing that Aktif Bank had requested this change—there is no evidence that Ziraat Bank knew or should have known that this requested change was part of an effort to defraud 3M.

Moreover, as beneficiary under the Amended HSBC Letter of Credit, Ziraat Bank was entitled to payment from HSBC after submitting "written demand via authenticated SWIFT . . . supported by [a] written statement certifying that [Ziraat Bank had] received a demand for . . . payment" on the standby letter of credit it had issued in favor of Aktif Bank, as long as Aktif Bank's demand was "in accordance with [the] terms [of the letter of credit Ziraat Bank had issued in favor of Aktif Bank]."

On July 18, 2016, Ziraat Bank sent a SWIFT message to HSBC requesting that its account be credited in the amount of $1 million, stating that it had "received a valid demand for payment for USD 1,000,000[] from Aktif Yatirm Bankasi under our stan[d]by letter of credit in accordance with its terms." This request facially conforms to the Amended HSBC Letter of Credit's drawing conditions.

3M argues, however, that Ziraat Bank's refusal to provide documentation of Aktif Bank's demand "is circumstantial evidence of fraud." 3M does not appear to dispute that Ziraat Bank received a demand on the letter of credit it had issued in favor of Aktif Bank, however. Instead, 3M argues that Ziraat Bank has "refused to provide to HSBC the documentation for its letter of credit in favor of Aktif Bank or the documentation of Aktif Bank's demand for payment to Ziraat Bank, all of which ha[s] been requested by 3M from HSBC."

The Amended HSBC Letter of Credit does not require Ziraat Bank to provide these documents in order to draw on the letter of credit, however. To the contrary, the Amended HSBC Letter of Credit is a "clean" letter of credit that requires only a demand and a "written statement [from Ziraat Bank] certifying that [Ziraat Bank] ha[s] received a demand for payment under [the letter of credit Ziraat Bank issued in favor of Aktif Bank] in accordance with [that letter of credit's] terms." HSBC determined that Ziraat Bank's demand conformed to the requirements of the Amended HSBC Letter of Credit, and under the independence principle, had an obligation to make payment.

The Court concludes that 3M has not demonstrated a likelihood of success on its claim that Ziraat Bank engaged in fraud in connection with the Amended HSBC Letter of Credit.

b. Fraud Imputed to Ziraat Bank

3M contends that fraud committed by PTT is sufficient to justify injunctive relief. 3M argues that where, as here, there are back-to-back letters of credit, and where "an intermediary bank beneficiary and an ultimate beneficiary [] are both part of the same government," fraud by the ultimate beneficiary can be imputed to the intermediary bank beneficiary.

According to 3M, PTT fraudulently drew on Aktif Bank's letter of credit long after Vendeka had (1) ceased working on the HGS Project; and (2) performed the obligations meant to be secured by the Aktif Bank letter of credit. In support of these allegations, 3M has submitted, *inter alia*, a declaration showing that a 3M employee was told by a PTT representative on August 6, 2016, that PTT "did not have a basis" to draw on the Aktif Bank letter of credit and that the $1 million should be returned to Aktif Bank.

3M's own submissions present a plausible, non-fraudulent explanation for PTT's draw, however. Pursuant to its contract with PTT, Vendeka agreed to post a performance guarantee in favor of PTT. Section 11.3.1 of the Vendeka-PTT contract provides that Vendeka will be entitled to the return of the performance bond "[u]pon the fulfillment of the contract in accordance with the provisions of the Agreement and tender documents, [and after] determining that [Vendeka] has no debts against the Administration . . . and [has] obtain[ed] [a] clearance certificate from [the] Social Security Institution."

In a June 22, 2016 letter to Vendeka, PTT explains that, under Turkish law,

> [i]n order to ensure the consummation of transactions without allowing performance bonds to expire because of delayed issuance of "no social security tax debt" statements by the Social Security Institution, the contractor's failure to submit a "no lien affidavit" obtained from the Social Security Institution . . . will result in the cashing of the performance bonds and [] credit[ing] . . . the contractor's debts and the return of the remainder, if any, back to the contractor. . . .

Because of the length of time required to obtain a "no lien affidavit," PTT asks Vendeka—in the same letter—to obtain an extension on the Aktif Bank letter of credit to avoid a drawdown. PTT subsequently justified its July 18, 2016 drawdown on the Aktif Bank letter of credit based on the fact that Vendeka had "declin[ed] [PTT's] request for [a] time extension of the guarantee letter." And—in accordance with the representations set forth in its June 22, 2016 letter—PTT returned the proceeds of the performance guarantee to Vendeka by wire transfer from Ziraat Bank on August 5, 2016. 3M has not responded to HSBC's argument on this point . . . .

3M's agreement to Ziraat Bank's proposed amendment to the HSBC Letter of Credit—which removed the reference to Section 4.2 of the Service Agreement—left it vulnerable, because the letter of credit it was providing was no longer tethered to its own performance. Under the Service Agreement with Vendeka, 3M was only obligated to post a letter of credit in favor of Vendeka to guarantee 3M's performance as subcontractor. But by consenting to the amendment of the HSBC Letter of Credit, 3M permitted the reference to these drawing conditions—tied to 3M's own performance in connection with the HGS Project—to be eliminated. 3M thereby left itself unprotected with respect to a drawdown by PTT on the Aktif Bank letter of credit, which in turn provoked Ziraat Bank's drawdown on the Amended HSBC Letter of Credit.

The Court concludes that 3M has not demonstrated a likelihood of success on its claim that PTT's draw on the Aktif Bank letter of credit was fraudulent. Material fraud under the New York Uniform Commercial Code exists where a beneficiary has "absolutely no basis in fact" to demand payment or where the circumstances "'plainly' show that the underlying contract forbids the beneficiary to call a letter of credit." *See* N.Y. U.C.C. §5-109, Official Comment 1. As discussed above, a basis in fact exists which 3M has not addressed, much less rebutted. Moreover, neither PTT nor Ziraat Bank kept the $1 million drawn on the Aktif Bank letter of credit. Under these circumstances, this Court is not persuaded that any fraud by PTT in drawing down on the Aktif Bank letter of credit can be imputed to Ziraat Bank.

. . .

Because 3M has not shown a likelihood of success on its claims of fraud, its application for a preliminary injunction must be denied.

B.   Problems in Standby Letter-of-Credit Transactions

Standby letter-of-credit transactions can raise many of the same issues as commercial letter-of-credit transactions, but the differences in context cause certain issues to be more important for standby letters of credit than they are for commercial letters of credit. For example, the likelihood that a draft will be presented against a standby letter of credit only when the beneficiary and applicant are at odds about the applicant's performance enhances the importance of the rules that obligate the issuer to pay when the applicant's performance is in doubt. The issuer's obligation to pay absent material fraud covered by UCC §5-109 leads to frequent litigation over application of the "material fraud" standard in the standby context. The nature of that standard, however, is no different here than it is in the commercial letter-of-credit context, discussed in Assignment 18.

In some areas, however, standby letters of credit present issues qualitatively different from the issues presented by commercial letters of credit. Generally, those issues arise from the difficulty of accommodating the form that the parties have selected (a letter of credit) to the substance of the underlying transaction (a guaranty). The remainder of this assignment discusses two of the most troubling problems: bankruptcy of the applicant and subrogation rights of the issuer.

1. Bankruptcy of the Applicant

The creditor that receives a standby letter of credit must take the possibility of bankruptcy by the applicant just as seriously as the creditor that receives a conventional guaranty must take the risk of bankruptcy by the principal obligor. As Assignment 15 explains, bankruptcy courts in recent years have shown some willingness to rely on bankruptcy of an obligor to justify deferring a creditor's right to pursue a guarantor. Accordingly, it should come as no surprise that in the early years of the Bankruptcy Code some bankruptcy judges concluded that they had a similar power to enjoin a creditor from collecting on a standby letter of credit after the applicant (the principal obligor) had filed for bankruptcy.

Those concerns were crystallized by the notorious decision in Twist Cap, Inc. v. Southeast Bank (In re Twist Cap, Inc.), 1 B.R. 284 (Bankr. M.D. Fla. 1979), handed down shortly after the 1978 enactment of the Bankruptcy Code. That case involved a typical standby letter-of-credit transaction. Two parties selling goods to Twist Cap obtained standby letters of credit to ensure that they would be paid for goods that they regularly shipped to Twist Cap. When Twist Cap filed for bankruptcy, the sellers predictably attempted to obtain payment from the still-solvent bank that had issued the letters of credit. The bankruptcy court enjoined the sellers from drawing on the letter of credit, vitiating the protection the sellers thought that they had obtained when they received the letters of credit.

Given the ready analogy of the standby letter of credit to a guaranty, the result in *Twist Cap* should not seem terribly surprising. The decision was, however, widely condemned in the financial and scholarly communities. The dominant perspective contended that the decision ignored the strong tradition in merchant circles that the bank's obligation on a letter of credit is entirely independent of the underlying obligation. As Douglas Baird states: "Parties that bargain for a letter of credit assume that regardless of war, revolution, or other catastrophe, the letter will be honored when the documents specified in the letter are presented." Douglas G. Baird, *Standby Letters of Credit in Bankruptcy*, 49 U. Chi. L. Rev. 130, 145 (1982). The willingness of the *Twist Cap* court to enjoin the sellers' attempts to draw on the letters of credit defied that tradition.

Also, the difference between this situation and the conventional guaranty situation (discussed in the preceding assignments) undermines the result in *Twist Cap*. As you should recall, in the conventional guaranty context, the intertwined relationship between a guarantor and a borrower is the principal justification for allowing the insolvency of a borrower to prevent a creditor from collecting on a relational guaranty. In the standby context, the creditor's decision to insist on an enhancement of the borrower's credit from a third-party bank makes it difficult to justify the rule in *Twist Cap*. Among other things, it ordinarily will be impossible to suggest that obtaining payment on the standby letter of credit will undermine the solvency of the borrower or its principal because the issuer of the letter of credit (ordinarily) is an independent party.

Thus, the principal legal argument available to debtors is that a draw on the letter of credit acts against "property of the debtor's estate." Using that approach, debtors argue that a draw on the letter of credit violates the automatic stay that bankruptcy imposes on all actions against property of a debtor's estate. 11 U.S.C. §362(a)(3). As the following decision suggests, those arguments have not been well received in recent years.

In re Ocana

151 B.R. 670 (S.D.N.Y. 1993)

LEVAL, District Judge.

[Latino Americano de Reaseguros, S.A. ("LARSA") entered into a series of reinsurance agreements pursuant to which it agreed to pay money to Hannover if Hannover experienced heavy losses on certain insurance policies. A Panamanian bank named Banco Cafetero issued a standby letter of credit backing up LARSA's obligations. In 1990, LARSA filed for statutory reorganization, a Panamanian procedure roughly equivalent to bankruptcy. Hannover brought suit against Banco Cafetero in the United States District Court for the Central District of California, arguing that Banco Cafetero was liable to Hannover on the letter of credit because LARSA had failed to pay Hannover about $1,700,000 that LARSA owed Hannover on the reinsurance agreements.

LARSA responded by filing a proceeding in the bankruptcy court in the United States District Court for the Southern District of New York, seeking to enjoin Hannover from collecting on Banco Cafetero's letter of credit. The bankruptcy court issued a stay of Hannover's action. Hannover appealed to the district court.]

The stay of Hannover's action against Banco Cafetero is based on an incorrect theory of law. Hannover's action against Banco Cafetero is not brought against the debtor (LARSA) nor against the debtor's property. The letter of credit is an irrevocable and unconditional promise on the part of Banco Cafetero to pay the beneficiary upon the presentation of specified documents. The beneficiary's action is against the bank, not the account party, and the money to be used in making the payment is the bank's money. The fact that the issuing bank holds collateral of the debtor to secure the bank's extension of credit to LARSA has no bearing on the beneficiary's right to receive payment from the bank on the bank's contract. . . .

Moreover, allowing the debtor's bankruptcy to interfere with payment on clean, irrevocable letters of credit would vitiate the purpose of such letters. Letters of credit are an ingenious device of international commerce. By interposing the bank between buyer and seller, as an independent party, they permit a seller to ship merchandise abroad with confidence that payment is guaranteed by a bank; and permit the purchaser to pay with assurance that the payment will not be released to the seller unless the seller delivers proof of the shipment of the goods. One of the principal purposes of letters of credit is to relieve the seller-shipper from worry as to the purchaser's solvency, for the seller looks not to the purchaser, but to the bank, for payment. If the payment of letters of credit could be stayed, as here, merely because the account party had obtained the protection of a bankruptcy court, this would do incalculable harm to international commerce. Letters of credit would no longer reliably perform the function they were designed for.

———————

Judge Leval's reference to the collateral held by Banco Cafetero points to the true significance of the controversy. If the seller cannot collect on the letter of credit, the seller ordinarily will have an unsecured claim for payment of the purchase price for the goods that it has sold to the debtor. Unless the seller can establish some Article 2 right of reclamation, that claim will not succeed in the bankruptcy, where all or almost all of the debtor's assets usually are distributed to pay secured creditors and the administrative costs of the bankruptcy. The seller's unsecured claim is limited to a pro rata share of any remaining assets, which will bring little or nothing in most cases. On the other hand, if the seller does collect on the letter of credit, the issuing bank then will have a claim for reimbursement. As in *Ocana*, the issuing bank frequently will have collateral that secures its claim for reimbursement. That collateral will enable the issuing bank to obtain full payment on its claim, even though the seller's pre-letter-of-credit claim would have received marginal payment at best. Thus, the decision in *Ocana* essentially transforms an unsecured claim with little chance of payment into a secured claim that is highly likely to be paid. As a practical matter, that transformation redistributes money away from creditors with general unsecured claims (by removing from the estate the funds that are used to pay the bank that issued the letter of credit). That redistribution does not directly benefit the party paid on the letter of credit, but by ensuring that the bank that pays the claim is paid in full, it certainly enhances the willingness of banks to pay such claims.

In the end, those rules largely insulate the beneficiary from the risk of insolvency by the applicant. They do not, however, protect the beneficiary from the risk of insolvency by the issuer. Indeed, upon the insolvency of a bank that has issued a standby letter of credit, the beneficiary's claim on the letter of credit is not even entitled to a payment from the Federal Deposit Insurance Corporation's insurance fund. Rather, the beneficiary loses its claim entirely upon the failure of the bank that issued the letter of credit. See FDIC v. Philadelphia Gear Corp., 476 U.S. 426, 430-440 (1986) (holding that a beneficiary's claim on a standby letter of credit is not a "deposit" entitled to recovery from the FDIC insurance fund).

2. The Issuer's Right of Subrogation

Another situation that frequently leads to litigation arises when an issuer that has honored a draft on a standby letter of credit attempts to use subrogation to recover the funds that it has paid on that draft. As explained in the preceding chapter, a guarantor that pays a creditor on behalf of the obligor ordinarily is subrogated to any rights that the creditor had against the obligor. Treatment of the standby letter of credit as analogous to a guaranty would recognize a right of subrogation for the issuer. Notwithstanding that functional similarity, many courts have focused on technicalities of the letter-of-credit form to deny that right of subrogation. The following case provides a cogent explanation of the problem.

CCF, Inc. v. First National Bank (In re Slamans)

175 B.R. 762 (N.D. Okla. 1994)

ELLISON, Chief Judge.

Debtor Thomas William Slamans operated gas stations. On December 4, 1990, Slamans gave First Capital Corporation a revolving credit note for $750,000. Appellant CCF, Inc. ("CCF") is the successor-in-interest to First Capital Corporation.

On December 20, 1994, Slamans entered into a distribution agreement with Sun Company ("Sun") for the purchase of oil products. Under the agreement, Slamans purchased the oil products from Sun on credit and then sold the products either for cash or by credit-card purchase. [When Slamans sold the products by means of a credit card, he sent the proceeds of the credit-card sales directly to Sun, without regard to the current status of his account. If Sun determined that Slamans's account was current, Sun returned the appropriate portion of those proceeds to Slamans.] The agreement [also] required Slamans to obtain a letter of credit.

On February 6, 1991, Appellee First National Bank [FNB] issued a standby letter of credit to Slamans in favor of Sun. The letter provided that FNB agreed to pay Sun up to $200,000 if Slamans defaulted under the distributor agreement. The letter of credit was secured by a note, mortgage and security agreement covering Slamans's accounts receivable [that is, sums that Slamans's customers owed to him].

On February 28, 1992, Slamans filed bankruptcy. On March 9, 1992, Sun—because Slamans had not paid [it]—requested $192,433.15 from FNB pursuant to the letter of credit. On March 11, 1992, FNB paid Sun the money. Also, at that time, FNB demanded the $111,053.41 in proceeds from credit card sales in Sun's possession. [Sun held those proceeds pursuant to the distribution agreement discussed above. If it had not been paid on the letter of credit, Sun could have asserted a right in Slamans's bankruptcy proceeding to keep those funds pursuant to the distribution agreement. In any event,] Sun did not turn the money over to FNB; instead it filed an interpleader complaint with the Bankruptcy Court. . . .

The dispute itself is straight-forward: Should FNB have received the $111,053.41 from Sun pursuant to 11 U.S.C. §509 of the Bankruptcy Code? Section 509 states: "Except as provided in subsection (b) or (c) of this section, an entity that is liable with the debtor on, or that has secured, a claim of a creditor against the debtor, and that pays such claim, is subrogated to the rights of such creditor to the extent of such payment."

The initial issue is whether FNB was "liable with" Slamans on the debt to Sun. Two divergent lines of authority address this issue. The first line, and what appears to be the majority position, is that only a party that is "secondarily liable," such as a guarantor, can be "liable with" the debtor under §509. Issuers of letters of credit, such as FNB, do not fit into the Section 509 "liable with" language because they are primarily liable, according to this reasoning. The distinctions between a guarantor and letters of credit issuers are based, in part, on the legal characteristics of each. One court explains:

> The key distinction between letters of credit and guarantees is that the issuer's obligation under a letter of credit is primary whereas a guarantor's obligation is secondary—the guarantor is only obligated to pay if the principal defaults on the debt the principal owes. In contrast, while the issuing bank in the letter of credit situation may be secondarily liable in the temporal sense, since its obligation to pay does not arise until after its customer fails to satisfy some obligation, it is satisfying its own absolute and primary obligation to make payment rather than satisfying an obligation of its customer. Having paid its own debt, as it has contractually undertaken to do, the issuer cannot then step into the shoes of the creditor to seek subrogation, reimbursement or contribution. . . . The only exception would be where the parties reach an agreement. Tudor Development Group, Inc. v. United States Fidelity & Guaranty Co., 968 F.2d 357, 362 (3d Cir. 1992).

Tudor is a non-bankruptcy case, but several bankruptcy courts have applied the same reasoning. These courts, in effect, emphasize that a letter of credit issuer has a separate legal obligation (and remedy) than the debtor. This means they have a primary liability—not a secondary one. Guarantors, on the other hand, are only secondarily liable and, as a result, can obtain Section 509 subrogation. In re Kaiser Steel Corporation, 89 B.R. 150 (Bankr. D. Colo. 1988).

A second group of cases spurn the foregoing reasoning. They conclude that, for the purposes of Section 509 subrogation, issuers of letters of credit and guarantors should both be eligible for subrogation. For example, [one] court states: "While a letter of credit may require conformity with certain obligations and formalities which are not required of a guarantee . . ., precluding the assertion of subrogation rights to issuers of standby letters of credit while allowing guarantors to assert them would be no more than an exercise in honoring form over substance." [In re Minnesota Kicks, 48 B.R. 93, 104 (Bankr. D. Minn. 1985).] . . .

[T]he undersigned rejects a rule that, in effect, states that, absent an agreement by the parties, an issuer of a letter of credit can never be eligible for Section 509 subrogation. . . .

Slamans obtained a letter of credit, at Sun's request, from FNB. Slamans filed bankruptcy, owing Sun $192,433.15. Sun drew upon the letter of credit for that amount, which FNB paid. FNB then requested that Sun turn over $111,053.41, which was owed to Slamans. The Bankruptcy Court subrogated FNB into Slamans' shoes, awarding the $111,053.41 under Section 509. That ruling was both equitably and legally well-founded, and, as a result, the Bankruptcy Court's decision is AFFIRMED.

The conclusion of the *Slamans* court did not survive an appeal to the United States Court of Appeals for the Tenth Circuit. Still, the *Slamans* rule is the rule reflected in current law. The revised version of Article 5 states in UCC §5-117(a) that an issuer of a letter of credit "is subrogated to the rights of the beneficiary to the same extent as if the issuer were a secondary obligor of the underlying obligation owed to the beneficiary." Comment 1 goes so far as to state that the statute is designed (like *Slamans*) to adopt the reasoning of Judge Becker's dissent from the decision of the Third Circuit in *Tudor Development*. Accordingly, the widespread adoption of the revised Article 5 makes it clear that issuers of letters of credit are entitled to subrogation under Article 5 of the UCC.

In light of that result, it would be appropriate for bankruptcy courts to follow the same rule in bankruptcy. Such a holding would rest on the idea that banks issuing letters of credit on behalf of applicants that subsequently become bankrupt are "liable with" the applicant on the underlying obligation for purposes of 11 U.S.C. §509(a). Accordingly, they should be entitled to use Section 509(a) to assert subrogation in the bankruptcy to the same extent that they would be entitled to assert subrogation under Article 5 outside the bankruptcy.

Just to be clear, the basic problem in *Tudor Development* only scratches the surface of the complex suretyship problems that arise in standby transactions. Consider the following case as a cautionary tale.

CRM Collateral II, Inc. v. Tri-County Metropolitan Transportation District

669 F.3d 963 (9th Cir. 2012)

Before WALLACE TASHIMA, M. MARGARET MCKEOWN, and RICHARD C. TALLMAN, Circuit Judges.

TALLMAN, Circuit Judge:

Appellant Tri-County Metropolitan Transportation District of Oregon ("TriMet") provides bus, light rail, and commuter rail service in the Portland metropolitan area. TriMet contracted with Colorado Railcar Manufacturing, LLC ("Colorado Railcar") for the manufacture of light railcars. The contract ("Railcar Contract") required Colorado Railcar to secure a $3 million standby letter of credit, which Colorado Railcar arranged through CRM Collateral II, Inc. ("Collateral II"), a bankruptcy remote entity. TriMet certified Collateral II's default and drew on the Letter of Credit when Colorado Railcar defaulted. We consider whether Collateral II was a surety to Colorado Railcar, entitled to the defense of discharge. We hold that it was not.

. . .

I

In November 2005, TriMet entered into the Railcar Contract with Colorado Railcar to build and deliver three light railcars and one trailer for TriMet's use in connection with its new Westside Express Service between Beaverton and Wilsonville, Oregon. The final price for the railcars and trailer was $17,299,135. The Contract required Colorado Railcar to maintain an irrevocable standby letter of credit in the amount of $3 million from the time Colorado Railcar issued notification that manufacture would begin to the final delivery of the railcars and trailer to TriMet. The parties had considered other methods of securing the contract, such as a performance bond. But, due to Colorado Railcar's credit history and financial health, TriMet agreed that a letter of credit would be an attainable and less expensive form of security.

Collateral II was formed, in part, for the purpose of fulfilling Colorado Railcar's letter of credit obligation under the contract. Thomas Rader, CEO of Colorado Railcar, was named one of Collateral II's corporate directors along with Scott State, who was also Collateral II's sole corporate officer, serving as both President and Treasurer. John Thompson, Colorado Railcar's CFO, was Collateral II's registered agent at the time of incorporation.

Colorado Railcar, Collateral II, and certain investors entered into an Investment Agreement whereby Colorado Railcar provided quarterly interest payments to the investors for pledging collateral as security for the purchase of a letter of credit in satisfaction of Colorado Railcar's obligation to provide the standby letter of credit. As a result, Collateral II purchased Irrevocable Standby Letter of Credit No. 312084 ("Letter of Credit") from KeyBank for the benefit of TriMet. The Letter of Credit provided that $3 million was available to TriMet upon its presentation of a sight draft accompanied by a signed and dated document "stating the amount requested and containing a statement that reads as follows: 'The undersigned Officer or Director of TriMet hereby certifies that the Applicant is in default under Contract . . . .'" The Letter of Credit was initially set to expire on November 15, 2007.

TriMet first learned that Collateral II, and not Colorado Railcar, was the applicant on the Letter of Credit several months after arrangements were finalized with KeyBank. [To solve the problem that the draft required a statement that Collateral II was in default on a contract to which it was not a party, the parties modified the Railcar Contract (in a document referred to as Modification No. 1) to make Collateral II a party] for the sole purpose of equating a default by Colorado Railcar under the Railcar Contract to a default by Collateral II for purposes of drawing on the Letter of Credit. The modification was clear that Collateral II had no rights under the Railcar Contract, nor did it undertake any new obligations.

In January 2008, TriMet and Colorado Railcar entered into a separate Project Monitoring Agreement ("PMA"), which modified their rights and obligations under the Railcar Contract in an effort to address Colorado Railcar's continuing financial problems. TriMet feared that Colorado Railcar's financial woes would jeopardize its ability to complete the light railcars. After evaluating the feasibility of engaging substitute contractors, TriMet determined that it would be less costly and would reduce delay to financially support Colorado Railcar to the extent needed to ensure completion of the railcars. Thus, under the PMA, TriMet was to make "special contract payments" to or on behalf of Colorado Railcar, including payments not previously provided for under the Railcar Contract. Under the PMA, TriMet was authorized to draw on the Letter of Credit to fund these payments or to compensate itself for any special payments that Colorado Railcar failed to repay. . . .

Colorado Railcar and TriMet did not inform Collateral II of these negotiations nor obtain its consent to the PMA. . . .

. . .

Between the date of the amended PMA and the completed manufacture of the railcars and trailer in October 2008, TriMet advanced more than $5.5 million in special contract payments to Colorado Railcar. On October 22, 2008, TriMet attempted to draw on the Letter of Credit to reimburse itself for $3 million of those special contract payments. In response, Collateral II filed an action against TriMet and KeyBank in the District of Oregon (the "lead action"), [alleging, among other things, that TriMet had defrauded Collateral II and seeking to enjoin KeyBank from honoring the draw. The district court at first granted a temporary injunction, but eventually permitted the draw.]

In the proceedings that followed, the district court held that Modification No. 1 created a suretyship between the parties whereby Collateral II became secondarily liable for Colorado Railcar's obligations under the Railcar Contract. Given Collateral II's status as a surety, the court concluded as a matter of law that the surety defense of discharge was available because the PMA had materially increased the risk Collateral II faced as a surety without Collateral II's consent. On these grounds the court granted summary judgment in Collateral II's favor on TriMet's counterclaim for a declaration that Collateral II was in default on the Railcar Contract. [Eventually, the district court held that the same suretyship defense excused its obligation to reimburse KeyBank for the payment it made on the letter of credit.]

II

. . .

A

TriMet contends that Collateral II should not have been characterized as a surety, and thus was not entitled to the surety defense of discharge. Review of the law of letters of credit and the structure of letter of credit transactions is necessary for proper evaluation of the parties' relationships.

[UCC §5-102(a)] defines "letter of credit" as a "definite undertaking . . . by an issuer to a beneficiary at the request or for the account of an applicant or, in the case of a financial institution, to itself or for its own account, to honor a documentary presentation by payment or delivery of an item of value." An applicant is the "person at whose request or for whose account the letter of credit is issued[,]" sometimes also referred to as the customer. The issuer is the bank or other party that issues the letter of credit. The beneficiary is the party entitled to payment on the letter of credit upon proper presentation of documents. In our case, Collateral II is the applicant, KeyBank the issuer, and TriMet the beneficiary.

At issue here is a standby letter of credit. Unlike a traditional commercial letter of credit, which is commonly used in commercial sales to reduce the risk of nonpayment for goods, standby letters of credit are used in the non-sale setting and serve to reduce the risk of nonperformance under a performance contract. To draw on the letter, the beneficiary is typically required to produce documents certifying the applicant has defaulted on its underlying obligation to the beneficiary. The letter of credit transaction typically involves two contracts and the letter of credit. First, there is the underlying contract for services or goods between the applicant and beneficiary. Second, there is a reimbursement contract between the applicant and issuer, requiring the applicant to reimburse the issuer for any payments made on the letter of credit. Lastly, there is the issuer's obligation under the letter of credit itself.

Unlike the typical letter of credit transaction, in this transaction there was no underlying contract for goods or services between Collateral II and TriMet. Instead the performance contract was between Colorado Railcar and TriMet. Because Colorado Railcar fulfilled its obligation to secure a letter of credit by employing Collateral II as applicant, Collateral II and TriMet did not initially contract with each other. Instead, each separately contracted with a third-party: Colorado Railcar. This fourth relationship is the basis for Collateral II's claim that it should be characterized as a surety.

We first note that a standby letter of credit itself does not create a suretyship. A standby letter of credit functions somewhat like a guaranty, given that it is the applicant's default that triggers the beneficiary's ability to draw on the letter of credit. James J. White & Robert S. Summers, Uniform Commercial Code §26-1 (5th ed. 2002). "But a true letter of credit arrangement is not a guaranty." *Id.* at §26-2. First and foremost, the issuer's obligation to pay upon presentation of conforming documents is a primary obligation, not a secondary one. Although default may trigger a draw, it is only upon proper certification of the applicant's default that the issuer is obligated to pay.

Furthermore, the independence principle controls the relationship between the issuer and beneficiary. Under this principle, the issuer must pay upon proper certification — with limited exceptions for fraud — even if the beneficiary has breached the underlying contract with the applicant. . . . Given these distinct features of the letter of credit, it is widely recognized that the issuer is not a guarantor.

Here, however, it is not the issuer that is claiming surety status. It is the applicant — Collateral II. Oregon courts look to the *Restatement (Third) of Suretyship & Guaranty* as authoritative on suretyship law. The *Restatement* states:

> (1) [A] secondary obligor has suretyship status whenever:
> (a) pursuant to contract (the "secondary obligation"), an obligee has recourse against a person (the "secondary obligor") or that person's property with respect to the obligation (the "underlying obligation") of another person (the "principal obligor") to that obligee; and
> (b) to the extent that the underlying obligation or the secondary obligation is performed the obligee is not entitled to performance of the other obligation; and
> (c) as between the principal obligor and the secondary obligor, it is the principal obligor who ought to perform the underlying obligation or bear the cost of performance.
>
> (2) An obligee has recourse against a secondary obligor . . . whenever:
> . . .
> (b) pursuant to the secondary obligation, either:
> ([i]) the secondary obligor has a duty to effect, in whole or in part, the performance that is the subject of the underlying obligation; or
> (ii) the obligee has recourse against the secondary obligor or its property in the event of the failure of the principal obligor to perform the underlying obligation[.]

Rest. (Third) Sur. & Guar. §1.

. . .

[T]he district court erred when it stated that Collateral II "arguably became a surety" when KeyBank issued the Letter of Credit. As we outlined above and as the district court correctly noted, the law on letters of credit is clear that simply entering into a letter of credit transaction does not a suretyship make. The hallmark of the surety is a secondary obligation. When we examine the three relationships in a letter of credit transaction there is typically no secondary liability. Instead, the applicant and beneficiary owe each other primary obligations on the underlying contract, the issuer is primarily obligated to honor the beneficiary's proper draw request, and the applicant is primarily obligated to reimburse the issuer for any payments made to the beneficiary. Under normal circumstances, and as contemplated by the Railcar Contract, Colorado Railcar would be the applicant and TriMet the beneficiary. Despite the fact that this transaction does not mirror normal circumstances, Collateral II's status as the applicant (on behalf of Colorado Railcar) on the Letter of Credit does not make it a surety because it has undertaken no secondary obligation in connection with the transaction. Agreeing to purchase the Letter of Credit for Colorado Railcar only resulted in a primary liability to Colorado Railcar, just as purchasing the Letter only made Collateral II primarily liable for reimbursing KeyBank if it honored a draw on the Letter.

. . .

. . . Contrary to the district court's conclusion, Modification No. 1 does not indisputably create a surety relationship.

When we look to the definition of a surety, what is lacking here is recourse. Although Collateral II purchased the Letter of Credit and its investors pledged their property as security, these obligations run strictly to KeyBank. Collateral II owes no duty to TriMet under either the Letter of Credit or Modification No. 1. The only right those instruments give TriMet is the right to draw on the Letter of Credit provided by KeyBank; they do not give TriMet recourse against Collateral II for Colorado Railcar's default on its primary obligations for TriMet's loss in excess of the $3 million stipulated in the Letter of Credit.

Being bound to the principal obligation is the defining feature of a surety:

> Although the relation of principal and surety generally springs from some agreement by which one person becomes personally bound for the debt of another, it may likewise grow out of a transaction whereby a person's property becomes security for payment of a debt or the performance of an act by another . . . . Conversely, the parties to an instrument given as collateral security for the payment of a debt due by others are not subject to the law which governs sureties since they are not bound for the principal debt and their engagement is independent of it.

74 Am. Jur. 2d *Suretyship* §10 (2005).

Modification No. 1 could not have created a surety relationship because it does not bind Collateral II to the primary obligations of Colorado Railcar. If, for example, the Letter of Credit . . . had expired in November 2007, TriMet would have had no right to pursue Collateral II for the $3 million in the later event of Colorado Railcar's default on the Railcar Contract. Nothing in Modification No. 1 changes this. Collateral II's participation was independent of Colorado Railcar's duties under the Railcar Contract because it had no additional duties to perform or fulfill if Colorado Railcar failed to perform its primary obligation. Simply purchasing a letter of credit for security as part of another's performance contract does not raise the purchaser to the status of surety, entitled to assert attendant defenses.

This modification was entered into for the purpose of allowing "TriMet to draw on the [letter of credit] in the event of default under [the Railcar] contract by [Colorado Railcar]." It specifically limited Collateral II's participation to define the event triggering the right to draw and did not grant any rights or impose any additional obligations on Collateral II. Modification No. 1 did nothing more than give effect to the original intent of TriMet and Colorado Railcar by clarifying the terms of default under the Letter of Credit—Collateral II did not undertake any new obligation to which it was not already bound before Modification No. 1 was executed. With or without Modification No. 1, Collateral II was primarily obligated to reimburse KeyBank for any payments made honoring a proper draw on the Letter of Credit.

The fact that, prior to Modification No. 1, the Letter of Credit required TriMet to certify Collateral II's default without reference to Colorado Railcar does not change this result. A disagreement over whether Collateral II could or could not have actually been in default would not have relieved KeyBank of its duty to pay TriMet because disagreements between the applicant and the beneficiary do not prevent the issuer from honoring a proper draw in the absence of fraud [UCC §5-103(d)] ("Rights and obligations of an issuer to a beneficiary . . . under a letter of credit are independent of the existence, performance or nonperformance of a contract or arrangement out of which the letter of credit arises or which underlies it, including contracts or arrangements between the . . . applicant and the beneficiary."). Thus, even without Modification No. 1, upon proper certification of Collateral II's default, KeyBank was obligated to honor the draw—the very hallmark and beauty of letters of credit. *See* Dolan, [The Law of Letters of Credit] ¶¶1.05, 3.06 [(4th ed. 2007)] (noting the "pay-now-argue-later" nature of standby letters of credit and the relative ease and cheapness of obtaining them).

Undoubtedly, without Modification No. 1 litigation regarding the default term could have—and likely would have—ensued, given that Collateral II was not a party to the original Railcar Contract. *See* White & Summers, *supra*, at §26-7 (noting that once the issuer has honored the draw, the independence principle no longer controls and it would be acceptable for the applicant to sue the beneficiary for violations of any underlying agreement). To give effect to the original intent of the parties, and presumably in an attempt to avoid delay and litigation if a draw was necessary, Modification No. 1 simply clarified that—for purposes of certifying Collateral II's default under the terms of the Letter of Credit—Collateral II would be in default should Colorado Railcar fail to meet its obligations. This does not create a secondary obligation to TriMet or to KeyBank. Before and after Modification No. 1, Collateral II was primarily liable on the reimbursement contract and nothing in the language of Modification No. 1 changed that obligation.

B

Because the district court incorrectly concluded that Collateral II was a surety, Collateral II was erroneously permitted to assert the defense of discharge. . . .

Problem Set 19

19.1.   Archie Moon (a book-dealer friend that you've been representing for some time) sends you an e-mail one morning that includes a proposed agreement with one of his major suppliers. The agreement states that Archie "at all times will maintain a clean standby letter of credit from a bank reasonably satisfactory to Seller." Archie has called his banker at Safety Central Bank, who has agreed to issue a letter of credit in the appropriate amount if Archie allows the bank to maintain possession of some certificates of deposit that Archie owns. Archie has no problem with that arrangement and wants to know if you have any concerns about the letter-of-credit provision quoted above.

19.2.   Bulstrode issues a standby letter of credit related to an issue of bonds by General Motors. The letter of credit incorporates ISP98 by reference. The letter of credit conditions payment on presentation of a draft described as follows: "The draft must include the exact wording that follows: 'Jeneral Motors has failed to make a payment on its Series C 20-year bonds maturing January 1, 2006.'"

General Motors defaults on the bonds. Subsequently, the beneficiary of the letter of credit submits a draft that states: "General Motors has failed to make a payment on its Series C 20-year bonds maturing January 1, 2006." Is Bulstrode obligated to pay? UCC §5-108(a) & comment 1; UCP art. 14; ISP98 Rule 4.09.

19.3.   Jodi Kay is working on a possible construction loan to Chancellor Investments, a long-time developer in her area that has suffered some hard times recently. Because Jodi has never done any business with Chancellor before, she is highly motivated to get the transaction for her bank. Jodi's bank ordinarily insists on a personal guaranty for at least one-quarter of the construction-loan amount, even for the most attractive projects from the most reputable developers.

Jodi's concern is that the principal of Chancellor Investments (Olive Chancellor) has suffered some financial reverses during the last several years that make Jodi doubt Olive's ability to cover the $500,000 guaranty that would be standard in this transaction. When Jodi raised that concern with Olive, Olive responded that she understood Jodi's concern. Olive asked if Jodi would be willing, in lieu of the guaranty, to accept a $500,000 letter of credit from SecondCity Bank, Chancellor's principal bank. Olive e-mailed SecondCity's letter-of-credit form to Jodi, who says it is identical to a form that you have approved in the past. Jodi is completely satisfied with SecondCity's financial strength. Is there any other reason that you can see why Jodi should be concerned about accepting a standby letter of credit as a substitute for a guaranty?

19.4.   Jodi followed your advice in Problem 19.3, and the loan transaction went forward without incident. Several months later, however, you read in the newspaper one morning of a bankruptcy filing by Chancellor Investments. Accordingly, you are not surprised later that afternoon to receive a phone call from Jodi. She tells you that she has just spoken with the general contractor on the project, who tells her that he could finish the project for $300,000. Jodi started by calling Olive to tell her that she plans to pursue her remedies as forcefully as possible to get the $300,000. Jodi became concerned when she received an e-mailed letter from Olive's attorney, advising her that any action against Olive or the SecondCity letter of credit would violate the Bankruptcy Code's automatic stay. What do you advise? 11 U.S.C. §§105, 362(a)(3).

19.5.   Stacy Vye (the Wessex Bank loan officer) calls you about a $400,000 standby letter of credit that one of her less experienced loan officers issued several weeks ago. The letter of credit was issued for the benefit of Timothy Fairway at the behest of Stacy's customer Damon Wildeve. Fairway had sold Wildeve an industrial tub grinder. (You might recall the *Diamond Z* case in Assignment 16.) This morning Fairway called Stacy to tell her that Fairway would be drawing on the letter of credit because Wildeve refused to pay when Fairway went by yesterday to collect payment. When Stacy called Wildeve, Wildeve told Stacy that he was sorry, but that his business had done so poorly that he had no money to pay Fairway. A few minutes ago Fairway appeared at Stacy's office with a draft on the letter of credit. Because the draft appeared to be in order, Stacy paid it.

Stacy is concerned because the loan officer who issued the letter of credit (Clym Yeobright) arranged for reimbursement by having Wildeve pledge $500,000 of Wildeve's stock in Tram Whirl Airlines (TWA). Because of TWA's bankruptcy last week, that stock is now completely worthless. Stacy wants to know what she can do to get paid if, as appears likely, Wildeve has no money to pay her. UCC §§2-702(2), 5-117(a); 11 U.S.C. §§509(a), 546(c).

19.6.   Do you think the result in *CRM* matches the intent of the parties—is this something to which the parties would have agreed if they had discussed the topic up front? In any event, can you see any steps that the attorneys could have taken to forestall litigation on this topic?

Part Three
Liquidity Systems

Chapter 7.   Negotiability

Assignment 20:   Negotiable Instruments

A.   Negotiability and Liquidity

The concept of liquidity is central to the "big picture" of financial transactions. Generally, liquidity refers to the ease with which an asset can be sold at a price that reflects the asset's economic value. For example, a certificate for 100 shares of stock traded on the New York Stock Exchange is one of the most liquid of all assets: Under normal conditions, a call to a stockbroker can produce a sale in a matter of minutes. Conversely, a partnership interest in a two-person general partnership is very illiquid: The uniqueness of that kind of asset precludes the establishment of any organized market for its sale. The lack of a market makes a sale difficult because it forces a prospective seller to expend considerable effort to locate a buyer and educate the buyer about the value of the asset.

Liquidity is as useful for payment obligations as it is for other assets. If a payment obligation is highly liquid, the payee easily can sell the obligation and thus convert it to cash. The ease of transferring the obligation makes it considerably more valuable; as Chris Desan puts it, liquidity is like a "lubricating layer of value around" the asset. By providing a ready source of cash, an active market for payment obligations aids the financial position of operating businesses that generate payment obligations when they sell things to their customers. Many businesses (especially small ones) prefer to have immediate cash rather than waiting for payment from their customers. Indeed, many businesses prefer immediate cash even if they have to sell their payment obligations at a discount. To put it in economic terms, liquidity allows those businesses to shift financial risks to third parties.

That process also enhances the general efficiency of financial markets by making it easier to form financial businesses that specialize in bearing the financial risks that operating businesses want to trade for cash. In turn, a system that encourages the formation of those financial enterprises allows specialization in evaluating, monitoring, and collecting those obligations. Specialization can lead to administration of those obligations that is cheaper and more effective than administration under a system in which each business holds and monitors all of the payment obligations that its sales generate.

Putting aside money, the negotiable instrument is the oldest device for enhancing liquidity with any role in modern commerce. Rules related to negotiability enhance liquidity in two distinct ways. First, negotiable instruments offer an easy way for verifying a party's power to transfer an enforceable interest in the instrument. As you will see in the assignments to come, all the relevant information appears on the two sides of the instrument. That means (at least in theory) that the only thing that a purchaser of a negotiable instrument needs to do to determine that the purported seller can transfer a right to enforce the instrument is look at the instrument and verify the identity of the party with whom it is dealing. The prospective purchaser's title search need not include inquiries to the payor or to any public or private records. Indeed, if the instrument is "bearer" paper (discussed below), the purchaser acquires a right to enforce the instrument even if the seller is a thief!

The second liquidity-enhancing feature of negotiable instruments arises from a defense-stripping rule that makes a negotiable instrument more valuable in the hands of a purchaser than it was in the hands of the payee that sold it. Upon compliance with that rule, a transfer of a negotiable instrument strips away most of the defenses to payment that the payor could have asserted against the original payee. In the common terminology, a purchaser that becomes a "holder in due course" takes the instrument free from all "personal" defenses. Thus, a holder in due course could force Carl to repay a negotiable instrument that he issued even if Carl had a defense to payment against the original payee. By stripping away the payor's defenses to payment, that rule enhances the likelihood that the purchaser will be entitled to payment from the payor. Accordingly (at least theoretically), those rules make the purchase of a negotiable instrument a more attractive investment, which in turn makes such instruments more liquid.

As the previous paragraphs suggest, the subject of the negotiability system is a piece of paper, a physical writing that evidences the payment obligation. That piece of paper is central to both of the rules mentioned above. The evidence of transfer takes the form of physical signatures (indorsements) on the instrument. Similarly, holder-in-due-course status can be attained only by a person who has possession of the instrument. Every student who has worked through the first part of this book should understand that no system that requires manipulation and transmission of physical documents can survive undiminished in the computer age. As systems for electronic transmission of information become less expensive and more reliable, the increasing relative expense of systems that rely on physical documents generates pressures that diminish wide use of any document-based system. Indeed, the pressures of a modernizing economy began to limit the use of negotiable instruments even before the computer age. Thus, as this chapter explains, a variety of practical considerations already have made negotiable instruments considerably less common than they were even a generation ago.

That is not to say that the negotiability system is a useless relic. Negotiable instruments still play some role in commerce, especially in the banking system. Furthermore, newer and more sophisticated systems for enhancing liquidity (such as securitization) are likely to draw heavily on the concepts developed in the negotiability system. Thus, an understanding of negotiability and how it works will be helpful in keeping pace with the changing mechanisms of commerce in the decades to come.

The remainder of this assignment discusses the basic framework of the negotiability system: the rules that determine whether any particular payment obligation constitutes a negotiable instrument. The next two assignments discuss other aspects of the system, including the two liquidity-enhancing features of negotiable instruments described above (free transferability and holder-in-due-course status), explaining how they work and discussing the concerns that have begun to limit their role in modern commerce. The chapter closes with a discussion of documentary draft transactions, a common modern transaction that uses both negotiability and letters of credit.

B. A Typical Transaction

To get a feel for how a negotiable instrument could be used in commerce, consider the following transaction. It is a simple international sale-of-goods transaction, both because it is easy to understand and because this context is one common use of negotiable instruments in commerce today. The parties to the transaction are B.K. Werner, a St. Louis businessman, and Neville Russell, a London bookseller.* Werner has purchased some engineering textbooks from Russell at an agreed price of 1,500 British pounds. Werner could pay by mailing a check on his account, but it would take several weeks for Russell to obtain payment for that check if he deposited it with his bank in Britain. Furthermore, unless Werner is a man of impressive solvency, Russell might doubt the value of Werner's check and thus refuse to ship the books until the check has cleared. Werner also could pay by means of a wire transfer or letter of credit, which would satisfy Russell with prompt and sure funding. Wire transfers and letters of credit, however, tend to be too expensive for small transactions like the one in question. Accordingly, unless Russell is in such a rush that he needs to provide payment on a same-day basis, it would be plausible for him to select a draft as the best mechanism for payment (see Figure 20.1).

Figure 20.1
Sample Negotiable Draft

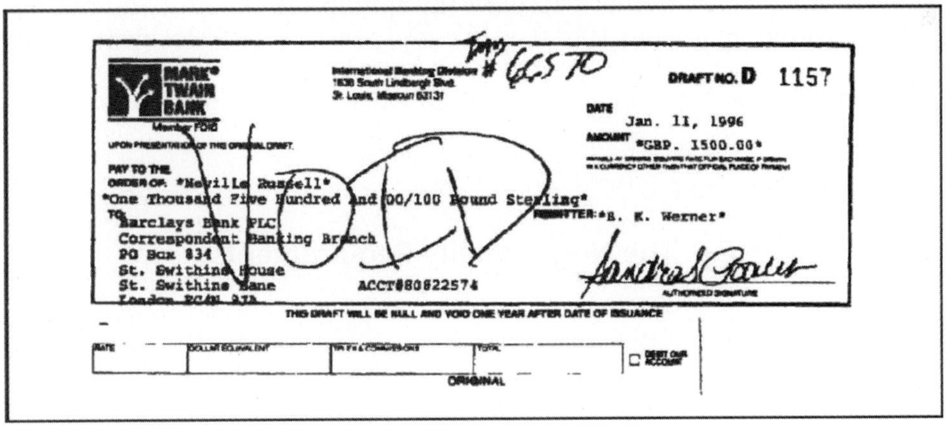

* The names identify real individuals, taken from a sample draft kindly provided to me by Mercantile Bank (then Mark Twain Bank). The remainder of the example is fictional, based on interviews with several bankers about common uses of drafts.

To pay with a draft, Werner goes to his bank (in this instance, Mark Twain Bank) to purchase the draft. Although the stylized form of the draft obscures the substance of what it says, careful study reveals something like a letter addressed to Barclays Bank (in London), asking Barclays to pay Neville Russell the agreed upon sum:

> January 11, 1996. Upon presentation of this original draft, pay to the order of Neville Russell One Thousand Five Hundred and 00/100 Pound Sterling. To Barclays Bank PLC.
>
> [Authorized Signature for Mark Twain]

If all goes as planned, Werner transmits the draft to Russell in the ordinary course of business. Russell, in turn, could present the draft directly to Barclays or sell it to his own bank in London (in which case Russell's bank would present the draft to Barclays). Meanwhile, Mark Twain notifies Barclays by telex that it has issued the draft so that Barclays recognizes the draft as valid when it is presented. When Barclays receives the draft, Barclays pays the money to Russell (or Russell's bank, as the case may be) and deducts the money from an account that Mark Twain maintains with Barclays for the purpose of handling such transactions. The result is the same as if Werner had paid Russell directly, except that the bank draft expedited the payment transaction.

If Werner is a large customer that engages in numerous draft transactions, Mark Twain could expedite the process further by allowing Werner to issue drafts directly, which would eliminate the need for Werner to come to the bank to purchase drafts. In that arrangement, Mark Twain authorizes specified officers of Werner's company to sign drafts that would be binding on Mark Twain and provides Werner with the paper stock on which drafts are issued. The final piece of the arrangement is software provided by Mark Twain that prints drafts at Werner's direction and notifies Mark Twain electronically as each draft is issued. Upon receipt of each electronic notice, Mark Twain charges Werner's account the appropriate amount and notifies Barclays (or the analogous Mark Twain correspondent in the locale to which Werner plans to send the draft) that it has issued the draft. At that point, the remote bank is prepared to honor the draft when it is presented for payment by the payee.

C.   The Negotiability Requirements

Although rules about negotiability originally developed through judicial decisions, they now have been codified into a formal and rigid statutory framework that appears in Article 3 of the Uniform Commercial Code.

Because of the formality of the rules set forth in Article 3, it is important to start with some basic terms used by Article 3 to identify the various parties to a transaction involving an instrument. Referring back to the Russell-Werner example, Article 3 calls the party that directs the payment (Mark Twain in this case) the "drawer" (UCC §3-103(a)(3)) or the "issuer" (UCC §3-105(c)).

Werner, the person who caused the draft to be issued, is called the "remitter" (UCC §3-103(a)(15)) because of the understanding that Werner will remit the draft to the payee Russell. Neville Russell, to whom the payment is to be made, is the "payee." Barclays, the person directed to make payment (the person on whom the draft is drawn, as it were), is the "drawee" (UCC §3-103(a)(2)).

As explained above, the foundation of negotiability is a physical object: the negotiable instrument. The text of Article 3 uses a two-stage framework to set out the rules for determining whether any particular obligation is negotiable. The first stage is a general definition of a negotiable instrument, which appears in UCC §3-104(a). The second stage is contained in an array of provisions scattered throughout Article 1 and other provisions in Part 1 of Article 3, which provide detailed definitions of many of the terms that appear in UCC §3-104.

UCC §3-104 sets forth seven requirements for negotiability (see Figure 20.2). An obligation that satisfies all seven requirements is a negotiable instrument, or (at least in Article 3) simply an "instrument." See UCC §3-104(b) ("'Instrument' means a negotiable instrument."). If an obligation fails to meet any of the seven requirements, then (with one minor exception discussed below) none of the substantive rules set forth in Article 3 applies. The paragraphs that follow discuss each of those seven requirements in turn.

1. The Promise or Order Requirement

The introductory paragraph of UCC §3-104(a) limits negotiability to obligations that are either a "promise" or an "order." Those terms are defined and distinguished in UCC §§3-103(a)(8) (defining "order") and 3-103(a)(12) (defining "promise"). Because each of the definitions requires that the obligation be in writing, the promise or order requirement implicitly requires all negotiable instruments to be in writing. Although the UCC includes a broad definition of "writing," it still requires an "intentional reduction to tangible form." UCC §1-201(b)(43). Accordingly, obligations reflected only in electronic form cannot be negotiable. However much that "tangible-form" requirement may limit use of the system in the future, it would be hard to dispense with it and maintain anything like the current system, which relies on physical signatures as a means for transfer and physical possession as the touchstone for enforcement. A future system might recognize indorsements made by electronic signatures attached to payment messages, but implementing such a system would require a significant conceptual reworking of Articles 3 and 4 of the UCC.

In addition to the writing requirement, the promise or order requirement limits the scope of Article 3 by limiting the types of obligations that it covers: If the obligation is not a "promise" or an "order," it cannot qualify. A "promise" is a direct commitment to pay. UCC §3-103(a)(12). The party that makes a promise is called a "maker," UCC §3-103(a)(7); the instrument that contains a promise is called a "note," UCC §3-104(e). An "order," by contrast, does not contain a direct promise to pay. Rather, an order is an instruction by one person (the "drawer," as described above, see UCC §3-103(a)(5)) directing some other party to pay (the "drawee," as described above, see UCC §3-103(a)(4)). An instrument that contains an order is called a "draft," UCC §3-104(e), the

Figure 20.2
The Negotiability Requirements

	REQUIREMENT	STATUTORY REFERENCES
1.	The obligation must be a written promise or order.	UCC §§3-104(a), 1-201(43), 3-103(a)(2), (3), (5), (6) & (9), 3-104(e), (f), (g) & (h)
2.	The obligation must be unconditional.	UCC §§3-104(a), 3-106
3.	The obligation must require payment of money.	UCC §§3-104(a), 1-201(b)(24), 3-107
4.	The amount of the obligation must be fixed.	UCC §§3-104(a), 3-112(b)
5.	The obligation must be payable to bearer or order.	UCC §§3-104(a)(1) & (c) 3-109, 3-115 comment 2
6.	The obligation must be payable on demand or at a definite time.	UCC §§3-104(a)(2), 3-108
7.	The obligation must not contain any extraneous undertakings by the issuer.	UCC §3-104(a)(3)

type of negotiable instrument illustrated by the Werner draft in Figure 20.1. UCC §3-104(f), (g), (h) defines three of the most common types of drafts. The first is a check, which is simply a draft drawn on a bank. UCC §3-104(f); see UCC §1-201(b)(4) (defining a "bank" as "any person engaged in the business of banking"). Thus, the Werner draft could be characterized as a check (although the transnational relationship would make that characterization unusual). The second is a cashier's check, a type of check in which the drawer and drawee are the same bank. UCC §3-104(g). For example, if Mark Twain had given Werner a draft drawn on itself, rather than on Barclays, the draft would have been a cashier's check. The third is a teller's check, a draft drawn by one bank on another bank. UCC §3-104(h). Because the Werner draft was issued by Mark Twain and drawn on Barclays, it technically would be correct (albeit unusual, as mentioned above) to describe that instrument as a teller's check.

2.   The Unconditional Requirement

The introductory paragraph of UCC §3-104(a) also requires negotiable instruments to be "unconditional," a term that UCC §3-106 defines in detail. That requirement generally limits negotiability to instruments that are absolute and include on their face all of the terms of payment. Thus, if a document includes a promise to pay that is subject to a condition, the instrument cannot be negotiable. UCC §3-106(a)(i). For example, the draft in Figure 20.1 would not be negotiable if it included a notation stating that it was "valid only upon remitter's receipt of the agreed-upon merchandise." That notation would make the obligation conditional because the drawer's instruction would be ineffective if Werner did not receive the promised books.

By excluding conditional promises, that provision obviates the need for potential purchasers of instruments to evaluate the likelihood that the issuer will become obligated to pay; if the issuer is unwilling to create an unconditional obligation to pay, the document is not negotiable. At the same time, that provision significantly limits the utility of the negotiability system because it excludes from the system any transaction that calls for a conditional payment obligation.

The unconditional requirement also addresses the related concern that the terms of payment be evident from the face of the document itself. Thus, under clauses (ii) and (iii) of UCC §3-106(a), a document is not negotiable if it states that it "is subject to or governed by" another writing or if it states "that rights or obligations with respect to [the document] are stated in another writing." Thus, the Werner draft would not be negotiable if it included the notation that it was "to be paid as stated in remitter's agreement with payee." A document that required potential purchasers to search other documents to discover the terms of payments would be too cumbersome for the negotiability system.

UCC §3-106(b) sets forth two important exceptions to the unconditional requirement. The first recognizes the reality that a note for which the maker gives collateral often includes references to other writings (such as a loan agreement, security agreement, or mortgage) describing rights related to the collateral and to the payee's remedies upon default. Those types of terms ordinarily do not limit the rights of the payee as a condition would. Rather, they tend to enhance the rights of the payee by giving the payee a greater ability to enforce payment than the payee would have without collateral or without the remedies stated in the ancillary documents. Accordingly, a strong case could be made that inclusion of those terms would not make a document conditional in the first instance. In any event, UCC §3-106(b)(i) resolves any concern by stating expressly that inclusion of such terms does not undermine negotiability.

The second provision is qualitatively different because it permits terms that directly limit the enforceability of the instrument. Specifically, UCC §3-106(b)(ii) extends negotiability to documents in which "payment is limited to resort to a particular fund or source." The most common example would be a "nonrecourse" real-estate note, which limits the payee's remedies to the mortgaged real estate and bars any suit directly against the maker of the note. Under UCC §3-106(b)(ii), that nonrecourse provision would not preclude negotiability.

The last paragraph of UCC §3-106 comment 1 states that particular-fund provisions should not undermine negotiability because the market can evaluate the effect those terms have on the value of the underlying obligation. That explanation, however, would justify a complete abandonment of the unconditional requirement. As explained above, the basic rationale for the unconditional requirement is the idea that purchasers of instruments should not have to evaluate the effect of conditions on the value of obligations. There is no logical reason a condition permitted by the "particular fund" exception (like the common "nonrecourse" requirement) is any easier to evaluate than other possible conditions (such as a condition that payment be made only if the stock market rises a specified amount). A more plausible explanation is that particular-fund conditions are so common that a rule excluding them would exclude a large class of potentially negotiable instruments for which conditions do not pose a serious problem. By allowing inclusion of those instruments, UCC §3-106(b)(ii) permits some broadening of the use of negotiable instruments without unduly compromising the streamlining that characterizes the system.

3.   The Money Requirement

The third requirement contained in the introductory paragraph of UCC §3-104(a) requires the promise or order to be for the payment of money. That requirement excludes obligations to deliver commodities other than money. For example: "The undersigned promises to deliver 100 tons of wheat on June 1, 2007." The UCC's concept of "money," however, is a broad one, which includes both domestic and foreign currency. UCC §1-201(b)(24); see UCC §3-107 comment (stating that an instrument can be payable in foreign currency). Thus, there is nothing unusual or disqualifying about the provision in the Werner draft calling for payment in pounds sterling rather than dollars.

4.   The Fixed-Amount Requirement

The fourth (and last) requirement embedded in the introductory paragraph of UCC §3-104(a) requires the amount of the obligation to be fixed. That rule excludes promises to pay unspecified sums of money ("I promise to pay to payee one-half of the 2002 profits from sales of my casebooks."). In commercial transactions, an instrument that includes a promise to pay a fixed sum often also includes a promise to pay interest and other charges that accrue on a debt. Like provisions related to collateral, provisions obligating the maker to pay interest or other charges only enhance the value of the instrument. Accordingly, a rule excluding documents with such provisions from the system would exclude a large class of obligations in which there is little doubt as to the amount due. UCC §3-104(a) expressly includes them by stating that the fixed amount can be "with or without interest or other charges described in the [instrument]."

   The principal topic of litigation about interest provisions has been whether a provision providing for a variable rate of interest violates the fixed-amount-of-money requirement. There was considerable litigation of that point in the 1980s, resulting in a number of decisions holding that variable-rate notes could not be negotiable instruments. The revised Article 3 rejects those decisions in UCC §3-112(b). This section states that interest "may be stated in an instrument as a fixed or variable amount of money or it may be expressed as a fixed or variable rate or rates." Those provisions may impose some doubt on the purchaser (by requiring it to ascertain the rate at which interest accrues), but their wide use in financial markets convinced the revisers of Article 3 to include them as instruments.

5.   *The Payable-to-Bearer-or-Order Requirement*

In addition to the four requirements set forth in the introductory paragraph to UCC §3-104(a), three more requirements appear in the three numbered subparagraphs of UCC §3-104(a). The first of those three (the fifth requirement overall) appears in UCC §3-104(a)(1): The document must be payable to "bearer" or "order." That provision refers to hoary terms of art detailed in UCC §3-109, an area where the formalism of Article 3 reaches its height. If an instrument does not contain the precise words required to satisfy the tests set forth in UCC §3-109, it is not an instrument. Accordingly, it is important to look carefully at the precise words authorized by the statute.

An instrument can be made payable to bearer in two general ways. The first way is the obvious one: The instrument can state that it is "payable to bearer" or "payable to the order of bearer." The closing phrase of UCC §3-109(a)(1) states that an instrument also can be payable to bearer if it "otherwise indicates that the person in possession of the promise or order is entitled to payment," but it seems unlikely that an instrument would satisfy that test if it did not contain the word "bearer" or some other phrase quite close to the words of the statute.

The second type of bearer paper is paper that is not payable to any particular identifiable person, which is covered in the second and third subsections of UCC §3-109(a). Subsection (a)(2) covers the simplest case, an instrument that does not state a payee. Imagine an instrument where the maker fails to fill in the name of the payee: "Pay to the order of _____."

Article 3 treats that instrument as payable to bearer. UCC §§3-109(a)(2), 3-109 comment 2, 3-115 comment 2. Subsection (a)(3) offers the same rule for instruments made payable "to cash." UCC §3-109(a)(3) & comment 2.

If an instrument is not payable to bearer, it can be made payable to order in one of two ways. First, under UCC §3-109(b)(i), the document can state that it is payable to the order of an identified person: "Pay to the order of Dan Keating." Second, under UCC §3-109(b)(ii), it can state that it is payable to an identified person or order: "Pay to Dan Keating or order."

The reference in UCC §3-109(b)(ii) to an "identified person or order" contains an unfortunate ambiguity. As written, it could be construed to include two types of instruments: instruments payable "to an identified person" and instruments payable "to order." That reading is incorrect. The statute should be read as if there were quotation marks around the entire phrase: A promise or order is payable to order if it is payable "to an identified person or order." An instrument satisfies that provision only if it includes the entire phrase, both the name of the identified person and the "order" language. An instrument that is payable "to Dan Keating" is not payable to order. Indeed, it is not an instrument at all because it fails the bearer-or-order requirement. Nor does order paper include an instrument made payable simply "to order." That instrument's failure to identify the payee would make it bearer paper under UCC §3-109(a)(2).

Finally, the practicalities of the checking system call for an exception to the bearer-or-order requirement for checks. Specifically, a check that fails the bearer-or-order requirement, but satisfies all of the remaining negotiability requirements, qualifies as an instrument despite that failure. UCC §3-104(c). Comment 2 succinctly explains the motivation for that exception:

> [I]t is good policy to treat checks, which are payment instruments, as negotiable instruments whether or not they contain the words "to the order of." These words are almost always pre-printed on the check form. Occasionally the drawer of a check may strike out these words before issuing the check. . . . Absence of the quoted words can easily be overlooked and should not affect the rights of holders who may pay money or give credit for a check without being aware that it is not in the conventional form.

6.   The Demand or Definite-Time Requirement

The sixth requirement appears in UCC §3-104(a)(2): The obligation must be payable on demand or at a definite time. UCC §3-108 defines those terms so broadly that they include all significant payment obligations. First, a demand obligation includes not only an obligation that is payable "on demand" (or "at sight," which is the same thing), but also an obligation that states no time for payment. UCC §3-108(a). The "no-time" provision allows the system to cover checks (which typically prescribe no specific time for payment). Second, the "definite time" category includes not only the conventional obligation that is due on a particular date or particular schedule of dates, but also documents that allow the holder a right to extend the date of payment, UCC §3-108(b)(iii). As the comment to UCC §3-108 explains, the rationale for that rule is that a provision giving the holder the option to extend should not undermine negotiability because the holder always could extend the time for payment even if the document did not include such a provision.

UCC §3-108(b) also permits provisions that alter the time of payment to permit acceleration and prepayment. Indeed, the statute even permits extensions at the option of the maker (if the instrument limits extension "to a further definite time") or "automatically upon or after a specified act or event." Apparently, the only obligation that would fail that rule would be a document giving the issuer either a completely unqualified option to extend or a qualified option to extend that did not state a date to which the extension would run.

7.   The No-Extraneous-Undertakings Requirement

The last requirement for negotiability is the requirement in UCC §3-104(a)(3) that forbids inclusion of a promise calling for something other than the payment of money. For historical reasons (that do not seem to have much explanatory value), that requirement typically is referred to as the "courier without luggage" requirement. The general concept is that a document cannot be negotiable if it includes any nonmonetary promises. Thus, a document cannot be an instrument if it includes provisions in which the maker not only promises to pay $100,000, but also promises to deliver 100 tons of wheat by a specified date.

The three numbered clauses at the end of UCC §3-104(a)(3) articulate three exceptions to the no-extraneous-undertakings requirement, identifying provisions that are so customary that the statute permits their inclusion even if they are not, strictly speaking, monetary promises. The first, which resonates with the provisions related to collateral in UCC §3-106(b)(i), permits "an undertaking or power to give, maintain, or protect collateral to secure payment." UCC §3-104(a)(3)(i). Thus, an instrument can be negotiable even if it includes provisions in which the maker promises to provide collateral to secure the debt evidenced by the instrument. Second, UCC §3-104(a)(3)(ii) permits "an authorization or power to the holder to confess judgment or realize on or dispose of collateral." That provision is intended to validate the provisions common in older promissory notes in some jurisdictions in which a maker authorizes the holder to obtain a default judgment on the note; in some cases, such a provision gives the holder procedural advantages that expedite enforcement of the instrument. Finally, UCC §3-104(a)(3)(iii) permits conditions in which the borrower waives laws intended for the benefit or protection of the borrower or obligor. That clause validates a group of common provisions in which borrowers waive various common-law protections — requirements of presentment, dishonor, notice of dishonor, and the like — that would hinder the holder's collection of the instrument.

This requirement has been the most controversial, because the increasing complexities of modern lending practice have led to the inclusion of a variety of common provisions that at least implicate the "courier-without-luggage" rule. The following case illustrates the most salient controversy about that provision.

In re Walker

466 B.R. 271 (Bankr. E.D. Pa. 2012)

Eric L. Frank, Bankruptcy Judge.

I.   INTRODUCTION

In this chapter 13 bankruptcy case, Debtor Janice Walker has filed an objection ("the Objection") to the secured proof of claim ("the Proof of Claim") of the Certificateholders CWALT, Inc., Alternative Loan Trust 2005-J14 Mortgage Pass Through Certificates ("the Trust"). The Trust filed the Proof of Claim through its trustee, the Bank of New York Mellon ("BNYM").

The Debtor's primary challenge to the validity of BNYM's claim is based on alleged defects in the process by which the underlying mortgage loan was "securitized" and became an asset of the Trust. . . .

. . .

As explained below, I conclude that . . . the underlying loan note is a negotiable instrument under Pennsylvania's version of article 3 of the Uniform Commercial Code . . . .

II. PROCEDURAL HISTORY

The Debtor commenced this chapter 13 bankruptcy case on March 31, 2010. The Debtor's proposed chapter 13 plan provides for the Debtor to make post-petition payments on her residential mortgage and to cure the pre-petition delinquency on the mortgage through her chapter 13 plan payments to the chapter 13 trustee.

On September 17, 2010, BNYM filed a secured proof of claim in the amount of $264,855.72 ("the Proof of Claim") [and the debtor promptly objected.]

III. STATEMENT OF UNDISPUTED FACTS

1. The Debtor is the owner of the residential real property located at 63 Buttonwood Drive Exton, PA 19341 ("the Property").

2. On August 31, 2005, the Debtor entered into a loan transaction ("the Loan") with Allied Mortgage Group, Inc. ("Allied").

3. The Debtor executed a note ("the Note") in the amount of $248,000.00 payable to Allied.

4. The Note provides for the Debtor to repay the loan of $248,000.00 by making monthly payments of $1,567.53 beginning on November 1, 2005 and ending on October 1, 2035.

5. Paragraph 4 of the Note states that the Debtor may prepay principal at any time, but requires the Debtor "to tell the Note Holder in writing that [she is] doing so."

. . .

V. DISCUSSION

A. Overview

The Debtor does not deny that she is obligated to repay the Note she signed when she entered into the mortgage loan transaction with Allied in 2005. Nor does she contest the amount of either the total secured claim or the pre-petition arrears stated in the Proof of Claim. Nevertheless, she objects to BNYM's claim because she asserts that the Trust is not the party to whom she is obliged to pay under the Note, *i.e.,* she disputes the Trust's right to enforce her repayment obligation under the Note. In effect, she contends that BNYM is not her "true" creditor.

The Debtor's argument is premised on the general, indisputable proposition that for a creditor to have an allowable claim in a bankruptcy case (be it secured or unsecured), the creditor must have a "right to payment." *See* 11 U.S.C. §101(5)(A). Thus, 11 U.S.C. §502(b)(1) requires the court to disallow a claim to the extent that it is "unenforceable against the debtor . . . under any agreement or applicable law for a reason other than because such claim is contingent or unmatured."

The Debtor's challenge to the Proof of Claim focuses on BNYM's rights under the Note, not the Mortgage. The Debtor contends that BNYM has not established that it has "an enforceable interest in the [N]ote." Thus, properly understood, in this contested matter, the Debtor disputes the right of a record mortgagee to assert a bankruptcy claim, *i.e.*, a right to payment, based on an asserted defect relating to BNYM's right to enforce the Note that is secured by the mortgage.

The Debtor makes two (2) arguments in support of the Objection.

First, the Debtor contends that, assuming the Pa. UCC is applicable, BNYM has not established under the UCC that it is the party with the right to enforce the Note.

[The court concludes that the creditor's rights are determined under the Note and the UCC rather than under the securitization documents.]

2. The Note Is a Negotiable Instrument

The term "negotiable instrument" is defined in Pa. UCC §3104. There is abundant legal authority for the proposition that mortgage notes, such as the one involved in this matter, are negotiable instruments governed by article 3 of the UCC. *See, e.g.,* In re Carmichael, 448 B.R. 690, 693-94 (Bankr. E.D. Pa. 2011) (collecting cases); *see also* In re AppOnline.com, Inc., 321 B.R. 614, 621-24 (E.D.N.Y. 2003), *aff'd on other grounds*, 128 Fed. Appx. 171 (2d Cir. 2005); J.S. Judge & Co. v. Lilley, 28 Pa. D & C. 3 (Phila. Mun. Ct. 1937).

In her initial Memorandum, the Debtor appears to assume that the Pa. UCC governs the analysis. However, in her Sur-Reply Memorandum, the Debtor questions, for the first time, whether the Note is a negotiable instrument under Article 3 (and, presumably whether Article 3 even applies).

In making this argument, the Debtor does not dispute that the Note satisfies the requirements of Pa. UCC §3104(a)(1) and (2). Her position is based entirely on

> (1) the requirement in Pa. UCC §3104(a)(3) that the Note impose no obligation or undertaking on the Debtor other than the payment of money, and
>
> (2) Paragraph 4 of the Note, which provides that in the event the Debtor makes a prepayment of principal (which is authorized by the Note), the Debtor must "tell the Note Holder in writing that [she is] doing so." (Ex. A).

The Debtor asserts that her non-monetary obligation to give the note holder notice of a prepayment of principal strips the Note of its status as a negotiable instrument. She cites no authority in support of her argument except for two (2) law review articles. *See* Dale A. Whitman, *How Negotiability Has Fouled up the Secondary Mortgage Market, and What to Do About It*, 37 Pepp. L. Rev. 737, 749-51 (2010); Ronald J. Mann, *Searching for Negotiability in Payment and Credit Systems*, 44 UCLA L. Rev. 951, 969-73 (1997).

There is no binding precedent on this issue. Indeed, there is very little case law at all. In my research, I have found only three (3) reported decisions. All three of them reject the Debtor's position. *See* Picatinny Fed. Credit Union v. Fed., National Mortgage Assoc., 2011 WL 1337507, at *7 (D.N.J. Apr. 7, 2011); In re Edwards, 2011 WL 6754073, at *5 (Bankr. E.D. Wis. Dec. 23, 2011); HSBC Bank USA, N.A. v. Gouda, 2010 WL 5128666, at *2-3 (N.J. Super. A.D. Dec. 17, 2010).

The most fulsome explanation for the courts' holdings is provided by *Gouda*:

> The right of defendants, under the note, to prepay part of the principal does not constitute an "additional undertaking or instruction" that adversely affects the negotiability of the note. Quite the opposite, the right of prepayment is a voluntary option that defendants may elect to exercise solely at their discretion. Indeed, such an allowance confers a benefit, not a burden, upon defendants, who can freely choose to decline the opportunity. The fact that defendants must notify the lender in the event they opt for prepayment imposes no additional liability on them and is not a condition placed on defendants' promise to pay. Rather, *notification is simply a requirement of the exercise of the right of prepayment which, as noted, defendants are free to reject.* This requirement does not render the note in issue non-negotiable.

[Emphasis added by *Walker* court.]

I find the *Gouda* court's analysis of the issue persuasive and I will follow its holding. Therefore, I reject the Debtor's sole ground for her contention that the Note is not a negotiable instrument. It follows from this conclusion that the Pa. UCC is presumptively the appropriate source of law to consult in determining the respective rights of the Debtor and BNYM under the Note.

. . .

VI.   CONCLUSION

For the reasons set forth above, I conclude that because the underlying source of BNYM's right to payment (the Note) is a negotiable instrument and BNYM is the holder of the Note, the Debtor lacks standing to object to BNYM's Proof of Claim on the ground that BNYM failed to comply with all of the requirements of the PSA. As the party with the right to enforce the Note, BNYM has a right to payment that is an allowable bankruptcy claim, regardless of whether BNYM is the party ultimately entitled to the economic benefit of the Debtor's repayment of the Note. As the Debtor has raised no other basis for disallowing the Proof of Claim, the Objection will be overruled.

Problem Set 20

20.1. Jodi Kay (your long-standing client from CountryBank) has started work on a project to sell a number of the bank's less desirable miscellaneous assets. The first item that comes to hand is a corporate bond issued by HAL Corp., in the following (standard) form:

HAL Corp.
Albany, New York
8 percent Bond
Due January 1, 2050

For value received, HAL Corp., a New York corporation (the "Corporation"), promises to pay to Mark Henry, or registered assigns, on January 1, 2050, the principal sum of $1,000 in lawful money of the United States of America. The Corporation further promises to pay interest on the principal sum from January 1, 2020, at the rate of 8 percent per annum in lawful money of the United States of America. Interest will be paid semiannually on July 1 and January 1 of each year after January 1, 2020, until the principal sum hereof has been paid or provision for its payment has been made.

The principal of this Bond will be payable at the principal office of the Corporation (or at whatever other place may be designated in writing by the Corporation from time to time) upon the presentation and surrender hereof. The semiannual interest payments will be mailed to the registered holder hereof at the address last furnished in writing to the Corporation.

This bond is registered both as to principal and interest and is transferable only on the books of the Corporation by the presentation and surrender hereof accompanied by an assignment form duly completed and executed by the registered holder hereof or a duly authorized attorney.

IN WITNESS WHEREOF, the Corporation has caused this Bond to be signed by its duly authorized officers on January 1, 2020.

Trying to determine exactly what she can say about it, she emails you a copy of the bond asking you to get back to her as soon as possible. She is trying to fill out a form that requires her to state whether each asset is a negotiable instrument. Does the bond qualify? UCC §§3-104(a), 3-109.

20.2. Pleased with your thoughtful advice in Problem 20.1, Jodi emails you another one. This time it's a commercial form note, set out as an appendix to this assignment. What is your opinion? UCC §§3-103(a), 3-104(a), 3-106(a), 3-108, 3-109, 3-112(b).

20.3. Late in the evening, Jodi calls to tell you that she has "just one more" for you to look at. She tells you that she has a cache of several hundred home-mortgage notes, all of which are on identical forms. She emails you the form, which appears to be the standard form promulgated by the Federal National Mortgage Association and the Federal Home Loan Mortgage Corp. It includes the following provisions:

4. Borrower's Right to Prepay I have the right to make payments of principal at any time before they are due. A payment of principal only is known as a "prepayment." When I make a prepayment, I will tell the Note Holder in writing that I am doing so. . . .

10. Uniform Secured Note . . . In addition to the protections given to the Note Holder under this Note, a Mortgage, Deed of Trust, or Security Deed (the "Security Instrument"), dated the same date as this Note, protects the Note Holder from possible losses which might result if I do not keep the promises which I make in this Note. That Security Instrument describes how and under what conditions I may be required to make immediate payment in full of all amounts I owe under this Note.

Do those provisions prevent the home-mortgage notes from being negotiable? UCC §§3-104(a), 3-106, 3-108. Do you agree with *In re Walker?*

20.4. Ben Darrow (your rural banker friend) calls you to ask about an unusual item that has landed on his desk. This morning's ATM deposits included a $12,000 check where the drawer (Carol Long) had crossed out the printed words "to order of" and written in pen "only to." The result is that the check states: "Pay only to Jasmine Ball." It appears from the back of the check that Ball cashed the check at Ovco Drugs in downtown Matacora. Ovco Drugs, in turn, deposited the check into its account at First State Bank of Matacora (Darrow's bank). Darrow wants to know if the check is valid and what advice you have as to what he should do. He tells you that Long is a valued customer, so he does not want to do anything wrong. UCC §§3-104(c), 4-301(a).

20.5. An old law-school classmate of yours named Doug Kahan works for the Internal Revenue Service (IRS). While you are reminiscing with him one afternoon, he asks you about a funny incident that came up the preceding week. He tells you that he's always heard stories about taxpayers mailing in their payments written on shirts, the "shirt off their back," as it were. Because he had never seen such a thing in all his years at the IRS, he had dismissed those tales as nothing but a common urban myth. This week, however, he received just such a package: a box including a (somewhat worn) white dress shirt, with the following written in black ink across the back of the shirt: "Pay to the order of the Internal Revenue Service $150,000." The taxpayer had scrawled a signature below that sentence and written "SecondBank" and a series of numbers to the left of the signature. Those numbers appear to identify the taxpayer's account at SecondBank.

Doug's assistant took the shirt to a branch of SecondBank a few blocks away. SecondBank, however, refused to honor the shirt-check. It acknowledged that the taxpayer had an account at SecondBank, that the shirt properly identified the taxpayer's account number, and that the account contained funds adequate to cover the specified payment. The bank explained, however, that it had a policy of honoring checks only if they were written on forms supplied by the bank.

Doug is frustrated because he has been attempting to collect payment from that particular taxpayer for several years. He tells you that the shirt-check story he's heard always ended with the statement that the shirt is a valid instrument. Is that right? If so, doesn't the bank have to pay it? What do you tell him? UCC §§3-103(a), 3-104(a), 3-104(e), 3-104(f), 3-108(a), 3-408.

<u>PROMISSORY NOTE</u>

$2,000,000.00 Houston, Texas   January __, 2016

FOR VALUE RECEIVED, the undersigned, BORROWER, INC., a Delaware corporation ("***Maker***"), hereby unconditionally promises to pay to the order of **LENDER, INC.**, a Delaware corporation ("***Payee***") at [Address], or such other address given to Maker by Payee, the principal sum of TWO MILLION **AND 00/100 DOLLARS** ($2,000,000.00), or so much thereof as may be advanced hereunder prior to maturity, in lawful money of the United States of America, together with interest (calculated on the basis of a 360day year) on the unpaid principal balance from day to day remaining, computed from the date of advance until maturity at the rate per annum which shall from day to day be equal to the lesser of (a) the Maximum Rate, or (b) seven percent (7.00%).

1. Definitions. When used in this Note, the following terms shall have the respective meanings specified herein or in the section referred to:

"***Business Day***" means a day upon which business is transacted by national banks in Houston, Texas.

"***Collateral***" has the meaning set forth in the Security Agreement.

"***Default***" has the meaning ascribed to it in ***Section 7*** hereof.

"***Loan Documents***" means this Note, the Security Agreement, the Guaranty, and any agreements, documents (and with respect to this Note, the Security Agreement and such other agreements and documents, any modifications, amendments, renewals, extensions, or restatements thereof), or certificates at any time executed or delivered pursuant to the terms of this Note.

"***Material Adverse Effect***" means (a) a material adverse change in, or a material adverse effect upon, the operations, business, properties, liabilities (actual or contingent), condition (financial or otherwise) or prospects of Maker; (b) a material impairment of the ability of Maker to perform its obligations under any Loan Document; or (c) a material adverse effect upon the legality, validity, binding effect or enforceability against Maker of any Loan Document.

"***Maximum Rate***" means, with respect to the holder hereof, the maximum non-usurious rate of interest which, under all legal requirements, such holder is permitted to contract for, charge, take, reserve, or receive on this Note. If the laws of the State of Texas are applicable for purposes of determining the "*Maximum Rate,*" then such term means the "*weekly ceiling*" from time to time in effect under *Texas Finance Code §303.001*, as amended, as limited by *Texas Finance Code §303.009.*

"***Obligation***" means all indebtedness, liabilities, and obligations, of every kind and character, of Maker, now or hereafter existing in favor of Payee, regardless of whether the same may, prior to their acquisition by Payee, be or have been payable to some other person or entity, including, but not limited to, all indebtedness, liabilities, and obligations arising under this Note.

"***Person***" means an individual, sole proprietorship, joint venture, association, trust, estate, business trust, corporation, non-profit corporation, partnership, sovereign government or agency, instrumentality, or political subdivision thereof, or any similar entity or organization.

"***Security Agreement***" means that certain Pledge, Assignment, and Security Agreement of even date herewith, pursuant to which Maker pledges and assigns in favor of Payee the collateral described therein.

2. Payment. The unpaid principal and interest of this Note shall be payable in sixty (60) equal monthly installments of $[_____], commencing on February 1, 2016 and continuing on the same day of each successive month thereafter, with a final payment in the amount of $[_____] (including any and all unpaid principal and interest thereon) on January 1, 2021. No principal amount repaid may be reborrowed.

All payments of principal and interest of this Note shall be made by Maker to Payee in federal or other immediately available funds. Payments made to Payee by Maker hereunder shall be applied first to accrued interest and then to principal.

Should the principal of, or any installment of the principal of or interest upon, this Note become due and payable on any day other than a Business Day, the maturity thereof shall be extended to the next succeeding Business Day, and interest shall be payable with respect to such extension.

All past due principal of and, to the extent permitted by applicable law, interest upon this Note shall bear interest at the Maximum Rate, or if no Maximum Rate is established by applicable law, then at the rate per annum which shall from day to day be equal to eighteen percent (18%).

3. Waivers. Maker and each surety, endorser, guarantor, and other party ever liable for payment of any sums of money payable upon this Note, jointly and severally waive presentment, demand, protest, notice of protest and nonpayment or other notice of default, notice of acceleration and intention to accelerate, or other notice of any kind, and agree that their liability under this Note shall not be affected by any renewal or extension in the time of payment hereof, or in any indulgences, or by any release or change in any security for the payment of this Note, and hereby consent to any and all renewals, extensions, indulgences, releases, or changes, regardless of the number of such renewals, extensions, indulgences, releases, or changes.

No waiver by Payee of any of its rights or remedies hereunder or under any other document evidencing or securing this Note or otherwise, shall be considered a waiver of any other subsequent right or remedy of Payee; no delay or omission in the exercise or enforcement by Payee of any rights or remedies shall ever be construed as a waiver of any right or remedy of Payee; and no exercise or enforcement of any such rights or remedies shall ever be held to exhaust any right or remedy of Payee.

4. Representations and Warranties. Maker hereby represents and warrants to Payee as follows:

(a) Maker is a limited liability company, duly organized, validly existing and in good standing under the laws of Delaware and has the power and authority to own its property and to carry on its business in each jurisdiction in which it does business.

(b) Maker has full power and authority to execute and deliver the Loan Documents and to incur and perform the obligations provided for therein, all of which have been duly authorized by all proper and necessary action of the appropriate governing body of Maker. No consent or approval of any public authority or other third party is required as a condition to the validity of any Loan Document, and Maker is in compliance with all laws and regulatory requirements to which it is subject.

(c) This Note and the other Loan Documents executed by Maker constitute valid and legally binding obligations of Maker, enforceable in accordance with their terms, except as enforceability may be limited by applicable bankruptcy, insolvency, or similar laws affecting the rights of creditors generally.

(d) There is no proceeding involving Maker pending or, to the knowledge of Maker, threatened before any court or governmental authority, agency or arbitration authority, except as disclosed to Payee in writing and acknowledged by Payee prior to the date hereof.

(e) There is no certificate of formation, membership provision, operating agreement or other document pertaining to the organization, power or authority of Maker and no provision of any existing agreement, mortgage, indenture or contract binding on Maker or affecting Maker's property, which would conflict with or in any way prevent the execution, delivery or carrying out of the terms of this Note and the other Loan Documents.

(f) Maker has good title to its properties and assets, and its properties and assets are free and clear of liens, except those granted to Payee or otherwise disclosed to Payee in writing prior to the date of this Note.

(g) All taxes and assessments due and payable by Maker have been paid or are being contested in good faith by appropriate proceedings and Maker has filed all tax returns which it is required to file.

(h) There has been no material adverse change in the financial condition or operations of Maker since formation. All factual information furnished by Maker to Payee in connection with this Note and any other loan documents executed in connection with this Note is and will be accurate and complete on the date as of which such information is delivered to Payee and is not and will not be incomplete by the omission of any material fact necessary to make such information not misleading.

(i) The principal office, chief executive office and principal place of business of Maker is at [Address].

(j) Maker maintains insurance on its present and future properties, assets, and businesses against such casualties, risks, and contingencies, and in such types and amounts, as are consistent with customary industry practices and standards.

(k) Maker will use the proceeds of this Note to purchase that certain drill press equipment, conveyor equipment, and sludge pad as are more particularly described in the Security Agreement.

(l) Maker has no subsidiaries and owns no equity interests in any other Person.

(m) To the best of Maker's knowledge, none of the Loan Documents, nor any document, financial statement, credit information, certificate or other statement required herein furnished to Payee by Maker contains any untrue statement of a material fact or omits to state a material fact relating to the Collateral or any matter covered by the Loan Documents. To the best of Maker's knowledge, no document, financial statement, credit information, certificate or other statement prepared by any party other than Maker and furnished to Payee contains any untrue statement of a material fact or omits to state a material fact relating to the Collateral or Loan Documents. To the best of Maker's knowledge, there is no fact that Maker has not disclosed to Payee in writing that could result in a Material Adverse Effect.

5. Affirmative Covenants. Until full payment and performance of the Obligation, Maker will, unless Payee consents otherwise in writing (and without limiting any requirement of any other Loan Document):

(a) Deliver to Payee: (i) (A) as soon as reasonably available and in any event within one hundred twenty (120) days after the end of each fiscal year of Maker, financial statements of Maker, including a balance sheet of Maker as of the end of such fiscal year and the related statements of operations for such fiscal year; and (B) as soon as available and in any event within sixty (60) days after the end of each of the first three quarters of each fiscal year of Maker, a balance sheet of Maker as of the end of such quarter and the related statements of operations for such quarter and for the portion of Maker's fiscal year ended at the end of such quarter; and (ii) simultaneously with the delivery of each set of financial statements referred to in *clause (i)* above, a certificate from an officer of Maker certifying that no Default then exists.

(b) Maintain insurance with responsible insurance companies on such of its properties, in such amounts and against such risks as is customarily maintained by similar businesses operating in the same vicinity, with such companies and in such amounts as are satisfactory to Payee.

(c) Maintain its existence, good standing and qualification to do business where required and comply with all laws, regulations and governmental requirements, including, without limitation, environmental laws applicable to it or to its properties and business operations.

(d) Pay all of its taxes, assessments and other obligations, including, but not limited to taxes, costs or other expenses arising out of this transaction, as the same become due and payable, except to the extent the same are being contested in good faith by appropriate proceedings in a diligent manner.

(e) Take all reasonable action to maintain all rights, privileges, permits, licenses and franchises necessary or desirable in the normal conduct of its business, except to the extent that failure to do so could not reasonably be expected to have a Material Adverse Effect.

(f) Deliver to Payee prompt notice of any Material Adverse Effect.

(g) Deliver to Payee, promptly upon request, such other information with respect to the operation or financial affairs of Maker as may be reasonably requested by Payee.

6. Negative Covenants. Until full payment and performance of the Obligation, Maker will not, without the prior written consent of Payee (and without limiting any requirement of any other Loan Documents):

(a) Sell, assign, lease, transfer or otherwise dispose of any part of Maker's business or assets, except in the ordinary course of its business; *provided, that* on the date of such sale, transfer, or other disposition, Maker shall prepay the Obligation in an amount equal to the proceeds therefrom.

(b) Grant, suffer or permit any lien on or security interest in the Collateral, except in favor of Payee, and other liens that have been disclosed to Payee in writing on or prior to the date hereof.

(c) Change the general character of business as conducted at the date hereof, or engage in any type of business not reasonably related to its business as presently conducted.

(d) Voluntarily liquidate, dissolve or suspend its business.

(e) Incur additional indebtedness, other than customary trade payables paid within sixty (60) days after they are incurred.

7. Default and Remedies.

(a) A *"**Default**"* shall exist hereunder if any one or more of the following events shall occur and be continuing: (i) Maker shall fail to pay any principal of, or interest upon, this Note or the Obligation within five (5) days when due; (ii) any representation or warranty made by Maker to Payee herein or in any of the Loan Documents shall prove to be untrue or inaccurate in any material respect; (iii) a material breach or any default shall occur in the performance of any of the covenants or agreements of Maker contained herein or in the Loan Documents; (iv) default shall occur in the payment of indebtedness of Maker in the principal amount of at least $300,000, or any such indebtedness shall become due before its stated maturity by acceleration of the maturity thereof or otherwise or shall become due by its terms and shall not be promptly paid or extended; (v) any of the Loan Documents shall cease to be legal, valid, binding agreements enforceable against any party executing the same in accordance with the respective terms thereof or shall in any way be terminated or become or be declared ineffective or inoperative or shall in any way whatsoever cease to give or provide the respective liens, security interests, rights, titles, interests, remedies, powers or privileges intended to be created thereby; (vi) Maker shall (A) apply for or consent to the appointment of a receiver, trustee, intervenor, custodian or liquidator of itself or of all or a substantial part of its assets, (B) be adjudicated a bankrupt or insolvent or file a voluntary petition for bankruptcy or admit in writing that it is unable to pay its debts as they become due, (C) make a general assignment for the benefit of creditors, (D) file a petition or answer seeking reorganization or an arrangement with creditors or to take advantage of any bankruptcy or insolvency laws, or (E) file an answer admitting the material allegations of, or consent to, or default in answering, a petition filed against it in any bankruptcy, reorganization or insolvency proceeding, or take corporate action for the purpose of effecting any of the foregoing; (vii) an order, judgment or decree shall be entered by any court of competent jurisdiction or other competent authority approving a petition seeking reorganization of Maker or appointing a receiver, trustee, intervenor or liquidator of any such person, or of all or substantially all of its or their assets, and such order, judgment or decree shall continue unstayed and in effect for a period of sixty (60) days; (viii) Payee's liens, mortgages or security interests in any of the Collateral should become unenforceable, or cease to be first priority liens, mortgages or security interests; or (ix) any final judgment(s) for the payment of money shall be rendered against Maker in excess of $100,000 (net insured amounts) that is not stayed pending appeal or otherwise contested in good faith.

(b) Upon the occurrence of any Default hereunder or under any other Loan Document, Payee may, at its option, (i) declare the entire unpaid balance of principal and accrued interest of the Obligation to be immediately due and payable without presentment or notice of any kind, which Maker waives pursuant to **Section 3** herein, (ii) reduce any claim to judgment, and/or (iii) pursue and enforce any of Payee's rights and remedies available pursuant to any applicable law or agreement including, without limitation, foreclosing all liens and security interests securing payment thereof or any part thereof; *provided, however*, in the case of any Default specified in *(vi)* or *(vii)* of **Section 7(a)** above with respect to Maker, without any notice to Maker or any other act by Payee, the principal of and interest accrued on this Note shall become immediately due and payable without presentment, demand, protest, or other notice of any kind, all of which are hereby waived by Maker.

8. Voluntary Prepayment. Maker reserves the right to prepay the outstanding principal balance of this Note, in whole or in part, at any time and from time to time, without premium or penalty, in increments of $100,000. Any such prepayment shall be made together with payment of interest accrued on the amount of principal being prepaid through the date of such prepayment.

9. Usury Laws. It is expressly stipulated and agreed to be the intent of Maker and Payee at all times to comply strictly with the applicable Texas law governing the maximum rate or amount of interest payable on the indebtedness evidenced by this Note (or applicable United States federal law to the extent that it permits Payee to contract for, charge, take, reserve or receive a greater amount of interest than under Texas law). If the applicable law is ever judicially interpreted so as to render usurious any amount (a) contracted for, charged, taken, reserved or received pursuant to this Note, any of the other Loan Documents or any other communication or writing by or between Maker and Payee related to the transaction or transactions that are the subject matter of the Loan Documents, (b) contracted for, charged, taken, reserved or received by reason of Payee's exercise of the option to accelerate the maturity of this Note, or (c) Maker will have paid or Payee will have received by reason of any voluntary prepayment by Maker of this Note, then it is Maker's and Payee's express intent that all amounts charged in excess of the Maximum Rate shall be automatically canceled, ab initio, and all amounts in excess of the Maximum Rate theretofore collected by Payee shall be credited on the principal balance of this Note (or, if this Note has been or would thereby be paid in full, refunded to Maker), and the provisions of this Note and the other Loan Documents shall immediately be deemed reformed and the amounts thereafter collectible hereunder and thereunder reduced, without the necessity of the execution of any new document, so as to comply with the applicable law, but so as to permit the recovery of the fullest amount otherwise called for hereunder and thereunder; provided, however, if this Note has been paid in full before the end of the stated term of this Note, then Maker and Payee agree that Payee shall, with reasonable promptness after Payee discovers or is advised by Maker that interest was received in an amount in excess of the Maximum Rate, either refund such excess interest to Maker and/or credit such excess interest against this Note then owing by Maker to Payee. Maker hereby agrees that as a condition precedent to any claim seeking usury penalties against Payee, Maker will provide written notice to Payee, advising Payee in reasonable detail of the nature and amount of the violation, and Payee shall have sixty (60) days after receipt of such notice in which to correct such usury violation, if any, by either refunding such excess interest to Maker or crediting such excess interest against this Note then owing by Maker to Payee. All sums contracted for, charged, taken, reserved or received by Payee for the use, forbearance or detention of any debt evidenced by this Note shall, to the extent permitted by applicable law, be amortized or spread, using the actuarial method, throughout the stated term of this Note (including any and all renewal and extension periods) until payment in full so that the rate or amount of interest on account of this Note does not exceed the Maximum Rate from time to time in effect and applicable to this Note for so long as debt is outstanding. In no event shall the provisions of Chapter 346 of the Texas Finance Code (which regulates certain revolving credit loan accounts and revolving triparty accounts) apply to this Note. Notwithstanding anything to the contrary contained herein or in any of the other Loan Documents, it is not the intention of Payee to accelerate the maturity of any interest that has not accrued at the time of such acceleration or to collect unearned interest at the time of such acceleration.

10. Costs and Expenses. If this Note is placed in the hands of an attorney for collection, or if it is collected through any legal proceeding at law or in equity, or in bankruptcy, receivership or other court proceedings, Maker agrees to pay all costs of collection, including, but not limited to, court costs and reasonable attorneys' fees, including all costs of appeal. In addition, Maker covenants and agrees to pay or reimburse Payee on demand all reasonable costs and expenses of Payee (including reasonable attorneys' fees and expenses) incurred by Payee in connection with the transactions contemplated by the Loan Documents.

11. Notices. Any notice that may be given by either Maker or Payee shall be in writing and shall be deemed given upon the earlier of the time of receipt thereof by the person entitled to receive such notice, or if mailed by registered or certified mail or with a recognized overnight mail courier upon two (2) days after deposit with the United States Post Office or one (1) day after deposit with such overnight mail courier, if postage is prepaid and mailing is addressed to Maker or Payee, as the case may be, at the following addresses, or to a different address previously given in a written notice to the other party:

```
To Maker:        Borrower, Inc.
                 [Address]
                 [City, State]
                 Attention: President
                 To Payee: Lender, Inc.
                 [Address]
                 [City, State]
                 Attention: Vice President and Treasurer
```

12. GOVERNING LAW. THIS INSTRUMENT AND ALL ISSUES AND CLAIMS ARISING IN CONNECTION WITH OR RELATING TO THE INDEBTEDNESS EVIDENCED HEREBY SHALL BE GOVERNED AND CONSTRUED IN ACCORDANCE WITH THE LAWS OF THE STATE OF TEXAS AND THE APPLICABLE LAWS OF THE UNITED STATES OF AMERICA.

13. JURY TRIAL. TO THE FULLEST EXTENT PERMITTED BY APPLICABLE LAW, MAKER HEREBY IRREVOCABLY AND EXPRESSLY WAIVES ALL RIGHT TO A TRIAL BY JURY IN ANY ACTION, PROCEEDING, OR COUNTERCLAIM (WHETHER BASED UPON CONTRACT, TORT, OR OTHERWISE) ARISING OUT OF OR RELATING TO ANY OF THIS NOTE OR THE OTHER LOAN DOCUMENTS OR THE TRANSACTIONS CONTEMPLATED HEREBY OR THEREBY, OR THE ACTIONS OF PAYEE IN THE NEGOTIATION, ADMINISTRATION, OR ENFORCEMENT THEREOF. THIS WAIVER OF RIGHT TO TRIAL BY JURY IS

GIVEN KNOWINGLY AND VOLUNTARILY BY MAKER, AND IS INTENDED TO ENCOMPASS INDIVIDUALLY EACH INSTANCE AND EACH ISSUE AS TO WHICH THE RIGHT TO A TRIAL BY JURY WOULD OTHERWISE ACCRUE. PAYEE IS HEREBY AUTHORIZED TO FILE A COPY OF THIS PARAGRAPH IN ANY PROCEEDING AS A CONCLUSIVE EVIDENCE OF THIS WAIVER BY MAKER.

14. ENTIRETY. THE PROVISIONS OF THIS NOTE AND THE LOAN DOCUMENTS MAY BE AMENDED OR REVISED ONLY BY AN INSTRUMENT IN WRITING SIGNED BY MAKER AND PAYEE. THIS NOTE AND ALL THE OTHER LOAN DOCUMENTS EMBODY THE FINAL, ENTIRE AGREEMENT OF MAKER AND PAYEE AND SUPERSEDE ANY AND ALL PRIOR COMMITMENTS, AGREEMENTS, REPRESENTATIONS, AND UNDERSTANDINGS, WHETHER WRITTEN OR ORAL, RELATING TO THE SUBJECT MATTER HEREOF AND THEREOF AND MAY NOT BE CONTRADICTED OR VARIED BY EVIDENCE OF PRIOR, CONTEMPORANEOUS, OR SUBSEQUENT ORAL AGREEMENTS OR DISCUSSIONS OF MAKER AND PAYEE. THERE ARE NO ORAL AGREEMENTS BETWEEN MAKER AND PAYEE.

MAKER:

BORROWER, INC.,
a Delaware corporation

By: _____

Name:

Title: _____

Assignment 21: Transfer and Enforcement of Negotiable Instruments

A. Transferring a Negotiable Instrument

One of the advantages of negotiable instruments is the ease with which an owner of a negotiable instrument can transfer clean and verifiable title: A transfer of a negotiable instrument never requires anything more than delivery of the instrument and a signature by the transferor. Furthermore, by examining the chain of signatures on the instrument (a topic discussed below), the purchaser generally can verify that the transfer is effective, in the sense that it will give the purchaser the ability to enforce the instrument. The ability to make a clean, complete, and verifiable transfer without the aid of any public official or recording of notice in a centralized record system substantially enhances the liquidity of negotiable instruments.

1. Negotiation and Status as a Holder

Two concepts are central to the rules for transferring negotiable instruments: the "holder" that possesses the instrument and has a right to enforce it (UCC §3-301(i)) and the act of "negotiation" by which it is transferred to a new holder. The UCC's definition of "negotiation" is not enlightening: it defines negotiation as any transfer of possession (even an involuntary transfer) by a person other than the original issuer that causes the transferee to become a holder. UCC §3-201(a). To make any sense out of that definition, you have to consider the UCC's definition of the "holder" in §1-201(b)(21).

One aspect of the document-centered focus of the negotiability system is the importance of possession of the physical document. Possession is the sine qua non of holder status: No person can be a holder without possession of the instrument. Thus, if an owner loses possession of an instrument (whether through inadvertence or theft), it loses its status as a holder at the same time. If an instrument is bearer paper (as defined in UCC §3-109), then possession is determinative. Any person in possession of bearer paper is a holder, however tenuous (or nonexistent) that person's claim to ownership of the instrument. UCC §1-201(b)(21). That rule is absolute: thieves that steal bearer paper become the holders of those instruments even though they are not the rightful owners. See UCC §3-203 comment 1 ("A thief who steals a check payable to bearer becomes the holder of the check and a person entitled to enforce it."). Accordingly, a prospective purchaser that examines an instrument and determines that it is bearer paper can purchase the instrument safe in the knowledge that it will be entitled to enforce the instrument as soon as it obtains possession.

Determining whether someone holds a piece of order paper is only slightly more complicated. As defined in UCC §3-109, order paper always must be payable to some particular, identified person. That identified person is the only person that can be a holder. UCC §1-201(b)(21). Thus, order paper in the possession of that identified person will have a holder (the identified person), but order paper in the possession of any other person will not have a holder. To put it another way, order paper has a holder only when the person in possession and the identified person "match up."

A variety of complications can arise in determining the precise party who is the identified person for a particular instrument. For example, checks frequently are payable to more than one person (such as a husband and wife). Article 3 relies on the precise words used on the instrument to decide whether one or both of the two is the holder. If the instrument is payable to "Husband or Wife," then it is treated as payable to them "alternatively," so that either of them that had possession would be a holder. UCC §3-110(d) and comment 4. The opposite rule applies if an instrument is payable to "Husband and Wife." In that case, the instrument is payable to them "not alternatively," so that "[n]either person, acting alone, can be the holder of the instrument." UCC §3-310(d) and comment 4.

Another common problem arises when the instrument is made payable to an account identified by number. That would happen if, for example, a person indorsed a check by writing an account number on the back and signing the check. In that case, the UCC treats the owner of the account as the identified person. UCC §3-110(c)(1). As you should recall from Assignment 12's discussion of wire-transfer errors, a likely problem in that area would be for the indorsement to identify an account both by name and by number, but for the account to be owned by somebody other than the named individual. In that case, Article 3 recognizes the named individual as the identified person, even if the named individual does not own the identified account. UCC §3-110(c)(1).

2.   *Special and Blank Indorsements*

The requirement that a holder of order paper be the identified person to whom that paper is payable means that a transfer of possession standing alone is not sufficient to make the purchaser a holder of order paper. If the seller is the identified person, then a transfer of possession with nothing more destroys the seller's holder status (because the seller no longer has possession) without giving the purchaser holder status (because the seller is still the "identified person").

To make the purchaser the identified person (and thus the holder), the seller must indorse the instrument. An indorsement can be as simple as a signature on an instrument. Indeed, the UCC presumes that any signature that appears on an instrument is an indorsement unless the circumstances "unambiguously indicate that the signature was made for a purpose other than indorsement." UCC §3-204(a). The most common contrary indication is the location of a signature in the lower right-hand corner of the face of an instrument. (Think of the place where you sign a check.) Courts recognize a signature in that location as the signature of an issuer (the maker of a note or the drawer of a draft), even without any specific written indication of purpose. UCC §3-204 comment 1, paragraph 2, sentence 14. Absent some specific written indication of contrary intent, a signature in any other place (even on the front) ordinarily will be treated as an indorsement.

A holder transferring an instrument can use two different types of indorsements to make the purchaser the holder of the instrument. The first is a special indorsement, which identifies a person to whom the instrument is to be paid. If Carl Eben had a check that he wished to transfer to Jodi Kay, he could indorse it by writing: "Pay to Jodi Kay, /s/ Carl Eben." If Carl held the instrument as the identified person at the time he made that indorsement, the indorsement would make Jodi the identified person. UCC §3-205(a). Thus, the instrument would remain order paper, but now the identified person would have changed to Jodi, so that a transfer of possession to Jodi would make Jodi the holder. If Carl held the instrument as bearer paper, the special indorsement would change the instrument to order paper, again with Jodi as the identified person, and thus the holder. UCC §§3-109(c), 3-205(a).

The second main type of indorsement is a blank indorsement. A blank indorsement is any indorsement made by a holder that does not indicate an identified person. For example, if Carl Eben had signed his name to the instrument, without more, he would have made a blank indorsement. A blank indorsement transforms order paper to bearer paper, so that any person in possession is a holder. UCC §§3-109(c), 3-205(b). Hence, if Carl made a blank indorsement and gave the instrument to Jodi, Jodi would be the holder solely because of her possession of the instrument. A blank indorsement on bearer paper has no effect on the character of the instrument, although (as discussed in Assignment 9 and later in this assignment) it does create liability for the indorser under UCC §3-415.

To accommodate the automated procedures used for processing the large volume of checks transferred to banks, the system includes a variety of special rules for checks that depart from the rules outlined above. First, Article 4 generally dispenses with the requirement of indorsements for transfers of checks in the check-collection system. Thus, a depositary bank automatically becomes a holder of a check deposited by its customer, even if the check was order paper and the customer failed to indorse it to the bank at the time of deposit. UCC §4-205(1). Similarly, a bank need not indorse the check when it transfers it to any other bank. Instead, "[a]ny agreed method that identifies the transferor bank is sufficient." UCC §4-206. See also 12 C.F.R. §229.35(a) (setting federal standards for indorsement under Regulation CC).

Similarly, to limit the potential for fraudulent enforcement of checks stolen during the course of collection, Regulation CC provides that no party other than a bank can become the holder of a check once it has been indorsed by a bank. Thus, even if a bank indorsed a check in blank (so that it was bearer paper), an employee that stole the check from a check-sorting machine could not become the holder of the check. The only way that a party other than a bank can become a holder of such a check is for the bank to specially indorse the check to a nonbank party or for the bank to return the check to the person that deposited it (presumably because the check was dishonored). Regulation CC, 12 C.F.R. §229.35(c); see also UCC §4-201(b) (articulating a similar rule that applies when a check is indorsed "pay any bank").

3.   *Restrictive and Anomalous Indorsements*

Article 3 also discusses two other kinds of indorsements. The first is a restrictive indorsement, an indorsement that purports to limit the indorsee's ability to deal with the instrument: "Pay to Jodi Kay, but only if the Astros win the World Series in 2018. /s/ Carl Eben." Article 3 invalidates most types of restrictive indorsements. UCC §3-206(a), (b). It does, however, respect the common restrictive indorsements of an instrument "for deposit only" or "for collection." If an instrument bears one of those indorsements, a party that pays or purchases the instrument commits conversion unless the proceeds of the instrument are received by the indorser or applied consistently with the indorsement. UCC §3-206(c). Thus, a bank can give a payee cash for a check, even if the payee mistakenly indorsed the check "for deposit only," but the bank would commit conversion if it deposited the funds in somebody else's account or cashed the check for a third party.

The last type of indorsement discussed in Article 3 is an anomalous indorsement. An indorsement is anomalous when it is made by a person that was not a holder at the time it made the indorsement. UCC §3-205(d). For example, if Kay Eben signed the back of a check payable to Carl Eben and Carl then negotiated the instrument to Jodi Kay, the signature by Kay Eben would be an anomalous indorsement. An indorsement by a party that is not a holder plays no role in negotiation of the instrument because only a holder can make a blank indorsement or a special indorsement. For example, if Kay Eben signed the back of the check "Pay to Jodi Kay," the instrument would remain order paper payable to Carl. Because anomalous indorsements play no role in negotiation, Article 3 gives them another purpose. It presumes that they were made for "accommodation," so that the anomalous indorser becomes a guarantor of the instrument. UCC §3-419. In Article 3 terminology, the anomalous indorser becomes an "accommodation" party. The rules governing that status are similar to the standard guaranty rules discussed in the chapter on guaranties. See UCC §§3-419, 3-605.

B.   Enforcement and Collection of Instruments

1.   *The Right to Enforce an Instrument*

The principal legal attribute of status as a holder is the right to enforce the instrument. Thus, any person that holds an instrument is a "[p]erson entitled to enforce the instrument" under UCC §3-301(i). What that means is that the holder has the legal right to call for payment from any party obligated to pay the instrument. Because a party can become a holder without actually owning the instrument (consider a thief in possession of bearer paper), the holder's absolute right to enforce the instrument means that Article 3 permits a party to enforce an instrument even if the party has no lawful right to payment. The system accepts that occasional injustice because of the benefits that the absolute rule brings in streamlining the process for determining whether a party has a right to enforce the instrument. A lawsuit to enforce a negotiable instrument requires proof of only the simple facts necessary to establish holder status; the holder need not establish the facts necessary to prove the underlying right to payment.

To be sure, it is not necessary to be a holder to become a person entitled to enforce an instrument. For example, one party that is a holder can transfer its rights to enforce an instrument to another party by selling the instrument to the second party. Under ordinary property rules, the transferee acquires whatever rights in the instrument the transferor had before the sale, whether or not the parties complied with the special Article 3 rules for making the transferee a holder. UCC §3-203(b). Thus, if Carl Eben sold a check to Jodi Kay without indorsing it, Jodi Kay would not become a holder herself, but she would obtain Carl's rights to enforce the instrument and thus would become a person entitled to enforce the instrument. UCC §3-301(ii). Moreover, because that circumstance generally would arise only because of the seller's inadvertent failure to indorse the instrument at the time of the sale, UCC §3-203(c) grants the purchaser a right to force the seller to indorse the instrument at any time after the sale. That indorsement, in turn, would make the purchaser a holder as of the time of the indorsement. Although those principles seem relatively pedestrian, the rapidity of transfers of home mortgage notes has raised interesting problems in this area since the early years of the century.

In re Kang Jin Hwang

396 B.R. 757 (Bankr. C.D. Cal. 2008)

Before Bufford, United States Bankruptcy Judge.

I.   INTRODUCTION

IndyMac Federal Bank ("IndyMac Federal") brings this motion, which the court grants, to reconsider its denial of relief from the §362 automatic stay to foreclose on real property belonging to debtor Kang Jin Hwang in Las Vegas. The property is security for a promissory note that was sold to the Federal Home Loan Mortgage Corp. ("Freddie Mac"), which has not joined and is not a party to this motion. Freddie Mac, in turn, has most likely sold the note to unknown third parties for securitization.

After trial on the motion for relief from stay, and several rounds of briefing, the question remains: to whom is the debt owed (i.e., who owns the promissory note)? The court denies the motion on two procedural grounds: IndyMac Federal is not the real party in interest pursuant to Rule 17 of the Federal Rules of Civil Procedure, and the joinder of the owner of the note is required by Rule 19.

Subject to these procedural infirmities, the court finds that IndyMac Federal is entitled to enforce the note under California law (and the Uniform Commercial Code ("UCC")): IndyMac Federal remains the holder of the note, notwithstanding the sale, because it has possession of the note and the note is payable to its predecessor IndyMac Bank, F.S.E. ("IndyMac Bank").

II. RELEVANT FACTS

Kang Jin Hwang filed this chapter 7 case on April 22, 2008. Hwang's residence in Las Vegas, Nevada is encumbered by a first deed of trust recorded on February 1, 2007, supporting a promissory note in the amount of $376,000. The original payee on the promissory note, as well as the beneficiary of the deed of trust, is Mortgageit, Inc. ("Mortgageit"). Apparently, at some time before this case was filed, Mortgageit transferred the note to IndyMac Bank. After this motion was filed, IndyMac Bank was taken over by the Federal Deposit Insurance Corporation ("FDIC") and put into a conservatorship that now operates under the name IndyMac Federal, which has substituted into this motion. . . .

IndyMac sold the note to unidentified "investors" through Freddie Mac, apparently at some time prior to the filing of this bankruptcy case. Most likely, Freddie Mac sold the note into a securitization trust. IndyMac does not know who owns the note today, although it still has possession of the note and there is nothing on the note to indicate that it has been transferred. Neither Freddie Mac nor any of the investors has joined in this motion. In addition, IndyMac has failed to provide any documents showing its sale of the note or its status as a servicing agent for the note's new owner.

IndyMac filed this motion for relief from the automatic stay. . . . The motion included a declaration by Erica A. Johnson-Sect, an IndyMac vice president, providing the factual grounds for the motion. Copies of the promissory note and the deed of trust are attached to her declaration. . . .

Erica A. Johnson-Sect, a Vice President of IndyMac, testified at the trial on this motion on July 15, 2008, and brought the original note to court. While the court was satisfied with the declarant's testimony on the accuracy of the payment records, she testified that IndyMac no longer owned the note, but had sold it to investors through Freddie Mac. The court finds her testimony credible on this point.

Ms. Johnson-Sect also testified that IndyMac has brought this motion as the duly authorized servicing agent for the new owner of the note. The court disbelieves this testimony, particularly in view of (a) her testimony that she does not know who owns the note at the present time, and (b) the failure to offer in evidence any servicing agreement with the new owner.

III. DISCUSSION

IndyMac argues that it is entitled to enforce the note because it possesses the note and the note shows it as transferee and no indorsement transferring it to any other party. IndyMac also argues that the court may not raise *sua sponte* any deficiencies in the evidence it has presented to the court.

A motion for relief from the automatic stay must satisfy both substantive and procedural requirements. The substantive requirements are provided by §362(d). The procedural requirements are imposed by the United States Constitution (due process) and the Federal Rules of Bankruptcy Procedure (which mostly incorporate the Federal Rules of Civil Procedure). The applicable rules here are the "real party in interest" rule and the "required joinder" rule.

The court finds that IndyMac is entitled to enforce the note, notwithstanding the sale to Freddie Mac. However, in coming to federal court, IndyMac must comply with the applicable procedures in this court. Two of these rules, the real party in interest rule and the required joinder rule, each requires IndyMac to join the present owner of the note in this motion for relief from stay, which it has refused to do.

A.   Right to Enforce the Note

Since a party (such as IndyMac in this case) that seeks relief under §362(d) does so in order to enforce rights that have been stayed by §362(a), it is necessary to consider who is entitled to enforce the note under the substantive law that governs those rights. Thus, for a relief from stay motion based on a promissory note, the court must look to the substantive law that governs promissory notes.

Bankruptcy law does not provide for the enforcement of promissory notes generally. In the absence of bankruptcy law, the legal obligations of the parties are determined by the applicable non-bankruptcy law, which is usually state law. *See,* e.g., United States v. Butner, 440 U.S. 48, 54-55 (1979).

In the United States, the law of promissory notes is not unified at the federal level. Instead, each state has its own law on promissory notes. However, every state has adopted a version of the UCC to govern negotiable promissory notes. Thus, we turn to the California Commercial Code ("CComC"), the California version of the UCC.

1.   Relevant Law of Negotiable Instruments

The substantive California law that governs negotiable instruments is CComC Division 3 (the California version of UCC Article 3). . . .

An instrument (including a secured note) may only be enforced by the "holder" of the note (with minor exceptions not relevant to this case). *See* UCC §3-301. For an instrument payable to an identified person (such as the note in this case), there are two requirements for a person to qualify as a holder: (a) the person must be in possession of the instrument, and (b) the instrument must be payable to that person. *See* UCC §1-201[(b)(21)].

The payee of an instrument may negotiate it by indorsing it and delivering it to another person, who then becomes its holder (and entitled to enforce it). . . .

A fundamental feature of negotiable instruments is that they are transferred by the delivery of possession, not by contract or assignment. The transfer of an instrument "vests in the transferee any right of the transferor to enforce the instrument. . . . "

UCC §3-203(b). Thus, the right to enforce a negotiable instrument is only transferable by delivery of the instrument itself. UCC §3-203.

The transfer of a negotiable instrument has an additional requirement: the transferor must indorse the instrument to make it payable to the transferee. *See* UCC §3-205(a). Alternatively, the transferor may indorse the instrument in blank, and thereby make it enforceable by anyone in its possession (much like paper currency). *See* UCC §3-205(b). If the transferor makes a transfer without indorsing the instrument, the transferee has a right to demand indorsement by the transferor. *See* UCC §3-203(c).

2.   Who May Enforce the Note in This Case

IndyMac contends, and the court assumes without deciding, that the note here at issue is a negotiable instrument, as defined in [UCC §3-104]. The note is on a standard printed form that is used in the finance industry for notes that are freely bought and sold in a manner inconsistent with treating it as a non-negotiable note. Thus IndyMac must be the holder of the note to entitle it to enforce the note (including bringing this relief from stay motion).

In this case, the note is payable to IndyMac (pursuant to its negotiation from Mortgageit to IndyMac), and IndyMac had possession of the note at the time that the motion was filed. Under these facts, IndyMac qualifies as the holder of the note.

There is a second scenario, not supported by the evidence in this case, in which IndyMac would have a right to enforce the note. If IndyMac held the note on behalf of the new owner (Freddie Mac or its subsequent transferee), this would constitute possession by the new owner, and IndyMac would be entitled to seek relief from stay on the new owner's behalf (provided that it joined the new owner in the motion).

Notably, however, IndyMac does not contend that it holds the note as an agent on behalf of Freddie Mac or its transferee. Indeed, it is doubtful that IndyMac could make such a claim, because IndyMac does not know who owns the note. Thus, this argument is not available.

3.   Sale of the Note to Freddie Mac

In this case IndyMac sold the note to Freddie Mac, which in turn most likely sold it again as part of a securitization transaction. Insofar as the record before the court discloses, the owner of the note today is unknown.

In this case, IndyMac has not delivered the note to Freddie Mac (or its successor): IndyMac still possesses the note. In addition, the note bears no indication of a transfer: it still shows IndyMac as the payee (pursuant to the indorsement from Mortgageit). In consequence, IndyMac remains the holder of the note and is entitled to enforce it under CComC §3301(a) (UCC §3-301): the right to enforce the note has not yet passed to Freddie Mac or its successor owner of the note. This interpretation of §3203 is supported by Note 1, which states in relevant part:

[A] person who has an ownership right in an instrument might not be a person entitled to enforce the instrument. For example, suppose X is the owner and holder of an instrument payable to X. X sells the instrument to Y but is unable to deliver immediate possession to Y. Instead, X signs a document conveying all of X's right, title, and interest in the instrument to Y. Although the document may be effective to give Y a claim to ownership of the instrument, Y is not a person entitled to enforce the instrument until Y obtains possession of the instrument. No transfer of the instrument occurs under Section 3203(a) until it is delivered to Y.

An instrument is a reified right to payment. The right is represented by the instrument itself. The right to payment is transferred by delivery of possession of the instrument "by a person other than its issuer for the purpose of giving to the person receiving delivery the right to enforce the instrument."

The foregoing makes it clear that no successor to IndyMac presently has a right to enforce the note, because IndyMac still has possession of the note.

This raises the question of who, if anybody, is presently entitled to enforce the note in these circumstances. Two alternatives are available. First, there may be no entity that is entitled to enforce the note until its delivery to its new rightful owner is accomplished. Second, because IndyMac continues to possess the note, it may be entitled to enforce the note, even though the note is owned by another entity.

There are good policy reasons for adopting the first alternative. Disabling the transferor from enforcing the note upon its sale to a new owner encourages the parties to complete the transaction by delivery of the instrument to the new owner. In the present configuration of the home mortgage industry, this policy can be important: it would discourage an apparently common practice in the secondary mortgage market of failure to deliver notes when they are sold, often numerous times, so that the possessor of the note may be far removed from the real owner of the note.

The second alternative also has substantial policy support. A note supporting a home mortgage ought to be enforceable, and the homeowner should be required to make the payments owing. If the owner fails to pay, the markets rely on the ability of the noteholder to bring foreclosure proceedings to realize the value of the note. . . .

Interposing a hiatus on the right to foreclose (apart from the automatic stay resulting from the filing of a bankruptcy case) interferes with the security of lenders in the home mortgage market. In addition, the noteholder is in position to cancel the note upon payment and to deliver the canceled note to the obligor.

IndyMac cites no case holding that, after selling (but not delivering) a secured note to an unrelated third party, the seller is entitled to enforce the note for its own account. The court's independent research has discovered two such cases, both involving transfers to corporations wholly owned by the sellers: Edwards v. Mesch, 107 N.M. 704, 763 P.2d 1169 (N.M. 1988); Spears v. Sutherland, 37 N.M. 356, 23 P.2d 622 (N.M. 1933). Both cases involved transfers to corporations owned by the sellers (100% in the *Edwards* case; 95% in the *Spears* case). The sale of a note to an unrelated third party, as in this case, is a very different situation.

In the court's view, the second alternative is the better view: the holder of a note is entitled to enforce it, notwithstanding sale of the note to another party, until the note is delivered to the purchaser (after indorsement, if appropriate). This assures that, notwithstanding the sale of the note and the failure to deliver the note pursuant to the sale, a holder exists that may enforce the note against the obligor. Thus, the court holds that, notwithstanding the sale of the note, IndyMac remains the holder of the note and is entitled to enforce it.

The debtor is not at risk in making payments on the note to IndyMac instead of the owner of the note. CComC §3602 (UCC §3-602) provides that any payment to a "person entitled to enforce the instrument" must be credited against the note, even if the debtor knows that a different party is claiming ownership of or an interest in the note. . . .

B.   Real Party in Interest

IndyMac's substantive right to enforce the note, as the holder, does not dispose of the motion before the court. In coming to federal court to enforce this right, IndyMac must comply with the applicable procedures of federal court. Two such procedures stand in the way of granting the motion for relief from stay in this case. The first procedural problem arises from the real party in interest rule. [Ultimately, the Court concludes that IndyMac is not entitled to relief from the stay because it is not the real party in interest and because that party has not been joined in the litigation.]

IV.   CONCLUSION

In conclusion, the court finds upon reconsideration that IndyMac is entitled to enforce the secured note here at issue. However, it must satisfy the procedural requirements of federal law in seeking relief from the automatic stay for this purpose. These requirements include joining the owner of the note on two separate grounds: it is the real party in interest under Rule 17, and it is a required party under Rule 19.

Because IndyMac has failed and refused to join the owner of the secured note, the motion for relief from stay is denied.

The disarray evident in *Kang Jin Hwang* is not unusual. Rather, the problems of managing paper transfers for tangible home-mortgage notes largely overwhelmed the system in the years before the 2009 financial crisis; you will read in Assignment 24 how similar pressures overwhelmed the securities transactions system in the 1960s. In any event, the system for home-mortgage notes apparently is now moving toward a registry system, much like the system adopted in Revised Article 8 (the topic of Assignment 24). Presently, the Federal Reserve is drafting a National Mortgage Note Repository Act, which would create a repository to hold home-mortgage notes; a UCC drafting committee is preparing parallel revisions to UCC Articles 1, 3, and 9. If implemented, those revisions would bring to an end the era of paper-based transfers as a method of documenting ownership of home-mortgage notes.

2.   Presentment and Dishonor

Article 3 codifies a formalistic two-step process for the collection of instruments established under common-law divisions that predate the UCC. The first step, presentment, is taken by the holder. Presentment is nothing more than a demand for payment made by a person entitled to enforce an instrument. UCC §3-501(a). If the instrument is a note, the demand ordinarily is made to the maker of the note. If the instrument is a draft, the demand ordinarily is made to the drawee. UCC §3-501(a). The demand is called "presentment" because the party to whom the demand is made is entitled to insist that the holder exhibit the instrument — "present" it, in the language of bills and notes. UCC §3-501(b)(2).

The second step in the collection process is the response of the party to whom presentment is made. It has a choice of honoring the instrument or dishonoring it. In most cases, the system assumes that a party intends to dishonor an instrument if it does not take an affirmative action to honor it. Thus, if the instrument is payable at the time of presentment, in most cases it is dishonored if it is not paid on the date of presentment. UCC §3-502(a)(1), (b)(2). If it is a check, however, the opposite rule applies: The drawee is assumed to honor the check unless it acts promptly to dishonor it. UCC §3-502(b)(1). Although dishonor usually has no immediate consequences as between the holder and the dishonoring party (because dishonor does not alter the dishonoring party's liability on the instrument), you will see later in the assignment that dishonor has a number of important consequences for the liability of indorsers of the instrument and the enforceability of the obligation for which the instrument was given.

3.   Defenses to Enforcement

Although Article 3 includes detailed rules regarding the steps that a party must take to become a person entitled to enforce an instrument, it is completely agnostic about that person's success in enforcing that instrument. As long as the person entitled to enforce the instrument is not a holder in due course (a status discussed in the next assignment), Article 3 allows the obligor to interpose a wide variety of defenses, which includes not only any defense created by Article 3, but also any claim that the obligor has against the payee with respect to the original transaction. UCC §§3-305(a)(2), (3). The following case illustrates what probably is the most common defense interposed by parties seeking to withhold payment of an instrument: failure of the payee to provide the goods and services for which the instrument was given.

Turman v. Ward's Home Improvement, Inc.
26 U.C.C. Rep. Serv. 2d 175 (Va. Cir. Ct. 1995)

HALEY, J.

I.

The question here for resolution is whether an assignee of the payee of a negotiable instrument is a holder in due course, and as such immune to the defenses that the makers might raise against the payee of the negotiable instrument.

II.

The pertinent facts can be concisely stated.

G. Michael Turman and Carolyn May Cash Turman (hereafter "Turman") executed a deed of trust note dated February 23, 1993 for $107,500.00 payable to Ward's Home Improvement, Inc. (hereafter "Ward"). The note was consideration for a contract by which Ward was to construct a home on property [owned] by Turman. . . . On that same date, Ward executed a separate written assignment of that note to Robert L. Pomerantz (herafter "Pomerantz"). This document specifically uses the word "assigns." Ward did not endorse the note to Pomerantz or otherwise write upon the note. Ward apparently received $95,000.00 for the assignment from Pomerantz. Ward failed to complete the house and to do so will require the expenditure of an additional $42,000.00. Pomerantz maintains that he is a holder in due course of the $107,500.00 note and has demanded payment. . . .

IV.

[UCC §3-201(b)] states that ". . . if an instrument is payable to an identified person, negotiation requires its indorsement by the holder." An assignment is not an endorsement. Accordingly, such a transfer is not a negotiation. And the transferee is not a holder. Official Comment 2 to Code §[3-]203(b).

An assignment does, however, vest ". . . in the transferee any right of the transferor to enforce the instrument . . . (under Code §[3]-301)." Code §[3]-203(b). The transferee's rights are derivative of the transferor's. Accordingly, and pursuant to Code §[3]-305(a)(2), a maker may assert a defense ". . . that would be available if the person entitled to enforce the instrument were enforcing a right to payment under a simple contract." In short, the assignee of a negotiable instrument is subject to defenses the maker can raise against the original payee/assignor. And such a defense is failure of consideration. See Code §[3]-303(b) ". . . If an instrument is issued for a promise of performance, the issuer has a defense to the extent performance of the promise is due and the promise has not been performed."

In light of the foregoing . . . the court holds Pomerantz is not a holder in due course and is subject to the defenses to payment of the $107,500.00 note that Turman could raise against Ward.

C.   Liability on an Instrument

A key part of a system for the enforcement of instruments is a set of rules deciding which parties are liable on any particular instrument. Part 4 of Article 3 sets out a series of rules on that point, which are relatively straightforward. First, UCC §3-401 articulates a general rule of exclusion. Except for the transfer and presentment warranty liability discussed in Chapter 3, no party is liable on an instrument unless it has signed the instrument. Two major difficulties arise in applying that rule. The first occurs when a party has applied some authenticating mark to a document that does not include a formal written signature. On that point, Article 3 follows general UCC principles by applying a broad definition of signature that includes "any name, including a trade or assumed name," as well as "a word, mark, or symbol executed or adopted by a person with present intention to authenticate a writing." UCC §3-401(b); see UCC §1-201(b)(37) (similar definition of "signed").

The more challenging issues arise in cases where an individual signing an instrument arguably is acting as an agent or representative of another individual. For example, Carl Eben might sign a note for Riverfront Tools, Inc. Two sets of issues arise: whether the signing individual (Carl) is liable and whether the nonsigning individual or entity (Riverfront Tools, Inc.) is liable. UCC §3-402 includes a series of rules to resolve those questions. In reading these rules, you should note that the UCC describes the signing party (Carl) as the "representative" and the nonsigning party (Riverfront Tools, Inc.) as the "represented person."

To decide whether the represented person is liable, Article 3 defers to customary principles of agency law: The UCC itself does not undertake to define these principles; it simply states that when "a representative signs an instrument . . ., the represented person is bound by the signature to the same extent the represented person would be bound if the signature were on a simple contract." UCC §3-402(a). To see how that would work, assume that Carl signed an instrument as "Carl Eben, President, Riverfront Tools, Inc." and that Carl had sufficient authority under ordinary principles of agency law to bind Riverfront Tools, Inc., to the contract. In that event, Riverfront Tools, Inc., would be just as liable on the instrument as an ordinary individual that had signed the instrument directly.

To decide whether the representative that signs is liable, Article 3 looks to the form of the signature. Generally, Carl is not liable if (a) the signature shows unambiguously that he is signing on behalf of the represented person *and* (b) the instrument identifies the represented person. Thus, Carl would not be liable on the signature set out in the preceding paragraph. UCC §3-402(b)(1). Conversely, if the signature fails either one of those tests, then Carl will be personally liable on the instrument unless he can prove that the original parties did not intend for him to be bound. UCC §3-402(b)(2).

To determine the liability of the parties that have signed the instrument, Article 3 includes a series of four separate rules to cover each of the capacities in which a party can sign an instrument. The first type of liability is absolute. The party that issues a note is directly and unconditionally liable on the instrument. UCC §3-412. That rule makes sense because the party issuing a note has agreed by issuing the note to accept liability; that is the purpose of the note.

State Bank v. Smith

2014 WL 6088513 (Mich. Ct. App. 2014)

Before Whitbeck, P.J., and Fitzgerald and Murray, JJ.
Per Curiam.

In this wrongful dishonor case, plaintiff/counter-defendant, The State Bank ("plaintiff"), appeals as of right an order granting summary disposition . . . in favor of defendant, J.P. Morgan Chase Bank, N.A. ("Chase"). We affirm.

I.   FACTS

On March 26, 2012, defendant/counter-plaintiff, Dale M. Smith ("Smith"), presented a cashier's check in the amount of $294,500.99 for deposit in his IOLTA [i.e., Interest on Lawyer Trust Account] account with plaintiff. The check appeared to be a cashier's check drawn on Chase [B]ank. Plaintiff accepted the check for deposit. The following day, March 27, 2012, Smith requested that plaintiff wire approximately $275,000 from his account to an account in Japan. Before performing this transfer, plaintiff contacted a local Chase branch and spoke to a representative. According to plaintiff, this representative "confirmed the check number, the account number, verified the amount in the check and represented there were no stop-payment orders placed on the item. Plaintiff processed the wire transfer request.

On March 28, 2012, Chase returned the check to plaintiff with the notation "refer to maker." Plaintiff presented the check to Chase for payment a second time, and Chase again returned the check to plaintiff. According to Elizabeth Roush, a Vice President and Reconciliation Manager for Chase, the cashier's check was "different from the form of official cashier's checks issued by Chase." The check number had an incorrect number of digits, did not include "a printed audit number to indicate its validity[,]" did not have the proper signature, and was missing a security symbol. At her deposition, Roush explained that only one authorized signature exists for all cashier's checks drawn on the account number printed on the cashier's check. This signature is electronically printed on all checks issued by Chase retail branches. Roush was immediately able to identify that the check was not issued by Chase because the signature was not an authorized signature for that account. Roush did not know who signed the check.

On May 16, 2012, plaintiff filed a complaint against Smith and Chase. In its only count against Chase, plaintiff alleged that Chase wrongfully dishonored the check. Chase filed a motion for summary disposition, arguing that it was not obligated to pay the check because the check did not contain a signature authorized by Chase. Plaintiff responded, arguing that, because it was a holder in due course of the check, Chase was obligated to pay the check regardless of whether the signature was authorized. . . . The trial court granted Chase's motion, ruling that even if plaintiff was a holder in due course, because the signature on the check was unauthorized, Chase was not obligated by it. . . .

II.   DISCUSSION

A.   Chase's Obligation on the Instrument

Plaintiff first argues that the trial court erred when it determined that, despite its unchallenged status as a holder in due course of the check, Chase had no obligation to pay the check because it did not contain an authorized signature. We disagree.

. . .

A cashier's check is a type of instrument recognized by Michigan's Uniform Commercial Code ("UCC"). Pursuant to [UCC §3-]401(1) "A person is not liable on an instrument unless (*i*) the person signed the instrument, or (*ii*) the person is represented by an agent or representative who signed the instrument and the signature is binding on the represented person under [UCC §3-]402." As the official comment to this provision explains, "Obligation on an instrument depends on a signature that is binding on the obligor." [UCC §3-]401, comment 1. [UCC §3-]403(1) further states, "Unless otherwise provided in this article or article 4, [[UCC §4-]101 et seq.,] an unauthorized signature is ineffective except as the signature of the unauthorized signer in favor of a person who in good faith pays the instrument or takes it for value. An unauthorized signature may be ratified for all purposes of this article."

It is undisputed that the cashier's check contains only an unauthorized signature. Chase attached to its motion the affidavit of Roush, who explained that the check did "not have the proper signature on it[.]" At her deposition, Roush explained that there was only one authorized signature for all cashier's checks issued by Chase retail banks. Roush stated that she immediately knew the check was not issued by Chase because the signature on the check was not the authorized signature. As there is no evidence that the check was authorized by Chase, Chase cannot be obligated to pay the check. [UCC §3-]401(1). The only person obligated by the check is the unknown individual who actually signed it, and only if plaintiff, in good faith, paid the check or took it for value. [UCC §3-]403(1).

Relying upon [UCC §3-]305(1), plaintiff argues that it was a holder in due course of the cashier's check, and as such, is entitled to enforce it, despite the lack of an authorized signature. Plaintiff's argument is without merit. . . .

Plaintiff argues that Chase is obligated to pay the check because forgery is not one of the defenses listed under [UCC §3-]305(1)(a), the defenses which may be raised against a holder in due course, [UCC §3-]305(2). Accordingly, plaintiff believes Chase may not defend against enforcement of the check on the basis of forgery because plaintiff is a holder in due course, and forgery is not a defense listed in [UCC §3-]305(1)(a). Plaintiff errs by ignoring that the defenses stated in [UCC §3-]305(1)(a)-(c) are only relevant when "the right to enforce the *obligation of a party to pay an instrument*" is at issue. [UCC §3-]305(1) (emphasis supplied). [UCC §3-]305(2) discusses when certain defenses are available or unavailable to an *obligor*, i.e., someone who is first obligated to pay an instrument, against a holder in due course. As explained, Chase has no obligation to pay the check because it did not sign the check, nor did it authorize the signature that appears on the check. [UCC §3-]401(1). Thus, Chase is not an obligor, and has no need for any of the defenses discussed in [UCC §3-]305. Whether plaintiff is a holder in due course is entirely irrelevant, as that fact only becomes relevant if there is an obligation to enforce. [UCC §3-]305(2).

. . .

Plaintiff argues that [UCC §3-]412 obligates Chase to pay the cashier's check "regardless of whether or not it actually issued the item because [plaintiff] is a holder in due course." . . . This statute simply defines the precise obligations of one who is obligated to pay a cashier's check. It does not attempt to redefine what must exist before one becomes obligated to pay a cashier's check — an authorized signature. [UCC §3-]401(1).

Plaintiff primarily relies upon comment 2 to [UCC §3-]412, which states, "Under [[UCC §3-]105(2)] nonissuance of either a complete or incomplete instrument is a defense by a maker or drawer against a person that is not a holder in due course." [UCC §3-]412, comment 2. It appears that plaintiff believes that "nonissuance" means that the party did not actually create or authorize the check, and accordingly, Chase may not refuse to honor the check against a holder in due course on the ground that it did not create or authorize the check. [UCC §3-]105(1) defines "issue" as "the first delivery of an instrument by the maker or drawer, whether to a holder or nonholder, for the purpose of giving rights on the instrument." In short, "issue" does not refer to creation or authorization, it refers to delivery. [UCC §3-]105(1). Chase does not argue, and the trial court did not decide, that Chase did not issue, i.e., deliver, the check. Rather, Chase argued, and the trial court agreed, that Chase was not obligated by the check because it did not sign it. Accordingly, [UCC §3-]105, and the citation to this statute in comment 2 to [UCC §3-]412, are of no relevance.

. . .

Affirmed.

The other three types of liability all depend on some occurrence after the issuance of the draft. The first of those three deals with the liability of the drawee of a draft. As you should recall from your study of the checking system, a drawee of a draft has no liability on a draft at the time it is issued. UCC §3-408. If it accepts the draft (which requires nothing but a signature, UCC §3-409(a)), however, the drawee at that point becomes directly liable on the draft. UCC §3-413(a).

The last two types of liability are conditioned on dishonor. Thus, except for drafts on which the drawer and the drawee are the same person (cashier's checks and the like), the drawer of a draft is not liable on the draft unless it is dishonored. UCC §3-414(b). Moreover, the drawer's liability is discharged if a bank accepts the draft (because the holder of the draft then can look to the bank for payment). UCC §3-414(c). The rules for indorser liability are quite similar. First, the indorser is liable only if the instrument is dishonored. UCC §3-415(a). Second, the indorser's liability is discharged if a bank accepts the instrument after it has been indorsed. UCC §3-415(d). Finally, an indorser (or a drawer of any type of draft other than a check) can limit its liability by indicating that it is signing the instrument "without recourse." UCC §§3-414(e), 3-415(b).

D. The Effect of the Instrument on the Underlying Obligation

The last topic related to liability on an instrument is the relation between the liability parties have on an instrument and the underlying obligation for which the instrument is given. Outside the loan context, payment obligations ordinarily are given in satisfaction of some underlying obligation. For example, if a tenant writes a check for rent, the tenant offers the check to satisfy the tenant's obligation to pay rent under its lease. As discussed above, the issuer of a negotiable instrument incurs liability on the instrument without regard to the terms of the underlying transaction. Accordingly, when a party issues a negotiable instrument, it incurs liability separate from its liability on any underlying obligation. If that liability is conditional, it is conditional only as indicated by the Article 3 rules discussed above.

The first problem in this area is the effect of the instrument on the ability of the payee to enforce the underlying obligation. If the issuer or drawer issues an instrument offering full payment of an obligation, it seems somehow unfair to allow the payee to continue to enforce the underlying obligation: It would be nonsensical to allow a landlord to sue for rent the day after the landlord accepts a check for the rent. On the other hand, it is not clear that issuance of the instrument should discharge the underlying obligation. If the check bounces, shouldn't the landlord then be able to sue for the rent?

UCC §3-310 sets out the rules governing the relation between liability on the instrument and liability on the underlying obligation. Those rules divide instruments into two classes: near-cash instruments (governed by UCC §3-310(a), (c)) and ordinary instruments (governed by UCC §3-310(b)).

The near-cash instruments governed by UCC §3-310(a) are certified checks, cashier's checks, and teller's checks. Each of those instruments is an instrument on which a bank has incurred liability. Cashier's checks and teller's checks are checks on which a bank is the drawer, so the bank has liability under UCC §3-412 (for cashier's checks) and UCC §3-414(b) (for teller's checks). A certified check is a check that a bank otherwise has agreed to pay. UCC §3-409(d). UCC §3-310(c)(i) provides that the near-cash rules set out in UCC §3-310(a) also apply to any other instrument on which a bank is liable as maker or acceptor.

Because of the bank's obligation to pay, most parties that accept such an instrument view themselves as having received final payment; the principal risk of nonpayment is the risk that the bank will become insolvent. Reflecting that perception, UCC §3-310(a) and (c) provide (absent a contrary agreement) that the underlying obligation is discharged when the obligee takes one of those near-cash instruments. That rule imposes no substantial burden on the obligee because the obligee that doubts the solvency of the relevant bank could protect itself by refusing to accept the instrument or agreeing with the payor that the underlying obligation will remain in effect. Absent such an action, though, it makes good sense to treat the underlying obligation as discharged when the obligee accepts the instrument.

UCC §3-310(b) sets out the rules for ordinary instruments such as notes and uncertified checks. Because a bank has not agreed to pay those instruments, the likelihood of nonpayment is considerably higher. Accordingly, UCC §3-310(b), unlike UCC §3-310(a), does not immediately discharge the underlying obligation. Instead, when an obligee takes an ordinary instrument, the underlying obligation is suspended. UCC §§3-310(b)(1), (2). That suspension continues until the instrument is dishonored or paid. If the instrument is paid, the underlying obligation is discharged. UCC §3-310(b)(1), (2). If the instrument is dishonored, the suspension terminates, and the obligee has the option to enforce either the instrument or the underlying obligation. UCC §3-310(b)(3). Thus, if a tenant's rent check bounces, the landlord can sue the tenant either on the check (for which the tenant would be liable as a drawer under UCC §3-414(b)) or on the underlying rent obligation (taking advantage of any remedies available under the lease).

A discharge of the underlying obligation under UCC §3-310 is effective only to the extent of the amount of the instrument. UCC §3-310(a), (b). In some cases, however, a party will try to use an instrument to pay an obligation for which the parties dispute the amount. For example, if Lydgate and Bulstrode disagree regarding the amount that Lydgate owes on a promissory note, Lydgate might write a check for half of the disputed amount, mark the check "PAID IN FULL," and tender the check to Bulstrode, hoping that Bulstrode's acceptance of the check will satisfy the entire amount of the disputed obligation. UCC §3-311 generally supports that use of instruments to resolve disputes. Specifically, such a "paid in full" check will discharge Lydgate's entire obligation (even if the obligation is for more than the instrument) if (a) the instrument is tendered as full satisfaction of a disputed claim, (b) the payor conspicuously notifies the payee that it intends the instrument to constitute full satisfaction of the claim, and (c) the payee successfully obtains payment of the instrument. UCC §3-311(a), (b).

Problem Set 21

21.1. This morning you meet with a new client named Tom Mae. Tom has operated billiard halls on the west side of town for several years and recently started to operate a check-cashing business, with counters in each of his billiard halls. The check-cashing business operates as Tom's Kash Outlet (TKO). The business has been successful; Tom is cashing about 150 checks a day. A long-time regular at one of the locations suggested to Tom that he see a lawyer to make sure that Tom was handling his checks properly.

Tom tells you that his normal practice requires the customers to sign the top end of the reverse of the check. Like most check-cashing services, Tom's business has a policy against cashing checks for parties other than the named payee. Accordingly, his clerks always check to make sure that the name with which the customer signs matches the name of the payee on the front of the check. The clerks then examine a driver's license to ensure that the signer is in fact the payee. Finally, his clerks stamp the top end of the reverse of each check, just below the signature by the customer. The clerks use a rubber stamp that reads "Tom's Kash Outlet."

a. Tom first wants to know if his procedures expose him to any undue risks. What do you think? UCC §§1-201(b)(21), (37) & (39), 3-109(c), 3-204(a), 3-205(b) & (c), 3-206(c), 3-401(b), 3-401 comment 2, 3-402(a).

b. Tom also wants to know what additional risks he would face if he began accepting third-party checks. He says that customers frequently try to cash checks that have been indorsed to them by the named payee. If the check appears to have been specially indorsed by the named payee and is submitted for cashing by the person to whom the named payee indorsed the check, what risk does Tom face in cashing the check? UCC §§1-201(b)(21), 3-415(a), 3-416(a)(1), 3-417(a)(1), 3-420(a).

c. What advantages would TKO gain if it altered the stamp with a line above its name that said, "For Deposit Only"?

21.2. While Tom is in your office, you get a call from Doug Kahan, who wants to follow up on your analysis of Problem 20.5 (the problem where Doug could not get a taxpayer's bank to honor a check written on the back of the taxpayer's shirt). What Doug wants to know is this: If the IRS can't make the bank pay the check, can the IRS at least sue the taxpayer on the shirt-check? UCC §§1-201(b)(21), 3-301(i), 3-310(b)(1) & (3), 3-414(b).

21.3. While having lunch with your friend Bill Robertson (a grocery-store operator and real-estate developer that you've represented on a variety of matters), Bill's assistant Jan Brown asks you about a problem she has. She has a particularly difficult tenant that has been complaining constantly about problems with the space it leases from Bill. Finally, Jan received from the tenant this morning a check for exactly half of what she believes the tenant owes, including a notation on the check that it constitutes "Full Payment for All Past-Due Rent." In the past, Jan has had a practice of drawing a line through such a notation and depositing the check. Her view is that the tenant cannot unilaterally decide that the check constitutes full payment and that drawing a line through the full-payment notation is adequate evidence of her rejection of the tenant's position. Jan wants to know what you think of her practice. What do you say? UCC §3-311.

21.4. Pleased with the thoughtful advice that you provided in Problem 21.1, Tom calls you back a few weeks later to ask whether you would be interested in doing some work for him collecting checks that payor banks dishonor after he cashes them. For the first installment of the project, Tom wants to know whom he could sue on the following four checks:

a. The first check was written by Dorothea Drawer and payable to Paul Payee. Tom's employee took the check in accordance with Tom's procedures. Thus, the check bears an indorsement that purports to be the signature of Paul Payee. It turns out, though, that the person that cashed the check actually was Ingrid Interloper. Ingrid had mugged Paul and stolen his wallet, including Paul's driver's license and the check.

Ingrid indorsed the check as requested by Tom's clerk. Tom's clerk did not understand that Ingrid in fact was not Paul. When Dorothea heard of the attack on Paul, she stopped payment on the check. Dorothea's bank dishonored the check, so it eventually was returned to Tom. Can Tom sue Paul on the check? Ingrid? Dorothea? UCC §§1-201(b)(21), 3-205(a), 3-301(i), 3-401(a), 3-403(a), 3-414(b), 3-415(a), 3-416(a)(1).

b. Same facts as question a, except that the check was written by Dorothea as "Pay to the order of cash." Ingrid brought the check into one of Tom's facilities. Because Tom's clerk could not figure out whose signature to get, the clerk simply paid Ingrid cash for the check and took possession of it without obtaining any indorsement at all. The bank dishonored the check and returned it to Tom. Can Tom sue Paul? Ingrid? Dorothea? UCC §§1-201(b)(21), 3-109, 3-301(i), 3-401(a), 3-414(b), 3-416(a)(1).

c. Same facts as question b, but now the clerk got Ingrid's signature when she brought the check in. UCC §§3-414, 3-415, 3-416.

21.5. One Friday morning you get a call from Jodi Kay (your friend and longtime client from CountryBank). She has a question from an irate customer named Ishmael Chambers. Chambers wrote a $3,400 check to purchase a new stereo system from Alan's Stereo Service. When Chambers put the stereo together the next day, the stereo would not work. Chambers called Alan's and asked if Chambers could return the stereo, but could not get an answer on the phone. Chambers then drove by the store and observed prominent "going out of business" signs. Chambers promptly called the bank and asked Jodi to stop payment on the check. Jodi told Chambers that Jodi could not stop payment because she already had paid the check. Chambers asked Jodi if he could come in and look at the check.

When Chambers came in, he looked at the back of the check and saw that there was no indorsement by Alan's, only a stamp by BigTown Bank (which appeared to be Alan's depositary bank). Bragging of his undergraduate business-law class, Chambers told Jodi that Jodi had acted improperly in paying the check. He insisted that BigTown Bank was not the holder of the check because of Alan's failure to indorse the check. Accordingly, he said that Jodi has to give him back the money. Jodi wants to know if Chambers is correct. What do you say? UCC §§1-201(b)(21), 4-205(1), 4-401, 4-401 comment 1.

21.6. Cliff Janeway (your book-dealer client dating back to Assignment 1) calls you with a question about a payment he just received from one of his large customers named Clydell Slater. Janeway's normal arrangement with Slater requires Slater to pay him once a month for all of the books that Slater bought during the preceding month. Slater's recent purchases, however, have been much larger than usual: They totaled $12,000 during the last two weeks. Accordingly, Janeway called Slater last week and asked Slater to forward payment immediately. Today in the mail Janeway received an odd-looking check for $12,000: It appears to be drawn on the Third State Bank of Yakima, but also is signed by that bank in the lower right-hand corner. In the lower left-hand corner, it lists Clydell Slater as "remitter." Cliff thinks he recently heard some negative news about that bank and worries that Slater might be trying to pull something on him. Cliff asks you what he should do. What do you say? UCC §§3-103(a)(15), 3-104(g), 3-310, 3-412, 3-414(a).

Assignment 22: Holders in Due Course

A. Holder-in-Due-Course Status

The most distinctive feature of negotiable instruments is the concept of the holder in due course, a specially favored type of transferee that is immune from most defenses that the issuer of an instrument could raise against the original payee. As discussed in the preceding assignment, holder-in-due-course status implements the idea — dating to common-law decisions that predate the American Revolution — that enhancing the ability of transferees to enforce instruments increases the liquidity of negotiable instruments by making negotiable instruments more attractive investments.

1. The Requirements for Holder-in-Due-Course Status

To become a holder in due course, the purchaser of an instrument must satisfy two sets of rules. First, it must obtain the instrument through the process of negotiation described in the preceding assignment so that it becomes a holder. A person that acquires an instrument through some other process (such as a simple sale without negotiation) will not become a holder and thus cannot become a holder in due course.

The second set of rules is a set of the qualifications that elevate an ordinary holder to the favored status of a holder in due course. Like the definition of instrument in Part 1 of Article 3, the definition of holder in due course in Part 3 of Article 3 is set out in two stages, a general definition (in UCC §3-302(a)), followed by a series of sections with definitions of the terms that appear in the basic definition in UCC §3-302(a). Generally, the holder must satisfy three tests to become a holder in due course: It must take the instrument for value, in good faith, and without notice of certain problems with the instrument.

The "value" requirement appears in UCC §3-302(a)(2)(i) and is defined in UCC §3-303(a). That requirement generally excludes transfers that are made as a gift or for some other insignificant reason. The value requirement is closely related to, but slightly more strict than, the classic concept of consideration: An instrument can be transferred for consideration and still fail the value requirement. The statute distinguishes Article 3's definition of value from the standard definition of "value" in UCC §1-204, which states that value includes "any consideration sufficient to support a simple contract." UCC §1-204(4). The Article 1 definition does not apply in Article 3.

Ordinary payment easily qualifies as value, as does the release by the purchaser of a preexisting claim against the seller. UCC §3-303(a)(3). On the other hand, a promise of future performance ordinarily will constitute consideration, but it will not constitute value until performance has occurred. UCC §3-303(a)(1). Thus, if Carl Eben transfers an instrument to Jodi Kay in return for Jodi's offer to provide consulting services to Carl's business, Jodi does not give value until she performs the services.

The "good faith" requirement appears in UCC §3-302(a)(2)(ii). The key point here is that, at least since its revision in 1990, Article 3 has used the modern UCC definition of good faith, which requires not only "honesty in fact," but also "the observance of reasonable commercial standards of fair dealing." See UCC §§1-201(b)(20), 3-103(a)(4). Thus, a plaintiff challenging a claim of holder-in-due-course status need not establish that the potential holder in due course acquired the instrument dishonestly. It is enough to establish that the actions of the claimed holder in due course failed to conform to reasonable commercial standards of fair dealing.

The most common claims regarding the good-faith requirement have challenged long-term relationships between lenders purchasing negotiable instruments, on the one hand, and their clients (operating businesses that sell the instruments), on the other hand. Essentially, those lenders are funding the operations of their clients by financing the sales that the clients make to retail purchasers. The issuers of those instruments (typically the retail purchasers from the operating businesses) have had considerable success arguing that those lender-client relationships can become so close that the lender acts in bad faith when it tries to use holder-in-due-course status to insulate itself from defenses that would have been valid against its longtime client. E.g., General Inv. Corp. v. Angelini, 278 A.2d 193 (N.J. 1971) (denying holder-in-due-course status to a financier of home improvement contracts on a loan purchased from an aluminum siding contractor that provided 10 percent of the financier's business).

In a related line of cases, courts do not rely explicitly on the good-faith provision, but simply say that there is such a "close connection" between the purchaser and the seller of the note that there has been no cognizable sale at all, leaving the purported purchaser subject to all defenses that could have been asserted against the seller. E.g., St. James v. Diversified Commercial Fin. Corp., 714 P.2d 179 (Nev. 1986) (denying holder-in-due-course status to a financier that supplied preprinted forms for the customers of its client the originating lender). Collectively, those cases have made it difficult for lenders to rely on holder-in-due-course status for instruments that they acquire from entities with whom they deal regularly.

The last requirement for holder-in-due-course status is the notice requirement, which appears in clauses (iii) through (vi) of UCC §3-302(a)(2). That requirement reflects the notion that a person that purchases an instrument with notice of a problem cannot use holder-in-due-course status to protect itself from that problem. Holder-in-due-course status rests on the paradigm of an anonymous unknowing purchaser that knows nothing about the underlying transaction and thus cannot fairly be charged with problems in that transaction. When that paradigm collapses because the transferee had notice of a problem when it purchased the instrument, holder-in-due-course status collapses as well.

The first salient point about the notice requirement is the distinction that the UCC draws between "notice" and "knowledge." As defined in UCC §1-202(a), a person has "notice" of a fact not only when it has actual knowledge of the fact (UCC §1-202(a)(1)), but also when it "has reason to know" of the fact based on "all the facts and circumstances known to [it] at the time" (UCC §1-202(a)(3)). Thus, a plaintiff can defeat holder-in-due-course status without proving that the purported holder in due course actually knew about the problem; it is enough to prove that the purported holder in due course had reason to know about the problem.

The second salient point about the notice requirement is that it is not enough to prove that the holder generally had notice that something was wrong in the abstract with the instrument, the maker, or the payee. Rather, the maker must prove notice of one of the four problems listed in the clauses that close UCC §3-302(a)(2): The instrument is overdue, has been dishonored, or is in default (UCC §3-302(a)(2)(iii)); the instrument has a forgery or an alteration (UCC §§3-302(a)(1), 3-302(a)(2)(iv)); a third party claims to own all or part of the instrument (UCC §3-302(a)(2)(v)); or one of the obligors has a defense or claim that would limit or bar enforcement of the instrument by the original payee (UCC §3-302(a)(2)(vi)). If the notice does not fall within one of those four classes, the notice is relevant only if it is sufficiently damaging to undermine the holder's good faith in acquiring the instrument.

The most intricate interpretive question about those notice requirements is whether an instrument is overdue or has been dishonored. UCC §3-304 explains the circumstances that make an instrument overdue. For demand instruments, an instrument becomes overdue if it is not paid on the day after demand is made; checks automatically become overdue 90 days after their date. Instruments payable at a definite time become overdue upon any failure to make a scheduled payment of principal or upon any other event that results in acceleration of the date of maturity of the instrument. As explained in Assignment 21, dishonor generally occurs under UCC §3-502 when an instrument is presented to a party obligated to pay and that party fails to pay the instrument in accordance with its obligation.

2. Rights of Holders in Due Course

Unlike a simple holder, a holder in due course takes the instrument free of all of the most significant defenses to payment. Most important, a holder in due course is immune from most ordinary contract claims or defenses (described by the UCC as claims "in recoupment"). Thus, if Carl Eben gave Jodi Kay an instrument as payment for consulting services that Jodi had agreed to provide Carl, and if Jodi had sold the instrument to Bulstrode Bank, so that Bulstrode became a holder in due course, Bulstrode could force Carl to pay even if Jodi never provided the agreed-on services. UCC §3-305(b). Assuming Jodi gave value, Carl's sole remedy for Jodi's failure to perform would be a suit against

Jodi; Carl would have no defense against the bank. Similarly, if a thief that stole a piece of bearer paper from Carl sold the instrument to Bulstrode, Bulstrode as a holder in due course would be immune from any attempt by Carl to recover the note. UCC §3-306. Carl's only remedy would be a suit against the thief.

The only defenses that bind a holder in due course are the four "real" defenses described in UCC §3-305(a)(1). The inclusion of those defenses reflects a pragmatic recognition of strong public policies that in a few unusual circumstances can override the concerns about free transferability that justify holder-in-due-course status. The first is infancy: Even a holder in due course cannot enforce an instrument issued by a minor that has no capacity under state law to bind itself to a simple contract. UCC §§3-305(a)(1)(i), 3-305 comment 1.

The second real defense encompasses duress, lack of legal capacity, and illegality. UCC §3-305(a)(1)(ii). Again, the holder in due course cannot enforce an instrument if the underlying transaction in which the instrument was issued occurred under circumstances that would make the original obligation completely void. Courts traditionally have interpreted that exception narrowly. For example, one notable case upheld holder-in-due-course status with respect to an instrument allegedly induced by bribery, relying on the theory that the crime of bribery only rendered the instrument voidable, not void. Bankers Tr. Co. v. Litton Sys., Inc., 599 F.2d 488 (2d Cir. 1979); see UCC §3-305 comment 1 paragraph 4 (stating that laws vitiate holder-in-due-course status only if they render obligations "entirely null and void").

The third real defense is fraud that induced issuance of the instrument "with neither knowledge nor reasonable opportunity to learn of its character or essential terms." UCC §3-305(a)(1)(iii). As with the previous exceptions, courts have interpreted that exception quite narrowly. For example, in one leading case that predates the UCC, a farmer who signed an instrument while working in his field claimed that he should not be bound by the instrument because he did not have his glasses when he signed the instrument and also because he barely could read even with his glasses. In an opinion by future United States Supreme Court Justice David Brewer, the Kansas Supreme Court rejected the farmer's claim that he did not understand that he was signing a promissory note. The court placed the blame squarely on the farmer: "If he has eyes, and can see, he ought to examine; if he can read, he ought to read. . . . If he relies upon the word of a stranger he makes that stranger his agent . . . and . . . cannot disaffirm the acts of that agent." Ort v. Fowler, 2 P. 580, 583 (Kan. 1884).

The final real defense is discharge of the obligor in insolvency proceedings. UCC §3-305(a)(1)(iv). That defense accepts the reality of the supremacy of federal law. Whatever state law might say, a discharge of liability under the federal bankruptcy laws bars enforcement of that same liability under Article 3 (or any other state law).

Because the real defenses are so limited, the ability of a holder to claim holder-in-due-course status significantly limits the ability of a party liable on an instrument to interpose a defense to enforcement of an instrument. The following case is illustrative.

State Street Bank & Trust Co. v. Strawser

908 F. Supp. 249 (M.D. Pa. 1995)

CALDWELL, District Judge. . . .

I.   BACKGROUND

On December 19, 1986, the Defendants, Chester L. and Connie M. Strawser, executed an Adjustable Rate Note ("the Note") in favor of Homestead Savings Association ("Homestead"), in consideration of and as security for a loan in the amount of $350,000.00. Pursuant to a Security Agreement executed at the same time, the Note was secured by a mortgage on four parcels of real property, and by farming and industrial equipment. The Note is payable in monthly installments with the balance, if any, due January 1, 1997. On March 22, 1993, the Note and Mortgage were assigned to Plaintiff, State Street Bank & Trust Company ("State Street"). . . .

. . . In paragraph 7(C), the Note provides that "[i]f I am in default, the Note Holder may send me a written notice telling me that if I do not pay the overdue amount by a certain date, the Note Holder may require me to pay immediately the full amount of principal which has not been paid and all the interest that I owe on that amount."

On October 17, 1994, State Street sent a Notice of Default to Defendants, indicating that if Defendants did not pay the past due principal and interest within thirty days, State Street would exercise the acceleration clause in paragraph 7(C), causing the entire balance and per diem interest to become due immediately. State Street asserts that it received no response from Defendants as a result of this demand.

On January 23, 1995, State Street instituted this action for breach of contract, alleging that the Strawsers have not made monthly payments since April 1, 1993, and are thus in default under . . . the Note. State Street seeks the balance due on the Note, per diem interest, late charges, and attorneys' fees pursuant to paragraph 7(E) of the Note. In their answer, Defendants deny that they are in default and assert an affirmative defense that State Street's claim is barred by the doctrine of illegality because the Note and Mortgage were obtained in violation of 7 P.S. §311(e). . . .

II.   LAW AND DISCUSSION . . .

B.   Breach of Contract

Because our jurisdiction is premised on diversity of citizenship, we apply the substantive law of Pennsylvania. In this case, we look to the Pennsylvania Commercial Code ("the Code"), which provides that the holder of an instrument has a right to enforce that instrument, subject to certain enumerated exceptions. 13 Pa. C.S.A. §§3104, 3301, 3305. Here, the Note is an instrument, as that term is defined in the

Code, State Street is a holder of the Note, and, as such, has a right to enforce the Note subject to the limitations of section 3305 of the Code. 13 Pa. C.S.A. §3301.

Additionally, State Street asserts that it is a "holder in due course," and is therefore entitled to enforce the Note free from all defenses that the Strawsers may assert. 13 Pa. C.S.A. §3302. . . .

The Defendants contend that Plaintiff is not a holder in due course because it had notice of a potential defense under section 3305(a). . . . The potential defense raised by the Strawsers is the alleged violation of 7 P.S. §311(e) by Homestead and its president, Gary Holman. Plaintiff had notice of this potential violation, Defendants argue, as a result of a letter from Defendants' former counsel to Homestead. However, even assuming that section 311(e) was violated and is a defense under section 3305 of the Code, Plaintiff is a holder in due course and therefore entitled to enforce the Note.[5.]

Admittedly, if State Street had notice of a potential defense, it could not assert the rights of a holder in due course. 13 Pa. C.S.A. §3302(a)(2)(vi). However, there is no evidence in the record to indicate that State Street had notice of the letter relied on by the Defendants when the assignment occurred on March 22, 1993. . . .

Here, the letter is addressed to Homestead. Defendants submitted no evidence that could establish that Plaintiff had actual knowledge of the letter, or that it received timely notification of the contents. Further, there is nothing in the record to support a finding that State Street had reason to know of a potential violation of 7 P.S. §311(e), particularly since the Letter of Commitment, Note, Security Agreement, and Appraisals indicate that the appraised value of the collateral exceeded one hundred twenty percent of the indebtedness. We conclude that State Street is a holder in due course.[6.]

The evidence produced by Plaintiff establishes that Defendants have not made monthly payments since April, 1993. Although Defendants deny that they are in default, they have failed to submit any evidence of payment to State Street since that time. Defendants have breached their contract and Plaintiff is entitled to summary judgment.

---

5. Section 311(e) provides that

[a]n institution shall not extend credit, directly or indirectly, for the purpose of enabling a customer to acquire or hold shares of stock or capital securities issued by the institution unless all indebtedness incurred for that purpose is secured by other readily marketable collateral with a value not less than one hundred twenty percent of the indebtedness.

7 P.S. §311(e). Defendants, allegedly at Holman's urging, used some of the proceeds from the loan to purchase shares of stock in Homestead. Apparently, Defendants contend that the market value of the property securing the loan was not 120 percent of the total indebtedness.

6. In any event, we reject Defendants' argument that the Note and Mortgage were obtained in violation of 7 P.S. §311(e) and that such violation is a defense under §3305(a)(2). The record is replete with evidence that the market value of the collateral that secured the Note was "not less than one hundred twenty percent of the indebtedness" as required by Section 311(e), and Defendants have not submitted evidence to contradict those values. Thus, even assuming Plaintiff was not a holder in due course, Defendants have not set forth any grounds to deny Plaintiff's right to enforce the Note.

The *Strawser* case is illustrative not only because it provides a rare modern example of a case explaining the benefits of holder-in-due-course status, but also because it helps to show why holder-in-due-course status has so little continuing relevance. Here, as in most cases involving litigation to enforce instruments, there is no reason to believe that the court would have found for the defendants even in the absence of holder-in-due-course status. The crux of the case is the defendants' failure to articulate any substantial defense. Without any substantial defense, the makers of the note would have lost regardless of whether the plaintiff was a holder in due course.

At this point, probably the most important outcome-determinative application of the holder-in-due-course doctrine comes from a doctrine that protects federal regulators, codifying decisions of the Supreme Court that had recognized such a doctrine. As you will see, the federal doctrine is even more protective than the doctrine codified in the Uniform Commercial Code.

Langley v. FDIC

484 U.S. 86 (1987)

Justice SCALIA delivered the opinion of the Court.

Petitioners W.T. and Maryanne Grimes Langley seek reversal of a decision by the United States Court of Appeals for the Fifth Circuit granting the Federal Deposit Insurance Corporation (FDIC) summary judgment on its claim for payment of a promissory note signed by petitioners. The Fifth Circuit rejected petitioners' contention that a defense of misrepresentation of existing facts is not barred by 12 U.S.C. §1823(e) because such a representation is not an "agreement" under that section. We granted certiorari to resolve a conflict in the Courts of Appeals.

I

The Langleys purchased land in Pointe Coupee Parish, Louisiana, in 1980. To finance the purchase, they borrowed $450,000 from Planters Trust & Savings Bank of Opelousas, Louisiana, a bank insured by the FDIC. In consideration for the loan, they executed a note, a collateral mortgage, and personal guarantees. The note was renewed several times, the last renewal being in March 1982, for the principal amount of $468,124.41.

In October 1983, after the Langleys had failed to pay the first installment due on the last renewal of the note, Planters brought the present suit for principal and interest in a Louisiana state trial court. The Langleys removed the suit, on grounds of diversity, to the United States District Court for the Middle District of Louisiana, where it was consolidated with a suit by the Langleys seeking more than $5 million in damages from Planters and others. The Langleys alleged as one of the grounds of complaint in their own suit, and as a defense against Planters' claim in the present suit, that the 1980 land purchase and the notes had been procured by misrepresentations. In particular, they alleged that the notes had been procured by the bank's misrepresentations that the property conveyed in the land purchase consisted of 1,628.4 acres, when in fact it consisted of only 1,522, that the property included 400 mineral acres, when in fact it contained only 75, and that there were no outstanding mineral leases on the property, when in fact there were. No reference to these representations appears in the documents executed by the Langleys, in the bank's records, or in the minutes of the bank's board of directors or loan committee.

In April 1984, the FDIC conducted an examination of Planters during which it learned of the substance of the lawsuits with the Langleys, including the allegations of Planters' misrepresentations. On May 18, 1984, the Commissioner of Financial Institutions for the State of Louisiana closed Planters because of its unsound condition and appointed the FDIC as receiver. The FDIC thereupon undertook the financing of a purchase and assumption transaction pursuant to 12 U.S.C. §1823(c)(2), in which all the deposit liabilities and most of the assets of Planters were assumed by another FDIC-insured bank in the community. Because the amount of the liabilities greatly exceeded the value of the assets, the FDIC paid the assuming bank $36,992,000, in consideration for which the FDIC received, *inter alia*, the Langleys' March 1982 note.

In October 1984, the FDIC was substituted as a plaintiff in this lawsuit, and moved for summary judgment on its claim. The District Court granted the motion, and was sustained on appeal. The Fifth Circuit held that the word "agreement" in 12 U.S.C. §1823(e) encompassed the kinds of material terms or warranties asserted by the Langleys in their misrepresentation defenses and, because the requirements of §1823(e) were not met, those defenses were barred. We granted the Langleys' petition for certiorari on the issue whether, in an action brought by the FDIC in its corporate capacity for payment of a note, §1823(e) bars the defense that the note was procured by fraud in the inducement even when the fraud did not take the form of an express promise.

II

The Federal Deposit Insurance Act of 1950, §13(e), 12 U.S.C. §1823(e), provides:

> No agreement which tends to diminish or defeat the right, title or interest of the Corporation [FDIC] in any asset acquired by it under this section, either as security for a loan or by purchase, shall be valid against the Corporation unless such agreement (1) shall be in writing, (2) shall have been executed by the bank and the person or persons claiming an adverse interest thereunder, including the obligor, contemporaneously with the acquisition of the asset by the bank, (3) shall have been approved by the board of directors of the bank or its loan committee, which approval shall be reflected in the minutes of said board or committee, and (4) shall have been, continuously from the time of its execution, an official record of the bank.

A

Petitioners' principal contention is that the word "agreement" in the foregoing provision encompasses only an express promise to perform an act in the future. We do not agree.

As a matter of contractual analysis, the essence of petitioners' defense against the note is that the bank made certain warranties regarding the land, the truthfulness of which was a condition to performance of their obligation to repay the loan. See 1 A. Corbin, Contracts §14, p. 31 (1963) ("[T]ruth [of the warranty] is a condition precedent to the duty of the other party."); accord, 5 S. Williston, Contracts §673, pp. 168-171 (3d ed. 1961); J. Murray, Contracts §136, pp. 275-276 (2d rev. ed. 1974). As used in commercial and contract law, the term "agreement" often has "a wider meaning than . . . promise," Restatement (Second) of Contracts §3, Comment *a* (1981), and embraces such a condition upon performance. The Uniform Commercial Code, for example, defines agreement as "the bargain of the parties in fact as found in their language or by implication from other circumstances . . . ." U.C.C. §1-201(3), 1 U.L.A. 44 (1976). Quite obviously, the parties' bargain cannot be reflected without including the conditions upon their performance, one of the two principal elements of which contracts are constructed. Cf. E. Farnsworth, Contracts §8.2, p. 537 (1982) ("[P]romises, which impose duties, and conditions, which make duties conditional, are the main components of agreements"). It seems to us that this common meaning of the word "agreement" must be assigned to its usage in §1823(e) if that section is to fulfill its intended purposes.

One purpose of §1823(e) is to allow federal and state bank examiners to rely on a bank's records in evaluating the worth of the bank's assets. Such evaluations are necessary when a bank is examined for fiscal soundness by state or federal authorities, see 12 U.S.C. §§1817(a)(2), 1820(b), and when the FDIC is deciding whether to liquidate a failed bank, see §1821(d), or to provide financing for purchase of its assets (and assumption of its liabilities) by another bank, see §§1823(c)(2), (c)(4)(A). The last kind of evaluation, in particular, must be made "with great speed, usually overnight, in order to preserve the going concern value of the failed bank and avoid an interruption in banking services." [Citation omitted.] Neither the FDIC nor state banking authorities would be able to make reliable evaluations if bank records contained seemingly unqualified notes that are in fact subject to undisclosed conditions.

A second purpose of §1823(e) is implicit in its requirement that the "agreement" not merely be on file in the bank's records at the time of an examination, but also have been executed and become a bank record "contemporaneously" with the making of the note and have been approved by officially recorded action of the bank's board or loan committee. These latter requirements ensure mature consideration of unusual loan transactions by senior bank officials, and prevent fraudulent insertion of new terms, with the collusion of bank employees, when a bank appears headed for failure. Neither purpose can be adequately fulfilled if an element of a loan agreement so fundamental as a condition upon the obligation to repay is excluded from the meaning of "agreement."

That "agreement" in §1823(e) covers more than promises to perform acts in the future is confirmed by examination of the leading case in this area prior to enactment of §1823(e) in 1950. In D'Oench, Duhme & Co. v. FDIC, 315 U.S. 447 (1942), the FDIC acquired a note in a purchase and assumption transaction. The maker asserted a defense of failure of consideration (that is, the failure to perform a promise that was a condition precedent to the maker's performance), based on an undisclosed agreement between it and the failed bank that the note would not be called for payment. The Court held that this "secret agreement" could not be a defense to suit by the FDIC because it would tend to deceive the banking authorities. The Court stated that when the maker "lent himself to a *scheme or arrangement* whereby the banking authority . . . was likely to be misled," that scheme or arrangement could not be the basis for a defense against the FDIC. *Ibid.* (emphasis added). We can safely assume that Congress did not mean "agreement" in §1823(e) to be interpreted so much more narrowly than its permissible meaning as to disserve the principle of the leading case applying that term to FDIC-acquired notes. Certainly, one who signs a facially unqualified note subject to an unwritten and unrecorded condition upon its repayment has lent himself to a scheme or arrangement that is likely to mislead the banking authorities, whether the condition consists of performance of a counterpromise (as in *D'Oench, Duhme*) or of the truthfulness of a warranted fact.

B

Petitioners' fallback position is that even if a misrepresentation concerning an existing fact can sometimes constitute an agreement covered by §1823(e), it at least does not do so when the misrepresentation was fraudulent and the FDIC had knowledge of the asserted defense at the time it acquired the note. We conclude, however, that neither fraud in the inducement nor knowledge by the FDIC is relevant to the section's application.

No conceivable reading of the word "agreement" in §1823(e) could cause it to cover a representation or warranty that is bona fide but to exclude one that is fraudulent. Petitioners effectively acknowledge this when they concede that the fraudulent nature of a *promise* would not cause it to lose its status as an "agreement." The presence of fraud could be relevant, however, to another requirement of §1823(e), namely, the requirement that the agreement in question "ten[ds] to diminish or defeat the right, title or interest" of the FDIC in the asset.

Respondent conceded at oral argument that the real defense of fraud in the factum — that is, the sort of fraud that procures a party's signature to an instrument without knowledge of its true nature or contents, see U.C.C. §3-305(2)(c), Comment 7, 2 U.L.A. 241 (1977) — would take the instrument out of §1823(e), because it would render the instrument entirely void, see Restatement (Second) of Contracts §163 and Comments *a, c*; Farnsworth §4.10, at 235, thus leaving no "right, title or interest" that could be "diminish[ed] or defeat[ed]." Petitioners have never contended, however, nor could they have successfully, that the alleged misrepresentations about acreage or mineral interests constituted fraud in the factum. It is clear that they would constitute only fraud in the inducement, which renders the note voidable but not void. *See* U.C.C. §3-201(1), 2 U.L.A. 127; Restatement (Second) of Contracts §163, Comment *c*; Farnsworth §4.10, at 235-236. The bank therefore had and could transfer to the FDIC voidable title, which is enough to constitute "title *or* interest" in the note. This conclusion is not only textually compelled, but produces the only result in accord with the purposes of the statute. If voidable title were not an "interest" under §1823(e), the FDIC would be subject not only to undisclosed fraud defenses but also to a wide range of other undisclosed defenses that make a contract voidable, such as certain kinds of mistakes and innocent but material misrepresentations. See Restatement (Second) of Contracts §§152-153, 164.

Finally, knowledge of the misrepresentation by the FDIC prior to its acquisition of the note is not relevant to whether §1823(e) applies. Nothing in the text would support the suggestion that it is: An agreement is an agreement whether or not the FDIC knows of it; and a voidable interest is transferable whether or not the transferee knows of the misrepresentation or fraud that produces the voidability. See Farnsworth §11.8, at 780-781; cf. U.C.C. §3-201(1), 2 U.L.A. 127. Petitioners are really urging us to engraft an equitable exception upon the plain terms of the statute. Even if we had the power to do so, the equities petitioners invoke are not the equities the statute regards as predominant. While the borrower who has relied upon an erroneous or even fraudulent unrecorded representation has some claim to consideration, so do those who are harmed by his failure to protect himself by assuring that his agreement is approved and recorded in accordance with the statute. Harm to the FDIC (and those who rely upon the solvency of its fund) is not avoided by knowledge at the time of acquiring the note. The FDIC is an insurer of the bank, and is liable for the depositors' insured losses whether or not it decides to acquire the note. Cf. 12 U.S.C. §1821(f). The harm to the FDIC caused by the failure to record occurs no later than the time at which it conducts its first bank examination that is unable to detect the unrecorded agreement and to prompt the invocation of available protective measures, including termination of the bank's deposit insurance. See §1818. Thus, insofar as the recording provision is concerned, the state of the FDIC's knowledge at that time is what is crucial. But as we discussed earlier, §1823(e) is meant to ensure more than just the FDIC's ability to rely on bank records at the time of an examination or acquisition. The statutory requirements that an agreement be approved by the bank's board or loan committee and filed contemporaneously in the bank's records assure prudent consideration of the loan before it is made, and protect against collusive reconstruction of loan terms by bank officials and borrowers (whose interests may well coincide when a bank is about to fail). Knowledge by the FDIC could substitute for the latter protection only if it existed at the very moment the agreement was concluded, and could substitute for the former assurance not at all.

The short of the matter is that Congress opted for the certainty of the requirements set forth in §1823(e). An agreement that meets them prevails even if the FDIC did not know of it; and an agreement that does not meet them fails even if the FDIC knew. It would be rewriting the statute to hold otherwise. Such a categorical recording scheme is of course not unusual. Under Article 9 of the U.C.C., for example, a filing secured creditor prevails even over those unrecorded security interests of which he was aware. [The court cites cases and treatises discussing the predecessor to UCC §9-322.]

A condition to payment of a note, including the truth of an express warranty, is part of the "agreement" to which the writing, approval, and filing requirements of 12 U.S.C. §1823(e) attach. Because the representations alleged by petitioners constitute such a condition and did not meet the requirements of the statute, they cannot be asserted as defenses here. The judgment of the Court of Appeals is

Affirmed.

3.   *Payment and Discharge*

The defenses of payment and discharge require special rules because an instrument can be paid in part, or a party can be discharged, even without any default or other problem with the instrument. For example, the fact that a party has partially paid an instrument by making scheduled monthly payments does not suggest a problem that should bar holder-in-due-course status. Similarly, the fact that one party has been discharged from liability does not indicate a problem with enforcing the note against remaining parties. Thus, as you should recall, an accommodation party might be discharged under UCC §3-605 when a holder grants the borrower an extension of the due date. There is no reason that a subsequent purchaser with knowledge of that fact should not become a holder in due course able to enforce the instrument against the principal obligor.

Article 3 offers a two-step solution to that problem. First, UCC §3-302(b) states that holder-in-due-course status is not precluded by notice of payment or discharge (other than the real defense of discharge in insolvency proceedings mentioned above). Second, any whole or partial discharge is effective against a person that takes with notice of the discharge. UCC §3-302(b). Returning to the examples of the preceding paragraph, consider a party that purchases an installment note, knowing that the maker has made the first two years' worth of payments. The purchaser could become a holder in due course free from personal defenses of the maker, but the purchaser would be bound to recognize the decrease in the amount owed on the note caused by the payments of which the purchaser had notice. Similarly, assume that a financier purchases a note from which an accommodation party has been released under the guarantor-protective rules of UCC §3-605. If the financier was on notice of that discharge (perhaps because the documents included an amendment extending the due date but did not indicate that the accommodation party had consented to the extension), the discharge of the accommodation party would be binding on the holder in due course. UCC §3-302(b).

Conversely, a discharge would not be binding on a holder in due course that took without notice of the discharge. UCC §3-601(b). For example, if a party selling an instrument misled a purchaser into believing that an accommodation party had consented to an extension (and thus had not been discharged by it), the purchaser would take free of the discharge. UCC §3-601(b). In that case, the holder in due course could enforce an instrument against an accommodation party even if the accommodation party would not have been liable to the prior holder of the instrument. *A fortiori*, a party that purchased an instrument would take free of a payment that a borrower made to the transferor after the date of the transfer (even if the borrower had no idea that the instrument had been transferred): How could the transferee take with knowledge of a payment that had not been made at the time of the transfer?

Those rules pose significant difficulties for parties that want to make sure that their payments and discharges are effective to bind subsequent holders of an instrument. Article 3 offers several ways in which obligors can protect themselves, but none of them is particularly practical. The simplest applies to a party that obtains a discharge. As the preceding paragraphs suggest, the discharged party can make the discharge effective only if the discharged party takes steps to make sure that subsequent parties cannot acquire the instrument without notice of the discharge. The most obvious device would be to obtain possession of the note and destroy it at the time of payment. By forcing the lender to produce the instrument, the borrower could ensure that the lender was still the holder. By destroying the instrument, the borrower could ensure that no subsequent party could become a holder of the note (because no subsequent party could obtain possession of the destroyed instrument). The UCC does obligate a holder to surrender an instrument when it receives full payment (UCC §3-501(b)(2)(iii)), but in practice a modern institutional lender with thousands of borrowers spread around the country may not locate the original instrument until weeks (if not months) after the borrower makes the final payment.

If a discharge is only partial (such as the partial discharge based on a monthly payment), the borrower obviously is not entitled to destroy the instrument. In that case, however, the statute offers the maker the ability to protect itself by forcing the holder to indicate on the instrument that the payment has been made. UCC §3-501(b)(2)(iii). That procedure would protect the maker because it would allow the maker to verify that the lender still was the holder, limiting the risk of making a payment to the wrong person. Also, at least in theory, no subsequent party could take without notice of the payment because subsequent parties would be on notice of the facts indicated by notations on the face of the instrument. See UCC §1-202(a)(3).

The problem with that solution is that it contemplates the borrower requiring the lender to produce the promissory note for examination by the borrower each month as a payment is due. The practical reality is that borrowers make their payments every month without insisting that lenders produce the original notes. Imagine the chaos of a system in which every homeowner went to the lender's office to view the promissory note before making each monthly mortgage payment!

The practical difficulties summarized in the foregoing paragraphs have motivated strong criticism of the traditional rules set out in Article 3. In the real-estate area, for example, the Restatement of Mortgages rejects those rules and provides instead that a payment by a borrower to a party that the borrower believes to be the holder is valid even if the supposed holder already has transferred the note to a third party. Restatement of Mortgages §5.5. Article 3, however, retained the traditional rule under which a payment is valid only if it is made to a person entitled to enforce the instrument at the time of the payment. UCC §3-602(a)(ii). Only the 2002 amendments to Section 3-602 reversed the rule of the 1990 version of Article 3 and brought Article 3 into conformity with the conventional rule articulated in the Restatement of Mortgages. Those revisions, though, were adopted in only 13 jurisdictions; thus many of the important commercial states (including New York, Massachusetts, Illinois, and California) retain the traditional rule. To the extent that revision does not provide relief, 2009 revisions to the Truth in Lending Act (enacted as part of the Helping Families Save Their Home Act) imposed an obligation on all purchasers of home mortgages to notify their borrowers, enforceable by the private right of action in the Truth in Lending Act. See Truth in Lending Act §131(g), 15 U.S.C. §1641(g).

4.   Transferees Without Holder-in-Due-Course Status

For the reasons explained in the preceding section, it frequently happens that a party acquires a negotiable instrument without becoming a holder in due course. As the preceding assignment suggests, the position of a purchaser without holder-in-due-course status is not so bad: The worst problem the purchaser faces from the absence of holder-in-due-course status is its exposure to defenses that would have been effective against the original payee of the instrument. Frequently, as in *Strawser*, the issuer will have no such defense. Nevertheless, Article 3 includes two rules that make the position of the purchaser that is not a holder in due course even better than that of the purchaser of a nonnegotiable obligation.

The first rule applies when the only problem is the purchaser's failure to obtain an indorsement from the seller. As discussed in the preceding assignment, a purchaser of order paper cannot become a holder of the instrument unless it obtains an indorsement from the previous holder. Thus, a purchaser that gave value for order paper and purchased it in good faith and without notice of any problems would not become a holder in due course unless it also obtained the requisite indorsement. You learned in that assignment that UCC §3-203(c) protects that purchaser by obligating the seller to provide the indorsement upon request, which elevates the purchaser to the status of a holder. If the purchaser satisfies the value, good-faith, and notice requirements, that same rule makes the purchaser a holder in due course as well.

The second rule is the "shelter rule." That rule implements the basic property principle that a purchaser of property obtains all of the rights that its seller had in the purchased property. That is the same rule that applied above to allow a party that purchased an instrument without negotiation to obtain all of the rights that the seller had to enforce the instrument. In this context, that rule allows a purchaser that fails to obtain its own holder-in-due-course status to assert any holder-in-due-course rights that the seller had before the sale. UCC §3-203(b). For example, going back to Carl's note to Jodi, assume that Jodi negotiated that note to Bulstrode Bank, which became a holder in due course. If Bulstrode donated the note as a charitable contribution to Wessex College, the college's failure to give value would prevent the college from obtaining its own holder-in-due-course status. The shelter rule, however, would allow the college to assert Bulstrode's rights as a holder in due course. The result grants the college protection that is nearly the same as the protection the college would have had if it had purchased the note and attained its own holder-in-due-course status.

B.   The Fading Role of Negotiability

No picture of negotiability is complete without a comment on its current significance. Although it might be unfair to declare negotiability dead, it is clear that a combination of consumer-protective regulation and the pressures of the modern commercial world have limited substantially the areas where negotiability has any real importance. The decline has two facets: the declining use of negotiable instruments and the declining significance of negotiability concepts in the processing of the negotiable instruments that remain.

1.   The Declining Use of Negotiable Instruments

For several reasons, the sphere within which negotiable instruments are used has contracted significantly during the last several decades. Two of the most significant reasons rest directly on legal reforms. The first of those involves credit for consumer sales transactions. To protect consumers from being forced to pay for goods and services that they do not actually receive, the Federal Trade Commission (FTC) promulgated a regulation that absolutely bars holder-in-due-course status for consumer credit transactions. That rule operates by declaring it an unfair trade practice to receive a promissory note in a consumer credit sale transaction unless the note includes the following legend:

> Any holder of this consumer credit contract is subject to all claims and defenses which the debtor could assert against the seller of goods and services obtained pursuant hereto or with the proceeds hereof. Recovery hereunder by the debtor shall not exceed amounts paid by the debtor hereunder.

16 C.F.R. §433.2(a). If a lender violates that rule, the FTC is authorized to impose a penalty of up to $10,000 for each violation. 15 U.S.C. §45(*l*).

Because that requirement conditions the maker's obligation to pay on the absence of defenses against the seller, it places consumer credit contracts outside the normal scope of negotiability. UCC §3-106(d) does provide that such a note still can be characterized as an instrument even though it is, strictly speaking, conditional. See UCC §3-106 comment 3. Article 3 makes it clear, however, that the note's status as an instrument is merely technical because "there cannot be a holder in due course of the instrument." UCC §3-106(d). Thus, holder-in-due-course status has no role in the financing of credit for consumer sales transactions. To make that point even clearer, the 2002 amendments to UCC §3-405 specify that a note that should contain the FTC statement will be construed as if it had the statement even when it is omitted! See UCC §3-405(e).

Commercial pressures also have hampered the use of negotiable instruments. If negotiability was an important feature of commercial lending transactions, you would expect that the notes in question would use provisions that left no doubt regarding negotiability. As you saw in Problem Set 21, however, many common commercial payment obligations include provisions that cast considerable doubt on their negotiability. There are two general reasons for this. The first is the increasing complexity of modern commercial transactions. That complexity makes it difficult for commercial parties to stick to the simple and absolute terminology for which the law of negotiable instruments is framed. As a practical matter, most commercial entities are much more interested in producing documents that accurately reflect their agreement than they are in ensuring that the documents satisfy the technical rules for negotiability. Indeed, in recent years commercial lenders have begun to dispense with notes entirely, relying on loan agreements to define the relevant payment obligations.

The second reason for the declining importance of negotiable instruments is the ease with which parties can protect themselves from surprise defenses even without negotiable instruments. If the purchaser of a commercial payment obligation perceives a significant risk that the maker will assert defenses to payment, the purchaser can insist that the seller retain the risk that the maker will interpose any such defense. For example, the seller of the note might agree to indemnify the purchaser from any such defenses or, alternatively, to repurchase the note if the maker refuses to pay as required by the terms of the note. A less accommodating seller could provide the purchaser a statement from the maker (often called an estoppel certificate) in which the maker waives any defenses based on events that occurred before the sale, or even obligate the seller to repurchase the note (a common practice in the mortgage industry). Any of those approaches provides a close substitute for the benefits of holder-in-due-course status because each protects the purchaser from defenses related to events that took place before the purchaser's acquisition of the instrument. Indeed, given the difficulties a purchaser faces in being sure that it will attain holder-in-due-course status, it is plausible to say that those approaches give the purchaser a position superior to the position in which the purchaser would be if the purchaser attempted to rely on holder-in-due-course status alone.

2.   The Decreasing Relevance of Negotiability to Negotiable Instruments

Practical constraints also have limited the role of negotiability even in cases in which the documents are negotiable. For example, the check certainly is the dominant form of negotiable instrument in our economy. Yet neither of the key negotiability concepts — negotiation by indorsement and holder-in-due-course status — plays any significant role in the processing and enforcement of checks. First, as the preceding assignment explained, the checking system includes a series of special rules that allow the processing and collection of checks to proceed without indorsement. Thus, when a customer deposits a check in its account, the bank becomes a holder whether or not the customer indorses the check. UCC §4-205(1). Similarly, at least as far as Article 4 is concerned, the bank need not indorse the check to transfer it in the check-collection process; any method of identification is adequate. UCC §4-206. See also 12 C.F.R. §229.35(a) (setting federal standards for indorsement under Regulation CC). Moreover, given the huge volume of checks that banks must process in the modern checking system, it is no longer practical for banks to examine indorsements to ensure that their customers have complied with the technical transfer rules contemplated by the rules of

Article 3. In sum, indorsements play no significant role in the modern check-processing system.

Nor does holder-in-due-course status play a significant role in the checking system. Consider the ordinary transaction in which a payee deposits a check into its bank account. In that case, the depositary bank becomes a holder in due course of the check when it allows the customer access to the funds represented by the check. UCC §4-210. If the payor bank refuses to pay the check, the depositary bank's status as a holder in due course gives the depositary bank the legal right to proceed directly against the issuer of the check without fearing the issuer's ability to assert defenses arising out of the issuer's transaction with the customer. In practice, however, that almost never happens. Instead, it is much more likely that the depositary bank will charge the check back to the account of the customer that deposited it. UCC §4-214. The ease and simplicity of the charge-back make the lawsuit against the (often insolvent) issuer a relatively impractical remedy. That impractical and uncommon remedy, however, provides the principal opportunity for using holder-in-due-course status in the checking system.

Consider also the Werner draft transaction outlined at the introduction to this chapter. The decision of the drawee (Barclays) to pay the draft did not depend at all on the proper appearance of the indorsements on the instrument; its decision to pay rested on a direct message from the drawer advising it of the draft. Similarly, holder-in-due-course rules have little significance to the successful functioning of those drafts. The ability of the payee and its depositary bank to obtain holder-in-due-course status against the issuer of a draft has no relevance to the transaction because there is no significant chance that Mark Twain will use some personal defense as a basis for denying payment. Mark Twain made the payment decision when its customer purchased the draft. The only thing likely to hinder Mark Twain's payment would be its insolvency, a real defense against which holder-in-due-course status would offer no protection.

The rise of a public secondary market for payment obligations has presented yet another obstacle to continued reliance on negotiability concepts. For example, consider the home-mortgage note. Most home-mortgage lenders do not retain ownership of the notes generated by their businesses. Instead, as you will see in Chapter 8, those lenders commonly sell those notes to other institutions, which package large groups of the notes for resale on public securities markets. Although that transaction involves the repeated transfers that once would have been the classic case for the use of negotiability, the size of the transactions makes it impractical for the parties to use the document-based transfer system offered by Article 3. To use the system as it was designed, the originating lender would have to indorse each of its notes separately and then deliver the notes to the purchasing institution; that institution, in turn, would have to indorse each note and deliver it to the (usually numerous) parties purchasing interests in the note. Then, whenever the maker of the note repaid the note, those parties would have to return the note to the maker to surrender it.

Not surprisingly, the industry has abandoned the cumbersome transfers contemplated by a pure negotiability system, moving instead to a much more streamlined system in which the actual documents remain in a single place, "warehoused" with a servicer (often the original lender) or some other custodian. The system facially addresses Article 3's requirement that a holder take possession by providing a complicated network of custody agreements under which the party that has physical possession agrees that it is holding the instrument as agent for the actual holder (or holders). The need to maintain those cumbersome devices illustrates just how outmoded the negotiability system's focus on possession of a physical document has become.

Finally, advances in electronic and computer technology can only accelerate the obsolescence of the negotiability system. As the checking system illustrates, advances in technology are continuously making it cheaper, easier, and more reliable to transmit information electronically than on paper. Those advances inevitably force a contraction in the use of systems that rely on the physical transmission of paper objects. Thus, just as the checking system already is moving to electronic presentment and truncated nondocumentary processing, there is every reason to believe that any other areas that still use negotiable instruments will make similar advances. Accordingly, even if parties continue to execute documents that are negotiable on their face, the processes for their transfer and collection will take less and less account of the "advantages" afforded by the document- and possession-based negotiability system.

Problem Set 22

22.1. When you come into the office Monday morning, you find a telephone message from Stacy Vye (from Wessex Bank), asking you to call her about a package of promissory notes that she wants to acquire. None of the notes matures during the next five years, but in each of them the borrower has missed one or more of the recent scheduled monthly payments. The seller of the notes has not yet accelerated the dates of maturity of the notes or otherwise responded to the defaults. Wessex Bank plans to acquire a package of the notes at a deeply discounted purchase price, reflecting the fact that the notes currently are in default. Stacy says that she does not need you to examine the notes to determine whether they are negotiable in form. Instead, assuming that they are negotiable in form, that the seller of the notes is the current holder of the notes, and that Stacy obtains proper indorsements in connection with the purchase, she wants you to tell her whether her knowledge that the borrowers have missed payments will prevent her from becoming a holder in due course of the notes.

Stacy tells you that she does these transactions "all the time," that the notes have two different types of payment schedules. Some call for a series of amortizing monthly payments (part interest and part principal), while others call for monthly payments of interest only, with the entire principal due in a single "balloon" payment on the date of maturity. What do you tell her? UCC §§3-302(a)(2)(iii), 3-304, 3-304 comment 2. Would it matter to your answer if she told you that she was buying the notes from the FDIC, which acquired them when it took control of the assets of a failed bank? 12 U.S.C. §1823(e).

22.2. Your friends at the World Wilderness Fund (WWF) call you for some advice about a gift that they recently received. They explain that the problem arises out of a transaction between Diggory Venn and Clym Yeobright. Venn operates a dyeing business, under which he dyes clothes a bright red that (he claims) is permanent and impervious to extremes of heat and cold. Clym Yeobright asked Venn to dye for him a set of 20 uniforms that Yeobright planned to sell to the local fire department. Yeobright agreed to pay for the work with a negotiable promissory note in the amount of $3,000, payable to the order of Venn in equal monthly installments over two years. When Venn finished the uniforms, Yeobright delivered the note. Venn promptly took the note to Stacy Vye at Wessex Bank. She agreed to purchase the note from Venn for $2,800. Venn added a special indorsement, as follows:

Pay to Wessex Bank
/s/ Diggory Venn

Venn then gave the note to Stacy. A few weeks later Stacy called your friends at WWF and told them that Wessex wanted to donate the note to WWF. She delivered the note to them, with a special qualified indorsement, as follows:

Pay to WWF, Without Recourse
Wessex Bank,
by /s/ Eustacia Vye
Vice President

It turns out that Venn did a poor job of the dyeing. The dye washed out of the uniforms the first time that they got wet. Accordingly, Yeobright refuses to pay the note. WWF got a letter today from Yeobright's lawyer, asserting that WWF could not force Yeobright to pay because WWF is not a holder in due course. WWF wants to know your opinion. What do you say? UCC §§3-203(b), 3-204, 3-205, 3-302(a)(2), 3-303(a), 3-305(a)(3), 3-305(b), 3-412.

22.3. Following up on your successful work in Problem Set 21, you take an afternoon field trip to visit your client Tom Mae at his pool-hall checkcashing service. While there, he asks you about a traveler's check that he recently cashed for a customer. The check was issued by Hunt Bank and payable to "bearer," but required a countersignature from Jane Kingsley as a condition to payment. It turns out that the customer for whom he cashed the check had stolen the check from Kingsley. The customer forged the Jane Kingsley countersignature. Because Kingsley had notified Hunt Bank of the theft before the check was processed, Hunt Bank refused to honor the check. Accordingly, Tom is stuck with the check. Not surprisingly, Tom cannot locate the customer for whom his employee cashed the check. Tom points out to you that he did not really do anything wrong. Because the forgery was quite good, he could not plausibly have known that there was a problem. Why can't he rely on holder-in-due-course status to enforce the check against Hunt Bank? UCC §§1-202, 3-104(a), 3-106(c), 3-106 comment 2, 3-305(a)(2).

22.4. You have lunch today with Bill Robertson, the grocery-store operator whom you have represented on a variety of matters. He tells you that he has gotten into a dispute with Bulstrode Bank over a $2,000,000 promissory note that Bill issued to Texas American Bank (TAB) in connection with a mortgage of his recent project "Shops at Four Corners." Bill tells you that he paid off the TAB note last month with a lump-sum payment of $2,000,000, made by a wire transfer directly to TAB. Accordingly, Bill was surprised yesterday to receive a telephone call from Bulstrode Bank informing Bill of the address to which Bill should send this month's payment. When Bill told the officer from Bulstrode (Nicholas Bulstrode) that Bill already had paid off the TAB note last month, Bulstrode laughed and said that wasn't his problem because Bulstrode purchased the TAB note from TAB six weeks ago (two weeks before Bill made the $2,000,000 payment). Bill can't believe that he might be liable to Bulstrode for a note that Bill already has paid. What do you tell him? UCC §§3-302(b), 3-601(b), 3-602(a); TILA §131(g).

22.5. Jodi Kay (from CountryBank) calls with a problem about a cashier's check that her bank has issued. It appears that one of her customers (Fluffy Feed Corporation) issued a check for $10,000 payable to Flatiron Linen. Because Fluffy Feed's account did not have $10,000 on the day that the check was presented for payment, Jodi's bank dishonored the Fluffy Feed check. A few days later Fluffy Feed sent Jodi a stop-payment order covering the check. Three months later the president of Flatiron walked into a branch of CountryBank and asked the teller if the teller would exchange the Fluffy Feed check for a cashier's check payable to Flatiron. Because Fluffy Feed's account at that time had a balance of far more than $10,000, the teller happily complied.

Minutes later the teller's supervisor noticed that payment had been stopped for the check the teller had taken in exchange for the cashier's check. The supervisor immediately called Flatiron and told the president that CountryBank would dishonor the check. Flatiron insists that the bank must honor its cashier's check. The matter is now on Jodi's desk and seems headed for litigation. What do you tell her? UCC §§3-302, 3-303, 3-305, 3-412 & comment 2, 3-418 & comment 2.

22.6. Consider again the facts of Problem 8.3, in which Bud Lassen wrote Carol Long a $15,000 check for some kitchen equipment that was too large for his kitchen and then stopped payment on the check in an effort to avoid payment. Suppose that instead of cashing the check at the First State Bank of Matacora (as Carol did in Problem 8.3), Carol properly indorsed the check and deposited it into an account at her own bank (the Nazareth National Bank). Now suppose that the Matacora bank (on which the check was drawn) dishonored the check the next day based on the stop-payment request and returned it to Nazareth before the funds were available to Carol under Nazareth's customary funds availability policies. What can Nazareth do to recover the funds that it has credited to Carol's account? (You might assume that Carol independently owes Nazareth far more than the existing balance of her account.) UCC §§1-201(b)(21), 3-302, 3-303(a)(2), 3-305(b), 4-105(5), 4-210, 4-211, 4-214.

Assignment 23: Documents of Title

Although the rules for negotiable instruments are the most prominent example of a legal system that uses negotiability, it is not the only legal system that uses negotiability. Indeed, as Assignment 22 explains, negotiable instruments are relatively insignificant in current commerce. There is one area, however, in which negotiability continues to have commercial import: documents of title covered by Article 7 of the Uniform Commercial Code. This assignment first summarizes the basic mechanics of the document-of-title system implemented by Article 7 and then describes how that system is used in commercial transactions.

A. The Mechanics of Documents of Title

As explained in the opening pages of the chapter, negotiability provides a general system for enhancing the value of assets by making them more liquid. The last three assignments showed how that concept worked for instruments that reflect rights to intangible payment obligations. This assignment shows how negotiability works for documents of title, which reflect rights to ordinary tangible personal property. Essentially, documents of title facilitate transactions in which a seller uses a common carrier to transport goods to a buyer. The basic system contemplates two separate events: a transfer of the goods from the seller/sender (a "consignor" in Article 7 terms) to the carrier (a "bailee" in Article 7 terms) and a delivery of the goods from the carrier to the buyer/recipient (the "consignee" in Article 7 terms).

1. Delivering Goods to a Carrier

A document-of-title transaction starts when a party that wishes to send goods (typically a seller) delivers the goods to a carrier for transportation to a remote location. Two sources of law govern those transactions: the Federal Bills of Lading Act, 49 U.S.C. §§80101 et seq. (the FBLA) and Article 7 of the Uniform Commercial Code. The FBLA preempts Article 7 when it applies, which includes any transaction that involves a shipment between American states or from one country to another country. FBLA §80102. Because the FBLA does not apply to shipments from a foreign country into the United States, Article 7 applies to those shipments. The distinction between the bodies of law is not important, because both include rules similar to the rules under the old Uniform Bills of Lading Act.

Because negotiability works by concentrating rights of ownership and possession in a writing (or record), a seller and carrier that wish to use those rules must create a writing (or record) that reflects the right to possession of the goods (analogous to the "instrument" that Article 3 uses to reflect a right to payment). Article 7 uses the term "document" or "document of title" to refer to that writing. UCC §§1-201(b)(16), 7-102(e).

The most important question is what formalities a writing must satisfy to qualify as a document for purposes of Article 7. In contrast to the complicated and formalistic rules that characterize Article 3, the UCC provisions on documents of title are relatively simple. Moreover, in contrast to the "magic words" approach that dominates Article 3, rules about documents of title are much more deferential to commercial practice. Essentially, there are only two requirements. First, the writing must be a document that "in the regular course of business or financing is treated as adequately evidencing that the person in possession of it is entitled to receive . . . the goods it covers." UCC §1-201(b)(6). The same provision helpfully provides a safe-harbor rule by stating specifically that bills of lading always qualify as documents of title. A related definitional provision states that the term "bill of lading" includes any document "evidencing the receipt of goods for shipment issued by a person engaged in the business of transporting or forwarding goods." UCC §1-201(b)(6). Thus, the term "bill of lading" (and indirectly the term "document of title") includes documents issued by all types of common carriers, whether trucking firms, railway carriers, ocean-going vessels, airlines, or some combination of them. UCC §1-201(b)(6).

The second requirement is similarly functional: The document "must purport to be issued by or addressed to a bailee and purport to cover goods in the bailee's possession which are either identified or are fungible portions of an identified mass." UCC §1-201(b)(16). That requirement reflects the types of transactions for which the documents are designed, transactions in which goods will be transported by a party that does not own the goods.

As a practical matter, those documents tend to be highly standardized forms prepared and maintained by the carrier, with blanks for insertion of the names of the parties, a description of the goods, and the particulars (destination and the like) of the shipment contract. For example, if Toy Exporter is shipping some toys from Los Angeles by boat, it might deliver the toys to Vessel at a dock in Los Angeles. At the dock, an employee of Vessel would fill out one of Vessel's standard bills of lading to describe the containers in which the toys were delivered to Vessel, give one or more counterparts for Toy Exporter, and retain one or more counterparts for Vessel's internal uses. One counterpart would be designated as the original and would serve as the document of title.

The only further requirement for a document to be negotiable is that the bill include words of negotiability. In particular, the bill needs to state "by its terms [that] the goods are to be delivered to bearer or to the order of a named person." UCC §7-104(b); FBLA §80103.

The most common practice is to indicate negotiability not in the form of the bill, but simply by the way in which the blanks on the bill are filled out. Thus, instead of typing the name of the recipient in the blank for the consignee, the carrier could type "order of shipper." For example, in the bill illustrated

Figure 23.1
Form Bill of Lading

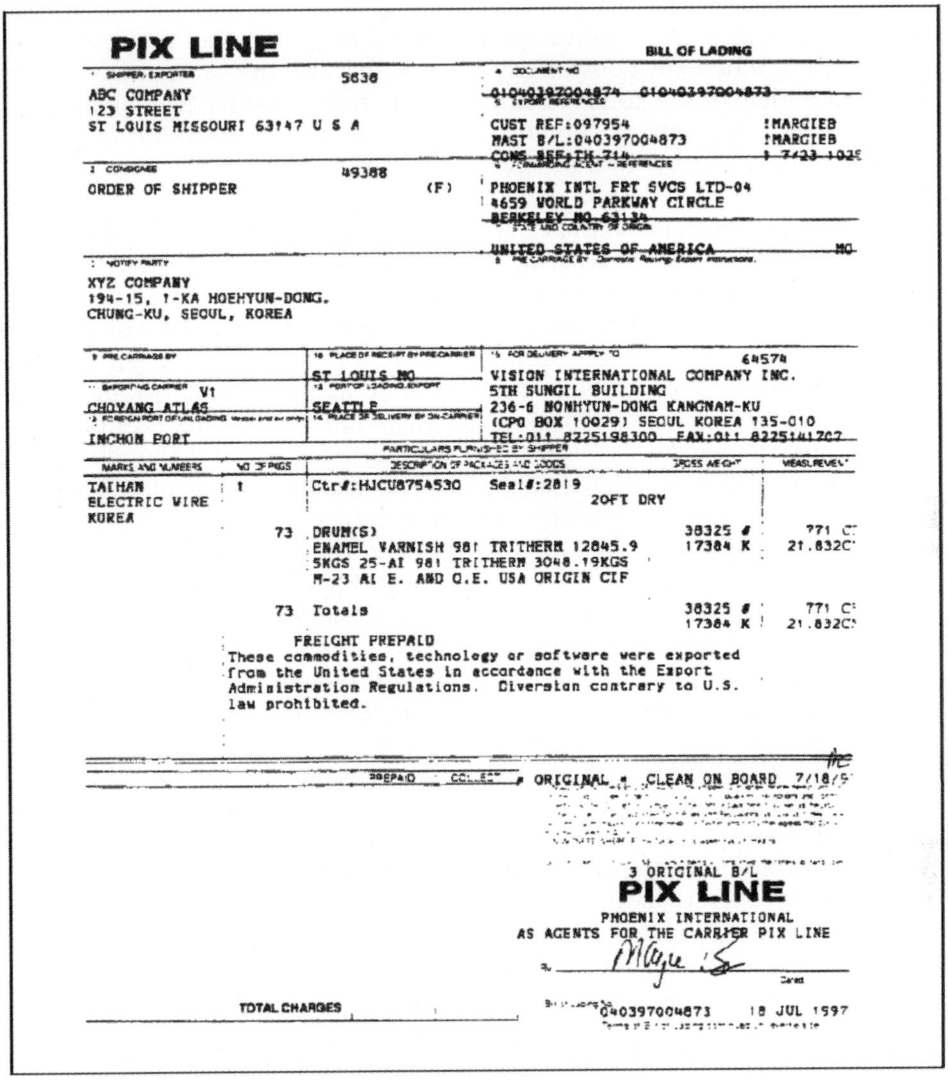

PIX LINE

BILL OF LADING

SHIPPER, EXPORTER 5638
ABC COMPANY
123 STREET
ST LOUIS MISSOURI 63147 U S A

DOCUMENT NO
~~01040397004874 01040397004873~~

EXPORT REFERENCES
CUST REF:097954 !MARCIEB
MAST B/L:040397004873 !MARCIEB
~~CONS REF:TH-714~~ ~~7/23 1025~~

CONSIGNEE 49388
ORDER OF SHIPPER (F)

FORWARDING AGENT – REFERENCES
PHOENIX INTL FRT SVCS LTD-04
4659 WORLD PARKWAY CIRCLE
~~BERKELEY MO 63134~~

STATE AND COUNTRY OF ORIGIN
~~UNITED STATES OF AMERICA~~ MO

NOTIFY PARTY
XYZ COMPANY
194-15, 1-KA HOEHYUN-DONG.
CHUNG-KU, SEOUL, KOREA

PRE-CARRIAGE BY

PLACE OF RECEIPT BY PRE-CARRIER
ST LOUIS MO

FOR DELIVERY APPLY TO 64574
VISION INTERNATIONAL COMPANY INC.
5TH SUNGIL BUILDING
236-6 NONHYUN-DONG KANGNAM-KU
(CPO BOX 10029) SEOUL KOREA 135-010
TEL:011 8225198300 FAX:011 8225141707

EXPORTING CARRIER V1
CHOYANG ATLAS

PORT OF LOADING/EXPORT
SEATTLE

FOREIGN PORT OF UNLOADING
INCHON PORT

PLACE OF DELIVERY BY ON-CARRIER

PARTICULARS FURNISHED BY SHIPPER

MARKS AND NUMBERS	NO. OF PKGS	DESCRIPTION OF PACKAGES AND GOODS	GROSS WEIGHT	MEASUREMENT
TAIHAN ELECTRIC WIRE KOREA	1	Ctr#:HJCU8754530 Seal#:2819 20FT DRY		
	73	DRUM(S) ENAMEL VARNISH 981 TRITHERM 12845.9 5KGS 25-AI 981 TRITHERM 3048.19KGS M-23 AI E. AND O.E. USA ORIGIN CIF	38325 # 17384 K	771 C 21.832C
	73	Totals	38325 # 17384 K	771 C 21.832C

FREIGHT PREPAID
These commodities, technology or software were exported from the United States in accordance with the Export Administration Regulations. Diversion contrary to U.S. law prohibited.

PREPAID COLLECT ORIGINAL CLEAN ON BOARD 7/18/9

3 ORIGINAL B/L
PIX LINE
PHOENIX INTERNATIONAL
AS AGENTS FOR THE CARRIER PIX LINE

TOTAL CHARGES

040397004873 18 JUL 1997

in Figure 23.1, ABC Company (the shipper is the party sending the goods, not the party carrying the goods) is shipping one container containing 73 drums of enamel varnish to XYZ Company (identified as the party to be notified), but the bill lists "order of shipper" as the consignee.

If a bill does not satisfy that test (as many do not), it is still a document covered by Article 7, even if it is a nonnegotiable document. UCC §7-104(c). In practice, especially in domestic commerce, many carriers never use negotiable bills. For example, air carriers rarely use negotiable bills because it is difficult for the documents to be transmitted to the recipient at the destination site any faster than the carrier could transport the goods. Those carriers do not, however, leave the nonnegotiable character of the bills in doubt. Instead, they ordinarily have a statement on the face of their bills indicating specifically that they are "nonnegotiable."

2.   Recovering Goods from a Carrier

Like an instrument, a document generally reflects the right to the underlying assets (in this case a right to possession of the goods that the document
covers). Thus, when the goods reach the destination, the carrier generally is
obligated to deliver the goods to the "person entitled under the document."
UCC §7-403(a). As with instruments, the negotiability of the bill is crucial to
determining the identity of the "entitled" person.

(a)   Nonnegotiable Documents. If the document is nonnegotiable, the
carrier's obligation usually is set by the terms of the original document: The
general rule (subject to numerous exceptions discussed below) is that the carrier must deliver the goods to the person identified as the recipient on the bill
(the consignee). UCC §7-403. Although that statement of the rule sounds
simple and direct, the statutory phrasing that states the rule is a model of
misdirection. The key provision is UCC §7-403(a), which provides that the
carrier "must deliver the goods to a person entitled under a document if the
person complies with subsections (b) and (c), unless [one of several exceptions
applies]." The easiest way to read that section is to start with subsection (a) as
stating a general rule that the carrier *must* deliver the goods to the person entitled to the goods under the document, subject to two groups of exceptions.
The first group of exceptions covers the failure of the entitled person to comply
with the rules in subsections (b) and (c) of UCC §7-403. The second group of
exceptions is the seven miscellaneous exceptions set forth in the numbered
subparagraphs (1) through (7) of subsection (a) of UCC §7-403. Because it
ordinarily is quite simple to determine the identity of the person entitled
under a nonnegotiable document — the consignee/buyer named in the document — the key practical question under all of this verbiage is the nature of
the exceptions.

The most common exception that justifies the carrier in delivering the goods
to somebody other than the consignee/buyer is when the instructions are
changed while the goods are en route. If the seller and buyer agree on what to do
with the goods, a change of instructions should present no difficulty. The carrier
obviously should be, and is, free to comply. UCC §§7-303(a)(2) & (3), 7-403(a)(5).

On the other hand, it is not so easy to determine how the carrier should
proceed if it receives conflicting instructions, a likely occurrence in cases in
which the buyer and seller become engaged in a dispute while the goods are
in transit. The UCC recognizes that the carrier is not in a position to determine which of the parties (seller/consignor, buyer/consignee) actually is entitled to the goods. Accordingly, the UCC absolves the carrier from liability if it
takes one of two courses. First, in cases involving nonnegotiable bills, the carrier always is free to comply with the seller's instructions. UCC §7-303(a)(2).
Second, if the goods already have reached their destination, the carrier can
deliver the goods to the buyer (unless the seller objects). UCC §7-303(a)(3).
The concept is that the carrier should be entitled to dispose of the goods in
some reasonable manner, leaving the seller and the buyer to resolve the actual
entitlement to the goods between themselves. See UCC §7-303 comment 2.

Another exception to the "deliver to consignee" rule allows the carrier to ignore instructions on the bill in cases where, notwithstanding the
instructions on the bill, some party other than the listed buyer actually is entitled to the goods. That could happen for a variety of reasons. For example,

suppose that a thief stole goods and immediately attempted to dispose of them by shipping them overseas. If the true owner established its claim, the carrier properly could deliver the goods to the true owner on the theory that the true owner was entitled to the goods as against both the seller and the buyer. UCC §7-403(a)(1) & comment 2.

The final significant exception to the carrier's obligation to deliver goods to the consignee protects the carrier's right to payment. The UCC gives the carrier a lien on the goods covered by the bill to cover the carrier's charges for shipment and storage. UCC §7-307. No party is entitled to possession of the goods from the carrier until those charges have been paid. UCC §7-403(b).

(b)   Negotiable Documents.   The rules for negotiable documents are similar, in that they also start from the baseline rule that the carrier must deliver the goods to a person entitled under the document. When the document is negotiable, however, two additional rules apply, reflecting the document-centered emphasis of the concept of negotiability. The first rule requires the claimant to surrender the document, a rule that implicitly requires the claimant to be in possession of the bill. UCC §7-403(c).

The second special rule for negotiable documents relates to the identity of the person entitled under the document. When the bill is negotiable, only a holder can be entitled under the document. UCC §7-102(a)(9). To be a holder, a party must satisfy two tests quite similar to the tests for holder status under Article 3. First, it must be in possession of the bill (a requirement implicitly imposed by UCC §7-403(c), as mentioned above). Second, unless the bill provides that the goods are deliverable to bearer, the party must be the person identified in the bill as entitled to possession. UCC §1-201(b)(21).

The key question for negotiable bills is how the parties can transfer the right to receive goods under the bill. As with instruments, the process is quite simple. For bills running to bearer, delivery alone is sufficient to transfer the bill (and entitlement under the bill). UCC §7-501(a)(2). When the bill provides that the goods are deliverable to the order of a named person, delivery of the bill to that person also is sufficient to make that person a holder of the bill. UCC §7-501(a)(3); see UCC §1-201(b)(21). Indorsement is required only if the parties wish to transfer an "order" bill to a party other than the named person. In that case, the currently named person must indorse the bill and transfer it to the new holder. UCC §7-501(a)(1). For example, suppose that Seller ships goods with Carrier, receiving a bill stating that the goods are deliverable to the order of shipper. Bank could transmit the bill to its branch in the destination city. Then, when Buyer pays for the goods, Bank could indorse the bill to Buyer and deliver it to Buyer, making Buyer a holder and thus allowing Buyer to obtain the goods from Carrier.

Implicit in the foregoing is the concept that the decision to cover goods by a negotiable bill substantially limits the ability of a seller to stop a shipment. When goods are covered by a negotiable document, a holder that acquires the bill by "due negotiation" (the analogue of a holder in due course under Article 3, see UCC §3-302) obtains an almost absolute right to the goods, which cannot be defeated by any decision of the seller to stop the shipment. UCC §7-502(a), (b). The only significant claimant that can defeat a party that becomes a holder of a negotiable bill by due negotiation is a prior owner (or lienholder) that neither participated nor acquiesced in the delivery of the goods to the bailee. UCC §7-503(a). For example, if a thief consigned goods to a shipper in return for a negotiable bill of lading, the true owner's right to the goods would defeat the claim of the holder of the bill, even if the holder of the bill paid full value for the goods and had no knowledge of the theft. Like holder-in-due-course status, obtaining a bill by due negotiation solves a lot of problems, but it doesn't solve everything.

B.   Transactions with Documentary Drafts

1.   *The Role of Documentary Draft Transactions*

Documents of title have a wide variety of relatively mundane uses, starting with the nonnegotiable bill torn from ubiquitous overnight mail packages. Similarly, businesses and consumers use UPS and competing domestic freight services to ship goods with nonnegotiable bills of lading when no payment is due for the goods or when the seller has made a credit decision to ship the goods without first obtaining payment. Going a step further, the seller can ship the goods to a buyer using a C.O.D. term, in which case the goods will be returned to the seller if the buyer does not pay.

In some cases, however, especially in international trade, sellers are reluctant to ship goods without obtaining a more concrete assurance that buyers will pay for the goods. Conversely, buyers are reluctant to send payment overseas for goods that have not yet been shipped to them. As discussed in the materials on letters of credit, letters of credit offer businesses one way to solve that dilemma: The buyer causes its financial institution to issue a letter of credit committing to pay the seller for the goods upon shipment. A glance at the standard form letter of credit in those materials shows the role that documents of title play in that process. The document of title (in that case a set of ocean bills of lading) is one of the documents that the seller must provide to demonstrate that it actually has shipped the goods. Accordingly, the buyer must honor the draft in order to obtain possession of the bill of lading, without which the buyer cannot obtain the shipped goods.

Letters of credit, however, are relatively expensive. Banks that issue letters of credit accept the ultimate obligation to pay for the goods, which frequently involves some risk that the bank will incur a loss if the applicant does not reimburse the bank for payments under the letter of credit. Moreover, even if a bank obtains a firm assurance that the buyer/applicant will reimburse the bank when it pays on the letter of credit, the task of reviewing the documents submitted with a draft on a letter of credit is quite time-consuming. Accordingly, banks typically charge fees that might amount to 1 percent of the purchase price for providing a letter of credit and paying on it in the course of the transaction.

Thus, even in international transactions, businesses involved in relatively small shipments frequently agree to ship goods without obtaining a letter of credit, especially when the parties have a relationship that gives the seller confidence that the buyer actually will pay when the goods arrive. In very small transactions, parties might use a simple draft like the Werner draft copied at the beginning of the chapter. In midsize transactions (in the range of $3,000 to $300,000), the most common mechanism substituting for a letter of credit is a documentary draft transaction, in which the seller obtains a negotiable document of title covering the goods and uses a draft to which those documents are attached to collect payment from the buyer.

One final preliminary point relates to the international character of such transactions. As always when commercial transactions cross national boundaries, the lawyer must consider the possibility that unfamiliar foreign practices will disrupt arrangements that would work smoothly under familiar domestic laws. Negotiability is not an area where that problem is particularly serious. Although there is no single overarching enactment to provide the certainty that the ICC publications give to letter-of-credit transactions, there is some possibility in the longer term that uniformity will come from the adoption of an international convention. The most likely candidate is the UNCITRAL Convention on International Bills of Exchange and International Promissory Notes. Promulgated by UNCITRAL in 1988, it has been adopted by the United States, Canada, Mexico, Russia, Gabon, Guinea, Honduras, and Liberia, but will not become effective until adopted by ten countries.

In any event, even without the UNCITRAL convention, all the major commercial nations enforce rules governing negotiability that for present purposes can be treated as functionally identical to the rules set out in Articles 3 and 7 of the UCC. Accordingly, it is convenient to explain documentary draft transactions by using the rules set forth in the UCC, even if those rules would not directly apply in some cases.

2.   Steps in the Transaction

(a)   *Preliminaries — Sale Contract, Shipment, and Issuance of the Draft.*   As should be clear from the discussion above, the first step in any documentary draft transaction is for the seller and buyer to agree on a sales contract. When the time for shipment comes, the seller delivers the goods to a carrier and obtains a bill of lading for the goods. If the seller wishes to obtain payment through a documentary draft, the seller then issues a draft in a form that qualifies as a negotiable instrument under Article 3. As illustrated in Figure 23.2, the draft typically is payable to the order of the seller. The draft is addressed to, and drawn on, the buyer (the party that ultimately should pay for the goods). The draft can be a sight draft or a time draft, but in the typical case, where the seller does not wish to extend credit to the buyer, the draft is a sight draft, which contemplates payment by the buyer promptly after the draft is presented to it. See UCC §3-502(c) (documentary drafts are dishonored if not paid by the close of the third business day after the day of presentment).

The draft also should include some identification of the buyer's bank (information that the seller should have obtained from the buyer at the time of the contract) so that the seller's bank will know how to collect payment. Often that information is provided by a notation that the draft is payable "through" buyer's bank. See UCC §4-106 (stating that a "payable through" draft can be "presented for payment only by or through" the identified bank).

(b)   *Processing by the Remitting Bank.*   Once the seller has all of the documents prepared, the seller takes the documents to the seller's bank, including an instruction letter detailing the terms of the transaction (identity of the buyer, identity of the buyer's bank, amount of payment, and the like). That letter ordinarily is prepared on a form provided by the bank. The seller then

Figure 23.2

Sight Draft for Documentary Collection

At Sight	Any City, KS	May 2, 2016

Pay to the order of **Seller**   US$10,000.00

Ten thousand and no/ 100 U.S. Dollars_____

Through <u>Banco di Roma</u>_____

Buyer   /S/ Seller

Any City, Italy

indorses the draft to its bank so that the bank becomes a holder of the draft. The seller also gives the bank the documents related to the shipping, usually including an invoice and (most crucial) the negotiable bill of lading. The seller also adds any indorsement necessary to make the bank a holder of that bill. Finally, the seller pays its bank a fixed fee regardless of the size of the transaction, usually in the range of $50–$100; that fee, you should notice, is much less than the typical 1 percent letter-of-credit fee that would be charged for transactions in the six-figure range for which documentary drafts are typical.

The seller's bank often is called the remitting bank because it is the bank that remits the draft for collection. See UCC §3-103(a)(15) (defining "remitter"). Once the remitting bank receives the documents, it prepares a collection document or instruction describing the terms of the transaction for the buyer's bank; if the seller prepared its instruction on the bank's form, the bank can use the document provided by the seller. Because the buyer's bank will present the draft to the buyer, the buyer's bank usually is described as the presenting bank. Among other things, the collection document ordinarily will incorporate by reference the provisions of International Chamber of Commerce Publication No. 522, Uniform Rules for Collections, which provides a standardized set of procedures for documentary collections and requires the collection document to include standardized details about the identity of the principal seeking payment (the seller), the identity of the drawee from whom payment is to be obtained (the buyer), and the amount and currency of the payment to be obtained.

Most importantly, the collection document must state the terms on which the documents are to be delivered to the buyer. Usually, the collection document states that the underlying documents are to be "delivered against payment," which means that the presenting bank is not authorized to release the documents until it obtains payment from the buyer. After placing the appropriate instructions on the collection document, the remitting bank indorses the draft and the bill in blank and transmits the entire package (including the collection document, the invoice and bill of lading, and the draft) to the presenting bank.

See UCC §7-501(a)(1) (after "indorsement in blank or to bearer," a bill can be negotiated "by delivery alone"). The documents typically are sent by overnight courier. In either case, the bank ordinarily passes the out-of-pocket shipping charges back to the seller (in addition to the fee mentioned above).

(c)   Processing by the Presenting Bank.   When the presenting bank receives the documents, it notifies the party indicated in the collection document. Under Article 6 of ICC Publication 522, the presenting bank is obligated to "make presentation . . . without delay," which ordinarily takes no more than a few days. At that point, the buyer must make arrangements with the presenting bank to pay the amount specified in the documents in order to receive the goods. If the buyer has a credit line with the presenting bank, it might draw against that credit line to pay for the goods. If not, the buyer will have to obtain funds from another source. Once the buyer pays the presenting bank, the presenting bank releases the documents, including the bill of lading. At that point, the buyer can use the bill of lading to obtain the goods from the shipper. Meanwhile, the presenting bank transmits the funds it received from the buyer back to the remitting bank. The remitting bank puts those funds in the seller's account, at which point the transaction is complete.

To make that summary more concrete, refer to Figure 23.1. When the presenting bank notifies XYZ Company that the presenting bank has the bill of lading illustrated in Figure 23.1, XYZ Company pays the bank for the drums of varnish. At that point, the presenting bank sends the funds back to ABC Company's bank to pay for the goods and gives the original bill of lading to XYZ Company. Notice that all of this is likely to occur while the *Choyang Atlas* is still in the middle of the Pacific, long before the goods arrive in Korea or XYZ Company has an opportunity to inspect them. The concept is that the negotiable document (bolstered by a considerable amount of confidence in the reliability of the seller, ABC Company) is enough to convince XYZ Company to pay before the goods arrive. When the goods do arrive in Korea, XYZ Company can present the bill to the vessel *Choyang Atlas* in Inchon, Korea (the particular destination indicated on the bill). At that point, the vessel releases the goods to XYZ Company and the transaction is complete.

Things would work somewhat differently in a case involving a time draft instead of a sight draft; a seller would use a time draft in a case in which the seller is willing to allow the buyer to obtain the goods immediately even though payment is to be deferred. In that case, the collection document would state that the documents are to be "delivered against acceptance." As you should recall from the discussion of liability on instruments in the materials above, the buyer's acceptance of the draft obligates it to pay the draft. See UCC §3-409(a). The UNCITRAL convention expressly codifies identical rules. Article 40(1) states that "[t]he drawee is not liable on a bill until he accepts it." And Article 40(2) states that "[t]he acceptor engages that he will pay the bill in accordance with the terms of his acceptance." Thus, a simple unqualified acceptance obligates the drawee completely; we call that accepted draft a bill of exchange. Accordingly, because the buyer's acceptance of the draft reflects the buyer's agreement to make the deferred payment, the presenting bank would be authorized to release the documents to the buyer when the documents reach the destination, allowing the buyer to obtain the goods at that time.

The ease with which documentary draft transactions can facilitate either immediate payment (with sight drafts) or deferred payment (with time drafts) helps to show the distinction between two separate functions that the documentary draft transaction is accommodating. The first is the sale of the goods — transferring possession and title from the seller to the buyer — which almost invariably happens at the time of transportation to the buyer. The second is payment, which can happen either simultaneously with the sale (with a sight draft) or later (with a time draft). The case that follows provides a recent example of a typical transaction.

Korea Export Insurance Corp. v. Audiobahn, Inc.

67 U.C.C. Rep. Serv. 2d 339 (Cal. Ct. App. 2008)

ARONSON, J.

Plaintiff Korea Export Insurance Corporation (KEIC) underwrites bills of exchange purchased by Korean banks from Korean exporters to finance their shipments of goods to other countries, including the United States. When defendant Audiobahn, Inc., failed to satisfy bills of exchange it had accepted for a shipment of electronic parts, KEIC paid the payee bank and asserted subrogation rights against Audiobahn. In a bench trial, the court found the payee bank to be a holder in due course of the bills of exchange, and that KEIC stood in the bank's shoes as subrogee. The court nonetheless entered judgment for Audiobahn, holding a notice provision in an assignment agreement between the shipper and KEIC imposed a condition subsequent upon KEIC's status as a holder in due course, and KEIC failed to satisfy this condition.

We conclude the trial court erred in imposing the condition subsequent. The assignment agreement did not purport to affect KEIC's right to enforce the bills of exchange, and nothing in the agreement could reasonably be read as imposing a condition subsequent. Accordingly, we reverse, and remand with instructions that the trial court enter judgment for KEIC.

I.

FACTUAL AND PROCEDURAL BACKGROUND

Under a sales agreement, exporter Mega Power, Inc. (Mega Power), agreed to ship electronic goods from Korea to importer Audiobahn in America. Mega Power sold its right to receive Audiobahn's payment for the shipment to Kookmin Bank by issuing bills of exchange, in the amounts of $256,414.98 and $63,254.40, respectively. The bills of exchange specified Kookmin Bank as payee, payable within a specified period of time upon acceptance by Audiobahn. Mega Power also provided Kookmin Bank with bills of lading for the shipped goods, so that Audiobahn would receive title to the shipped goods only after it had accepted the bills of exchange. Audiobahn accepted the bills of exchange, thus obligating itself to pay for the shipped goods.

Audiobahn failed to satisfy the bills of exchange, first because of cash flow problems, and later because of offsets arising from previous disputes it had with Mega Power and related companies. Because Audiobahn failed to pay the bills of exchange, KEIC, as underwriter, paid the amount owed to Kookmin Bank. KEIC also obtained from Mega Power letters of assignment giving KEIC Mega Power's rights under its sales agreement with Audiobahn.

Asserting its subrogation and assignment rights, KEIC sued Audiobahn for the two unpaid letters of exchange. Following a bench trial, the court determined that Kookmin Bank was a holder in due course of the letters of exchange, and that KEIC stood in Kookmin's shoes. The court, however, determined that KEIC was required to provide Audiobahn notice of KEIC's rights to receive payment "at its earliest opportunity." Relying on "the intention of mechanics lien law" and a notice provision in the letters of assignment, the court held that prompt notice to Audiobahn was a condition subsequent to KEIC maintaining its holder in due course status. Finding neither Mega Power nor KEIC provided prompt notice of KEIC's interest, the trial court entered judgment in Autobahn's favor. KEIC now appeals.

II.

DISCUSSION

NEITHER THE STATUTES NOR THE ASSIGNMENT AGREEMENT
CREATED A CONDITION SUBSEQUENT TO KEIC'S RIGHTS TO
ENFORCE THE BILLS OF EXCHANGE

KEIC contends the trial court erred in holding that prompt notice was a condition subsequent to enforcement of KEIC's subrogation rights. We agree.

[UCC §3-305(b)] provides that a holder in due course of a negotiable instrument, such as a bill of exchange, is subject only to defenses of duress, incapacity, illegality, fraud in the execution, or discharge in insolvency proceedings. [UCC §3-203(b)] provides that "[t]ransfer of an instrument, whether or not the transfer is a negotiation, vests in the transferee any right of the transferor to enforce the instrument, including any right as a holder in due course. . . ." Accordingly, the trial court's findings that Kookmin Bank was a holder in due course, and that KEIC stood in Kookmin's shoes preclude Audiobahn from contesting the bills of exchange because it was entitled to an offset from Mega Power.

The trial court, however, imposed a condition subsequent on KEIC's right to enforce the bills of exchange as a holder in due course. Aside from the trial court's reference to mechanic's lien law, which it expressly recognized did not apply, the only basis for the court's imposition of a condition subsequent was a notice provision in Mega Power's letters of assignment to KEIC. The notice provision does not support the trial court's rulings for two reasons.

First, the letters of assignment have nothing to do with KEIC's rights to enforce the bills of exchange. The letters of assignment between Mega Power and KEIC simply assigned Mega Power's rights to enforce its sales contract against Audiobahn. Mega Power, however, already had sold its right to receive payment from Audiobahn under the sales contracts when Mega Power issued the bills of exchange to Kookmin Bank. . . .

Second, the letters of assignment do not contain a condition subsequent. The provision cited by the trial court reads: "The Exporter hereby agrees to notify the Importer of the fact of assignment hereunder immediately after the signing of this Letter of Assignment. The Exporter hereby agrees that the notification shall be made by such methods as will make the assignment hereunder fully effective and valid with respect to the Importer and any third parties. Without prejudice to the above obligation to notify the importer of the assignment hereunder, the Exporter hereby grants to KEIC the full power and authority to notify the Importer of the assignment on behalf of the Exporter."

Nothing in the foregoing provision requires KEIC to notify Audiobahn of the assignment; although KEIC may give notice, only Mega Power is contractually obligated to do so. Moreover, the agreement does not state or even suggest the assignment automatically fails unless notice is given. The agreement's requirement that "notification shall be made by such methods as will make the assignment hereunder fully effective and valid with respect to the Importer and any third parties," simply recognizes that a debtor receives a discharge for any payments made to the assignor before notice of the assignment. [Ed.: Compare UCC §3-602.] Although Mega Power breached its contractual duty to give immediate notice of the assignment to Audiobahn, this failure did not affect the validity of the assignment because Audiobahn admitted it had made no payments on the shipment to Mega Power. Thus, the letters of assignment do not defeat KEIC's rights to enforce the bills of assignment.

In ruling in Audiobahn's favor, the trial court expressed concern for the financial harm Audiobahn would suffer by losing its offsets against Mega Power, which had declared bankruptcy. But this concern does not support the abrogation of KEIC's statutory rights. Accordingly, we reverse.

C.   Credit Transactions and Banker's Acceptances

The last transaction of import is an international sale of goods transaction in which the buyer wants to use the documents not only to facilitate immediate payment to the seller, but also to obtain credit that allows the buyer to defer payment: The buyer wants the seller to be paid now so that the buyer can obtain the goods now, but the buyer wants to pay for the goods later. The traditional format for such a transaction results in an instrument known as a banker's acceptance, which provides immediate payment to the seller while allowing the buyer to defer payment for 60 to 90 days. That arrangement gives the buyer in such a transaction an opportunity to resell the goods before paying for them so that it can use the funds from its resale of the goods to pay for them in the first instance.

That transaction starts out just like the documentary draft transaction discussed above, with three significant differences. First, the draft that the seller executes is not a sight draft for which it hopes to obtain immediate payment from the buyer. Instead, even though the seller anticipates immediate payment, the document is structured as a time draft, calling for deferred payment (the 60- to 90-day agreed-on period for which the buyer can defer payment), drawn on the buyer's bank, rather than the buyer itself. The buyer's bank arranges for credit (through either its own investment department or some third-party investor) that will allow the buyer to defer payment and yet allow the seller's bank (and the seller) to obtain immediate payment for the goods.

With all of those preliminary arrangements in place, the actual transaction proceeds as follows. When the seller ships the goods, the seller's bank sends the draft to the buyer's bank. The draft is drawn by the seller on the buyer's bank and includes the documents of title covering the goods, just as the drafts discussed above. The buyer's bank accepts the draft, which obligates that bank directly to pay for the goods at the scheduled time. See UCC §3-409. At that point, the buyer's bank releases the documents to the buyer, allowing the buyer to obtain the goods. The buyer's bank relies for reimbursement on the credit agreement with the buyer it obtained in connection with its original acceptance of the draft.

The next step is to provide payment to the seller. That payment comes from the time draft that the buyer's bank has accepted (which now is called a banker's acceptance). At the time of the shipment, the draft is indorsed to the bank in return for a payment to the seller from that bank. Because the buyer's bank is directly liable on this draft, it is a valuable financial instrument; accordingly, the buyer's bank can sell the draft to obtain the funds that it uses to pay the seller. Ordinarily, this sale is at a discount (reflecting the time period scheduled to elapse before the payment is made). In some cases, the investment department of the bank that has accepted the draft purchases the draft and pays the seller itself. Frequently, however, the buyer's bank sells the draft to a third-party investor on the open market. In that case, the draft is indorsed over to that investor. Finally, at the end of the stated 60- to 90-day period, the buyer's bank pays the owner of the draft the amount due on the draft. When the holder of the draft obtains payment from the buyer, the transaction is complete.

Although the market for banker's acceptances has declined significantly in the last few decades, tens of billions of dollars of them remain outstanding at any given time. The main attraction of banker's acceptances as an investment is the low risk. Industry sources report that during the approximately 75 years that banker's acceptances have been traded in the United States, no investor has ever suffered a loss of principal. Few investment opportunities offer that level of reliability.

Problem Set 23

23.1.   This week you have a new client, Bob Puget from Puget Shipping Company. His first question relates to Puget's form bill of lading, which is identical to the form set out in Figure 23.1. Puget tells you that a recent audit of Puget's files indicated that several recent shipments were made in which the bill was completed by an inexperienced clerk. Contrary to Puget's customary practices, the clerk typed the name and address of the consignee into blank 2 (designating that party as the consignee by name). If the bills were completed in that manner, do they constitute documents of title? Are they negotiable? UCC §§1-201(b)(6) and (b)(16), 7-102(a)(1), 7-104; FBLA §80103(a).

23.2.   You get an e-mail this morning from Archie Moon (your importer client from Chapter 6). He tells you that he got a call from his bank this morning about a draft it has received on one of the letters of credit it has issued on Archie's behalf. The draft apparently does not comply, because it includes only two counterparts of the invoice rather than the "triplicate" counterparts that the letter of credit specifies. Archie has heard some troubling things about the shipper (Asia Pulp and Paper, a large Indonesian paper company), so he is a little worried about the quality of the product in question, which is on a boat approaching Seattle. He wants to run by you his idea that he should seize on the defect in the letter-of-credit draft as a basis for dishonoring the draft. Then, when the paper gets here, he can look it over and forward payment if the quality appears appropriate. Assuming that the documentary requirements of the letter of credit are typical, do you foresee any problems with his plan? UCC §§ 4-104(a)(6), 4-503.

23.3. Puget's second question involves a shipment of two containers of air movers (a type of industrial machinery used to cool factory workers) from Seattle to Brasileira Lumber, in Rio de Janeiro. The seller was Guterson Pneumatic Tools. At the time of the shipment, Puget issued a negotiable bill of lading stating that the goods were consigned to the "order of shipper" (that is, to the order of Guterson, the seller). The vessel on which the goods are being shipped currently is located in Los Angeles. This morning Puget received an urgent telephone call from the captain of the vessel. The captain says that an attorney for Olympia National Bank has just served papers on him claiming that it has a lien on all of Guterson's assets. The attorney wants Puget to hand the goods over to Olympia.

When Puget called Brasileira Lumber and advised it of the situation, Brasileira told Puget that it intended to pay for the goods as contracted and that Brasileira would be displeased if Puget did not deliver the goods as agreed. It appears that the original bill of lading currently is in an overnight mail package on the way to Banco de Janeiro (Brasileira's bank). What should Puget do? UCC §§7-104(b), 7-403, 7-602; FBLA §§80105, 80110, 80115. Would your answer be any different if the bill was not negotiable?

23.4.   Later in the day, Puget calls you back with one final question about the Guterson shipment from Problem 23.3. He is frustrated because he has just discovered that the check Guterson gave him for the shipping charges has bounced. When Puget tried to telephone Guterson about paying for the charges, Puget listened to a recording stating that Guterson's number had been disconnected. When he went to Guterson's business, he saw that the warehouse was completely boarded up. When you question Puget about his charges, he explains that he always notes the charges on the bill, but ordinarily does not insist on payment until he delivers the goods. In this case, his understanding was that the seller Guterson would pay him before the goods arrived. Do you have any suggestions for how Puget can obtain payment? UCC §§7-307, 7-403(b); FBLA §80109.

23.5.   You get a call this morning from a new client, Giles Winterborne, who runs a gourmet apple company with customers worldwide. He came by this afternoon to consult about a shipment of apples that he sent to Grace Melbury (in Paris), using a standard documentary draft transaction to protect his right to payment. When the draft arrived in Paris, Melbury called up Winterborne, told Winterborne that she had changed her mind and no longer wanted the apples, and advised Winterborne that she would not pay for the apples. Later that afternoon Safety Pacific (Winterborne's bank) called to advise Winterborne that it had been notified by telex that Melbury had dishonored the draft. Winterborne comes to you confused. Can't he force Melbury to pay the draft? If he can't, he wants to know what the point of all of the documents and drafts is? UCC §§3-401, 3-408. How would his position differ if he had shipped the apples with a nonnegotiable document of title consigning the apples to Melbury? (In this problem and the rest of the problems in this assignment, you should assume that rights on the drafts in question are determined either under Article 3 or under foreign rules that are substantively identical to Article 3.) See UNCITRAL Conv. art. 40.

23.6.   Satisfied by the frank advice that you rendered in Problem 23.5, Winterborne returns to you the next day with a new problem. His question involves another documentary draft shipment, this time to Edred Fitzpiers in Hintock, England. The collection document was in the customary form, calling for delivery of the documents "against payment." For reasons that are unclear to you and Winterborne, Hintock Bank and Trust (Fitzpiers's bank) released the documents to Fitzpiers without obtaining payment from Fitzpiers. Accordingly, Fitzpiers now has the apples, and Winterborne has not been paid. What can Winterborne do to obtain payment? Convention on Contracts for the International Sale of Goods 62; UCC §2-709; ICC 522 arts. 7-17.

23.7.   A week later Winterborne comes to you with another problem. This one involves a banker's acceptance transaction in which he sold some apples several months ago to Marty South, drawing a draft on the same Hintock Bank and Trust. Hintock accepted the draft and sold it to Barclays Bank on the open market. Unfortunately (for reasons that should be obvious from Hintock's conduct in Problem 23.6), British regulatory authorities recently closed Hintock. Thus, Hintock did not pay the banker's acceptance when it came due. Barclays has now approached Winterborne, seeking payment from him as "drawer" of the draft. Winterborne can't understand what possible claim Barclays has against him. "I shipped apples to Marty South. She got the apples. I got paid. What's the problem?" Does he have anything to fear? UCC §§3-414, 3-415; Convention on International Bills of Exchange and Promissory Notes art. 38.

23.8. Consider again the facts of *Korea Export*. Do you think the result accords with what the parties would have expected before the transaction? That Audiobahn would have to pay for the goods even if it had unfulfilled outstanding claims against a bankrupt seller?

Chapter 8. Securities

Assignment 24: Securities

A. Securitization and Liquidity

Negotiability is not the only system for making commercial assets liquid. Indeed, it is not even the most common system. In the modern economy, the most important group of liquid assets (aside from cash itself) is securities.

Although it might not be obvious at first glance, securities serve much the same function as negotiable instruments: They enhance the value of assets by increasing their liquidity. The technique here, however, is to take a single asset (or pool of assets), divide it into a large number of identical shares (or groups of identical shares), and then sell the individual shares; each of those shares is a security.

Securitization enhances liquidity in two related ways. The simplest rests on the relation between the size of an asset and its liquidity. On the one hand, all other things being equal, smaller assets tend to be more liquid than larger assets because the universe of potential purchasers for small assets is larger than the universe of potential purchasers for large assets. For example, compare the number of people that you know that could consider investing $10,000 in a company with the number that could consider investing $100,000,000. And the difference does not rest simply on the smaller number of people that have $100,000,000 to invest. It also rests on the notion of portfolio diversification. Most people prefer to limit risk by investing in a wide variety of assets so that a misfortune on one investment will not have a serious impact on the entire portfolio. The desire of investors to diversify their portfolios significantly limits the willingness of even large investors to purchase assets that have very high prices. On the other hand, the larger the asset, the easier it is for businesses like stockbrokers and investment banks to profit by acquiring, analyzing, and promulgating the kind of information that makes it easier for investors to make an informed assessment of the value of an investment in the asset.

Securitization responds to that dichotomy by taking very large assets (large enough to reward investigation into their value) and dividing them up into very small pieces (small enough to be suitable purchases for investors). Because securitization divides the single asset into a large number of small pieces, each of the smaller pieces has a much lower purchase price than the entire asset, yet each of the smaller pieces retains the financial characteristics (the same risk, return, maturity date, and the like) of the asset out of which the securities have been carved.

Securitization also enhances liquidity by enhancing the potential for an organized market in which assets can be bought and sold. If a potential purchaser must purchase an entire company (or an entire building or an entire loan), then sales of interests in the company will be relatively infrequent because they will occur only when that single purchaser wishes to make a sale. Accordingly, it is unlikely that there will be any organized market for making such a sale. Thus, the seller will incur substantial time, effort, and cost in locating and reaching an agreement with a purchaser.

By contrast, if the ownership of the company is divided into a large number of small interests (securities), sales will occur more frequently because they will occur whenever any one of the many owners wishes to sell some portion of its interest. Because sales are more frequent, it is easier for a regular market to develop, which will display a market price around which potential sellers and purchasers can focus their discussions. The result of the process is a market in which the transaction costs of a sale (essentially a broker's commission) are much smaller than in a conventional market without securities. Indeed, in many cases, the securities seller can complete a sale within minutes (or seconds) with nothing more than a simple telephone call or a few keystrokes at a computer terminal.

B. The Rise of Securitization

Although securitization probably is not as ancient as negotiability, it is certainly not novel. Organized securities markets have existed for at least three centuries, dating to the late seventeenth century in England. But for almost all of that time, securitization has been limited to a narrow range of assets: debt and equity interests in the largest and most creditworthy businesses and governmental entities. Thus, until the 1960s, there were really only two major types of securities, which can be referred to loosely as stocks and bonds. If a large company wished to securitize its equity ownership interests, it could issue stock in the company, so that the individual shareholders would own the company. Similarly, if an entity (like the United States government) wished to securitize a portion of its debt, it could issue the debt in the form of securities, distributing a large number of relatively small but identical debt instruments (bonds) rather than a single large promissory note that would be purchased by a single investor. Thus, as a tool to provide liquidity to debt obligations, securitization is a direct alternative to negotiability.

On that point, it is important to distinguish between a securitized debt and a secured debt. Although the terms sound similar, they have quite different implications. A securitized debt is a debt (like an issue of bonds) that has been divided up into a large number of identical pieces. A secured debt is a debt for which the borrower has given collateral, like a home mortgage or a car loan; the collateral is said to "secure" the borrower's obligation to repay the debt. A securitized debt can be secured or not; a secured debt can be securitized or held intact and undivided.

Since the 1960s the use of securitization has spread into many contexts other than the traditional issues of stocks and bonds by large creditworthy companies. Many of the newer uses involve relatively small payment obligations, for which negotiability once would have played an important role. The first significant advance (and still the most important one) occurred in the market for home-mortgage notes. Starting with the 1970 creation of the Federal Home

Loan Mortgage Corporation (colloquially referred to as Freddie Mac), the federal government has supervised the creation of a variety of quasigovernmental entities that have succeeded in securitizing hundreds of billions of dollars of home-mortgage notes. By 2005, those entities (which now include not only Freddie Mac, but also the Federal National Mortgage Association (Fannie Mae) and the Government National Mortgage Association (Ginnie Mae)) were securitizing almost all conforming mortgages in this country.

The key concept necessary to extend securitization to home-mortgage notes was asset pooling. Taken one by one, home-mortgage notes are not at all liquid because a careful assessment of the value of an individual note would require evaluation of not only the home for which the money was used, but also the credit characteristics of the borrower. Given the relatively small size of the typical home-mortgage note, it is relatively expensive to perform that assessment on a case-by-case basis. The law of large numbers, however, suggests that a large pool of home mortgages can be evaluated quite accurately at a relatively low cost. That is true because the total return for a large pool of mortgages will not be affected significantly by a small number of unusual unfortunate occurrences.

To implement that insight, Freddie Mac, Fannie Mae, and Ginnie Mae (joined now by a number of large banks and other investors) purchase huge numbers of home-mortgage notes as soon as borrowers sign them, collect similar notes into large pools, and then issue massive numbers of securities reflecting minuscule interests in each of those pools. A large and thriving market for those securities makes them an asset that is in practice not significantly less liquid than a stock traded on the New York Stock Exchange. The collapse of that market in 2008 may have reflected serious failure in monitoring origination and in assessing the quality of underwriting the complex securities into which the mortgages were converted, but it does not undermine the effectiveness of the securitization model as a vehicle for enhancing liquidity.

That same pooling concept has been applied in a variety of other areas, the most notable of which involves credit-card receivables. In that context, major credit-card issuers collect pools of their outstanding credit-card receivables and securitize them. Just as with home-mortgage notes, an individual credit-card receivable is not at all liquid; its value depends on the vagaries of the individual cardholder's repayment patterns. But the repayment pattern of a large pool of credit-card receivables is sufficiently predictable to make it easy to find investors willing to invest in small shares of such a pool.

C. Investment Securities and Article 8

The average student (or lawyer) thinking of legal rules for securities thinks immediately of the extensive federal regime of securities regulation reflected in the Securities Act, the Securities Exchange Act, and the voluminous regulations issued by the Securities and Exchange Commission (SEC).

Although those rules obviously are crucial to a complete picture of the market for securities, they are not directly relevant here. For the most part, they respond to the potential for fraud or sharp dealing in the issuance and sale of securities. Thus, they require a large variety of registrations and disclosures as a condition to the issuance of certain types of securities. Similarly, they closely regulate securities exchanges to ensure that those exchanges provide fair venues for the purchase and sale of securities. The concern here, however, is not with the fairness of the market in which securities are sold, but with the way in which the mechanisms for effecting their issuance and sale can enhance their liquidity. The primary legal rules relevant to that topic appear in the revised version of Article 8 of the Uniform Commercial Code. Adopted by the American Law Institute in 1994, that statute has been enacted in all 50 states. Moreover, pursuant to the "TRADES regulations" issued by the Treasury Department, similar rules govern book-entry securities issued by the United States Treasury. 31 C.F.R. Part 357. Parallel (and largely similar) rules govern the securities issued by major government-sponsored entities such as the Federal National Mortgage Association ("Fannie Mae"), Federal Home Loan Mortgage Corporation ("Freddie Mac"), and Government National Mortgage Association ("Ginnie Mae"). The following case is a good illustration of the basic commercial-law problems for which Article 8 provides responses.

Davis v. Stern, Agee & Leach, Inc.

965 So. 2d 1076 (Ala. 2007)

STUART, Justice.

Mary Davis [("Davis")] sued Sterne, Agee & Leach, Inc. (hereinafter "Sterne Agee"), and her two stepsons, Robert Davis, Jr., and Frank R. Davis (hereinafter "the sons"), alleging claims of fraud by forgery, conversion, negligence or wantonness, conspiracy, unjust enrichment, fraudulent misrepresentation, and fraudulent suppression, regarding the disbursement of the proceeds of the individual retirement account ("IRA") belonging to her late husband Robert E. Davis, Sr., and serviced by Sterne Agee. Sterne Agee and the sons moved separately for summary judgments. The trial court entered a summary judgment for Sterne Agee and the sons as to all claims. Davis appeals. We affirm in part, reverse in part, and remand.

FACTS AND PROCEDURAL HISTORY

Mr. Davis owned an IRA that was serviced by Sterne Agee and one of its financial advisors, Linda Daniel. During Mr. Davis's life, he changed the named beneficiary on this IRA four times. Each time the named beneficiary was either Davis or the sons.

In December 2001, Daniel received in the mail a change-of-beneficiary ("COB") form allegedly signed by Mr. Davis, changing the beneficiary of his IRA from Davis to his sons. Daniel did not compare the signature on this form to other known signatures of Mr. Davis to confirm its validity.

Mr. Davis died in February 2002. After his death, Davis contacted Daniel to inquire about the disbursement of the proceeds in the IRA. Daniel informed Davis that she was not the designated beneficiary on the IRA, and she refused to disclose information about the account. The sons also contacted Daniel. Because they were the designated beneficiaries, Daniel provided information about the IRA to them and pursuant to their request began to liquidate the IRA and to distribute the proceeds to the sons.

In July 2002, Davis, believing that the signature on the COB form dated December 8, 2001, had been forged, requested copies of the last three COB forms allegedly executed by Mr. Davis. Daniel released the documentation. After Davis had the signatures on the forms evaluated, Davis concluded that the signature on the COB form dated December 8, 2001 was not that of Mr. Davis.

On June 22, 2004, Davis filed her complaint in the circuit court, naming Sterne Agee and the sons as defendants. The sons completely liquidated the IRA after receiving notice of the lawsuit.

Sterne Agee and the sons answered the complaint. In June 2005 Sterne Agee moved for a summary judgment. . . . In support of its motion, Sterne Agee provided an affidavit from Daniel; that affidavit stated:

> I received what turned out to be a final designation of beneficiary from [Mr. Davis] in December 2001. This form was completed and executed and directed that the beneficiaries on the IRA account be [the sons]. I was surprised when I received the form because Mr. Davis had not recently requested a form and I had not recently sent him a form. It was during the holidays and I had already planned to call Mr. Davis and wish him a happy holiday. When I called to wish him happy holidays, I also asked him about the December 2001 beneficiary change, to verify that he wanted his sons to be his beneficiaries. [Mr. Davis] confirmed that he did in fact want his sons to be the beneficiaries and had sent the form to me to effectuate the change.
>
> If I had suspected, or if there had been any hint of a forgery, I would have reported it immediately to the branch manager. As to the December 2001 final beneficiary change, although the form had not been requested [by or sent to] Mr. Davis immediately prior to the change in beneficiary, I called [Mr. Davis] and verified that the completed and executed designation I received, indicating he wanted his sons to be the beneficiaries of his IRA account, was correct. [Mr. Davis] confirmed that he wanted his sons to be the beneficiaries of his IRA account as he had previously stated on a number of occasions.

Sterne Agee also included excerpts from Daniel's deposition conducted in February 2005 in which she testified that she had had numerous conversations with Mr. Davis about changing the designated beneficiary of his IRA. She stated that she could not recall when she last spoke with Mr. Davis about the designation of a beneficiary for his IRA. Additionally, Sterne Agee submitted deposition testimony from Davis in which Davis admitted that she did not have any facts to support her contention that Sterne Agee and the sons had conspired to deprive her of the proceeds of Mr. Davis's account and that she was not aware of any conversations between Sterne Agee and the sons. Sterne Agee also attached excerpts from the deposition testimony of the sons, which indicated that they did not have contact with Sterne Agee or Daniel until after Mr. Davis had died. Last, Sterne Agee attached excerpts from the deposition testimony of Steven A. Slyter, Davis's expert

witness on handwriting analysis, establishing that he believed an expert's assistance would be required to analyze Mr. Davis's signatures on the three COB forms
to conclude that the signature on the December 8, 2001, COB form was not that
of Mr. Davis.

In opposition to Sterne Agee's motion for a summary judgment, . . . Davis
presented evidence, in the form of the testimony of Slyter, that the signature on
the December 2001 COB form was not that of Mr. Davis. She argued that a genuine issue of material fact was created as to whether the signature on the document was forged and whether Sterne Agee had breached its duty of care in disbursing the proceeds of the IRA. She also argued that Sterne Agee had presented
no evidence to refute Slyter's testimony that the signature on the December 2001
COB form was not Mr. Davis's and that Daniel and Sterne Agee had breached the
standard of care in servicing Mr. Davis's IRA. Last, to counter statements in Daniel's
affidavit regarding Mr. Davis's intent, she attached an affidavit from Beverly Scott,
a former nurse of Mr. Davis's, who stated:

> At one time he told me that he had changed the beneficiary of his IRA account to his
> [sons]. He then said that he felt bad about it and started crying. He said that he loved
> [Davis] and that he wanted to change the beneficiary back to her. He changed the
> beneficiary back to [Davis] because I saw him sign the change form and I placed it in
> the mailbox. He intended for [Davis] to be the beneficiary of that account. He never
> said anything about changing the beneficiary back to his [sons]. . . .

After conducting a hearing on the summary-judgment motions, the trial court
entered a summary judgment for Sterne Agee and the sons as to all claims. . . .

Davis appeals.

LEGAL ANALYSIS

Davis contends that the trial court erred in entering a summary judgment for
Sterne Agee because, she says, [UCC §8-115] does not protect Sterne Agee from
liability when it improperly relied on a forged December 2001 COB form to pay
the proceeds of Mr. Davis's IRA to the sons.

The parties agree that this case involves a "financial asset" as that term is defined
in [UCC §8-102(a)(9)]. Thus, this transaction is governed by Title 7, Ala. Code
1975, this state's version of the Uniform Commercial Code, which includes an
article entitled Investment Securities. [Article 8] governs the rights and obligations
of entitlement holders, i.e., those who own financial assets, and the holders and
servicers, i.e., security intermediaries, of those financial assets. . . .

[I]n order to determine whether [UCC §8-115] protects Sterne Agee from the
adverse claims of Davis, this Court must first determine whether Sterne Agee's distribution of the proceeds of Mr. Davis's IRA to his sons was done at "the direction
of Mr. Davis."

[UCC §8-107(b)] provides:

> An indorsement, instruction, or entitlement order is effective if:
> (1) it is made by the appropriate person;

(2) it is made by a person who has power under the law of agency to transfer the security or financial asset on behalf of the appropriate person . . .; or

(3) the appropriate person has ratified it or is otherwise precluded from asserting its ineffectiveness.

An "'appropriate person' means . . . with respect to an instruction, the registered owner of an uncertificated security [or financial asset]." [UCC §8-107(a)(2)].

According to Davis, Mr. Davis's signature on the December 2001 COB form was forged; therefore, she maintains, Sterne Agee did not act at Mr. Davis's "directive" when it distributed the proceeds of the IRA to the sons pursuant to the forged COB form. Sterne Agee argues that because it distributed the proceeds of the IRA pursuant to Mr. Davis's direction as indicated on the December 2001 COB form, [§8-115] protects it from liability from Davis's adverse claims. Whether a COB form, allegedly not executed by the owner of the account or his agent, directing a change of beneficiary on an investment account is an effective directive as provided in [§8-115], is an issue of first impression in Alabama.

[Section] 8-115 and its comments were adopted verbatim from §8-115 of the Uniform Commercial Code. Very few cases have addressed whether a document that is not executed by the owner of the financial asset or his agent or representative and that provides directions to a securities intermediary is an effective directive. Powers v. American Express Financial Advisors, Inc., 82 F. Supp. 2d 448 (D. Md. 2000), however, is one of these rare cases. In *Powers*, Powers and her boyfriend entered into a mutual-fund investment, in joint-and-survivor form, with American Express Financial Advisors, Inc. The contract with American Express required the signatures of both Powers and the boyfriend for any redemption request over $50,000. Powers and the boyfriend terminated their relationship and, pursuant to an agreement, "froze" the account while they determined how to distribute the proceeds.

Some months later, American Express received a letter, signed purportedly by Powers and the boyfriend, directing American Express to release the freeze on the account and to transfer the proceeds of the account, amounting to over $50,000, to another financial agency. The signatures on the letter were notarized. A financial worker at American Express compared the signature on the letter with an exemplar of Powers's signature, verified the signature as Powers's, and transferred the proceeds of the mutual fund. 82 F. Supp. 2d at 451. The evidence presented to the district court, however, established that the signature was not that of Powers but was forged by her ex-boyfriend. Additionally, no evidence was presented indicating that the ex-boyfriend had authority to affix Powers's signature to the letter or that Powers had ratified the forgery. The district court held that, even if American Express exercised due care in accordance to accepted standards in the business, American Express was "still liable to Powers, because the order, for which she never gave any form of authorization or ratified, was 'ineffective.'" 82 F. Supp. 2d at 452. . . .

In Watson v. Sears, 766 N.E.2d 784 (Ind. Ct. App. 2002), the Court of Appeals of Indiana, citing *Powers*, also came to the conclusion that a securities intermediary is liable for a wrongful transfer when it acts pursuant to a forged instruction. The *Watson* court, adopting the rationale of *Powers*, held that a forged document does not qualify as an effective directive, stating: "Simply put, if the appropriate person does not make the order to transfer assets, then the order is ineffective."

This Court adopts the rationale of *Powers* and *Watson* and holds that a forged directive, *i.e.*, one not executed by the owner of the financial asset, his agent, or his representative, or one that is not ratified by the owner, his agent, or his representative, is not an effective instruction. Thus, a securities intermediary acting upon such an ineffective directive is not protected from liability by [§8-115].

Our holding is consistent with the examples provided in [§8-115]. Each of the examples involves a situation wherein the securities intermediary has acted pursuant to an effective directive from the customer. When the securities intermediary acts pursuant to an effective directive, then the protections of [§8-115] clearly apply. . . .

[The court declines the invitation to analogize to insurance law.] The language in [the relevant insurance statute] is distinguishable from the language in [§8-115]. Insurance law is different from investment-securities law. In insurance law, there is an accepted premise that the insurer is not under any duty to determine whether the change of beneficiary was procured or induced by improper means where it has no reason to believe or know that such was the case. [Citations and quotation marks omitted.] There is also an established good-faith exception in light of the presumption that insurance benefits might be paid to someone with an inferior claim. [Citation omitted.] No such general premise, good-faith exception, or presumption exists with regard to investment-securities law. For example, [§8-507] recognizes that a securities intermediary has a duty to comply with an effective entitlement order and provides the consequences for the securities intermediary when it acts pursuant to an ineffective entitlement order, stating:

> If a securities intermediary transfers a financial asset pursuant to an ineffective entitlement order, the securities intermediary shall reestablish a security entitlement in favor of the person entitled to it, and pay or credit any payments or distributions that the person did not receive as a result of the wrongful transfer. If the securities intermediary does not reestablish a security entitlement, the securities intermediary is liable to the entitlement holder for damages.

Thus, because the language in Art. 8 does not lend itself to a good-faith exception and no such presumptions exist as they do in insurance law, we refuse to interpret [§8-115] so broadly when nothing in the caselaw or the language of the statute lends itself to such a broad interpretation. Indeed, in light of the facts of this case, we can perceive of situations in which such a broad interpretation of [§8-115] would be inequitable and unjust.

Now, we must determine whether there is substantial evidence creating a genuine issue of material fact as to whether Sterne Agee distributed the proceeds of Mr. Davis's IRA pursuant to an ineffective directive. In other words, we must determine whether Davis produced substantial evidence that Mr. Davis's signature was forged or that Mr. Davis did not ratify the directive. . . .

Here, Davis presented evidence, in the form of Slyter's opinion, indicating that the signature on the December 2001 COB form was not that of Mr. Davis. The evidence established that Slyter examined the signature purported to be Mr. Davis's on the December 2001 COB form and compared it to other known exemplars of Mr. Davis's signature. In Slyter's expert opinion, the December

2001 COB form was not signed by Mr. Davis. Thus, Davis produced substantial evidence that Mr. Davis did not sign the December 2001 COB form, creating a genuine issue of material fact as to whether Sterne Agee, relying on the December 2001 COB form, was acting pursuant to an effective directive from Mr. Davis.

Sterne Agee, however, argues that even if Mr. Davis did not sign the December 2001 COB form, summary judgment is nonetheless proper as to it because Mr. Davis made the directive effective by confirming it in a telephone conversation with Daniel. Sterne Agee submitted an affidavit from Daniel executed in June 2005, in which she stated that she verified with Mr. Davis "that the completed and executed [December 2001] designation . . ., indicating he wanted his sons to be the beneficiaries of his IRA account, was correct." Daniel specifically stated in her affidavit that "[Mr. Davis] confirmed that he wanted his sons to be the beneficiaries of his IRA account as he had previously stated on a number of occasions."

[The court ultimately concludes that the dispute presents a genuine issue of material fact.]

Because Davis has created a genuine issue of material fact as to whether Sterne Agee acted pursuant to an effective directive, the trial court erred in entering a summary judgment for Sterne Agee on Davis's conversion claim. . . .

CONCLUSION

Based on the foregoing, the trial court's judgment is affirmed in part and reversed in part, and this cause is remanded for proceedings consistent with this opinion.

NABERS, C.J., and LYONS, HARWOOD, SMITH, and PARKER, JJ., concur. BOLIN, J., concurs in the result.

SEE and WOODALL, JJ., concur in part and dissent in part. [The dissents relate to the court's disposition of fraud claims that do not involve UCC Article 8 and are not reprinted above.]

The best way to provide a general picture of the system is to summarize the basic coverage and terminology of Article 8. After that introduction, the assignment closes by discussing the obligations of the issuer and the two separate systems for holding and transferring securities: the traditional direct holding system (in which each investor deals directly with the issuer) and the modern indirect holding system (in which a few intermediaries hold each issuer's shares on behalf of investors at large).

1. The Subject Matter: What Is a Security?

The basic subject matter of Article 8 is the "security," a term defined in UCC §§8-102(a)(15) and 8-103. The most important thing to remember about that definition is that it has nothing to do with the federal securities laws or the relatively vague definition of "security" found there. Although most assets that are securities under Article 8 will be securities under the federal securities laws, and vice versa, the Article 8 definition is distinct.

The Article 8 definition includes four separate requirements. The first three requirements are simple descriptive requirements that implement the concept of a security described in the opening pages of the assignment. First, under the introductory clause to UCC §8-102(a)(15), the item must be either an obligation of an issuer (such as a bond) or a share or other interest in the issuer (such as a share of stock). Second, under UCC §8-102(a)(15)(ii), the item must be divided or divisible into a class or series of shares. Thus, Article 8 applies to a series of bonds, but it does not apply to a single undivided promissory note.

Third, under UCC §8-102(a)(15)(iii), the item either must be of a type that is traded on securities exchanges or markets or must expressly provide that it is governed by Article 8. To limit the ambiguity in the question whether assets satisfy that test, UCC §8-103 includes several bright-line rules that govern the most common types of investment assets. For example, any "share or similar equity interest issued by a corporation, business trust, joint stock company, or similar entity is a security." UCC §8-103(a). Conversely, except for a special rule related to federally regulated investment companies, "[a]n interest in a partnership or limited liability company is not a security unless it is dealt in or traded on securities exchanges or in securities markets [or] its terms expressly provide that it is a security governed by this Article." UCC §8-103(c).

The fourth requirement (UCC §8-102(a)(15)(i)) is the only one that presents any significant complexity. That requirement governs the form in which the security exists. Specifically, Article 8 applies only if the security appears in one of three forms. The first two forms involve certificated securities, that is, securities represented by a physical piece of paper, a certificate. UCC §8-102(a)(4). Certificated securities can appear in either bearer form or registered form. To be in bearer form, the certificate must provide that the security is payable to the bearer of the certificate. UCC §8-102(a)(2). For reasons explained in Assignment 22, bearer securities are no longer common; this assignment will not discuss them further. To be in registered form, the certificate must specify a person entitled to the security and provide that the security can be transferred on books maintained by (or on behalf of) the issuer. That provision was the subject of the controversial decision of the New York Court of Appeals in Highland Capital Management, L.P. v. Schneider, 866 N.E.2d 1020 (N.Y. 2007) (on questions certified from the Second Circuit). That case concluded that an obligation was a "registered" security solely because the issuer happened to maintain books on which it recorded transfers. Proposed revisions to UCC §8-103, however, adopt the reasoning of the *Highland Capital* dissent that a security is "registered" for Article 8 purposes only if the relevant records are maintained specifically for the purposes of registering transfers. The corporate bond in Problem 20.1 is a registered certificated security.

The third permissible form is the uncertificated security, a security for which there is no physical certificate. UCC §8-102(a)(18). Because there is no certificate to reflect the ownership interest, those securities necessarily must be transferred by entries on books maintained by (or on behalf of) the issuer. UCC §8-102(a)(15)(i). Again, because uncertificated securities are uncommon, I discuss them no further here.

The last significant point about the definition of the Article 8 security applies to documents that qualify as both a security under Article 8 and an instrument under Article 3. Under UCC §8-103(d), such documents are treated as securities, not instruments.

2.   The Obligation of the Issuer

Investors ordinarily do not purchase securities because of their interest in the form of the certificate. Rather, they are interested in the monetary return that will come from the security. Accordingly, the nature of the obligation that the security represents is central to the system.

Unlike Article 3's treatment of instruments, Article 8 does not itself impose an obligation to pay a security. Instead, it accepts the obligation imposed by the laws governing contracts and business associations and uses the term "issuer" to describe the entity obligated under those laws. If the security is a bond or some other debt instrument, the issuer is the party obligated to pay the debt. If the security is stock or some other ownership interest, the issuer is the party in which the security creates an interest. UCC §8-201.

Article 8 does, however, have much to say about enforcement of that obligation. Most importantly, Article 8 includes a series of rules (parallel to the rules that govern holder-in-due-course status) that limit the defenses an issuer can impose to the obligation created by the security. Following the reasoning of the negotiability system, Article 8 accepts the premise that strict limitation of the defenses that an issuer can interpose enhances the value of securities by improving their liquidity. Thus, with only two exceptions discussed below, Article 8 generally bars issuers from asserting defenses against any party that purchases a security for value and without notice of the defense. UCC §8-202(d).

The "notice" that is adequate to allow interposition of a defense is the standard UCC concept of notice set forth in UCC §1-202(a), which extends to all facts of which a person "has reason to know" based on "all the facts and circumstances known to [it]." Thus, a person might have notice under UCC §1-202(a), and be subject to a defense on a security, even if the person had no actual knowledge of the defense, so long as the person had reason to know of the defense. UCC §8-202 amplifies that point by stating expressly that a purchaser (even if it technically does not have "notice") is bound by terms stated on a certificated security, by terms incorporated into the security by reference, and by terms stated in any applicable legal rule governing the issuance of the security. UCC §8-202(a).

The "value" that a purchaser must give to take advantage of that rule also refers to the standard UCC definition, which includes "any consideration sufficient to support a simple contract." UCC §1-204(4). That concept is conspicuously broader — easier to satisfy — than the concept of value that must be given for a party to become a holder in due course of a negotiable instrument under Article 3. As Assignment 22 explains, the value that a purchaser must give to become a holder in due course of a negotiable instrument excludes a variety of things that would constitute consideration (and thus value under Article 8), the most important of which probably is a commitment to provide future services. See UCC §3-303(a)(1).

The first of the two defenses valid against a purchaser for value without notice is a claim that the security is counterfeit. UCC §8-202(c). The second exception is more complicated. It relates to defenses that go to the validity of the initial issuance of the security. If the security is issued by a person that is not a governmental entity, Article 8 allows a defense of invalidity to be asserted against purchasers for value without notice only if the defense arises from constitutional provisions. Even then, the defense can be asserted only against a party that purchased the security at its original issuance. UCC §8-202(b)(1).

Governmental issuers are permitted considerably more leeway. Thus, to defeat a defense of invalidity interposed by a governmental issuer, a purchaser must not only overcome the private-issuer standard articulated in UCC §8-202(b)(1), but also demonstrate one of two things: that the security was issued in "substantial compliance" with the applicable legal requirements, or that the issuer received a substantial consideration for the securities and that the "stated purpose of the issue is one for which the issuer has power to borrow money or issue the security." UCC §8-202(b)(2). Although those rules do give governmental issuers a greater opportunity to disavow their securities than private issuers, they are not exceptionally onerous. After all, a purchaser can be safe in purchasing a security without examining every aspect of the issuer's conduct in issuing the securities. It is enough to determine that the issuer "substantial[ly] compli[ed]" with the applicable laws. Similarly, even if it is not practical for the purchaser to evaluate the issuer's compliance with applicable rules governing the issue, it ordinarily would not be difficult for a purchaser (or, more likely, a broker marketing the securities to the purchaser) to determine that the issuer actually received funds from the issue and that the stated purpose of the issue is a legitimate one.

Although the special rules for governmental issuers are not particularly onerous, and admittedly have a long history, they are difficult to justify as a policy matter. The premise of Article 8 is that general rules barring issuers from interposing defenses enhance the liquidity of all securities by enhancing the reliability of the obligation that they present. If that premise is correct, then special rules giving governmental issuers a greater right to disavow their securities should diminish the liquidity of the securities that they issue, thus lowering the price that purchasers will pay for those securities.

That problem is particularly troubling, given this country's long and sordid record of local disavowal of securitized obligations. Detroit's willingness to file for bankruptcy may be the most recent instance in which a major governmental entity chose not to meet its obligations to the financial markets, but other jurisdictions frequently have used the less direct tactic of interposing technical claims of invalidity, to which state courts on occasion have been receptive. Article 8's continuation of that tradition is regrettable.

3. *The Two Holding Systems*

Just as the Article 8 rules limiting the defenses of the issuer are analogous to the holder-in-due-course provisions in the negotiability system, the Article 8 rules regarding systems for holding and transferring securities are analogous to the mechanisms by which the negotiability system facilitates the easy transfer of negotiable instruments and documents. Article 8 recognizes the same underlying premise regarding transferability as the negotiability system: A cheap and reliable system for transferring assets enhances their liquidity. Indeed, people often refer to securities as "negotiable" to describe the freedom with which they can be transferred.

The revised version of Article 8 deals with the transferability issue by recognizing two separate systems for holding and transferring securities. The first is the direct holding system, a traditional system in which the issuer deals directly with the purchaser of the security. The second is the more modern indirect holding system, in which the purchaser holds the security through an intermediary.

(a) The Direct Holding System. The best place to start in understanding the way in which securities are held and sold is with the traditional direct holding system. To see how that system works, you should consider two issues: what it takes for a transfer to be effective against the issuer of the security, and what it takes for a transfer to cut off the claims that third parties might have to the security.

(i) Making the Transfer Effective Against the Issuer. An issuer generally is free to ignore the transfer of a security until the transfer is registered on the books of the issuer. To put it another way, the issuer of a security has a broad right to treat the registered owner as the true owner of a security, even if the registered owner no longer has possession of or actual title to the security. UCC §8-207(a). Accordingly, a party that purchases a security has a powerful incentive not only to take delivery of the security, but also to have itself registered as the owner of the security on the books of the issuer.

To obtain registration as the owner of a security, the purchaser must notify the issuer (or a designated transfer agent that acts for the issuer) that it has purchased the security and must provide adequate evidence of the purchase. Ordinarily, this is done by obtaining an indorsement of the security from the seller. See UCC §§8-401(a)(2) (allowing issuer to condition registration on an indorsement or instruction from the "appropriate person"), 8-107(a)(1) (specifying the "appropriate person" as the currently registered owner). Even if the purchaser neglects to obtain that indorsement at the time of the transaction, Article 8 grants it a right to obtain the indorsement later upon demand. UCC §8-304(d); see UCC §8-307 (obligating the seller to provide "proof of authority or any other requisite necessary to obtain registration of the transfer").

Although UCC §8-401 offers a long list of potential problems that could allow the issuer to refuse to register a security, the presentation of a security that bears a signature purporting to be the signature of the previously registered owner ordinarily is sufficient to induce the issuer to register the security in the name of the purchaser. If the security is uncertificated, the issuer's notation of the transfer on its books finishes the registration. If the security is certificated, the issuer completes the registration by issuing a new certificate in the name of the purchaser.

(ii) The Effect of a Transfer on Third Parties. Under UCC §8-302(a), a purchaser of a security obtains all of the rights that its transferor had to the security. But the desire for clean and irrevocable transfers is as powerful for securities as it is for negotiable instruments. Accordingly, Article 8 includes rules analogous to Article 3's holder-in-due-course rules, which allow certain parties to take free of claims that third parties might have to a security. As you know from the earlier sections of the assignment, Article 8 imposes strict limits on defenses that issuers can interpose against all purchasers (even those that dealt directly with the issuer). Thus, the main concern is not the ability of a transferee to take free of a defense to enforcement of the security (because Article 8 already has removed most of those defenses); the main concern is the ability of the purchaser to cut off adverse claims to the security. The classic problem is a sale of a stolen security: When does a party that buys a security from a thief take free of the claim of the (previously) true owner?

The Article 8 answer is that the purchaser takes free of the adverse claim if the purchaser qualifies as a "protected purchaser." UCC §8-303(b). The rules for protected purchaser status are considerably simpler than the Article 3 holder-in-due-course rules; Article 8 requires only that the purchaser give value without notice of the claim and obtain control of the security. As mentioned above, the Article 8 concept of value is much broader than the Article 3 definition, extending to any consideration sufficient to support a simple contract. UCC §§8-303 comment 2, 1-204. The notice requirement incorporates the familiar standard from UCC §1-202(a), which includes not only claims of which the purchaser has actual knowledge, but also claims of which the purchaser has reason to know from all the facts and circumstances. The only new requirement is the control requirement. The purchaser can satisfy that requirement if it both obtains possession of the security (which constitutes delivery under UCC §8-301) and obtains either an indorsement of the security or a registration in its own name. UCC §8-106(b), (c).

The last component of the system is a shelter rule that mirrors the shelter rule in UCC §3-203(b) (which should be familiar to you from Assignment 22). Under basic property principles, a transferee of a security acquires all of the rights of its transferor. Accordingly, if one protected purchaser (insulated from an adverse claim to a security) delivers the security to another purchaser, the second purchaser is as insulated from the claim as the previous owner would have been, even if the second purchaser fails to obtain protected-purchaser status in its own right. UCC §8-302(a) & comment 1. For example, assume that a thief sells a security to a person that becomes a protected purchaser. If the protected purchaser contributes the security to a charity, the charity's failure to give value would deprive it of protected-purchaser status. The shelter rule nevertheless would let the charity take free of the claim of the (previously) true owner.

The case that follows illustrates how those provisions operate.

Meadow Homes Development Corp. v. Bowens

211 P.3d 743 (Colo. Ct. App. 2009)

This case involves competing claims to a bond: a "security" covered by Revised Article 8 of the Uniform Commercial Code (UCC). The parties who had or claimed interests in the bond were: (A) the original owners of the bond (collectively the Horvats); (B) appellee Meadow Homes Development Corp., the entity that was entitled to purchase the bond if the Horvats failed to close on the underlying property development; and (C) appellant Ronald R. Bowens, who purchased the bond from the Horvats. This opinion sometimes refers, as does the UCC commentary relied on by appellant, to the parties as A (the Horvats), B (Meadow Homes), and C (Bowens).

The issue arises because A fraudulently transferred the bond to C. C relies on the UCC's "protected purchaser" (formerly "bona fide purchaser") provision to claim he acquired greater interests than A actually had and thereby trumped B's interests. Because C had notice of B's property interests in the bond, he was not a protected purchaser. We affirm the judgment that B (Meadow Homes), not C (Bowens), was entitled to the bond.

I.   BACKGROUND

The bond, issued by the Greatrock North Water and Sanitation District, was created by agreement of all parties during a multi-phase development of land in Adams County. It is a limited tax bond covering the costs of acquiring domestic water improvements for the development.

The agreement provided that A would retain the bond if it closed on the relevant phase of the property development but "[i]f [A] does not acquire and develop [that property], [it] shall sell to [B] and [B] shall purchase from [A] the Bond for $50,000." A ultimately failed to close on the property. B received notice of A's default, closed on the property, and demanded the bond from A. A declined B's demand because, unbeknownst to B, A had transferred the bond to C through a series of intermediary transactions.

The ensuing litigation spawned plethoric claims, counterclaims, and cross-claims among numerous parties. It suffices for our purposes to note that B sued A and C for a declaratory judgment and order entitling it to the bond upon payment of the agreed-upon $50,000.

After a four-day bench trial, the trial court ruled B could recover the bond from C by paying $50,000. It found A had transferred the bond to C in derogation of B's rights. And it rejected C's contention that he should take the bond as a "protected purchaser" under UCC §8-303. The court found C was not a protected purchaser because he had notice of B's adverse claim when he obtained the bond. Only C has appealed the ruling.

II.   THE MERITS

This appeal raises issues of first impression under Revised UCC Article 8 (Investment Securities), which have not previously been considered in Colorado and have received surprisingly little attention elsewhere. . . .

A.   The General Rule Is That a Purchaser Cannot Obtain Greater Rights Than the Seller Had to Transfer

A purchaser generally "takes only such title as his seller has and is authorized to transfer"; "he acquires precisely the interest which the seller owns, and no other or greater." *Rocky Mountain Fuel Co. v. George N. Sparling Coal Co.*, 143 P. 815, 818 (1914); accord *Commerce Bank v. Chrysler Realty Corp.*, 244 F.3d 777, 783-84 (10th Cir. 2001) (predicting Kansas courts under UCC Article 9 would apply the "basic principle of commercial law encapsulated in the Latin phrase *nemo dat qui non habet*": "He who hath not cannot give," which establishes the "basic concept" that "a transferee's rights are no better than those held by his transferor"); Russell A. Hakes, *UCC Article 8: Will the Indirect Holding of Securities Survive the Light of Day?*, 35 Loy. L.A. L. Rev. 661, 673 (2002) (discussing same rule in present context). This rule is codified in UCC 8-302(a), which provides (with two exceptions not applicable here) that a purchaser "acquires all rights in the security that the transferor had or had power to transfer."

There is no longer any dispute that, as between A and B, B is entitled to the bond. A was required to sell the bond to B if: A failed to close on the property; B closed instead; and B made proper demand. All those events occurred. Absent some exception to the general rule, purchaser C stands in the shoes of seller A and must now sell the bond to B for the agreed-upon price of $50,000.

B.   The Purchaser Here Was Not a "Protected Purchaser" Acquiring Rights Greater Than the Seller Held Because He Had Prior Notice of Another's Adverse Claim

Purchaser C could have obtained rights greater than seller A had against B only if C qualified as a "protected purchaser" under UCC 8-303(b) (such a purchaser acquires not only the rights of the seller but "also acquires its interest in the security free of any adverse claim"). This provision: (1) "allocat[es] the burden and risk of pursuing the bad actor transferor between two groups of innocents," see *In re Enron Corp.*, 379 B.R. 425, 448 (S.D.N.Y. 2007) (discussing similar provision); and (2) helps ensure marketability of investment securities by bringing "finality" to transactions. See James Steven Rogers, *Policy Perspectives on Revised U.C.C. Article 8*, 43 UCLA L. Rev. 1431, 1462 (1996).

The three requirements for protected purchaser status are that the purchaser has: (1) "[g]ive[n] value"; (2) "not ha[d] notice of any adverse claim to the security"; and (3) "[o]btain[ed] control of" the security. UCC 8-303(a), §4-8-303(a). To "qualify as a protected purchaser there must be a time at which all [three] of the requirements are satisfied." UCC 8-303(a) official cmt. 2. While Article 8 could be clearer on this point, there is general agreement that the burden of proving each of these requirements is on the party claiming protected purchaser status.

The trial court assumed, without expressly finding, that C satisfied the first requirement by giving value to A for the bond. Nor is the third requirement disputed because C plainly obtained control of the bond. The trial court's ultimately dispositive ruling was that C did not satisfy the second requirement because it had notice of B's adverse claim at the time it obtained control of the bond.

1.   C Had Notice of B's Interest in the Bond

What constitutes "[n]otice of [an] adverse claim" is set forth in UCC §8-105(a). As relevant here, a purchaser has notice if he either: (1) has actual knowledge of the adverse claim; or (2) "is aware of facts sufficient to indicate that there is a significant probability that the adverse claim exists and deliberately avoids information that would establish the existence of the adverse claim." The latter is "intended to codify the 'willful blindness' test." UCC §8-105(a) official cmt. 4. Notice requires not just awareness that someone other than the transferor has a property interest in the security but also that "the transfer violates the other party's property interest." Official cmt. 2.

The trial court found C had notice of B's adverse claim to the bond. While C professes not to challenge any of the trial court's factual findings, he nonetheless denies having notice of B's adverse claim. . . .

Even the limited appellate record provided by C reveals ample support for finding that C, at the very least, was willfully blind to the fact that the transfer was adverse to B's rights in the bond. C, after all, *signed* the settlement agreement that created A's and B's respective interests in the bond. As such, he indisputably had actual knowledge of B's right to demand the bond if A failed to close on the property.

C argues he was never shown to have known that B had continuing interests in the bond, particularly because C obtained the bond a couple of months after the scheduled closing date when C should have been free to assume either that A had closed or that B's interests otherwise had terminated. Given C's involvement in the agreement creating A's and B's respective interests, however, he had the ability to determine the status of B's continued interests before acquiring the bond from A. Even if C lacked actual knowledge of those interests (a generous assumption on this record), he could be found to have willfully blinded himself to those interests. There was no error in the trial court's finding that C had notice of B's adverse claim.

2.   B Had a Protectable Property Interest in the Bond

C's more substantial argument is that B's claim to the bond did not rise to the level of a "property interest" sufficient to constitute an adverse claim. This argument relies on the legal definition of "adverse claim" in UCC §8-102(a)(1), and its accompanying commentary.

The UCC §8-102(a)(1) definition of an "adverse claim" requires that a claimant "has a property interest in a financial asset" (emphasis omitted). The commentary explains that this definition, as amended in the 1994 revisions . . ., was intended to reject case law that "might have been read to suggest that any wrongful action concerning a security, even a simple breach of contract, gave rise to an adverse claim." UCC §8-102(a)(1) official cmt. 1 (rejecting such reading of Pentech International, Inc. v. Wall Street Clearing Co., 983 F.2d 441 (2d Cir. 1993), and

Fallon v. Wall Street Clearing Co., 182 A.D.2d 245 (1992)). C deems this case "nearly identical" to a hypothetical in the commentary, which states (using the same "A-B-C" shorthand references to parties we have used):

> Suppose, for example, that A contracts to sell or deliver securities to B, but fails to do so and instead sells or pledges the securities to C. B, the promisee, has an action against A for breach of contract, but absent unusual circumstances the action for breach would not give rise to a property interest in the securities. Accordingly, B does not have an adverse claim.

Thus, "absent *unusual circumstances*," "a *simple* breach of contract" does not by itself establish a "property interest" required for an adverse claim to a security. The language we have emphasized is significant, as the official UCC commentary goes on to explain: "An adverse claim might, however, be based upon principles of equitable remedies that give rise to property claims."

The present case involves "unusual circumstances" entitling B to "equitable remedies." While A clearly did breach its contract with B, "the fact that the action involves a breach of contract can hardly be enough to prove relief is not equitable." Sereboff v. Mid Atlantic Medical Services, Inc., 547 U.S. 356, 363 (2006). In the language of the UCC commentary, A's inequitable actions toward B involve much more than "a simple breach of contract."

At least two factors make this an unusual case in which B had more than a simple breach of contract action. Given these factors, we hold the trial court properly ruled that B was entitled to the bond itself and was not limited to seeking monetary damages.

First, when it transferred the bond to C, A did more than simply breach a contract: the trial court found A acted "in a fraudulent manner" that "was intended to hinder and defraud the rights of [B]." In support of this ultimate finding, the court found the transfer was concealed from B, represented substantially all of A's assets, and rendered A insolvent.

Second, this particular bond was sufficiently unique to give rise to an equitable property interest in favor of B. The bond was not a fungible investment security. Rather, it was created as part of a land development project, and ownership of the bond pivoted on which party ultimately bought and developed the land. We cannot assume the parties acted fortuitously in deciding to tie bond ownership to land development. Because B ultimately bought and was responsible for developing the land, its interest in and right to the bond outweighed any competing claim of C.

The court's equitable remedy, awarding B the bond itself, was in the nature of a constructive trust: a flexible equitable remedy that may be imposed to prevent unjust enrichment by enabling the restitution of property that in equity and good conscience does not belong to the defendant. [Brackets, citation, and quotation marks omitted.] C's legal argument — that B had only contractual, not property, interests — might carry the day in another case because a transferor's simple breach of contract does not outweigh the need for finality in securities transfers. But, under the circumstances of this case, equity overrides the legal argument.

We finally reject C's argument that B could not have had a property interest because its right to the bond had not yet ripened at the time of transfer. A property interest may exist even where an owner's rights are contingent on future events. . . .

IV. CONCLUSION

The judgment is affirmed, and the case is remanded for the trial court to assess and award against Bowens the attorney fees reasonably incurred by Meadow Homes in this appeal.

(b) The Indirect Holding System.

(i) The Basic Framework. For a variety of reasons, the direct holding system described above is no longer the principal method for holding securities. Among other things, that system was doomed by its requirement that each sale of a security be registered on the books of the issuer. It is not practical for each sale of a security to be completed by transportation of a paper certificate to the issuer, registration of the transfer by the issuer, and issuance of a new certificate to the purchaser. Indeed, during the 1960s (when that system still was widely used), the major securities exchanges frequently experienced considerable disruptions of trading because of backlogs in the process of delivering certificates to settle previous trades.

To be sure, that problem could have been solved to some extent by the issuance of uncertificated securities. By abandoning the paper certificate, an issuer of uncertificated securities saves the bulk of the transaction costs contemplated by the classic paper-based system. But abandonment of certificates — dematerialization of securities — would have required each separate issuer (or some agent on its behalf) to maintain procedures for processing transfers of securities on a daily basis. And so the issuance of uncertificated securities has not been the dominant response to the inconveniences of the paper-based system. The most common response has been a system of indirect holding of securities — immobilization — in which the overwhelming majority of securities that are in circulation are immobilized in the custody of a small number of intermediaries. Trades among the vast number of retail purchasers of securities are consummated by entries on the books of these intermediaries. The following explanation by the Reporter for the revised Article 8 is illuminating:

> If one examined the shareholder records of large corporations whose shares are publicly traded on the exchanges or in the over-the-counter market, one would find that one entity — Cede & Co. — is listed as the shareholder of record of somewhere in the range of sixty to eighty per cent of the outstanding shares of all publicly traded companies. Cede & Co. is the nominee used by The Depository Trust Company ("DTC"), a limited purpose trust company organized under New York law for the purpose of acting as a depository to hold securities for the benefit of its participants, some six hundred or so broker-dealers and banks. Essentially all the trading in publicly held companies is executed through the broker-dealers who are participants in DTC, and the great bulk of public securities — the sixty to eighty per cent figure noted above — is held by these broker-dealers and banks on behalf of their customers. If all of these broker-dealers and banks held physical certificates, then as trades were executed each day it would be necessary to deliver the certificates back and forth among these broker-dealers and banks. By handing

all of their securities over to a common depository, all of these deliveries can be eliminated. Transfers can be accomplished by adjustments to the participants' DTC accounts. . . .

The development of the book-entry system of settlement seems to have accomplished the objective of ensuring that the settlement system has adequate operational capacity to process current trading volumes. At the time of the "paperwork crunch" in the late 1960s, the trading volume on the New York Stock Exchange that so seriously strained the capacities of the clearance and settlement system was in the range of ten million shares per day. Today, the system can easily handle trading volume on routine days of hundreds of millions of shares. Even during the October 1987 market break, when daily trading volume reached the current record level of six hundred eight million shares, the clearance and settlement system functioned relatively smoothly.

James Steven Rogers, *Policy Perspectives on Revised U.C.C. Article 8*, 43 UCLA L. Rev. 1431, 1443-1445 (1996).

In the indirect holding system, transfers of securities rarely require either physical delivery of a certificate or registration on the books of the issuer. On the contrary, most transfers can be made by the book-entry method, which requires nothing more than entries on the accounts of the various intermediaries at a central depository. For example, assume that Edward Casaubon has purchased 100 shares of stock in ABC Corp. Like most investors, Casaubon never received a stock certificate. He purchased the stock through his broker Bullish Broker and monitors the transaction (and the securities that he "owns") only through the Bullish Web site. In fact, it may be that Bullish also has no certificates, but instead has an account at DTC that contains 100,000 shares in ABC Corp. DTC, in turn, has certificates representing 3,000,000 shares in ABC Corp. If Casaubon sells his stock to Dorothea Brooke, nothing will happen to any of the certificates. Instead, Bullish will simply transfer some shares from its DTC account to the DTC account of Dorothea's broker, which will hold those shares in Dorothea's account. Alternatively, if Bullish also is Dorothea's broker, then Bullish need only transfer the shares from Dorothea's account to Casaubon's account. DTC need take no action. Most important, the issuer takes no action in either case.

The revised Article 8 expressly recognizes the indirect holding system and includes a variety of rules to facilitate transactions using that system. Working from the classic holding system, it would be possible to construct rules that would treat the retail purchasers as owning individual stock certificates, based on the intermediaries' status as agents for the retail purchasers. And Article 8 still permits that result, but only if the intermediaries register their individual purchasers' transactions with the issuer. UCC §§8-301(a)(3), 8-301(b)(2).For the most part, however, Article 8 dispenses with such a cumbersome framework and instead attempts to articulate functional rules that more directly reflect the true relationships of the parties. These rules reflect the absence of any direct relationship between Casaubon and Brooke, on the one hand, and the issuer, on the other. Instead, the only relationship that has any substance is the relationship between the retail purchaser and the intermediary with which it deals. Part 5 of Article 8 establishes a legal framework to govern that relationship. In that framework, Casaubon's right to the securities makes him an "entitlement holder" (defined in UCC §8-102(a)(7)). His right to the shares of ABC Corp. is a "security entitlement" (defined in UCC §8-102(a)(17)). Bullish, the party against which Casaubon holds this entitlement, is a "securities intermediary" (defined in UCC §8-102(a)(14)). The same rules apply at each tier of the holding system, so that Bullish also is an entitlement holder with a security entitlement against DTC based on the shares in Bullish's account at DTC. To illustrate the basic features of that framework, the remainder of the assignment discusses two topics: the rights of the entitlement holder against its securities intermediary and the rights of the entitlement holder against third parties.Although the historical genesis of the indirect holding rules in Part 5 of Article 8 was the market for conventional publicly traded securities, it is important to note the intentional decision of the drafters to extend the system more broadly. The definition of securities entitlement is broad enough to cover any asset that a securities intermediary might carry in a securities account — whether or not the asset bears any of the typical features of what we would consider securities. See UCC §§8-102(a)(9) (defining "financial asset" as anything held in a securities account by a securities intermediary), 8-102(a)(14) (defining "securities intermediary" to mean any person that holds a securities account, whether or not the entity is a regulated financial institution).

(ii)   Rights Against the Intermediary.   The best place to start in examining the relationship between the entitlement holder and its securities intermediary is to see how an entitlement holder can obtain an entitlement that is valid against its securities intermediary: How does Casaubon get the stock into his account at Bullish in the first place? Article 8 uses two separate, overlapping functional tests. The first test focuses on Bullish's conduct and recognizes that Casaubon has a security entitlement if Bullish agrees that Casaubon has one, that is, if Bullish "indicates by book entry that a financial asset has been credited to the person's securities account." UCC §8-501(b)(1). The second test focuses on actions that other parties take that should lead to the same result. If Bullish receives securities on Casaubon's behalf, Casaubon has a security entitlement to the extent of those securities. UCC §8-501(b)(2). That test might seem straightforward, but the following case illustrates some of the attendant complications.

Rider v. Estate of Rider (In re Estate of Rider)

756 S.E.2d 136 (S.C. 2014)

Justice BEATTY.
  This Court granted a petition for a writ of certiorari to review the decision of the Court of Appeals, which applied the common law of agency to hold that certain financial assets were part of the decedent's probate estate. The decedent had directed his bank to transfer specified assets in his investment account to a new account for his spouse, but died before all of the assets were credited to her account. At issue in this case of first impression is whether South Carolina's Uniform Commercial Code ("UCC") or the common law of agency controls the transfer. We reverse.

I.   FACTS

Charles Galen Rider ("Husband") executed an Investment Agency Agreement/ Discretionary Account ("Account Agreement") with First Union National Bank of North Carolina ("First Union"), a predecessor of Wachovia Bank, N.A. ("Wachovia"), on September 27, 1993. The Account Agreement authorized First Union "to open and maintain an Agency Account" for Husband and "to hold therein, as [his] Agent, all cash, stocks, bonds, securities and other property . . . subject to" Husband's current and future written instructions. The Account Agreement stated First Union was "to provide investment review and management of the Account, taking such action as [the bank], in [its] discretion, deem[s] best . . . as though [the bank] were the owner of such property." This discretionary authority permitted First Union to buy, sell, and exercise certain rights regarding the securities in accordance with the overall investment objective selected by Husband. The terms of the Account Agreement called for its termination upon the bank acquiring actual knowledge of Husband's death, but that Husband's death "shall not affect the validity of any prior actions."

On June 8, 2005, Husband called Ruth DiLella in the Capital Management Group of what was then Wachovia and informed her that he had met with his estate attorney, who had advised him to transfer some assets to his spouse, Carolyn S. Rider ("Wife"). Husband was suffering from terminal cancer and reportedly wanted Wife to have sufficient funds to maintain her standard of living during the inevitable time that probate would be going on. Husband instructed DiLella to move $2 million in securities from his account at Wachovia and place them in a new account in Wife's name. DiLella told Husband that Wachovia would send him a list of specific securities to transfer, along with a signature page for him to sign to approve the transfer. The same day, DiLella e-mailed a list of assets totaling $2 million to Wachovia's trust department, along with Husband's instruction, so it could prepare a letter and asset listing for the client's approval.

On June 17, 2005, Husband signed the letter and returned it to the attention of Wachovia's trust administrator. The letter provided: "Please accept this letter as my authority and direction to transfer the assets listed on the following page to a new agency account to be opened for my wife, Carolyn Sue Rider." A total of $2 million in assets were listed, which included specific securities and a small sum of cash.

In response, Wachovia made a series of four transfers from June to October 2005. On June 21, 2005, four days after Husband's signing of the June 17th directive, Wachovia made the first transfer of $733,228.00 in securities (stocks) to Wife's account. On July 8, 2005, Wachovia transferred $39,672.00 in securities (stocks). That afternoon, Husband passed away in Charlotte, North Carolina, and Husband's daughter, respondent Deborah Rider McClure, notified Wachovia the same day. The next business day, Monday, July 11, 2005, Wachovia transferred $935,032.64 in securities (mutual funds) to Wife's account, and on October 20, 2005, Wachovia made a fourth and final transfer of $304,182.46 in securities (mutual funds). The total amount transferred to Wife's account was $2,012,115.00, the excess being due to the appreciation in the value of the securities.

In 2006, Thomas M. Grady, as personal representative of Husband's estate ("PR"), instituted this declaratory judgment action in the probate court for Beaufort County asking the court to determine either (1) that the securities transferred pursuant to Husband's June 17, 2005 letter to Wachovia were completed transfers on June 17, 2005 and, thus, were not includible in Husband's probate estate; or (2) that the securities transferred after Husband's death on July 8, 2005 were incomplete transfers and were includible in Husband's probate estate. The PR did not take a position, but sought guidance as to whether the UCC or the law of agency under the South Carolina common law controlled the outcome.

In its order, the probate court stated much of the argument in this case centered on whether the UCC's provision on Investment Securities applies to the securities transfer directed by Husband on June 17, 2005. The probate court stated Wife argued the UCC applies, Husband's June 17, 2005 directive was an "entitlement order" under the applicable definition in the UCC found in [§]8-102, the transfer was effectuated on June 17, 2005, and it was unaffected by Husband's death before completion of the transfers. In contrast, Husband's two daughters from his prior marriage, Deborah Rider McClure and Ginger C. McClure, and his two grandsons, Christian McClure and Austin McClure (collectively, "the McClure Respondents") argued, *inter alia*, that the UCC did not apply and, even if it did, it did not supplant the law of agency that governed the parties' Account Agreement. Either way, Wachovia's authority to make the transfers ended when it acquired actual knowledge of Husband's death and the disputed assets belonged to Husband's probate estate.

The probate court found the UCC controlled this securities transaction, that Husband's June 17, 2005 directive was an "entitlement order," and Wachovia was a "securities intermediary." However, it determined an entitlement order's "effective date" is a distinguishable concept from when an entitlement order is "effectuated." The probate court agreed with Wife that Husband's entitlement order was "effective" upon its issuance to Wachovia on June 17, 2005, but reasoned it still had to be carried out by Wachovia, the securities intermediary, to be "effectuated," and the UCC did not supplant the laws of property or agency, nor did it vitiate the terms of the Account Agreement.

The probate court noted Wachovia received actual notice of Husband's death on Friday, July 8th, that the second transfer of $39,672.00 was posted to Wife's account that day, and that the third transfer of $935,032.64 was posted to Wife's account the next business day, Monday, July 11th. The court stated the credible testimony at trial persuaded it that Wachovia took the necessary actions to effectuate the second and third transfers before it knew of Husband's death. The court observed, "In the commercial context of the transactions, it would be unreasonable to conclude otherwise."

The probate court concluded the first three transfers, totaling $1,707,932.64, which were posted to Wife's account on June 21, July 8, and July 11, 2005, respectively, were carried out and effectuated before Husband's death and are not part of his probate estate. However, the securities posted to Wife's account on October 20, 2005 in the amount of $304,082.46 belonged to Husband's probate estate because it was not effectuated until after Husband's death, when Wachovia's authority to act had already terminated.

Wife appealed to the circuit court, which affirmed in an order adopting the probate court's factual findings and legal conclusions. Wife appealed to the Court of Appeals, which found both the third and fourth transfers properly belonged to Husband's probate estate because they occurred after the bank had actual knowledge of Husband's death . . ., so it too affirmed. The Court of Appeals also distinguished the "effective date" of Husband's entitlement order from the date it was "effectuated" and found the latter determinative of the question of ownership. This Court granted Wife's petition for a writ of certiorari to review the decision of the Court of Appeals.

. . .

III. LAW/ANALYSIS

Wife contends the UCC addresses the subject matter at issue in this appeal, arguing only where the UCC is incomplete does the common law provide the applicable rule. *See* [§]1-103 ("Unless displaced by the particular provisions of this act [Title 36, the UCC], the principles of law and equity, including . . . the law relative to capacity to contract, principal and agent, estoppel, fraud, . . . or other validating or invalidating cause shall supplement its provisions.").

Chapter 8 of our state's UCC governs "Investment Securities." S.C. Code Ann. §36-8-101 (2003). It is based on the state's adoption of the revised Article 8 contained in the model Uniform Commercial Code prepared by the American Law Institute in collaboration with the National Conference of Commissioners on Uniform State Laws. Its primary purposes are to provide uniformity in the securities industry and to provide an accurate description of the realities of the securities markets, and secondarily to enhance the value-adding factors of liquidity and certainty in securities transactions. [§§]8-101 to -511 cmt. Part 5 of Chapter 8, entitled "Security Entitlements," specifically governs the "indirect holding system," whereby purchasers of securities deal with intermediaries who hold securities for others, as compared to the traditional system whereby purchasers deal directly with the issuers of those securities. It is noted in the Introductory Comment that these provisions "supplant a pastiche of common law rules and agreed practices." *Id.*

In the current matter, Wachovia held certain financial assets (securities) for Husband and managed those assets, subject to his oversight, pursuant to the Account Agreement, by which the bank acted as Husband's agent. This relationship thus implicates the indirect holding system set forth in Part 5 as well as general UCC provisions. Under the terms of the UCC, Husband was an "entitlement holder" with a "security entitlement" to the "financial assets" in a "securities account" maintained and managed by Wachovia for Husband's benefit in its capacity as a "securities intermediary." . . .

. . .

Wachovia is a "securities intermediary," which is defined to include "a bank . . . that in the ordinary course of its business maintains securities accounts for others and is acting in that capacity." [§]8-102(a)(14)(ii).

Husband was the "entitlement holder," which the UCC defines as follows: "A person identified in the records of a security intermediary as the person having a security entitlement against the securities intermediary. If a person acquires a security entitlement by virtue of Section 36-8-501(b)(2) or (3), that person is the entitlement holder." [§]8-102(a)(7).

A "security entitlement" consists of "the rights and property interest of an entitlement holder with respect to a financial asset specified in Part 5." [§]8-102(a)(17).

Section [8]-501(b) of the UCC provides a person generally acquires a security entitlement if a securities intermediary does any of the following three things: "(1) indicates by book entry that a financial asset has been credited to the person's securities account; (2) receives a financial asset from the person or acquires a financial asset for the person and, in either case, accepts it for credit to the person's securities account; or (3) becomes obligated under other law, regulation, or rule to credit a financial asset to the person's securities account."

Husband, as the entitlement holder, retained the right to direct Wachovia to make changes in his account by issuing an "entitlement order," i.e., "a notification communicated to a securities intermediary directing transfer or redemption of a financial asset to which the entitlement holder has a security entitlement." [§]8-102(a)(8).

Wachovia was statutorily required to respond to an appropriate entitlement order. *See* [§]8-506 ("A securities intermediary shall exercise rights with respect to a financial asset if directed to do so by an entitlement holder."); [§]8-507(a) ("A securities intermediary *shall comply* with an entitlement order if [1] the entitlement order is *originated by the appropriate person*, [2] the securities intermediary has had reasonable opportunity to assure itself that the entitlement order is genuine and authorized, and [3] the securities intermediary has had *reasonable opportunity to comply* with the entitlement order." (emphasis added)).

An "appropriate person" with respect to an entitlement order is the entitlement holder. [§]8-107(a)(3). However, if the person "is deceased, the designated person's successor taking under other law or the designated person's personal representative acting for the estate of the decedent" is an appropriate person to initiate an entitlement order. [§]8-107(a)(4).

The UCC further provides that "[e]ffectiveness of an . . . entitlement order is determined as of the date the . . . entitlement order *is made*, and an . . . entitlement order *does not become ineffective by reason of any later change in circumstances.*" [§]8-107(e) (emphasis added). Subsection (e) clarifies the protection from liability of securities intermediaries who rely on appropriate persons, and "[t]his protection reflects the policy of revised Article 8 to enhance liquidity and finality in securities transactions." [§]8-107 cmt.

. . .

In the Court of Appeals, the court first reviewed the terms of the Account Agreement and found the "prior actions" clause therein refers to both Husband's and Wachovia's conduct and that the plain language of the agreement showed Wachovia's authority ended upon actual knowledge of Husband's death. Rider v. Estate of Rider, 394 S.C. 84, 91, 713 S.E.2d 643, 646-47 (Ct. App. 2011). The court stated the determination whether the securities in the fourth transfer were part of Husband's estate was, therefore, determined by whether Husband's and Wachovia's conduct was sufficient to complete the transfers before Wachovia learned of Husband's death. *Id.* at 91, 713 S.E.2d at 647.

Wife argued the general agency rule that an agent lacks authority to act for a principal after a principal's death, relied upon by the McClure Respondents, does not apply to this situation because Husband's June 17, 2005 directive was an effective entitlement order under Article 8 of the UCC. Wife contended (1) an effective entitlement order transfers the right to financial assets the date it is made and, (2) even if it does not, an entitlement order *remains effective* pursuant to the

UCC provision above, which displaces the agency rule under the common law, so that actions taken to comply with the entitlement order may be completed regardless of later changes in circumstances.

The Court of Appeals rejected both of Wife's contentions and determined "the probate court properly found the [securities in] the fourth transfer are part of [Husband's] estate." In reaching this conclusion, the Court of Appeals stated the UCC applied, but nevertheless found the UCC's rule as to the effective date of an entitlement order contained in [Section] 8-107(e) of the UCC did not fully address the subject, so it did not displace the relevant agency rule.

Applying the common law of agency, the Court of Appeals reasoned that an entitlement order does not complete a transfer of financial assets at the time it is made, so like other orders to agents, it is an instruction to act in the manner the principal desires, and the request is terminated by the principal's death . . . .

The court distinguished the effective date of the entitlement order from the date it was completed by Wachovia, which it defined as when the assets were credited to Wife's account, and it found the fourth transfer at issue was completed by Wachovia in October 2005, citing [§]8-501(b)(1) (providing a book entry by the securities intermediary to a person's account establishes a security entitlement). As a result, the court held the securities in the fourth transfer, having been credited after the bank's knowledge of Husband's death, are properly part of Husband's probate estate because the bank's authority under the Account Agreement had ended.

Several jurisdictions have observed there is a dearth of authority addressing the unique problems arising under Article 8 of the UCC. *See, e.g.,* Meadow Homes Dev. Corp. v. Bowens, 211 P.3d 743, 745 (Colo. Ct. App. 2009) (stating the "appeal raises issues of first impression under Revised UCC Article 8 (Investment Securities)" that had not previously been considered in the jurisdiction and that "have received surprisingly little attention elsewhere"); Watson v. Sears, 766 N.E.2d 784, 788 (Ind. Ct. App. 2002) ("Unfortunately, there is no discernible case law anywhere under revised Article 8 of the U.C.C. (Title 8 in Maryland) — and very little commentary — dealing with the question of the effect of an entitlement order that is authorized by only one of the entitlement holders on a joint account.").

As one legal commentator has opined, a significant body of case law has not developed for the indirect holding system, and the reported cases generally have applied whatever principles were necessary to protect an innocent investor, so they did not create well-reasoned legal doctrines to resolve the competing policies unique to the indirect holding system. Russell A. Hakes, *UCC Article 8: Will the Indirect Holding of Securities Survive the Light of Day?,* 35 Loy. L.A. L. Rev. 661, 678 (2002). "The drafters [of UCC Article 8] had the benefit of effectively starting with a clean slate." "Troubling precedents could be overruled by the adoption of contrary concepts that matched the perceptions of those most familiar with the operation of the system-securities professionals." "The interest and experience of securities professionals were essential to an Article 8 that could successfully govern the indirect holding system."

"The securities industry did not want to use principles of bailment, agency, or trust law to describe the basic operations of the indirect holding system, even though agency law governs much in the relationship between the securities industry and its customers." "One important goal in revising Article 8 was to simplify transfer rules for the indirect holding system." Moreover, "[t]he drafters also caution courts not to use 'mechanical jurisprudence' but to interpret the definitions based upon the suitability of applying Article 8's substantive rules."

We agree with the Court of Appeals that the UCC does not invalidate all general principles of agency, but, as noted by the commentator above, those principles must be viewed in light of the unique nature of the indirect holding system. The UCC provisions were created to provide a uniform method of resolving issues in order to promote liquidity and finality, to be supplemented by (not thwarted by) the rules of agency and other applicable laws.

In relying upon agency law to mandate that both Husband's execution of the entitlement order and full compliance by the securities intermediary exist prior to Husband's death, the Court of Appeals has created an additional requirement that does not exist under the UCC and that thwarts the purpose of the language in [Section] 8-107(e) establishing a uniform effective date for entitlement orders, regardless of subsequent events. Moreover, it also overlooks the fact that under UCC [§]8-501(b), the making of a "book entry" is but one of several means by which Wife can acquire an interest in the securities.

Once Husband issued the entitlement order and was the appropriate person, Wachovia was obligated by the UCC and the parties' Account Agreement to obey his directive. Wachovia had set up a new investment account in Wife's name and commenced the transfer of securities within a few days of Husband's request, so at that point, Wife already had a recognizable interest, even though Wachovia had not posted all of the securities to her account. The Court of Appeals, in focusing solely on the date of the "book entry," which it took to mean the date the securities were credited or posted to Wife's account, seemed to view this as the exclusive means for obtaining an interest in the securities. However, a security entitlement is created if a securities intermediary does *any* of the following three things:

> (1) indicates by book entry that a financial asset has been credited to the person's securities account;
> (2) receives a financial asset from the person or acquires a financial asset for the person and, in either case, accepts it for credit to the person's securities account; or
> (3) becomes obligated under other law, regulation, or rule to credit a financial asset to the person's securities account.

[§]8-501(b).

In this case, while the Court of Appeals relied on book entry under subsection (b)(1), we agree with Wife that under subsection (b)(3), Wachovia had a legal obligation to credit the securities to Wife's account.[4.] As noted in the Official Comment to §8-501 of the Uniform Act:

> Paragraph (3) of subsection (b) sets out a residual test, to avoid any implication that the failure of an intermediary to make the appropriate entries to credit a position to a customer's securities account would prevent the customer from acquiring the rights of an entitlement holder under Part 5. As is the case with the paragraph (2) test, the

---

4. At oral argument, the parties agreed the UCC does not define the term "book entry," so the drafters intended it to have a broad meaning. In addition, although not necessary to our disposition, we believe the transfer in this case also falls within the ambits of subsection (b)(2), as Wachovia received and accepted financial assets for credit to Wife's securities account.

paragraph (3) test would not be needed for the ordinary cases, since they are covered by paragraph (1).

Wachovia's failure to more quickly make the last posting to Wife's account clearly is not the ordinary case, and it falls squarely within the parameters of the residual provision in [Section] 8-501(b)(3). Although the Court of Appeals treats the transfers as separate, unrelated events subject to termination under general agency law, we conclude Husband's execution of an entitlement order directing Wachovia to transfer certain specified securities to Wife is a singular act that falls squarely within the "prior act" language of the parties' agreement. Further, Wachovia's obligation to comply with Husband's entitlement order is supported by the UCC provisions examined above and comports with Article 8's goals of liquidity and finality in securities transactions. Consequently, we hold the disputed assets in this case properly belong to Wife and are not includible in Husband's probate estate.

IV. CONCLUSION

For the foregoing reasons, the decision of the Court of Appeals is reversed.

Once Casaubon obtains a security entitlement, Article 8 imposes a variety of duties on Bullish with respect to the entitlement. The most important duty is a duty to maintain assets sufficient to cover the entitlement. Because Article 8 recognizes an entitlement for Casaubon immediately upon Bullish's crediting Casaubon's account, it is entirely possible for Casaubon to acquire an entitlement against Bullish to stock of ABC Corp. without Bullish obtaining a corresponding amount of ABC Corp. stock. UCC §8-504(a) obligates Bullish to "promptly obtain and thereafter maintain a financial asset in a quantity corresponding to the aggregate of all security entitlements it has established in favor of its entitlement holders with respect to that financial asset." Thus, when Casaubon acquired the stock, Bullish was obligated to make sure that it had enough ABC Corp. stock in its portfolio to cover that purchase. If it did not, it would have to acquire more shares of that stock to bring its balance of that stock up to the level of the entitlements of its customers. As the discussion above suggests, Bullish ordinarily would satisfy that duty by increasing the amount of stock in its account at DTC (which it would do by purchasing stock from some other securities intermediary), not by obtaining additional physical certificates.

The second major duty of the securities intermediary relates to administration of the security. Generally, the securities intermediary is obligated to take all steps necessary to protect the rights of the entitlement holder with respect to the security so that the entitlement holder will be in the same position as if it held the security directly. Among other things, the securities intermediary is obligated to "take action to obtain" all payments that the issuer of the security makes with respect to the security. UCC §8-505(a). Thus, if ABC Corp. issues a dividend (or makes a payment on its bonds), Bullish has to take steps to obtain that payment. Then Bullish must forward to Casaubon all of the payments that it receives with respect to Casaubon's security entitlements. UCC §8-505(b).

In the same way, Bullish is obligated to act for Casaubon with respect to voting rights and other rights related to the securities (such as rights to redeem securities). UCC §8-506. With respect to those matters, Bullish can either take the steps necessary to allow Casaubon to vote on his own behalf (to "exercise the rights directly," UCC §8-506(1)) or act for Casaubon, provided that it "exercises due care in accordance with reasonable commercial standards to follow the direction of the entitlement holder," UCC §8-506(2).

Finally, as the cases above underscore, the securities intermediary is obligated to follow the instructions of the entitlement holder regarding sale or other disposition of the security entitlement. UCC §§8-507(a) (obligating securities intermediary to comply with an "entitlement order"), 8-102(a)(8) (defining "entitlement order"). A common problem arises when a third party asserts a claim to the securities reflected by the security entitlement. If the securities intermediary proceeded to sell the securities pursuant to the instructions of its customer (the entitlement holder), the third party would be likely to assert a claim against the securities intermediary, contending that the intermediary should not have allowed the entitlement holder to sell the securities. To ensure liquidity of securities, UCC §8-115 bars any such claim against the securities intermediary except in three narrow cases: where the creditor obtains an injunction barring transfer of the securities (UCC §8-115(1)), where the intermediary "acted in collusion with the wrongdoer" (UCC §8-115(2)), or where the securities intermediary has notice of a claim that the applicable security certificate constitutes stolen property (UCC §8-115(3)). The last exception obviously could arise only in the relatively unusual case in which the securities intermediary received a stock certificate as the basis for the entitlement instead of an entry in the securities intermediary's account at a higher-level securities intermediary.

(iii)   Rights Against Third Parties. The indirect holding system must deal with two logically distinct claims that third parties can interpose against an entitlement holder: claims that third parties assert against a particular security and claims that third parties assert against the securities intermediary.

The first topic is a simple one, as to which the indirect holding system uses rules much like those of the direct holding system. Specifically, an entitlement holder that acquires a security entitlement for value and without notice of an adverse claim takes free of the claim, just as a protected purchaser would in the direct holding system. UCC §§8-502, 8-503(e). That is true even though the entitlement holder does not obtain "control" of any particular certificate representing the security in question. It is enough for the entitlement holder to obtain a security entitlement that is valid under UCC §8-501.

The second topic is considerably more difficult. Because Article 8 recognizes security entitlements that are not backed by specific stock certificates, it is possible for a securities intermediary to incur obligations that exceed the amount of the securities that it owns. Of course, the system includes a wide variety of safeguards designed to limit the possibility of such losses. For one thing, most securities intermediaries are subject to considerable regulatory oversight, which substantially diminishes the risk of malfeasance that would result in such a shortage. Moreover, all brokers and dealers in securities are required to join the Securities Investor Protection Corporation (SIPC). The SIPC provides retail purchasers insurance analogous to the deposit insurance provided by the FDIC. That insurance currently covers up to a $500,000 shortfall that a customer experiences upon a liquidation of the assets of a securities intermediary. For example, if a customer had $1,500,000 in its account, but received only $900,000 upon liquidation of the intermediary, the SIPC insurance would provide $500,000, leaving the customer short "only" $100,000. Although investors lost a great deal in scandals such as the Bernie Madoff affair in 2009, the SIPC has provided full recovery in many of the best-known brokerage failures because the brokerage houses were acquired and did not technically become insolvent.

Nevertheless, the possibility of shortages remains, and a functioning system must devise rules to deal with those situations. Hence, the inevitable question remains: If the securities that the intermediary owns are inadequate to satisfy all of the claims against the intermediary, which creditors are entitled to the securities that are on hand? Essentially, Article 8 resolves the problem by recognizing three different types of claims a creditor might have against a securities intermediary: an ordinary creditor's claim, a security entitlement, and a controlling security interest in the intermediary's security entitlements.

The first category of claimants includes most creditors of the securities intermediary. These could be employees of the intermediary, suppliers of services or equipment, or financial institutions that have loaned money to the intermediary. Because those entities hold no security entitlements, their claims against the securities held by the securities intermediary are subordinate to the claims of customers that hold security entitlements against the securities intermediary. UCC §8-503(a). Thus, if a shortage of securities held by the securities intermediary means that there are not enough securities to satisfy all of the entitlement holders, the general unsecured creditors will have no claim against any of the securities that the intermediary does have. The same rule would apply even to creditors that had a security interest in the securities, except in the situation (discussed below) in which the creditors took control of the securities. UCC §8-511(a) (entitlement holders have priority over secured creditors that do not have control of securities).

The second category of claimants is entitlement holders. In the event of a shortage, Article 8 puts all entitlement holders on an equal footing, without regard to the time that they acquired their individual entitlements. UCC §8-503(b). Thus, all entitlement holders would receive pro rata shares of whatever securities were available to satisfy their claims. If the securities intermediary held 70 percent of the ABC Corp. securities for which its customers held security entitlements, then liquidation of the assets of the securities intermediary would give each of the entitlement holders 70 percent of its security entitlements to shares of ABC Corp.

The only claimants that can defeat claims of the entitlement holders are secured creditors that hold liens against the securities in question. For a variety of reasons, that situation should be unusual, even in the context of insolvent securities intermediaries. Among other things, UCC §8-504(b) expressly prohibits an intermediary from "grant[ing] any security interests in a financial asset it is obligated to maintain [to cover the security entitlements of its entitlement holders]." Accordingly, creditors will not have such interests in the ordinary course of financing the operations of a securities intermediary. Those interests should arise only through the coincidence of a shortage that occurs for other reasons with the existence of a creditor that has a security interest in securities of the securities intermediary.

Nevertheless, if that situation occurs, and if the holder of the security interest has control of the securities in question, the holder of the security interest prevails over the customer of the entitlement holder. UCC §8-511(b). Although that result might seem counterintuitive from the perspective of the customer, it was one of the most thoroughly debated issues in the revision of Article 8. In the end, the drafters decided that traditional practices related to the purchase of securities required recognition of the rights of secured creditors in that limited circumstance. The key to that outcome is the part of the rule stating that a creditor can prevail only if it has "control" of the security. To have control of the security under UCC §8-106, the creditor would have to have a directly held security indorsed over to it or registered in its name. If the securities intermediary itself held the security indirectly (as it usually would, through an account at DTC), the creditor would have to obtain control by having the securities transferred to it, so that the creditor would become the entitlement holder. Thus, for CountryBank to obtain control of securities held by Bullish in the form of a security entitlement at DTC, CountryBank would have to cause DTC to transfer the entitlement to CountryBank.

At that point, Bullish technically would remain the owner of the securities as against CountryBank, in the sense that CountryBank would return the entitlement to Bullish if Bullish repaid the loan. But there is no real sense in which Bullish still retains the securities: No stock certificates show Bullish's ownership, and Bullish has no entitlements against any securities intermediary. Because the securities industry operates on the practical understanding that acquisition of control of a security cuts off adverse claims to the security (a rule that receives broad application throughout Article 8), the drafters concluded that it would be too disruptive to adopt a rule allowing Bullish's customers to recover securities from creditors in that situation.

Problem Set 24

24.1. Pleased with your fine analysis in the matter of Problem 22.4, Bill Robertson comes to you this Monday morning with a similar problem. This one involves one of a series of bonds issued by Bill's company, Pearland Holdings, Inc. Each of the bonds states that it is payable to the order of the initial purchaser (identified by name on each bond). The bonds also state that transfers of the bonds can be registered on Pearland's books. This particular bond was issued to Texas American Bank. Like the note in Problem 22.4, the bond was acquired from Texas American Bank by Bulstrode with an appropriate indorsement from Texas American Bank. Bulstrode did not, however, register its acquisition with Pearland or otherwise notify Pearland of its ownership of the bond. Accordingly, Pearland has made the last two payments on the bond to Texas American Bank, rather than Bulstrode.

Bulstrode has written Pearland demanding the two payments that Pearland has made to Texas American Bank that were due after the date on which Bulstrode acquired the bond. Is Pearland obligated to Bulstrode for those payments? UCC §§3-302(b), 3-601(b), 3-602(a), 8-102(a)(13), 8-102(a)(15), 8-103(d), 8-207(a).

24.2.   Following up on the advice that you rendered in the discussion of negotiability, Jodi Kay calls you to ask about a few problems with some securities that CountryBank has purchased. On the first one, she sends you a telecopy of a bond issued by Chiripada Investment Trust (CIT). The bond states on its face that the entire series of bonds is governed by Article 8, includes standard provisions for registering transfers on CIT's books, and recites that it was issued pursuant to and in accordance with the provisions of the New Mexico Investment Trust Company Act. Jodi received a letter last week from CIT, stating that CIT intends to stop making payments on the bonds. The letter states that the bonds are invalid because they were issued without a unanimous vote of the trust managers of CIT. The letter asserts that the New Mexico Investment Trust Company Act requires such a vote for a trust validly to issue securities and that all purchasers of the securities are on notice of that requirement because of the reference to that statute on the face of the securities.

Jodi tells you that she was personally responsible for CountryBank's investment in the CIT securities, so she is directly interested in establishing their validity. Assuming that the letter from CIT accurately describes the provisions of the New Mexico statute, does CIT's letter establish a defense that is valid against CountryBank? UCC §§1-202 (formerly §1-201(25)), 8-102(a)(13), 8-102(a)(15), 8-202.

24.3.   Jodi's other question relates to a bond that she purchased about a month ago from one of her customers (Harlan Smythe). Because the bond is in a registered form, she tried last week to register her purchase with the issuer, but failed when she discovered that she had neglected to obtain an indorsement from Smythe at the time that she purchased the bond. She became concerned when yesterday's newspaper included a detailed article describing a federal indictment alleging that one J.R. McDonald has engaged in a wide-ranging scheme to defraud his creditors by selling securities that he already has pledged to his lenders. Under the scheme, McDonald would obtain possession of a security from his lender on the pretext of using it for internal auditing purposes. Instead of returning the security to the lender, however, he would sell it to a third party, hoping to purchase a substitute security to return to the creditor within a few days.

Because Jodi could tell from a McDonald indorsement on the bond that Smythe had purchased the bond from McDonald the day before Smythe sold the bond to CountryBank, Jodi was concerned that one of McDonald's creditors might assert a claim against CountryBank. Accordingly, she went down to Smythe's office yesterday and obtained his indorsement on the bond. Does that indorsement protect her from the claims of McDonald's creditors?

If not, does Jodi have any other way to defeat that claim? UCC §§8-102(a)(4), 8-106, 8-301(a), 8-302(a), 8-303, 8-304(d).

24.4. Edward Casaubon comes to you to ask you a question about a potential problem that he has with his broker (Bullish Broker). Casaubon tells you that he asked his contact at Bullish last week to purchase 10,000 shares of stock in Advanced Tactical Devices, Inc. (ATDI). The contact advised Casaubon that the purchase had been completed. Furthermore, Casaubon has ascertained by examining his account record from his home computer that Bullish credited Casaubon's account with the ATDI stock on the date of the purchase.

While talking to his broker this morning, Casaubon was upset by a comment to the effect that the broker had not yet been able to obtain the ATDI securities that Casaubon thought he had purchased last week. Casaubon wants to know if he has anything to be worried about. Does Casaubon own the securities or not? Does Bullish have any obligation to remedy the situation? UCC §§8-102(a)(7), 8-102(a)(14), 8-102(a)(17), 8-501(b), 8-503(a), 8-503(b), 8-504(a).

24.5. A few weeks later Casaubon calls you back to tell you that the situation has deteriorated at Bullish Broker. Apparently because of large investments in Southeast Asian municipal bonds, Bullish has become insolvent. This morning it was closed for liquidation. Casaubon's broker tells him that Bullish's portfolio will be inadequate to cover the accounts of many of its customers. Among other things, Bullish owns only 180,000 shares of ATDI stock, although its customers have accounts for 200,000 shares. Also, the broker has told Casaubon that 120,000 of the 200,000 shares in the accounts were acquired by the entitlement holders before Casaubon acquired his entitlement. Finally, the broker has told Casaubon that Bullish in the aggregate has only 75 percent of the securities that would be necessary to cover all of the various types of securities in all of its customers' accounts.

a. Assuming that the broker's statements are accurate, what will Casaubon receive upon liquidation of Bullish? UCC §8-503(b) & comment 1.
b. How would your answer change if 80,000 of the ATDI shares were pledged to ThirdBank? Would the mechanics by which ThirdBank acquired its interest affect your answer? UCC §§8-106, 8-503(a), 8-511(a), (b).

24.6. Think again of the Argentine bond litigation discussed in Problem 14.6. Argentina has a proposal to issue Argentine bonds in exchange for the bonds on which it cannot make payment. It would issue them in Argentina and make payment in Argentina. The only activity outside Argentina would be that the holders accepting the exchange offer would have to transfer their bonds back to Argentina to receive the new bonds. Do you foresee any difficulties? UCC §§8-112, 8-502.

Table of Cases

Italics indicate principal cases.

Table of Statutes and Regulations

Table of Uniform Commercial Code

UCC §		Article 3	132, 137, 148, 149, 152,
			153, 158, 169, 170, 176, 303,
Article 1	429, 458, 469		428–429, 432, 433, 436, 437,
1-103	156, 181, 371, 528		450, 452, 453, 455, 458, 459,
1-105(1)	374		461, 462, 465, 469, 470, 472,
1-201(3)[]*	477		480, 481, 483, 485, 486,
1-201(25)	536		490, 493, 495, 503, 515, 518
1-201(43)	430, 491	3-103	72, 170
1-201(b)(4)	430	3-103(a)	439, 440
1-201(b)(6)	490, 502	3-103(a)(2)	131, 429, 430, 491
1-201(b)(16)	490, 502	3-103(a)(3)	131, 428, 430, 491
1-201(b)(20)	146, 470	3-103(a)(4)	162, 429, 470
1-201(b)(21)	139, 449, 450,	3-103(a)(5)	429, 430, 491
	455, 467, 468, 488, 493	3-103(a)(6)	430, 491
1-201(b)(24)	430, 432, 491	3-103(a)(7)	163, 176, 208, 429
1-201(b)(25)	132	3-103(a)(8)	429
1-201(b)(27)	132	3-103(a)(9)	430, 491
1-201(b)(36)	184	3-103(a)(12)	429
1-201(b)(37)	461, 467	3-103(a)(15)	429, 468, 496
1-201(b)(39)	467	3-103 comment 4	170, 171
1-201(b)(43)	429	3-104	72, 429, 456
1-202	151, 487, 536	3-104(a)	349, 429, 430, 432,
1-202(a)	471, 515, 518		433, 439, 440, 487, 491
1-202(a)(1)	471	3-104(a)(1)	430, 433, 491
1-202(a)(3)	471, 481	3-104(a)(2)	430, 434, 491
1-204	469, 518	3-104(a)(3)	430, 434, 435, 491
1-204(4)	469, 515	3-104(a)(3)(i)	435
1-304	250, 293	3-104(a)(3)(ii)	435
Article 2	137, 312, 412	3-104(a)(3)(iii)	435
2-313(a)(1)	20	3-104(b)	429
2-601	390	3-104(c)	430, 434, 440, 491
2-702	312	3-104(e)	429, 430, 440, 491
2-702(2)	422	3-104(f)	430, 440, 491
2-709	503	3-104(g)	179, 430, 468, 491
2-711	390	3-104(h)	179, 430, 491

* Editor's note: This table includes former citations to the UCC, which sometimes—as shown here in §1-201—have a number subsection before a letter. In the current UCC, the corresponding definitions are found in §1-201(b). The table also includes some state-adopted UCC counterparts that also designate the first subsection as a number followed by a letter, when the current version of the UCC is vice versa. In those citations, the number (1) in the state version corresponds to the letter (a) in the UCC, and lower-level subsections alternate letters and numbers on the same "level" as their UCC counterparts. All citations to former or state-adopted UCC sections with different numbering are listed separately in this table as shown in the extracts themselves and as designated in the state statutes, with initial number subsections listed before the current UCC's initial letter subsections.

Index